INTERNATIONAL CRIMINAL LAW PRACTITIONER LIBRARY

Volume II of the International Criminal Law Practitioner Library series focuses on the core categories of international crimes: crimes against humanity, genocide, and war crimes. The authors present a comprehensive and critical review of the law on the elements of these crimes and their underlying offences, and examine how they interact with the forms of responsibility discussed in Volume I. They also consider the effect of the focus in early ICTY and ICTR proceedings on relatively low-level accused for the development of legal definitions that are sometimes ill-suited for leadership cases, where the accused had little or no physical involvement in the crimes. The book's main focus is the jurisprudence of the ad hoc Tribunals, but the approaches of the ICC and the various hybrid tribunals are also given significant attention. The relevant jurisprudence up to 1 December 2007 has been surveyed, making this a highly useful and timely work.

GIDEON BOAS, a former Senior Legal Officer at the ICTY, is a Senior Lecturer in Law at Monash University Law Faculty and an international law consultant.

JAMES L. BISCHOFF, a former Associate Legal Officer at the ICTY, is an Attorney-Adviser in the Office of the Legal Adviser of the United States Department of State.

NATALIE L. REID, a former Associate Legal Officer at the ICTY, is an Associate with Debevoise & Plimpton LLP, New York.

ELEMENTS OF CRIMES UNDER INTERNATIONAL LAW

International Criminal Law Practitioner Library Series

VOLUME II

GIDEON BOAS
JAMES L. BISCHOFF
NATALIE L. REID

The views expressed in this book are those of the authors alone. They do not necessarily reflect the views or official positions of the International Criminal Tribunal for the former Yugoslavia, the United Nations in general, the United States Department of State, or the United States government.

CAMBRIDGE
UNIVERSITY PRESS

CAMBRIDGE UNIVERSITY PRESS
Cambridge, New York, Melbourne, Madrid, Cape Town, Singapore, São Paulo,
Delhi, Tokyo, Mexico City

Cambridge University Press
The Edinburgh Building, Cambridge CB2 8RU, UK

Published in the United States of America by Cambridge University Press, New York

www.cambridge.org
Information on this title: www.cambridge.org/9780521878302

First published 2008
3rd printing 2011

Printed in the United Kingdom at the University Press, Cambridge

A catalogue record for this publication is available from the British Library

Library of Congress Cataloguing in Publication data
Boas, Gideon.
Elements of crimes under international law / Gideon Boas, James L. Bischoff, Natalie L. Reid.
p. cm. – (International criminal law practitioner library series; v. 2)
ISBN 978-0-521-87830-2 (hardback)
1. International offenses. 2. Crimes against humanity. 3. Genocide. 4. War crimes.
I. Bischoff, James L., J. D. II. Reid, Natalie L. III. Title.
K5301.B627 2008
345′.0235–dc22
2008028118

ISBN 978-0-521-87830-2 hardback

Contents

Foreword

International criminal law has developed substantially in the past two decades largely due to the creation of the *ad hoc* Tribunals for the former Yugoslavia and Rwanda and the International Criminal Court. Although much attention has been devoted to the International Criminal Court (ICC) since 1998, on the ground that it is a truly international tribunal, international criminal law has developed mainly through the jurisprudence of the International Criminal Tribunal for the former Yugoslavia (ICTY) and the International Criminal Tribunal for Rwanda (ICTR). Unlike the ICC, which at the time of writing has delivered few judgments, the *ad hoc* Tribunals have been operating actively as criminal law tribunals for more than a decade. Lengthy, carefully researched, and thoroughly reasoned judgments have been handed down by judges from different countries with different judicial experience. These judgments have created a new international or transnational criminal law that draws on the experience of the Nuremberg and Tokyo Tribunals and national courts, and successfully integrates national and international criminal law, humanitarian law and human rights law.

The ICTY and ICTR have succeeded in developing both procedural law and substantive international criminal law. A host of orders have been given on questions of procedure designed to ensure that due process of law is respected; and many judgments have been rendered on questions of substantive law that advance international criminal justice. The first two volumes of the *International Criminal Law Practitioner Library*, written by three young international criminal lawyers who have all worked in the ICTY and been directly involved in the evolution of the law before this tribunal, deal largely with issues of substantive law. Volume I examined the law of individual criminal responsibility and focused on joint criminal enterprise, superior orders, aiding and abetting, and the planning and instigation of international crime. Volume II – *Elements of Crimes Under International Law* – examines the jurisprudence of the core crimes of international criminal law: genocide, crimes against humanity, and war crimes, and the subject of cumulative convictions and sentencing. Although the ICTY and ICTR provide much of the jurisprudence described in the present volume, the jurisprudence of other tribunals is not ignored. The law of Nuremberg and Tokyo features prominently, and the law and structure of other international and internationalised tribunals – the Special Court for Sierra Leone (SCSL), the Special Panels for Serious Crimes in East Timor (SPSC), the Supreme Iraqi Criminal Tribunal (SICT), the Extraordinary Chambers of the Courts of Cambodia (ECCC) and, of course, the International Criminal Court – are also examined.

Most of Volume II is devoted to a study of the core crimes of crimes against humanity, genocide, and war crimes, as applied and interpreted by the ICTY and ICTR. The evolution of each crime and its elements are addressed in the context of the jurisprudence of the *ad hoc* Tribunals, and then considered in the light of decisions of other international tribunals. Contemporary history in the form of the major criminal trials of the past two decades involving events in the Balkans, Rwanda, and Iraq are brought alive in the language of the law.

Volume II also contains a very useful Annex of the elements of core international crimes and sample combinations with forms of responsibility. This Annex will prove of great assistance to the practitioner. It will also assist the student as its detailed portrayal of the elements of each crime serves to underscore the complexities of these crimes in a jigsaw-like puzzle from which a coherent picture of each crime emerges.

The final part of Volume II deals with the vexed question of cumulative convictions and sentencing. Like national criminal courts, the ICTY, and to a lesser extent the ICTR, have grappled with the problem of cumulative and alternative charging and cumulative convictions. Whether the tribunals have reached satisfactory solutions on these subjects is carefully examined – and doubted – by the authors. The coherency – or incoherency! – of sentencing practice and policy is also described and analysed.

The authors provide an accurate portrayal and description of the law. But their study achieves much more. The approaches of different tribunals, and the approaches of different judges within the same tribunal, are contrasted and compared; and decisions are carefully analysed and criticised. This makes the study a critical portrayal of the jurisprudence of the *ad hoc* Tribunals. One need not agree with all the criticisms of the authors (indeed this writer does not!), but one must welcome their reasoned criticisms. For too long, scholars have sought to protect international tribunals (both criminal and non-criminal) from criticism on the ground that the novel and fragile nature of these institutions requires them to be sheltered from criticism to enable them to survive in the harsh world of international politics. There is no substance in such a view. International judicial institutions, like national courts, must not be beyond criticism if they are to grow and prosper. Careful and reasoned criticism, of the kind found in this volume, contributes to the development of international criminal law and is to be welcomed.

Gideon Boas, James Bischoff and Natalie Reid are to be congratulated on a study that informs us about the content and complexities of the core crimes, and the problems of cumulative convictions and sentencing, but which at the same time makes us aware that international criminal law, like other branches of the law, is the product of the judicial search for reason and coherence in the context of legal sources and legal principle.

John Dugard
The Hague, July 2008

Table of Authorities

International Criminal Tribunal for the Former Yugoslavia (ICTY) materials

International Criminal Tribunal for Rwanda (ICTR) materials

International Criminal Court (ICC) materials

Special Court for Sierra Leone (SCSL) materials

Special Panels for Serious Crimes (SPSC, East Timor) materials

Extraordinary Chambers in the Courts of Cambodia (ECCC) materials

Supreme Iraqi Criminal Tribunal (SICT) materials

Other international cases

National cases and legislation

Treaties and other international agreements

Other international and United Nations materials

Selected secondary sources

Mark B. Harmon and Fergal Gaynor, 'Ordinary Sentences for Extraordinary Crimes', (2007) 5 *Journal of International Criminal Justice* 683, 362

Herman von Hebel and Darryl Robinson, 'Crimes with the Jurisdiction of the Court' in Roy S. Lee (ed.), *The International Criminal Court: The Making of the Rome Statute* (1999) 68–69, 105–106, 107

Hersch Lauterpacht, 'The Problem of the Revision of the Law of War', (1952) 29 *British Yearbook of International Law* 360 230, 267

Raphaël Lemkin, *Axis Rule in Occupied Europe* (1944) 145, 147, 169, 178–181

Francis Lieber, *Instructions for the Government of Armies of the United States in the Field* ('Lieber Code') (1881) 223, 243–256

Timothy L. H. McCormack, 'From Sun Tzu to the Sixth Committee: the Evolution of an International Criminal Regime', in Timothy H. L. McCormack and Gerry J. Simpson (eds.), *The Law of War Crimes: National and International Approaches* (1997) 220, 232

Allison Marston Danner, 'Constructing a Hierarchy of Crimes in International Criminal Law', (2001) 87 *Virginia Law Review* 415, 365

Guénaël Mettraux, *International Crimes and the* Ad Hoc *Tribunals* (2005) 141, 153–154, 358

Valerie Oosterveld, 'The Elements of Genocide: Introduction', in Roy S. Lee (ed.), *The International Criminal Court: Elements of Crimes and Rules of Procedure and Evidence* (2001) 202

Dianne F. Orentlicher, 'The Law of Universal Conscience: Genocide and Crimes Against Humanity', paper presented at the conference Genocide and Crimes Against Humanity: Early Warning and Prevention on 9 December 1998 16, 19, 23, 24, 32–41

Jean Pictet (ed.), *Commentary I Geneva Convention for the Amelioration of the Condition of the Wounded and Sick in Armed Forces in the Field* (1952) 251

Jean Pictet (ed.), *Commentary II Geneva Convention for the Amelioration of the Condition of theWounded, Sick and Shipwrecked Members of Armed Forces at Sea (1960)*

Jean Pictet (ed.), *Commentary IV Geneva Convention Relative to the Protection of Civilian Persons in Time of War* (1958) 44, 72, 254

Report of the *Ad Hoc* Committee on Genocide, UN ESCOR, 7th Sess., UN Doc. E/74 (1948) 147, 148, 178, 181–183

Steven R. Ratner and Jason S. Abrams, *Accountability for Human Rights Atrocities in International Law: Beyond the Nuremberg Legacy* (2nd edn 2001) 130

Darryl Robinson, 'The Elements of Crimes Against Humanity', in Roy S. Lee (ed.), *The International Criminal Court: Elements of Crimes and Rules of Procedure and Evidence* (2001). 112, 113

Jean-Jacques Rousseau, *On the Social Contract* (1772) 222, 238–239

1

An overview of crimes under international law

Yves Sandoz once wrote: 'It has often been said that one of the most pressing tasks for international criminal law is to set out clearly what violations are punishable under that law and to define them in specific terms.'[1] This second volume in the *International Criminal Law Practitioner Library* examines the elements of crimes under international law, primarily as they have been defined in the jurisprudence of the International Criminal Tribunal for the former Yugoslavia (ICTY) and the International Criminal Tribunal for Rwanda (ICTR) (collectively, the '*ad hoc* Tribunals'). This jurisprudence has contributed greatly to the nuanced definitions of the core categories of crimes under international law applied in current and future international adjudication, and is the richest body of contemporary applications of the law on elements to the actual facts of cases. Despite this contribution, the specificity referred to by Sandoz appears elusive: the case law is frequently contradictory or obscure, and thus requires analysis to explain the legal principle clearly, or at least to identify what is unclear and in need of further jurisprudential development. Such an analysis is the fundamental goal of this book, as it is of this series.

Two consequences flow from our focus on the judicial interpretation of the scope and content of crimes under international law. First, like the first volume in this series, this volume does not seek to repeat the extensive and well-considered literature on the Statute and Elements of Crimes of the International Criminal Court (ICC), although each chapter contains a brief examination of how those instruments and those of the Special Court for Sierra Leone (SCSL), the East Timor Special Panels for Serious

[1] Yves Sandoz, 'Penal Aspects of International Humanitarian Law', in M. Cherif Bassiouni, *International Criminal Law* (2nd edn 1998), p. 406.

Crimes (SPSC), the Extraordinary Chambers in the Courts of Cambodia (ECCC), and the Supreme Iraqi Criminal Tribunal (SICT)[2] define crimes, and highlights the important differences between the approaches of the *ad hoc* Tribunals and those of the other tribunals. Second, this volume only discusses the crimes or categories of crimes against the person or against property that are provided for in the Statutes of the *ad hoc* Tribunals. As will be seen in the sections of Chapters 2 and 4 dealing with the ICC and the internationalised criminal tribunals, the respective lists of underlying offences of crimes against humanity and war crimes vary somewhat from tribunal to tribunal. While there is considerable academic literature on some of the offences that do not appear in the *ad hoc* Statutes – especially the many additional offences in the lengthy war crimes provision of the Rome Statute of the ICC – these offences have not, as yet, been the subject of much judicial interpretation. To the extent that they have been the subject of judicial interpretation, this jurisprudence is touched upon in the respective sections on the ICC and the internationalised tribunals in Chapters 2 to 4.

On one view, an international crime could be defined as any offence that requires international cooperation for its prosecution and therefore involves more than one domestic jurisdiction, or which requires cross-border movements or transactions, such as money laundering or trafficking in narcotics. This book, however, focuses on crimes under international law – that is, conduct that violates international law, and is punishable as such with the imposition of individual criminal liability – rather than all crimes that have an international aspect. Moreover, it is not an exhaustive analysis of all conduct that may constitute a crime under international law, but rather a focused study of those 'core' categories of crimes – crimes against humanity, genocide, and war crimes – for which a wealth of judicial exposition exists.

The question of what constitutes the corpus of law with which international criminal law is concerned is not definitively settled. While the Nuremberg and

[2] The Iraqi National Assembly changed this Tribunal's name from its original appellation, 'Iraqi Special Tribunal', and there has been confusion about how to translate the new Arabic name into English. See Michael P. Scharf and Gregory S. McNeal (eds.), *Saddam on Trial: Understanding and Debating the Iraqi High Tribunal* (2006), p. 57. The Tribunal's name in Arabic is al-Mahkama al-Jina'iya al-'Iraqiya al-'Uliya. These words translate as 'Iraqi', 'High' or 'Higher', and 'Criminal Court' or 'Tribunal'. According to Scharf and McNeal, the Tribunal subsequently issued an official statement in which it said its name in English is 'Iraqi High Tribunal' (although they provide no citation to this official statement), and this is the name Scharf and McNeal chose to use in their book. *Ibid.* By contrast, M. Cherif Bassiouni and Michael Wahid Hanna use the translation 'Iraqi High Criminal Court' in their article. See M. Cherif Bassiouni and Michael Wahid Hanna, 'Ceding the High Ground: The Iraqi High Criminal Court Statute and the Trial of Saddam Hussein', (2006–07) 39 *Case Western Reserve Journal of International Law* 21, 57. For consistency with Volume I of this series, we follow the practice of Human Rights Watch in employing the translation 'Supreme Iraqi Criminal Tribunal'. See Human Rights Watch, World Report 2006, Iraq, available at www.hrw.org/english/docs/2006/01/18/iraq12215.htm. Although the SICT is not, strictly speaking, a hybrid or internationalised tribunal, it is included in these comparative analyses because it has jurisdiction over the core crimes under international law, and the definitions of these crimes in its Statute are clearly modelled on those of the Rome Statute of the ICC. Though its practice and jurisprudence are limited, and its proceedings criticised and often chaotic, discussion of the manner in which the law on the core crimes has been applied by the SICT is nevertheless useful for illustrating the difficulties of adapting international practice and jurisprudence to a particular kind of domestic context.

Tokyo Charters included the crime of aggression, modern international criminal law – as embodied in the Statutes of the ICTY, ICTR, ICC, and other international and internationalised tribunals, and developed in their jurisprudence – tends to focus exclusively on the three core categories of crimes: crimes against humanity, genocide, and war crimes.[3] Because these crimes are almost invariably (although not necessarily) prosecuted in the context of an armed conflict, the proposition that 'international humanitarian law' is synonymous with these core crimes holds some attraction.

International humanitarian law is generally understood to cover two bodies of law: first, 'Geneva Law', which derives from a range of Geneva Conventions dating back to 1864, but in particular the Geneva Conventions of 1949 and their Additional Protocols of 1977; and which seeks to ameliorate the suffering of those not directly involved in combat;[4] and second, 'Hague Law', which derives mainly from a number of the Hague Conventions, particularly those of 1899 and 1907, as well as Additional Protocol I of 1977; and which seeks to regulate the means and methods by which war is conducted.[5] Crimes against humanity and genocide have traditionally been viewed as outside the definition of international humanitarian law, and separately associated with international criminal law because their proscription gives rise to individual criminal responsibility. This is no doubt in part because these categories of crimes can occur in times of peace as well as war, and because they were developed in the post-Second World War context of the Nuremberg and subsequent post-war trials as distinct species of criminality from war crimes proper, which are violations of international humanitarian law considered to be so serious that they entail not only state responsibility, but also individual criminal responsibility.[6]

3 Accordingly, we will not discuss aggression (also labelled 'crimes against peace'), even though that crime is included in the Rome Statute of the ICC and the International Law Commission's latest Draft Code of Crimes Against the Peace and Security of Mankind. See Draft Code of Crimes Against the Peace and Security of Mankind, in Report of the International Law Commission on the Work of Its Forty-eighth Session, UN Doc. A/51/10 (1996) ('1996 ILC Draft Code'), Art. 16; Rome Statute of the International Criminal Court, 17 July 1998, entered into force 1 July 2002, UN Doc. A/CONF. 183/9, 37 ILM 1002 (1998), 2187 UNTS 90 ('Rome Statute'), Art. 5(2) (providing that the ICC 'shall exercise jurisdiction over the crime of aggression once a provision is adopted in accordance with articles 121 and 123 defining the crime and setting out the conditions under which the Court shall exercise jurisdiction with respect to this crime').

4 For a detailed discussion of Geneva Law, see Chapter 4, text accompanying notes 43–45, and 58–63.

5 For a detailed discussion of Hague Law, see Chapter 4, text accompanying notes 43–57. Frits Kalshoven writes that the term 'international humanitarian law' came into common usage around the time of the 1949 Geneva Conventions, and that the International Committee of the Red Cross used the term to refer to Geneva Law, but not Hague Law or crimes against humanity, let alone genocide. See Frits Kalshoven, 'From International Humanitarian Law to International Criminal Law', (2004) 3 *Chinese Journal of International Law* 151, 153. Additional Protocol I of 1977 finally dissipated any real distinction between Geneva Law and Hague Law, fusing legal rules concerning the protection and treatment of civilians, prisoners of war, and persons *hors de combat* with those regulating the use of certain weapons and certain means of warfare; it thereby merged these two historically distinct strands of law into one. See Kalshoven, *supra*, p. 153; see also Chapter 4, note 45.

6 See Chapter 2, section 2.1 (discussing the origins and evolution of crimes against humanity); Chapter 3, section 3.1 (discussing the origins and evolution of genocide); Chapter 4, section 4.1 (discussing the origins and evolution of war crimes).

There is sense in the treatment of these categories of genocide and crimes against humanity as not falling within the realm of international humanitarian law. The overwhelming bulk of international humanitarian law concerns the responsibility of states (and, sometimes, armed rebel groups) in respect of armed conflict, and has nothing to do with individual criminal responsibility, whereas genocide and crimes against humanity, strictly speaking, are in the first instance categories of international crimes, that may also give rise to state responsibility in certain circumstances. Nevertheless, genocide and crimes against humanity are much more likely to occur in the context of an armed conflict than in times of peace, so they invariably overlap considerably with international humanitarian law. As such, they have increasingly come to be considered as forming part of that body of law, *de facto* if not *de jure*. A salient example can be seen in the Statutes of some of the international and internationalised criminal courts and tribunals, which provide for jurisdiction over 'serious violations of international humanitarian law', understood in those instruments to cover not only war crimes, but also crimes against humanity and genocide.[7] The jurisprudence of the *ad hoc* Tribunals and the SCSL has reinforced this conceptualisation of international humanitarian law on many occasions.[8] It may well be that, as international criminal law evolves, the distinctions between these differently conceived bodies of law will gradually disappear.

It is no surprise that crimes against humanity, genocide, and war crimes have been included within the jurisdiction of the contemporary international and internationalised

[7] This point is well made by Kalshoven, *supra* note 5, pp. 153–4. See also Statute of the International Criminal Tribunal for the Prosecution of Persons Responsible for Serious Violations of International Humanitarian Law Committed in the Territory of the former Yugoslavia since 1991, (1993) 32 ILM 1159, as amended by Security Council Resolution 1660 of 28 February 2006 ('ICTY Statute'), Art. 9(1); Statute of the International Criminal Tribunal for Rwanda, (1994) 33 ILM 1602, as amended by Security Council Resolution 1534 of 26 March 2004 ('ICTR Statute'), Art. 1; Statute of the Special Court for Sierra Leone, 2178 UNTS 138, UN Doc. S/2002/246, 16 January 2002, Appendix II ('SCSL Statute'), Art. 1(1); see also Law on the Establishment of the Extraordinary Chambers in the Courts of Cambodia for the Prosecution of Crimes Committed During the Period of Democratic Kampuchea, as amended on 27 October 2004, Doc. No. NS/RKM/1004/006, unofficial translation by the Council of Jurists and the Secretariat of the Task Force, revised on 26 August 2007 ('ECCC Law'), Art. 2 new. Perhaps tellingly, however, the Rome Statute of the ICC does not use the term 'serious violations of international humanitarian law' in this sense, preferring instead the terms 'most serious crimes of concern to the international community' or, simply, 'international crimes'. See Rome Statute, *supra* note 3, preambular paras. 4, 6. The constitutive instrument of the East Timor SPSC similarly employs the term 'serious criminal offences'. See United Nations Transitional Administration in East Timor, Regulation No. 2000/15 on the Establishment of Panels with Exclusive Jurisdiction over Serious Criminal Offences, UN Doc. UNTAET/REG/2000/15, 6 June 2000 ('UNTAET Regulation'), Section 1.3.

[8] See, e.g., *Prosecutor* v. *Blagojević and Jokić*, Case No. IT-02-60-T, Judgement, 17 January 2005, para. 834 (noting that '[a]ll crimes falling within the jurisdiction of this Tribunal are characterise[d] as "serious violations of international humanitarian law"', and that '[t]he crimes for which the Accused in this case have been convicted' – that is, complicity in genocide, several crimes against humanity, and murder as a violation of the laws or customs of war – 'clearly warrant such a label'); *Prosecutor* v. *Simba*, Case No. ICTR-2001-76-T, Judgement, 13 December 2005, para. 431 ('All crimes under the [ICTR] Statute are serious violations of international humanitarian law.'); *Prosecutor* v. *Fofana and Kondewa*, Case No. SCSL-04-14-J, Judgement, 2 August 2007, para. 93 (noting that, as '[n]o crimes under Sierra Leonean law [had been] charged in the Indictment … , [t]he Chamber [would] therefore consider only serious violations of international humanitarian law', by which it meant war crimes and crimes against humanity).

courts and tribunals, for they represent the worst excesses and atrocities in human conflict, and have characterised to varying degrees the situations to which each of the temporary courts reviewed in this volume is a response.[9] In addition, as outlined below and discussed in detail at the beginning of Chapters 2, 3, and 4, the development and codification of the rules of international law underlying these crimes has been one of the hallmarks of the progressive development of international law over the last century. It is in prohibiting the conduct that constitutes these crimes, and in providing effective means to enforce those prohibitions with individual penal sanctions, that international criminal law seeks to contribute to an international rule of law.

1.1 Legal sources for definitions of crimes under international law

The classic statement of the sources of international law, in Article 38(1) of the Statute of the International Court of Justice, refers to three primary sources and one subsidiary source: international agreements, treaties, or conventions (collectively, 'conventional international law'); customary international law, or the consistent practice of states undertaken in the belief that the conduct is permitted, required, or prohibited by international law; the general principles of law recognised by, and typically derived from the domestic legal systems of, states; and the subsidiary source of the collected commentaries on international law provided by judicial decisions and academic writings of the 'most highly qualified publicists'.[10] International criminal law demonstrates the interplay among these different sources, and thus provides a particularly robust example of how these types of legal instruments and practices relate to and build on each other in the effort to define and enforce the core categories of crimes under international law.

[9] In the constitutive instruments of the courts and tribunals discussed in this series, these core categories include other offences that are also given separate treatment under international law. Certain of the internationalised tribunals in fact include some of these offences as separate crimes. See, e.g., UNTAET Regulation, *supra* note 7, Section 7 (freestanding torture provision); ECCC Law, *supra* note 7, Art. 8 (provision on crimes against diplomatic staff). Except to the extent that breaches of norms of international law constitute war crimes or underlying offences of crimes against humanity, this volume will generally not discuss other international norms – such as the prohibitions against torture, hostage-taking, enforced disappearance, apartheid, the various manifestations of slavery, forced labour, and acts of terrorism – indicating or suggesting that individuals may or should be held responsible for their breach, and that such responsibility may or should be criminal. Other norms of this nature, also not treated in this volume, include mercenarism and piracy.

[10] Statute of the International Court of Justice, (1945) 39 *AJIL Supp.* 215, Art. 38(1). This traditional list of the sources of international law has been criticised as under-inclusive and overly focused on the role of states as international actors, as it is now generally accepted that there are other entities and persons that have international legal personality and should therefore play a role in providing the content and shaping the development of international law. See, e.g., Maurice H. Mendelson, 'Formation of Customary International Law', in (1998) 272 *Recueil des Cours* 165, 188, 203; Jonathan Charney, 'Universal International Law', (1993) 87 *American Journal of International Law* 529 ('Rather than state practice and *opinio juris*, multilateral forums [where representatives of states and other interested groups come together to address important international problems of mutual concern] often play a central role in the creation and shaping of contemporary [customary] international law.'). In particular, the role of international and non-governmental organisations in the field of international criminal law has been especially pronounced in the preparations for, establishment, and initial functioning of the ICC.

International treaties from the turn of the last century represent the earliest efforts to create a code of conduct for interstate hostilities, while post-war agreements between and among victor and vanquished states at the end of the First and Second World Wars laid the foundations for individual criminal liability for violations of that code, and the first comprehensive international effort to bring the worst individual offenders to justice.[11] Developments before, between, and after the major wars of the twentieth century were reflected in burgeoning norms of customary international law, which were in turn codified in later international treaties. In particular, growing acceptance of the need for clearer restrictions on permissible military tactics and protection of vulnerable populations led to the 1949 Geneva Conventions,[12] while widespread revulsion at the Holocaust resulted in the rapid drafting and entry into force of the 1948 Genocide Convention.[13]

Yet the international criminal tribunals, from Nuremberg up to the creation of the ICC and the internationalised tribunals, have experienced some difficulty in marrying these traditional sources of international law with their jurisdictional peculiarities as criminal courts. Perhaps the most important issue confronting their legitimacy has been the fact that their constitutive statutes, which give them jurisdiction and set forth much of the law they must apply, were all promulgated after the commission of the alleged crimes that are the subject of prosecutions,[14] with one exception and one partial exception: (1) the ICC, which has jurisdiction only over crimes committed subsequent to the Court's July 2002 establishment;[15] and (2) the ICTY, with respect to crimes allegedly committed after the 1993 promulgation of that Tribunal's Statute, most notably in and around Srebrenica in 1995 and Kosovo in 1999. Consequently, the Statutes of the various courts and tribunals, drawing inspiration from the Nuremberg Tribunal,[16] grant jurisdiction over certain international crimes but do not themselves prohibit criminal conduct or

[11] See Chapter 2, section 2.1; Chapter 3, section 3.1; Chapter 4, section 4.1; see also Gideon Boas, James L. Bischoff, and Natalie L. Reid, *Forms of Responsibility in International Criminal Law* (2007), pp. 145–8.

[12] See Chapter 4, section 4.1.2. [13] See Chapter 3, section 3.1.1.

[14] See ICTY Statute, *supra* note 7, Art. 8 (temporal jurisdiction from 1 January 1991 onward); ICTR Statute, *supra* note 7, Art. 7 (temporal jurisdiction from 1 January 1994 to 31 December 1994); UNTAET Regulation, *supra* note 7, Section 2.3 (SPSC temporal jurisdiction from 1 January 1999 to 25 October 1999); ECCC Law, *supra* note 7, Art. 2 new (temporal jurisdiction from 17 April 1975 to 6 January 1979); Law No. 10 (2005), Law of the Iraqi Higher Criminal Court, 18 October 2005, reprinted in Scharf and McNeal (eds.), *supra* note 2, pp. 283 *et seq*., Art.1(2) (temporal jurisdiction from 17 July 1968 to 1 May 2003); SCSL Statute, *supra* note 7, Art. 1(1) (temporal jurisdiction from November 1996 onward). The SCSL has already indicted all of its accused, all for crimes allegedly committed before the Court's establishment.

[15] Rome Statute, *supra* note 3, Art. 24(1) ('No person shall be criminally responsible under this Statute for conduct prior to the entry into force of the Statute.').

[16] The indictment at Nuremberg listed a number of international treaties as a basis for the law the Charter included in the Tribunal's jurisdiction, most notably the 1899 and 1907 Hague Conventions. See *France, Union of Soviet Socialist Republics, United Kingdom, and United States* v. *Göring, Bormann, Dönitz, Frank, Frick, Fritzsche, Funk, Hess, Jodl, Kaltenbrunner, Keitel, von Bohlen und Halbach, Ley, von Neurath, von Papen, Raeder, von Ribbentrop, Rosenberg, Sauckel, Schacht, von Schirach, Seyss-Inquart, Speer, and Streicher*, *International Military Tribunal, Judgment and Sentence*, 1 October 1946, in *Trial of the Major War Criminals Before the International Military Tribunal, Nuremberg*, vol. 1, pp. 84–92.

create individual liability.[17] Rather, the primary prohibitive rules, generally identifying the conduct that violates international law, and secondary attributive rules, identifying which individuals may be held personally responsible for those violations, must usually exist in customary international law before they may be enforced.[18] A significant part of the body of decisional law of the *ad hoc* Tribunals is therefore an exercise in divining and clarifying customary international law, and the effect the Tribunals will have on the jurisprudence of the ICC will further advance that project.

The Rome Statute of the ICC is arguably the most important treaty in contemporary international criminal law, owing to its relative comprehensiveness and to the fact that it was agreed upon by a large body of states. In addition, because the Court enjoys only prospective jurisdiction, the legal basis for its jurisdiction is far less controversial than that of its predecessors.[19] Like the *ad hoc* Tribunals, the ICC owes a significant debt to customary international law.[20] First, the *travaux préparatoires* of the Rome Statute at times reveal intense debate between a range of international actors over how far a specific requirement or prohibition had developed in customary international law,[21] with the result that the final text represents a partial codification of custom, partial progressive development of the

[17] As such, it is important to note that judgements of the *ad hoc* Tribunals are technically incorrect, and certainly imprecise, when they refer to alleged crimes as 'violating' a given Article of their Statutes.

[18] For the ICTY and the ICTR, see Boas, Bischoff, and Reid, *supra* note 11, pp. 27 & n. 100, 112–13 & n. 640; Report of the Secretary-General Pursuant to Paragraph 2 of Security Council Resolution 808 (1993), UN Doc. S/25704, 3 May 1993, ('Secretary-General's ICTY Report'), para. 33 (noting that the subject matter jurisdiction of the ICTY includes international humanitarian law, which 'exists in the form of both conventional law and customary law', and that 'while there is international customary law which is not laid down in conventions, some of the major conventional humanitarian law has become part of customary international law'); *ibid.*, para. 35 (explaining that 'the part of conventional international humanitarian law which has beyond doubt become part of international customary law' includes the Geneva Conventions and the Genocide Convention); Letter Dated 1 October 1994 from the Secretary-General Addressed to the President of the Security Council, UN Doc. S/1994/1125, 4 October 1994 (attaching the report of the Commission of Experts appointed to investigate the events in Rwanda, and noting the Commission's conclusion that violations of the Geneva Conventions and the Genocide Convention, as well as crimes against humanity, were committed in Rwanda). While the ICTY Appeals Chamber has held that the relevant legal rules may also be found in conventional international law binding on Yugoslavia at the time of the alleged crimes, see, e.g., *Prosecutor* v. *Kordić and Čerkez*, Case No. IT-95-14/2-A, Judgement, 17 December 2004, paras. 43–46, chambers at both levels in both *ad hoc* Tribunals generally also undertake or rely on analyses of customary international law. See *Prosecutor* v. *Galić*, Case No. IT-98-29-A, Judgement, 30 November 2006, para. 83 (noting that 'in most cases, treaty provisions will only provide for the prohibition of a certain conduct, not for its criminalisation, or … will not sufficiently define the elements of the prohibition they criminalise and customary international law must be looked at for the definition of those elements').

[19] See Alexander Zahar and Göran Sluiter, *International Criminal Law: A Critical Introduction* (2007), pp. 80–91.

[20] The Rome Statute was adopted by the United Nations Diplomatic Conference of Plenipotentiaries on the Establishment of an International Criminal Court and opened for signature by all states on 17 July 1998. It entered into force on 1 July 2002, and as of 1 December 2007 had 139 signatories and 105 parties. See Multilateral Treaties Deposited with the Secretary-General, available at http://untreaty.un.org/ENGLISH/bible/englishinternetbible/partI/chapterXVIII/treaty11.asp. One of the main bodies of the ICC is the Assembly of States Parties, in which each state party is represented and to which signatories may send observers. See Rome Statute, supra note 3, Art. 112.

[21] See, e.g., Chapter 2, notes 476–477 and accompanying text; Chapter 3, notes 323–329, 346 and accompanying text; Chapter 4 notes 439–445, 459–464, 474–477 and accompanying text.

law, and a partial compromise between the different participants in the process. Second, much of the content of the Statute and the accompanying Elements of Crimes is derived from or influenced by the jurisprudence of the *ad hoc* Tribunals.

The role that states play in the lawmaking process at the international level is complemented by the contribution that their domestic criminal legal systems make to the growing sophistication of international criminal law. Although relatively few prosecutions for crimes under international law have taken place at the domestic level,[22] the procedural rules of international criminal adjudication are based on – and are in fact an attempt to take the best practices from – the rules in the principal legal systems of the world.[23] Moreover, the most fundamental principles of international criminal law are in fact derived from the general principles of criminal law accepted in domestic legal systems. *Nullum crimen sine lege* and *nulla poena sine lege* are the principles that no conduct can be subject to criminal sanction unless prohibited and penalised by law.[24] In the context of international criminal law, these principles are interpreted as requiring that, at the time the alleged conduct was committed, it was a breach of international law and was subject to the imposition of individual criminal penalties.[25] As such, they are important limiting principles that guide judicial findings and pronouncements of guilt or innocence. In particular, they require that chambers at the *ad hoc* Tribunals ground their analysis firmly in customary international law – a responsibility that is observed to varying degrees by different chambers.[26]

[22] See, e.g., *Fédération Nationale des Déportés et Internés Résistants et Patriotes et Autres* v. *Barbie* (French Cour de Cassation, Chambre Criminelle, 20 December 1985), 1985 Bull. Crim. No. 407, 1053, (1990) 78 ILR 124; Affaire *Touvier* (French Cour de Cassation, Chambre Criminelle, 27 November 1992), 1992 Bull. Crim. No. 294, 1085; *Public Prosecutor* v. *Menten* (Dutch Hoge Raad 1981), 75 ILR 362, 362–363; *Regina* v. *Finta* (Canadian Supreme Court 1994), 1 SCR 701, 814; *Chilean Genocide* case (Spanish Audiencia Nacional, 5 November 1998), *translation reprinted in* Reed Brody and Michael Ratner (eds.), *The Pinochet Papers: The Case of Augusto Pinochet in Spain and Britain* (2000); see also Chapter 2, note 53 (citing crimes against humanity cases in Canada, Australia, Germany, Austria, and Israel).

[23] See generally Patrick L. Robinson, 'Fair but Expeditious Trials', in Hirad Abtahi and Gideon Boas (eds.), *The Dynamics of International Criminal Justice: Essays in Honour of Sir Richard May* (2005), p. 169; Gideon Boas, 'A Code of Evidence and Procedure for International Criminal Law? The Rules of the ICTY', in Gideon Boas and William A. Schabas (eds.), *International Criminal Law Developments in the Case Law of the ICTY* (2002), pp. 31–33; Daryl A. Mundis, 'From "Common Law" Towards "Civil Law": The Evolution of the ICTY Rules of Procedure and Evidence', (2001) 14 *Leiden Journal of International Law* 367.

[24] See generally Guillaume Endo, '*Nullum crimen nulla poena sine lege* principle and the ICTY and ICTR', (2002) 15 *Revue québécoise de droit international* 205.

[25] See, e.g., Robert Cryer, Håkan Friman, Darryl Robinson, and Elizabeth Wilmshurst, *International Criminal Law and Procedure* (2007), pp. 12–16; William A. Schabas, *The UN International Criminal Tribunals: The Former Yugoslavia, Rwanda and Sierra Leone* (2006), pp. 155–156; Gerhard Werle, *Principles of International Criminal Law* (2005), pp. 190–195; Salvatore Zappalà, *Human Rights in International Criminal Proceedings* (2003), pp. 195–197; Christoph Safferling, *Towards an International Criminal Procedure* (2001), p. 88.

[26] See Theodor Meron, 'Reflections on the Prosecution of War Crimes by International Tribunals', (2006) 100 *American Journal of International Law* 551, 566–567 (asserting that 'to forestall … criticisms' similar to those levelled at the Nuremburg trials, 'the *ad hoc* tribunals take pains to explain the customary and conventional underpinnings of their decisions', and that '[c]onsequently, judgments of the ICTY are helping to revitalize customary law and to anchor international law firmly in both codified law and judicial decisions'); Secretary-General's ICTY Report, *supra* note 18, para. 34 (expressing the view that the *nullum crimen sine lege* principle

Finally, the efforts of renowned international scholars – most notably in the form of the work of the International Law Commission (ILC) – cannot be underestimated. In 1950, the ILC presented its codification of the Principles of International Law Recognized in the Charter of the Nürnberg Tribunal and in the Judgment of the Tribunal;[27] in 1954, its first draft criminal code, the Draft Code of Offences against the Peace and Security of Mankind;[28] in 1991, a revised and updated version of that Code;[29] in 1994, the Draft Statute for an International Criminal Court that was eventually considered by the conference of plenipotentiaries in Rome;[30] and in 1996, the revised Draft Code of Crimes against the Peace and Security of Mankind.[31] Each of these documents included invaluable commentaries that explored and explained the relevant principles of the nascent and developing field of international criminal law. Collectively, they have had a remarkable influence on the establishing instruments and the evolving case law of the contemporary international and internationalised criminal courts and tribunals.

1.2 Structure of crimes under international law

The complex variety of sources from which international criminal law derives its substantive content is matched by the complicated structure of the crimes themselves. In certain domestic criminal regimes, for example, each crime is typically a comprehensive description of the conduct justifying the imposition of penal sanctions, bundling together the physical act or omission, the accused's role in the crime, and sometimes any aggravating or mitigating factors.[32] In international criminal law, however, those components are disaggregated, and must be independently evaluated and then combined in order to determine whether the accused on trial

'requires that the international tribunal should apply rules of international humanitarian law which are beyond any doubt part of customary law so that the problem of adherence of some but not all states to specific conventions does not arise'). But see, e.g., Chapter 3, note 178 and accompanying text (noting, for example, that the *Akayesu* Trial Chamber cited almost no authority for its descriptions of the various bases on which a protected group under the Genocide Convention may be defined).

27 5 UN GAOR Supp. (No. 12) at 11, UN Doc. A/1316 (1950).

28 See Report of the International Law Commission on the Work of Its Sixth Session, UN Doc. A/2963 (1954).

29 See Report of the International Law Commission on the Work of Its Forty-third Session, UN Doc. A/46/10 (1991).

30 See Report of the International Law Commission on the Work of Its Forty-sixth Session, UN Doc. A/49/10 (1994).

31 See 1996 ILC Draft Code, *supra* note 3.

32 See, e.g., Carl Erik Herlitz, *Parties to a Crime and the Notion of a Complicity Object* (1992), p. 89 (describing the traditional common-law structure of felonies, which distinguished between the participants in a crime by, *inter alia*, the concepts of first-degree and second-degree principals; for murder, for example, those who physically committed the crime would be guilty of first-degree murder, while those who were merely present and aided its commission would be guilty of second-degree murder); *American Jurisprudence*: *Criminal Law*, vol. 21 § 187 (2nd edn 2007) (treatise on criminal law in the United States, noting that while '[s]ome jurisdictions today continue the common-law distinction in liability' between the participants in a crime, in most state jurisdictions, no such distinction is recognised, and '[a]ll persons involved in the crime are equally guilty of the completed offense, and all are liable for the conduct of each person').

may be convicted. As will be seen below and throughout this volume, the result is that the various elements of an international crime may, in the circumstances, be fulfilled by different actors involved in the bringing to fruition of a given crime.

Broadly speaking, there are three substantive components to international crimes: (1) the underlying offence; (2) the general requirements of each core category of crimes under international law; and (3) the specific requirements for certain crimes. A fourth component – the form of responsibility, or method through which a given individual participates in the crime – must be supplied before an accused can be subject to criminal penalties. This critical fourth component is the subject of the first volume in this series.[33] Though all the elements of a crime may be satisfied by the accused's conduct, international law does not require that a person physically commit the offence in order to be held responsible for the crime. With limited exceptions for certain requirements where their satisfaction may be determined as a matter of law,[34] the prosecution must prove all elements of all four components beyond reasonable doubt before a conviction may be entered.

The **underlying offence** is the conduct that produces the result, or is intended to produce the result, that is prohibited by international law. Such conduct is usually also prohibited by domestic law. Examples include murder; rape; physical assault or beating; and theft or destruction of property. In the contexts in which international crimes are generally committed, such as international or non-international armed conflicts, or actions by military or security services against civilian populations, there are frequently many people at different levels in the political or military hierarchy who are involved in the preparation and execution of the criminal activity. In such circumstances, it is often the lowest-level actor, the foot soldier, who carries out the underlying offence. In order to form the basis of an international crime, such conduct will almost always have to be criminal itself;[35] as such, it will have its own physical and mental elements. In order to avoid confusion, we restrict the use of the terms '*actus reus*' and '*mens rea*' to these physical and mental elements of the underlying offences.

The **general requirements** are the elements that must be satisfied before an underlying offence constitutes a crime of international significance. These elements vary according to which core category of crimes is alleged, and generally correspond to the context in which the underlying offence was committed or the intent that accompanies the offence: for example, war crimes must occur in an armed

[33] See generally Boas, Bischoff, and Reid, *supra* note 11.

[34] For example, the equal gravity requirement for persecution as a crime against humanity, and the gravity requirement for violations of the laws or customs of war. See Chapter 2, text accompanying note 399; Chapter 4, section 4.2.1.5.2.

[35] The sole exception being certain forms of persecution as a crime against humanity. See Chapter 2, note 397 and accompanying text.

conflict;[36] crimes against humanity must be committed in the context of a widespread or systematic attack on a civilian population;[37] and the defining element of genocide is the specific intent to partially or completely destroy a national, ethnic, racial, or religious group (a 'protected group').[38] The general requirements are the elements that distinguish each category of crimes; that is, any underlying offence must satisfy one set of general requirements if it is to constitute a war crime, a different set of general requirements before it becomes a crime against humanity, and yet another set of general requirements if it is to qualify as genocide.[39] Using one example from the paragraph above, the underlying offence of murder is a crime against humanity if the victim is a civilian, the murder is committed in the context of a widespread or systematic attack directed against a civilian population, and either the physical perpetrator[40] or another relevant actor knows that the murder is part of that attack.[41] That same underlying offence becomes the war crime of wilful killing, a grave breach of the Geneva Conventions, if it is committed in territory controlled by one of the parties to an international conflict, is closely related to that conflict, and the victim is a person protected by the Geneva Conventions.[42] Finally, this underlying offence constitutes genocide by killing if the physical perpetrator or other relevant actor intends by that murder (and presumably, others) to contribute to the partial or complete destruction of a protected group.[43]

The **specific requirements** are elements that must also be fulfilled if an underlying offence is to constitute one of a small subset of international crimes that are characterised by unique physical and mental elements, such as discriminatory intent and discrimination in fact for persecution, or the three cumulative criteria for 'other

[36] See generally Chapter 4, section 4.2.1.1. There are also subcategories of war crimes, each defined by its own additional general requirements. See *ibid.*, sections 4.2.1.3–4.2.1.5.

[37] See generally Chapter 2, sections 2.2.2.2, 2.2.2.4.

[38] See generally Chapter 3, section 3.2.1.2.

[39] Under the Statutes of the *ad hoc* Tribunals, the elements that characterise each category of crimes include certain jurisdictional requirements that do not exist in customary international law. See Chapter 2, section 2.2.1. In addition, the ICTY Statute has two separate provisions on war crimes; Article 2 grants jurisdiction over grave breaches of the Geneva Conventions, and Article 3 over violations of the laws or customs of war. There are therefore several references in *ad hoc* judgements to the fact that these articles share certain general or *chapeau* requirements – referring to the *chapeau* paragraph of each article. See, e.g., *Prosecutor* v. *Brđanin*, Case No. IT-99-36-T, Judgement, 1 September 2004, paras. 139–143 (making 'findings in respect of the general requirements common to Articles 2, 3 and 5'). Under customary international law, however, each core category of crimes is characterised by a distinct set of general requirements.

[40] As in Volume I of this series, the term physical perpetrator is used throughout this volume to refer to the person who physically carries out the *actus reus* of the underlying offence. See Boas, Bischoff, and Reid, *supra* note 11, p. 5 (citing judgements alternatively deeming this person the 'principal perpetrator', the 'principal offender', the 'immediate perpetrator', and the 'physical perpetrator'). Recently, the ICTY Appeals Chamber expressed its preference for the term 'principal perpetrator'. See *Prosecutor* v. *Brđanin*, Case No. IT-99-36-A, Judgement, 3 April 2007, para. 362. We choose to retain our terminology, as the word 'principal' may erroneously imply that this person must be one of the more important persons involved in a criminal transaction, when in fact he may occupy a very low place in the hierarchy.

[41] See generally Chapter 2, section 2.2.2; see also Annex, section 2.2.

[42] See generally Chapter 4, sections 4.2.1.1–4.2.1.3, 4.2.2.4; see also Annex, section 4.13.

[43] See generally Chapter 3, section 3.2.1; see also Annex, section 3.2.

inhumane acts'.[44] Both these examples are crimes against humanity, and an underlying offence must satisfy both the general requirements for crimes against humanity and these additional specific requirements before it may constitute either of these crimes. Again using the example of the underlying offence of murder, in order to qualify as murder as a form of persecution as a crime against humanity, the following general and specific requirements must be satisfied: it must be committed in the context of a widespread or systematic attack directed against a civilian population; either the physical perpetrator or another relevant actor must know that the murder is part of that attack; the victim must be a civilian; and he or she must be targeted on the basis of political, racial, or religious identity.[45] These crimes, and the specific requirements that distinguish them, are among the most difficult aspects of international criminal law to understand and apply correctly. This difficulty is compounded by the inconsistent and confusing manner in which the chambers of the *ad hoc* Tribunals have treated these crimes, in particular persecution as a crime against humanity.[46] In our view, persecution as a crime against humanity is not a single undifferentiated crime, but rather a convenient label that is applied to a cluster of underlying offences that share those distinguishing characteristics. In order to determine whether an accused charged with responsibility for 'rape as a form of persecution as a crime against humanity' may be convicted, a trial chamber must first determine whether the crime occurred; in order to do that, it must evaluate the elements of each component of the crime, that is, the elements of the underlying offence (in this example, rape), the specific requirements for persecution, and the general requirements for crimes against humanity. It is a daunting and time-consuming task, but it is one that must be executed assiduously, or an accused could be unfairly punished, or a fundamental breach of international law go unrecognised.

As mentioned above, the fourth component to an international crime is the form of responsibility, which describes the manner and extent of an individual's participation in the realisation of the crime. Before they may convict an accused of a crime under international law, the courts and tribunals discussed in this series must combine the elements of the underlying offence, the general requirements for the charged category of crimes, any specific requirements for particular crimes, and the elements of the charged form or forms of responsibility. For example, in order to conclude that an accused aided and abetted the commission of murder as a form of

[44] See Chapter 2, sections 2.2.3.8.1, 2.2.3.9.1.

[45] See Chapter 2, sections 2.2.2, 2.2.3.8.1; see also Annex, section 2.9.b. As explained in Chapter 2, the jurisprudence is not very clear on whether the victim must actually be a member of a group defined by one of these characteristics, or whether the subjective belief of the physical perpetrator or other relevant actor is sufficient. See Chapter 2, text accompanying notes 408–415.

[46] See Chapter 5, section 5.2.4.1.

persecution as a crime against humanity,[47] a trial chamber must find that (1) murder was committed, that is, that the death of an individual (the 'victim') was caused by the conduct of another person (the 'physical perpetrator' or 'killer'), who acted with intent to kill or intent to harm with acceptance of the reasonable likelihood of death; (2) the murder was part of a widespread or systematic attack directed at a predominantly civilian population, and either the killer or another relevant actor knew that it was a part of that attack; (3) the victim was targeted on the basis of his or her of political, racial, or religious identity; and (4) the accused was aware of the essential elements of the crime, including the persecutory elements, and intentionally lent practical assistance, encouragement, or moral support to the killer, with knowledge or awareness that it would have a substantial effect on the commission of the murder.[48] As increasingly higher-ranking accused are charged and tried in international criminal proceedings, international courts and tribunals will have to grapple directly with the question of which elements of crimes must be fulfilled by the accused in front of them, and which may be satisfied by the conduct of the physical perpetrator, an intermediate civilian superior or military commander, or another relevant actor.[49] The annex to this volume, which combines the elements of the forms of responsibility and the elements of the crimes, will specify which elements must be satisfied by an accused in order to hold him responsible for a particular crime under a particular form of responsibility.

Notwithstanding – or perhaps because of – the completion strategies at the two *ad hoc* Tribunals,[50] their chambers remain extremely active, releasing interlocutory decisions and judgements relevant to the core crimes at least once a month. In addition, the newer courts and tribunals have begun to, or will soon, produce relevant jurisprudence and judgements. As a consequence, readers should note that this analysis is current as of 1 December 2007.

[47] The elements of the various components of the crime listed in this sentence generally follow the jurisprudence of the *ad hoc* Tribunals. See Chapter 2, sections 2.2.2, 2.2.3.1, 2.2.3.8.1; see also Annex, section 5.2.5. There are minor variations in the definitions, both within the Tribunals and in the instruments and case law of the other courts and tribunals discussed in this series.

[48] See generally Boas, Bischoff, and Reid, *supra* note 11, pp. 303–327.

[49] See Chapter 2, section 2.2.2.1; Chapter 3, section 3.2.1.1.

[50] See Security Council Resolution 1534, UN Doc. S/RES/1534 (2004), 26 March 2004, p. 2, para. 5; Security Council Resolution 1503 UN Doc. S/RES/1503 (2003), 28 August 2003, pp. 1–2.

2

Crimes against humanity

A crime against humanity is one of several specific offences[1] – such as murder, extermination, deportation, or rape – committed as part of a widespread or systematic attack on a civilian population,[2] and at least one of the relevant actors involved in the commission of the crime must know that the offence forms part of such an attack.[3] It is these circumstances and knowledge which elevate an otherwise 'ordinary' offence to the level of an international crime. This category of crimes, first enunciated by the post-Second World War tribunals, but having roots in treaties and state practice from earlier in the twentieth century, is distinguished from war crimes by three principal characteristics: the context in which the crime occurs, which under customary international law need not be during or connected to armed conflict; the scale of the criminal conduct, which cannot be isolated but must necessarily form part of a broader attack; and who may be considered a victim of the crime – according to most authorities, only civilians. Unlike other international crimes, the elements and application of crimes against humanity have evolved in a

[1] For a number of historical reasons described below, there is no single, authoritative definition of crimes against humanity. The relevant provisions in the statutes of the various international and internationalised courts and tribunals consequently vary from one another in some important respects. The most commonly listed underlying offences are those first enunciated in the Charter of the International Military Tribunal at Nuremberg: murder, extermination, enslavement, deportation, persecution, and other inhumane acts. See Agreement for the Prosecution and Punishment of Major War Criminals of the European Axis, and Establishing the Charter of the International Military Tribunal, Annex, 8 August 1945 ('IMT Charter'), 82 UNTS 279, Art. 6(c).

[2] By its nature or consequences, the act or omission constituting the underlying offence must objectively be part of the attack. See *infra* section 2.2.2.5 (discussing this general requirement). The attack must be widespread or systematic, but need not be both. See *infra* section 2.2.2.4 (discussing this general requirement). The population need only be *predominantly* civilian. See *infra* section 2.2.2.3.2 (discussing this general requirement).

[3] The question of who, among the potentially large pool of relevant actors involved in the commission of crimes against humanity, must have knowledge of the attack is complicated and is informed by the law on the forms of responsibility. This question is discussed below in section 2.2.2.1. For the requirement of knowledge that the offence forms part of the attack, see *infra* section 2.2.2.6.

convoluted and confusing manner, rendering their definition complex and at times difficult to understand.

These complexities derive from the delicate legal birth of this crime in the work of the International Military Tribunal at Nuremberg (IMT), and its less-than-uniform development thereafter. The recent work of the *ad hoc* Tribunals has contributed enormously to solidifying of the content and meaning of crimes against humanity, but this work has also given rise to other vexing questions. Perhaps the most salient of these is who, among the potentially very large pool of persons involved in bringing to fruition a crime against humanity, must engage in the conduct that forms part of the attack on a civilian population, and who must have knowledge that such conduct forms part of the larger attack. Is it the accused whose conduct must form part of the attack, or the physical perpetrator acting at his behest, or another relevant actor involved in the commission of the crime? Is it the accused, the physical perpetrator, or someone else who must have knowledge that such conduct forms part of the larger attack? Unfortunately, most chambers of the Tribunals, inspired by older jurisprudence not drawing the distinction between an accused and a physical perpetrator, have failed to answer these critical questions clearly and coherently. We will propose in this chapter a clarification of the definition of crimes against humanity that takes account not only of the simple case of a perpetrator-accused, but also those of high-ranking accused far removed from the perpetration of offences on the ground.[4]

Crimes against humanity are critically important because they are usually regarded as the main weapon in the arsenal of international prosecutors dealing with massive criminal activity. They are certainly the most commonly charged crime in the indictments of the International Criminal Tribunal for the former Yugoslavia (ICTY), and appear in most indictments issued by the International Criminal Tribunal for Rwanda (ICTR), the International Criminal Court (ICC), and the internationalised tribunals. Indeed, in 1999 William Fenrick, then a key legal advisor in the ICTY Office of the Prosecutor, commented that the Office 'ha[s] used crimes against humanity charges whenever it has been practicable to do so, including in connection with combat incidents'.[5] One reason for the ubiquity of crimes against humanity charges is that their elements are generally easier to prove than those of genocide, a point well illustrated by the sensible decision of former ICTY Prosecutor Louise Arbour to charge Slobodan Milošević with crimes against

[4] See *infra* section 2.2.2.1.

[5] William J. Fenrick, 'Should Crimes Against Humanity Replace War Crimes?', (1999) 37 *Columbia Journal of Transnational Law* 767, 785 ('Fenrick, "Replace War Crimes"'). See also William J. Fenrick, 'The Crime Against Humanity of Persecution in the Jurisprudence of the ICTY', (2001) 32 *Netherlands Yearbook of International Law* 89, 90 ('Just as genocide has become the offence which represents what happened in Rwanda during 1994 so the crime against humanity of persecution has come to typify what happened in the territory of the former Yugoslavia.').

humanity, and not genocide, in respect of alleged criminal conduct perpetrated by Yugoslav forces in Kosovo. Another reason is that, in all international and internationalised courts and tribunals except the ICTY, crimes against humanity, unlike war crimes, do not require proof of the existence of an armed conflict.[6]

Section 2.1 discusses the historical evolution of crimes against humanity, from their conception in the early twentieth century to their inclusion in the IMT Charter and the jurisdiction of other post-Second World War tribunals; their incremental development in the post-war era – including through the work of the International Law Commission (ILC) and a handful of domestic prosecutions; and their inclusion in the jurisdiction of the ICTY and ICTR in the 1990s. Section 2.2 then considers the substantial development of crimes against humanity in the case law of the ICTY and ICTR, setting out and analysing the elements of this category of crimes and suggesting ways to clarify the applicable law. Finally, the treatment of crimes against humanity in the ICC and in various internationalised criminal tribunals – including the Special Court for Sierra Leone (SCSL), the Special Panels for Serious Crimes in East Timor (SPSC), the Extraordinary Chambers in the Courts of Cambodia (ECCC), and the Supreme Iraqi Criminal Tribunal (SICT)[7] – are considered in Section 2.3.

2.1 Evolution of crimes against humanity

2.1.1 Development through the Second World War

It is often said that crimes against humanity are as old as humanity itself.[8] The Martens Clause, which appeared in the preamble to the 1899 Hague Convention II and the 1907 Hague Convention IV and in many key international humanitarian law treaties thereafter,[9] probably stands as the earliest identifiable legal foundation for

[6] For both of these reasons it is anticipated that the bulk of the work of the ECCC will concern crimes against humanity, and not genocide or war crimes, even though these latter crimes are also in the Chambers' jurisdiction. See *infra* text accompanying notes 655–658.

[7] Also known as the Iraqi High Tribunal (IHT). See Chapter 1, note 2 (discussing the different English translations of the Tribunal's name).

[8] See, e.g., Jean Graven, 'Les crimes contre l'humanité', (1950) 76 *Recueil des Cours* 427, 433. See also Beth van Schaack, 'The Definition of Crimes Against Humanity: Resolving the Incoherence', (1999) 37 *Columbia Journal of Transnational Law* 787, 789; Steven R. Ratner and Jason S. Abrams, *Accountability for Human Rights Atrocities in International Law: Beyond the Nuremberg Legacy* (2nd edn 2001), p. 46.

[9] See, e.g., Hague Convention (II) with Respect to the Laws and Customs of War on Land and Its Annex: Regulations Concerning the Laws and Customs of War on Land, 22 July 1899, entered into force 4 September 1900, 26 *Martens Nouveau Recueil* (ser. 2) 949, 187 Consol. T.S. 429 ('1899 Hague Convention II'), preambular para. 9; Hague Convention (IV) Respecting the Laws and Customs of War on Land and Its Annex: Regulation Concerning the Laws and Customs of War on Land, 18 October 1907, entered into force 26 January 1910, 3 *Martens Nouveau Recueil* (ser. 3) 461, 187 Consol. T.S. 227, preambular para. 8; Geneva Convention IV Relative to the Protection of Civilian Persons in Time of War, 12 August 1949, entered into force 21 October 1950, 75 UNTS 287 ('Geneva Convention IV'), Art. 158; Protocol I Additional to the Geneva Conventions of 12 August 1949, and Relating to the Protection of Victims of International Armed Conflicts, 12 December 1977, entered into force 7 December 1978, 1125 UNTS 3 ('Additional Protocol I'), Art. 1(2); Protocol II Additional to the Geneva

crimes against humanity.[10] In relevant part, that clause states that 'populations and belligerents remain under the protection and empire of the principles of international law, as they result from the usages established between civilized nations, from the *laws of humanity* and the requirements of the public conscience'.[11]

The notion of an international crime against humanity appears to have been rooted in the developing idea that individual rights warranted protection outside (and more importantly, on account of) the state structure – particularly in the obvious circumstances of a state's massive violation of the human rights of a group or groups of its own citizens.[12] Although 1915 is generally considered to be the first time that the term 'crimes against humanity' was used in the context we now recognise as giving rise to individual criminal responsibility under international law, Dianne Orentlicher claims that the term first appeared in the late nineteenth century when an American lawyer, historian, and minister, George W. Williams, commented that King Leopold's Belgium was, in his view, guilty of 'crimes against humanity' for atrocities committed in the Congo.[13] M. Cherif Bassiouni traces the roots of the crime to sources often used also to refer to the development of the laws of war, reaching as far back as the fifth-century B.C. Chinese scholar Sun Tzu.[14] For his part, Tristan Gilbertson argues that the evolution of specific provisions for the protection of civilians in the context of developing war crimes treaties in the nineteenth and early twentieth centuries suggests that 'moral'

Conventions of 12 August 1949, and Relating to the Protection of Victims of Non-International Armed Conflicts, 12 December 1977, entered into force 7 December 1978, 1125 UNTS 609 ('Additional Protocol II'), preambular para. 4. For a discussion about the Martens Clause and its role in international law, see generally, J. B. Scott (ed.), *The Hague Conventions and Declarations of 1899 and 1907* (1915), p. 101; Christopher Greenwood, 'Historical Developments and Legal Basis', in Dieter Fleck (ed.), *The Handbook of Humanitarian Law in Armed Conflicts* (1995), pp. 28–29; Theodor Meron, 'Francis Lieber's Code and Principles of Humanity', (1997) 36 *Columbia Journal of Transnational Law* 269; Antonio Cassese, 'The Martens Clause: Half a Loaf or Simply Pie in the Sky?', (2000) 11 *European Journal of International Law* 187; Dianne F. Orentlicher, 'The Law of Universal Conscience: Genocide and Crimes Against Humanity', paper presented at the conference Genocide and Crimes Against Humanity: Early Warning and Prevention on 9 December 1998, available at www.ushmm.org/conscience/analysis/details/1998-12-09/orentlicher.pdf.

10 See M. Cherif Bassiouni, 'Crimes Against Humanity', in M. Cherif Bassiouni, *International Criminal Law* (2d edn 1998), p. 522.

11 1899 Hague Convention II, *supra* note 9, preambular para. 9.

12 For a discussion of this proposition and the evolution of crimes against humanity and their international prosecution, see Geoffrey Robertson, *Crimes Against Humanity: The Struggle for Global Justice* (3rd edn 2006) (especially ch. 1); Larry May, *Crimes Against Humanity: A Normative Account* (2005), pp. 11–13 (arguing that the basis for breaching the Westphalian idea of intractable state sovereignty, through the application of international criminal law, emerges where a society has failed to secure the safety of its members, thereby crossing the 'minimalist position in international law where the limit of toleration and sovereignty is reached').

13 Orentlicher, *supra* note 9, p. 8.

14 See M. Cherif Bassiouni, *Crimes Against Humanity in International Criminal Law* (2nd edn 1998), pp. 44–60. For other scholarly discussion on ancient examples of the evolution of the laws of war that incorporated concepts relating to the protection of civilians, see generally Greenwood, *supra* note 9, ch. 1; Timothy L. H. McCormack, 'From Sun Tzu to the Sixth Committee: The Evolution of an International Criminal Law Regime', in Timothy L. H. McCormack and Gerry J. Simpson (eds.), *The Law of War Crimes: National and International Approaches* (1997).

concepts relating to the laws of humanity were in fact a developing legal foundation for crimes against humanity.[15]

It is clear, however, that the modern concept of crimes against humanity emerged out of responses to the conduct of Germany and the other Central Powers during the First World War, in particular what has become known as the Armenian genocide undertaken by the Ottoman government of the time.[16] In 1915, a joint declaration was issued by the French, British, and Russian governments, condemning the massive and widespread deportation and extermination of over one million Christian Armenians by the Ottoman government, stating:

> In view of these new crimes of Turkey against humanity and civilisation, the Allied governments announce publicly to the *Sublime Porte* that they will hold personally responsible [for] these crimes all members of the Ottoman Government and those of their agents who are implicated in such massacres.[17]

The Commission on the Responsibility of the Authors of War and on Enforcement of Penalties reported to the 1919 Preliminary Peace Conference that Germany and its Allies had committed numerous acts in violation of established laws and customs of war 'and the elementary laws of humanity',[18] the latter reference being identified as offences committed by the Central Powers against their own nationals.[19] The legal and procedural difficulty that arose concerned a critical lacuna in the laws of war, which were then understood as applying only to the treatment of the armed forces or civilians of an enemy or occupied territory. This meant that any conduct concerning the treatment by a state of its own nationals was outside the established grounds for legal intervention by foreign powers, acting alone, in compact, or conceptually as the 'international community'. The fact that a collective of states – even in the exercise of a form of 'victor's justice' – began seriously to consider the idea that some construct of a 'law of humanity' might give rise to new legal rights

[15] Tristan Gilbertson, 'War Crimes', (1995) 25 *Victoria University Wellington Law Review*, pp. 315, 317–322.

[16] Chapter 3 discusses these matters in the context of the crime of genocide. See Chapter 3, text accompanying note 30.

[17] United Nations War Crimes Commission, *History of the United Nations War Crimes Commission and the Developments of the Laws of War* (1948), p. 35. See also Robert Cryer, Håkan Friman, Darryl Robinson, and Elizabeth Wilmshurst, *An Introduction to International Criminal Law and Procedure* (2007), pp. 187–188; Antonio Cassese, *International Criminal Law* (2003), p. 67; Machteld Boot, *Genocide, Crimes Against Humanity, War Crimes: Nullum Crimen Sine Lege and the Subject Matter Jurisdiction of the International Criminal Court* (2002), p. 458; Roger S. Clark, 'Crimes Against Humanity at Nuremberg', in George Ginsburgs and V. N. Kudriavtzev (eds.), *The Nuremberg Trials and International Law* (1990); Egon Schwelb, 'Crimes Against Humanity', (1946) 23 *British Yearbook of International Law* 181; van Schaack, *supra* note 8, p. 796.

[18] Commission on the Responsibility of the Authors of War and on Enforcement of Penalties, 'Report Presented to the Preliminary Peace Conference, March 29, 1919', reprinted in (1920) 95 *American Journal of International Law* 115 ('Preliminary Peace Conference Report'). See also Ratner and Abrams, *supra* note 8, pp. 46–47; William A. Schabas, *Genocide in International Law* (2000), pp. 17–20; Boot, *supra* note 17, pp. 457–458; Bassiouni, *supra* note 14, ch. 2; Schwelb, *supra* note 17, p. 181.

[19] See Boot, *supra* note 17, p. 458.

and obligations that overrode the sanctity of state sovereignty was exciting, if, as it turned out, somewhat premature.

What followed was an unsurprisingly flawed attempt to hold senior and lesser officials of these defeated states to account for this newly conceived species of crime, as well as for more traditionally accepted violations of the laws of war. The Treaty of Versailles represents the most advanced attempt to prosecute crimes committed by Germans – even providing for the establishment of an international criminal tribunal in Articles 228 to 230[20] – although by the time the Treaty's text was finalised, the American delegation had managed to exclude any reference to 'crimes against humanity'.[21] In the drafting of this and other treaties in the aftermath of the First World War, the Americans had criticised the legal merit of 'laws of humanity' as providing no basis for punishment by a court of justice, arguing instead that it was a concept of moral law and lacking 'any fixed and universal standard'.[22] Given the tentative manner in which the IMT would later prosecute 'crimes against humanity' following the Second World War,[23] it is possible that the American position was not, in the context of the time it was held, as restrictive as it seems today.

The original draft peace treaty with Turkey – the Treaty of Sèvres – was, like the Treaty of Versailles, intended in part to provide for the prosecution of those most responsible for crimes committed by the Ottoman government against the Armenian minority, crimes later recognised as 'crimes against humanity' or 'genocide'.[24] The Treaty was never signed.[25] In its place, the Treaty of Lausanne was ratified with no reference to an international tribunal or account for 'crimes against humanity and civilisation'.[26] The reason for this omission was the declaration of amnesty provided to members of the Ottoman leadership as part of the treaty negotiations.[27] Bassiouni makes an interesting observation, however, on the (no doubt unintended) legal

20 Treaty of Peace Between the Allied and Associated Powers and Germany, 28 June 1919, 226 Consol. T.S. 188 ('Treaty of Versailles'), Arts. 228–230. For a discussion of the evolution of this aspect of the treaty, see Schabas, *supra* note 18, pp. 17–22; Howard Ball, *Prosecuting War Crimes and Genocide* (1999), pp. 19–22.

21 See van Schaack, *supra* note 8, p. 797.

22 In its 'Memorandum of Reservations', the United States stated: 'The laws and principles of humanity vary with the individual.' Preliminary Peace Conference Report, *supra* note 18, p. 64. See also Schabas, *supra* note 18, pp. 17–20; Bassiouni, *supra* note 14, ch. 2.

23 See *infra* text accompanying notes 41–43.

24 See John Shamsey, '80 Years Too Late: The International Criminal Court and the 20th Century's First Genocide', (2002) 11 *Journal of Transnational Law and Policy* 327, 371; Ball, *supra* note 20, pp. 26–30; Vahakn N. Dadrian, 'The Historical and Legal Interconnections Between the Armenian Genocide and the Jewish Holocaust: From Impunity to Retributive Justice', (1998) 23 *Yale Journal of International Law* 503, 510.

25 Articles 226 to 230 of the draft Treaty of Sèvres were similar to Articles 228 to 230 of the Treaty of Versailles. Compare Treaty of Peace Between the Allied and Associated Powers and Turkey (Treaty of Sèvres), 10 August 1920, reprinted in (1921) 15 *AJIL Supp.* 179, Arts. 226–230, with Treaty of Versailles, *supra* note 20, Arts. 228–230.

26 See Treaty of Peace Between the Allied Powers and Turkey (Treaty of Lausanne), 24 July 1923, 28 LNTS 11, reprinted in (1924) 18 *AJIL Supp.* 1.

27 See Schwelb, *supra* note 17, p. 182; Bassiouni, *supra* note 14, p. 68.

consequences of the granting of amnesty by the Allies in respect of crimes committed by Turkey, including crimes against humanity:

> Such a clearly politically motivated decision did not … alter the fact that criminal responsibility had been recognized, though actual prosecution of individual offenders was subsequently foregone. Moreover, it is noteworthy that an amnesty can only be for a crime. Clearly, the fact that a crime was not prosecuted does not negate its legal existence. Indeed, the only reason to provide an amnesty was the existence of a crime whose prosecution was waived.[28]

Nonetheless, at the conclusion of the First World War the practical reality of the status of crimes against humanity was reflected in the position taken by the Americans, at least for the time being.[29] As it turned out, no international trials were ever held in the interwar period, although a few domestic prosecutions for war-related crimes were undertaken by the German, Turkish, and other defeated governments. Lamentably, these prosecutions were either politically motivated scapegoat trials or show trials, the results of which were an affront to any idea of genuine justice.[30] A chilling and well-documented reminder of the consequences of the Allies' hollow threats of international prosecution for crimes committed during the First World War came in the form of Hitler's oft-quoted briefing to his generals on the eve of the invasion of Poland in 1941: 'Who, after all, speaks of the annihilation of the Armenians?'[31]

2.1.2 Post-Second World War development

Article 6(c) of the IMT Charter was the first international instrument to define crimes against humanity as a positive crime punishable under international law.[32] Clearly, the Holocaust and other atrocities perpetrated by Germany and its allies towards their own nationals during the Second World War caused an American

[28] Bassiouni, *supra* note 14, pp. 68–69.

[29] Preliminary Peace Conference Report, *supra* note 18, p. 144. See also Ratner and Abrams, *supra* note 8, p. 47. For a discussion of the post-First World War trials and their failings, see Timothy L. H. McCormack, '*Their* Atrocities and *Our* Misdemeanours: The Reticence of States to Try Their "Own Nationals" for International Crimes', in Mark Lattimer and Philippe Sands (eds.), *Justice for Crimes Against Humanity* (2003), pp. 121–125.

[30] For a discussion of these trials, see, e.g., Robertson, *supra* note 12, pp. 243, 501; McCormack, *supra* note 14, pp. 45–48; Gerry Simpson, *Law, War and Crime* (2007), pp. 40–41.

[31] See Schabas, *supra* note 18, p. 1 n. 2 (quoting Hitler). The genocide of the Armenians has been called 'a terrible harbinger of worse things to come'. Jay Winter and Blaine Baggett, *The Great War and the Shaping of the 20th Century* (1996), cited in Ball, *supra* note 20, p. 30.

[32] See Bassiouni, *supra* note 10, p. 521; Antonio Cassese, 'Crimes Against Humanity', in Antonio Cassese, Paola Gaeta, and John R. W. D. Jones (eds.), *The Rome Statute of the International Criminal Court: A Commentary* (2001), vol. I, p. 353; Fenrick, 'Replace War Crimes', *supra* note 5, p. 769; Ratner and Abrams, *supra* note 8, ch. 3; Mohamed Elewa Badar, 'From the Nuremberg Charter to the Rome Statute: Defining the Elements of Crimes Against Humanity', (2004) 5 *San Diego International Law Journal* 73, 80–83.

change of heart, creating what Orentlicher describes as a 'moral impulse'.[33] The fear that accepted categories of war crimes would not capture many of the atrocities of the Nazis led to an (albeit tremulous) inclusion of crimes against humanity in Article 6 of the IMT Charter:

> The following acts, or any of them, are crimes coming within the jurisdiction of the Tribunal for which there shall be individual responsibility:
>
> ...
>
> (c) Crimes against humanity: namely, murder, extermination, enslavement, deportation, and other inhumane acts committed against any civilian population, before or during the war; or persecutions on political, racial or religious grounds in execution of or in connection with any crime within the jurisdiction of the Tribunal, whether or not in violation of the domestic law of the country where perpetrated.[34]

The language of Article 6(c) gave rise to some initial confusion. This category of crimes was clearly intended to encompass pre-war conduct ('before or during the war'), although the appearance of a semicolon after the word 'war' in the French and English versions of the Charter had the potential to create different legal requirements for what scholars have labelled 'murder-type' crimes against humanity, on one hand, and 'persecution-type' crimes against humanity, on the other. The words 'in execution of or in connection with any crime within the jurisdiction of the Tribunal' following reference to persecutions indicated that, for such crimes to be punishable, they had to be tied materially to a war-related crime – that is, either war crimes or crimes against peace (aggression), the other two crimes in the IMT Charter. The semicolon, on one reading, had the effect of rendering the murder-type crimes against humanity free of any requirement that there be a connection with the war[35] – an approach initially proposed by the French and apparently rejected.[36] However, the Allies clearly did not intend to abolish this 'war nexus' or 'armed

[33] Orentlicher, *supra* note 9, p. 9. American concerns, apparently based on the principle of legality, gave rise (over French resistance) to the 'war nexus' or 'armed conflict' requirement contained in the final version of Article 6(c) of the IMT Charter. Van Schaack, *supra* note 8, pp. 798–801. See also *infra* note 55 (discussing the war nexus in the ICTY Statute, and its absence from the statutes of other tribunals); text accompanying notes 38–43 (IMT armed conflict requirement); text accompanying notes 44–47 (Control Council Law No. 10 absence of armed conflict requirement); text accompanying notes 479–482 (ICC absence of armed conflict requirement); text accompanying note 559 (SCSL absence of armed conflict requirement).

[34] IMT Charter, *supra* note 1, Art. 6(c). While the International Military Tribunal for the Far East indicted twenty-five Japanese leaders for war crimes and crimes against humanity, only war crimes were addressed in the judgement. See Ken Roberts, 'Striving for Definition: The Law of Persecution from Its Origins to the ICTY', in Hirad Abtahi and Gideon Boas, *The Dynamics of International Criminal Justice: Essays in Honour of Sir Richard May* (2006), pp. 263–264; Robert Cryer, *Prosecuting International Crimes: Selectivity and the International Criminal Law Regime* (2005), p. 249.

[35] Roberts, *supra* note 34, p. 263; Bassiouni, *supra* note 14, p. 25.

[36] For a discussion of the drafting and correction of Article 6(c), see G. I. A. D. Draper, 'The Modern Pattern of War Criminality', (1976) 6 *Israel Yearbook of Human Rights* 19, 26; Clark, *supra* note 17, p. 192; van Schaack, *supra* note 8, pp. 801–803.

conflict' requirement in relation to murder-type crimes against humanity, and by the time of the Berlin Protocol of 6 October 1945, any confusion about the meaning of Article 6(c) of the IMT Charter was resolved by the insertion of a comma in place of the semicolon.[37]

The requirement that crimes against humanity be committed 'in execution of or in connection with' war crimes or crimes against peace essentially extinguished any genuine avenue for the IMT to convict for crimes committed before the war, unless those pre-war crimes were intimately linked with the waging, or conduct, of the war effort.[38] The nexus to an armed conflict was apparently considered necessary by the drafters of the IMT Charter – and, as emerges from the judgement, the IMT itself – as required 'to justify the extension of international jurisdiction to what would otherwise be acts within the domestic jurisdiction of a state'.[39] As Orentlicher puts it, the armed conflict requirement 'provided the principal legal rationalization for what would otherwise be an extreme assault on the citadel of state sovereignty'.[40] This concern not to – or at least not appear to – tread on state sovereignty permeated the Tribunal's decision-making in respect of crimes against humanity, a reluctance that no doubt resonated from the American position on the matter during and immediately after the First World War. While the IMT tried twenty-two senior German officials and convicted nineteen of them, only two – Julius Streicher and Baldur von Schirach – were convicted of crimes against humanity, and only in connection with the commission of war crimes.[41] On one view, clearly expressed later by the French judge at Nuremberg, Donnedieu de Varbres,[42] the IMT applied crimes against humanity ostensibly as 'a subsidiary or accessory to the traditional types of war crimes'.[43]

Shortly after the war, the Allied Powers enacted Control Council Law No. 10, which provided for the prosecution of lesser Nazi officials by military tribunals of the individual victorious states. Article II(c) of the Law removed any armed conflict

[37] See Report of Robert H. Jackson, United States Representative to the International Conference on Military Tribunals (1945), vol. 22, doc. IV, cited in van Schaack, *supra* note 8, pp. 798, 801.

[38] See Schwelb, *supra* note 17, p. 207; Cassese, *supra* note 17, p. 69.

[39] van Schaack, *supra* note 8, p. 791. [40] Orentlicher, *supra* note 9, p. 11.

[41] See *France, Union of Soviet Socialist Republics, United Kingdom, and United States v. Göring, Bormann, Dönitz, Frank, Frick, Fritzsche, Funk, Hess, Jodl, Kaltenbrunner, Keitel, von Bohlen und Halbach, Ley, von Neurath, von Papen, Raeder, von Ribbentrop, Rosenberg, Sauckel, Schacht, von Schirach, Seyss-Inquart, Speer, and Streicher*, International Military Tribunal, Judgment and Sentence, 1 October 1946, in *Trial of the Major War Criminals Before the International Military Tribunal, Nuremberg* ('Nuremberg Judgement'), vol. 1, pp. 547–549, 563–566. The reticence of the IMT in convicting accused of crimes against humanity without a nexus to either crimes against peace or war crimes is discussed at length in the literature. See, e.g., Cassese, *supra* note 17, pp. 69–74; Bassiouni, *supra* note 14, pp. 78–79; van Schaack, *supra* note 8, pp. 804–805.

[42] de Varbres later wrote that crimes against humanity also constituted war crimes, thereby not breaching the *nullum crimen sine lege* principle. See Cassese, *supra* note 17, p. 71 n. 14 (citing de Varbres).

[43] Schwelb, *supra* note 17, p. 207 (quoting de Varbres).

requirement from the definition of crimes against humanity.[44] However, despite the apparent opening of the door to the prosecution of crimes against humanity committed in circumstances entirely unrelated to the commission of war crimes or crimes against peace, subsequent trials under the Law – with a few exceptions – consistently maintained the armed conflict requirement.[45] Antonio Cassese explains this diffidence on the part of the IMT and subsequent military tribunals as a tacit acknowledgement that what was being applied here was new law. While these tribunals dismissed defence arguments that crimes against humanity constituted *ex post facto* criminal law, preferring to characterise it as a crystallisation or codification of a nascent rule of international law,[46] Cassese argues: 'It seems more correct to contend that the provision constituted *new* law. This explains both the limitations to which the new notion was subjected … and the extreme caution and indeed reticence of the IMT.'[47]

[44] Control Council Law No. 10, Punishment of Persons Guilty of War Crimes, Crimes Against Peace and Against Humanity, *Trials of War Criminals Before the Nuernberg Military Tribunals Under Control Council Law No. 10*, (1997 Hein ed.), vol. I, pp. xvi–xix. Control Council Law No 10 was issued by the Allied Control Council on 20 December 1945, and empowered any of the occupying authorities to try suspected war criminals in their respective occupation zones. Article II(c) of the Law defines crimes against humanity as follows:

> Atrocities and offences, including but not limited to murder, extermination, enslavement, deportation, imprisonment, torture, rape, or other inhumane acts committed against any civilian population, or persecutions on political, racial or religious grounds whether or not in violation of the domestic laws of the country where perpetrated.

Absent from this text is the IMT formulation's explicit requirement of a connection between crimes against humanity and crimes against peace or war crimes. It added the term 'atrocities and offences', inserted the broad reference to underlying offences as 'including but not limited to' the specified acts, and specifically included the offences of 'imprisonment' and 'rape'. Bassiouni asserts that these offences were already encompassed in the IMT Charter by 'other inhumane acts'. See Bassiouni, *supra* note 10, pp. 564–565 (also arguing that removal of the armed conflict requirement strains, to a greater degree than the IMT Charter, the principle of legality, but that this might be cured by viewing Control Council Law No. 10 as a national, not an international, instrument).

[45] The overwhelming majority of the post-IMT Control Council Law No. 10 judgements required the link to be made. See, e.g., *United States* v. *Flick, Steinbrinck, Weiss, Burkart, Kaletsch, and Terberger*, in *Trials of War Criminals Before the Nuernberg Military Tribunals Under Control Council Law No. 10* (1950) ('*Flick* case'), vol. 6, p. 1194; *United States v. Karl Brandt, Becker-Freyseng, Beiglböck, Blome, Brack, Rudolf Brandt, Fischer, Gebhardt, Genzken, Handloser, Hoven, Mrugowsky, Oberheuser, Pokorny, Poppendick, Rombert, Rose, Rostick, Ruff, Schäfer, Schröder, Sievers, and Weltz*, in *Trials of War Criminals Before the Nuernberg Military Tribunals Under Control Council Law No. 10* (1950) ('*Medical* case'), vol. 2, p. 181; *United States v. Weizsäcker, Steengracht von Moyland, Keppler, Bohle. Wörmann, Ritter, von Erdmannsdorf, Veesenmayer, Lammers, Stuckart, Darré, Meissner, Dietrich, Berger, Schellenberg, von Krosigk, Puhl, Raschke, Kömer, Pleiger, and Kehrl*, in *Trials of War Criminals Before the Nuernberg Military Tribunals Under Control Council Law No. 10* (1950) ('*Ministries* case'), vol. 14, p. 322. For a detailed discussion of the cases and verdicts in respect of this issue, see van Schaack, *supra* note 8, pp. 807–819; Fenrick, 'Replace War Crimes', *supra* note 5, p. 775; Cassese, *supra* note 17, pp. 70–71; Cryer, Friman, Robinson, and Wilmshurst, *supra* note 17, p. 191; Matthew Lippman, 'Crimes Against Humanity', (1997) 17 *Boston College Third World Law Journal* 171, 270.

[46] See, e.g., Nuremberg Judgement, *supra* note 41, pp. 497–498; *Flick* case, *supra* note 45, pp. 36–39.

[47] See Cassese, *supra* note 17, p. 70 (emphasis in original). Cassese has also noted that the creation of *ex post facto* laws was not, at that time, strictly prohibited in international law. See *ibid.*, pp. 71–72. In the *Flick* and *Ministries* cases, however, the Tribunals maintained the armed conflict requirement on the basis of the *nullum crimen sine lege* principle. See Gilbertson, *supra* note 15, pp. 323–327. There is much scholarly debate about whether the inclusion of crimes against humanity in the Charters of the IMT and Tokyo Tribunal – as well as Control Council Law No. 10, which omitted the armed conflict requirement – violated the principle of legality. See, e.g., Bassiouni, *supra* note 14, ch. 4; Gilbertson, *supra* note 15, p. 326 (suggesting that the IMT Charter only truly diverged from existing international law when it applied crimes against humanity to '*any* civilian population'); Cryer, *supra* note 34, p. 248 (suggesting that disquiet about the applicability of crimes against humanity in peacetime 'was more to do with a fear of allegations of *tu quoque* than fears about *nullum crimen sine lege*').

Whatever the precise contours of crimes against humanity immediately following the Second World War, and whether or not such crimes were truly established in customary international law by 1945, the IMT and subsequent post-war tribunals entrenched the notion that they were punishable under international law. Neither the IMT Charter nor Control Council Law No. 10 explicitly defined crimes against humanity as implicating mass or systematised criminality, or requiring some sort of policy on the part of government or formalised authorities. Nevertheless, the United Nations War Crimes Commission reviewing these instruments in 1948 interpreted them as follows:

> Isolated offences did not fall within the notion of crimes against humanity. As a rule systematic mass action, particularly if it was authoritative, was necessary to transfer a common crime, punishable only under municipal law, into a crime against humanity, which thus became also the concern of international law. Only crimes which either by their magnitude and savagery or by their large number or by the fact that a similar pattern was applied at different times and places, endangered the international community or shocked the conscience of mankind, warranted intervention by states other than that on whose territory the crimes had been committed, or whose subjects had become their victims.[48]

These important elements of crimes against humanity – which encapsulate state involvement, acquiescence or encouragement, and the requirement that these crimes be widespread or systematic – were ultimately to be the subject of significant jurisprudential and scholarly development in the fifty ensuing years.[49]

2.1.3 Developments through the ad hoc *Tribunals and beyond*

While genocide was quickly codified in the Genocide Convention of 1948,[50] and the detailed articulation of war crimes that predated the Second World War continued apace,[51] there has not been a great deal of treaty activity[52] or state

Some domestic law jurisprudence has considered this question. For example, the Australian High Court has held, by majority, that crimes against humanity existed in customary international law by 1945. See *Polyukhovich* v. *Commonwealth*, (1991) 101 ALR 545, 661–662. The Canadian Supreme Court has held, by majority, that crimes against humanity were retroactively but appropriately criminalised in the IMT Charter. See *Regina* v. *Finta*, (1994) 104 ILR 285, 336–337, 402.

48 United Nations War Crimes Commission, *supra* note 17, p. 178.

49 See *infra* note 55 (discussing the armed conflict requirement in the various international and internationalised courts and tribunals); note 59 (discussing the requirement of a state or organisational policy); note 60 (discussing the requirement of a discriminatory attack for all crimes against humanity).

50 See Convention on the Prevention and Punishment of the Crime of Genocide, 9 December 1948, entered into force 12 January 1951, 78 UNTS 277 ('Genocide Convention'), Arts. II–III. See also Chapter 3, section 3.1.2 (extensive discussion of the Genocide Convention).

51 See especially Geneva Convention for the Amelioration of the Condition of the Wounded and Sick in Armed Forces in the Field, 12 August 1949, entered into force 21 October 1950, 75 UNTS 31; Geneva Convention for the Amelioration of the Condition of Wounded, Sick and Shipwrecked Members of Armed Forces at Sea, 12 August 1949, entered into force 21 October 1950, 75 UNTS 85; Geneva Convention Relative to the Treatment of Prisoners of War, 12 August 1949, entered into force 21 October 1950, 75 UNTS 135 ('Geneva Convention III'); Geneva Convention IV, *supra* note 9; Additional Protocol I, *supra* note 9; Additional Protocol II, *supra* note 9.

52 See *infra* notes 54–55 (citing treaties dealing in some way with crimes against humanity).

practice[53] with respect to crimes against humanity since the Second World War, and no specific convention on crimes against humanity has ever been developed.[54] Nevertheless, in keeping with the rapid abandonment of the IMT Charter's armed conflict requirement by the drafters of Control Council Law No. 10, it is now widely acknowledged that, in customary international law, crimes against humanity can be committed in times of peace and war, and that custom does not require that such crimes have a nexus to an armed conflict.[55]

[53] There have been some domestic prosecutions for crimes against humanity that have helped confirm their existence, their customary status, and the potential for basing domestic prosecutions for them on universal jurisdiction. For example, Bassiouni notes that in Germany between 1947 and 1990, some 60,000 prosecutions took place, as well as some 28,000 in Austria. Moreover, a limited number of prosecutions have been reported in other European countries, Canada, Israel, and Australia. See *ibid.*, pp. 584–586; see also *infra* text accompanying notes 70–72 (discussing universal jurisdiction to prosecute crimes against humanity); *supra* note 47 (citing crimes against humanity cases in Canada and Australia); Sharon A. Williams, 'Laudable Principles Lacking Application: The Prosecution of War Criminals in Canada', in McCormack and Simpson (eds.), *supra* note 14, pp. 151–170; Gillian Triggs, 'Australia's War Crimes Trials: All Pity Choked', in McCormack and Simpson (eds.), *supra* note 14, pp. 124–149; *Attorney-General of the Government of Israel* v. *Eichmann*, District Court of Jerusalem, 12 December 1961, (1961) 36 ILM 5; Jonathan M. Wenig, 'Enforcing the Lessons of History: Israel Judges the Holocaust', in McCormack and Simpson (eds.), *supra* note 14, pp. 103–122; *Fédération Nationale des Déportés et Internés Résistants et Patriotes et autres* v. *Barbie*, 1985 Bull. Crim. No. 407, 1053, (1990) 78 ILR 124; Benedetto Conforti, *International Law and the Role of Domestic Legal Systems* (1993); Richard A. Falk, *The Role of Domestic Courts in the International Legal Order* (1964).

[54] See Bassiouni, *supra* note 10, p. 574 (listing post-IMT Charter treaties dealing in some way with crimes against humanity); M. Cherif Bassiouni, 'Crimes Against Humanity: The Need for a Specialised Convention', (1994) 31 *Columbia Journal of Transnational Law* 457. Nevertheless, it should be noted that, while no treaty (with the important exception of the Rome Statute of the ICC) specifically proscribes crimes against humanity, a number of treaties contain penal provisions proscribing conduct that embodies prohibitions contained in some definitions of crimes against humanity. See, e.g., International Convention on the Suppression and Punishment of the Crime of Apartheid, General Assembly Resolution 3068 (XXVIII) (1973), 30 November 1973, entered into force 18 July 1976, 1015 UNTS 243 ('Apartheid Convention'), Art. II; Inter-American Convention on Forced Disappearance of Persons, 9 June 1994, entered into force 28 March 1996, reprinted in (1994) 33 *International Legal Materials* 1529 (1994) ('Forced Disappearance Convention'), Art. II. Apartheid and enforced disappearance as crimes against humanity in the jurisdiction of the ICC are discussed at notes 510–518, *infra*.

[55] See, e.g., Convention on the Non-Applicability of Statutory Limitations to War Crimes and Crimes Against Humanity, 26 November 1968, entered into force 11 November 1970, 754 UNTS 73 ('Convention on Non-Applicability of Statutory Limitations'), Art. I(b) (no statute of limitations for '[c]rimes against humanity *whether committed in time of war or in time of peace*') (emphasis added); Draft Code of Crimes Against the Peace and Security of Mankind (1996), in Report of the International Law Commission on the Work of Its Forty-eighth Session, UN Doc. A/51/10 (1996) ('1996 ILC Draft Code with Commentaries'), p. 48; Cassese, *supra* note 17, p. 73 (citing national codifications of crimes against humanity lacking the armed conflict requirement); Dianne Orentlicher, 'Settling Accounts: The Duty to Prosecute Human Rights Violations of a Prior Regime', (1991) 100 *Yale Law Journal* 2537, 2589–2591. Interestingly, some delegates during the preparatory work for the Rome Statute of the ICC tried to resuscitate the armed conflict requirement, but this effort failed. See *infra* text accompanying notes 479–482. The armed conflict requirement is absent from the statutes of all other international and internationalised tribunals except the ICTY. See, e.g., *infra* text accompanying note 559 (SCSL); text accompanying note 656 (ECCC). Oddly enough, the ICTY Statute reproduces the armed conflict requirement. See Statute of the International Criminal Tribunal for the Prosecution of Persons Responsible for Serious Violations of International Humanitarian Law Committed in the Territory of the former Yugoslavia since 1991, (1993) 32 ILM 1159, as amended by Security Council Resolution 1660 of 28 February 2006 ('ICTY Statute'), Art. 5 ('The International Tribunal shall have the power to prosecute persons responsible for the following crimes *when committed in armed conflict* ...') (emphasis added). Nevertheless, even the ICTY Appeals Chamber has observed, in line with overwhelming scholarly opinion, that the armed conflict requirement had disappeared as an element of crimes against humanity by the time of the events in the former Yugoslavia, and that the armed conflict requirement is peculiar to the jurisdiction of the ICTY. See *infra* section 2.2.1.1. The Appeals Chamber in *Tadić* observed that the armed conflict requirement in the ICTY Statute was

The absence of a treaty on crimes against humanity is probably partially explained by the forty-year-long debate in the ILC on these crimes during the production and amendment of the Draft Code of Crimes Against the Peace and Security of Mankind.[56] In its first 1954 Draft Code, the ILC set out what Bassiouni describes as a 'broad generic definitional approach' to crimes against humanity, with clear 'gaps and insufficiencies'.[57] The armed conflict requirement that had existed in the IMT Charter and in an earlier draft of the Code was removed and replaced with a reference to such crimes being carried out 'under the instigation or toleration of the authorities', and motivated by 'political, social, racial, religious, or cultural grounds'.[58] Both these notions – that some sort of state or organisational involvement in a crime against humanity is required,[59] and that all crimes against

inconsistent with customary international law. See *Prosecutor* v. *Tadić*, Decision on Defence Motion for Interlocutory Appeal on Jurisdiction, Case No. IT-94-1-AR72, 2 October 1995 ('*Tadić* Jurisdiction Appeal Decision'), para. 251. Later, in the *Šešelj* case, the Appeals Chamber explained that the Security Council had included this additional jurisdictional requirement because it intended to limit the Tribunal's jurisdiction to those crimes committed in the context of armed conflict in the former Yugoslavia. See *Prosecutor* v. *Šešelj*, Decision on the Interlocutory Appeal Concerning Jurisdiction, Case No. IT-03-67-AR72.1, 31 August 2004 ('*Šešelj* Jurisdiction Appeal Decision'), para. 13. Schabas argues, however, that this interpretation reads too much into the sparse record of the intent of the Security Council, and that it is more likely that the Council adhered to the Secretary-General's apparent view that prosecuting crimes against humanity without the armed conflict connection would violate the principle of *nullum crimen sine lege*. See William A. Schabas, *The UN International Criminal Tribunals: The Former Yugoslavia, Rwanda and Sierra Leone* (2006), pp. 187–188. Perhaps even more strikingly, a trial panel of the East Timor SPSC held that a connection to an armed conflict must be proven for crimes against humanity, even though such a requirement does not appear in the constitutive document of the SPSC. See *infra* text accompanying notes 626–630 (discussing and criticising this holding). For more on the armed conflict requirement, see Guénaël Mettraux, *International Crimes and the Ad Hoc Tribunals* (2005), pp. 148–152; Cryer, *supra* note 34, pp. 250–251; Larry D. Johnson, 'Ten Years Later: Reflections on the Drafting', (2004) 2 *Journal of International Criminal Justice* 368, 371–372; Virginia Morris and Michael Scharf, *An Insider's Guide to the International Criminal Tribunal for the former Yugoslavia* (1995), p. 239; Alexander Zahar and Göran Sluiter, *International Criminal Law: A Critical Introduction* (2007), pp. 204–205.

56 The General Assembly voted to create the ILC in 1947, and tasked it with formulating principles of international law as recognised in the IMT Charter and Judgement. See GA Res. 174, UN Doc. A/RES/174(II) (1947); GA Res. 177, UN Doc. A/RES/177(II) (1947).

57 Bassiouni, *supra* note 14, p. 185. See also Draft Code of Offences Against the Peace and Security of Mankind (1954), in Report of the International Law Commission on the Work of Its Sixth Session, UN Doc. A/2963 (1954) ('1954 ILC Draft Code'), Art. 2(11):

> The following acts are offences against the peace and security of mankind: … Inhuman acts such as murder, extermination, enslavement, deportation or persecutions, committed against any civilian population on social, political, racial, religious or cultural grounds by the authorities of a State or by private individuals acting at the instigation or with the toleration of such authorities.

58 1954 ILC Draft Code, *supra* note 57, Art. 2(11). For a discussion of the ILC drafting process, see Bassiouni, *supra* note 14, ch. 5; van Schaack, *supra* note 8, pp. 821–826. For more on the armed conflict requirement, see *supra* note 55.

59 The Rome Statute of the ICC and the ICC Elements of Crimes require that the widespread or systematic attack be committed pursuant to a state or organisational policy. Rome Statute of the International Criminal Court, 17 July 1998, entered into force 1 July 2002, UN Doc. A/CONF. 183/9 (1998) ('Rome Statute'), Art. 7(1). See also *infra* text accompanying notes 493–496, 532–534 (discussing the difficult negotiations leading up to the inclusion of a policy requirement in the Rome Statute and the Elements of Crimes). The Statute of the SICT, following the lead of the Rome Statute, also requires such a policy, and a trial chamber of that Tribunal has confirmed this requirement. See *infra* text accompanying note 692. Even though no such requirement exists in the SPSC's constitutive document, an SPSC trial panel has likewise held that such a requirement exists. See *infra* text accompanying notes 590–592 (Rome Statute's formulation followed in SPSC, with the exception of the definition containing the policy requirement); text accompanying note 621 (trial panel holding that policy

humanity must be committed with discriminatory intent[60] – would make their way into the statutes of certain of the later international and internationalised courts and tribunals. Work on the Draft Code virtually ceased thereafter pending the determination of a definition of the crime of aggression, and did not resume in earnest until the 1980s.[61]

The final Draft Code was concluded in 1996.[62] Changes made during the drafting of earlier versions included explicit reference to the application of crimes against humanity in times of war and peace, to the violation of human rights as a constitutive element of the crime, and to the crime being committed 'systematically' and in respect of a 'segment of the population'.[63] Although in many ways the 1996 Draft Code's definition of crimes against humanity resembles that of the *ad hoc* Tribunals as developed in their jurisprudence – most notably in that the punishable conduct must be committed, as the ILC draft puts it, 'in a systematic manner or on a large

requirement exists). By contrast, the *ad hoc* Tribunals and the SCSL have unequivocally rejected the notion of a policy requirement. See *infra* text accompanying notes 180–181 (rejection in the ICTY and ICTR); text accompanying notes 559–560 (rejection in the SCSL).

60 The ICTR Statute requires that the widespread or systematic attack be committed 'on national, political, ethnic, racial or religious grounds'. Statute of the International Criminal Tribunal for Rwanda, (1994) 33 ILM 1602, as amended by Security Council Resolution 1534 of 26 March 2004 ('ICTR Statute'), Art. 3. See also *infra* section 2.2.1.2 (discussing ICTR jurisprudence holding that this is a jurisdictional requirement unique to the ICTR). The constitutive document of the ECCC copies the ICTR crimes against humanity formulation and thus reproduces this requirement of a discriminatory attack for all crimes against humanity. See *infra* text accompanying notes 649–655 (also positing a theory why such a requirement exists uniquely in the ICTR and ECCC, the so-called 'genocide tribunals'); Chapter 6, section 6.2 (discussing this theory further). No other international or internationalised court or tribunal statute contains such a requirement, and this requirement was considered and rejected at the meetings leading up to the conclusion of the Rome Statute of the ICC. See *infra* text accompanying notes 483–484 (especially note 484, listing the reasons for such rejection). According to William Schabas, the probable reason for the inclusion of this requirement in the ICTR Statute was that the Statute's drafters actually believed it to be a requirement for all crimes against humanity, and preferred to spell it out explicitly in the ICTR Statute, instead of leaving it implicit, as they considered themselves to have done in the ICTY Statute. Schabas, *supra* note 55, p. 197. Despite this assertion, the ICTR has made it clear that customary international law does not require that all crimes against humanity be committed with discriminatory intent. See *Prosecutor* v. *Akayesu*, Case No. ICTR-96-4-A, Judgement, 1 June 2001 ('*Akayesu* Appeal Judgement'), paras. 464–465.

61 Ratner and Abrams, *supra* note 8, p. 49; Robertson, *supra* note 12, pp. 43 *et seq.*

62 See 1996 ILC Draft Code with Commentaries, *supra* note 55. Article 18 of the 1996 Draft Code, on crimes against humanity, provides:

> A crime against humanity means any of the following acts, when committed in a systematic manner or on a large scale and instigated or directed by a Government or by any organization or group:
>
> (a) Murder;
> (b) Extermination;
> (c) Torture;
> (d) Enslavement;
> (e) Persecution on political, racial, religious or ethnic grounds;
> (f) Institutionalized discrimination on racial, ethnic or religious grounds involving the violation of fundamental human rights and freedoms and resulting in seriously disadvantaging a part of the population;
> (g) Arbitrary deportation or forcible transfer of population;
> (h) Arbitrary imprisonment;
> (i) Forced disappearance of persons;
> (j) Rape, enforced prostitution and other forms of sexual abuse;
> (k) Other inhumane acts which severely damage physical or mental integrity, health or human dignity, such as mutilation and severe bodily harm.

63 For a detailed discussion of the evolution of the drafts, see Bassiouni, *supra* note 14, ch. 5.

scale'[64] – there are also some important differences, some of which have been reproduced in the instruments of subsequent international and internationalised courts and tribunals.[65]

While genocide started life as a crime against humanity – albeit a particularly egregious one[66] – soon after the Second World War it took a different path in its international legal development. Genocide was codified in its own Convention in 1948[67] and, as discussed in Chapter 3, was the subject of significant jurisprudential review in the International Court of Justice (ICJ) in 1951.[68] Meanwhile crimes against humanity, as noted above, were referred to the ILC for clarification and development over the course of some forty years.[69] This differing procedural evolution resulted in a distinct customary status for the two crimes. While the prohibition of genocide is overwhelmingly viewed as a *jus cogens* norm to which universal jurisdiction attaches,[70] it is less clear whether crimes against humanity qualify for similar treatment. On one hand, there is considerable scholarly argument – and some jurisprudence of the post-Second World War tribunals, domestic courts, and the *ad hoc* Tribunals – supporting the view that crimes against humanity violate *jus cogens* norms and give rise to universal jurisdiction.[71] On the other hand, the

[64] 1996 ILC Draft Code with Commentaries, *supra* note 55, Art. 18.

[65] For example, unlike the ICTY Statute but in line with the statutes of the ICTR and all subsequent courts and tribunals, the 1996 ILC Draft Code contains no armed conflict requirement. See *supra* note 55 (discussing the armed conflict requirement, or the absence thereof, in the different courts and tribunals). Moreover, unlike the *ad hoc* Tribunals' jurisprudence, but in line with the statutes of the ICC and the SICT, the 1996 Draft Code stipulates that crimes against humanity must be 'instigated or directed by a Government or by any organization or group'. *Ibid.*; see also *supra* note 59 (discussing the policy requirement, or the absence thereof, in the different courts and tribunals). Curiously, in contrast to all the courts and tribunals, the 1996 Draft Code makes no mention of the 'systematic' or 'large scale' conduct being part of an attack directed against a civilian population. Furthermore, the Code lists a number of underlying offences not present in the *ad hoc* Statutes, but which were later included, in one form or another, in the statutes of later courts and tribunals: institutionalised discrimination (seemingly akin to apartheid), enforced prostitution and other sexual offences besides rape, enforced disappearance, and persecution committed not only on political, racial, or religious grounds, but also on ethnic grounds. See *infra* text accompanying notes 499, 508–511 (discussing ICC underlying offences); text accompanying notes 556, 564–568 (SCSL underlying offences); text accompanying note 590 (SPSC underlying offences); text accompanying notes 647–648 (ECCC underlying offences); text accompanying note 675 (SICT underlying offences).

[66] United Nations War Crimes Commission, *supra* note 17, pp. 196–97. See also Chapter 3, text accompanying notes 35–41 (discussing references made to the nascent idea of an international crime known as 'genocide' in arguments before the IMT and in the Tribunal's Judgement, as well as the judgements of the tribunals operating pursuant to Control Council Law No. 10).

[67] See Genocide Convention, *supra* note 50, Art. II. [68] See Chapter 3, text accompanying note 69.

[69] See *supra* text accompanying notes 56–65. [70] See Chapter 3, text accompanying notes 76–78.

[71] See, e.g., May, *supra* note 12, pp. 24–39 (containing a well-reasoned and in-depth account); Bassiouni, *supra* note 14, pp. 210–217, 227–242; Gilbertson, *supra* note 15, pp. 327–328. In the *Einsatzgruppen* case, the U.S. Military Tribunal evoked sentiment that crimes against humanity might be subjected to a kind of universal jurisdiction: '[T]he inalienable and fundamental rights of common man need not lack for a court ... Those who are indicted [for crimes against humanity] are answering to humanity itself, humanity which has no political boundaries and no geographical limitations.' *United States* v. *Ohlendorf, Jost, Naumann, Rasch, Schulz, Six, Blobel, Blume, Sandberger, Seibert, Steimle, Biberstein, Braune, Hänsch, Nosske, Ott, Strauch, Haussmann, Klingelhöfer, Fendler, von Radetzky, Rühl, Schubert, and Graf*, in *Trials of War Criminals Before the Nuernberg Military Tribunals Under Control Council Law No. 10* (1950), vol. 4, p. 498. Some domestic cases have also acknowledged that crimes against humanity give rise to universal jurisdiction. See, e.g., *Polyukhovich* v. *Commonwealth*, *supra* note 47, p. 661 (High Court of Australia observing that 'there appears to be general agreement that war crimes and crimes against humanity are now within the category subject to universal

ICJ's 2002 Judgement in the *Arrest Warrant* case suggests that, while crimes against humanity are no doubt prohibited under customary international law, the notion that they violate *jus cogens* norms and give rise to universal jurisdiction may at this stage be more aspirational.[72]

Three and two years respectively before the conclusion of the 1996 Draft Code, the UN Security Council enacted the ICTY and ICTR Statutes, thereby creating two largely comprehensible positive formulations of the crime.[73] Despite the inclusion of jurisdictional features that are not required by customary international law, the jurisprudence of the *ad hoc* Tribunals serves as the single richest source for the development of the legal elements of crimes against humanity. At the same time, that jurisprudence has created some confusion and inconsistencies that would benefit from reconsideration.

2.2 Elements of crimes against humanity

Article 5 of the ICTY Statute, entitled 'Crimes against humanity', grants the Tribunal jurisdiction 'to prosecute persons responsible for [certain listed] crimes when committed in armed conflict, whether international or internal in character, and directed against any civilian population'. Article 3 of the ICTR Statute does not include a requirement that the crimes be committed in an armed conflict, but provides that the Tribunal has jurisdiction over certain listed crimes 'when committed as part of a widespread or systematic attack against any civilian population on national, political, ethnic, racial or religious grounds'. Both Statutes thus go beyond the definition of crimes against humanity under customary international law by including qualifying language that imposes additional requirements: for the ICTY, it is the requirement that the crimes be committed in armed conflict; for the ICTR, it is the requirement that the attack be committed on the basis of any of the five listed grounds.

jurisdiction'); *Israel* v. *Eichmann*, (1962) 36 ILR 277, 282–283 (Israeli Supreme Court); *Demjanjuk* v. *Petrovsky*, 776 F.2d 571, 582–583 (6th Cir. 1985) (U.S. federal court of appeals). Some ICTY judgements also make vague reference to the universal character of 'international crimes', including torture, war crimes, crimes against humanity, and genocide. See, e.g., *Prosecutor* v. *Furundžija*, Case No. IT-95-17/1-T, Judgement, 10 December 1998 ('*Furundžija* Trial Judgement'), para. 56; *Prosecutor* v. *Kupreškić, Kupreškić, Kupreškić, Josipović, Papić, and Šantić*, Case No. IT-95-16-T, Judgement, 14 January 2000 ('*Kupreškić et al.* Trial Judgement'), para. 520.

72 See Case Concerning the Arrest Warrant of 11 April 2000 (*Democratic Republic of the Congo* v. *Belgium*), (2002) ICJ Rep. 3, para. 71. See also *ibid.*, Joint Separate Opinion of Judges Higgins, Kooijmans and Buergenthal, paras. 42–51 (carefully considered analysis of whether universal jurisdiction attaches to crimes against humanity). See also Robert Jennings and Arthur Watts, *Oppenheim's International Law* (9th edn 1997), p. 998 (noting that 'there are clear indications pointing to the gradual evolution' of the principle that crimes against humanity give rise to universal jurisdiction). According to the ICJ, at least, this point has not yet been reached.

73 See *infra* text accompanying notes 74 and 81 for the full text of these provisions.

2.2.1 *Requirements unique to the* ad hoc *Tribunals*

2.2.1.1 ICTY: armed conflict as a jurisdictional requirement

Article 5 of the ICTY Statute provides:

The International Tribunal shall have the power to prosecute persons responsible for the following crimes when committed in armed conflict, whether international or internal in character, and directed against any civilian population:

(a) murder;
(b) extermination;
(c) enslavement;
(d) deportation;
(e) imprisonment;
(f) torture;
(g) rape;
(h) persecutions on political, racial and religious grounds;
(i) other inhumane acts.[74]

The ICTY's armed conflict requirement for crimes against humanity is not equivalent to the requirement for war crimes that the acts be closely related to an armed conflict, which is essential to the very definition of those crimes under international humanitarian law.[75] Instead, it is a jurisdictional requirement unique to that Tribunal,[76] and is satisfied by proof of two elements: (1) there was an armed conflict, whether internal or international; and (2) the offences charged in the indictment are objectively linked, both geographically and temporally, with the armed conflict.[77] As the ICTY Appeals Chamber has explained:

[74] ICTY Statute, *supra* note 55, Art. 5.

[75] See Chapter 4, section 4.2.1.2. See also *Tadić* Jurisdiction Appeal Decision, *supra* note 55, paras. 137, 141–142 (holding that although it is 'a settled rule of customary international law that crimes against humanity do not require a connection to international armed conflict', Article 5 of the Statute does impose a jurisdictional requirement of an armed conflict) (quotation at para. 141); *Prosecutor* v. *Tadić*, Case No. IT-94-1-A, Judgement, 15 July 1999 ('*Tadić* Appeal Judgement'), para. 251 ('The armed conflict requirement is satisfied by proof that there was an armed conflict; that is all that the Statute requires, and in so doing, it requires more than does customary international law.'); *Prosecutor* v. *Kunarac, Kovač, and Vuković*, Case Nos. IT-96-23 & IT-96-23/1-A, Judgement, 12 June 2002 ('*Kunarac et al.* Appeal Judgement'), para. 83. Accord, e.g., *Prosecutor* v. *Martić*, Case No. IT-95-11-T, Judgement, 12 June 2007 ('*Martić* Trial Judgement'), para. 48; *Prosecutor* v. *Limaj, Bala, and Musliu*, Case No. IT-03–66-T, Judgement, 30 November 2005 ('*Limaj et al.* Trial Judgement'), para. 180; *Prosecutor* v. *Blagojević and Jokić*, Case No. IT-02-60-T, Judgement, 17 January 2005, ('*Blagojević and Jokić* Trial Judgement'), para. 541; *Prosecutor* v. *Kordić and Čerkez*, Case No. IT-95-14/2-T, Judgement, 26 February 2001 ('*Kordić and Čerkez* Trial Judgement'), para. 23.

[76] See *supra* note 55 (discussing different explanations for the inclusion of the armed conflict requirement).

[77] See *Prosecutor* v. *Mrkšić, Radić, and Šljivančanin*, Case No. IT-95-13/1-T, Judgement, 27 September 2007 ('*Mrkšić et al.* Trial Judgement'), paras. 431–432 (noting that 'instruments adopted after the Statute of the Tribunal … no longer require such nexus') (quotation at para. 431); *Kunarac et al.* Appeal Judgement, *supra* note 75, paras. 83, 89; *Tadić* Appeal Judgement, *supra* note 75, paras. 249, 251; *Kupreškić et al.* Trial Judgement, *supra* note 71, para. 546; *Prosecutor* v. *Tadić*, Case No. IT-94-1-T, Judgement, 14 July 1997 ('*Tadić* Trial Judgement'), para. 632.

the jurisdictional requirement of Article 5 requires the existence of an armed conflict at the time and place relevant to the indictment, but it does not mandate any material nexus between the acts [charged in the indictment] and the armed conflict. While this interpretation itself offers little guidance on the meaning of 'time and place relevant to the indictment', the Tribunal's jurisprudence on the application of Article 5 of the Statute points towards a broad interpretation. For example, there is no requirement that an attack directed against a civilian population be related to the armed conflict.[78]

The test for the existence of an armed conflict for the purposes of this jurisdictional requirement is the same as that used by the ICTY in the context of grave breaches and other violations of the laws or customs of war under Articles 2 and 3 of the Statute:[79] a resort to armed force between states; or protracted armed violence between governmental authorities and organised armed groups or between such groups within a state.[80]

2.2.1.2 ICTR: discriminatory basis as a jurisdictional requirement

Article 3 of the ICTR Statute provides:

The International Tribunal for Rwanda shall have the power to prosecute persons responsible for the following crimes when committed as part of a widespread or systematic attack against any civilian population on national, political, ethnic, racial or religious grounds:

(a) Murder;
(b) Extermination;
(c) Enslavement;
(d) Deportation;
(e) Imprisonment;
(f) Torture;
(g) Rape;
(h) Persecutions on political, racial and religious grounds;
(i) Other inhumane acts.[81]

[78] *Šešelj* Jurisdiction Appeal Decision, *supra* note 55, para. 13 (citing *Tadić* Appeal Judgement, *supra* note 75, paras. 249, 251). See also *ibid.*, para. 14 (concluding, for example, that the jurisdictional requirement is satisfied in 'situations where an armed conflict is ongoing in one state and ethnic civilians of one of the warring sides, resident in another state, become victims of a widespread and systematic attack in response to that armed conflict').

[79] See, e.g., *Prosecutor* v. *Šešelj*, Case No. IT-03-67-AR72.1, Decision on Motion for Reconsideration of the 'Decision on the Interlocutory Appeal Concerning Jurisdiction Dated 31 August 2004', 15 June 2006 ('*Šešelj* Decision on Reconsideration'), para. 24 (citing and quoting with approval the prosecution's submission that 'there is no basis for according a more restrictive scope to the term "armed conflict" in Article 5 than the one enunciated by the Appeals Chamber for Articles 2 and 3'); *Prosecutor* v. *Milošević*, Case No. IT-02-54-T, Decision on Motion for Judgement of Acquittal, 16 June 2004 ('*Milošević* Rule 98 *bis* Decision'), para. 15.

[80] See Chapter 4, section 4.2.1.1; *Kunarac et al.* Appeal Judgement, *supra* note 75, para. 56; accord *Prosecutor* v. *Brđanin*, Case No. IT-99-36-T, Judgement, 1 September 2004 ('*Brđanin* Trial Judgement'), para. 122; *Prosecutor* v. *Stakić*, Case No. IT-97-24-T, Judgement, 31 July 2003 ('*Stakić* Trial Judgement'), para. 568; cf. *Tadić* Jurisdiction Appeal Decision, *supra* note 55, para. 70 (defining armed conflict for the purposes of war crimes).

[81] ICTR Statute, *supra* note 60, Art. 3.

Unlike most of the provisions on crimes and forms of responsibility, therefore, the article in the ICTR Statute governing crimes against humanity is not identical to the corresponding article in the ICTY Statute. The ICTR provision differs in two respects: first, it corresponds more closely to the definition of the category of crimes under customary international law, by explicitly requiring that the conduct be part of a widespread or systematic attack on a civilian population; second, it replaces the ICTY's armed conflict requirement with its own additional jurisdictional criterion, that the attack has been committed on national, political, ethnic, racial or religious grounds.[82]

In the first ICTR appeal judgement on the merits, the *Akayesu* Appeals Chamber concluded that the additional requirement in the Statute did not mandate that each crime against humanity be committed with discriminatory intent, and therefore did not impermissibly depart from the established definition of the crimes in this category.[83] It found that the statutory text 'narrows the scope of the jurisdiction, [but] introduces no additional element in the legal ingredients of the crime as these are known in customary international law'.[84] Thus the ICTR jurisdictional requirement for crimes against humanity is satisfied, 'even if the accused did not have a discriminatory intent when he committed the act charged against a particular victim', if 'he nevertheless knew that his act could further a discriminatory attack against a civilian population; the attack could even be perpetrated by other persons and the accused could even object to it.'[85]

As the ICTY Appeals Chamber had concluded in *Tadić*, the *Akayesu* Appeals Chamber confirmed that specific discriminatory intent is required under customary international law, and under the *ad hoc* Statutes, only for persecution as a crime against humanity.[86] Subsequent ICTR trial judgements have confirmed that the

[82] See *supra* note 60 (discussing the explanation offered by Schabas for the inclusion of this requirement).

[83] The Appeals Chamber noted with approval the earlier decision of the ICTY Appeals Chamber in *Tadić*, in which that Chamber had concluded that neither Article 5 of the ICTY Statute nor customary international law required discriminatory intent for all crimes against humanity, only persecution. *Akayesu* Appeal Judgement, *supra* note 60, para. 461. Observing that the differences in the statutory text rendered that holding helpful, but not dispositive, *ibid.*, paras. 462–463, the *Akayesu* Chamber set forth its own textual and legal analysis of the ICTR provision.

[84] *Ibid.*, para. 465. Accord, e.g., *Prosecutor* v. *Muvunyi*, Case No. ICTR-00-55A-T, Judgement, 11 September 2006 ('*Muvunyi* Trial Judgement'), para. 514.

[85] *Akayesu* Appeal Judgement, *supra* note 60, para. 466. Accord, e.g., *Prosecutor* v. *Gacumbitsi*, Case No. ICTR-2001–64-T, Judgement, 14 June 2004 ('*Gacumbitsi* Trial Judgement'), para. 301; *Prosecutor* v. *Semanza*, Case No. ICTR-97-20-T, Judgement and Sentence, 15 May 2003 ('*Semanza* Trial Judgement'), para. 331. The references to 'accused' in the *Akayesu* quotation should more accurately be to the physical perpetrator, who may or may not be the accused. See *infra* section 2.2.2.1 for a detailed discussion of whose conduct and mental state may satisfy the general requirements for crimes against humanity.

[86] *Akayesu* Appeal Judgement, *supra* note 60, para. 466. Accord *Prosecutor* v. *Kajelijeli*, Case No. ICTR-98-44A-T, Judgement and Sentence, 1 December 2003 ('*Kajelijeli* Trial Judgement'), para. 879; *Semanza* Trial Judgement, *supra* note 85, para. 350. See *infra* section 2.2.3.8 for a detailed discussion of this specific requirement for persecution.

jurisdictional requirement of discrimination applies to the attack in general, not the specific underlying offences or crimes.[87]

2.2.2 *General requirements*

2.2.2.1 Preliminary question: whose conduct and mental state may satisfy the contextual general requirements?

In 2002, the *Kunarac* Appeals Chamber set forth what has become the definitive list of the general requirements that must be satisfied before an underlying offence qualifies as a crime against humanity:

(i) There must be an attack.
(ii) The acts of the perpetrator must be part of the attack.
(iii) The attack must be directed against any civilian population.
(iv) The attack must be widespread or systematic.
(v) The perpetrator must know that [there is] a pattern of widespread or systematic crimes directed against a civilian population and know that his acts fit into such a pattern.[88]

Two of the five general requirements outlined by the *Kunarac* Appeals Chamber concern the relationship between the underlying offence and the attack on the civilian population: commission of an act that, 'by its nature or consequences,' is objectively part of the attack; and knowledge that the act is part of the attack.[89] Throughout the Tribunals' jurisprudence on these two contextual general requirements, the terms 'perpetrator' and 'accused' have been used interchangeably and

[87] See, e.g., *Prosecutor* v. *Bagilishema*, Case No. ICTR-95-1A-T, Judgement, 7 June 2001 ('*Bagilishema* Trial Judgement'), para. 81 ('[T]he qualifier "on national, political, ethnic, racial or religious grounds," which is peculiar to the ICTR Statute should, as a matter of construction, be read as a characterisation of the nature of the "attack" rather than of the *mens rea* of the perpetrator.'); accord *Semanza* Trial Judgement, *supra* note 85, para. 331 ('Acts committed against persons outside the discriminatory categories may nevertheless form part of the attack where the act against the outsider supports or furthers or is intended to support or further the attack on the group discriminated against on one of the enumerated grounds.'); *Gacumbitsi* Trial Judgement, *supra* note 85, para. 301.

[88] See generally *Kunarac et al.* Appeal Judgement, *supra* note 75, para. 85. The unaltered text phrased the fifth general requirement as follows: 'The perpetrator must know that his acts *constitute part of* a pattern of widespread or systematic crimes directed against a civilian population and know that his acts fit into such a pattern.' *Ibid.* (emphasis added). It is apparent, however, that the italicised part of this statement is a drafting error, and it has been corrected in later judgements' restatement of the general requirements. See, e.g., *Prosecutor v. Blaškić*, Case No. IT-95-14-A, Judgement, 29 July 2004 ('*Blaškić* Appeal Judgement'), para. 126 (ICTY Appeals Chamber referring to its earlier case law and phrasing it as 'knowledge on the part of the accused that *there is* an attack') (emphasis added). It appears that, in affirming and restating the Trial Chamber's definition, the *Kunarac* Appeals Chamber intended to replace the lower chamber's vague terminology of 'wider context' with a more precise explanation of the requirement, but unwittingly introduced a redundancy. In order to avoid confusion in light of the discussion in this section of the chapter, we have not reproduced the apparent drafting error.

[89] *Kunarac et al.* Appeal Judgement, *supra* note 75, para. 99.

apparently unthinkingly, so it is unclear whose conduct must form part of the attack and who must have knowledge of the context in which the acts are committed.[90]

For instance, in one of the earliest discussions of the two contextual general requirements, the *Tadić* Appeals Chamber asserted, with little explanation, that:

> it may be inferred from the words 'directed against any civilian population' in Article 5 of the Statute that the acts of the *accused* must comprise part of a pattern of widespread or systematic crimes directed against a civilian population and that the *accused* must have known that his acts fit into such a pattern.[91]

The contention that the acts of the accused must comprise part of the pattern is described in the relevant footnote as 'already … recognised by this Tribunal in the *Vukovar Hospital* Rule 61 Decision'.[92] Any reference in that earlier decision to an accused, however, can only be read as describing an accused who is also the physical perpetrator of the crimes at issue:

> Crimes against humanity are to be distinguished from war crimes against individuals. In particular, they must be widespread or demonstrate a systematic character. However, as long as there is a link with the widespread or systematic attack against a civilian population, a single act could qualify as a crime against humanity. As such, *an individual committing a crime against a single victim or a limited number of victims* might be recognised as guilty of a crime against humanity if his acts were part of the specific context identified above.[93]

90 See, e.g., *ibid.*, paras. 85, 433–435 (referring to both 'the accused' and 'the perpetrator', and using the terms interchangeably); *Mrkšić et al.* Trial Judgement, *supra* note 77, paras. 438–439 (same); *Prosecutor* v. *Blaškić*, Case No. IT-95-14, Judgement, 3 March 2000 ('*Blaškić* Trial Judgement'), para. 257 (same); *Prosecutor* v. *Kunarac, Kovač, and Vuković*, Case No. IT-96-23-T & IT-96-23/1-T, Judgement, 22 February 2001 ('*Kunarac et al.* Trial Judgement'), para. 410 (using the term 'perpetrator', but citing *Tadić* Appeal Judgment, *supra* note 75, para. 248, which uses the term 'accused'); *ibid.*, para. 418 (restating the contextual general requirements as existing between 'the acts of the *accused* and the attack') (emphasis added); *Prosecutor* v. *Kayishema and Ruzindana*, Case No. ICTR 95-1-T, Judgement, 21 May 1999 ('*Kayishema and Ruzindana* Trial Judgement'), paras. 133–134 (holding that '*the perpetrator* must knowingly commit crimes against humanity in the sense that he must understand the overall context of his act' and that '*the accused* must have acted with knowledge of the broader context of the attack') (emphasis added).

91 *Tadić* Appeal Judgement, *supra* note 75, para. 248 (footnote omitted) (emphases added).

92 *Ibid.*, para. 248 n. 311.

93 *Prosecutor* v. *Mrkšić, Radić, and Šljivančanin*, Case No. IT-95-13-R61, Review of Indictment Pursuant to Rule 61 of the Rules of Procedure and Evidence, 3 April 1996 ('*Mrkšić et al.* Rule 61 Decision'), para. 30 (emphasis added). See also *ibid.*, para. 15 (noting that 'the responsibility of the accused for the acts for which they have been charged could be established not only because of their position of authority but also because of *their direct participation in the commission of those acts*') (emphasis added). Even the most persuasive explanations of the contextual general requirements by ICTR chambers suffer from the same flawed assumption that the accused is also the physical perpetrator. See, e.g., *Kayishema and Ruzindana* Trial Judgement, *supra* note 90, paras. 133–134 (emphasis added):

> The *perpetrator* must knowingly commit crimes against humanity in the sense that he must understand the overall context of his act … [T]he *accused* must have acted with knowledge of the broader context of the attack … Part of what transforms an individual's act(s) into a crime against humanity is the inclusion of the act within a greater dimension of criminal conduct; therefore an accused should be aware of this greater dimension in order to be culpable. Accordingly, actual or constructive knowledge of the broader context of the attack, meaning that the accused must know that his act(s) is part of a widespread or systematic attack on a civilian population and pursuant to some kind of policy or plan, is necessary to satisfy the requisite *mens rea* element of the accused.

In relying on the *Vukovar Hospital* decision to ground its assertion about an accused, the *Tadić* Appeals Chamber apparently failed to recognise the distinction between the physical perpetrator who stands trial, and another person who is charged with responsibility for the crime, but who did not physically commit it. In the early years of the Tribunals, particularly the ICTY, the cases brought to trial involved relatively low-ranking accused, who were frequently charged with physically committing some, if not all, of the crimes with which they were charged.[94] It is understandable, therefore, that the first *ad hoc* judgements saw no need to distinguish between an accused and a perpetrator; for the purposes of those cases, they were one and the same.

Yet the actual holdings of trial and appeal chambers over the years have demonstrated that the requirement that the conduct charged relate to the attack is satisfied by proof that the underlying offences comprise part of the attack, regardless of whether they are physically committed by the accused or by others in circumstances where he also bears responsibility.[95] Accordingly, the 'acts' in question are the

[94] Thus the first few trial judgements of the ICTY included those against Duško Tadić, a café owner, local politician, and reserve traffic police officer, who was found to have committed several offences, including beating Muslim prisoners and killing two Muslim policemen; Anto Furundžija, a local commander of the 'Jokers', a special unit of the Croatian Defence Council in Bosnia and Herzegovina, who was convicted of torture and outrages against personal dignity as violations of the laws or customs of war for interrogating two detainees while one was being raped by another soldier and the other forced to watch, and for personally assaulting one of the detainees; and Goran Jelisić, the self-described 'Serb Adolf', who personally killed, beat, and stole from Muslim detainees in and around Brčko. See *Tadić* Trial Judgement, *supra* note 77, paras. 181, 188, 190, 714; *Furundžija* Trial Judgement, *supra* note 71, paras. 2, 38, 124–130, 250–257, 276; *Prosecutor* v. *Jelisić*, Case No. IT-95-10-T, Judgement, 14 December 1999 ('*Jelisić* Trial Judgement'), paras. 3, 23–24. While the ICTR accused were usually of comparatively higher rank, because most of the low-level perpetrators remained in Rwandan custody, certain were also convicted of personally committing at least some of the crimes with which they were charged. See, e.g., *Prosecutor* v. *Akayesu*, Case No. ICTR-96-4-T, Judgement, 2 September 1998 ('*Akayesu* Trial Judgement'), paras. 680–683; *Prosecutor* v. *Ntakirutimana and Ntakirutimana*, Case Nos. ICTR-96-10 and ICTR-96-17-T, Judgement and Sentence ('*Ntakirutimana and Ntakirutimana* Trial Judgement'), paras. 791–795; *Prosecutor* v. *Niyitegeka*, Case No. ICTR 96-14-T, Judgement and Sentence, 16 May 2003 ('*Niyitegeka* Trial Judgement'), paras. 443–444.

[95] See, e.g., *Šešelj* Decision on Reconsideration, *supra* note 79, para. 25 (clarifying that the earlier jurisprudence 'establish[es] … that a nexus between the armed conflict and the accused's acts is not required and that all that is required is that the Prosecution establish a connection between the Article 5 crime itself and the armed conflict'); *Prosecutor* v. *Gacumbitsi*, Case No. ICTR-2001-64-A, Judgement, 7 July 2006 ('*Gacumbitsi* Appeal Judgement'), para. 102 (affirming the Trial Chamber's conclusion that the rapes for which the accused was held responsible, but which he was not alleged to have committed himself, formed part of the attack); *ibid*., para. 103 ('[T]he question is simply whether the totality of the evidence proves a nexus between the act and the widespread or systematic attack.'); *Prosecutor* v. *Ntakirutimana and Ntakirutimana*, Case Nos. ICTR-96-10-A and ICTR-96-17-A, Judgement, 13 December 2004 ('*Ntakirutimana and Ntakirutimana* Appeal Judgement'), para. 516 ('As a crime against humanity, for the purposes of the ICTR Statute, the *act of killing* must occur within the context of a widespread or systematic attack against the civilian population for national, political, ethnic, racial or religious grounds.') (emphasis added); *Blaškić* Trial Judgement, *supra* note 90, para. 429, p. 267 (noting that the accused did not physically commit the offences charged, and convicting him 'of having *ordered* a crime against humanity' for five categories of underlying offences) (emphasis added); *Blaškić* Appeal Judgement, *supra* note 88, paras. 98, 102 (endorsing the Trial Chamber's description of the first contextual general requirement, which had not specified whose conduct could constitute crimes against humanity); *Prosecutor* v. *Kordić and Čerkez*, Case No. IT-95-14/2-A, Judgement, 17 December 2004 ('*Kordić and Čerkez* Appeal Judgement'), para. 117 (recognising, in the context of inhumane acts as crimes against humanity, that the underlying offences may be committed by either the accused or his subordinate); *Akayesu* Trial Judgement,

elements of the underlying offences,[96] and the conduct of the accused is relevant only to the extent that he physically committed those offences. Discussions of the knowledge of the context[97] in which the underlying offence occurs have been both more uniform and less clear. Statements of the law tend to refer to the accused's knowledge that 'his acts' form part of the attack,[98] but there is little discussion in the actual findings of trial chambers, or the review by appellate benches, of whether the accused actually knew that the underlying offences are part of the attack, particularly in cases where the accused is not alleged to have physically committed any offences.[99] The most charitable explanation for this gap in the case law is that consideration of knowledge of the context is either implicit in the trial chambers' other factual findings on whether the offences constitute crimes against humanity, or is folded into the evaluation of whether the accused is responsible for the crimes. If the latter is true, however – if the acts considered by chambers are those underlying the form of responsibility through which the accused is held individually liable for

supra note 94, paras. 579, 585 (using the term 'acts' to refer to both the conduct that must form part of the attack and the crimes charged in the indictment); *Ntakirutimana and Ntakirutimana* Trial Judgement, *supra* note 94, para. 803 (same).

96 See, e.g., *Kupreškić et al.* Trial Judgement, *supra* note 71, para. 544 ('The following elements can be identified as comprising the core elements of crimes against humanity: … second, that the acts were part of a widespread or systematic occurrence of crimes directed against a civilian population').

97 The ICTY Appeals Chamber has implicitly disapproved of references to 'context' for the purposes of discussions of the general requirements for Article 5, at least with regard to the listing of those elements. See *supra* note 88. The term is used throughout this chapter in the interests of concision, to refer to the 'attack' or the pattern of widespread or systematic criminal conduct within which the underlying offences are committed. The full restatement of the general requirements for crimes against humanity is set forth in the Annex to this volume.

98 See, e.g., *Kordić and Čerkez* Appeal Judgement, *supra* note 95, paras. 99–100; *Semanza* Trial Judgement, *supra* note 85, para. 332; *Akayesu* Appeal Judgement, *supra* note 60, para. 467 (interpreting the discriminatory basis jurisdictional requirement, but presuming an accused who is also the physical perpetrator) (emphasis added):

> [E]ven if the accused did not have a discriminatory intent when he committed the act charged against a particular victim, he nevertheless knew that his act could further a discriminatory attack against a civilian population; the attack could even be perpetrated by other persons and the accused could even object to it. As a result, *where it is shown that the accused had knowledge of such objective nexus*, the Prosecutor is under no obligation to go forward with a showing that the crime charged was committed against a particular victim with a discriminatory intent.

But see, e.g., *Semanza* Trial Judgement, *supra* note 85, para. 447 (focusing on the physical perpetrators and finding that '*the attackers* at Musha church were aware that their actions in murdering Tutsi refugees formed part of the widespread attack; and therefore that 'the *principal perpetrators* committed murder as a crime against humanity') (emphases added); *ibid.*, para. 452 (same).

99 Among the few cases where such discussion occurs are those in which the accused is convicted of physically committing certain of the underlying offences. In those cases, the Trial Chambers emphasised the accused's knowledge that the offences he personally physically committed formed part of the attack. See, e.g., *Ntakirutimana and Ntakirutimana* Trial Judgement, *supra* note 94, para. 808 ('[T]he Chamber finds that in killing Charles Ukobizaba, Gérard Ntakirutimana had the requisite intent to kill him and knew that it was part of a widespread and systematic attack against the civilian Tutsi population on ethnic grounds[.]'); *Niyitegeka* Trial Judgement, *supra* note 94, para. 446 (finding that 'in killing the old man, the young boy and the young girl, the Accused had the requisite intent to kill them and knew that it was part of a widespread and systematic attack against the civilian Tutsi population on ethnic grounds'). But cf. *Ntakirutimana and Ntakirutimana* Appeal Judgement, *supra* note 95, para. 492 (holding, in respect of Gérard Ntakirutimana's conviction for genocide, that it was error for the Trial Chamber to base its conviction only on the underlying offences which he personally physically committed).

the crimes, such as aiding and abetting or instigating[100] – it risks conflating the issue of whether crimes within the jurisdiction of the Tribunals were committed with the separate question of individual criminal responsibility for those crimes.[101]

As these later cases have begun to demonstrate, the distinction between an accused and other persons involved in the realisation of a crime is extremely important in cases involving military and civilian leaders, where the prosecution rarely alleges that the accused personally and physically committed any of the acts charged in the indictments, but instead claims that the accused is individually liable for the conduct of others, through one or more of the forms of responsibility discussed in Volume I of this series. Such cases are increasingly becoming the focus of international and internationalised courts and tribunals, so it is crucial that trial and appeal chambers distinguish between cases in which an accused is charged with personally and physically committing a crime – where all the elements of a crime must be fulfilled by the accused – and those in which the elements can be satisfied by the physical perpetrator alone or in conjunction with another person involved in the crime.[102]

This legal inquiry should not simply be a question of choosing to focus on either the accused or the physical perpetrator. Crimes under international law, such as those committed in an armed conflict, typically involve a large number of persons whose conduct contributes to a greater or lesser degree to the realisation of the crime. Crimes against humanity are no exception; the requirement that an offence be part of a widespread or systematic attack makes it nearly inevitable that many different people, frequently at different levels in a *de jure* or *de facto* hierarchy, will be implicated in the charged conduct. It would thus be illogical and inconsistent with the very circumstances that international criminal law is intended to address to hold that only an accused or only a physical perpetrator may satisfy any of the

[100] For example, the 'act' of an accused convicted of aiding and abetting a crime against humanity could include providing practical assistance to the physical perpetrator, such as providing the weapons or other means used to commit the crime, while the 'act' for instigating would be the prompting of criminal conduct. See Gideon Boas, James L. Bischoff, and Natalie L. Reid, *Forms of Responsibility in International Criminal Law* (2007), pp. 305–306; 358–362. In neither case would the conduct of the accused be the actual underlying offence. Even if it forms part of the attack, the conduct underlying the form of responsibility should be a separate and independent inquiry from the question of whether a crime was committed. As a matter of law, the accused's possible responsibility for the conduct of others is irrelevant if that conduct is not itself criminal.

[101] See, e.g., *Blagojević and Jokić* Trial Judgement, *supra* note 75, para. 553 (in a case where neither accused was charged with physically committing any crimes):

> Both Accused were high-ranking officers in brigades which took part in the attack on the Srebrenica enclave and as such had knowledge of the wider context in which their own acts occurred. The Trial Chamber finds that it has been established beyond reasonable doubt that the acts of both Accused were part of the attack and that both Accused knew that their acts were part of the attack.

[102] See, e.g., Boas, Bischoff, and Reid, *supra* note 100, pp. 140–141 (discussing the effect of the completion strategies at the *ad hoc* Tribunals, where 'the active cases remaining in their dockets concentrate on the most senior leaders suspected of being most responsible for crimes within the jurisdiction of the relevant Tribunal') (internal quotation marks omitted).

elements of a crime.[103] For these reasons, we will use the terms 'physical perpetrator' or 'other relevant actor' when discussing the elements of the core international crimes. The term 'relevant actor' is deliberately broad enough to encompass the accused and any other person whose mental state and conduct should be relevant to the establishment of a crime, such as an intermediate civilian superior or military commander who plans, orders, or instigates a crime.

Under the settled law on forms of responsibility, however, persons responsible for crimes on the bases of the third category of joint criminal enterprise, aiding and abetting, or superior responsibility should not be able to supply the knowledge or intent element of a crime.[104] An accused convicted under the third category of joint criminal enterprise need not have the specific or general intent for the crime that lies outside the common criminal purpose of the enterprise; an aider or abettor need not share the intent of the physical perpetrator or other participants in the crime; and a superior need not have the intent required for the crime committed by his subordinates.[105] More importantly, even if an accused in any of these positions does have the intent required for the crime, that fact should be irrelevant to the question of whether the international crime in question was committed. If a person whose responsibility can only be characterised as an aider, abettor, or superior were the only actor linked to the charged conduct who actually intended that the prohibited result occur, then no crime under international law has been committed, because persons in these positions are incidental to the crime. The bases for their criminal responsibility lie in their assistance to, or failure to prevent or punish, the conduct. Similarly, if a person's liability for a given crime may only be described as falling under the third category of joint criminal enterprise, his intent with regard to that crime is irrelevant, because it is not shared by his co-participants; if it were, the crime would be within the common criminal purpose, and the appropriate basis for liability would be the first category of joint criminal enterprise.[106]

The same reasoning does not apply, however, to planning, instigating, and ordering. Although direct intent is one of two alternative mental states for these forms of responsibility,[107] if a person in this position is in fact the only actor with the required intent, the charged conduct should still qualify as a crime. In a very real sense, the planner, instigator, or orderer is the architect of the crime – in much the

[103] In order for an accused to be held individually liable, once it has been established that an international crime has in fact occurred, he must of course satisfy all of the elements of one or more of the forms of responsibility discussed in Volume I of this series, such as joint criminal enterprise, superior responsibility, or aiding and abetting.

[104] For a description of the law on these forms of responsibility, see generally Boas, Bischoff, and Reid, *supra* note 100, chs. 2–4.

[105] See *ibid.*, pp. 426–429 (laying out the elements of these forms of responsibility).

[106] See generally *ibid.*, p. 426 (laying out the elements of all categories of joint criminal enterprise, or JCE).

[107] See generally *ibid.*, pp. 428–429.

way that the Tribunals treat the first-category joint criminal enterprise – and the physical perpetrators merely the tools with which the crime is implemented.

With regard to the contextual general requirements, therefore, the preferable approach is that an underlying offence may constitute a crime against humanity in at least two sets of circumstances: first, where the physical perpetrator satisfies both requirements, because his acts or omissions form part of the attack, and he knows that his conduct is part of the attack; and second, even if the physical perpetrator is unaware of the context in which his conduct occurs, where another relevant actor – such as the orderer or planner of the physical perpetrator's conduct – knows that it forms part of the attack.[108] In both situations, the physical perpetrator or the other relevant actor could be the accused, but that should not be a required element of the crime.[109]

The relevant portion of the annex to this volume, which combines the elements of the forms of responsibility and the elements of the crimes, will specify which elements must be satisfied by an accused in order to hold him responsible for a particular crime under a particular form of responsibility.

2.2.2.2 *The attack requirement*

There is an attack.

An 'attack' for the purposes of crimes against humanity, which is distinct from an 'armed conflict' as the latter term has been developed and applied in the Tribunals' jurisprudence on war crimes,[110] has been simply and consistently described by *ad hoc* chambers as 'a course of conduct involving the commission of acts of violence';[111] in the ICTR, this definition is frequently restated as 'an unlawful act, event, or series of events of the kind listed in Article 3(a) through (i) of the Statute'.[112] Both Appeals Chambers have specified that, under customary international law, when crimes against humanity occur in the context of an armed conflict,

[108] Cf. *Stakić* Trial Judgement, *supra* note 80, para. 746 ('[I]n this context, it is immaterial whether or not the direct perpetrator had, or even shared, the intent of the indirect perpetrator who acts on a higher level. What counts is the discriminatory intent of the indirect perpetrator.'), quoted with approval in *Prosecutor* v. *Stakić*, Case No. IT-97-24-A, Judgement, 22 March 2006 ('*Stakić* Appeal Judgement'), para. 329.

[109] When quoting directly from trial or appeal judgements, however, we may retain the original language if alteration would lead to confusion.

[110] *Tadić* Appeal Judgement, *supra* note 75, para. 251; accord, e.g., *Prosecutor* v. *Nahimana, Barayagwiza, and Ngeze*, Case No. ITCR-99-52-A, Judgement, 28 November 2007 ('*Media* Appeal Judgement'), para. 916; *Martić* Trial Judgement, *supra* note 75, para. 49; *Limaj et al.* Trial Judgement, *supra* note 75, para. 182; *Prosecutor* v. *Galić*, Case No. IT-98-29, Judgement, 5 December 2003 ('*Galić* Trial Judgement'), para. 141. See Chapter 4, sections 4.2.1.1–4.2.1.2 for a discussion of the armed conflict and nexus requirements for war crimes.

[111] *Kunarac et al.* Trial Judgement, *supra* note 90, para. 415 (citing *Prosecutor* v. *Tadić*, Case No. IT-94-1-A, Decision on the Form of the Indictment, 14 November 1995, para. 11); accord, e.g., *Media* Appeal Judgement, *supra* note 110, para. 916; *Prosecutor* v. *Krnojelac*, Case No. IT-97-25-T, Judgement, 15 March 2002 ('*Krnojelac* Trial Judgement'), para. 54.

[112] See, e.g., *Gacumbitsi* Trial Judgement, *supra* note 85, para. 298 & nn. 272–273 (noting that '[t]his is the accepted definition in the Tribunal's case law').

the attack can precede, outlast, or continue during the armed conflict, but it need not be a part of it.[113] In particular, as both Tribunals have confirmed, an attack in the context of a crime against humanity is not limited to the use of armed force, but rather encompasses any mistreatment of the civilian population.[114] With cases arising out of the wars that accompanied the break-up of Yugoslavia, ICTY chambers have consistently held that, when considering whether there was an attack upon a particular civilian population, it is irrelevant that the other party to a conflict may have also committed atrocities against its opponent's civilian population.[115]

2.2.2.3 The targeting requirement

This attack is directed against any civilian population.

Both Tribunals have explained that the status of the victims as civilians is one of the characteristics of a crime against humanity.[116] The use of the word 'population' in the statutory provision, however:

> does not mean that the entire population of the geographical entity in which the attack is taking place must have been subjected to the attack. It is sufficient to show that enough individuals were targeted in the course of the attack, or that they were targeted in such a way as to satisfy the Chamber that the attack was in fact directed against a 'civilian population', rather than against a limited and randomly selected number of individuals.[117]

[113] *Kordić and Čerkez* Appeal Judgement, *supra* note 95, para. 666; *Kunarac et al.* Appeal Judgement, *supra* note 75, para. 86; *Tadić* Appeal Judgement, *supra* note 75, paras. 248, 251. Accord, e.g., *Media* Appeal Judgement, *supra* note 110, para. 916; *Limaj et al.* Trial Judgement, *supra* note 75, paras. 182, 194; *Prosecutor* v. *Naletilić and Martinović*, Case No. IT-98-34, Judgement, 31 March 2003 ('*Naletilić and Martinović* Trial Judgement'), para. 233.

[114] *Kunarac et al.* Appeal Judgement, *supra* note 75, para. 86. See also *Limaj et al.* Trial Judgement, *supra* note 75, para. 194 ('[T]o amount to an attack the relevant conduct need not amount to a military assault or forceful takeover; the evidence need only demonstrate a course of conduct directed against the civilian population that indicates a widespread or systematic reach.') (internal quotation marks omitted); *Blagojević and Jokić* Trial Judgement, *supra* note 75, para. 543 (citing *Kunarac et al.* Trial Judgement, *supra* note 90, para. 415, and holding that '"[a]ttack" in the context of a crime against humanity can be defined as a course of conduct involving the commission of acts of violence'); *Akayesu* Trial Judgement, *supra* note 94, para. 581 ('An attack may also be non violent in nature, like imposing a system of apartheid … or exerting pressure on the population to act in a particular manner.'); accord *Semanza* Trial Judgement, *supra* note 85, para. 327; *Prosecutor* v. *Musema*, Case No. ICTR-96-13-T, Judgement and Sentence, 27 January 2000 ('*Musema* Trial Judgement'), para. 205; *Prosecutor* v. *Rutaganda*, Case No. ICTR-96-3-T, Judgement and Sentence, 6 December 1999 ('*Rutaganda* Trial Judgement'), para. 70.

[115] See, e.g., *Kunarac et al.* Appeal Judgement, *supra* note 75, paras. 87–88; *Kupreškić et al.* Trial Judgement, *supra* note 71, para. 765; *Brđanin* Trial Judgement, *supra* note 80, para. 131; *Prosecutor* v. *Simić, Tadić, and Zarić*, Case No. IT-95-9-T, Judgement, 17 October 2003 ('*Simić et al.* Trial Judgement'), para. 40; see also *Prosecutor* v. *Kupreškić, Kupreškić, Kupreškić, Josipović, Papić, and Šantić*, Case No. IT-95-16-T, Decision on Evidence of the Good Character of the Accused and the Defence of *Tu Quoque*, 17 February 1999 (holding that 'evidence that Bosnian Muslims may have committed atrocities against Bosnian Croat civilians in villages in the vicinity of Ahmići or elsewhere in the Lašva River valley is … irrelevant because it does not tend to prove or disprove any of the allegations made in the indictment against the accused').

[116] See, e.g., *Blaškić* Appeal Judgement, *supra* note 88, para. 107; *Semanza* Trial Judgement, *supra* note 85, para. 330. See also *infra* note 120 and accompanying text.

[117] *Kunarac et al.* Appeal Judgement, *supra* note 75, para. 90; accord, e.g., *Kordić and Čerkez* Appeal Judgement, *supra* note 95, para. 95; *Blaškić* Appeal Judgement, *supra* note 88, para. 105; *Prosecutor v. Krajišnik*, Case No. IT-00-39-T, Judgement, 27 September 2006 ('*Krajišnik* Trial Judgement'), para. 706; *Bagilishema* Trial

An offence may constitute a crime against humanity even if some of the members of the targeted population were not civilians. Under the law of the Tribunals, '[a] population is considered a "civilian population" if it is predominantly civilian in nature',[118] and the presence of combatants within the population at issue does not alter its civilian character.[119]

Accordingly, as discussed below, the status of a particular victim is relevant in two different respects to the determination of whether a crime against humanity has been committed. On one hand, the victim must be a 'civilian' in order for an offence to be a crime against humanity.[120] On the other hand, as long as the targeted population in question is *predominantly* civilian, the fact that some of its members – and therefore some of the victims of the attack – were not civilians does not mean that it was not a 'civilian population' for the purposes of the law on crimes against humanity.

2.2.2.3.1 The definition of a 'civilian' In the context of international law, the term 'civilian' immediately conjures up a distinction with members of the armed forces. Since the legal difference between these two groups of individuals is most clearly codified in the Geneva Conventions of 1949, it is unsurprising that many *ad hoc* judgements either explicitly or implicitly adopt the terminology of those Conventions, or refer to their official commentaries or the Additional Protocols to the Conventions.[121] Thus the 1998 *Akayesu* Trial Judgement at the ICTR and the 2005 *Blagojević and Jokić* Trial Judgement at the ICTY use nearly identical language, based on Common Article 3 of the Conventions, to define the term 'civilian', noting that it

Judgement, *supra* note 87, para. 80 (noting also that 'the "population" element is intended to imply crimes of a collective nature and thus excludes single or isolated acts which, although possibly constituting crimes under national penal legislation, do not rise to the level of crimes against humanity'). See also *Kunarac et al.* Trial Judgement, *supra* note 90, para. 424 (giving the examples of 'a state, a municipality or another circumscribed area' as illustrations of the term 'geographical entity').

118 *Blagojević and Jokić* Trial Judgement, *supra* note 75, para. 544 (citing *Krnojelac* Trial Judgement, *supra* note 111, para. 56; *Tadić* Trial Judgement, *supra* note 77, para. 638); *Semanza* Trial Judgement, *supra* note 85, para. 330; *Kayishema and Ruzindana* Trial Judgement, *supra* note 90, para. 128.

119 See, e.g., *Limaj et al.* Trial Judgement, *supra* note 75, para. 186; *Galić* Trial Judgement, *supra* note 110, para. 143; *Bagilishema* Trial Judgement, *supra* note 87, para. 79; *Akayesu* Trial Judgement, *supra* note 94, para. 582. Accord *Blaškić* Appeal Judgement, *supra* note 88, para. 113.

120 See, e.g., *Mrkšić et al.* Trial Judgement, *supra* note 77, paras. 443–464 (reviewing the parties' submissions and discussing the question at length before concluding that both the ICTY's jurisprudence and customary international law require that the victim be a civilian); see also *Krnojelac* Trial Judgement, *supra* note 111, para. 56; *Kupreškić et al.* Trial Judgement, *supra* note 71, para. 547; *Tadić* Trial Judgement, *supra* note 77, paras. 636, 638. But see *Tadić* Trial Judgement, *supra* note 77, paras. 640, 641 (recognising post-Second World War commentary and practice supporting inclusion of traditional combatants within those who may be the victims of a crime against humanity); *ibid.*, para. 643 (holding that members of resistance forces can be victims of crimes against humanity); *Kupreškić et al.* Trial Judgement, *supra* note 71, para. 547 (arguing that the limitation of Article 5 of the ICTY Statute to civilians 'constitutes a departure from customary international law'); Cassese, *supra* note 17, p. 91 (arguing that, under customary international law, the victim of a crime against humanity may be a combatant). It is also worth noting that Professor Cassese presided over the *Kupreškić* Trial Chamber in his capacity as judge of the ICTY.

121 For example, the holding that the presence of non-civilians within a civilian population does not deprive it of its civilian character, see *supra* text accompanying note 119, *infra* section 2.2.2.3.2, is based directly on Article 50 (3) of Additional Protocol I, *supra* note 9.

encompasses persons 'who are not taking any active part in the hostilities, including members of the armed forces who laid down their arms and those persons placed *hors de combat* by sickness, wounds, detention or any other cause.'[122]

In two separate judgements in 2004, however, the ICTY Appeals Chamber noted that, in light of its 'obligation to ascertain the state of customary law in force at the time the crimes were committed', it would refer to the definition of civilians and civilian population contained in Article 50 of Additional Protocol I to the Conventions, which it determined reflected customary international law.[123] Contrary to the approach suggested by reliance on Common Article 3, the *Blaškić* Appeals Chamber emphasised that 'the specific situation of the victim at the time the crimes are committed may not be determinative of his civilian or non-civilian status'; if the victim is a 'member of an armed organization, the fact that he is not armed or in combat at the time of the … crimes does not accord him civilian status'.[124]

Each of these approaches to defining a civilian for the purposes of crimes against humanity takes its point of departure from a different aspect of international humanitarian law, and each thus identifies a different group of persons who may be the victims of these crimes. As the official commentaries to the Geneva Conventions make clear, the purpose of Common Article 3 was to encapsulate the basic principles animating all four Conventions, by setting forth 'the rules of humanity that are recognized as essential by civilized nations' and describing the persons to whom these essential protections would be extended.[125] The concern in Common Article 3 was therefore less to distinguish between categories of persons and more to ensure that these protections were ensured for anyone not actively participating in the fighting.[126]

On the other hand, a primary preoccupation behind Additional Protocol I was the elaboration of more detailed rules with regard to one of the most fundamental tenets of international humanitarian law: the principle of distinction between combatants and civilians, that is, those who can legitimately be considered the targets of military

[122] *Akayesu* Trial Judgement, *supra* note 94, para. 582 (quoting Common Article 3); *Blagojević and Jokić* Trial Judgement, *supra* note 75, para. 544 (same). Accord *Naletilić and Martinović* Trial Judgement, *supra* note 113, para. 235; *Musema* Trial Judgement, *supra* note 114, para. 207; *Jelisić* Trial Judgement, *supra* note 94, para. 54; *Rutaganda* Trial Judgement, *supra* note 114, para. 72.

[123] *Kordić and Čerkez* Appeal Judgement, *supra* note 95, para. 97; *Blaškić* Appeal Judgement, *supra* note 88, para. 110.

[124] *Blaškić* Appeal Judgement, *supra* note 88, para. 114.

[125] See, e.g., Jean Pictet (ed.), *Commentary IV Geneva Convention Relative to the Protection of Civilian Persons in Time of War* (1958) ('ICRC Commentary to Geneva Convention IV'), p. 34 (stating also that 'Article 3 is like a Convention in miniature') (quotation marks omitted).

[126] See *Mrkšić et al.* Trial Judgement, *supra* note 77, para. 450 (discussing the line of authority relying on Common Article 3 and explaining that '[t]he implication of this reasoning was that those who were members of a resistance movement or former combatants … who were no longer taking part in the hostilities when the crimes were committed could qualify as victims of crimes against humanity').

action, and those who cannot.[127] In so doing, Article 50(1) of the Additional Protocol relies on the definition of combatants laid out in Geneva Convention III, which regulates the treatment of prisoners of war.[128] The Additional Protocol's definition is therefore arrived at through a process of exclusion: a 'civilian' is anyone who is neither a member of the armed forces of a party to a conflict, as defined by Geneva Convention III or the Additional Protocol itself; nor a member of a group of '[i]nhabitants of a non-occupied territory, who on the approach of the enemy spontaneously take up arms to resist the invading forces, without having had time to form themselves into regular armed units'.[129]

Though this last provision – Article 4(A)(6) of Geneva Convention III – is generally interpreted as referring to the theoretical notion of a *levée en masse*,[130] there is nonetheless some tension between its labelling such persons as combatants (and therefore deserving of prisoner-of-war status), and the observations in the Report of the Commission of Experts created prior to the establishment of the ICTY, cited in the *Tadić* Trial Judgement in its discussion of the scope of Article 5 of the ICTY Statute:

> It seems obvious that article 5 applies first and foremost to civilians, meaning people who are not combatants. This, however, should not lead to any quick conclusions concerning people who at one particular point in time did bear arms. One practical example: in the former Yugoslavia, large-scale arbitrary killings were one of the hallmarks of attacks by a given group. Information about such arbitrary killings was then used by the same group to instill fear and demand total subjugation of the other group in other areas as well. Many of the most barbarous onslaughts on villages started with heavy artillery bombardments followed by the villages being stormed by infantry in tandem, while paramilitary groups sought the inhabitants in each and every house. A head of family who under such circumstances tries to protect his family, gun in hand, does not thereby lose his status as a civilian.

[127] See, e.g., Yves Sandoz, Christophe Swinarski and Bruno Zimmerman (eds.), *Commentary on the Additional Protocols of 8 June 1977 to the Geneva Conventions of 12 August 1949* (1987) ('ICRC Commentary to the Additional Protocols'), p. 586, para. 1826 ('Protection of civilians from arbitrary and oppressive enemy action, outlined in 1899, and later in 1907, was expressed in its most complete form in the Fourth Geneva Convention of 1949, which is now supplemented by this Protocol.'). See also Chapter 4, text accompanying notes 43–45.

[128] Additional Protocol I, *supra* note 9, Art. 50(1) ('A civilian is any person who does not belong to one of the categories of persons referred to in Article 4 (A) (1), (2), (3) and (6) of the Third Convention and in Article 43 of this Protocol.'); see also Geneva Convention III, *supra* note 51, Art. 4(A) (defining the following categories as prisoners of war when they fall into the hands of the enemy: '[m]embers of the armed forces of a Party to the conflict, as well as members of militias or volunteer corps forming part of such armed forces' (Article 4(A)(1)); with certain prerequisites, '[m]embers of other militias and members of other volunteer corps … belonging to a Party to the conflict and operating in or outside their own territory, even if this territory is occupied' (Article 4 (A)(2)); and '[m]embers of regular armed forces who profess allegiance to a government or an authority not recognized by the Detaining Power' (Article 4(A)(3))). See also Additional Protocol I, *supra* note 9, Art. 43(1) ('The armed forces of a Party to a conflict consist of all organized armed forces, groups and units which are under a command responsible to that Party for the conduct or its subordinates, even if that Party is represented by a government or an authority not recognized by an adverse Party.').

[129] Geneva Convention III, *supra* note 51, Article 4(A)(6).

[130] See *Prosecutor* v. *Halilović*, Case No. IT-01-48-T, Judgement, 16 November 2005 ('*Halilović* Trial Judgement'), para. 34 n. 79.

Maybe the same is the case for the sole policeman or local defence guard doing the same, even if they joined hands to try to prevent the cataclysm. Information of the overall circumstances is relevant for the interpretation of the provision in a spirit consistent with its purpose. Under such circumstances, the distinction between improvised self-defence and actual military defence may be subtle, but none the less important.[131]

To be sure, Article 50(1) of Additional Protocol I explicitly notes that '[i]n case of doubt whether a person is a civilian, that person shall be considered to be a civilian.'[132] In the view of the *Blaškić* Appeals Chamber, however, that 'imperative ... is limited to the expected conduct of a member of the military'; when an accused's 'criminal responsibility is at issue, the burden of proof as to whether a person is a civilian rests on the Prosecution'.[133] Under the *Blaškić*-Additional Protocol definition, if an alleged victim was a member of an organised armed force, even if he was unarmed or *hors de combat* at the time of the commission of the offence, the offence cannot be considered a crime against humanity.[134]

The clearest example of the consequences of such an approach is in the *Mrkšić* Trial Judgement. The Trial Chamber rejected the prosecution's assertion that Article 5's reference to civilians was intended to invoke Common Article 3, and instead adopted the *Blaškić*-Additional Protocol definition and concluded that 'the term "civilian" in Article 5 ... does not include combatants or fighters *hors de combat*'.[135] Reasoning in light of the weight of ICTY jurisprudence that a victim of a crime against humanity must be a civilian,[136] the Chamber ultimately held that the crimes charged in the indictment – including the infamous massacre of injured men taken from Vukovar Hospital in November 1991 – were not crimes against humanity, even though they took place in the context of 'a widespread and systematic attack by the [Yugoslav National Army] and other Serb forces directed against the Croat and other non-Serb civilian population',[137] because in the executioners' 'awareness of the factual circumstances, the victims were prisoners of war, not civilians.'[138] The Chamber's reasoning appears flawed in at least two respects. First, it is based on the erroneous conclusion that 'the civilian status of the victims is only

[131] Final Report of the Commission of Experts Established Pursuant to Security Council Resolution 780 (1992), annexed to UN Doc. S/1994/674 (1994), para. 78 (emphasis added) (cited and quoted with approval in *Tadić* Trial Judgement, *supra* note 77, para. 640).

[132] Additional Protocol I, *supra* note 9, Art. 50(1). [133] *Blaškić* Appeal Judgement, *supra* note 88, para. 111.

[134] See, e.g., *Prosecutor* v. *Galić*, Case No. IT-98-29-A, Judgement, 30 November 2006 ('*Galić* Appeal Judgement'), para. 144 n. 437 (following *Blaškić*, disapproving of the Trial Chamber's definition of 'civilian' for the purposes of a crime against humanity, and noting that '[e]ven *hors de combat* [persons] would still be members of the armed forces of a party to the conflict ... ; as such they are not civilians in the context of Article 50(1) of Additional Protocol I').

[135] *Mrkšić et al.* Trial Judgement, *supra* note 77, para. 461. In many respects, the *Mrkšić* Trial Chamber's analysis of the issues is more detailed and persuasive than any of the appeal judgements which it was bound to follow. See, e.g., *ibid.*, para. 458 (citing the fact that certain crimes listed in Article 5 of the ICTY Statute 'can only be committed against civilians, not against combatants' as further proof that the definition should not include members of the armed forces, regardless of their situation at the time of the crimes).

[136] *Ibid.*, para. 463. [137] *Ibid.*, para. 472. [138] *Ibid.*, para. 480.

a jurisdictional requirement and not an element of the crime',[139] so 'it is sufficient for the perpetrator to have been aware of the factual circumstances that established the status of the victim'.[140] Second, and as a result, it abjures the stronger basis for finding that no crimes against humanity were committed – the failure of the prosecution to prove that the victims were civilians[141] – for the weak, and likely insufficient, basis that the victims were 'in Serb eyes … war crimes suspects'.[142] Nevertheless, the judgement is a clear demonstration that it is possible for a chamber, applying ICTY appellate jurisprudence, to conclude that the general requirements for crimes against humanity have been satisfied, but the particular offence alleged is not a crime against humanity.[143]

Notwithstanding some internal inconsistencies in the reasoning of the ICTY Appeals Chamber,[144] the more restrictive approach to the definition of a civilian has generally been applied by that Chamber since its judgement in *Blaškić*.[145] It has not, however, been consistently employed by Trial Chambers.[146] Anchoring itself in a long line of pre-*Blaškić* authority,[147] the Trial Chamber in the November 2005 *Limaj* Judgement opined that 'the definition of "civilian" employed in the laws of war cannot be imported wholesale into discussions of crimes against humanity',[148] and recalled the *Tadić* Trial Chamber's earlier reminder that the terms of Common

139 *Ibid.*, para. 464. This holding is both illogical, in light of the Chamber's conclusion in the immediately preceding paragraph that 'a crime listed in Article 5 … does not qualify as a crime against humanity if the victims were non-civilians', and inconsistent with binding appellate jurisprudence. See *supra* note 133 and accompanying text. See also Boas, Bischoff, and Reid, *supra* note 100, p. 26 n. 94 (discussing the binding nature of *ad hoc* appellate jurisprudence).

140 *Mrkšić et al.* Trial Judgement, *supra* note 77, para. 464.

141 See *ibid.*, para. 480 (noting the 'evidentiary difficulties' and 'the absence of adequate evidence before this Chamber to establish a role of a few of the victims in the Croat forces in Vukovar', and concluding that '[t]hose matters cannot be resolved on the available evidence').

142 *Ibid.* It is difficult to reconcile the Chamber's emphasis on the subjective belief of the physical perpetrators with the 'imperative' contained in Article 50(3) of Additional Protocol I and incorporated into the ICTY's jurisprudence by the *Blaškić* Appeals Chamber, which imposes an obligation on combatants to err on the side of presuming that an individual is a civilian. A better formulation of what the Chamber may have been attempting to articulate appears in Mettraux's pre-*Mrkšić* restatement of the law on this point, where he asserts that to obtain a conviction, 'the Prosecutor must demonstrate that the accused could not reasonably have believed that the victim was a member of the armed forces in the particular circumstances of the case'. Mettraux, *supra* note 55, p. 170 (citing *Kunarac et al.* Trial Judgement, *supra* note 90, para. 435).

143 As the *Mrkšić* Trial Chamber noted, depending on the circumstances, that offence might constitute a war crime, and would therefore still be a crime under international law. See *Mrkšić et al.* Trial Judgement, *supra* note 77, para. 460 (noting also that, if committed in peacetime, such offences would likely be punishable under national law).

144 See, e.g., *Kordić and Čerkez* Appeal Judgement, *supra* note 95, para. 97 (reprising the Additional Protocol definition and citing *Blaškić*). But see *ibid.*, para. 421 (concluding that the murders of certain soldiers placed *hors de combat* were crimes against humanity because they were 'civilians').

145 See, e.g., *ibid.*, para. 97; *Galić* Appeal Judgement, *supra* note 134, para. 144.

146 Other than the *Mrkšić* Trial Judgement, the only trial judgement to apply the restrictive *Blaškić* definition of civilians has been that in the *Martić* case. See *Martić* Trial Judgement, *supra* note 75, paras. 50–56.

147 See *supra* note 122; see also, e.g., *Mrkšić et al.* Rule 61 Decision, *supra* note 93, para. 29; *Tadić* Trial Judgement, *supra* note 77, paras. 641, 643; *Galić* Trial Judgement, *supra* note 110, para. 143; *Kupreškić et al.* Trial Judgement, *supra* note 71, para. 549 (holding that 'those actively involved in a resistance movement can qualify as victims of crimes against humanity')

148 *Limaj et al.* Trial Judgement, *supra* note 75, para. 223.

Article 3, Additional Protocol I, and the commentary to Geneva Convention IV 'can only be applied by analogy'.[149] The Chamber ultimately applied the more expansive definition based on Common Article 3.[150] Similarly, the September 2004 *Brđanin* Trial Judgement and the January 2005 *Blagojević and Jokić* Trial Judgement still used the Common Article 3 terminology to define the term 'civilian';[151] the September 2006 *Krajišnik* Trial Judgement explicitly eschewed a 'narrowly defined' interpretation of civilian status in favour of the Common Article 3 approach;[152] and the November 2005 *Halilović* Trial Judgement reverted to an emphasis on the specific situation of the victim at the time the crime was committed.[153] Nor has the restrictive *Blaškić* approach been explicitly adopted by ICTR Trial Chambers, some of which place no particular emphasis on the definition of 'civilian',[154] and others of which refer only to ICTR jurisprudence that pre-dates the *Blaškić* Appeal Judgement.[155]

One reason for the intermittent reluctance of *ad hoc* chambers to rely too heavily on the definitions of international humanitarian law may be that such reliance could emphasise a tension between the sometimes exacting details of those definitions and the desire expressed in the Tribunals' jurisprudence to adopt very broad definitions of 'civilian', so as to ensure the broadest possible protection for persons who may become the victims of crimes against humanity.[156] For example, the *Kayishema and Ruzindana* Trial Judgement observed that, since crimes against humanity need not occur during an armed conflict, 'the term civilian must be understood within the context of war as well as relative peace'. Deciding to apply as broad a definition as possible, the Chamber found that the term 'includes all persons except those who have the duty to maintain public order and have the legitimate means to exercise force.'[157] The broader approach of the *Kayishema and Ruzindana* Trial Chamber, and of the trial chambers applying the Common Article 3 definition, appears more

[149] *Tadić* Trial Judgement, *supra* note 77, para. 639.

[150] *Limaj et al.* Trial Judgement, *supra* note 75, para. 186.

[151] See *Brđanin* Trial Judgement, *supra* note 80, para. 134 (holding that the civilian population 'may include … individuals *hors de combat*'); see also *supra* note 122 (noting the *Blagojević and Jokić* holding).

[152] *Krajišnik* Trial Judgement, *supra* note 117, para. 706.

[153] *Halilović* Trial Judgement, *supra* note 130, para. 34.

[154] See, e.g., *Prosecutor* v. *Simba*, Case No. ICTR-01-76-T, Judgement and Sentence, 13 December 2005 ('*Simba* Trial Judgement'), para. 421 (noting merely that it is a general requirement for crimes against humanity that there be a widespread or systematic attack directed against a civilian population).

[155] See, e.g., *Muvunyi* Trial Judgement, *supra* note 84, para. 512 (referring to the *Akayesu* and *Bagilishema* Trial Judgements, both predating the *Blaškić* Appeal Judgement, for its definition of 'civilian').

[156] See, e.g., *Kupreškić et al.* Trial Judgement, *supra* note 71, para. 547 (lamenting the limitation that crimes against humanity must be directed against a civilian population, and holding that 'a broad interpretation should nevertheless be placed on the word "civilians"'). See also *Limaj et al.* Trial Judgement, *supra* note 75, para. 186 (holding that 'the term "civilian population" must be interpreted broadly'); accord *Jelisić* Trial Judgement, *supra* note 94, para. 54; *Tadić* Trial Judgement, *supra* note 77, para. 639.

[157] *Kayishema and Ruzindana* Trial Judgement, *supra* note 90, para. 127 (giving the examples of members of the Forces Armées Rwandaises, the Rwandan Armed Forces (FAR); the Rwandan Patriotic Front (RPF); the police; and the Gendarmerie Nationale).

consonant with the definition of crimes against humanity under customary international law.[158] Indeed, the caution expressed by the *Tadić* and *Limaj* Trial Chambers against importing concepts from international humanitarian law into the law on crimes against humanity seems particularly appropriate, given that the armed conflict requirement that is present in the ICTY Statute – and which perhaps unduly colours its approach to the issue – is not an element of the crimes under customary international law.

2.2.2.3.2 The definition of a 'civilian population' For the definition of a civilian population, the *ad hoc* chambers have uniformly adopted the approach of subparagraphs (2) and (3) of Article 50 of Additional Protocol I, which provide:

2. The civilian population comprises all persons who are civilians.
3. The presence within the civilian population of individuals who do not come within the definition of civilians does not deprive the population of its civilian character.[159]

Trial and appeals chambers of both Tribunals have held, on the basis of this provision, that the population in question need only be predominantly civilian in order to satisfy this general requirement for crimes against humanity.[160] Thus the *Blagojević and Jokić* Trial Chamber concluded that a particular attack was undoubtedly directed against a civilian population, notwithstanding the presence of combatants among the targeted:

> The attack was clearly directed against the Bosnian Muslim civilian population in the Srebrenica enclave. The Trial Chamber has heard evidence that the 28th Division of the [Army of Bosnia-Herzegovina] was located in the Srebrenica enclave and that members of that division were among the men that formed the column. However, the Trial Chamber finds that the estimated number of members of the [Army of Bosnia-Herzegovina] present in the enclave and among the column, ranging from about 1,000 soldiers to 4,000 soldiers do[es] not amount to such numbers that the civilian character of the population would be affected, as the vast majority of the people present in the enclave itself and in the column were civilians.[161]

Perhaps out of a desire to keep the applicable law as flexible as possible, neither Tribunal has to date attempted to articulate a more precise standard for determining whether a particular mixed combatant-civilian population is sufficiently civilian to qualify as a target of crimes against humanity. In considering whether there is a

[158] For example, the ICC's Elements of Crimes do not appear to require that the victim be a civilian. See, e.g., Assembly of States Parties to the Rome Statute of the International Criminal Court, First Session: Official Records, Part II(B): Elements of Crimes, UN Doc. ICC-ASP/1/3 (2002) ('ICC Elements of Crimes'), Art. 7(1)(a), Element 1 (defining the relevant element of murder as a crime against humanity as the killing of 'one or more persons', without further elaboration). See also *infra* text accompanying note 542 (noting that there is no definition of the term 'civilian population' or 'civilian' in the Rome Statute or Elements of Crimes).

[159] Additional Protocol I, *supra* note 9, Art. 50.

[160] See *supra* notes 118–119.

[161] *Blagojević and Jokić* Trial Judgement, *supra* note 75, para. 552.

threshold at which the presence of combatants deprived a population of its civilian character, the *Blaškić* Appeals Chamber quoted the official commentary to Article 50, which had noted that 'in wartime conditions it is inevitable that individuals belonging to the category of combatants become intermingled with the civilian population, for example, soldiers on leave visiting their families'.[162] With no further elaboration on the commentary's observation, the Appeals Chamber then held that 'in order to determine whether the presence of soldiers within a civilian population deprives the population of its civilian character, the number of soldiers, as well as whether they are on leave, must be examined'.[163]

Finally, the chambers of the ICTY have repeatedly emphasised that customary international law protects any and all civilian populations, so it is unnecessary to prove that the targeted population at issue was linked with one or the other party to an armed conflict.[164]

2.2.2.3.3 The meaning of 'directed against' The expression 'directed against' indicates that in the context of a crime against humanity, the civilian population must be the primary object of the attack.[165] To determine whether an alleged attack was targeted in this manner, the settled jurisprudence of the Tribunals directs trial chambers to consider several factors including:

> the means and method used in the course of the attack; the status of the victims; their number; the discriminatory nature of the attack; the nature of the crimes committed in the course of the attack; the resistance to the assailants at the time; and the extent to which the attacking force may be said to have complied or attempted to comply with the precautionary requirements of the laws of war.[166]

Certain ICTY judgements have held that, in order to constitute part of an attack 'directed against' a civilian population, the acts in question cannot be capable of characterisation as offences directed at random individuals, even if those individuals

162 ICRC Commentary to the Additional Protocols, *supra* note 127, p. 612, para. 1922.

163 *Blaškić* Appeal Judgement, *supra* note 88, paras. 113–115 (footnotes omitted); accord, e.g., *Limaj et al.* Trial Judgement, *supra* note 75, para. 186; *Brđanin* Trial Judgement, *supra* note 80, para. 134.

164 See, e.g., *Limaj et al.* Trial Judgement, *supra* note 75, para. 186; *Blagojević and Jokić* Trial Judgement, *supra* note 75, para. 544; *Prosecutor* v. *Vasiljević*, Case No. IT-98-32-T, Judgement, 29 November 2002 ('*Vasiljević* Trial Judgement'), para. 33. See also *Semanza* Trial Judgement, *supra* note 85, para. 326 (also referring to 'any civilian population').

165 *Kunarac et al.* Appeal Judgement, *supra* note 75, para. 91; accord *Blaškić* Appeal Judgement, *supra* note 88, para. 106; *Limaj et al.* Trial Judgment, *supra* note 75, para. 185; *Stakić* Trial Judgement, *supra* note 80, para. 624; *Semanza* Trial Judgement, *supra* note 85, para. 330.

166 *Kunarac et al.* Appeal Judgement, *supra* note 75, para. 91 (directing also that '[t]o the extent that the alleged crimes against humanity were committed in the course of an armed conflict, the laws of war provide a benchmark against which the Chamber may assess the nature of the attack and the legality of the acts committed in its midst') (footnote omitted); accord *Kordić and Čerkez* Appeal Judgement, *supra* note 95, para. 96; *Blaškić* Appeal Judgement, *supra* note 88, para. 105.

are civilians. The *Stakić* Trial Judgement concluded, after evaluating the evidence presented at trial, that:

the events which took place in Prijedor municipality between 30 April and 30 September 1992 constitute an attack directed against a civilian population. The scale of the attack was such that it cannot be characterised as having been directed against only a limited and randomly selected group of individuals. Rather, most of the non-Serb population in the Municipality of Prijedor was directly affected.[167]

Conversely, the *Limaj* Trial Chamber ruled that, although the evidence established that the Kosovo Liberation Army had abducted and in some cases killed Serbian civilians, there was insufficient evidence to establish that these occurrences were coordinated actions targeting the population as such, instead of those individuals in particular:

The evidence does not allow a determination in most cases as to why some were released, but others not. Clearly, in many cases there was a process of decision by the KLA. On what basis that process of decision turned is not, however, established by the evidence ... Whatever was the basis, the existence of a process of decision which affected the consequences of KLA abduction tells with some force against the existence and perpetration of a general KLA strategy of abduction of the Serbian civilian population of Kosovo. The evidence does not establish that the abduction, detention or mistreatment of Serbian civilians was on a scale or frequency such that the attack could be considered to have been directed against a civilian population.[168]

2.2.2.4 The 'widespread or systematic' requirement

This attack is widespread or systematic.

Under the *ad hoc* Tribunals' jurisprudence, the attack must constitute 'a pattern of widespread or systematic crimes', so that crimes against humanity are distinguished from isolated or unconnected crimes against individuals.[169] Applying the terminology used in this series,[170] it is more accurate to state that the attack must consist of widespread or systematic *underlying offences*, not crimes, because it is the evaluation of whether the relevant general requirements are satisfied that will determine whether a given offence qualifies as an international crime within the jurisdiction of the Tribunals.

167 *Stakić* Trial Judgement, *supra* note 80, para. 627.

168 *Limaj et al.* Trial Judgement, *supra* note 75, para. 225.

169 *Blaškić* Appeal Judgement, *supra* note 88, para. 98; *Kordić and Čerkez* Appeal Judgement, *supra* note 95, para. 93; *Kunarac et al.* Appeal Judgement, *supra* note 75, para. 85; *Tadić* Appeal Judgement, *supra* note 75, para. 248; *Muvunyi* Trial Judgement, *supra* note 84, para. 514 ('"[S]ystematic" reflects the organized nature of the attack, excludes acts of random violence, and does not require a policy or plan.'); *Semanza* Trial Judgement, *supra* note 85, para. 329 (same). See also *Mrkšić et al.* Rule 61 Decision, *supra* note 93, para. 30; Report of the Secretary-General Pursuant to Paragraph 2 of Security Council Resolution 808, UN Doc. S/25704, 3 May 1993, para. 48 ('Crimes against humanity refer to inhumane acts of a very serious nature, such as wilful killing, torture or rape, *committed as part of a widespread or systematic attack* against any civilian population on national, political, ethnic, racial or religious grounds.') (emphasis added).

170 See Chapter 1, section 1.2.

The requirement that the attack be widespread or systematic is disjunctive;[171] once a chamber concludes that either requirement is met, it need not consider whether the alternative qualifier is also satisfied.[172] The term 'widespread' refers to the large-scale nature of the attack and the number of targeted persons,[173] while the term 'systematic' refers to the organised nature of the underlying offences and the unlikelihood of their random occurrence.[174] As the *Kunarac* Trial Chamber noted, in an oft-repeated observation, 'patterns of crimes – that is the non-accidental repetition of similar criminal conduct on a regular basis – are a common expression of such systematic occurrence.'[175]

The assessment of what constitutes a 'widespread' or 'systematic' attack is a fact-dependent exercise, that is influenced by the civilian population that was attacked.[176] Trial chambers must therefore 'first identify the population which is the object of the attack and, in light of the means, methods, resources and result of

[171] See, e.g., *Ntakirutimana and Ntakirutimana* Appeal Judgement, *supra* note 95, para. 516; *Kunarac et al.* Appeal Judgement, *supra* note 75, para. 93; *Tadić* Appeal Judgement, *supra* note 75, para 248.

[172] See, e.g., *Ntakirutimana and Ntakirutimana* Appeal Judgement, *supra* note 95, para. 516; *Kunarac et al.* Appeal Judgement, *supra* note 75, para. 93; see also *Akayesu* Trial Judgement, *supra* note 94, para. 579 (noting also, in footnote 144, that the French version of the ICTR Statute presents these as cumulative criteria, but '[s]ince Customary International Law requires only that the attack be either widespread or systematic, there are sufficient reasons to assume that the French version suffers from an error in translation'); accord *Media* Appeal Judgement, *supra* note 110, para. 920; *Ntakirutimana and Ntakirutimana* Appeal Judgement, *supra* note 95, para. 516 n. 883; *Semanza* Trial Judgement, *supra* note 85, para. 328 and n. 548 (collecting ICTR trial judgements and observing that 'this jurisprudence does not fully articulate the basis of such a custom', but following the uniform practice of both Tribunals); *ibid.*, para. 442 ('Having found that the attack was widespread, the Chamber need not consider whether it was also systematic.'); see also *Kunarac et al.* Trial Judgement, *supra* note 90, para. 578 (finding that the attack was systematic without also determining whether it was widespread); *Blagojević and Jokić* Trial Judgement, *supra* note 75, para. 551 (finding that the attack was 'widespread or systematic', but not specifying whether it was both); *Brđanin* Trial Judgement, *supra* note 80, para. 157 (same). Many trial judgements, of course, conclude that both of the alternative requirements are satisfied. See, e.g., *Niyitegeka* Trial Judgement, *supra* note 94, para. 440 (finding that '[t]he attacks were methodical, organized and on a large scale, involving many armed attackers', and therefore that 'there was a widespread and systematic attack against the civilian Tutsi population' in the relevant geographical area); see also *infra* note 497 and accompanying text.

[173] *Gacumbitsi* Appeal Judgement, *supra* note 95, para. 101 (approving of the Trial Chamber's definition, which held that '[t]he attack must be massive or large scale, involving many victims') (quoting *Gacumbitsi* Trial Judgement, *supra* note 85, para. 299) (internal quotation marks omitted); accord *Kordić and Čerkez* Appeal Judgement, *supra* note 95, para. 94; *Blaškić* Appeal Judgement, *supra* note 88, para. 101; *Kunarac et al.* Appeal Judgement, *supra* note 75, para. 94. See also *Akayesu* Trial Judgement, *supra* note 94, para. 580 ('The concept of "widespread" may be defined as massive, frequent, large scale action, carried out collectively with considerable seriousness and directed against a multiplicity of victims.'); accord *Media* Appeal Judgement, *supra* note 110, para. 920; *Ntakirutimana and Ntakirutimana* Trial Judgement, *supra* note 94, para. 804; *Niyitegeka* Trial Judgement, *supra* note 94, para. 439; *Semanza* Trial Judgement, *supra* note 85, para. 329.

[174] *Kordić and Čerkez* Appeal Judgement, *supra* note 95, para. 94; *Blaškić* Appeal Judgement, *supra* note 88, para. 101; *Kunarac et al.* Appeal Judgement, *supra* note 75, para. 94; see also *Akayesu* Trial Judgement, *supra* note 94, para. 580 (holding that '"systematic" may be defined [*inter alia*] as thoroughly organised and following a regular pattern'); accord *Media* Appeal Judgement, *supra* note 110, para. 920; *Gacumbitsi* Appeal Judgement, *supra* note 95, para. 101; *Ntakirutimana and Ntakirutimana* Trial Judgement, *supra* note 94, para. 804; *Niyitegeka* Trial Judgement, *supra* note 94, para. 439; *Semanza* Trial Judgement, *supra* note 85, para. 329.

[175] *Kunarac et al.* Trial Judgment, *supra* note 90, para. 429, quoted in *Kunarac et al.* Appeal Judgement, *supra* note 75, para. 94, paraphrased in *Blaškić* Appeal Judgement, *supra* note 88, para. 101; *Kordić and Čerkez* Appeal Judgement, *supra* note 95, para. 94. Accord *Gacumbitsi* Appeal Judgement, *supra* note 95, para. 101.

[176] See *Kunarac et al.* Appeal Judgement, *supra* note 75, para. 95 (citing *Kunarac et al.* Trial Judgement, *supra* note 90, para. 430).

the attack upon the population, ascertain whether the attack was indeed widespread or systematic'.[177] The consequences of the attack upon the targeted population, the number of victims, the nature of the acts, the possible participation of officials or authorities, or any identifiable patterns of underlying offences are among the factors that could be taken into account to determine whether the attack satisfies either or both requirements of a 'widespread' or 'systematic' attack with respect to a given civilian population.[178] Accordingly, after consideration of the evidence, the *Niyitegeka* Trial Chamber held:

> There is evidence of daily attacks in Bisesero against the Tutsi seeking shelter there, leading to thousands of Tutsi being killed, and of a large number of corpses in Kibuye town at the relevant time, the corpses being that of Tutsi refugees. The evidence further shows that the Tutsi being targeted were of all ages and both sexes. The attacks were methodical, organized and on a large scale, involving many armed attackers, especially those on 13 and 14 May 1994. Therefore, the Chamber finds that there was a widespread and systematic attack against the civilian Tutsi population on ethnic grounds in Kibuye Prefecture, in particular, in Bisesero, from April to July 1994.[179]

Proof of a plan or policy is not required for crimes against humanity,[180] although it may be relevant in evaluating the evidence presented to prove that an attack was directed against a civilian population and that it was widespread or systematic.[181]

2.2.2.5 The first contextual requirement: the underlying offence as part of the attack

The conduct of the physical perpetrator forms part of this attack.

In its first judgement on the merits, the ICTY Appeals Chamber concluded in *Tadić* that the underlying offences of crimes against humanity 'must comprise part of a pattern of widespread or systematic crimes directed against a civilian population'.[182] It clarified that those acts must have an objective nexus to the attack, but

[177] *Ibid.* [178] See *ibid.* [179] *Niyitegeka* Trial Judgement, *supra* note 94, para. 440

[180] See *Gacumbitsi* Appeal Judgement, *supra* note 95, para. 84 (affirming the Trial Chamber's holding that 'the existence of a policy or plan can be evidentially relevant, but it is not a separate legal element of a crime against humanity'); accord *Media* Appeal Judgement, *supra* note 110, para. 922; *Blaškić* Appeal Judgement, *supra* note 88, paras. 120, 126; *Prosecutor* v. *Krstić*, Case No. IT-98-33-A, Judgement, 19 April 2004 ('*Krstić* Appeal Judgement'), para. 225; *Kunarac et al.* Appeal Judgement, *supra* note 75, para. 98 n. 114. See also *Martić* Trial Judgement, *supra* note 75, para. 49 ('It is settled jurisprudence that the existence of a plan need not be proven.'); accord *Blagojević and Jokić* Trial Judgement, *supra* note 75, para. 546. See also *supra* note 59 and accompanying text (discussing the policy requirement in the 1954 ILC Draft Code, and comparing the respective positions of the different international and internationalised tribunals on whether there is a requirement); *infra* text accompanying notes 493–496 (discussing the policy requirement in the ICC).

[181] *Media* Appeal Judgement, *supra* note 110, para. 920; *Gacumbitsi* Appeal Judgement, *supra* note 95, paras. 84, 101; *Prosecutor* v. *Semanza*, Case No. ICTR-97-20A, Judgement, para. 269; *Kordić and Čerkez* Appeal Judgement, *supra* note 95, para. 98; *Blaškić* Appeal Judgement, *supra* note 88, para. 120; *Kunarac et al.* Appeal Judgement, *supra* note 75, para. 98. Accord, e.g., *Limaj et al.* Trial Judgement, *supra* note 75, paras. 184, 212; *Brđanin* Trial Judgement, *supra* note 80, para. 137.

[182] *Tadić* Appeal Judgement, *supra* note 75, para. 248.

they need not have a similar link to the armed conflict as a whole.[183] As later judgements make clear, moreover, the offences need not be committed in the midst of an attack on a civilian population in order to be considered part of that attack. An offence which is committed before or after the main attack against the civilian population or away from it could still, if sufficiently connected, be part of that attack.[184] While the determination of whether a given offence is sufficiently connected to the attack will depend on the facts of the case, it is clear that the offence cannot be an isolated act: it cannot be so far removed from the attack that, having considered the context and circumstances in which it was committed, it cannot reasonably be said to have been part of that attack.[185]

There is no minimum threshold requirement: the conduct of the physical perpetrator need only be a part of the attack, and all other conditions being met, a single or relatively limited number of offences would qualify as a crime against humanity, unless those offences are isolated or random.[186]

2.2.2.6 The second contextual requirement: the knowledge that the offence is part of the attack

The physical perpetrator, or other relevant actor, knows of this attack, and knows that the conduct of the physical perpetrator forms part of this attack.[187]

The general mental element requirement for crimes against humanity can be broken down into two sub-elements: the physical perpetrator or other relevant

183 *Ibid.*, para. 251; accord, e.g., *Mrkšić et al.* Trial Judgement, *supra* note 77, para. 433; *Kunarac et al.* Trial Judgement, *supra* note 90, para. 413, affirmed in *Kunarac et al.* Appeal Judgement, *supra* note 75, paras. 82–83, 99; *Stakić* Trial Judgement, *supra* note 80, para. 570. See *supra* section 2.2.1.1 for a discussion of the armed conflict requirement in the context of Article 5 of the ICTY Statute.

184 See, e.g., *Kunarac et al.* Appeal Judgement, *supra* note 75, para. 100; *Semanza* Trial Judgement, *supra* note 85, para. 326 ('Although the [underlying offence] need not be committed at the same time and place as the attack or share all of the features of the attack, it must, by its characteristics, aims, nature, or consequence objectively form part of the … attack.').

185 *Kunarac et al.* Appeal Judgement, *supra* note 75, para. 100; *Kupreškić et al.* Trial Judgement, *supra* note 71, para. 550. See also *Semanza* Trial Judgement, *supra* note 85, para. 330 ('[T]he victim(s) of the [underlying offence] need not necessarily share geographic or other defining features with the civilian population that forms the primary target of the … attack, but such characteristics may be used to demonstrate that the [underlying offence] forms part of the attack.'); *Krnojelac* Trial Judgement, *supra* note 111, para. 55 ('A crime committed several months after, or several kilometres away from, the main attack against the civilian population could still, if sufficiently connected, be part of that attack.') (citing *Kunarac et al.* Trial Judgment, *supra* note 90, paras. 417 *et seq.*).

186 See *Media* Appeal Judgement, *supra* note 110, paras. 923–924 (with the exception of extermination, rejecting the assertion that offences must be committed against a multiplicity of victims in order to constitute crimes against humanity); *Blaškić* Appeal Judgement, *supra* note 88, para. 101; *Kordić and Čerkez* Appeal Judgement, *supra* note 95, para. 94; *Kunarac et al.* Appeal Judgement, *supra* note 75, para. 96. See especially *Blagojević and Jokić* Trial Judgement, *supra* note 75, para. 545 ('A crime may be widespread by the "cumulative effect of a series of inhumane acts or the singular effect of an inhumane act of extraordinary magnitude[.]"') (quoting 1996 ILC Draft Code with Commentaries, *supra* note 55, p. 47).

187 In practical terms, of course, a finding that the physical perpetrator or other relevant actor knew that the acts charged formed part of the attack would necessarily require a finding that he knew of the attack, while conversely, if it could not be shown that he knew the acts charged formed part of the attack, his knowledge of the attack itself is insufficient and likely irrelevant.

actor[188] (1) knows that there is a widespread or systematic attack on the civilian population, and (2) knows that the underlying offences comprise part of that attack.[189] This requirement does not demand knowledge of the particular details of the attack.[190] Earlier restatements of this requirement, including the 2002 *Kunarac* Appeal Judgement, included the alternative that the person committing the offences 'took the risk' that his acts formed part of the attack.[191] The next time either *ad hoc* Appeals Chamber considered the question was in the 2004 *Blaškić* Judgement; there, the ICTY Appeals Chamber held that the Trial Chamber had erred when it followed the *Kunarac* line of authority to hold that 'it suffices that [the accused or physical perpetrator] knowingly took the risk of participating' in the attack.[192] Even though the *Blaškić* Appeals Chamber offered no reason for its abrupt limitation of the permissible mental states for crimes against humanity to actual knowledge that the underlying offences were part of the attack, subsequent judgements have generally applied the more restrictive formulation of this general requirement.[193]

As a matter of law, this mental element requirement is distinct from the motives the physical perpetrator may have had for taking part in the attack, which are irrelevant, and a crime against humanity may be committed for 'purely personal' reasons.[194] Both Appeals Chambers have emphasised that 'even in the event that personal motivations can be identified in the [physical perpetrator's] carrying out of an act, it does not necessarily follow that the required nexus with the attack on a

188 Such as the person who planned, ordered, or instigated the conduct of the physical perpetrator. See *supra* section 2.2.2.1 (discussing our use of the term 'other relevant actor' in this context).

189 See *Kunarac et al.* Appeal Judgement, *supra* note 75, paras. 85, 99, 102–103; *Tadić* Appeal Judgement, *supra* note 75, paras. 248, 251, 271; see also generally *Blaškić* Appeal Judgement, *supra* note 88, paras. 121–127; *Kordić and Čerkez* Appeal Judgement, *supra* note 95, para. 99.

190 See, e.g., *Kunarac et al.* Appeal Judgement, *supra* note 75, para. 102; *Mrkšić et al.* Trial Judgement, *supra* note 77, para. 439; *Martić* Trial Judgement, *supra* note 75, para. 49.

191 See, e.g., *Kunarac et al.* Appeal Judgement, *supra* note 75, para. 102 (explicitly affirming the Trial Chamber's formulation and quoting its language, including the alternative that 'the accused … took the risk that his acts were part of the attack') (quoting *Kunarac et al.* Trial Judgement, *supra* note 90, para. 434); *Simić* et al. Trial Judgement, *supra* note 115, para. 46; *Stakić* Trial Judgement, *supra* note 80, para. 626; *Vasiljević* Trial Judgement, *supra* note 164, para. 37; *Krnojelac* Trial Judgement, *supra* note 111, para. 59.

192 *Blaškić* Appeal Judgement, *supra* note 88, para. 126 (quoting with disapproval *Blaškić* Trial Judgement, *supra* note 90, para. 257).

193 See, e.g., *Krajišnik* Trial Judgement, *supra* note 117, para. 705 (following the *Blaškić* Appeal Judgement); *Limaj et al.* Trial Judgement, *supra* note 75, para. 190 (same); *Blagojević and Jokić* Trial Judgement, *supra* note 75, paras. 541, 547 (following *Blaškić*, but only citing *Kunarac*); *Brđanin* Trial Judgement, *supra* note 80, para. 130 (same). But see *Mrkšić et al.* Trial Judgement, *supra* note 77, paras. 435, 439 (initially omitting the mental elements entirely from its list of the general requirements, but then reprising the *Kunarac* Appeal Judgement's 'took the risk' alternative without acknowledging the intervening *Blaškić* Appeal Judgement); *Martić* Trial Judgement, *supra* note 75, para. 49 (also retaining the 'took the risk' alternative). This partial failure to apply the *Blaškić* holding is perhaps surprising, because ICTY trial chambers are obliged to apply the decisions of the appellate chamber. See *Prosecutor* v. *Aleksovski*, Case No. IT-95-14/1-A, Judgement, 24 March 2000 ('*Aleksovski* Appeal Judgement'), para. 113; see also Boas, Bischoff, and Reid, *supra* note 100, p. 26 n. 94 (discussing the binding nature of *ad hoc* appellate jurisprudence).

194 See *Kunarac et al.* Appeal Judgement, *supra* note 75, para. 103; *Tadić* Appeal Judgement, *supra* note 75, paras. 248, 252, 272.

civilian population must also inevitably be lacking'.[195] The physical perpetrator need not share the purpose or goal behind the attack,[196] and it is irrelevant whether he intended the underlying offences to be directed against the targeted population or merely against the victim or victims concerned.[197] It is the attack, not the underlying offences, which must be directed against the target population, and the physical perpetrator or other relevant actor need only know that the conduct for which he is responsible is part of that attack.[198]

The *Blaškić* Appeals Chamber held that evidence of this knowledge 'depends on the facts of a particular case … , [so] the manner in which this legal element may be proved may vary from case to case'; the Chamber therefore declined 'to set out a list of evidentiary elements which, if proved, would establish the requisite knowledge'.[199]

2.2.3 Underlying offences

Unlike the open-ended design of Article 3 of the ICTY Statute and Article 4 of the ICTR Statute, which both explicitly state that their lists of war crimes are not exhaustive, the list of crimes in Article 5 of the ICTY Statute and Article 3 of the ICTR Statute is comprehensive, so the offence charged must fall within the scope of the article's subparagraphs in order for it to be considered a crime against humanity in the Tribunals' jurisdiction.[200] That said, one category of offences punishable under the article – inhumane acts – is clearly designed as a residual provision *internal to* the article.[201] In order to qualify as a crime against humanity, however, an offence charged as an inhumane act must nevertheless be of a gravity similar to the enumerated crimes in the article.[202]

Each subsection below discusses the elements of the underlying offence or offences for each crime against humanity within the jurisdiction of the *ad hoc*

[195] *Gacumbitsi* Appeal Judgement, *supra* note 95, para. 103 (quoting and citing *Tadić* Appeal Judgement, *supra* note 75, para. 252) (internal quotation marks omitted).

[196] See *Kordić and Čerkez* Appeal Judgement, *supra* note 95, para. 99; *Blaškić* Appeal Judgement, *supra* note 88, para. 124; *Kunarac et al.* Appeal Judgement, *supra* note 75, para. 103; accord, e.g., *Blagojević and Jokić* Trial Judgement, *supra* note 75, para. 548; *Galić* Trial Judgement, *supra* note 110, para. 148.

[197] See *Kunarac et al.* Appeal Judgement, *supra* note 75, para. 103; accord, e.g., *Mrkšić et al.* Trial Judgement, *supra* note 77, para. 439.

[198] See *Kunarac et al.* Appeal Judgement, *supra* note 75, paras. 102, 103; *Blaškić* Appeal Judgement, *supra* note 88, paras. 121–127.

[199] *Blaškić* Appeal Judgement, *supra* note 88, para. 126. See also Mettraux, *supra* note 55, p. 173 (listing several factors that chambers have considered in determining 'the perpetrator's awareness of his participation' in the attack).

[200] We therefore disagree with the *Muvunyi* Trial Judgement, *supra* note 84, para. 515, which asserts that 'Article 3 of the [ICTR] Statute lays down a non-exhaustive list of acts that constitute crimes against humanity'.

[201] See *Kordić and Čerkez* Appeal Judgement, *supra* note 95, para. 117 (quoting and endorsing *Kupreškić et al.* Trial Judgement, *supra* note 71, para. 563, for the proposition that 'inhumane acts as crimes against humanity were deliberately designed as a residual category, as it was felt undesirable for this category to be exhaustively enumerated') (internal quotation marks omitted).

[202] See, e.g., *Krnojelac* Trial Judgement, *supra* note 111, para. 130; *Tadić* Trial Judgement, *supra* note 77, para. 729. For more detail, see *infra* section 2.2.3.9.1.

Tribunals. Two of the subparagraphs in the article actually list subcategories of underlying offences, namely persecution and inhumane acts.[203] The corresponding subsections of the following analysis will first discuss the specific requirements that must be satisfied before an underlying offence may fall within those subcategories, and then outline the elements of each such offence as it has been defined in the Tribunals' jurisprudence.

2.2.3.1 Murder

The conduct of the physical perpetrator caused the death of an individual (the 'victim'), and the physical perpetrator either intended to kill the victim or intended to inflict harm in the reasonable knowledge that the conduct was likely to cause death. It is unclear whether the conduct must be premeditated.

Chambers of both *ad hoc* Tribunals have generally presented a consistent definition of the physical elements of murder as a crime against humanity, listing them as (1) the death of a person, frequently termed the 'victim', (2) as a result of (3) the conduct of the physical perpetrator.[204] Most judgements state that the conduct causing death must be that of the accused,[205] or of someone for whose conduct the accused bears criminal responsibility.[206] Both formulations are incorrect. First, focusing the definition on the accused is overly restrictive and inconsistent with the actual practice of the Tribunals, because it fails to acknowledge the findings in cases where the accused are not charged with physically committing the crimes in the indictment.[207] Second, importing the question of individual criminal responsibility into the definition of the crime conflates two distinct legal questions: 'was a crime committed?' and 'is the accused responsible?'. Although the conduct leading to the

[203] As explained below, an underlying offence may qualify as persecution even if it is neither listed in the *ad hoc* Statutes nor qualifies as a crime under international law. See *infra* text accompanying notes 395–398. Although one could therefore argue that persecution should also be considered as a residual category, the key distinction between persecution and inhumane acts is that the former is characterised by unique and heightened specific requirements, while the only restriction on the latter is that the offence be of similar gravity to those already listed in the Statute. As such, only inhumane acts may appropriately be termed the residual or 'catchall' subcategory of offences that may constitute crimes against humanity.

[204] ICTY judgements frequently observe that the elements of the underlying offence of murder are identical, regardless of the particular category of international crime charged – that is, crimes against humanity, genocide, or war crimes. See, e.g., *Brđanin* Trial Judgement, *supra* note 80, paras. 380–381; *Blagojević and Jokić* Trial Judgement, *supra* note 75, para. 556; *Kordić and Čerkez* Trial Judgement, *supra* note 75, para. 236. While generally true, this observation glosses over differences in the permissible scope of the *mens rea* for murder. As discussed in Chapter 3, *ad hoc* jurisprudence has generally held that only intentional murder may be an underlying offence of genocide. See Chapter 3, section 3.2.2.1.2. As discussed below, the ICTR definition of murder as a crime against humanity has an additional element that the standard ICTY definition does not. See *infra* text accompanying notes 214–222.

[205] See, e.g., *Blagojević and Jokić* Trial Judgement, *supra* note 75, para. 556; *Bagilishema* Trial Judgement, *supra* note 87, para. 84.

[206] See, e.g., *Brđanin* Trial Judgement, *supra* note 80, para. 381; *Akayesu* Trial Judgement, *supra* note 94, para. 589.

[207] See, e.g., *Blagojević and Jokić* Trial Judgement, *supra* note 75, para. 569 (concluding that the acts of the 'direct perpetrators' satisfied the elements of the underlying offence of murder).

death cannot be the basis for a conviction in a particular case if it is not committed by the accused in that case, or a person for whom he bears responsibility, that does not mean that it is not murder. If the trial chamber decides, as many do, to have separate findings on the elements of the crimes and the accused's responsibility for those crimes, it may indeed conclude that a murder as a crime against humanity was committed, but that the accused is not liable for the murder because he was not the superior of the physical perpetrators, or did not aid and abet the murder, for example. It is thus incorrect to define the crime in such a manner as to assume that the only circumstances in which the conduct is criminal is if it is committed by the accused or someone for whose conduct he is responsible.[208]

In order to prove beyond reasonable doubt that a victim is dead, the prosecution need not establish that the body has been recovered, and a trial chamber may conclude that death occurred from circumstantial evidence presented at trial, as long as that conclusion is the only reasonable inference that may be drawn.[209] The requirement that death occur 'as a result of' the physical perpetrator's conduct has not been interpreted as a rule of 'but-for' causation, and the prosecution need only prove that the conduct was a substantial contributing factor in the victim's death.[210] Thus the *Krnojelac* Trial Chamber held that, as a matter of law, the accused could be convicted of murder as a crime against humanity for an individual's suicide if the physical perpetrator's conduct caused the victim to take his own life, and 'the [a] ccused, or those for whom he bears criminal responsibility … intended by that act or omission to cause the suicide of the victim, or have known that the suicide of the victim was a likely and foreseeable result of the act or omission.'[211]

In contrast to the near-uniformity of the definition of the physical elements, there is a clear split in the *ad hoc* jurisprudence at the trial level about the *mens rea* for murder as a crime against humanity. Although there is some disagreement or inconsistency within the judgements of each Tribunal, most ICTR trial judgements state that in order to constitute an underlying offence for a crime against humanity, the murder must be premeditated, while most ICTY judgements are either silent or explicitly reject a premeditation requirement.

[208] See also *infra* note 307 (discussing this issue with respect to imprisonment as a crime against humanity).

[209] See, e.g., *Tadić* Trial Judgement, *supra* note 77, para. 240 (refusing to find that certain named victims were killed because the prosecution had failed to provide 'evidence to link injuries received to a resulting death', and emphasising that '[w]hen there is more than one conclusion reasonably open on the evidence, it is not for this Trial Chamber to draw the conclusion least favourable to the accused'); accord *Brđanin* Trial Judgement, *supra* note 80, paras. 383, 385; *Krnojelac* Trial Judgement, *supra* note 111, para. 326; *Prosecutor* v. *Ngeze*, Case No. ICTR-97-27, Oral Decision, 21 June 2001 (cited in *Brđanin* Trial Judgement, *supra* note 80, para. 384).

[210] See, e.g., *Brđanin* Trial Judgement, *supra* note 80, para. 382.

[211] *Krnojelac* Trial Judgement, *supra* note 111, para. 329. Ultimately, the Trial Chamber concluded that the prosecution had not established that the individual in question committed suicide as a result of the severe beating and other mistreatment he suffered at the hands of the guards at the prison where Krnojelac was warden. *Ibid.*, para. 342.

In *Akayesu*, the Trial Chamber noted that the English version of the ICTR's Statute listed murder as a crime against humanity, but that the equivalent French provision listed '*assassinat'*. Without explaining that the distinction between the two is that the latter requires premeditation, the Chamber concluded that since 'Customary International Law dictates that it is the act of "Murder" that constitutes a crime against humanity', the *mens rea* requirement for this underlying offence would be satisfied by a showing that the physical perpetrator 'had the intention to kill or inflict grievous bodily harm on the deceased having known that such bodily harm is likely to cause the victim's death, and is reckless whether death [ensues] or not'.[212] Two subsequent trial judgements adopted this reasoning,[213] but the different approach of the *Kayishema and Ruzindana* Trial Judgement has proved much more persuasive to other ICTR chambers. Emphasising that it is a matter of textual interpretation, the *Kayishema and Ruzindana* Chamber concluded that the difference between the English and French versions of the Statute 'should be decided in favour of the accused', which required the inclusion of the additional element of premeditation and thus a higher *mens rea* standard.[214] As the *Semanza* Trial Chamber later explained, '[p]remeditation requires that, at a minimum, the [physical perpetrator] held a deliberate plan to kill prior to the act causing death, rather than forming the intention simultaneously with the act … a cool moment of reflection is sufficient'.[215] Under the higher standard applied by almost all ICTR Trial Chambers, an intent merely to cause harm to the victim would be insufficient.

In the ICTY, on the other hand, only the *Kupreškić* Trial Chamber has held that 'the standard of *mens rea* required is intentional and premeditated killing', although it did also state in the same paragraph that the standard is satisfied by 'the intent to inflict serious injury in reckless disregard of human life'.[216] Other ICTY trial judgements have either explicitly rejected the notion that premeditation is required for murder as a crime against humanity,[217] or omitted it from their recitation of the elements of the offence.[218] The description in the *Brđanin* Trial Judgement is thus

[212] *Akayesu* Trial Judgement, *supra* note 94, para. 588.

[213] See *Rutaganda* Trial Judgement, *supra* note 114, para. 79; *Musema* Trial Judgement, *supra* note 114, para. 214.

[214] *Kayishema and Ruzindana* Trial Judgement, *supra* note 90, paras. 137–140. Accord, e.g., *Prosecutor* v. *Muhimana*, Case No. ICTR- 95–1B-T, Judgement and Sentence, 28 April 2005 ('*Muhimana* Trial Judgement'), para. 569; *Semanza* Trial Judgement, *supra* note 85, paras. 334–339; *Bagilishema* Trial Judgement, *supra* note 87, para. 84.

[215] *Semanza* Trial Judgement, *supra* note 85, para. 339.

[216] *Kupreškić et al.* Trial Judgement, *supra* note 71, para. 561.

[217] See, e.g., *Kordić and Čerkez* Trial Judgement, *supra* note 75, para. 235; *Blaškić* Trial Judgement, *supra* note 90, para. 216; *Jelisić* Trial Judgement, *supra* note 94, para. 51.

[218] See, e.g., *Blagojević and Jokić* Trial Judgement, *supra* note 75, para. 556; *Prosecutor* v. *Krstić*, Case No. IT-98-33-T, Judgement, 2 August 2001 ('*Krstić* Trial Judgement'), para. 485 (incorrectly stating that its definition was the standard one used in both Tribunals).

typical of ICTY trial judgements defining murder as an underlying offence for an international crime within the jurisdiction of the Tribunal:[219]

1. The victim is dead;
2. The death was caused by an act or omission of the accused, or of a person or persons for whose acts or omissions the accused bears criminal responsibility; and
3. The act was done, or the omission was made, by the accused, or a person or persons for whose acts or omissions he bears criminal responsibility, with an intention:
   - to kill, or
   - to inflict grievous bodily harm or serious injury, in the reasonable knowledge that such act or omission was likely to cause death.[220]

The Appeals Chambers have not yet clarified whether premeditation is a requirement for murder as a crime against humanity, either under customary international law or the Tribunals' Statutes. Indeed, it is not always clear that the Appeals Chambers are aware of the variations in the definitions of murder as an underlying offence;[221] it does not appear that any party has raised this particular issue on appeal, and appellate benches have affirmed convictions based on both approaches to the *mens rea* standard.[222]

2.2.3.2 Extermination

The conduct of the physical perpetrator caused the death of an individual or individuals who are part of a numerically significant group of victims; and the physical perpetrator either intended to kill the individual(s) or intended to inflict harm in the reasonable knowledge that the conduct was likely to cause death, and also intended to participate in causing mass death.

Extermination as a crime against humanity shares the same underlying offence as murder as a crime against humanity: the death of an individual caused by the

219 See *supra* note 204 (citing examples of judgements holding that the underlying offence of murder has the same elements regardless of the international crime at issue, but noting that this assertion appears to ignore the stricter standard for genocide and the disagreement between ICTY and ICTR trial chambers for murder as a crime against humanity). See also *supra* text accompanying note 208 (explaining why references to the accused or someone for whose conduct he bears responsibility are incorrect in the definitions of crimes).

220 *Brđanin* Trial Judgement, *supra* note 80, para. 381.

221 See, e.g., *Kordić and Čerkez* Appeal Judgement, *supra* note 95, para. 113 (asserting that '[t]he elements of murder as a crime against humanity are undisputed'); *ibid.*, paras. 36–38 (comparing the definitions of wilful killing as a grave breach of the Geneva Conventions and murder as a violation of the laws or customs of war, which have different *mens rea* standards in the recitation presented by the Appeals Chamber, but then stating that the only material difference between the two is that the former requires that the victim be a protected person under the Geneva Conventions).

222 See, e.g., *Prosecutor* v. *Kupreškić, Kupreškić, Kupreškić, Josipović, Papić, and Šantić*, Case No. IT-95-16-A, Appeal Judgement, 23 October 2001 ('*Kupreškić et al.* Appeal Judgement'), p. 172 (affirming one accused's conviction for murder as a crime against humanity; the issue of the definition does not appear to have been raised on appeal); *Kordić and Čerkez* Appeal Judgement, *supra* note 95, para. 113 (affirming the Trial Chamber's definition, which was identical to the *Blaškić* definition quoted above).

conduct of a physical perpetrator who either intended to kill the victim or intended to inflict harm with knowledge and acceptance of the reasonable likelihood that death would ensue.[223] In order to qualify as extermination, two additional elements must be proved, and both are related to the massive scale of the crime. First, by his conduct, the physical perpetrator must participate in causing the deaths of a massive number of victims; second, he must intend to participate in causing the mass deaths.[224]

From the early years of the ICTR, its trial chambers have emphasised that the deaths need not be caused by direct killing, and that the creation of conditions of life leading to mass death will also satisfy the *actus reus* requirements for extermination.[225] This holding has been echoed in the ICTY's jurisprudence.[226] Such fatal conditions could be caused by, for example, the withholding of basic necessities required to sustain life, such as food and medicine.[227] Although both Tribunals have held that the key feature of extermination as a crime against humanity is that it is *mass* murder – a crime that is collective in nature, and which involves more than singling out individual victims[228] – they have also emphasised that there is no precise threshold requirement for the number of victims.[229] There must be a numerically significant group of victims for the deaths to constitute

[223] See, e.g., *Ntakirutimana and Ntakirutimana* Appeal Judgement, *supra* note 95, para. 522; *Blagojević and Jokić* Trial Judgement, *supra* note 75, para. 571; *Stakić* Trial Judgement, *supra* note 80, para. 229.

[224] See *supra* note 223; see also, e.g., *Prosecutor v. Mpambara*, Case No. ICTR-01-65-T, Judgement, 11 September 2006 ('*Mpambara* Trial Judgement'), para. 9; *Simba* Trial Judgement, *supra* note 154, para. 422; *Brđanin* Trial Judgement, *supra* note 80, para. 388; *Prosecutor* v. *Ndindabahizi*, Case No. ICTR-2001-71-T, Judgement and Sentence, 15 July 2004 ('*Ndindabahizi* Trial Judgement'), para. 479; *Vasiljević* Trial Judgement, *supra* note 164, para. 229.

[225] See, e.g., *Rutaganda* Trial Judgement, *supra* note 114, para. 84; *Kayishema and Ruzindana* Trial Judgement, *supra* note 90, para. 144; *Bagilishema* Trial Judgement, *supra* note 87, para. 89. Accord *Mpambara* Trial Judgement, *supra* note 224, para. 9; *Simba* Trial Judgement, *supra* note 154, para. 422.

[226] See, e.g., *Brđanin* Trial Judgement, *supra* note 80, para. 389 (citing *Krstić* Trial Judgement, *supra* note 218, para. 498, which in turn relied on Rome Statute, *supra* note 59, Art. 7(2)(b)).

[227] See, e.g., *Kayishema and Ruzindana* Trial Judgement, *supra* note 90, para. 146. This alternative *actus reus* for extermination thus echoes the underlying offence for genocide of 'deliberately inflicting on the group conditions of life calculated to bring about its physical destruction in whole or in part'. See Chapter 3, section 3.2.2.3 (discussing the elements of this underlying offence).

[228] See, e.g., *Mpambara* Trial Judgement, *supra* note 224, para. 8; *Blagojević and Jokić* Trial Judgement, *supra* note 75, para. 572; *Brđanin* Trial Judgement, *supra* note 80, para. 388; *Ndindabahizi* Trial Judgement, *supra* note 224, para. 479; *Stakić* Trial Judgement, *supra* note 80, para. 638. But see *Prosecutor* v. *Nahimana, Barayagwiza, and Ngeze*, Case No. ICTR-99-52-T, Judgement and Sentence, 3 December 2003 ('*Media* Trial Judgement'), para. 1061 (holding that the mass element is only part of the distinction between murder and extermination as crimes against humanity, and that there is also a conceptual distinction relating to the victims and the manner in which they are targeted).

[229] See, e.g., *Ntakirutimana and Ntakirutimana* Appeal Judgement, *supra* note 95, para. 516; *Stakić* Appeal Judgement, *supra* note 108, para. 260 (affirming *Stakić* Trial Judgement, *supra* note 80, para. 640); *Kayishema and Ruzindana* Trial Judgement, *supra* note 90, para. 145; *Krstić* Trial Judgement, *supra* note 218, para. 501; *Bagilishema* Trial Judgement, *supra* note 87, para. 87; *Kajelijeli* Trial Judgement, *supra* note 86, para. 891; *Media* Trial Judgement, *supra* note 228, para. 1044; *Prosecutor v. Kamuhanda*, Case No. ICTR-99-54A-T, Judgement and Sentence, 22 January 2003 ('*Kamuhanda* Trial Judgement'), para. 692; *Vasiljević* Trial Judgement, *supra* note 164, para. 227.

extermination,[230] but the element of massiveness should be evaluated in the context of each case.[231]

Qualifying its holding that 'extermination could only be established by proving killing on a massive scale', the *Kayishema and Ruzindana* Trial Chamber observed in a footnote that 'an accused may be guilty of extermination … when sufficient evidence is produced that he or she killed a single person as long as this killing was a part of a mass killing event'.[232] Taking issue with that assertion, the *Vasiljević* and *Brđanin* Trial Chambers averred that customary international law does not support the conclusion that a single killing may qualify as extermination, regardless of its context.[233] Even accepting the disquiet expressed by the *Vasiljević* Chamber that 'the adoption of a more lenient definition [that would cover a single killing] would be prejudicial to the accused',[234] that concern seems misplaced given the predominant profile of the cases before international and internationalised courts and tribunals, where the accused is not the physical perpetrator, but is rather alleged to have been responsible for the conduct of a number of perpetrators. If there are a large number of alleged killers, there would seem to be no logical reason why a single intentional killing by an individual perpetrator may not be an underlying offence of extermination.

Notwithstanding the oft-repeated concern about relaxed standards in the definitions of international crimes, the *Brđanin* Trial Judgement took a decidedly broad approach to the determination of whether the deaths charged met the massiveness requirement. Reiterating a point it had made in its earlier decision on the accused's motion for acquittal,[235] the Trial Chamber stated that 'the element of massiveness of the crime allows for the possibility to establish the evidence of the *actus reus* of extermination on an accumulation of separate and unrelated incidents, meaning on an aggregated basis'.[236] The Appeals Chamber did not explicitly disagree with this

[230] See, e.g., *Media* Appeal Judgement, *supra* note 110, para. 924 & n. 2092 (noting that extermination requires a large number of victims, and citing *Stakić* Appeal Judgement, *supra* note 108, para. 259; *Ntakirutimana and Ntakirutimana* Appeal Judgement, *supra* note 95, paras. 521–522).

[231] *Krstić* Trial Judgement, *supra* note 218, para. 503; *Stakić* Trial Judgement, *supra* note 80, para. 640; *Bagilishema* Trial Judgement, *supra* note 87, para. 87; *Kayishema and Ruzindana* Trial Judgement, *supra* note 90, para. 142; *Kajelijeli* Trial Judgement, *supra* note 86, para. 891; *Kamuhanda* Trial Judgement, *supra* note 229, para. 692.

[232] *Kayishema and Ruzindana* Trial Judgement, *supra* note 90, para. 645 n. 8. See also *ibid.*, para. 147 (same).

[233] See *Vasiljević* Trial Judgement, *supra* note 164, para. 227; *Brđanin* Trial Judgement, *supra* note 80, para. 391 n. 926.

[234] *Vasiljević* Trial Judgement, *supra* note 164, para. 227 n. 586.

[235] See *Prosecutor* v. *Brđanin*, Case No. IT-99-36-T, Decision on Motion for Acquittal Pursuant to Rule 98 *bis*, 28 November 2003, para. 72.

[236] *Brđanin* Trial Judgement, *supra* note 80, para. 391. This approach is not inconsistent with the manner in which *ad hoc* chambers have held that individual incidents may be considered for the purposes of determining whether there was an attack, and if the offence in question was part of that attack. See *supra* text accompanying notes 182–184.

aggregation approach, but also noted that each of the separate incidents charged would have independently satisfied the massiveness requirement:

> Since the parties do not challenge the Trial Chamber's decision to consider all of the killings in the territory of the ARK as a whole rather than to distinguish them by location and incident, the Appeals Chamber need not consider this issue. Suffice it to say that, with respect to those specific incidents cited by the Prosecution which involved the killing of between 68 and 300 people in each of the five locations, the Appeals Chamber is satisfied that the *actus reus* of the crime of extermination was made out. The Appeals Chamber considers that the scale of the killings, in light of the circumstances in which they occurred, meets the required threshold of massiveness for the purposes of extermination.[237]

Similarly, the *Stakić* Appeals Chamber appeared to affirm the position taken by the Trial Chamber in that case, which had rejected the accused's argument that extermination requires killings on a vast scale in a concentrated location over a short period of time.[238] The requirement that the offences be part of a broader attack on a civilian population in order to qualify as crimes against humanity[239] may serve to reduce the likelihood that these holdings would support a finding of extermination based on the amalgamation of a number of otherwise unrelated incidents.

The definition of the *mens rea* for extermination shows a degree of inconsistency and disagreement among the chambers of both *ad hoc* Tribunals that is similar to that for murder as a crime against humanity. The September 2004 *Brđanin* Trial Judgement outlined three of the different approaches to articulating the standard for the appropriate mental state for extermination:[240] (1) the *Kayishema and Ruzindana* Trial Chamber's standard, under which the killing may be intentional, reckless, or grossly negligent;[241] (2) the approach of the *Krstić* and *Stakić* Trial Chambers, which held that the *mens rea* for extermination should be the same as for murder as a crime against humanity, and therefore be restricted to direct and indirect intent;[242] and (3) the interpretation of the *Vasiljević* Trial Chamber, which had imposed a requirement that the person committing the killing know 'that his action is part of a vast murderous enterprise'.[243] In addition, noting the divergence between the *Krstić*

[237] *Prosecutor* v. *Brđanin*, Case No. IT-99-36-A, Judgement, 3 April 2007 ('*Brđanin* Appeal Judgement'), para. 472.

[238] See *Stakić* Trial Judgement, *supra* note 80, para. 640; *Stakić* Appeal Judgement, *supra* note 108, paras. 258–264 (rejecting each of the accused-appellant's challenges to the Trial Chamber's treatment of extermination).

[239] See *supra* section 2.2.2.5.

[240] See generally *Brđanin* Trial Judgement, *supra* note 80, paras. 392–393.

[241] *Kayishema and Ruzindana* Trial Judgement, *supra* note 90, para. 144; accord *Bagilishema* Trial Judgement, *supra* note 87, para. 89, *Rutaganda* Trial Judgement, *supra* note 114, para. 80; *Musema* Trial Judgement, *supra* note 114, para. 218. Neither the *Kayishema and Ruzindana* Trial Chamber nor any other chamber to follow its lead on this issue attempted to reconcile this more relaxed mental standard with the insistence that murder as a crime against humanity be intentional and premeditated. See *supra* note 214 and accompanying text.

[242] *Krstić* Trial Judgement, *supra* note 218, para. 495; *Stakić* Trial Judgement, *supra* note 80, para. 642 (using the civil law terms of *dolus directus* and *dolus eventualis* for direct intent and intent to cause harm with acceptance of reasonable likelihood of death).

[243] *Vasiljević* Trial Judgement, *supra* note 164, para. 229.

and *Kayishema and Ruzindana* definitions, and that neither Appeals Chamber had yet clarified which was appropriate, the *Semanza* Trial Chamber developed a fourth approach: expressing the view that 'in the absence of express authority in the Statute or in customary international law, international criminal liability should be ascribed only on the basis of intentional conduct', the Chamber held that 'the mental element for extermination is the intent to perpetrate or participate in a mass killing'.[244] The more recent appeal judgements appear to endorse this fourth approach, but they neither explicitly nor implicitly deal with the other approaches to defining the mental element.[245] It is hoped that the Appeals Chambers of both Tribunals take advantage of the remaining cases in which extermination is alleged to articulate a clear and consistent mental standard for both murder and extermination as crimes against humanity.[246] In the absence of clear direction from either appellate body,[247] we expect most trial judgements will either restrict the *mens rea* to direct intent, or adopt the 'murder plus' approach to defining extermination – that is, add the elements of massiveness to both the *actus reus* and *mens rea* for the underlying offence of murder.

If extermination has generally been treated as 'murder plus' by the *ad hoc* jurisprudence, it seems it has also been viewed as 'genocide minus' by many chambers.

[244] *Semanza* Trial Judgement, *supra* note 85, para. 341; accord *Kajelijeli* Trial Judgement, *supra* note 86, para. 894; *Kamuhanda* Trial Judgement, *supra* note 229, para. 696.

[245] See, e.g., *Gacumbitsi* Appeal Judgement, *supra* note 95, para. 86 (referring with approval to the holdings of the *Ntakirutimana and Ntakirutimana* Appeal Judgement and the *Stakić* Appeal Judgement, and quoting the former judgement). See *infra* note 246. But see *Stakić* Appeal Judgement, *supra* note 108, paras. 99–103 (considering and summarily rejecting Stakić's challenge to the simultaneous use of a form of responsibility and a mental element for crimes that expand the possible factual basis for conviction, where the mental element for extermination was *dolus eventualis* (acceptance of the likelihood that the prohibited result will occur, even if not directly intended), and thereby implicitly affirming the Trial Chamber's inclusion of this alternative mental state for extermination).

[246] In two of the most recent appeal judgements, the Appeals Chambers have appeared to hold that the *mens rea* for extermination is limited to direct intent. See *Stakić* Appeal Judgement, *supra* note 108, para. 260 (holding, in an apparent combination of the elements of the underlying offence and the general requirements for crimes against humanity, that 'the *mens rea* of extermination clearly requires the intention to kill on a large scale or to systematically subject a large number of people to conditions of living that would lead to their deaths', and citing *Ntakirutimana and Ntakirutimana* Appeal Judgement as support); *Ntakirutimana and Ntakirutimana* Appeal Judgement, *supra* note 95, para. 522 (holding simply that 'the crime of extermination requires proof that the accused participated in a widespread or systematic killing or in subjecting a widespread number of people or systematically subjecting a number of people to conditions of living that would inevitably lead to death, and that *the accused intended by his acts or omissions this result*') (emphasis added). Neither judgement appears to consider the variation in the definition of the *mens rea* described above, or seems to reflect a considered definition of the crime that is intended to cover the situation where the accused is not the alleged physical perpetrator. Moreover, the *Ntakirutimana and Ntakirutimana* Appeal Judgement's definition combines the elements of the crime with the general requirements for crimes against humanity in a manner that makes it difficult to isolate the various elements.

[247] The *Vasiljević* approach has been rejected by the Appeals Chamber in *Stakić*. See *Stakić* Appeal Judgement, *supra* note 108, para. 258; see also *Krstić* Appeal Judgement, *supra* note 180, para. 225 (holding that the existence of a plan or policy is not a requirement for crimes against humanity in general, or extermination in particular, and citing similar holdings in other appeal judgements); accord *Brđanin* Trial Judgement, *supra* note 80, para. 394. To date, however, there has been no considered discussion in the appellate case law in an attempt to clarify or correct the divergent jurisprudence.

That is, while both crimes address the situation where mass deaths are inflicted on a targeted population, certain chambers have either emphasised the more lenient requirements of extermination, or highlighted the characteristics it shares with genocide that serve to distinguish it from other crimes against humanity. For example, extermination does not require the intent to destroy a national, ethnic, racial, or religious group, merely that the victims constitute a numerically significant part of a civilian population. The victims of extermination as a crime against humanity need share no common characteristics beyond a general geographic location; most importantly, unlike the targets of genocide, extermination victims can be defined negatively, such as all non-Serbs.[248] On the other hand, both ICTY and ICTR chambers have placed great weight on the collective nature of extermination, going so far as to assert that a single killing should not be considered as an instance of extermination, even if it took place in the context of a mass killing event.[249] Even the requirement of numerical significance resonates with the 'substantial part' requirement for genocide where the intent is to partially destroy the protected group.

2.2.3.3 Enslavement

The physical perpetrator intentionally exercised over another individual any or all of the powers attached to the right of ownership.

The prohibition against slavery is perhaps the oldest norm of customary international law that is directly concerned with the protection of human dignity.[250] Although it is a crime under international law in its own right, regardless of the context in which it occurs,[251] it appears in the Statutes of the *ad hoc* Tribunals only as one of the underlying offences that may constitute a crime within the core categories of war crimes and crimes against humanity.[252] As such, it must occur in circumstances that satisfy the general requirements for either category of crimes before either Tribunal may exercise jurisdiction in respect of an allegation of slavery. For crimes against humanity, the term of art applied to the underlying offence is 'enslavement'.

248 See, e.g., *Stakić* Trial Judgement, *supra* note 80, para. 639, affirmed in *Stakić* Appeal Judgement, *supra* note 108, paras. 96–97. See Chapter 3, text accompanying note 180 (discussing the jurisprudence rejecting a negative definition for victims of genocide).

249 See *supra* text accompanying notes 232–234.

250 See, e.g., James L. Bischoff, 'Forced Labour in Brazil: International Criminal Law as the *Ultima Ratio* Modality of Human Rights Protection', (2006) 19 *Leiden Journal of International Law* 151, 157–164 (discussing domestic and international instruments condemning and outlawing slavery and its related practices from the early nineteenth century to the present day, and the status of the prohibition against slavery and slavery-related practices as an *erga omnes* obligation and a *jus cogens* norm of customary international law).

251 See *ibid.*, pp. 164–166.

252 See *Simić et al.* Trial Judgement, *supra* note 115, para. 85 n. 147 (noting that ICTY case law 'has established that the offence of slavery under Article 3 of the Statute [as a violation of the laws or customs of war] is the same as the offence of enslavement under Article 5', and holding that '[b]oth offences require proof of the same elements and both terms can be used interchangeably') (citing *Kunarac et al.* Trial Judgement, *supra* note 90, para. 523; *Krnojelac* Trial Judgement, *supra* note 111, para. 356).

The clearest judicial statement of the elements of this underlying offence occurs in the *Kunarac* Trial Judgement. After an extensive review of several international instruments and cases in order to determine the definition under customary international law,[253] the Trial Chamber held that the *actus reus* of the offence is the 'exercise of any or all of the powers attaching to the right of ownership of a person', and the *mens rea* is the intention to so exercise those powers.[254] In affirming that definition, the *Kunarac* Appeals Chamber emphasised that the traditional concept of slavery had evolved beyond 'chattel slavery'[255] to include 'various contemporary forms of slavery [in which] the victim is not subject to the exercise of the more extreme rights of ownership' associated with that traditional form, 'but in all cases … there is some destruction of the juridical personality' as a result of the exercise by another person of any of the powers attaching to the right of ownership.[256] Although it generally approved of the Trial Chamber's description of the elements, the Appeals Chamber observed that a restatement that more closely tracked the language of the 1926 Slavery Convention was preferable; instead of a 'right of ownership over a person', the treaty refers to 'a person over whom any or all of the powers attaching to the right of ownership are exercised.'[257]

The *Kunarac* Appeals Chamber also approved the Trial Chamber's non-exhaustive list of eight indicia of enslavement, which may be applied to determine whether the alleged conduct qualified as the exercise of the powers of ownership over a human being:[258] control of the individual's movement; control of his or her physical environment; psychological control; measures taken to prevent or deter escape; actual or threatened force or coercion; assertion of exclusive control; subjection to cruel treatment and abuse; control of sexuality;[259] and forced labour. Both the Trial and Appeals Chamber in this case laid particular emphasis on forced or compulsory labour as conduct that would qualify as enslavement:[260] the Trial Chamber noted

[253] *Kunarac et al.* Trial Judgement, *supra* note 90, paras. 515–538. See especially *ibid.*, para. 516 (explaining that its review 'is not intended to be an exhaustive pronouncement on the law of enslavement' because it focuses on the particular conduct charged: the 'treatment of women and children and certain allegations of forced or compulsory labour or service').

[254] *Ibid.*, para. 540, affirmed in *Kunarac et al.* Appeal Judgement, *supra* note 75, para. 116; accord *Krnojelac* Trial Judgement, *supra* note 111, para. 350.

[255] As the ICTY Appeals Chamber explained in a footnote: '"Chattel slavery" is used to describe slave-like conditions. To be reduced to "chattel" generally refers to a form of movable property as opposed to property in land.' *Kunarac et al.* Appeal Judgement, *supra* note 75, para. 117 n. 145.

[256] *Ibid.*, para. 117 & n. 146. See also Bischoff, *supra* note 250, p. 187 (noting that the reference to contemporary forms of slavery 'encompassed not only chattel slavery, but also the slave trade, servitude, [and] forced labour').

[257] *Kunarac et al.* Appeal Judgement, *supra* note 75, para. 118 (citing and quoting Convention to Suppress the Slave Trade and Slavery, 25 September 1926, entered into force 9 March 1927, 212 UNTS 17, Art. 1(1)).

[258] *Ibid.*, para. 119 (citing and quoting *Kunarac et al.* Trial Judgement, *supra* note 90, paras. 542–543).

[259] The Trial Chamber noted that examples of such control include sex and prostitution. *Kunarac et al.* Trial Judgement, *supra* note 90, para. 542. Presumably, any sexual intercourse in this context would be non-consensual, and would thus qualify as rape, even under the limited definition applied in the *ad hoc* Tribunals. See *infra* section 2.2.3.7.

[260] This emphasis is probably explained by the fact, as noted above, that the indictment focused on allegations of forced labour. See *supra* note 253.

that 'the exaction of forced or compulsory labour or service, often without remuneration and often, though not necessarily, involving physical hardship' was an indication of enslavement,[261] while the Appeals Chamber quoted at length from the post-Second World War *Pohl* case to underscore that 'ill-treatment ... starvation, beatings, and other barbarous acts' are not indispensable prerequisites for a finding of enslavement, if the 'admitted fact of slavery – compulsory uncompensated labour [or] involuntary servitude' has been proved.[262]

While the duration of the exercise of the powers of ownership is a factor to be weighed in the overall evaluation, it is not an element of the offence of enslavement.[263] Similarly, lack of consent is not an element,[264] but may be relevant as evidence of whether the alleged conduct was in fact enslavement.[265] Unlike the offence of imprisonment,[266] even prolonged arbitrary detention is not sufficient for a finding of enslavement.[267]

Applying these statements of the law to the evidence before it, the *Kunarac* Trial Chamber found Dragoljub Kunarac, a Bosnian Serb commander in the Foča area, guilty of enslavement as a crime against humanity because, among other things, he and other soldiers detained two Muslim women in a house for five or six months; he and one other soldier raped these women continually during the period of their detention, and treated them as their personal property; Kunarac in particular forbade any other soldier to rape the woman whom he himself raped throughout the period; and the women performed household chores while being detained, and complied with any orders from the soldiers.[268] In sum, the Trial Chamber concluded that it was satisfied that the two women were 'denied any control over their lives by

261 *Kunarac et al.* Trial Judgement, *supra* note 90, para. 542.

262 *United States* v. *Pohl, Frank, Georg Lörner, Fanslau, Hans Lörner, Vogt, Tschentscher, Scheide, Kiefer, Eirenschmalz, Sommer, Pook, Baier, Hohberg, Volk, Mummenthey, Bobermin, and Klein*, in *Trials of War Criminals Before the Nuernberg Military Tribunals Under Control Council Law No. 10* (1950), vol. V, p. 970, quoted in *Kunarac et al.* Appeal Judgement, *supra* note 75, para. 123.

263 *Kunarac et al.* Appeal Judgement, *supra* note 75, para. 121; *Kunarac et al.* Trial Judgement, *supra* note 90, para. 542 (noting that the importance of this factor will depend on the existence of other indicia of enslavement).

264 See especially *Prosecutor* v. *Krnojelac*, Case No. IT-97-25-A, Judgement, 17 September 2003 ('*Krnojelac* Appeal Judgement'), para. 191 (describing 'involuntariness' as 'the definitional feature of forced or compulsory labour'); *ibid.*, paras. 194–196 (overturning the Trial Chamber's acquittal on the count alleging forced labour as a form of persecution, which had been based on the conclusion that the prosecution had not established certain victims' lack of consent, and holding that 'given the specific detention conditions of the non-Serb detainees ... a reasonable trier of fact should have arrived at the conclusion that the detainees' general situation negated any possibility of free consent') (quotation at para. 194).

265 *Kunarac et al.* Appeal Judgement, *supra* note 75, para. 120 (noting that the issue of consent 'may be relevant from an evidential point of view as going to the question whether the Prosecutor has established the [*actus reus*] of the crime', and holding that 'circumstances which render it impossible to express consent may be sufficient to presume the absence of consent'). Although the Appeals Chamber did not so state explicitly, this holding is probably best read as indicating that the prosecution need not prove lack of consent in order to obtain a conviction, but consent may be a defence to a charge of enslavement, depending on the circumstances of the case.

266 See *infra* section 2.2.3.5.

267 *Kunarac et al.* Trial Judgement, *supra* note 90, para. 542 ('Detaining or keeping someone in captivity, without more, would, depending on the circumstances of a case, usually not constitute enslavement.').

268 *Ibid.*, paras. 728–741. See also *ibid.*, para. 592 (concluding that the general requirements had been satisfied).

Dragoljub Kunarac and DP6 [the other soldier] during their stay there', and added that the victims:

> had no realistic option whatsoever to flee the house [in which they were kept] or to escape their assailants. They were subjected to other mistreatments, such as Kunarac inviting a soldier into the house so that he could rape [one of the victims] for 100 Deutschmark[s] if he so wished. On another occasion, Kunarac tried to rape [that victim] while in his hospital bed, in front of other soldiers. The two women were treated as the personal property of Kunarac and DP6. The Trial Chamber is satisfied that Kunarac established these living conditions for the victims in concert with DP6. Both men personally committed the act of enslavement.[269]

Similarly, the Trial Chamber concluded that one of Kunarac's co-accused, Radomir Kovač, also personally committed enslavement because, among other things, he personally detained two Muslim women in his apartment for approximately four months, during which time he had 'complete control over their movements, privacy and labour';[270] and he subjected them to beatings and humiliating treatment, including 'an almost daily regime of rapes and other abuses'.[271] Most tellingly, he actually sold both women to two Montenegrin soldiers in exchange for a sum of money,[272] leading to the Trial Chamber's conclusion that his conduct 'was wanton in abusing and humiliating [the victims] and in exercising his *de facto* power of ownership as it pleased him', and that he 'disposed of them in the same manner'.[273]

Although similar allegations of the detention, rape, and mistreatment of Tutsi women during the 1994 genocide were made,[274] it does not appear that enslavement as a crime against humanity has ever been charged, or been the subject of a trial or appeal judgement, at the ICTR.

2.2.3.4 Deportation

The physical perpetrator coercively displaced individuals from a place in which they were lawfully present, across an international border, without grounds permitted under international law.

Four crimes punishable under Articles 5 and 3, respectively, of the ICTY and ICTR Statutes ('Article 5/3') share the same underlying offence, which may be termed 'forcible displacement' – deportation as a crime against humanity punishable under

[269] *Ibid.*, para. 742. [270] *Ibid.*, para. 780. [271] *Ibid.*, paras. 777, 780.

[272] *Ibid.*, paras. 775–780. The consideration paid for the two victims was not definitively established at trial. There was some evidence that they were sold for 500 Deutschmarks each, and other evidence that the price paid included a 'truckload of washing powder'. *ibid.*, paras. 778, 779 (quotation at para. 778).

[273] *Ibid.*, para. 781. On appeal, the accused challenged both the legal definitions and the factual findings of the Trial Chamber in respect of enslavement. Having rejected all those arguments, the Appeals Chamber dismissed the challenges to the convictions for enslavement. See *Kunarac et al.* Appeal Judgement, *supra* note 75, paras. 124, 218, 229, 237, 246, 255–256.

[274] See, e.g., *Akayesu* Trial Judgement, *supra* note 94, paras. 434, 436 (testimony of one witness alleging that she had been kept in an apartment for two nights and one week on two separate occasions and repeatedly raped by a man); *ibid.*, para. 444 (a defence witness admitted in her statement that the Interahamwe were abducting beautiful Tutsi girls, taking them home as mistresses, and keeping them against their will).

Article 5/3(d), deportation and forcible transfer as forms of persecution as a crime against humanity punishable under Article 5/3(h), and forcible transfer as an inhumane act as a crime against humanity punishable under Article 5/3(i).

The elements of forcible displacement as an underlying offence do not change depending on the crime alleged.[275] The *actus reus* of forcible displacement is (1) the displacement of persons by expulsion or other coercive acts; (2) without grounds permitted under international law; (3) from an area in which they are lawfully present. Until relatively recently, the jurisprudence of the ICTY[276] also included a fourth element – the *mens rea* for the offence – which was that the displacement must have been performed with the intent that the removal of the persons be permanent. As discussed below, however, the ICTY Appeals Chamber has held that deportation, and thus any other crime for which forcible displacement is the underlying offence, does not require proof that the removal was intended to be permanent.

2.2.3.4.1 The displacement of persons was caused by expulsion or other coercive acts The defining feature of both deportation and forcible transfer is the involuntary nature of the displacement.[277] ICTY Chambers have consistently held that it is the absence of 'genuine choice' that makes a given act of displacement unlawful.[278] Expanding on this holding, the *Krnojelac* Appeals Chamber held that genuine choice cannot be inferred from the fact that consent was expressed where the circumstances deprive the consent of any value.[279] Thus consent induced by force or threat of force is not considered to be valid, and will not preclude the determination that forcible displacement was committed. The *Brđanin* Trial Chamber offered an even more expansive reading of consent, observing that 'even in cases where those displaced may have wished – and in fact may have even requested – to be removed, this does not necessarily mean that they had or exercised a genuine choice.'[280]

Consequently, chambers have inferred a lack of genuine choice from threatening and intimidating acts intended to deprive the civilian population of exercising its

275 See, e.g., *Simić et al.* Trial Judgment, *supra* note 115, para. 123; *Krnojelac* Trial Judgement, *supra* note 111, para. 473. The crimes of unlawful deportation or transfer of a civilian as grave breaches under Article 2(g) of the ICTY Statute also share the same core elements. See Chapter 4, section 4.2.2.13; Annex, section 4.29.

276 As of 1 December 2007, no ICTR chamber had discussed the elements of this crime. This lacuna is unsurprising, given that forced displacement of persons is an offence that is associated much more with the 'ethnic cleansing' that characterised the conflicts in the former Yugoslavia in the 1990s.

277 See, e.g., *Brđanin* Trial Judgement, *supra* note 80, para. 543; *Simić et al.* Trial Judgement, *supra* note 115, para. 125; *Stakić* Trial Judgement, *supra* note 80, para. 682; *Krstić* Trial Judgement, *supra* note 218, para. 529.

278 See, e.g., *Krnojelac* Appeal Judgment, *supra* note 264, para. 229; *Blagojević and Jokić* Trial Judgement, *supra* note 75, para. 596; *Brđanin* Trial Judgement, *supra* note 80, para. 543.

279 *Krnojelac* Appeal Judgment, *supra* note 264, para. 229. The Appeals Chamber held that 'the prohibition against forcible population displacements therefore aims at safeguarding the right and aspiration of individuals to live in their communities and homes without outside interference.' *Ibid.*, para. 218. See also *Milošević* Rule 98 *bis* Decision, *supra* note 79, para. 69; *Simić et al.* Trial Judgement, *supra* note 115, para. 125.

280 *Brđanin* Trial Judgment, *supra* note 80, para. 596; accord *Krnojelac* Appeal Judgement, *supra* note 264, para. 229.

free will, such as the shelling of civilian objects, the burning of civilian property, and other crimes 'calculated to terrify the population and make them flee the area with no hope of return'.[281] A person's genuine choice may be eliminated by physical force or 'threat of force or coercion, such as that caused by fear of violence, duress, detention, psychological oppression or abuse of power against such person or persons or another person, or by taking advantage of a coercive environment'.[282] A trier of fact must consider 'all relevant circumstances, including in particular the victims' vulnerability, when assessing whether the displaced victims had a genuine choice to remain or leave and thus whether the resultant displacement was unlawful'.[283] Applying these guidelines, the *Simić* Trial Chamber rejected arguments that the victims' alleged consent to be exchanged with civilians held by the opposing party to the conflict was voluntary:

> The Trial Chamber accepts the evidence that some of the non-Serb civilians who were to be exchanged were asked whether they wanted to cross over to the other side. This, however, does not necessarily indicate that these persons voluntarily agreed to be exchanged, as they could have been left without a genuine choice as to whether to leave or to remain in the area when they made their statement. In this context, the Trial Chamber notes the atmosphere of terror and fear created for the non-Serbs who were taken from their homes and held in various detention centres in the municipality of Bosanski Samač and in other locations. When these detainees had to state whether or not they wanted to be exchanged, they were not given guarantees that they would not be mistreated again. The Trial Chamber also accepts the evidence that some of the non-Serb civilians who were exchanged were not asked whether they wanted to be exchanged. In the view of the Trial Chamber, this is a strong indicator that these civilians were not voluntarily exchanged.[284]

In particular, the Trial Chamber concluded that the exchange of three prosecution witnesses from detention centres in Bosnia and Herzegovina to Croatia constituted deportation because 'the conditions under which they had to live did not provide them with a free choice'.[285]

2.2.3.4.2 The persons displaced were lawfully present in the area Although judgements routinely refer to the victims' lawful presence as an objective element of the underlying offence of forcible displacement, it does not appear to have been defined or analysed in any trial or appeal judgement to date. Instead, consideration of the

[281] *Krnojelac* Appeal Judgment, *supra* note 264, para. 126 (holding that threats to commit such crimes would also create a sufficiently coercive environment).

[282] *Simić et al.* Trial Judgment, *supra* note 115, para. 125 (quoting *Krnojelac* Trial Judgement, *supra* note 111, para. 475, *Krstić* Trial Judgement, *supra* note 218, para. 529, both in turn quoting the Report of the Preparatory Commission for the International Criminal Court, Finalised Draft Text of the Elements of the Crimes, UN Doc. PCNICC/200/INF/3/Add.2, 6 July 2000, p. 11). See also ICRC Commentary to the Additional Protocols, *supra* note 127, p. 1474, para. 4862 ('In our view, to get one or more people to leave the country by means of threats should also be considered as forced movement.').

[283] *Brđanin* Trial Judgement, *supra* note 80, para. 596.

[284] *Simić et al.* Trial Judgement, *supra* note 115, paras. 967, 968.

[285] *Ibid.*, para. 968.

issue has been folded into the examination of the forced displacement of the victims.[286] It is therefore not clear what legal authorities are to be consulted in order to determine whether the alleged victims were displaced from a location in which they were lawfully present. As a practical matter, the cases in which this offence is charged almost uniformly allege that the accused or physical perpetrators for whom he is responsible expelled civilians from their residences or forced them to leave their town, municipality, or country,[287] so it is understandable that the issue has received little attention.

2.2.3.4.3 The displacement occurred without grounds permitted under international law According to the jurisprudence of the ICTY, there are basically two grounds on which displacement of persons is legitimate under international law: the security of a civilian population, or imperative military reasons.[288] In either case, the chief distinction between an illegitimate forcible displacement and a permissible evacuation is that, in the case of the latter, 'persons thus evacuated [are] transferred back to their homes as soon as the hostilities in the area in question have ceased.'[289] International law thus prohibits the use of evacuation measures as a pretext to forcibly dislocate a population and seize control over a territory,[290] and this prohibition (as well as the more general prohibition of forcible displacement) cannot be

[286] See, e.g., *ibid.*, subsection VI(B) ('Displacement from the area in which they are lawfully present.') The *Simić* Trial Chamber did not address the element of the victims' lawful presence in the area from which they were displaced, but rather focused on the elements necessary to establish displacement. The question of the lawfulness of the victims' presence does not appear to have been a matter of dispute between the parties.

[287] See, e.g., *Blaškić* Trial Judgement, *supra* note 90, para. 550 (forcible transfer and forcible displacement, constituting persecution, of civilians from their towns and villages into other municipalities); *Blagojević and Jokić* Trial Judgement, *supra* note 75, para. 616 (forcible transfer of the population of Srebrenica from that municipality); *Brđanin* Trial Judgement, *supra* note 80, paras. 548–549 (deportation and forcible transfer from victims' villages and towns).

[288] See *Blagojević and Jokić* Trial Judgement, *supra* note 75, para. 597; *Brđanin* Trial Judgment, *supra* note 80, para. 556. Additional Protocol II lists the security of the population and imperative military reasons as the only justifications for evacuation of a civilian population. Additional Protocol II, *supra* note 9, Art. 17(1). In addition to these two exceptions, the *Blagojević and Jokić* Trial Chamber held that the law allows evacuations for humanitarian reasons. See *Blagojević and Jokić* Trial Judgement, *supra* note 75, para. 600 (referring to Additional Protocol II, *supra* note 9, Art. 17(1), which provides in relevant part that '[t]he displacement of the civilian population shall not be ordered for reasons related to the conflict'). The Commentary to Article 17 indicates other reasons that displacement of the civilian population may be lawfully carried out by the parties to the conflict. See ICRC Commentary to the Additional Protocols, *supra* note 127, p. 1473, para. 4855 (listing outbreak or risk of epidemics, natural disasters, or the existence of a generally untenable and life-threatening living situation).

[289] *Brđanin* Trial Judgment, *supra* note 80, para. 556 (quoting Geneva Convention IV, *supra* note 9, Art. 49). The official commentary notes that 'evacuation must not involve the movement of protected persons to places outside the occupied territory, unless it is physically impossible to do otherwise. Thus as a rule, evacuation must be to reception centres inside the territory.' ICRC Commentary to Geneva Convention IV, *supra* note 125, p. 280. See also Additional Protocol II, *supra* note 9, Art. 17(2); ICRC Commentary to the Additional Protocols, *supra* note 127, pp. 1471–1474, paras. 4847–4865.

[290] *Blagojević and Jokić* Trial Judgment, *supra* note 75, para. 597. See also ICRC Commentary to the Additional Protocols, *supra* note 127, p. 1473, para. 4854.

circumvented by agreements concluded by military commanders or other representatives of parties to a conflict.[291]

2.2.3.4.4 Is intent that the removal be permanent an element of forcible displacement? By early 2005, at least five separate trial judgements had held that the alleged conduct must be performed with the intent that the removal of the persons involved be permanent in order for it to constitute the underlying offence of forcible displacement.[292] In its review of the trial judgement in the *Stakić* case, however, the Appeals Chamber disagreed, noting:

> The Judgements requiring an intent to permanently remove the victims rely for their authority on a statement in the ICRC Commentary on Article 49 of Geneva Convention IV. The Commentary states that: [']Unlike deportation and forcible transfers, evacuation is a provisional measure entirely negative in character, and is, moreover, often taken in the interests of the protected persons themselves.['] The Trial Chamber in this case appears to have interpreted this statement to mean that 'the intent of the perpetrator must be that the victim is removed, which implies the aim that the person is not returning.'
>
> Article 49 of Geneva Convention IV itself, the underlying instrument prohibiting deportation regardless of the motive behind the act, contains no suggestion that deportation requires an intent that the deportees should not return. The Appeals Chamber is concerned that care should be taken not to read too much into the Commentary on Geneva Convention IV, and finds that the Commentary to Article 49 in particular is primarily an attempt to distinguish 'evacuation', a form of removal permitted by the Convention which is by definition provisional, from the crimes of deportation and forcible transfer.
>
> The Appeals Chamber therefore chooses to follow the text of Article 49 and concludes that deportation does not require an intent that the deportees should not return.[293]

The reluctance to 'read too much' into the official commentary to Geneva Convention IV seems odd, given that resort to such commentaries is common in the interpretation of treaties,[294] and has often been used by *ad hoc* chambers, including the ICTY Appeals Chamber itself.[295] Another basis for the Appeal Chamber's

[291] See *Simić et al.* Trial Judgment, *supra* note 115, para. 127; *Naletilić and Martinović* Trial Judgement, *supra* note 113, para. 523 (holding that '[m]ilitary commanders or political leaders cannot consent on behalf of the individual').

[292] See *Blagojević and Jokić* Trial Judgement, *supra* note 75, para. 601; *Brđanin* Trial Judgement, *supra* note 80, para. 545; *Simić et al.* Trial Judgement, *supra* note 115, paras. 132–134; *Stakić* Trial Judgement, *supra* note 80, para. 687; *Naletilić and Martinović* Trial Judgement, *supra* note 113, para. 520. See also *Krnojelac* Appeal Judgement, *supra* note 264, Separate Opinion of Judge Schomburg, para. 16.

[293] *Stakić* Appeal Judgement, *supra* note 108, paras. 305–307.

[294] See, e.g., Ian Brownlie, *Principles of Public International Law* (6th edn. 2003), pp. 602–603 (relying on the ILC's commentary to the Vienna Convention on the Law of Treaties for an explanation of the operation of that agreement's provisions on interpretation of treaties).

[295] See, e.g., *Aleksovski* Appeal Judgement, *supra* note 193, paras. 22, 27 (noting that its interpretation of an article in the Statute 'is confirmed by the International Committee of the Red Cross commentaries to the Geneva Conventions', and making a visible effort to interpret the Statute in concordance with the ICRC Commentaries) (quotation at para. 22); *Galić* Appeal Judgement, *supra* note 134, paras. 137–138 (ICTY Appeals Chamber relying on a holding from its *Blaškić* Judgement, which in turn relied on and approvingly quoted the ICRC Commentary to Geneva Convention IV).

conclusion, and one that runs less risk of inconsistency with past practice, is that the requirement of permanent removal is unnecessary if its purpose is to distinguish between lawful and unlawful displacements. One of the elements of forcible displacement as an underlying offence is that it must occur without justification under international law,[296] which would be sufficient to exclude any legitimate evacuation.

2.2.3.4.5 Additional element for deportation

The displacement took place across a de jure *or* de facto *international border.*

In 2001, the *Krstić* Trial Chamber summarised the state of the law on forcible displacement as it then stood, explaining that 'both deportation and forcible transfer relate to the involuntary and unlawful evacuation of individuals from the territory in which they reside. Yet, the two are not synonymous in customary international law. Deportation presumes transfer beyond State borders, whereas forcible transfer relates to displacements within a State'.[297] This view has generally prevailed at the ICTY,[298] notwithstanding the attempt by one trial chamber to eliminate forcible transfer as an inhumane act as a crime within the jurisdiction of the Tribunal,[299] and the sometimes confusing explanations of the ICTY Appeals Chamber.[300]

[296] See *supra* section 2.2.3.4.3. [297] *Krstić* Trial Judgment, *supra* note 218, para. 521.

[298] See, e.g., *Krnojelac* Trial Judgement, *supra* note 111, para. 474 (rejecting the prosecution's submission that forcible displacement within a state could constitute deportation); *ibid.*, para. 476 (considering 'it to be well established that forcible displacements of people within national boundaries are covered by the concept of forcible transfer', but noting that the indictment did not plead forcible transfer, only deportation and expulsion); *Krnojelac* Appeal Judgment, *supra* note 264, paras. 218, 222–224 (overturning the Trial Chamber on other grounds, but clearly holding that there is a distinction between displacements within a state and those across an international border); accord *Stakić* Appeal Judgement, *supra* note 108, paras. 288–303 (examining post-Second World War jurisprudence, Geneva Convention IV, the 1954 ILC Draft Code, and the customary international law study of the ICRC); *Blaškić* Appeal Judgement, *supra* note 88, paras. 152–153; *Simić et al.* Trial Judgement, *supra* note 115, para. 129; *Brđanin* Trial Judgement, *supra* note 80, para. 540; *Blagojević and Jokić* Trial Judgment, *supra* note 75, para. 595; *Milošević* Rule 98 *bis* Decision, *supra* note 79, para. 78 ('If, as a matter of fact, the result of the removal of the victim is the crossing of a[n inter]national border then the crime of deportation is committed; if there is no such crossing, the crime is forcible transfer.'). As discussed below, in the Rome Statute of the ICC the terms 'deportation' and 'forcible transfer' are not defined as legally distinct from one another, and deportation does not appear to require that the victim be transferred across a border; instead, the victim may be 'deported or forcibly transferred' 'to another State or location'. See *infra* text accompanying notes 540–541.

[299] See *Stakić* Trial Judgement, *supra* note 80, paras. 723–724 (concluding that forcible transfer as an inhumane act as a crime against humanity violated the principle of *nullum crimen sine lege certa*), reversed by *Stakić* Appeal Judgement, *supra* note 108, para. 317.

[300] See, e.g., *Prosecutor* v. *Naletilić and Martinović*, Case No. IT-98-34-A, Judgement, 3 May 2006 ('*Naletilić and Martinović* Appeal Judgement'), para. 154 (holding that 'whether "deportation" encompasses a border element is irrelevant for the purposes of liability under Article 5(h) of the Statute, because acts of forcible displacement are equally punishable as underlying acts of persecutions whether or not a border is crossed', and concluding that '[t]o the extent the Trial Chamber suggested otherwise, it erred in law') (citing *Krnojelac* Appeal Judgement, *supra* note 264, para. 218, which had held that '[t]he forced character of displacement and the forced uprooting of the inhabitants of a territory entail the criminal responsibility of the perpetrator, not the destination to which these inhabitants are sent'); accord *Prosecutor v. Simić*, Case No. IT-95-9-A, Judgement, 28 November 2006 ('*Simić* Appeal Judgement'), para. 172. The Appeals Chamber is certainly correct when it notes that forcible displacement, regardless of the destination, will give rise to criminal responsibility if all the necessary general and specific requirements are satisfied, but it seems incorrect to assert that the Trial Chamber had erred by concluding 'that there was no basis upon which it could find that persecutions was conducted by means of the underlying act of deportation' because 'the acts described in the Indictment contained no

The ICTY Appeals Chamber has adopted a relatively flexible interpretation of the cross-border requirement for deportation. As the *Stakić* Appeal Judgement explained:

> The default principle under customary international law with respect to the nature of the border is that there must be expulsion across a *de jure* border to another country, as illustrated in Article 49 of Geneva Convention IV and the other references set out above. Customary international law also recognises that displacement from 'occupied territory', as expressly set out in Article 49 of Geneva Convention IV and as recognised by numerous Security Council Resolutions, is also sufficient to amount to deportation. The Appeals Chamber also accepts that under certain circumstances displacement across a *de facto* border may be sufficient to amount to deportation. In general, the question whether a particular *de facto* border is sufficient for the purposes of the crime of deportation should be examined on a case by case basis in light of customary international law.[301]

Flexibility has its limits, however: the Appeals Chamber rejected the Trial Chamber's conclusion that deportation was established if persons were forcibly displaced across 'constantly changing frontlines', because it was 'clear from the facts of the case that the constantly changing frontlines in question are neither *de jure* state borders nor the *de facto* borders of occupied territory', and it could find no support in customary international law for the Trial Chamber's approach.[302] Reiterating that the principle of *nullum crimen sine lege* is a limitation on the potential legal creativity of international criminal adjudication, the Appeals Chamber emphasised that:

> such an approach is not legally justified, nor is it necessary – the application of the correct definition of deportation would not leave individuals without the protection of the law. Individuals who are displaced within the boundaries of the State or across *de facto* borders not within the definition of deportation, remain protected by the law, albeit not under the protections afforded by the offence of deportation. Punishment for such forcible transfers may be assured by the adoption of proper pleading practices in the Prosecution's indictments – it need not challenge existing concepts of international law.[303]

Although the language used in the Appeal Judgement was not always clear, it does not appear that the *Stakić* Appeals Chamber intended to remove the requirement that deportation must take place across an international border.[304] Instead, its efforts were directed at clarifying that the international border in question need not

allegations of cross-border transfer and no evidence had been introduced to that effect'. *Naletilić and Martinović* Appeal Judgement, *supra*, para. 149. Although the distinction between deportation and forcible transfer is somewhat artificial when both are alleged as forms of persecution, trial chambers should certainly not be discouraged from seeking precision from the prosecution in its charging instruments or using the appropriate legal terminology.

301 *Stakić* Appeal Judgement, *supra* note 108, para. 300. 302 *Ibid.*, paras. 301–302. 303 *Ibid.*, para. 302.

304 See, e.g., *ibid.*, paras. 300, 301 (referring to '*de facto* borders' and then '*de facto* borders of occupied territory'); *ibid.*, para. 300 n. 631 (quoting the portion of Geneva Convention IV regarding deportations of persons from occupied territory to the territory of the occupying party, which must necessarily be a different state, or the territory of any other country); *ibid.*, para. 302 (distinguishing between *de facto* borders that would fall within the definition of deportation, and those that would not).

be a formal, universally recognised demarcation. As indicated by the Appeals Chamber, if the additional element of displacement across an international border is not satisfied, the conduct in question would still qualify as forcible transfer, which is typically charged as an inhumane act as a crime against humanity at the ICTY.[305]

2.2.3.5 Imprisonment

The physical perpetrator arbitrarily deprived an individual of his or her liberty, and this conduct was either intentional or performed with knowledge of the reasonable likelihood that it would result in an arbitrary deprivation of liberty.

Just as *Kunarac* was the case that most closely focused on allegations of sexual slavery,[306] *Krnojelac* – which also arose out of events in and around Foča in Bosnia and Herzegovina in 1992 – was the case most closely focused on allegations of imprisonment. In *Krnojelac*, the ICTY Prosecutor sought to highlight a practice that, like enslavement and deportation, seemed emblematic of the Bosnian conflict: the arbitrary detention of non-Serb men and boys in makeshift camps. The case focused on one of the more notorious detention centres, the Kaznezno-Popravni Dom, or KP Dom, a prison in Foča, and alleged that Milorad Krnojelac had committed or been responsible for several crimes against humanity and war crimes as the prison's warden.[307] After a brief review of international instruments and the limited ICTY jurisprudence at the time, the Trial Chamber concluded that the elements of the underlying offence of imprisonment were as follows:

1. An individual is deprived of his or her liberty.
2. The deprivation of liberty is imposed arbitrarily, that is, no legal basis can be invoked to justify the deprivation of liberty.
3. The act or omission by which the individual is deprived of his or her physical liberty is performed by the [physical perpetrator] with the intent to deprive the individual arbitrarily of his or her physical liberty or in the reasonable knowledge that his act or omission is likely to cause arbitrary deprivation of physical liberty.[308]

[305] See *infra* section 2.2.3.9.2. [306] See *supra* section 2.2.3.3.

[307] See generally *Krnojelac* Trial Judgement, *supra* note 111, paras. 1–10.

[308] *Ibid.*, para. 115. Instead of the term 'physical perpetrator' in the third element, the original text used the phrase 'accused or a person or persons for whom the accused bears criminal responsibility'. Although this phrasing is consistent with what must be proved in order for the trial chamber to enter a conviction on this charge, it is not a correct statement of what is required simply to establish that the crime occurred. In order to avoid conflating the questions of the commission of a crime and the accused's responsibility for that crime, we instead use the term 'physical perpetrator'. See *supra* text accompanying notes 205–206 (discussing the same issue in the context of the underlying offence of murder); see also *Martić* Trial Judgement, *supra* note 75, para. 88 n. 163 (referring to this phrasing and considering that 'these words comprise definitions included in elements of Article 7(1) and 7(3) [the statutory provisions on forms of responsibility] and that there is no need to include them in the definition of a crime').

The definition propounded by the *Krnojelac* Trial Chamber was not challenged on appeal. See *Krnojelac* Appeal Judgement, *supra* note 264, paras. 38–41 (discussing and dismissing the accused-appellant's argument that the Trial Chamber erred by finding him guilty of aiding and abetting imprisonment as a form of persecution as a crime against humanity because it had not explained the basis for its conclusions on the form of responsibility).

This definition has been adopted in subsequent trial judgements.[309]

ICTY Chambers have repeatedly held that, except for the general requirements that characterise war crimes and crimes against humanity, the crimes of unlawful confinement as a grave breach and imprisonment as a crime against humanity are identical.[310] Accordingly, it is possible to isolate a single underlying offence, which may be termed arbitrary detention, that has the elements laid out above by the *Krnojelac* Trial Chamber and may qualify as either unlawful confinement as a war crime or imprisonment as a crime against humanity depending on whether the corresponding set of general requirements is fulfilled.[311]

In applying its definition to the evidence adduced at trial, the *Krnojelac* Trial Chamber concluded that imprisonment as a crime against humanity had been proved, relying in significant part on the failure of the Bosnian Serb physical perpetrators and commanders to observe or provide any of the guarantees required by international human rights law:

> [N]one of the non-Serb men was arrested on the basis of a valid arrest warrant … or informed orally of the reason for [his] arrest … After the initial arrest … they were detained at the KP Dom for periods ranging from four months to two and a half years.
>
> [O]nce detained at the KP Dom, none of the detainees was informed of the reason for his detention, the term of his detention or of any possibility of release … [I]nterrogations of those detained were conducted sometimes within a few days or weeks, sometimes only after months and, in some cases, never … A number of detainees were threatened in the course of the interrogations, and others heard fellow detainees being mistreated in neighbouring rooms. Many of the detainees were forced to sign written statements. None of the detainees was released from the KP Dom following interrogation, notwithstanding the individual outcome of the interview.
>
> [N]one of the detainees was ever actually charged, tried or convicted for any crime before being detained or while detained at the KP Dom. [N]one of the detainees was ever advised of [his] procedural rights before or during [his] detention.[312]

309 See, e.g., *Martić* Trial Judgement, *supra* note 75, paras. 87–88; *Simić et al.* Trial Judgement, *supra* note 115, para. 64. An alternative definition, put forth by the *Kordić and Čerkez* Trial Judgement, was rejected by the Appeals Chamber as inappropriate for use with respect to crimes against humanity. See *Kordić and Čerkez* Trial Judgement, *supra* note 75, para. 303 (invoking the provisions of Geneva Convention IV), overturned by *Kordić and Čerkez* Appeal Judgement, *supra* note 95, paras. 114–115 (finding that 'not all of these elements necessarily have to be met in order to establish liability for unlawful confinement pursuant to Article 5(e) of the Statute; the existence of an international armed conflict, an element of [the provisions invoked by the Trial Chamber], is not required'); accord *Krnojelac* Trial Judgement, *supra* note 111, para. 111 (explicitly rejecting the *Kordić and Čerkez* definition because it appeared to hold that 'imprisonment as a crime against humanity can *only* be established if the requirements of … Article 2 [on grave breaches of the Geneva Conventions] are met'). But see *infra* text accompanying note 310 (elements of underlying offence of arbitrary detention identical for war crimes and crimes against humanity).

310 See, e.g., *Kordić and Čerkez* Trial Judgement, *supra* note 75, paras. 298, 301; *Simić et al.* Trial Judgement, *supra* note 115, para. 63; see also *Krnojelac* Trial Judgement, *supra* note 111, para. 111.

311 See Chapter 4, section 4.2.2.12; Annex, sections 4.27, 4.28.

312 *Krnojelac* Trial Judgement, *supra* note 111, paras. 119–121.

In this and other judgements, ICTY chambers have placed particular emphasis on the arbitrary nature of the deprivation of liberty in order to distinguish it from potentially lawful conduct. For example, in *Kordić and Čerkez* the Trial Chamber held, and the Appeals Chamber affirmed, that 'the term imprisonment in Article 5(e) of the Statute should be understood as arbitrary imprisonment, that is ... the deprivation of liberty of the individual without due process of law'.[313] Thus the *Simić* Trial Chamber – in discussing its findings on allegations that the imprisonment of hundreds of Bosnian Croats, Bosnian Muslims, and other non-Serb civilians in the area of Bosanski Samač in 1992 were instances of persecution as a crime against humanity[314] – considered that:

> the non-Serb civilians who were detained in the camps in Zasavica, and for the short period in Crkvina, were detained arbitrarily, with no lawful basis. Non-Serb civilians were taken to the village of Zasavica where they were guarded and unable to leave. They were not brought before a judge to challenge the legality of their detention, nor were any lawful criminal proceedings conducted. There was no reasonable suspicion that they had committed any criminal offence. They were not informed of any accusation against them, but rather forced from their homes, rounded up and taken to Zasavica where they were prevented from leaving. This treatment constitutes arbitrary deprivation of their liberty.[315]

It appears that the only time imprisonment as a crime against humanity has been charged at the ICTR was in the '*Cyangugu*' case against André Ntagerura, Emmanuel Bagambiki, and Samuel Imanishimwe. The ICTR Prosecutor alleged that Bagambiki, the *préfet* or head of the Cyangugu *préfecture*, and Imanishimwe, a lieutenant in the Rwandan armed forces and the commander of the Cyangugu or Karambo barracks, had ordered and participated in the arrest and forcible detention

313 *Kordić and Čerkez* Trial Judgement, *supra* note 75, para. 302, quoted with approval in *Kordić and Čerkez* Appeal Judgement, *supra* note 95, para. 116. Accord *Martić* Trial Judgement, *supra* note 75, paras. 87–88; *Simić et al.* Trial Judgement, *supra* note 115, para. 64.

314 It is irrelevant for our purposes that the Trial Chamber was analysing imprisonment as a form of persecution, rather than as a simple crime against humanity under Article 5(e) of the ICTY Statute. First, its statement of the applicable law is based on cases discussing the crime under Article 5(e). See, e.g., *Simić et al.* Trial Judgement, *supra* note 115, para. 64. Second, as discussed below, examinations of the elements of any of the underlying offences of Article 5 of the ICTY Statute or Article 3 of the ICTR Statute as crimes against humanity, or as forms of persecution as a crime against humanity, differ only with regard to whether the specific requirements for persecution are also satisfied. See *infra* section 2.2.3.8.2; see also Chapter 5, note 152 and accompanying text.

315 *Simić et al.* Trial Judgement, *supra* note 115, para. 680. It does not appear that this factual finding was challenged on appeal. See, e.g., *Simić* Appeal Judgement, *supra* note 300, para. 118 (dismissing Simić's ground of appeal, which raised arguments based on the form of responsibility through which he was convicted, and affirming his conviction 'as an aider and abettor of persecutions for the unlawful arrests and detention of non-Serb civilians'). For another set of findings emphasising the arbitrary nature of the detention, see, e.g., *Krnojelac* Trial Judgement, *supra* note 111, paras. 116–122 (culminating in the findings, in paragraph 122, that 'there was no legal basis which could be relied upon to justify [the] deprivation of liberty [of the Muslims and other non-Serbs detained at the KP Dom] under national or international law', and that '[t]hose detained were not criminals under suspicion of having committed a crime or ever accused of having committed a crime under national and/or international law').

of Tutsi refugees in the barracks and in one or two stadiums in Cyangugu.[316] Although the Trial Chamber ultimately found in relation to two incidents that the prosecution had not proved the basic assertion that the alleged victims had been held against their will,[317] it nevertheless concluded that the evidence had established imprisonment as a crime against humanity in at least one set of circumstances, in which the 'arrests were not based on valid warrants, nor were the[] civilians ever formally charged and informed of their procedural rights'.[318]

2.2.3.6 Torture

The physical perpetrator intentionally inflicted severe mental or physical pain or suffering on an individual ('the victim') for a prohibited purpose, such as punishment, coercion, or intimidation of, obtaining information or a confession from, or discrimination against the victim or a third party.

The definition of torture applied in the *ad hoc* Tribunals is derived directly from the Convention Against Torture (CAT), which provides that:

> the term 'torture' means any act by which severe pain or suffering, whether physical or mental, is intentionally inflicted on a person for such purposes as obtaining from him or a third person information or a confession, punishing him for an act he or a third person has committed or is suspected of having committed, or intimidating or coercing him or a third person, or for any reason based on discrimination of any kind, *when such pain or suffering is inflicted by or at the instigation of or with the consent or acquiescence of a public official or other person acting in an official capacity.* It does not include pain or suffering arising only from, inherent in or incidental to lawful sanctions.[319]

Indeed, in the 1998 *Akayesu* Trial Judgement, the first from either Tribunal to deal with this underlying offence, the Trial Chamber simply applied the CAT definition – including the italicised text, which has been termed the 'official act' or 'public official' requirement – directly to the facts before it, and did not attempt to modify the definition in light of any developments in customary international law since the conclusion of the treaty.[320] This approach was largely mirrored by the Trial and Appeals Chambers in the

[316] See, e.g., *Prosecutor* v. *Ntagerura, Bagambiki, and Imanishimwe*, Case No. ICTR-99-46-T, Judgement and Sentence, 25 February 2004 ('*Cyangugu* Trial Judgement'), paras. 12, 13, 726, 751.

[317] See, e.g., *ibid.*, paras. 728, 751–753 (Trial Chamber observing for one incident that it 'lack[ed] sufficient reliable evidence to determine whether the refugees were held at the stadium against their will', and that 'the evidence was insufficient to determine whether the refugees' movement at the stadium was curtailed to incarcerate them or to ensure their protection'; and for the other incident that 'there [was] insufficient evidence to conclude that Côme Simugomwa and the seventeen refugees removed from Kamarampaka Stadium and Cyangugu Cathedral were imprisoned').

[318] *Ibid.*, para. 754.

[319] Convention Against Torture and Other Cruel, Inhuman or Degrading Treatment or Punishment, 10 December 1984, entered into force 26 June 1987, UN Doc. A/39/51 (1984), 1465 UNTS 85, Art. 1(1) (emphasis added). For a general discussion of torture in the *ad hoc* Tribunals, see Sandesh Sivakumaran, 'Torture in International Human Rights and International Humanitarian Law: The Actor and the *Ad Hoc* Tribunals', (2005) 18 *Leiden Journal of International Law* 541.

[320] See, e.g., *Akayesu* Trial Judgement, *supra* note 94, paras. 593–595, 681.

Furundžija case at the ICTY, in which the latter chamber concurred with the inclusion of the public official requirement in the definition of torture.[321]

In the 2002 *Kunarac* Appeal Judgement, however, the ICTY Appeals Chamber was confronted with a definition, developed by the Trial Chamber in that case after an extensive review of the customary international legal status of torture, that explicitly omitted the public official requirement.[322] The *Kunarac* Trial Chamber distinguished between the international conventions that incorporated this requirement, and the ICTY Statute where torture appears only as an underlying offence that may constitute a war crime or crime against humanity. The Trial Chamber concluded that the public official requirement is inapplicable in the context of international criminal law: unlike the treaties that seek to regulate the conduct of states,[323] 'the characteristic trait of the offence' for the purposes of international criminal law 'is to be found in the nature of the act committed rather than in the status of the person who committed it.'[324] The Appeals Chamber concurred, observing that the Trial Chamber was 'right in taking the position that the public official requirement is not a requirement under customary international law in relation to the criminal responsibility of an individual for torture outside of the Torture Convention'.[325] This definition of torture, without the public official requirement, has been uniformly applied by subsequent *ad hoc* chambers, which have also confirmed that the conduct alleged to be torture must be intentional.[326] Several chambers have held that the definition of torture as an underlying offence is the same regardless of the article of the Statute under which it is charged, that is, regardless of whether crimes against humanity or war crimes are alleged.[327]

Two elements of torture set it apart from other underlying offences involving physical or mental mistreatment: the first, a physical element, is that the mistreatment must cause severe pain or suffering;[328] the second, the defining mental

[321] See, e.g., *Prosecutor* v. *Furundžija*, Case No. IT-95-17/1-A, Judgement, 21 July 2000 ('*Furundžija* Appeal Judgement'), para. 111; *Furundžija* Trial Judgement, *supra* note 71, para. 162.

[322] See *Kunarac et al.* Trial Judgement, *supra* note 90, paras. 465–497.

[323] See *Kunarac et al.* Appeal Judgement, *supra* note 75, para. 146.

[324] *Kunarac et al.* Trial Judgement, *supra* note 90, para. 495 (citing, for support, the definition of torture included in the Rome Statute and the Elements of Crimes of the ICC); see *infra* section 2.3.1 (discussing crimes against humanity in the ICC); see also *infra* note 478 (noting that, unlike the *ad hoc* Tribunals, torture in the ICC need not be inflicted for a prohibited purpose); note 635 (panel of the SPSC finding an accused guilty of torture); notes 661–671 (torture charges in the ECCC); notes 687, 714 (torture charges in the SICT).

[325] *Kunarac et al.* Appeal Judgement, *supra* note 75, para. 148.

[326] See, e.g., *Mrkšić et al.* Trial Judgement, *supra* note 77, para. 513; *Cyangugu* Trial Judgement, *supra* note 316, para. 703; *Limaj et al.* Trial Judgement, *supra* note 75, para. 235; *Brđanin* Trial Judgement, *supra* note 80, paras. 481, 488–489, affirmed in *Brđanin* Appeal Judgement, *supra* note 237, para. 252; *Simić et al.* Trial Judgement, *supra* note 115, paras. 79, 82; *Stakić* Trial Judgement, *supra* note 80, para. 750; *Semanza* Trial Judgement, *supra* note 85, paras. 342–343; *Krnojelac* Trial Judgement, *supra* note 111, para. 179.

[327] See, e.g., *Brđanin* Trial Judgement, *supra* note 80, para. 482; *Simić et al.* Trial Judgement, *supra* note 115, para. 79; see also *Naletilić and Martinović* Trial Judgement, *supra* note 113, para. 336.

[328] See, e.g., *Brđanin* Trial Judgement, *supra* note 80, para. 483 ('The seriousness of the pain or suffering sets torture apart from other forms of mistreatment.').

element of torture, is that the pain or suffering must be inflicted for a specific and prohibited purpose.[329]

2.2.3.6.1 The severity requirement In 2004, the *Brđanin* Trial Judgement noted that the jurisprudence of the *ad hoc* Tribunals had not specified a particular threshold of pain or suffering that must be proved before it is sufficiently severe that the alleged conduct qualifies as torture. Attempting to bring both clarity and detail to the basic propositions outlined in previous judgements, the Trial Chamber noted:

> In assessing the seriousness of any mistreatment, the objective severity of the harm inflicted must be considered, including the nature, purpose and consistency of the acts committed. Subjective criteria, such as the physical or mental condition of the victim, the effect of the treatment and, in some cases, factors such as the victim's age, sex, state of health and position of inferiority will also be relevant in assessing the gravity of the harm. Permanent injury is not a requirement for torture; evidence of the suffering need not even be visible after the commission of the crime.[330]

The Chamber concluded that Bosnian Serb forces in the Autonomous Region of Krajina (ARK) had committed multiple acts of torture in various locations and detention centres throughout the region during and after attacks on non-Serb towns, villages and hamlets;[331] and that Radoslav Brđanin had aided and abetted that torture because, in his position as the highest political authority in the ARK, he 'rendered practical assistance and a substantial contribution to the Bosnian Serb forces carrying out these attacks', and was aware that these forces would commit torture in the course of these attacks.[332]

In his challenge to his conviction for torture as both a grave breach of the Geneva Conventions and a crime against humanity,[333] Brđanin attacked not only the Trial Chamber's findings on the form of responsibility, but also its conclusion that the acts charged in the indictment constituted torture. He argued that the current definition of torture in customary international law 'is best exemplified by a pronouncement from the Office of Legal Counsel of the United States Justice Department',[334] the infamous

[329] See, e.g., *ibid.*, para. 486; *Krnojelac* Trial Judgement, *supra* note 111, para. 180 ('"Torture" constitutes one of the most serious attacks upon a person's mental or physical integrity. The purpose and the seriousness of the attack upon the victim sets torture apart from other forms of mistreatment.').

[330] *Brđanin* Trial Judgement, *supra* note 80, para. 484 (citing *Kunarac et al.* Appeal Judgement, *supra* note 75, para. 150; *Krnojelac* Trial Judgement, *supra* note 111, para. 182; *Prosecutor* v. *Kvočka, Kos, Radić, Žigić, and Prcać*, Case No. IT-98-30/1-T, Judgement, 2 November 2001 ('*Kvočka et al.* Trial Judgement'), paras. 143, 148).

[331] See *ibid.*, paras. 535, 538 (summarising and referring to earlier findings).

[332] *Ibid.*, paras. 532–538 (finding that Brđanin also aided and abetted torture in detention camps). For more on aiding and abetting as a form of responsibility, see generally Boas, Bischoff, and Reid, *supra* note 100, ch. 4.

[333] See *supra* text accompanying note 327.

[334] *Prosecutor* v. *Brđanin*, Case No. IT-99–36-A, Appellant Brđanin's Brief on Appeal, 25 July 2005, quoted in *Brđanin* Appeal Judgement, *supra* note 237, para. 244.

Bybee Memorandum,[335] which claimed that an act could not constitute torture unless it inflicted physical pain 'of an intensity akin to that which accompanies serious physical injury such as death or organ failure', or mental pain resulting in 'lasting psychological harm, such as seen in mental disorders like posttraumatic stress disorder'.[336] Moreover, the memorandum asserted that the mental pain must be the result of one of the specific causes identified in a federal statute.[337]

The Appeals Chamber rejected this argument for three reasons. First, the Bybee Memorandum had been subsequently 'withdrawn' by the United States executive branch.[338] Second, even if the executive branch considered that the severity requirement could only be satisfied by pain that passed the threshold specified in the memorandum, that view 'would not suffice to make pain of such intensity a requirement for conviction under customary international law', as '[n]o matter how powerful or influential a country is, its practice does not automatically become customary international law'.[339] Third, and most importantly, the *travaux préparatoires* of the CAT indicate that the treaty's reference to 'severe pain or suffering, whether physical or mental' is not intended to be synonymous with 'extreme' pain or suffering, because that suggested revision was specifically rejected by the drafters.[340] With the limited exception of the public official requirement, the CAT is still regarded as 'declarative of customary international law' on the crime of torture,[341] and since the Appeals Chamber considered that 'severe' pain or suffering was necessarily less intense than 'extreme' pain and suffering, it held that 'it is therefore clear that, under customary international law, physical torture can

335 This memorandum, also known as the 'Torture Memo', takes its nickname from the then-head of the Office of Legal Counsel, Jay Bybee.

336 See Memorandum for Alberto R. Gonzales, Counsel to the President, Re: Standards of Conduct for Interrogation under 18 USC §§ 2340–2340A, 1 August 2002, available at www.humanrightsfirst.org/us_law/etn/gonzales/memos_dir/memo_20020801_JD_%20Gonz_.pdf, p. 46. Title 18 of the United States Code defines crimes within the jurisdiction of the U.S. federal courts.

337 *Ibid.*, pp. 9–12 (citing 18 U.S.C. § 2340 (2002)). Section 2340(2) provides:

> '[S]evere mental pain or suffering' means the prolonged mental harm caused by or resulting from–
>
> (A) the intentional infliction or threatened infliction of severe physical pain or suffering;
> (B) the administration or application, or threatened administration or application, of mind-altering substances or other procedures calculated to disrupt profoundly the senses or the personality;
> (C) the threat of imminent death; or
> (D) the threat that another person will imminently be subjected to death, severe physical pain or suffering, or the administration or application of mind-altering substances or other procedures calculated to disrupt profoundly the senses or personality[.]

338 *Brđanin* Appeal Judgement, *supra* note 237, para. 248 (referring to the 'Levin Memorandum'); see also Neil A. Lewis, 'Justice Dept. Toughens Rule on Torture', *New York Times*, 1 January 2005, p. A1 ('The Justice Department has broadened its definition of torture, significantly retreating from a memorandum in August 2002 that defined torture extremely narrowly … '). But see Scott Shane, David Johnston, and James Risen, 'Secret U.S. Endorsement of Severe Interrogations', *New York Times*, 4 October 2007, p. A1 ('[S]oon after Alberto R. Gonzales's arrival as attorney general in February 2005, the Justice Department issued another opinion, this one in secret. It was a very different document, according to officials briefed on it, an expansive endorsement of the harshest interrogation techniques ever used by the Central Intelligence Agency.').

339 *Brđanin* Appeal Judgement, *supra* note 237, para. 247. 340 *Ibid.*,

341 See generally *Kunarac et al.* Appeal Judgement, *supra* note 75, para. 147.

include acts inflicting physical pain or suffering less severe' than the level indicated in the Bybee Memorandum.[342] Although it rejected Brđanin's arguments regarding the severity of the pain required for torture, the Appeals Chamber partially reversed his conviction for this crime on other grounds, namely that the Trial Chamber had erred in holding him responsible for aiding and abetting torture in certain specified locations.[343]

The jurisprudence of the ICTY has consistently held that the evaluation of whether the charged conduct satisfies the severity requirement is a fact-dependent inquiry.[344] Accordingly, the *Brđanin* Appeal Judgement also reaffirmed the Chamber's earlier holding in *Naletilić and Martinović* that 'while the suffering inflicted by some acts may be so obvious that the acts amount *per se* to torture, in general allegations of torture must be considered on a case-by-case basis'.[345] Several chambers have concluded that rape or other sexual violence are among the acts that may cause effects so severe as to constitute torture *per se*;[346] in addition, in one of the earliest judgements at the ICTY, the *Čelebići* Trial Chamber included a lengthy list of acts that unequivocally qualified as torture, drawing on the work of the United Nations Special Rapporteur for Torture.[347] Other acts that have been held to constitute torture include telling a detainee that he would be killed;[348] and 'severe physical abuse in the course of interrogation … particularly when combined with acts designed to cause psychological torment, such as falsely informing a prisoner

342 *Brđanin* Appeal Judgement, *supra* note 237, para. 249. 343 *Ibid*., para. 288.

344 See, e.g., *Kunarac et al.* Appeal Judgement, *supra* note 75, para. 149; *Brđanin* Trial Judgement, *supra* note 80, para. 483; *Simić et al.* Trial Judgement, *supra* note 115, para. 80; *Krnojelac* Trial Judgement, *supra* note 111, para. 181; accord *Prosecutor* v. *Delalić, Mucić, Delić and Landžo*, Case No. IT-96-21, Judgement, 16 November 1998 ('*Čelebići* Trial Judgement'), para. 469 (noting that 'it is difficult to articulate with any degree of precision the threshold level of suffering at which other forms of mistreatment become torture'). Cf. *Naletilić and Martinović* Trial Judgement, *supra* note 113, para. 343 (similar holding in the context of wilfully causing great suffering or serious injury to body or health as a grave breach of the Geneva Conventions).

345 *Brđanin* Appeal Judgement, *supra* note 237, para. 251 (quoting *Naletilić and Martinović* Appeal Judgement, *supra* note 300, para. 299).

346 See, e.g., *Semanza* Trial Judgement, *supra* note 85, paras. 431–435 (holding that rape committed with discriminatory intent constitutes torture); *Kunarac et al.* Appeal Judgement, *supra* note 75, paras. 149–150; *Brđanin* Trial Judgement, *supra* note 80, para. 485; *Akayesu* Trial Judgement, *supra* note 94, paras. 596–598, 686–688; see also *Kvočka et al.* Trial Judgement, *supra* note 330, para. 145 (holding that rape 'may' constitute torture).

347 See *Čelebići* Trial Judgement, *supra* note 344, para. 467 (describing it as a 'a detailed, although not exhaustive, catalogue of those acts which involve the infliction of suffering severe enough to constitute the offence of torture'):

> [B]eating; extraction of nails, teeth, etc.; burns; electric shocks; suspension; suffocation; exposure to excessive light or noise; sexual aggression; administration of drugs in detention or psychiatric institutions; prolonged denial of rest or sleep; prolonged denial of food; prolonged denial of sufficient hygiene; prolonged denial of medical assistance; total isolation and sensory deprivation; being kept in constant uncertainty in terms of space and time; threats to torture or kill relatives; total abandonment; and simulated executions.

348 See, e.g., *Naletilić and Martinović* Trial Judgement, *supra* note 113, para. 449 ('[T]elling witness Z that he was a dead man and … ordering him to go back to his cell and pray and prepare to die … wilfully inflicted severe mental suffering on witness Z with the purpose to punish him for the alleged stealing of money from the safe.'), affirmed in *Naletilić and Martinović* Appeal Judgement, *supra* note 300, para. 300 (confirming that 'telling prisoners falsely that they will be executed, in a "brutal context" that makes the statement believable, can amount to wilfully causing great suffering').

that his father had been killed'.[349] On the other hand, among the acts that have been considered insufficiently serious to qualify as torture by themselves are simple interrogation;[350] 'minor contempt for the physical integrity of the victim';[351] imprisonment;[352] solitary confinement;[353] and deprivation of food.[354]

The *Naletilić and Martinović* Appeal Judgement also established that, although the duration of the charged conduct may affect a trial chamber's determination as to whether it qualifies as torture, it is not an element of the definition of the underlying offence that the conduct causing severe pain or suffering be of a particular duration.[355]

2.2.3.6.2 The prohibited purpose requirement The fact that the physical perpetrator's conduct causes severe pain and suffering is insufficient to render it torture; it must also be inflicted in order to achieve a particular result, or for a particular purpose.[356] The CAT lists five such purposes – punishment, coercion, intimidation, obtaining information or a confession, or discrimination directed at the victim or a third person – which are typically referred to as the 'prohibited purposes',[357] and which have generally been adopted and incorporated into the Tribunals' jurisprudence as part of customary international law.

349 *Naletilić and Martinović* Appeal Judgement, *supra* note 300, para. 300 (referring to and affirming the holding in *Naletilić and Martinović* Trial Judgement, *supra* note 113, paras. 446–447).

350 See, e.g., *Simić et al.* Trial Judgement, *supra* note 115, para. 80; *Krnojelac* Trial Judgement, *supra* note 111, para. 181.

351 *Krnojelac* Trial Judgement, *supra* note 111, para. 181. Though this holding has been reprised by other Trial Chambers, see, e.g., *Simić et al.* Trial Judgement, *supra* note 115, para. 80, none has explained what conduct would constitute only 'minor' contempt.

352 *Mrkšić et al.* Trial Judgement, *supra* note 77, para. 524 (observing that 'unlawful detention for prolonged periods' or imprisonment alone had never before been held to constitute torture or cruel treatment, and finding that in the circumstances of that case, the mere fact of imprisonment was not an act inflicting severe pain or suffering or constituting a serious attack on human dignity, within the meaning of torture or cruel treatment under Article 3 of the ICTY Statute).

353 *Krnojelac* Trial Judgement, *supra* note 111, para. 183 (noting, however, that 'in view of its strictness, its duration, and the object pursued, solitary confinement could cause great physical or mental suffering of the sort envisaged by this offence').

354 *Ibid.* (with similar qualification as for solitary confinement, *supra* note 353).

355 *Naletilić and Martinović* Appeal Judgement, *supra* note 300, para. 299. See also *Krnojelac* Trial Judgement, *supra* note 111, para. 182:

> [T]o the extent that an individual has been mistreated over a prolonged period of time, or that he or she has been subjected to repeated or various forms of mistreatment, the severity of the acts should be assessed as a whole to the extent that it can be shown that this lasting period or the repetition of acts are inter-related, follow a pattern or are directed towards the same prohibited goal.

356 See, e.g., *Brđanin* Trial Judgement, *supra* note 80, para. 486 (holding that 'in the absence of such purpose or goal, even a very severe infliction of pain would not qualify as torture'); accord *Krnojelac* Trial Judgement, *supra* note 111, para. 184. But see *infra* note 478 (noting that, in contrast to the *ad hoc* Tribunals, torture in the ICC need not be inflicted for a prohibited purpose). The jurisprudence does not explicitly state whether the intent in question must be that of the physical perpetrator, or whether another actor's intent may satisfy the requirement. Consistent with the analysis outlined above, it seems clear that the intent of the true author or authors of the crime – whether it be the physical perpetrator, or the planner, orderer, instigator, or first category JCE participant – is the object of this element of the crime. See *supra*, section 2.2.2.1.

357 See, e.g., *Čelibići* Trial Judgement, *supra* note 344, paras. 470–472.

There has been some disagreement, however, among ICTY chambers as to whether the listing in the CAT is intended to be exhaustive. Early on, the *Čelebići* Trial Chamber opined that the list was merely illustrative.[358] Other judgements have implicitly or explicitly restricted the prohibited purposes to those listed in the Convention,[359] while at least two have asserted that humiliation of the victim or a third person is also a prohibited purpose under customary international law.[360] It does not appear that the ICTY Appeals Chamber has specifically endorsed one of these approaches, even though it has generally approved of the definitions used by the Trial Chambers in each of these cases.[361]

Whether the list of purposes is open-ended or closed, it is evident that, as the *Krnojelac* Trial Chamber remarked, the fact that a purpose is 'prohibited' 'does not necessarily mean that [it] must be illegitimate. Several listed purposes, in particular obtaining information or a confession, may be perfectly legitimate on condition that appropriate methods are used to achieve them.'[362] Moreover, the prohibited purpose need not be the sole or even predominant reason for which the pain or suffering is inflicted; it need only be 'part of the motivation behind the conduct'.[363]

2.2.3.7 Rape

The penetration, without consent, of (a) the vagina or anus of an individual (the 'victim') by the penis of, or any other object used by, the physical perpetrator, or (b) the mouth of the victim by the penis of the physical perpetrator, committed with intent to effect that penetration and knowledge of either the victim's non-consent or the existence of coercive circumstances precluding the possibility of valid consent.

The definition of rape as an underlying offence offers a unique window into the relationship between the ICTY and the ICTR, and an interesting case study of the

358 *Čelebići* Trial Judgement, *supra* note 344, para. 470. Accord *Brđanin* Trial Judgement, *supra* note 80, para. 487. See also J. Herman Burgers and Hans Danielus, *The United Nations Convention Against Torture and Other Cruel, Inhuman or Degrading Treatment or Punishment* (1988), p. 46 ('[I]t was agreed that the enumeration of purposes … should not be exhaustive but merely indicate the most characteristic examples.').

359 See *Kunarac et al.* Trial Judgement, *supra* note 90, para. 485 (doubting 'whether other purposes have come to be recognized under customary international law'); *Krnojelac* Trial Judgement, *supra* note 111, paras. 185–186 (considering that only the purposes listed in the CAT have attained customary status, and refusing to expand the list because the *nullum crimen sine lege* principle required it to apply the law as it stood at the time the alleged crimes were committed). For a brief explanation of this principle, see Chapter 1, text accompanying notes 24–26.

360 See *Kvočka et al.* Trial Judgement, *supra* note 330, para. 162; *Furundžija* Trial Judgement, *supra* note 71, paras. 141, 152, 157.

361 See *Čelebići* Trial Judgement, *supra* note 344, paras. 499, 507 (upholding torture convictions against the accused's challenge alleging factual errors); *Kunarac et al.* Appeal Judgement, *supra* note 75, paras. 142, 144 (affirming and adopting the Trial Chamber's definition, which listed only the purposes in the Convention); *Furundžija* Appeal Judgement, *supra* note 321, para. 111 (approving of the Trial Chamber's definition, although quoting the section of the Trial Judgement that did not include the reference to humiliation).

362 *Krnojelac* Trial Judgement, *supra* note 111, para. 184.

363 *Čelebići* Trial Judgement, *supra* note 344, para. 470; accord, e.g., *Kunarac et al.* Appeal Judgement, *supra* note 75, para. 155; *Brđanin* Trial Judgement, *supra* note 80, para. 487; *Simić et al.* Trial Judgement, *supra* note 115, para. 81; *Semanza* Trial Judgement, *supra* note 85, para. 343.

tension between two basic themes of their jurisprudence: on one hand, the need to ensure that the conduct for which an accused is convicted was both prohibited and criminal at the time it was committed (the *nullum crimen sine lege* principle), and thus to have a firm basis in international law for the definitions of the crimes and forms of responsibility that are applied;[364] and on the other, the desire to articulate flexible definitions that can be applied to the entire range of circumstances that have given rise to the cases within their jurisdiction.[365]

The *Akayesu* Trial Judgement, the first international case ever to hold that rape could qualify as both genocide[366] and torture as a crime against humanity, was also the first from either Tribunal to attempt a definition of rape as a crime against humanity. Recognising that no clear definition of rape could be discerned under customary or conventional international law,[367] the Trial Chamber decided to apply what has been termed a 'conceptual' approach to defining the underlying offence.[368] That is, instead of trying to describe in detail the individual actions that comprise the *actus reus* of rape – rejecting any attempt to capture 'the central elements of rape ... in a mechanical description of objects and body parts'[369] – it defined rape broadly as 'a physical invasion of a sexual nature, committed on a person under circumstances which are coercive.'[370] Coercive circumstances, in turn:

> need not be evidenced by a show of physical force. Threats, intimidation, extortion and other forms of duress which prey on fear or desperation may constitute coercion, and coercion

[364] See Chapter 1, note 18; *ibid.*, text accompanying notes 24–26. For scholarly analysis of rape in the *ad hoc* Tribunals, see Karen Engle, 'Feminism and Its (Dis)contents: Criminalizing Wartime Rape in Bosnia and Herzegovina', (2005) 99 *American Journal of International Law* 778; Doris E. Buss, 'Prosecuting Mass Rape: *Prosecutor* v. *Dragoljub Kunarac, Radomir Kovač and Zoran Vuković*, (2002) 10 *Feminist Legal Studies* 91; Wolfgang Schomburg and Ines Peterson, 'Genuine Consent to Sexual Violence Under International Criminal Law', (2007) 101 *American Journal of International Law* 121.

[365] See, e.g., *supra* section 2.2.2.3.1 (discussing the debate over the definition of a civilian for purposes of crimes against humanity).

[366] Rape is not specifically listed in the Tribunals' Statutes as one of the underlying offences of genocide, but has generally been treated as conduct that may constitute genocide, if the general requirements are satisfied, because it causes serious physical and mental harm to the victims. See Chapter 3, section 3.2.2.2 (discussing serious bodily or mental harm as an underlying offence of genocide).

[367] *Akayesu* Trial Judgement, *supra* note 94, paras. 596, 686. See also *Čelebići* Trial Judgement, *supra* note 344, para. 478 ('Although the prohibition on rape under international humanitarian law is readily apparent, there is no convention or other international instrument containing a definition of the term itself.').

[368] See *Akayesu* Trial Judgement, *supra* note 94, paras. 597–598, 687 (analogising its approach to that of the CAT, which 'does not catalogue specific acts in its definition of torture, focusing rather on the conceptual framework of state sanctioned violence'); *Musema* Trial Judgement, *supra* note 114, para. 227 (characterising the *Akayesu* method as a 'conceptual approach').

[369] *Akayesu* Trial Judgement, *supra* note 94, paras. 597, 687.

[370] *Ibid.*, paras. 598, 688; see also *ibid.*, para. 686 (noting that 'while rape has been historically defined in national jurisdictions as non-consensual sexual intercourse, variations on the form of rape may include acts which involve the insertion of objects and/or the use of bodily orifices not considered to be intrinsically sexual'). The Chamber also considered rape to be one manifestation of sexual violence, which it defined as 'any act of a sexual nature which is committed on a person under circumstances which are coercive', and which 'is not limited to physical invasion of the human body and may include acts which do not involve penetration or even physical contact.' *Ibid.*, para. 688.

may be inherent in certain circumstances, such as armed conflict or the … presence of [militia members] among refugee Tutsi women at the *bureau communal*.[371]

This approach to defining rape was adopted by the first ICTY trial judgment to discuss rape, in the *Čelebići* case, where the Trial Chamber saw 'no reason to depart from the conclusion of the ICTR in the *Akayesu* Judgement on this issue.'[372]

Less than one month later, however, the *Furundžija* Trial Chamber disagreed. It also acknowledged the lack of a definition for rape under customary or conventional international law,[373] but concluded that the *nullum crimen sine lege* principle required it to determine whether a definition that would provide detail to the basic prohibition against rape under international law could be derived from an analysis of national jurisdictions.[374] The Chamber eventually concluded that the *actus reus* of rape was 'the sexual penetration, however slight[,] of the vagina or anus of the victim by the penis of the perpetrator or any other object used by the perpetrator; or of the mouth of the victim by the penis of the perpetrator' which must occur 'by coercion or force or threat of force against the victim or a third person'.[375] Although this definition focused on precisely the sort of mechanical description that the *Akayesu* Trial Chamber eschewed, the *Furundžija* Trial Chamber actually considered it a broadened definition that sought to promote 'the fundamental principle of protecting human dignity', because it explicitly included forcible oral sex, which is not included in the definition of rape in certain domestic jurisdictions.[376]

The first appeal judgements considering these opposing definitions did not resolve the conflict: the definition of rape was not an issue raised on appeal in *Akayesu*, while the *Furundžija* Appeal Judgement acknowledged the divergence, but concluded that since there had been no dispute between the parties on this question, 'the Trial Chamber was entitled to interpret the law as it stood.'[377] It was not until the *Kunarac* Appeal Judgement that either Appeals Chamber endorsed a particular definition of rape, and here again, it was in response to the initiative of the *Kunarac* Trial Chamber.[378] The Trial Chamber had accepted the *Furundžija* mechanical description, but had rejected the requirement of force as overly restrictive, because it ignored other factors 'which would render an act of sexual

[371] *Ibid.*

[372] *Čelebići* Trial Judgement, *supra* note 344, para. 479 (emphasis removed). Accord *Musema* Trial Judgement, *supra* note 114, para. 229 (explicitly rejecting the *Furundžija* definition described below).

[373] *Furundžija* Trial Judgement, *supra* note 71, para. 175.

[374] *Ibid.*, paras. 177–178 (holding that '[w]henever international criminal rules do not define a notion of criminal law, reliance upon national legislation is justified, subject to [certain specified] conditions'). The Trial Chamber referred to the animating legal principle as *nullum crimen sine lege stricta*, or the 'criminal law principle of specificity'. *Ibid.*, para. 177. See also *ibid.*, para. 176 (noting the different approach taken by the *Akayesu* Trial Chamber and adopted by the *Čelebići* Trial Chamber).

[375] *Ibid.*, para. 185. [376] *Ibid.*, paras. 183–184 (definition at para. 184).

[377] *Furundžija* Appeal Judgement, *supra* note 321, para. 212.

[378] See *supra* text accompanying note 322 (discussing the role of the *Kunarac* Trial Chamber in changing the definition of torture applied in the *ad hoc* Tribunals).

penetration non-consensual or non-voluntary on the part of the victim'.[379] Instead, in an approach subsequently approved by the ICTY Appeals Chamber, the Trial Chamber made 'the absence of consent the *conditio sine qua non* of rape',[380] defining the underlying offence as follows:

> [T]he *actus reus* of the crime of rape in international law is constituted by: the sexual penetration, however slight: (a) of the vagina or anus of the victim by the penis of the perpetrator or any other object used by the perpetrator; or (b) the mouth of the victim by the penis of the perpetrator; where such sexual penetration occurs *without the consent of the victim*. Consent for this purpose must be consent given voluntarily, as a result of the victim's free will, assessed in the context of the surrounding circumstances. The *mens rea* is the intention to effect this sexual penetration, and the knowledge that it occurs without the consent of the victim.[381]

The Appeals Chamber explained, in an aside that seemed to borrow from *Akayesu*, that the surrounding circumstances may be so inherently coercive, like those in the case before it,[382] 'as to negate any possibility of consent'.[383] Thus, if the prosecution establishes beyond a reasonable doubt that such were the prevailing circumstances, lack of consent may be presumed.[384]

Once approved by the ICTY Appeals Chamber, it is the *Kunarac* definition that has been generally applied by chambers of both Tribunals.[385] Subsequent ICTR Trial Judgements have strained to reconcile the *Furundžija-Kunarac* mechanical description and the *Akayesu* conceptual approach.[386] The *Kunarac* definition was recently reaffirmed, however, in the *Gacumbitsi* Judgement of the ICTR Appeals Chamber, which confirmed that both the victim's non-consent and the perpetrator's knowledge thereof are elements of the underlying offence, but that they may be

379 *Kunarac et al.* Trial Judgement, *supra* note 90, para. 438.

380 *Kunarac et al.* Appeal Judgement, *supra* note 75, para. 129.

381 *Kunarac et al.* Trial Judgement, *supra* note 90, para. 460 (emphasis added).

382 See *supra* text accompanying notes 268–273 for a description of the factual findings in this case.

383 *Kunarac et al.* Appeal Judgement, *supra* note 75, para 132. See also *ibid.*, paras. 129, 130 (referring to the possibility of perpetrators 'taking advantage of coercive circumstances without relying on physical force' and noting that 'true consent will not be possible' in the context of war crimes and crimes against humanity, where circumstances are 'almost universally coercive').

384 *Ibid.*, para. 131. Accord *Gacumbitsi* Appeal Judgement, *supra* note 95, para. 155.

385 See, e.g., *Muvunyi* Trial Judgement, *supra* note 84, paras. 517–522 (reviewing the 'rather chequered history of the definition of rape' in the Tribunals' jurisprudence); *Muhimana* Trial Judgement, *supra* note 214, para. 551 (purporting to reconcile the *Akayesu* and *Kunarac* definitions); *Brđanin* Trial Judgement, *supra* note 80, para. 1008; *Niyitegeka* Trial Judgement, *supra* note 94, para. 456 (same); *Semanza* Trial Judgement, *supra* note 85, paras. 344–345.

386 See, e.g., *Muhimana* Trial Judgement, *supra* note 214, para. 550 ('Whereas *Akayesu* referred broadly to a "physical invasion of a sexual nature", *Kunarac* went on to articulate the parameters of what would constitute a physical invasion of a sexual nature amounting to rape.'); *Muvunyi* Trial Judgement, *supra* note 84, para. 522 ('[B]oth the *Akayesu* and *Kunarac* definitions of rape reflect this objective of protecting individual sexual autonomy and therefore are not incompatible. The broad language in *Akayesu* that rape constitutes "physical invasion of a sexual nature", when properly interpreted, could include "sexual penetration" as stipulated in *Kunarac*.').

satisfied by proof of the coercive circumstances in which the alleged rape took place, and of the fact that the physical perpetrator 'was aware, or had reason to be aware, of the coercive circumstances that undermined the possibility of genuine consent'.[387]

2.2.3.8 Persecution on political, racial, and religious grounds

In statements of the law by chambers at both levels in both *ad hoc* Tribunals, persecution is often treated as if it were a single, undifferentiated crime that can be committed in a number of different ways: trial chambers frequently enter convictions for 'persecutions as a crime against humanity' without explicitly acknowledging the underlying offences that were alleged to constitute persecution, and majorities in the Appeals Chambers now routinely insist that the elements of a persecution conviction should not be considered as including the elements of the underlying offence.[388] As the charging practices of the Tribunals' Prosecutors and the factual findings of trial chambers demonstrate, however, that view of persecution fails to acknowledge the complicated structure of crimes under international law and the factual patterns of the cases. Indictments typically allege that persecution was committed through other underlying offences that may fall within the jurisdiction of the Tribunals, such as murder, rape, torture, forcible displacement, and destruction of personal or real property.[389] In determining whether the prosecution has proved its allegations beyond a reasonable doubt, trial chambers therefore uniformly apply both the elements of the particular underlying offence that is asserted to be an instance of persecution, and the specific requirements for persecution.[390] For this reason, a better view of persecution is that it is a label that is applied to underlying offences when they satisfy its specific requirements, which

[387] *Gacumbitsi* Appeal Judgement, *supra* note 95, paras. 155, 157. See also generally Schomburg and Peterson, *supra* note 364 (discussing the evolution of the definition of rape in *ad hoc* jurisprudence through the *Gacumbitsi* Appeal Judgement). As discussed below, the ICC and internationalised tribunals contain a longer catalogue of sexual underlying offences of crimes against humanity. See *infra* text accompanying note 508 (Rome Statute of the ICC lists rape, sexual slavery, enforced prostitution, forced pregnancy, enforced sterilisation, and 'any other form of sexual violence of comparable gravity'); notes 564–565 (SCSL Statute lists rape, sexual slavery, enforced prostitution, forced pregnancy, and 'any other form of sexual violence'); text accompanying note 579 (findings of rape in the SCSL); text accompanying note 590 (SPSC has the same list as the ICC); text accompanying note 674 (SICT has the same list as the ICC); but see *infra* text accompanying note 648 (crimes against humanity in the constitutive document of the ECCC modelled on the ICTR Statute, and the document thus explicitly lists only rape).

[388] See Chapter 5 for an analysis of cumulative convictions, the area of the law in which such discussions occur most frequently. See especially Chapter 5, text accompanying notes 95–142, 165–166. For a general discussion of persecution in the ICTY, see Ken Roberts, 'The Law of Persecution Before the International Criminal Tribunal for the Former Yugoslavia', (2002) 15 *Leiden Journal of International Law* 623.

[389] Indeed, chambers routinely demand that the prosecution amend indictments in order to specify the particular acts alleged to be persecution. See, e.g., *Blaškić* Appeal Judgement, *supra* note 88, para. 139; *Brđanin* Trial Judgement, *supra* note 80, para. 994; *Krnojelac* Trial Judgement, *supra* note 111, para. 433; see also *infra* note 391.

[390] See Chapter 5, text accompanying notes 99–101, 117–120, 152–155 and accompanying text, for illustrations of this practice; see also *supra* note 314.

are characterised by discrimination against particular groups of persons.[391] This conception of persecution applies equally to those instances of conduct that are not, strictly speaking, underlying offences because they are not necessarily criminal in and of themselves, but rather become so when they are imposed discriminatorily and are of a gravity comparable to the enumerated offences. There too, the task of the trier of fact is to determine first, whether the bare allegation of conduct has been proved, then whether it satisfies the specific requirements for persecution, and finally whether it also satisfies the general requirements for crimes against humanity.

Recognition of this three-step process for determining whether the prosecution has proved that particular conduct constituting persecution as a crime against humanity was committed would have two salutary effects on the jurisprudence of the Tribunals and other courts applying international criminal law. First, it would improve the quality of the jurisprudence by encouraging greater rigour in the factual findings of trial chambers and greater consistency in appellate review. Second, it would correct a critical and currently flawed aspect of the jurisprudence on cumulative convictions, in which trial and appellate chambers, failing to recognise that persecution is a collection of underlying offences and not a single crime, have entered unjustified convictions that may have had a number of negative consequences for the convicted persons, such as longer sentences, less eligibility for early release, and easier qualification for sentencing enhancements for subsequently committed crimes.[392]

2.2.3.8.1 Specific requirements for persecution as a crime against humanity In addition to the general requirements listed above for crimes against humanity, certain specific requirements must be satisfied in order for an underlying offence to qualify as persecution as a crime against humanity. In contrast to the general requirements for crimes against humanity and war crimes, which generally refer to the context in which the alleged offences occur, the specific requirements for persecution as a crime against humanity focus on the specific intent accompanying the underlying offences.[393]

The jurisprudence generally describes persecution as an act or omission that discriminates in fact, which denies or infringes upon a fundamental right laid down in customary or conventional international law, and which was committed

391 See, e.g., *Kupreškić et al.* Appeal Judgement, *supra* note 222, para. 98 (noting that persecution is an 'umbrella crime', and explaining that the prosecution must set forth the particular acts that it alleges to be instances of persecution even if is not 'required to lay a separate charge in respect of *each basic crime* that makes up the general charge of persecution') (emphasis added).

392 See Chapter 5, for a more detailed discussion of the jurisprudence on cumulative convictions; see especially Chapter 5, text accompanying notes 111–166, for a discussion of how this jurisprudence has unsatisfactorily characterised persecution as a crime against humanity.

393 In this regard, they are similar to the defining general requirement for genocide. See generally Chapter 3, section 3.2.1.2.

with the intent to so discriminate.[394] In addition to the mental element of discriminatory intent – the hallmark of persecution – this description refers to two distinct physical elements: first, the underlying conduct of the physical perpetrator must deny or infringe a fundamental right laid down in customary international law or treaty law; second, that conduct must discriminate in fact.

The equal gravity requirement

The act or omission alleged to be persecution is of the same gravity as the specifically listed underlying offences of crimes against humanity.

Mindful of their task in applying and clarifying international law, the Tribunals have made clear that not every denial or infringement of a fundamental right is sufficiently serious to qualify as a potential crime against humanity:[395] the act or omission underlying persecution as a crime against humanity must be of the same gravity as the offences listed in Article 5 of the ICTY Statute and Article 3 of the ICTR Statute,[396] though it need not constitute, on its own, a crime under international law.[397]

The conduct alleged to be persecution may be a specific offence arising under other articles of the Tribunals' Statutes, but it need not be explicitly mentioned in the Statutes.[398] It is clear that when the underlying offence otherwise appears in the

[394] See, e.g., *Media* Appeal Judgement, *supra* note 110, para. 985; *Blaškić* Appeal Judgement, *supra* note 88, para. 131; *Prosecutor* v. *Kvočka, Radić, Žigić, and Prcać*, Case No. IT-98-30/1-A, Judgement, 28 February 2005 ('*Kvočka et al.* Appeal Judgement'), para. 320; *Prosecutor* v. *Vasiljević*, Case No. IT-98-32-A, Judgement, 25 February 2004 ('*Vasiljević* Appeal Judgement'), para. 113; *Krnojelac* Appeal Judgement, *supra* note 264, paras. 185–186; accord *Krajišnik* Trial Judgement, *supra* note 117, para. 734; *Niyitegeka* Trial Judgement, *supra* note 94, para. 431; *Semanza* Trial Judgement, *supra* note 85, paras. 347, 350; *Prosecutor* v. *Ruggiu*, Case No. ICTR-97-32-I, Sentencing Judgement, 1 June 2000, para. 21; *Akayesu* Trial Judgement *supra* note 94, paras. 559–562; *Prosecutor* v. *Bagosora, Kabiligi, Ntabakuze, and Nsengiyumva*, Case No. ICTR-98-41-T, Decision on Motions for Judgement of Acquittal, 2 February 2005 ('*Military I* 98 *bis* Decision'), para. 32.

[395] See, e.g., *Media* Appeal Judgement, *supra* note 110, para. 985; *Krajišnik* Trial Judgement, *supra* note 117, para. 735; *Blagojević and Jokić* Trial Judgement, *supra* note 75, para. 580; *Brđanin* Trial Judgement, *supra* note 80, para. 995; *Simić et al.* Trial Judgement, *supra* note 115, para. 48; *Naletilić and Martinović* Trial Judgement, *supra* note 113, para. 635; *Krnojelac* Trial Judgement, *supra* note 111, para. 434; *Kupreškić et al.* Trial Judgement, *supra* note 71, para. 621.

[396] *Kvočka et al.* Appeal Judgement, *supra* note 394, para. 321; *Blaškić* Appeal Judgement, *supra* note 88, para. 135; *Krnojelac* Appeal Judgement, *supra* note 264, paras. 199, 221.

[397] *Kvočka et al.* Appeal Judgement, *supra* note 394, para. 323 (departing from *Blaškić* Appeal Judgement, *supra* note 88, para. 139; and *Kordić and Čerkez* Appeal Judgement, *supra* note 95, para. 103); accord *Stakić* Appeal Judgement, *supra* note 108, para. 296; *Media* Appeal Judgement, *supra* note 110, para. 985; *Brđanin* Appeal Judgement, *supra* note 237, para. 296; *Krajišnik* Trial Judgement, *supra* note 117, para. 735.

[398] *Kvočka et al.* Appeal Judgement, *supra* note 394, para. 323; *Krajišnik* Trial Judgement, *supra* note 117, para. 735; *Semanza* Trial Judgement, *supra* note 85, para. 349; *Naletilić and Martinović* Trial Judgement, *supra* note 113, para. 635; *Kupreškić et al.* Trial Judgement, *supra* note 71, para. 614; *Krnojelac* Trial Judgement, *supra* note 111, para. 434. While some ICTY trial judgements state that conduct constituting crimes under Articles 2 and 3 of the Statute are necessarily of sufficient gravity to constitute persecution, others indicate that offences enumerated under those Articles must be independently examined to determine if they rise to the same level of gravity as crimes enumerated under Article 5. Compare, e.g., *Krnojelac* Trial Judgement, *supra* note 111, para. 439, with *Brđanin* Trial Judgement, *supra* note 80, para. 995. The four most recent appeal judgements to discuss the physical element of persecution neither noted this difference of opinion nor took a position on the question. See *Kvočka et al.* Appeal Judgement, *supra* note 394, paras. 321–323; *Kordić and Čerkez* Appeal Judgement, *supra* note 95, para. 102; *Blaškić* Appeal Judgement, *supra* note 88, para. 135; *Krnojelac* Appeal Judgement, *supra* note 264, para. 199.

Statutes – such as murder or torture, for example – the equal gravity requirement is automatically satisfied as a matter of law.[399] It seems, therefore, that the purpose of the requirement is to ensure that other conduct, even if reprehensible, is not subject to criminal sanctions unless it is comparable to the type of conduct that is clearly criminal under international law.[400]

Other aspects of the case law support this interpretation. Although persecution often refers to a series of acts or a course of conduct, a single act or omission may be sufficient.[401] When applying the gravity requirement, however – particularly in respect of conduct that does not otherwise constitute an offence under the Statutes or a crime under international law – 'the acts must not be considered in isolation, but in context, by looking at their cumulative effect.'[402] Thus in its judgement in the *Media* case, the ICTR Appeals Chamber held that there was no need to consider whether hate speech could, by itself, constitute persecution as a crime against humanity; instead, the context in which the conduct occurred was especially important for determining its gravity.[403] Since the relevant hate speech in that case was accompanied by a call to commit genocide against the Tutsis, and all this communication took place in the context of a vast campaign directed against the Tutsi population that included murder, physical abuse, rape, and destruction of property, the Appeals Chamber concluded that the equal gravity requirement had been met.[404]

The requirement of discrimination 'in fact'

The conduct actually targets the members of a group defined on the basis of politics, race, or religion.

The specific requirements for persecution are frequently referred to as comprising a 'discriminatory act' coupled with 'discriminatory intent'.[405] In order to constitute

[399] See, e.g., *Brđanin* Trial Judgement, *supra* note 80, para. 995 (holding that 'acts or omissions under other sub-paragraphs of Article 5 are by definition serious enough' to constitute persecution).

[400] See, e.g., *Blaškić* Appeal Judgement, *supra* note 88, paras. 138–139 (rebuking the Trial Chamber for failing to specify that the conduct alleged must meet the equal gravity requirement, and holding that '[i]t is not the case that any type of act, if committed with the requisite discriminatory intent, amounts to persecutions as a crime against humanity'); *Krnojelac* Appeal Judgement, *supra* note 264, Separate Opinion of Judge Shahabuddeen, para. 7:

> It is possible that there can be persecution at different levels. It is here, I think, that it would be reasonable to say that the Statute is concerned only with cases in which the level of gravity of the proven persecution matches the level of the gravity of an enumerated crime.

[401] *Blaškić* Appeal Judgement, *supra* note 88, para. 165 (quoting *Vasiljević* Appeal Judgement, *supra* note 394, para. 113).

[402] *Kvočka et al.* Appeal Judgement, *supra* note 394, para 321 (citing, *inter alia*, *Kupreškić et al.* Trial Judgement, *supra* note 71, paras. 615(e), 622; *Krnojelac* Trial Judgement, *supra* note 111, para. 434). Accord *Semanza* Trial Judgement, *supra* note 85, para. 349.

[403] *Media* Appeal Judgement, *supra* note 110, para. 987.

[404] *Ibid.*, para. 988. Confusingly, the Chamber also concluded later in the paragraph that the hate speech and other communications calling for violence against Tutsis were themselves acts of persecution.

[405] See, e.g., *Vasiljević* Appeal Judgement, *supra* note 394, para. 146; *Krnojelac* Trial Judgement, *supra* note 111, para. 503. See also *Tadić* Trial Judgement, *supra* note 77, para. 715 (holding that the physical element for persecution is a discriminatory act).

a 'discriminatory act', the underlying conduct in question must 'discriminate in fact'[406] – in the words of one trial judgement, it must 'target the members of a group because they belong to a specific community'.[407]

The question of whether 'discrimination in fact' should be evaluated objectively or subjectively has been the subject of some dispute among ICTY trial chambers. The *Krnojelac* Trial Judgement, rendered in 2002, held that discrimination in fact requires an objective result; for example, if the group was targeted because of its ethnic or religious identity, then the victim must actually be of that ethnicity or that religion in order for the offence to qualify as persecution. Beyond the fact that this conclusion follows from the ordinary meaning of the term used in the jurisprudence, the Chamber considered that 'logic argues in favour of a ... such a requirement', because without it, 'an accused could be convicted of persecution without anyone actually having been persecuted'.[408] The Chamber continued:

> [T]he distinction between the crime of persecution and other crimes would be rendered virtually meaningless by depriving the crime of persecution of the qualities that distinguish it from other prohibited acts, such as murder and torture, which have as their object the protection of individuals irrespective of any group association. Although the Statute does not expressly require that the discrimination take place against a member of the targeted group, this is a necessary implication of the occurrence of an act or omission on a discriminatory basis.[409]

By way of illustration, the *Krnojelac* Trial Chamber presented the following hypothetical example:

[406] See *Media* Appeal Judgement, *supra* note 110, para. 985; *Blagojević and Jokić* Trial Judgement, *supra* note 75, para. 583; *Brđanin* Trial Judgement, *supra* note 80, para. 992; *Krnojelac* Trial Judgement, *supra* note 111, para. 431; *Stakić* Trial Judgement, *supra* note 80, para. 732; *Vasiljević* Trial Judgement, *supra* note 164, para. 244. See also *supra* note 394.

[407] *Blaškić* Trial Judgement, *supra* note 90, para. 220. See also *Blagojević and Jokić* Trial Judgement, *supra* note 75, para. 583:

> An act is discriminatory when a victim is targeted because of his membership in a group defined by the perpetrator on a political, racial or religious basis. The act or omission needs to discriminate in fact, *i.e.*, a discriminatory intent is not sufficient, but the act or omission must have discriminatory consequences.

> This specific requirement for persecution is therefore to be contrasted with the ICTR's unique jurisdictional requirement of a discriminatory basis for the general attack on the civilian population. See, e.g., *Muvunyi* Trial Judgement, *supra* note 84, para. 514 (noting that, insofar as the jurisdictional requirement of a discriminatory attack is concerned, 'it is irrelevant whether the *particular victim* of a crime against humanity was a member of a listed group if it can be proved that the perpetrator targeted the *civilian population* on one of the enumerated discriminatory grounds') (emphasis added) (citing *Akayesu* Trial Judgement, *supra* note 94, para. 584; *Muhimana* Trial Judgement, *supra* note 214, para. 529); accord *Gacumbitsi* Trial Judgement, *supra* note 85, para. 301, *Kajelijeli* Trial Judgement, *supra* note 86, paras. 877–878; *Semanza* Trial Judgement, *supra* note 85, para. 331. This jurisdictional requirement is discussed at section 2.2.1.2, *supra*; the treatment of the requirement in the ILC Draft Codes and other international and internationalised courts and tribunals is discussed at note 60, *supra*.

[408] *Krnojelac* Trial Judgement, *supra* note 111, para. 432 (explicitly rejecting the approach taken by the 2001 *Kvočka* Trial Judgement, which had dispensed with the need for discriminatory consequences, and dismissing that holding as unpersuasive).

[409] *Ibid.*

If a Serb deliberately murders someone on the basis that he is Muslim, it is clear that the object of the crime of persecution in that instance is to provide protection from such discriminatory acts to members of the Muslim religious group. If it turns out that the victim is not Muslim, to argue that this act amounts nonetheless to persecution if done with a discriminatory intent needlessly extends the protection afforded by that crime to a person who is not a member of the listed group requiring protection in that instance (Muslims).[410]

The *Naletilić and Martinović* Trial Judgement, rendered in 2003, rejected this reasoning in favour of a subjective approach, under which a victim is discriminated against in fact as long as the physical perpetrators believe – even incorrectly – that the victim is a member of the target group:

The targeted group must be interpreted broadly, and may, in particular, include such persons who are defined by the perpetrator as belonging to the victim group due to their close affiliations or sympathies for the victim group. The Chamber finds this interpretation consistent with the underlying ratio of the provision prohibiting persecution, as it is the perpetrator who defines the victim group while the targeted victims have no influence on the definition of their status.[411]

In what seems a strained attempt to reconcile its holding with the terms of the Tribunal's jurisprudence, the Chamber concluded that 'in such cases, a factual discrimination is given as the victims are discriminated in fact for who or what they are on the basis of the perception of the perpetrator'.[412]

Nevertheless, this awkward attempt at reconciling the subjective approach with the element of 'discrimination in fact' found favour with the ICTY Appeals Chamber, which appears to have settled the dispute over the application of this aspect of persecution in favour of the *Naletilić* approach. Rendering its decision on the merits in September 2003, the *Krnojelac* Appeals Chamber confirmed the *Krnojelac* Trial Chamber's definition of persecution, but rejected its objective approach to the physical element and instead endorsed the subjective approach:

The Appeals Chamber finds [the Trial Chamber's] assertion to be incorrect. It is an erroneous interpretation of the requirement for discrimination in fact (or a discriminatory act) established by the case-law. To use the example provided in the footnote [1293 of the Trial Judgement], the Appeals Chamber considers that a Serb mistaken for a Muslim may still be the victim of the crime of persecution. The Appeals Chamber considers that the act committed against him institutes discrimination in fact, *vis-à-vis* the other Serbs who were not subject to such acts, effected with the will to discriminate against a group on grounds of ethnicity.[413]

[410] *Ibid.*, para. 432 n. 1293. [411] *Naletilić and Martinović* Trial Judgement, *supra* note 113, para. 636.

[412] *Ibid.* It does not appear that the Chamber had need to apply the subjective approach to the facts before it: in all but one of the incidents it discusses in its factual findings on persecution, the victims were Bosnian Muslims and had been targeted on that basis. See generally *ibid.*, paras. 643–715. The sole exception was a Bosnian Croat who was married to a Bosnian Muslim, and the Trial Chamber's discussion suggests that this relationship was the reason for his persecution, not any subjective belief that he was in fact Muslim. See *ibid.*, paras. 679, 712.

[413] *Krnojelac* Appeal Judgement, *supra* note 264, para. 185.

To date, no other appeal judgement has opined on this particular issue.[414] The ICTY Appeals Chamber's endorsement of the subjective approach elevates the physical perpetrator's perception of identity, even if mistaken, above the objective fact of membership in a particular group.[415] As a result, and regardless of its continual recital as part of the elements of persecution, it appears that the 'discrimination in fact' requirement no longer has any independent weight, because if a physical perpetrator intends to discriminate against a victim on the basis of his political, racial, or religious identity, he necessarily believes that the victim is a member of a group defined by that identity. The defining characteristic of persecution in the jurisprudence of the Tribunals is thus discriminatory intent.

The discriminatory intent requirement

The physical perpetrator or other relevant actor intended to discriminate against an individual on the basis of his political, racial, or religious identity.

In order to constitute persecution, the underlying act or omission must have been carried out deliberately, with the intention to discriminate on one of the grounds listed in subparagraph (h): politics, race, or religion.[416] Although the requirement of discriminatory intent may not be satisfied merely by reference to the allegedly discriminatory nature of an attack characterised as a crime against humanity, it 'may be inferred from such a context as long as, in view of the facts of the case, circumstances surrounding the commission of the alleged acts substantiate the existence of such intent.'[417]

[414] This includes the *Blagojević and Jokić* Appeal Judgement, which did not correct the Trial Chamber's statement of the law, even though the latter took the objective approach to discrimination in fact. See *Blagojević and Jokić* Trial Judgement, *supra* note 75, para. 583 (holding that 'a discriminatory intent is not sufficient … the act or omission must have discriminatory consequences'); see also generally *Prosecutor* v. *Blagojević and Jokić*, Case No. IT-02-60-A, Judgement, 9 May 2007. The ICTY Appeals Chamber has, however, expressed a particular preference for the formulation of the definition of persecution it set forth in the same paragraph of the *Krnojelac* Appeal Judgement, thereby indirectly reaffirming the subjective approach. See *Kvočka et al.* Appeal Judgement, *supra* note 394, para. 320 (citing *Krnojelac* Appeal Judgement, *supra* note 264, para. 185).

[415] See, e.g., *Naletilić and Martinović* Trial Judgement, *supra* note 113, para. 636 n. 1572:

> In the view of the Chamber, a teleological interpretation of the element 'discriminatory basis' demands to take into account the fact that the power to define the 'targeted group' rests solely in the hands of the perpetrator group. If a certain person is defined by the perpetrator as belonging to the targeted group, this definition thus becomes 'discriminatory in fact' for the victim as it may not be rebutted, even if such classification may be incorrect under objective criteria.

[416] *Kvočka et al.* Appeal Judgement, *supra* note 394, para. 320; *Krnojelac* Appeal Judgement, *supra* note 264, para. 185; *Vasiljević* Appeal Judgement, *supra* note 394, para. 113; *Blaškić* Appeal Judgement, *supra* note 88, para. 131. See also *Krnojelac* Trial Judgement, *supra* note 111, para. 431 n. 1290 ('Although the Statute refers to the listed grounds in the conjunctive, it is settled in the jurisprudence of the Tribunal that the presence of discriminatory intent on any one of these grounds is sufficient to fulfil the *mens rea* requirement for persecution[.]') (citing *Tadić* Trial Judgement, *supra* note 77, para. 713); accord *Stakić* Trial Judgement, *supra* note 80, para. 732. It should be noted that, although the ICTR's jurisdictional requirement expands the discriminatory grounds for an attack on a civilian population, see *supra* section 2.2.1.2 and note 60, its specific provision on persecution retains only these three alternative grounds. See *supra* text accompanying note 81.

[417] *Blaškić* Appeal Judgement, *supra* note 88, para. 164 (citing *Krnojelac* Appeal Judgement, *supra* note 264, para. 184). In certain circumstances, the line between the elements of the crime charged and the form of responsibility

Discriminatory intent is a term of art that describes the 'specific intent to cause injury to a human being because he belongs to a particular community or group.'[418] The *Blaškić* Appeals Chamber clarified that there is no legal requirement of a 'persecutory intent' over and above discriminatory intent; that is, the intent to implement a particular plan or policy such as the removal of targeted persons from society or humanity is not required to satisfy the mental element of persecution as a crime against humanity.[419] Discriminatory intent may be inferred from the context in which the conduct of the physical perpetrator occurred,[420] but should not be presumed merely because the attack of which it is alleged to be a part is itself discriminatory.[421] When considering whether particular conduct was committed with discriminatory intent, the ICTY Appeals Chamber has directed, somewhat unhelpfully, that chambers look to whether crimes were committed systematically, and 'the general attitude of the alleged perpetrator as demonstrated by his behaviour.'[422] The first factor is redundant, because trial chambers will already consider it when determining whether the conduct qualifies as a crime against humanity, and potentially meaningless, because it therefore does not serve to distinguish potential forms of persecution from other crimes against humanity.

The Tribunal's jurisprudence on the mental element of persecution shows a confusion between the accused and the physical perpetrator similar to that explored above in respect of crimes against humanity in general.[423] One ICTY trial chamber, recognising the distinction, chose to deal with it by departing from the Tribunal's settled law on whether discriminatory intent must be proved with regard to the

can become especially thin. For example, the ICTY Appeals Chamber in one case held, on the facts then before it, that 'the intent to contribute to the joint criminal enterprise and discriminatory intent is one and the same thing'. *Kvočka et al.* Appeal Judgement, *supra* note 394, para. 347. See also *Naletilić and Martinović* Appeal Judgement, *supra* note 300, para. 129 (noting that discriminatory intent may be inferred from circumstances that sound strikingly similar to the usual context for the second category of joint criminal enterprise, that is, 'the operation of a prison, in particular the systematic nature of crimes committed against a particular group within the prison, and the general attitude of the alleged perpetrator as seen through his behaviour').

418 *Blaškić* Trial Judgement, *supra* note 90, para. 235, quoted with approval in *Blaškić* Appeal Judgement, *supra* note 88, para. 165.

419 *Blaškić* Appeal Judgement, *supra* note 88, para. 165. Accord *Brđanin* Trial Judgement, *supra* note 80, para. 997 (noting that 'in the event that such a policy is shown to have existed, the accused need [not] have taken part in the formulation of such discriminatory policy or practice'); *Blagojević and Jokić* Trial Judgement, *supra* note 75, para. 582; *Kupreškić et al.* Trial Judgement, *supra* note 71, para. 625.

420 See, e.g., *Kvočka et al.* Appeal Judgement, *supra* note 394, paras. 366, 460; *Blaškić* Appeal Judgement, *supra* note 88, para. 164; *Krnojelac* Appeal Judgement, *supra* note 264, para. 184.

421 See, e.g., *Kvočka et al.* Appeal Judgement, *supra* note 394, para. 460. See also *supra* text accompanying note 87 (noting that in the ICTR, the jurisdictional requirement of discrimination applies to the attack in general, not the specific underlying offences or crimes). As an element of persecution as a crime against humanity, therefore, discriminatory intent must still be proved by direct or circumstantial evidence.

422 *Kvočka et al.* Appeal Judgement, *supra* note 394, para. 460; accord *Krnojelac* Appeal Judgement, *supra* note 264, para. 184.

423 See, e.g., *Kordić and Čerkez* Appeal Judgement, *supra* note 95, para. 110 (reiterating that 'the *mens rea* of the perpetrator' requires evidence of the specific intent); *Blaškić* Appeal Judgement, *supra* note 88, para. 165 (referring to the intent of 'the perpetrator carrying out the underlying physical acts of persecutions'); *Stakić* Trial Judgement, *supra* note 80, para. 739 (referring to the specific intent for persecution as 'the requirement that an accused intend to discriminate'). See also *supra* text accompanying notes 90–108 (discussion of the similar issue for one of the general requirements for crimes against humanity).

alleged underlying offence. Grounding its jurisprudential disobedience on the fact that it considered the accused an 'indirect co-perpetrator' of the offences at issue,[424] the *Stakić* Trial Chamber asserted:

> In such a context, to require proof of the discriminatory intent of both the Accused and the acting individuals in relation to all the single acts committed would lead to an unjustifiable protection of superiors and would run counter to the meaning, spirit and purpose of the Statute of this International Tribunal. This Trial Chamber, therefore, holds that proof of a discriminatory attack against a civilian population is a sufficient basis to infer the discriminatory intent of an accused for the acts carried out as part of the attack in which he participated as a (co-)perpetrator.
>
> In cases of indirect perpetratorship, proof is required only of the general discriminatory intent of the indirect perpetrator in relation to the attack committed by the direct perpetrators/actors. Even if the direct perpetrator/actor did not act with a discriminatory intent, this, as such, does not exclude the fact that the same act may be considered part of a discriminatory attack if only the indirect perpetrator had the discriminatory intent.[425]

While the Chamber's attention to the position of the accused and his relation to the crimes is certainly welcome, its studied refusal to apply the Tribunals' law on persecution as a crime against humanity seems unnecessary.[426] A better approach would be to retain the requirement that discriminatory intent be proved with regard to each instance of alleged persecution, but recognise that the physical perpetrator may indeed be an ignorant actor implementing the plan or following the directions of another person. In order to prove that the alleged conduct is indeed a form of persecution, the prosecution should be required to establish that that other person had discriminatory intent with regard to that conduct.

For reasons similar to those outlined in a previous section of this chapter,[427] but different from those put forth by the *Stakić* Trial Chamber, we take the view that, if all the general requirements for a crime against humanity are met, conduct fulfilling the factual specific requirements outlined above should constitute persecution in at least two situations: first, where the physical perpetrator has discriminatory intent; and second, even if the physical perpetrator does not have discriminatory intent, where another relevant actor – the planner, orderer, or instigator of his conduct, or a first-category JCE participant who is the ultimate 'author' of the crime – has discriminatory intent.

[424] See Boas, Bischoff, and Reid, *supra* note 100, pp. 105–115 (discussing the *Stakić* Trial Chamber's definition and application of the purported form of responsibility 'indirect co-perpetratorship', and its subsequent rejection by the Appeals Chamber).

[425] *Stakić* Trial Judgement, *supra* note 80, paras. 742–743.

[426] Surprisingly, this approach seemed to go unchallenged on appeal. See *Stakić* Appeal Judgement, *supra* note 108, para. 339 (considering Stakić's arguments against his conviction for various offences as forms of persecution as a crime against humanity and concluding that 'the Trial Chamber did not err in its consideration of the evidence on the Appellant's *mens rea* for persecutions').

[427] See *supra* section 2.2.2.1.

2.2.3.8.2 Underlying offences qualifying as persecution as a crime against humanity As noted above,[428] any offence otherwise arising under an article in the Tribunals' Statutes may also constitute persecution if the specific requirements are satisfied. Accordingly, murder;[429] torture;[430] rape and other sexual violence;[431] forcible displacements both within and across (inter)national borders;[432] arbitrary arrest, detention, and confinement;[433] cruel or inhuman treatment;[434] physical

[428] See *supra* note 398 and accompanying text.

[429] Murder as an underlying offence appears in various guises in the Statutes: murder as a crime against humanity, extermination as a crime against humanity, genocide through killing, wilful killing as a grave breach of the Geneva Conventions, and murder as a violation of the laws or customs of war. See *supra* sections 2.2.3.1, 2.2.3.2; Chapter 3, section 3.2.2.1; Chapter 4, section 4.2.2.4. Cases in which murder has been held to constitute persecution include: *Blaškić* Appeal Judgement, *supra* note 88, para. 143 ('[T]he crime of persecutions has developed in customary international law to encompass acts that include murder, extermination, torture, and other serious acts on the person such as those presently enumerated in Article 5.') (internal quotation marks omitted); *Kordić and Čerkez* Appeal Judgement, *supra* note 95, para. 106; see also *ibid.*, paras. 667–669, 671–676 (concluding that evidence presented at trial, including that of individual killings or massacres of civilians in Central Bosnia, established that offences constituting persecution were carried out against the Bosnian Muslim population of this region).

[430] Torture appears as an underlying offence for both crimes against humanity and war crimes in both Tribunals. See *supra* section 2.2.3.6; Chapter 4, section 4.2.2.10. Cases in which torture has been held to constitute persecution include: *Blaškić* Appeal Judgement, *supra* note 88, para. 143; *Brđanin* Trial Judgement, *supra* note 80, para. 491 (holding that the treatment of Bosnian Muslim detainees constituted torture because they were 'singled out for … ill-treatment', such as 'being pricked … with knives on their legs, beat … with handcuffs, and stamped on … until some of them fainted' because their Bosnian Serb captors wished to punish them).

[431] Rape has been held to be an underlying offence for crimes against humanity, and an underlying offence of genocide as well as a form of torture, because it causes serious bodily or mental harm. See *supra* section 2.2.3.7; *supra* section 2.2.3.6; Chapter 3, section 3.2.2.2. Other sexual violence has been held to fall under other inhumane acts as crimes against humanity. For recognition that rape and other sexual violence may constitute persecution, see, e.g., *Brđanin* Trial Judgement, *supra* note 80, paras. 1008, 1012 (holding that rape and '[a]ny sexual assault falling short of rape may be punishable as persecution under international criminal law' and explaining that the latter offence 'embraces all serious abuses of a sexual nature inflicted upon the integrity of a person by means of coercion, threat of force or intimidation in a way that is humiliating and degrading to the victim's dignity'); accord *Semanza* Trial Judgement, *supra* note 85, para. 345. The Statutes of the ICC and some of the internationalised tribunals explicitly list several sexual underlying offences in addition to rape. See *infra* text accompanying note 508 (ICC); text accompanying notes 564–565 (SCSL); text accompanying note 590 (SPSC); text accompanying note 674 (SICT).

[432] Forcible displacement, whether termed deportation or forcible transfer, may constitute a crime against humanity either in its own right or as an inhumane act, or a war crime. See *supra* section 2.2.3.4; *infra* section 2.2.3.9.2; Chapter 4, section 4.2.2.13. Cases in which forcible displacement has been held to constitute persecution include: *Blaškić* Appeal Judgement, *supra* note 88, para. 153 ('[D]eportation, forcible transfer, and forcible displacement constitute[] crimes of equal gravity to other crimes listed in Article 5 of the Statute and therefore could amount to persecutions as a crime against humanity.'); *Brđanin* Trial Judgement, *supra* note 80, para. 570 (finding numerous instances of forcible transfer, including an incident where '[a]pproximately 2,500 Bosnian Muslim men, women and children were also transported to Travnik on 24 September 1992, following a public announcement made by the military police that all Bosnian Muslims would be transferred there').

[433] These underlying offences may constitute crimes against humanity or war crimes. See *supra* section 2.2.3.5; Chapter 4, section 4.2.2.12. Cases in which arbitrary arrest, detention, and confinement have been held to constitute persecution include: *Simić et al.* Trial Judgement, *supra* note 115, paras. 61–62 (holding that 'unlawful detention, confinement and imprisonment have each been considered acts of persecution and constituting crimes against humanity' and that when considered in context, together with unlawful detention or confinement, arbitrary arrest may constitute persecution); *Blaškić* Trial Judgement, *supra* note 90, paras. 234, 688 (holding that unlawful detention may constitute persecution, and finding that the imprisonment of male Muslim civilians qualified as this crime against humanity).

[434] Cruel treatment and inhuman treatment have been held to be war crimes if the relevant requirements are satisfied. See Chapter 4, section 4.2.2.3. Cases in which cruel or inhumane treatment have been held to constitute persecution include: *Blaškić* Appeal Judgement, *supra* note 88, para. 155; *Blagojević and Jokić*

violence;[435] serious mental harm;[436] terrorising the civilian population;[437] deliberate attacks on civilians or civilian objects;[438] forced labour and other forms of slavery;[439] hostage-taking and human shields;[440] and destruction of personal and real property[441] have all been held to constitute persecution in circumstances where they are committed with intent to discriminate on political, racial, or religious

Trial Judgement, *supra* note 75, paras. 605–610, 621; *Simić et al.* Trial Judgement, *supra* note 115, para. 771 (finding that beatings committed on discriminatory grounds constitute cruel and inhumane treatment as an underlying offence of persecution).

435 Physical violence may qualify as other inhumane acts as crimes against humanity if the specific requirements are satisfied. See *infra* section 2.2.3.9. Cases in which physical violence has been held to constitute persecution include: *Blaškić* Appeal Judgement, *supra* note 88, para. 155; *Stakić* Trial Judgement, *supra* note 80, para. 752 (defining physical violence broadly to include 'overcrowded conditions, deprivation of food, water and sufficient air, exposure to extreme heat or cold, random beating of detainees … and similar forms of physical assaults not amounting to torture', and concluding that this treatment satisfied the gravity requirement and therefore qualified as persecution).

436 Serious mental harm appears synonymous with mental suffering, which is one of the alternative characteristics of torture; it is also one of the specific requirements for other inhumane acts and an underlying offence of genocide. See *supra* section 2.2.3.6; *infra* section 2.2.3.9.1; Chapter 3, section 3.2.2.2. Cases in which causing serious mental harm has been held to constitute persecution include: *Kvočka et al.* Appeal Judgement, *supra* note 394, para. 324 ('The Appeals Chamber has no doubt that, in the context in which they were committed and taking into account their cumulative effect, the acts of harassment, humiliation and psychological abuse ascertained by the Trial Chamber are acts which by their gravity constitute material elements of the crime of persecution.'); *Kordić and Čerkez* Appeal Judgement, *supra* note 95, para. 107 (considering that the subjection of detained Bosnian Muslim civilians to 'physical and psychological abuse' qualified as persecution).

437 Deliberately inflicting terror on a civilian population has been held to be a violation of the laws or customs of war. See Chapter 4, section 4.2.2.9. For recognition that terrorising a civilian population may constitute persecution, see, e.g., *Blagojević and Jokić* Trial Judgement, *supra* note 75, paras. 592, 611–614, 620 (holding that numerous 'unlawful acts and threats of violence against the Bosnian Muslim civilians … were carried out with the primary purpose to create an atmosphere of extreme fear among the population', and finding that acts including 'the terrorising of the civilian population as described above constitute blatant denials of fundamental rights that had a severe impact on the victims and therefore amount to persecutions') (quotations at paras. 614 and 620, respectively).

438 Attacks on civilians and civilian objects are war crimes if the relevant requirements are satisfied. See Chapter 4, section 4.2.2.11. For holdings that attacks on civilians and civilian objects constitute persecution, see, e.g., *Blaškić* Appeal Judgement, *supra* note 88, para. 159 ('[A]ttacks in which civilians are targeted, as well as indiscriminate attacks on cities, towns, and villages, may constitute persecutions as a crime against humanity.'); accord *Kordić and Čerkez* Trial Judgement, *supra* note 75, para. 203.

439 Forced labour and other forms of slavery constitute either the crime against humanity of enslavement or war crimes if the respective requirements are fulfilled. See *supra* section 2.2.3.3; Chapter 4, section 4.2.2.8. For recognition that forced labour may constitute persecution, see, e.g. *Krnojelac* Appeal Judgement, *supra* note 264, para. 200 (concluding that 'there can be no doubt that the non-Serb prisoners were detained and forced to work on account of their ethnicity' and noting other circumstances 'particularly indicative of the discriminatory character of the acts of forced labour imposed upon the non-Serb detainees').

440 Hostage-taking and using individuals as human shields are war crimes if the relevant requirements are satisfied. See Chapter 4, section 4.2.2.2. Cases in which these underlying offences have been held to constitute persecution include: *Blaškić* Appeal Judgement, *supra* note 88, para. 155; *Kordić and Čerkez* Appeal Judgement, *supra* note 95, para. 107.

441 Destruction of property may constitute a war crime if the respective requirements are fulfilled. See Chapter 4, section 4.2.2.1. Cases in which destruction of property has been held to constitute persecution include: *Blaškić* Appeal Judgement, *supra* note 88, para. 149 (holding that 'destruction of property, depending on the nature and extent of the destruction, may constitute a crime of persecutions of equal gravity to other crimes listed in Article 5 of the Statute'); *Kupreškić et al.* Trial Judgement, *supra* note 71, para. 631 (holding that the extensive destruction of homes and property amounted to 'destruction of the livelihood of a certain population,' with the 'same inhumane consequences as a forced transfer or deportation', and therefore qualified as persecution); *Prosecutor* v. *Obrenović*, Case No. IT-02-60/2-S, Sentencing Judgement, 10 December 2003, para. 37 (recognising that the confiscation and destruction of personal property of the Bosnian Muslim prisoners from Srebrenica, including their identification documents, was a form of persecution).

grounds. In addition, although they do not appear in either Statute, the Tribunals have also found that following acts or omissions qualify as persecution in the circumstances of the particular cases: political, social, and economic rights violations;[442] and the issuance of discriminatory orders, decisions, or other policies.[443]

Conduct that *ad hoc* chambers ultimately found did not constitute persecution includes encouraging and promoting hatred on political grounds;[444] dismissing individuals from government positions;[445] and interrogations.[446]

2.2.3.9 Other inhumane acts

2.2.3.9.1 Specific requirements for inhumane acts as crimes against humanity As mentioned above, the Tribunals treat 'other inhumane acts' as a residual category of crimes against humanity that encompasses conduct that does not fall within the subparagraphs of Article 5 of the ICTY Statute or Article 3 of the ICTR Statute, but which is of similar gravity and may nevertheless constitute a crime against humanity if the general requirements are satisfied.[447] Together with 'inhuman treatment' as a grave breach of the 1949 Geneva Conventions and 'cruel treatment' as a violation of the laws or customs of war,[448] inhumane acts encompass certain serious transgressions against human dignity that are not specifically enumerated in the Tribunals' Statutes. Like persecution, 'other inhumane acts' functions as a subcategory of crimes against humanity, gathering underlying offences that share common characteristics and may qualify as crimes against humanity if they satisfy the general requirements of this category of crimes. These common characteristics – the specific requirements of inhumane acts – collectively set a standard high enough to justify

[442] See, e.g., *Kupreškić et al.* Trial Judgement, *supra* note 71, para. 615 (holding that '[p]ersecution can also involve a variety of other discriminatory acts, involving attacks on political, social, and economic rights').

[443] See, e.g., *Simić et al.* Trial Judgement, *supra* note 115, para. 58 ('[I]ssuance of discriminatory orders, policies, decisions or other regulations may constitute the *actus reus* of persecution, provided that these orders infringe upon a person's basic rights and that the violation reaches the level of gravity of the other crimes against humanity listed in Article 5 of the Statute.').

[444] See *ibid.*, para. 55; *Kordić and Čerkez* Trial Judgement, *supra* note 75, para. 209; but see *Media* Appeal Judgement, *supra* note 110, paras. 986–988 (explaining that hate speech or speech calling for violence against a population on the basis of ethnicity or other discriminatory grounds infringes the human rights to security and respect for human dignity, but not the rights to life, liberty, or physical integrity; and concluding that it need not reach the question of whether the violation of the former rights was sufficiently serious to constitute persecution because it was accompanied by calls for genocide, so the gravity test was satisfied by the aggregation of the charged acts).

[445] See *Simić et al.* Trial Judgement, *supra* note 115, para. 55; *Kordić and Čerkez* Trial Judgement, *supra* note 75, para. 210.

[446] See *Simić et al.* Trial Judgement, *supra* note 115, paras. 67, 69.

[447] See *supra* note 201 and accompanying text. See also *Kordić and Čerkez* Appeal Judgement, *supra* note 95, para. 117; *Muvunyi* Trial Judgement, *supra* note 84, para. 527; *Blagojević and Jokić* Trial Judgement, *supra* note 75, para. 625; *Galić* Trial Judgement, *supra* note 110, para. 152; *Naletilić and Martinović* Trial Judgement, *supra* note 113, para. 247; *Rutaganda* Trial Judgement, *supra* note 114, para. 77; *Akayesu* Trial Judgement, *supra* note 94, para. 585.

[448] See Chapter 4, section 4.2.2.3.

considering these offences as international crimes, but lower than the specific requirements for persecution.

The specific requirements for other inhumane acts, which are identical to those of inhuman treatment and cruel treatment,[449] are sometimes described as being three in number: (1) the physical perpetrator's conduct must cause serious mental or physical suffering to the victim or constitute a serious attack on human dignity; (2) such suffering or attack must be of similar gravity to the enumerated underlying offences that qualify as crimes against humanity; and (3) the physical perpetrator's conduct must be performed with the intent to inflict serious physical or mental harm upon the victim or commit a serious attack on human dignity, or with the knowledge that it would probably have that effect.[450]

The suffering or attack on dignity requirement

The conduct causes serious mental or physical suffering to the victim or constitutes a serious attack on human dignity.

It is well established in the jurisprudence of the ICTY that, when assessing whether an act or omission causes sufficiently serious suffering, or constitutes a sufficiently serious attack on human dignity, to give rise to liability for other inhumane acts, chambers must consider all the factual circumstances, such as the nature of conduct; the context in which it occurred; the age, sex, and health of the victim; and the physical, mental, and moral effects of the act or omission upon the victim.[451] The act or omission need not have caused long-term suffering, but a finding that the harm imposed had long-lasting effects would support a conclusion that the conduct was serious enough to qualify as inhumane acts.[452]

Early judgements at both Tribunals noted that an offence would constitute an inhumane act if it were a serious attack on the dignity of the victim or victims,[453] and

[449] See, e.g., *Simić et al.* Trial Judgement, *supra* note 115, para. 74; *Naletilić and Martinović* Trial Judgement, *supra* note 113, para. 246; *Vasiljević* Trial Judgement, *supra* note 164, para. 234; *Krnojelac* Trial Judgement, *supra* note 111, para. 130; *Kordić and Čerkez* Trial Judgement, *supra* note 75, para. 265; *Čelebići* Trial Judgement, *supra* note 344, para. 552.

[450] See, e.g., *Blagojević and Jokić* Trial Judgement, *supra* note 75, paras. 626, 628; *Vasiljević* Trial Judgement, *supra* note 164, para. 234.

[451] *Kordić and Čerkez* Appeal Judgement, *supra* note 95, para. 117; *Simić et al.* Trial Judgement, *supra* note 115, para. 75; *Vasiljević* Trial Judgement, *supra* note 164, para. 235; *Krnojelac* Trial Judgement, *supra* note 111, para. 131; *Kordić and Čerkez* Trial Judgement, *supra* note 75, para. 271; *Blaškić* Trial Judgement, *supra* note 90, para. 243. Although some Trial Chambers have held that these factors go toward evaluation of the similar seriousness requirement, see, e.g., *Blagojević and Jokić* Trial Judgement, *supra* note 75, para. 627, it seems clear that the satisfaction of the similar gravity requirement may be established as a matter of law. See *supra* note 399 and accompanying text. These factual circumstances, on the other hand, are relevant to whether the specific requirement of serious mental or physical suffering or a serious attack on human dignity has been fulfilled in the circumstances of the case under consideration.

[452] *Blagojević and Jokić* Trial Judgement, *supra* note 75, para. 627; *Simić et al.* Trial Judgement, *supra* note 115, para. 75; *Vasiljević* Trial Judgement, *supra* note 164, para. 235; *Krnojelac* Trial Judgement, *supra* note 111, para. 131.

[453] See, e.g., *Vasiljević* Trial Judgement, *supra* note 164, paras. 234, 239, affirmed in *Vasiljević* Appeal Judgement, *supra* note 394, para. 165; *Kayishema and Ruzindana* Trial Judgement, *supra* note 90, paras. 148–151.

found that degrading treatment may qualify as an inhumane act.[454] More recent restatements of the definition, however, have focused on mental or physical harm or suffering,[455] perhaps because they consider that an attack on human dignity inevitably causes mental harm or suffering.

The similar gravity requirement

The conduct is of similar gravity to the enumerated underlying offences for crimes against humanity.

Perhaps because it is the residual category for crimes against humanity, inhumane acts has received relatively little attention in the jurisprudence of either Tribunal. No effort has been made, for example, to explain exactly what the term 'serious' means in this context, even though it is used repeatedly in the list of the elements and their application to the facts in the findings of trial chambers. The requirement that the conduct be of 'similar gravity' to the other offences listed in Articles 5 and 3 of the ICTY and ICTR Statutes, respectively, is the best indication of the required level of seriousness. Nevertheless, because inhumane acts is intended to capture conduct that does not qualify as the other underlying offences, it is clear that the 'similar gravity' requirement is not interpreted strictly to mean that the charged conduct be necessarily of the same severity. For example, trial chambers at both Tribunals have clarified that sexual violence that falls short of rape, and physical mistreatment that falls short of torture, might qualify as other inhumane acts.[456]

Even with the yardstick of the other enumerated underlying offences, chambers at both the trial and appellate level have expressed concern over the 'potentially broad range' of conduct that may be covered by other inhumane acts,[457] and one trial chamber has emphasised that factfinders must 'exercise great caution in finding that an alleged act, not regulated elsewhere in [the relevant Article of] the Statute, forms part of this crime'.[458] Indeed, the *Stakić* Trial Judgement recalled the Chamber's earlier unease with other inhumane acts in its decision on the accused's motion for

[454] See, e.g., *Kvočka et al.* Trial Judgement, *supra* note 330, para. 208; *Akayesu* Trial Judgement, *supra* note 94, para. 688, 697 (holding that sexual violence may fall within other inhumane acts, and concluding that the forced undressing of women and forced public nudity of women, including forcing them to march or perform exercises naked, was sexual violence that qualified as inhumane acts as crimes against humanity).

[455] See, e.g., *Kordić and Čerkez* Appeal Judgement, *supra* note 95, para. 117; *Kordić and Čerkez* Trial Judgement, *supra* note 75, para. 271; *Blaškić* Trial Judgement, *supra* note 90, para. 373.

[456] See *infra* notes 467, 474 and accompanying text. See also *Semanza* Trial Judgement, *supra* note 85, paras. 344–345 (adopting the *Kunarac* definition of rape, discussed at text accompanying notes 378–385 *supra*, and noting that other acts of sexual violence can be prosecuted as other crimes against humanity, including inhumane acts); *Military I* 98 *bis* Decision, *supra* note 394, para. 35 (implicitly accepting the prosecution's argument that, as a matter of law, 'civilians endur[ing] deprivations of liberty falling short of detention' could constitute inhumane acts as crimes against humanity). The Statutes of the ICC and some of the internationalised tribunals explicitly list several sexual underlying offences in addition to rape. See *infra* text accompanying note 508 (ICC); text accompanying notes 564–565 (SCSL); text accompanying note 590 (SPSC); text accompanying note 674 (SICT).

[457] See *Kordić and Čerkez* Appeal Judgement, *supra* note 95, para. 117; accord *Stakić* Trial Judgement, *supra* note 80, para. 719.

[458] See *Blagojević and Jokić* Trial Judgement, *supra* note 75, para. 625.

acquittal, and reiterated that this subcategory, if not strictly construed, 'may well be considered to lack sufficient clarity, precision and definiteness [and] might violate the fundamental criminal law principle *nullum crimen sine lege certa*'.[459] On appeal, however, the *Stakić* Appeals Chamber rebuffed the Trial Chamber's concern, and reaffirmed that 'that the notion of "other inhumane acts" contained in Article 5(i) of the Statute cannot be regarded as a violation of the principle of *nullum crimen sine lege* as it forms part of customary international law'.[460] Even if the notion – the subcategory characterised by its specific requirements – has the status of customary international law, care should nevertheless be taken when considering whether particular alleged conduct should qualify, in the final analysis, as inhumane acts as a crime against humanity.[461]

The requirement of direct or indirect intent

The physical perpetrator must act with the intent to inflict serious physical or mental harm upon the victim or commit a serious attack on human dignity; or with the knowledge that his act or omission would probably cause serious physical or mental harm to the victim or constitute a serious attack on human dignity.

Chambers of both Tribunals have held that either direct or indirect intent is sufficient for inhumane acts: the physical perpetrator may act with intent to cause serious physical or mental harm or suffering, or to attack the human dignity of the victim; alternatively, he could act deliberately with the knowledge that his conduct is likely to have that effect.[462] In addition, in circumstances where the prosecution alleges that the suffering experienced was inflicted on third parties, such as persons forced to witness the commission of crimes on their friends, relatives, or other similarly situated persons, it must also prove that the physical perpetrator intended to cause suffering to the third party.[463]

2.2.3.9.2 Underlying offences qualifying as inhumane acts as crimes against humanity The jurisprudence of the Tribunals has identified a number of underlying

459 *Stakić* Trial Judgement, *supra* note 80, para. 719. See also *Kordić and Čerkez* Appeal Judgement, *supra* note 95, para. 117 (expressing similar concern, but considering that where all the alleged acts involved injuries to individuals, a breach of the *nullum crimen* principle was unlikely).

460 *Stakić* Appeal Judgement, *supra* note 108, para. 315.

461 See, e.g., Mettraux, *supra* note 55, p. 189 (cautioning that other inhumane acts 'should not serve as a mechanism to criminalize vaguely reprehensible conduct which does not satisfy the stricter requirement of other, better-defined criminal offences'); *Muvunyi* Trial Judgement, *supra* note 84, para. 527 ('Whether an act falls within the ambit of Article 3(i) [of the ICTR Statute] has to be determined on a case-by-case basis').

462 See, e.g., *Blagojević and Jokić* Trial Judgement, *supra* note 75, para. 628; *Galić* Trial Judgement, *supra* note 110, para. 154; *Krnojelac* Trial Judgement, *supra* note 111, para. 132; *Kayishema and Ruzindana* Trial Judgement, *supra* note 90, para. 153.

463 See *Kayishema and Ruzindana* Trial Judgement, *supra* note 90, para. 153 (holding therefore that if the physical perpetrator was 'unaware of the third party bearing witness to his act, then he cannot be held responsible for the mental suffering of the third party'). Accord *Muvunyi* Trial Judgement, *supra* note 84, para. 529; *Kamuhanda* Trial Judgement, *supra* note 229, para. 717; *Kajelijeli* Trial Judgement, *supra* note 86, para. 932.

offences which, if the conduct in question also fulfils the requisite general and specific requirements, can constitute inhumane acts as crimes against humanity. The forced displacements of civilian populations were one of the emblematic crimes of the wars accompanying the break-up of Yugoslavia, but those displacements did not always take place across a *de jure* or *de facto* international border. As a result, forcible transfer as an inhumane act as a crime against humanity is one of the most frequently charged crimes at the ICTY,[464] because it captures the criminal conduct involved in forcible displacements within national borders.[465] The elements of the underlying offence of forcible displacement, which are relatively straightforward, are outlined above.[466]

Other underlying offences qualifying as inhumane acts include physical mistreatment, such as beatings, which falls short of torture;[467] mutilation;[468] attempted murder;[469] forced trench-digging;[470] the use of persons as human shields;[471] forced

464 See, e.g., *Blagojević and Jokić* Trial Judgement, *supra* note 75, para. 629; *Brđanin* Trial Judgement, *supra* note 80, para. 544; *Kupreškić et al.* Trial Judgement, *supra* note 71, para. 566. But see *Stakić* Trial Judgement, *supra* note 80, paras. 723–724 (dismissing the count in the indictment charging forcible transfer as an inhumane act on the grounds that it does not 'reach[] the same level as other crimes listed under Article 5 of the Statute' and 'in this case might amount to an infringement of the principle *nullum crime*[*n*] *sine lege certa*'), reversed in *Stakić* Appeal Judgement, *supra* note 229, para. 317 (noting that 'acts of forcible transfer have been accepted in other cases before the Tribunal as specifically substantiating the notion of other inhumane acts pursuant to Article 5(i)', and holding that 'acts of forcible transfer may be sufficiently serious as to amount to other inhumane acts').

465 But see *supra* note 300 (discussing appellate jurisprudence disregarding the distinction between deportation and forcible transfer as forms of persecution). See also *supra* section 2.2.3.4.5 (discussing the requirement that deportation as a crime against humanity take place across a *de jure* or *de facto* international border).

466 See *supra* sections 2.2.3.4.1–2.2.3.4.4.

467 See *Naletilić and Martinović* Trial Judgement, *supra* note 113, para. 246; *Simić et al.* Trial Judgement, *supra* note 115, para. 78:

> Taking into consideration the requirements of Article 5 (i) of the Statute as set out above, the Trial Chamber finds that beatings constitute cruel and inhumane treatment if the following elements can be proved: (a) the beatings caused serious mental or physical suffering or injury or constituted a serious attack on human dignity, and (b) the beatings were performed deliberately.

See also *Krnojelac* Trial Judgement, *supra* note 111, para. 133:

> The Trial Chamber is satisfied that the brutal and deplorable living conditions imposed upon the non-Serb detainees at [the prison known as] the KP Dom … constituted acts and omissions of a seriousness comparable to the other crimes enumerated in Article 5 and Article 3 of the Tribunal's Statute, and thus warrants a finding that those acts and omissions constitute inhumane acts and cruel treatment under those Articles.

Accord *Muvunyi* Trial Judgement, *supra* note 84, para. 530; *Kordić and Čerkez* Trial Judgement, *supra* note 75, para. 270; *Kupreškić et al.* Trial Judgement, *supra* note 71, para. 566; *Tadić* Trial Judgement, *supra* note 77, para. 730.

468 See *Kajelijeli* Trial Judgement, *supra* note 86, para. 936 (holding that cutting off a woman's breast and piercing a woman's sexual organs with a spear qualify as inhumane acts as crimes against humanity); see also *Kordić and Čerkez* Trial Judgement, *supra* note 75, para. 270; *Tadić* Trial Judgement, *supra* note 77, para. 730.

469 See *Vasiljević* Trial Judgement, *supra* note 164, para. 239.

470 See *Kordić and Čerkez* Appeal Judgement, *supra* note 95, para. 39 n. 34 ('Trench-digging may under certain circumstances amount to cruel treatment [as a violation of the laws or customs of war] … The Appeals Chamber in this case considers that the same applies for inhuman treatment [as a crime against humanity].'); *Blaškić* Appeal Judgement, *supra* note 88, para. 597 ('Any order to compel protected persons to dig trenches or to prepare other forms of military installations … constitutes cruel treatment [as a violation of the laws or customs of war].').

471 See *Naletilić and Martinović* Trial Judgement, *supra* note 113, para. 334; *Kordić and Čerkez* Trial Judgement, *supra* note 75, para. 256.

disappearance;[472] forced prostitution;[473] and sexual violence upon a dead woman's body which causes suffering to onlookers.[474]

2.3 Crimes against humanity in the International Criminal Court and Internationalised Tribunals

2.3.1 The International Criminal Court

2.3.1.1 The Rome Statute

Article 7 of the Rome Statute of the ICC sets forth crimes against humanity in greater detail than its analogues in the ICTY and ICTR Statutes:

1. For the purpose of this Statute, 'crime against humanity' means any of the following acts when committed as part of a widespread or systematic attack directed against any civilian population, with knowledge of the attack:
   (a) Murder;
   (b) Extermination;
   (c) Enslavement;
   (d) Deportation or forcible transfer of population;
   (e) Imprisonment or other severe deprivation of physical liberty in violation of fundamental rules of international law;
   (f) Torture;
   (g) Rape, sexual slavery, enforced prostitution, forced pregnancy, enforced sterilisation, or any other form of sexual violence of comparable gravity;
   (h) Persecution against any identifiable group or collectivity on political, racial, national, ethnic, cultural, religious, gender … or other grounds that are universally recognised as impermissible under international law, in connection with any act referred to in this paragraph or any crime within the jurisdiction of the Court;
   (i) Enforced disappearance of persons;
   (j) The crime of apartheid;
   (k) Other inhumane acts of a similar character intentionally causing great suffering, or serious injury to body or to mental or physical health.
2. For the purpose of paragraph 1:
   (a) 'Attack directed against any civilian population' means a course of conduct involving the multiple commission of acts referred to in paragraph 1 against any civilian population, pursuant to or in furtherance of a State or organizational policy to commit such attack;

   …

[472] See *Kupreškić et al.* Trial Judgement, *supra* note 71, para. 566. [473] See *ibid.*
[474] See *Niyitegeka* Trial Judgement, *supra* note 94, paras. 465–467 (finding also that several acts performed on the body of a influential and well-liked Tutsi man – including decapitation, castration, and piercing his skull and placing it and his genitals on spikes in view of the public – constituted inhumane acts).

(g) 'Persecution' means the intentional and severe deprivation of fundamental rights contrary to international law by reason of the identity of the group or collectivity; ...[475]

Although the essence of this provision is similar to crimes against humanity in the *ad hoc* Statutes, there are also several significant differences, largely the result of intense negotiations among delegations at the various drafting meetings leading up to the conclusion of the Rome Statute.[476] A number of commentators close to the negotiations have discussed these differences and the resulting compromises at considerable length.[477] We focus here on four of the more salient features of the ICC formulation that differ in some respects from crimes against humanity in the *ad hoc* Tribunals.[478]

First, as discussed above, each of the respective *ad hoc* formulations contains a unique jurisdictional requirement in its *chapeau*: the armed conflict requirement for the ICTY,[479] and the discriminatory attack for the ICTR.[480] Over the opposition of a substantial minority,[481] the view prevailed at the ICC drafting meetings that customary international law did not mandate a nexus to an armed conflict.[482] The majority was also opposed to the idea of incorporating a requirement of discriminatory grounds for all crimes against humanity.[483] According to Herman von Hebel and Darryl Robinson, the majority was concerned that such a requirement 'would create an unnecessary burden for prosecutions, and could inadvertently exclude

[475] Rome Statute, *supra* note 59, Art. 7.

[476] See Report of the *Ad Hoc* Committee on the Establishment of an International Criminal Court, UN Doc. A/50/22, 6 September 1995 ('1995 *Ad Hoc* Committee Report'), paras. 77–80 (foreshadowing many of the points of disagreement that would be worked out over the course of the following three years).

[477] See especially Machteld Boot, Rodney Dixon, and Christopher K. Hall, 'Article 7: Crimes Against Humanity', in Otto Triffterer (ed.), *Commentary on the Rome Statute of the International Criminal Court* (1999), pp. 117–172; Herman von Hebel and Darryl Robinson, 'Crimes with the Jurisdiction of the Court', in Roy S. Lee (ed.), *The International Criminal Court: The Making of the Rome Statute* (1999) ('von Hebel and Robinson'), pp. 90–103; Darryl Robinson, 'Defining "Crimes Against Humanity" at the Rome Conference', (1999) 93 *American Journal of International Law* 43 ('Robinson'). See also Cassese, *supra* note 32, pp. 373–377; William A. Schabas, *An Introduction to the International Criminal Court* (2nd edn 2004), pp. 43–51.

[478] Other differences include the explicit definitions of extermination, enslavement, and deportation and forcible transfer in Article 7(2); the elimination of a requirement that torture must be inflicted for a prohibited purpose; and the specification in Article 7(1)'s *chapeau* that some relevant actor must have 'knowledge of the [widespread or systematic] attack' – a requirement developed in the *ad hoc* jurisprudence but present in neither Statute. See Cassese, *supra* note 32, pp. 373–374; von Hebel and Robinson, *supra* note 477, p. 99; *Kordić and Čerkez* Appeal Judgement, *supra* note 95, para. 99.

[479] See *supra* section 2.2.1.1. [480] See *supra* section 2.2.1.2.

[481] See von Hebel and Robinson, *supra* note 477, p. 92 n. 43 (noting that this view was advanced by 'several delegations of the Arab Group' and 'some other African and Asian delegations').

[482] See *ibid.*, p. 93. For a more detailed discussion on the armed conflict requirement, including a comparison of the respective positions of the different international and internationalised courts and tribunals, see *supra* note 55.

[483] An alternative *chapeau* formulation requiring all crimes against humanity to be committed 'on political, philosophical, racial, ethnic or religious grounds or any other arbitrarily defined grounds' was still on the table as late as the April 1998 draft version of the Rome Statute. See Report of the Preparatory Committee on the Establishment of an International Criminal Court, UN Doc. A/CONF.183/2/Add.1, 14 April 1998 ('1998 Preparatory Committee Report'), p. 26. See also *supra* note 60 and accompanying text (comparing the respective positions of the different international and internationalised tribunals on whether there is a requirement of a discriminatory attack for all crimes against humanity).

serious crimes against humanity.'[484] As a result, neither jurisdictional restriction appears in Article 7 of the Rome Statute.[485]

Second, like the ICTR Statute,[486] Article 7 states expressly that the attack must be 'widespread *or* systematic'.[487] This aspect of the definition was the most serious point of contention among the delegations:[488] while one group of states argued that, under customary international law, it was sufficient for the attack to be either widespread or systematic, a significant number of others – including many Arab and Asian states and the permanent members of the UN Security Council – were concerned that the disjunctive construction would render offences committed during a common 'crime wave' crimes against humanity, even though there may be no connection among such offences.[489] A difficult compromise was reached in the form of Article 7(2)(a), which defines 'attack directed against a civilian population'. William Schabas has suggested that this definition may serve effectively to render the 'widespread or systematic' language conjunctive:[490] the attack must 'involv[e] the *multiple commission of acts*'[491] – similar to the definition of 'widespread'[492] – and the attack must be carried out 'pursuant to or in furtherance of a State or organizational policy to commit such an attack'[493] – something akin to

[484] von Hebel and Robinson, *supra* note 477, p. 94. See also Report of the Preparatory Committee on the Establishment of an International Criminal Court, UN Doc. A/51/22, 13 September 1996 ('1996 Preparatory Committee Report'), vol. I, para. 87, listing some reasons given by the delegations opposing the ICTR restriction:

> [D]elegations expressed the view that the inclusion of such a criterion would complicate the task of the Prosecution by significantly increasing its burden of proof in requiring evidence of this subjective element; that crimes against humanity could be committed against other groups, including intellectuals and social, cultural or political groups; that it was important to include crimes against such groups since the definition of genocide might not be expanded to cover them; and that the criterion was not required under customary law, with attention being drawn to the Yugoslavia Tribunal Statute and the [ILC] draft Code.

[485] Compare 1998 Preparatory Committee Report, *supra* note 483, p. 26 (listing 'in armed conflict' in brackets for possible inclusion), with Committee of the Whole, Bureau, Discussion Paper, UN Doc. A/CONF.183/C.1/L.53, 6 July 1998, Part 2, p. 2 (not longer listing 'in armed conflict'). The non-binding Elements of Crimes also clarify that 'the acts need not constitute a military attack'. ICC Elements of Crimes, *supra* note 158, Art. 7, Introduction, para. 3. Accord *Kunarac et al.* Appeal Judgement, *supra* note 75, para. 86.

[486] ICTR Statute, *supra* note 60, Art. 3 (*chapeau* quoted at note 480). See also Schabas, *supra* note 477, p. 44 (noting that the push for a disjunctive formulation in the Rome Statute was supported by the then-recent May 1997 Trial Judgement in *Tadić*, which adopted such a formulation for the ICTY); *Tadić* Trial Judgement, *supra* note 77, para. 646 ('Either one of these is sufficient to exclude isolated or random acts.'); *supra* section 2.2.2.4 (discussing *ad hoc* jurisprudence on 'widespread or systematic attack').

[487] Rome Statute, *supra* note 59, Art. 7(1) (emphasis added).

[488] Robinson, *supra* note 477, p. 47.

[489] Von Hebel and Robinson, *supra* note 477, p. 94. See also *ibid.*, p. 97 ('It is the existence of a policy that unites otherwise unrelated inhumane acts, so that it may be said that in the aggregate they collectively form an "attack".'). See also 1998 Preparatory Committee Report, *supra* note 483, p. 25 (relatively late draft version of Statute still listing 'widespread and systematic' and 'widespread or systematic' as bracketed alternatives).

[490] See Schabas, *supra* note 477, p. 44 (calling the possible broadening of the threshold 'a deception').

[491] Rome Statute, *supra* note 59, Art. 7(2)(a).

[492] In *ad hoc* jurisprudence, 'widespread' connotes the large-scale nature of the attack and the number of targeted persons. See *supra* text accompanying note 173.

[493] Rome Statute, *supra* note 59, Art. 7(2)(a).

systematicity.[494] This second prong requiring a policy certainly goes beyond what has been required by the *ad hoc* Tribunals and the SCSL, which have explicitly rejected the existence of a plan or policy as a legal element of crimes against humanity.[495] Von Hebel and Robinson assert, however, that delegations understood each prong of the Article 7(2)(a) definition to be somewhat less demanding than 'widespread' or 'systematic': 'multiple commission of acts' was considered to involve a lower scale of violence than 'widespread', and 'systematic' was considered to involve not only a policy to effect an attack on a civilian population, 'but also a highly organized and orchestrated execution of those acts in accordance with a developed plan'.[496] As there is not yet any jurisprudence construing Article 7, whether the chambers of the Court will read the definition in this manner remains to be seen, although the question may not make much of a difference in reality: in actual cases, it is common for courts and tribunals to find the attack under analysis to be both widespread and systematic.[497]

Third, the definition of persecution in Articles 7(1)(h) and 7(2)(g) is more elaborate than its counterparts in the *ad hoc* Statutes,[498] specifying that the conduct in question may be committed not only on political, racial, or religious grounds, but also on national, ethnic, cultural, or gender grounds – or, indeed, any other ground 'universally recognized as impermissible under international law'.[499] This residual

494 In *ad hoc* jurisprudence, 'systematic' refers to the organised nature of the acts of violence and the improbability of their random occurrence, such as the non-accidental repetition of similar criminal conduct on a regular basis. See *supra* text accompanying note 174.

495 See *supra* text accompanying notes 180–181; *Prosecutor* v. *Fofana and Kondewa*, Case No. SCSL-04-14-J, Judgement, 2 August 2007 ('*CDF* Trial Judgement'), para. 113. Antonio Cassese rightly criticises the second prong in Article 7(2)(a) as going beyond what is required by custom. See Cassese, *supra* note 32, pp. 376–377; see also *infra* text accompanying notes 529–534 (discussing the policy requirement in the context of the Elements of Crimes); *supra* note 59 and accompanying text (discussing the policy requirement in the 1954 ILC Draft Code, and comparing the respective positions of the different international and internationalised tribunals on whether this is a requirement).

496 Von Hebel and Robinson, *supra* note 477, p. 97. See also Robinson, *supra* note 477, pp. 48–51 (explaining this point in considerable detail with reference to international and national precedent and scholarly works, and concluding that the resulting formulation 'reflects a middle ground between a conjunctive test (widespread and systematic), which was clearly too restrictive, and an unqualified disjunctive test (widespread or systematic), which was considered too expansive').

497 See e.g., *Mrkšić et al.* Trial Judgement, *supra* note 77, para. 472 (finding a 'widespread and systematic attack by the [Yugoslav army] and other Serb forces directed against the Croat and other non-Serb civilian population in the wider Vukovar area'); *Martić* Trial Judgement, *supra* note 75, para. 352; *Stakić* Trial Judgement, *supra* note 80, paras. 629–630; *Cyangugu* Trial Judgement, *supra* note 316, paras. 707–708; *Rutaganda* Trial Judgement, *supra* note 114, para. 516; *Prosecutor* v. *Brima, Kamara, and Kanu*, Case No. SCSL-04-16-T, Judgement, 20 June 2007 ('*AFRC* Trial Judgement'), paras. 232, 237–238. But see *CDF* Trial Judgement, *supra* note 495, para. 692 (finding that the attack was widespread, and considering it therefore unnecessary to also determine whether it was systematic); see also *supra* note 172 and sources cited therein.

498 See ICTY Statute, *supra* note 55, Art. 5(h); ICTR Statute, *supra* note 60, Art. 3(h); see also *supra* section 2.2.3.8.

499 Rome Statute, *supra* note 59, Art. 7(1)(h). Uniquely, 'gender' is explicitly defined in its own subparagraph with somewhat awkward wording: '[I]t is understood that the term "gender" refers to the two sexes, male and female, within the context of society. The term "gender" does not indicate any meaning different from the above.' *Ibid.*, Art. 7(3). For commentary on the debate surrounding the term 'gender', see Cate Steains, 'Gender Issues', in Lee (ed.), *supra* note 477, pp. 371–375; Valerie Oosterveld, 'The Definition of "Gender" in the Rome Statute of the International Criminal Court: A Step Forward or Back for International Criminal Justice?' (2005) 18 *Harvard Human Rights Journal* 55.

ground was the result of a compromise between delegations that advocated for an exhaustive list of grounds and those that wanted an illustrative list.[500] According to Antonio Cassese, the additional grounds take the ICC definition well beyond what would be justiciable under customary international law.[501] Article 7(2)(g) also specifies that the discriminatory conduct must constitute an 'intentional and severe deprivation of fundamental rights contrary to international law'[502] – a requirement essentially in line with *ad hoc* jurisprudence.[503] Yet in another respect, persecution in the Rome Statute is also more restrictive than it is in *ad hoc* jurisprudence or custom:[504] Article 7(1)(h) specifies that the offence must occur 'in connection with any act referred to in this paragraph or any crime within the jurisdiction of the Court'.[505] By contrast, the *ad hoc* Tribunals have held that the conduct constituting the form of persecution in a given case may be any act or omission – whether enumerated in the Statute or not – as long as it denies or infringes a fundamental right laid down in customary or treaty law and is carried out deliberately.[506] The more restrictive ICC formulation is the result of another compromise: some delegations insisted on a so-called 'connection requirement' as appeared in the Nuremberg and Tokyo Charters, even though such a requirement was absent from Control Council Law No. 10, the ILC Draft Codes, and the *ad hoc* Statutes.[507]

Fourth, there are additional underlying offences listed in Article 7(1) of the Rome Statute that do not expressly appear in the *ad hoc* Statutes. These include a number of sexual offences in addition to rape – sexual slavery, enforced prostitution, forced pregnancy, enforced sterilization, and 'any other form of sexual violence of comparable gravity'[508] –

[500] von Hebel and Robinson, *supra* note 477, p. 101. Several delegations opposed including persecution in the jurisdiction of the Court at all, considering it 'too vague a concept'. 1995 *ad hoc* Committee Report, *supra* note 476, para. 78. See also 1996 Preparatory Committee Report, *supra* note 484, vol. I, para. 99 (noting that some states still opposed including persecution at all).

[501] See Cassese, *supra* note 32, pp. 376–377.

[502] Rome Statute, *supra* note 59, Art. 7(2)(g).

[503] See *infra* note 506 and accompanying text.

[504] See Cassese, *supra* note 32, p. 376 ('It would seem that under customary international law … it is not necessary for persecution to consist of … conduct defined as a war crime[,] … a crime against humanity[,] [genocide, or aggression,] or linked to any such crime.').

[505] Rome Statute, *supra* note 59, Art. 7(1)(h).

[506] See *Krnojelac* Appeal Judgement, *supra* note 264, para. 186; *Tadić* Trial Judgement, *supra* note 77, para. 697 (persecution involves 'the violation of the right to equality *in some serious fashion* that infringes on the enjoyment of a basic or fundamental right') (emphasis added); see also *supra* section 2.2.3.8.

[507] von Hebel and Robinson, *supra* note 477, p. 101.

[508] Rome Statute, *supra* note 59, Art. 7(1)(g). See also *ibid.*, Art. 7(2)(f) (defining forced pregnancy). The debates over forced pregnancy met with particularly strong opposition from the Holy See and several Catholic and Arab States concerned that the inclusion of such an offence might be interpreted as obliging states to provide abortions to forcibly impregnated women. See von Hebel and Robinson, *supra* note 477, p. 100 nn. 67–69. The compromise result was a proviso: 'This definition shall not in any way be interpreted as affecting national laws relating to pregnancy'. Rome Statute, *supra* note 59, Art. 7(2)(f). As Schabas notes, the very substantial list of sexual offences in the Rome Statute stands in significant contrast to the Nuremberg Charter, which did not even include rape as an underlying offence of crimes against humanity. Schabas, *supra* note 477, p. 46. '[R]ape, enforced prostitution and other forms of sexual abuse' appeared as underlying offences of crimes against humanity in the 1996 ILC Draft Code of Crimes Against the Peace and Security of Mankind. See 1996 ILC Draft Code with Commentaries, *supra* note 55, Art. 18(j).

forcible transfer,[509] enforced disappearance,[510] and apartheid.[511] To the extent these offences have been charged by the *ad hoc* Prosecutors and considered in the jurisprudence, the chambers have usually channelled them through the residual underlying offence of 'other inhumane acts', or have regarded them as forms of persecution;[512] ICTY and recent ICTR chambers have adhered to a rather orthodox description of rape as non-consensual sexual penetration.[513] The inclusion of apartheid and enforced disappearance was prompted by two groups of particularly concerned states – African states for the former and Latin American states for the latter[514] – and the definitions of the offences in Article 7(2)(h) and (i) are loosely based on those in the 1973 Apartheid Convention and the 1994 Forced Disappearance Convention.[515] Notwithstanding references to these two treaty-based crimes as crimes against humanity in various instruments,[516] the notion that they could serve as underlying offences of crimes against humanity in an international court had probably not solidified into custom by the time of the Rome Statute's drafting.[517] Nevertheless, the proposed listing of these two underlying offences does not appear to have met a great deal of resistance. Proposals to include

509 Rome Statute, *supra* note 59, Arts. 7(1)(d), 7(2)(d).

510 *Ibid.*, Arts. 7(1)(i), 7(2)(i). '[F]orced disappearance of persons' also appeared as an underlying offence of crimes against humanity in the 1996 ILC Draft Code of Crimes Against the Peace and Security of Mankind. See 1996 ILC Draft Code with Commentaries, *supra* note 55, Art. 18(i).

511 Rome Statute, *supra* note 59, Arts. 7(1)(j), 7(2)(h). '[I]nstitutionalized discrimination on racial, ethnic or religious grounds' appeared as an underlying offence of crimes against humanity in the 1996 ILC Draft Code of Crimes Against the Peace and Security of Mankind. See 1996 ILC Draft Code with Commentaries, *supra* note 55, Art. 18(f). See also *supra* note 65 (comparing the list of underlying offences in the 1996 ILC Draft Code with those of the international and internationalised courts and tribunals).

512 For forcible transfer, see, e.g., *supra* text accompanying note 464. For sexual offences, see *supra* notes 431, 454. See also *Akayesu* Trial Judgement, *supra* note 94, paras. 688, 697 (convicting Akayesu for inhumane acts as a crime against humanity for the forced undressing and public display of naked women); *Kunarac et al.* Trial Judgement, *supra* note 90, paras. 728–729, 739, 744–745 (convicting Kunarac of enslavement as a crime against humanity for keeping two girls captive for several months and forcing them to obey his demands, including sexual demands).

513 See *supra* section 2.2.3.7. See also *supra* note 431 and accompanying text (sexual violence as a form of persecution as a crime against humanity in the *ad hoc* Tribunals); note 456 and accompanying text (sexual violence as an inhumane act as a crime against humanity in the *ad hoc* Tribunals).

514 Von Hebel and Robinson, *supra* note 477, p. 102 n. 75.

515 See Apartheid Convention, *supra* note 54, Art. II; Forced Disappearance Convention, *supra* note 54, Art. II. See also Convention on Non-Applicability of Statutory Limitations, *supra* note 55, Art. I(b) (listing 'eviction by armed attack or occupation and inhuman acts resulting from the policy of apartheid' as crimes for which there is no statute of limitations). The definition of enforced disappearance in the Rome Statute is broader than that which appears in the Forced Disappearance Convention, in that the crime against humanity can be committed not only with the authorisation, support or acquiescence of a state, but also 'a political organization'. Rome Statute, *supra* note 59, Art. 7(1)(i). The Rome Statute's definition of apartheid, on the other hand, is more narrow than that of the Apartheid Convention. See Boot, Dixon, and Hall, *supra* note 477, pp. 167–168 (Hall explaining the various differences).

516 See, e.g., 1996 ILC Draft Code with Commentaries, *supra* note 55, Art. 18(f) ('institutionalized discrimination on racial, ethnic or religious grounds' as a crime against humanity); *ibid.*, Art. 18(i) ('forced disappearance of persons' as a crime against humanity); Apartheid Convention, *supra* note 54, Art. I(1) (declaring apartheid 'a crime against humanity'); Forced Disappearance Convention, *supra* note 54, preambular para. 5 (recognising that enforced disappearance is 'in certain circumstances defined in international law' a crime against humanity); Declaration on the Protection of All Persons from Enforced Disappearance, General Assembly Resolution 47/133, UN Doc. A/47/49 (1992), p. 207, preambular para. 4 (considering that the systematic practice of enforced disappearance 'is of the nature of a crime against humanity').

517 See Cassese, *supra* note 32, p. 376.

several other underlying offences – including terrorism, mass starvation, and imposing economic embargo – were rejected.[518]

2.3.1.2 The Elements of Crimes

The Rome Statute provides for recourse by the Court to an instrument setting forth non-binding elements of crimes to 'assist ... in the interpretation and application of articles 6, 7 and 8' – that is, the respective articles on genocide, crimes against humanity, and war crimes.[519] The crimes against humanity provision of the Elements of Crimes is quite detailed, with a substantial number of explanatory footnotes reflecting difficult compromises reached by states in drafting the document.[520] Again, we focus on a few salient features.[521]

First, each underlying offence contains one or more *actus reus* elements that must be fulfilled by an individual referred to as the 'perpetrator', an element that such conduct be realised as part of a widespread or systematic attack, and a mental element whereby the 'perpetrator' must 'kn[o]w that the conduct was part of or intend[] the conduct to be part of a widespread or systematic attack'.[522] On its face, this approach appears not to accommodate the possibility – or indeed likelihood – that a given international crime may be brought to fruition through the contributions of a multiplicity of actors at different levels of a formal or informal hierarchy, with the relatively low-level physical perpetrator acting at the behest of someone in a higher position. This higher-level actor may be able to fulfil some of the mental elements of a given crime without the necessity of the physical perpetrator also fulfilling the element. A particularly compelling example of this is the requirement of knowledge of the widespread or systematic attack.[523] In determining the responsibility of mid- and high-level accused for crimes against humanity physically perpetrated by other, often far-removed individuals, the *ad hoc* Tribunals have

[518] Von Hebel and Robinson, *supra* note 477, pp. 102–103. Cuba proposed economic embargo; India, Sri Lanka, and Turkey proposed terrorism; Costa Rica proposed mass starvation. *Ibid.*, p. 103 nn. 78–80.

[519] Rome Statute, *supra* note 59, Art. 9(1). See also *ibid.*, Art. 21(1) (setting forth a hierarchy of sources of law containing, in the first place, the Elements of Crimes along with the Statute and Rules of Procedure and Evidence).

[520] See ICC Elements of Crimes, *supra* note 158, pp. 116–124. See also Maria Kelt and Herman von Hebel, 'The Making of the Elements of Crimes', in Roy S. Lee (ed.), *The International Criminal Court: Elements of Crimes and Rules of Procedure and Evidence* (2001), p. 11.

[521] The negotiations resulting in the crimes against humanity provision of the Elements have been considered at length elsewhere. See especially Philippe Kirsch, 'The Work of the Preparatory Commission', in Lee (ed.), *supra* note 520, pp. xlvii–xlix; Kelt and von Hebel, *supra* note 520, pp. 3–18; Darryl Robinson, 'The Elements of Crimes Against Humanity', in Lee (ed.), *supra* note 520, pp. 57–108.

[522] See, e.g., ICC Elements of Crimes, *supra* note 158, Art. 7(1)(a), Elements 1–3. The Introduction to the crimes against humanity provision specifies that this element 'should not be interpreted as requiring proof that the perpetrator had knowledge of all characteristics of the attack or the precise details of the plan or policy of the State or organization.' *ibid.*, Art. 7, Introduction, para. 2. See also *supra* note 478.

[523] Another compelling example is the requirement of genocidal intent for the crime of genocide, and who among the relevant actors must fulfil it. For the parallel discussion concerning genocide in the Elements of Crimes, see Chapter 3, text accompanying notes 354–364.

generally focused on whether the accused knew that the underlying offences – that is, the physical perpetrator's conduct – fit into the widespread or systematic attack.[524] As we have argued above, there are good reasons for extending this notion to allow for the conclusion that a crime against humanity was committed where the planner, instigator, or orderer of the physical perpetrator's conduct – whether or not this person is the accused – possesses such knowledge.[525]

The lack of detail on this point in the Elements of Crimes is perhaps understandable, given that the document was negotiated and concluded in an era when most accused before the *ad hoc* Tribunals were physical perpetrators – thus needing to fulfil all the elements of the charged crime themselves – or otherwise very close to the ground. Nevertheless, it is also clear that the delegates did have some appreciation for the general notion that the elements of an international crime may be fulfilled by different actors.[526] This appreciation is reflected in an explicit provision in the General Introduction to the Elements defining 'perpetrator' as a term of art:

> As used in the Elements of Crimes, the term 'perpetrator' is neutral as to guilt or innocence. The elements, including the appropriate mental elements, apply *mutatis mutandis* to all those whose criminal responsibility may fall under articles 25 and 28 of the Statute [setting forth the forms of responsibility].[527]

When faced with an accused who did not physically perpetrate the crimes against humanity with which he is charged, the Court will likely have to adopt a broad and varying interpretation of the term 'perpetrator': while it is indeed the physical perpetrator who must fulfil the *actus reus* of the underlying offence and whose conduct must form part of the widespread or systematic attack, the requirement of knowledge that this conduct is part of the attack may, in the circumstances, be fulfilled by the orderer, solicitor, or inducer of the conduct, whether or not this person is also the accused.[528]

Second, the Introduction to crimes against humanity in the Elements of Crimes features language not present in the introductions to genocide or war crimes:

[524] See *supra* text accompanying notes 95–96. [525] See *supra* section 2.2.2.1.

[526] See Kelt and von Hebel, *supra* note 520, pp. 17–18 (discussing the debate over what term should be used in this position, noting that delegates rejected 'accused' because the accused is not always the physical perpetrator, and that they rejected 'actor' as too vague a term).

[527] ICC Elements of Crimes, *supra* note 158, General Introduction, para. 8.

[528] See *supra* text accompanying note 108 (arguing that an underlying offence may qualify as a crime against humanity in at least two situations: first, where the physical perpetrator knows that his conduct is part of the attack; and second, even if the physical perpetrator lacks knowledge of the context in which his conduct occurs, where the planner, order, instigator, or person charged through the first category of JCE knows that it forms part of the attack). See also Rome Statute, *supra* note 59, Art. 25(3)(b), (d) (listing the forms of responsibility of ordering, soliciting, inducing, and common-purpose liability). As discussed in Volume I of this series, the Rome Statute does not contain the form of responsibility of 'planning', and 'inducing' can probably be regarded as synonymous with 'instigating' in the ICTY and ICTR Statutes. See Boas, Bischoff, and Reid, *supra* note 100, p. 371.

> [The] provisions [of article 7] … must be strictly construed, taking into account that crimes against humanity as defined in article 7 are among the most serious crimes of concern to the international community as a whole … and require conduct which is impermissible under generally applicable international law, as recognized by the principal legal systems of the world.[529]

This stipulation was part of a compromise reached after very difficult negotiations over the fears of some states that, especially since crimes against humanity may be committed in times of peace as well as times of war, politically motivated prosecutors and activist Western judges might use the law on crimes against humanity, in words of Darryl Robinson, 'as a tool of "social engineering"'[530] – that is, to scrutinise a state's human rights practices or religious and cultural traditions.[531] The other part of the compromise has been mentioned above: in contrast to the *ad hoc* Tribunals and the SCSL, crimes against humanity in the ICC must be committed pursuant to a state or organisational policy to commit an attack on a civilian population.[532] The Introduction to crimes against humanity in the Elements strengthens this requirement: '[T]he State or organization [must] actively promote or encourage such an attack'.[533] The states concerned about intervention in their domestic affairs clearly won the day with these restrictions, although the opposing group of states may have achieved a small concession in the perplexing footnote accompanying this text: 'A policy which has a civilian population as the object of the attack would be implemented by State or organizational action. Such a policy may, in exceptional circumstances, be implemented by a deliberate failure to take action, which is consciously aimed at encouraging such attack.'[534] Again, the precise import of and interaction between these terms awaits actual jurisprudence, although it should also be borne in mind that the Elements are non-binding.[535]

Third, with respect to persecution as a crime against humanity, the requirement of discriminatory intent appears to be spread across two separate elements:

[529] ICC Elements of Crimes, *supra* note 158, Art. 7, Introduction, para. 1.

[530] Robinson, *supra* note 521, p. 65; see also *ibid.*, pp. 69–71 (describing various aspects of the debate over paragraph 1).

[531] *Ibid.*, p. 65; Kirsch, *supra* note 521, p. xlix. For example, some Arab states were concerned that national laws making it more difficult for women to obtain divorce than men would be characterised as sexual slavery or imprisonment as crimes against humanity. Robinson, *supra* note 521, p. 65.

[532] Rome Statute, *supra* note 59, Art. 7(2)(a). See also *supra* text accompanying notes 493–496.

[533] ICC Elements of Crimes, *supra* note 158, Art. 7, Introduction, para. 3. See also *supra* note 59 and accompanying text (discussing the policy requirement in the 1954 ILC Draft Code, and comparing the respective positions of the different international and internationalised tribunals on whether this is a requirement).

[534] *Ibid.*, Art. 7, Introduction, para. 3 n. 6. Cassese argues that mere state or organisational tolerance or acquiescence of a widespread or systematic attack would suffice under custom. See Cassese, *supra* note 32, pp. 376–377. See also Robinson, *supra* note 521, pp. 74–76 (discussing in detail the debate over the 'action' requirement and the inclusion of the footnote).

[535] See Rome Statute, *supra* note 59, Art. 9(1).

2. The perpetrator targeted such person or persons by reason of the identity of a group or collectivity or targeted the group or collectivity as such.
3. Such targeting was based on political, racial, national, ethnic, cultural, religious, gender … or other grounds that are universally recognized as impermissible under international law.[536]

With the caveats identified above that the Rome Statute recognises more discriminatory grounds than the *ad hoc* Statutes,[537] and that the term 'perpetrator' may extend beyond the physical perpetrator to other relevant actors involved in the realisation of a crime,[538] this formulation does not appear to be materially different from the much simpler one developed in the *ad hoc* jurisprudence: the relevant actor intended to discriminate on one or more of the grounds of race, religion, or politics.[539]

Fourth, the terms 'deportation' and 'forcible transfer' are not defined as legally distinct from one another, and deportation does not appear to require that the victim be transferred across a border. Instead, the victim may be 'deported or forcibly transferred' 'to another State or location'.[540] This approach differs markedly from that of the *ad hoc* Tribunals, where deportation liability can only arise if the victim is transferred across a *de jure* or *de facto* international border, and where displacements within a state are analysed under the rubric of forcible transfer.[541]

Fifth and finally, it is interesting to note that a few critical terms are not defined at all, either in the Statute itself or in the Elements of Crimes: these include 'widespread', 'systematic', 'civilian', and 'civilian population'. Divining the meaning and scope of the term 'civilian' has proven particularly challenging for the *ad hoc* Tribunals.[542] According to Robinson, the delegations agreed that these complex terms should not be defined in the Elements, but should be left for resolution in the Court's case law.[543] This decision is certainly curious in light of the meticulous delineation of so many other aspects of crimes against humanity in the Statute and the Elements – including a great number of caveats and provisos – prompted largely by the anxieties of certain states that activist judges would meddle in their internal affairs.

As of 1 December 2007, there were few judicial pronouncements from the ICC on crimes against humanity. Arrest warrants have been issued against five members of the Lord's Resistance Army (LRA) in Uganda,[544] although proceedings were later

[536] ICC Elements of Crimes, *supra* note 158, Art. 7(1)(h), Elements 2–3.
[537] See *supra* text accompanying notes 498–501. [538] See *supra* text accompanying notes 526–528.
[539] See *supra* text accompanying note 416.
[540] *Ibid.*, Art. 7(1)(d), Element 1. See also *ibid.*, Element 1 n. 13 ('"Deported or forcibly transferred" is interchangeable with "forcibly displaced".').
[541] See *supra* section 2.2.3.4.5; see especially notes 297, 301–303 and accompanying text.
[542] See *supra* section 2.2.2.3.1. [543] Robinson, *supra* note 521, pp. 77–78.
[544] See *Situation in Uganda*, Case No. ICC-02/04-01/05, Warrant of Arrest for Joseph Kony issued on 8 July 2005 as amended on 27 September 2005, 27 September 2005 ('*Kony* Arrest Warrant'), paras. 42–44, 47–48 (pre-trial chamber finding that the information provided by the Prosecutor demonstrated reasonable grounds to believe that the accused was responsible for various crimes against humanity and war crimes, and issuing a warrant for his arrest); *ibid.*, Warrant of Arrest for Vincent Otti, 8 July 2005, paras. 42–44, 47–48 (same); *ibid.*, Warrant of

terminated with respect to one on account of his death.[545] In the heavily redacted public version of the indictment against Joseph Kony, the notorious leader of the LRA, the Pre-Trial Chamber finds reasons to believe him responsible for ordering rape,[546] enslavement,[547] sexual enslavement,[548] murder,[549] and inhumane acts.[550] The Court has also issued arrest warrants for two suspects with respect to the situation in Darfur, Sudan: Minister of State for Humanitarian Affairs Ahmad Harun and Ali Kushayb, a major Janjaweed militia leader, are suspected of common-purpose liability for a variety of crimes against humanity.[551] In both arrest warrants, the Pre-Trial Chamber finds reasonable grounds to believe that attacks by the Sudanese armed forces and the Janjaweed were widespread or systematic; were directed against civilians primarily from the Fur, Zaghawa, and Masalit populations; were carried out pursuant to a state or organisational policy to attack the civilian population; and that the armed forces and Janjaweed committed persecution, murder, forcible transfer, imprisonment or severe deprivation of liberty, torture, rape, and other inhumane acts against civilians primarily from these populations.[552] All the LRA and Sudanese suspects are still at large.[553] The Court has secured custody of two individuals with respect to the Situation in the Democratic Republic of the Congo. Thomas Lubanga – whose charges have been confirmed – is charged only with war crimes;[554] Germain Katanga was surrendered to the Court on 17 October 2007, and is suspected of responsibility for various war crimes and crimes against humanity allegedly committed in Ituri province in early 2003.[555]

Arrest for Raska Lukwiya, 8 July 2005, paras. 30–32, 35–36 (same); *ibid.*, Warrant of Arrest for Okot Odhiambo, 8 July 2005, paras. 32–34, 37–38 (same); *ibid.*, Warrant of Arrest for Dominic Ongwen, 8 July 2005, paras. 30–32, 35–36 (same).

545 See *Situation in Uganda*, Case No. ICC-02/04-01/05, Decision to Terminate the Proceedings Against Raska Lukwiya, 11 July 2007 ('Decision Terminating *Lukwiya* Proceedings'), p. 4.

546 *Kony* Arrest Warrant, *supra* note 544, p. 12 (Count 2).

547 *Ibid.*, p. 13 (Count 6); *ibid.*, p. 14 (Count 11); *ibid.*, p. 16 (Count 21); *ibid.*, p. 18 (Count 28).

548 *Ibid.*, p. 12 (Count 1).

549 *Ibid.*, p. 14 (Count 10); *ibid.*, p. 14 (Count 16); *ibid.*, p. 16 (Count 20); *ibid.*, p. 17 (Count 23); *ibid.*, p. 18 (Count 27).

550 *Ibid.*, p. 17 (Count 22); *ibid.*, p. 18 (Count 29).

551 *Situation in Darfur, Sudan*, Case No. ICC-02/05, Warrant of Arrest for Ahmad Harun, 27 April 2007 ('*Harun* Arrest Warrant'), pp. 6–15; *ibid.*, Warrant of Arrest for Ali Kushayb, 27 April 2007 ('*Kushayb* Arrest Warrant'), pp. 6–16. Kushayb is also suspected of co-perpetrating two campaigns of murder pursuant to Article 25(3)(a) of the Rome Statute. See *ibid.*, p. 11 (Count 25); *ibid.*, p. 12 (Count 29).

552 *Harun* Arrest Warrant, *supra* note 551, p. 4; *Kushayb* Arrest Warrant, *supra* note 551, p. 4.

553 For the Sudanese suspects, see 'Prosecutor briefs UN Security Council, calls for the arrest of Ahmed Harun and Ali Kushayb for crimes in Darfur', Press Release ICC-OTP-PR-20070607-222_EN, 7 June 2007, available at www.icc-cpi.int/press/pressreleases/251.html.

554 *Prosecutor* v. *Lubanga*, Case No. ICC-01/04-01/06, Decision on the Confirmation of Charges (public redacted version), 29 January 2007, pp. 156–157. See also Chapter 4, text accompanying notes 510–519 (discussing this decision in detail).

555 *Situation in the Democratic Republic of the Congo*, Case No. ICC-01/04-01/07, Warrant of Arrest for Germain Katanga, 2 July 2007, p. 6 (pre-trial chamber finding that the information provided by the Prosecutor demonstrated reasonable grounds to believe that the accused is responsible for murder, inhumane acts, and sexual slavery as crimes against humanity committed during an attack on the village of Bogoro in Ituri province in early 2003); *ibid.*, Decision to Unseal the Warrant of Arrest Against Germain Katanga, 18 October 2007, pp. 3–4 (lifting the confidentiality of the arrest warrant).

2.3.2 The Internationalised Tribunals

2.3.2.1 Special Court for Sierra Leone (SCSL)

Although the SCSL Statute postdates the Rome Statute, its crimes against humanity provision is inspired by that of the *ad hoc* Tribunals:

Article 2: Crimes Against Humanity
The Special Court shall have the power to prosecute persons who committed the following crimes as part of a widespread or systematic attack against any civilian population:

(a) Murder;
(b) Extermination;
(c) Enslavement;
(d) Deportation;
(e) Imprisonment;
(f) Torture;
(g) Rape, sexual slavery, enforced prostitution, forced pregnancy and any other form of sexual violence;
(h) Persecution on political, racial, ethnic or religious grounds;
(i) Other inhumane acts.[556]

This formulation is simpler than that of the ICC and both *ad hoc* Tribunals and, indeed, any of the other internationalised tribunals. In contrast to the ICTY, the *chapeau* of Article 2 lacks the armed conflict requirement;[557] it also lacks the ICTR's requirement that the attack be discriminatory.[558] Also absent are the definitions from Article 7(2) of the Rome Statute, including any notion that a crime against humanity must be committed as part of a plan or policy.[559] A chamber of the Special Court has since confirmed that no such requirement exists.[560] Robert Cryer characterises the SCSL formulation's simplicity in the face of the many provisos and

[556] Statute of the Special Court for Sierra Leone, 2178 UNTS 138, UN Doc. S/2002/246, 16 January 2002, Appendix II ('SCSL Statute'), Art. 2.

[557] For a more detailed discussion of the armed conflict requirement, including a comparison of the respective positions of the different international and internationalised courts and tribunals, see *supra* note 55.

[558] *AFRC* Trial Judgement, *supra* note 497, para. 212. See also *supra* text accompanying notes 55, 60 (discussing these requirements); notes 479–485 (discussing negotiations at the ICC drafting meetings resulting in the exclusion of either requirement from the Rome Statute); *infra* note 656 (Cambodia Group of Experts opining that armed conflict requirement is not part of custom). The *ad hoc* Appeals Chambers have clarified that these requirements do not form part of the customary definition of crimes against humanity, except for the requirement that persecution be committed with discriminatory intent. See *Tadić* Jurisdiction Appeal Decision, *supra* note 55, paras. 141–142; *Akayesu* Appeal Judgement, *supra* note 60, paras. 464–465; Schabas, *supra* note 55, p. 196 (absence of discriminatory grounds in SCSL *chapeau* '[r]eflect[s] evolving views on the subject'). See also *supra* note 60 and accompanying text (comparing the respective positions of the different international and internationalised tribunals on whether there is a requirement of a discriminatory attack for all crimes against humanity).

[559] See Rome Statute, *supra* note 59, Art. 7(2)(a). See also *supra* text accompanying notes 495–496.

[560] *CDF* Trial Judgement, *supra* note 495, para. 113. Accord Cassese, *supra* note 32, pp. 376–377 (policy requirement not part of custom). See also *supra* note 59 and accompanying text (discussing the policy requirement in the 1954 ILC Draft Code, and comparing the respective positions of the different international and internationalised tribunals on whether this is a requirement).

restrictive definitions in the Rome Statute as 'an implicit critique of the Rome definition'.[561] Of all the crimes against humanity formulations yet produced in the statutes of international and internationalised courts and tribunals, the SCSL formulation comes closest to reflecting the customary definition.[562] For this reason, it should be preferred as the model for future tribunals, particularly over the unduly complicated ICC formulation.

Article 2 contains the same standard catalogue of underlying offences that appears in the *ad hoc* Statutes, with two noteworthy exceptions.[563] The first exception is Article 2(g), which contains several sexual offences in addition to rape, and closely resembles the analogous subparagraphs in the Rome Statute and the 1996 ILC Draft Code.[564] The longer list of sexual offences was a response to the rampant commission of sexual violence as one of the hallmarks of the conflict.[565] This sort of definitional tailoring is also obvious in other provisions of the SCSL Statute – for example, in the inclusion of the war crime of conscripting, enlisting, or using child soldiers,[566] and in the included Sierra Leonean domestic crime of abuse of girls.[567] The second exception is that persecution in Article 2(h) may be committed not only on political, racial, or religious grounds, but also on ethnic grounds.[568]

Every accused before the SCSL has been charged with various crimes against humanity. In stark contrast to the ICTY, persecution does not appear in any current indictment, and was not charged against those whose judgements have already been handed down. On the other hand, and predictably, sexual crimes feature

561 Cryer, *supra* note 34, p. 261.

562 See *ibid.* (opining that the SCSL formulation's 'material coverage is essentially that of customary international law'); John Cerone, 'The Special Court for Sierra Leone: Establishing a New Approach to International Criminal Justice', (2002) 8 *ILSA Journal of International and Comparative Law* 379, 385 (SCSL formulation 'broadly in accord with … what is generally considered to be the definition under customary law'); *supra* text accompanying notes 514–517 (questioning whether apartheid and enforced disappearance have support in custom as underlying offences as crimes against humanity).

563 The SCSL formulation thus lacks the underlying offences of enforced disappearance and apartheid which, as discussed above, may not qualify as underlying offences of crimes against humanity in customary international law. See *supra* text accompanying notes 514–517; accord Cassese, *supra* note 477, p. 376.

564 See Rome Statute, *supra* note 59, Art. 7(1)(g); 1996 ILC Draft Code with Commentaries, *supra* note 55, Art. 18 (j). See also Micaela Frulli, 'The Special Court for Sierra Leone: Some Preliminary Comments', (2000) 11 *European Journal of International Law* 857, 863–864; *supra* note 65 (comparing the list of underlying offences in the 1996 ILC Draft Code with those of the international and internationalised courts and tribunals).

565 See Report of the Secretary-General on the Establishment of a Special Court for Sierra Leone, UN Doc. S/2000/915, 4 October 2000 ('Report on the Establishment of the SCSL'), para. 12 (noting a number of the 'most egregious practices' of the conflict, including sexual violence against girls and women and sexual slavery); Nsongurua J. Udombana, 'Globalization of Justice and the Special Court for Sierra Leone's War Crimes', (2003) 17 *Emory International Law Review* 55, 73–74 (citing estimates that Sierra Leone had 'the highest rate of sexual violence in the world, with thousands of women and girls raped and killed, or abducted and forced to live as sexual slaves by rebel groups in the country's civil war').

566 SCSL Statute, *supra* note 556, Art. 4(c). See also Chapter 4, section 4.3.2.1.

567 SCSL Statute, *supra* note 556, Art. 5(a). See also Report on the Establishment of the SCSL, *supra* note 565, para. 19.

568 SCSL Statute, *supra* note 556, Art. 2(h).

prominently,[569] including in the indictment of former Liberian President Charles Taylor, the highest-ranking of the Special Court's indictees.[570]

The SCSL Statute provides that '[t]he judges of the Appeals Chamber of the Special Court shall be guided by the decisions of the Appeals Chamber of the International Tribunals for the former Yugoslavia and for Rwanda'.[571] This statement has since been held equally applicable to trial chambers.[572] The aversion to 'reinventing the wheel' is understandable, especially given the developed stage of *ad hoc* Tribunal jurisprudence. The two trial judgements issued by the Special Court as of 1 December 2007 – in the so-called *AFRC* and *CDF* cases – reveal heavy reliance on *ad hoc* precedent in their definitions of crimes against humanity. Both recite the general requirements of crimes against humanity by near exclusive reference to ICTY cases, with no significant variation.[573] In the same vein, the elements of the underlying offences are usually taken directly from ICTY or ICTR jurisprudence,[574] although the *AFRC* Trial Chamber seems also to have had recourse to the ICC Elements of Crimes in defining the elements of certain underlying offences.[575] Still, one wonders whether the *AFRC* and *CDF* Chambers should

[569] See *AFRC* Trial Judgement, *supra* note 497, para. 14 (Brima, Kamara, and Kanu charged with murder, extermination, rape, sexual slavery, other forms of sexual violence, inhumane acts, and enslavement as crimes against humanity); *Prosecutor* v. *Sesay, Kallon, and Gbao*, Case No. SCSL-2004–15-PT, Corrected Amended Consolidated Indictment, 2 August 2006, p. 12 (extermination and murder); *ibid.*, p. 14 (rape); *ibid.*, p. 15 (sexual slavery and other inhumane acts); *ibid.*, p. 17 (other inhumane acts); *ibid.*, p. 22 (murder); *Prosecutor* v. *Koroma*, Case No. SCSL-2003-03-I, Indictment, 7 March 2003, p. 7 (extermination and murder); *ibid.*, p. 10 (rape and sexual slavery); *ibid.*, p. 11 (other inhumane acts); *ibid.*, p. 13 (enslavement); *ibid.*, p. 14 (murder). The CDF accused were not charged with sexual crimes.

[570] *Prosecutor* v. *Taylor*, Case No. SCSL-2003-01-PT, Second Amended Indictment, 29 May 2007, paras. 14–17 (alleging that rebel forces 'assisted and encouraged by, acting in concert with, under the direction and/or control of, and/or subordinate to [Taylor]', raped an unknown number of women and girls in several locations throughout Sierra Leone from November 1996 to January 2002, and abducted many others to use as sexual slaves) (quotation at para. 14). For this conduct, Taylor is charged with responsibility for rape and sexual slavery as crimes against humanity. *Ibid.*, p. 4 (Counts 4 and 5). The indictment also charges Taylor with responsibility for the crimes against humanity of murder, *ibid.*, p. 3 (Count 2), inhumane acts, *ibid.*, p. 6 (Count 8), and enslavement, *ibid.* (Count 10), through all the forms of responsibility in the SCSL Statute, including joint criminal enterprise, see *ibid.*, paras. 33–34. Taylor's trial began on 4 June 2007, but was thereafter suspended until 7 January 2008 to allow the new defence team time to prepare. See *Prosecutor* v. *Taylor*, Case No. SCSL-2003-01-T, Trial Transcript, 20 August 2007, p. 34.

[571] SCSL Statute, *supra* note 556, Art. 20(3).

[572] *AFRC* Trial Judgement, *supra* note 497, para. 639 n. 1269 ('[T]he Trial Chamber finds that as a matter of course, the provision equally applies to triers of fact at first instance.').

[573] See *CDF* Trial Judgement, *supra* note 495, paras. 111–121; *AFRC* Trial Judgement, *supra* note 497, paras. 214–222. Oddly but understandably given that it was rendered just six weeks after the *AFRC* Trial Judgement, the *CDF* Trial Judgement does not cite the *AFRC* Trial Judgement as precedent for its holdings. See also Chapter 4, text accompanying notes 542–551 (discussing how the mutually independent analyses of the two judgements led to apparently conflicting definitions for the war crime of conscripting child soldiers).

[574] See *CDF* Trial Judgement, *supra* note 495, para. 143 (murder, citing earlier SCSL decisions and *Kordić and Čerkez* Trial Judgement, *supra* note 75, para. 236); *ibid.*, paras. 150, 153 (other inhumane acts, citing earlier SCSL decisions and, *inter alia*, *Vasiljević* Trial Judgement, *supra* note 164, para. 234); *AFRC* Trial Judgement, *supra* note 497, paras. 693–694 (rape, relying on *Kunarac et al.* Appeal Judgement, *supra* note 75, paras. 127–130).

[575] At times, the *AFRC* Trial Chamber's list of a set of elements appears to be an amalgam of *ad hoc* and ICC elements. See, e.g., *AFRC* Trial Judgement, *supra* note 497, paras. 683–684 (extermination, citing, *inter alia*, *Kayishema and Ruzindana* Trial Judgement, *supra* note 90, paras. 137–147, and *Prosecutor* v. *Brima, Kamara, and Kanu*, Case No. SCSL-04-16-T, Decision on Motions for Judgement of Acquittal Pursuant to Rule 98,

have put greater thought into certain aspects of ICTY and ICTR jurisprudence before unquestioningly endorsing it for the Special Court. For example, both Chambers perpetuate the lack of distinction between 'accused' and 'perpetrator' in discussing which of the actors involved in the realisation of a crime against humanity must have knowledge of the widespread or systematic attack, and which actor must engage in conduct that forms part of the attack,[576] even though in both cases the accused held high positions in the hierarchy and did not usually physically perpetrate the charged crimes themselves.[577]

In the *CDF* case, the two accused were acquitted of the crimes against humanity with which they were charged (murder and other inhumane acts) because the Trial Chamber found that, even though fighters under the direction of the accused engaged in a widespread attack, rebel forces – not civilians – were the primary object of the attack.[578] In the *AFRC* case, the three accused were found

31 March 2006 ('*AFRC* Rule 98 Decision'), para. 73, which itself seems to rely on ICC Elements of Crimes, *supra* note 158, Art. 7(1)(b), Elements 1–2); *ibid.*, paras. 688–690 (murder, citing, *inter alia*, *Prosecutor* v. *Orić*, Case No. IT-03-68-T, Judgement, 30 June 2006, paras. 347–348, and *AFRC* Rule 98 Decision, *supra*, para. 74, which itself seems to rely on ICC Elements of Crimes, *supra* note 158, Art. 7(1)(a), Element 1). Other times, the Trial Chamber has taken its elements directly from the ICC Elements. *ibid.*, para. 708 (sexual slavery, relying on ICC Elements of Crimes, *supra* note 158, Art. 7(1)(g)-2, Elements 1–2); *ibid.*, para. 698 (other inhumane acts, relying on ICC Elements of Crimes, *supra* note 158, Art. 7(1)(k), Elements 1–3).

576 See, e.g., *AFRC* Trial Judgement, *supra* note 497, paras. 220–221 (acts of 'perpetrator' must be part of attack and 'perpetrator' must have knowledge of attack); *CDF* Trial Judgement, *supra* note 495, paras. 120–121 ('Accused' fulfils both requirements). The *CDF* Chamber seems to have recognised the need to differentiate among the possibly many relevant actors who may fulfil the different elements of a crime against humanity, but adopted the unsatisfactory solution of the ICC Elements of Crimes:

> The Chamber notes that the term 'Accused' … was chosen for purposes of convenience and should be understood in a broad sense. The general requirements, including the appropriate mental elements therein, apply, *mutatis mutandis*, to the direct perpetrator of the crime as well as all those whose criminal responsibility may fall under Article 6(1) and (3) of the Statute [on forms of responsibility].

Ibid., para. 109 (copying ICC Elements of Crimes, *supra* note 158, General Introduction, para. 8, as described at text accompanying notes 527–528, *supra*). By virtue of this caveat, the Trial Chamber apparently felt free to eschew precision in describing who may fulfil which element, and instead used the term 'Accused' in describing general requirements and elements of underlying offences. See, e.g., *ibid.*, para. 143 (for murder, 'Accused' must have caused victim's death). See generally *supra* section 2.2.2.1 and text accompanying notes 4, 95–109, on who among the relevant actors must fulfil which element of a crime against humanity.

577 See, e.g., *CDF* Trial Judgement, *supra* note 495, paras. 721–746 (Fofana and Kondewa 'key and essential components' of the Civil Defence Forces leadership structure whose decisions and orders were carried out by pro-government fighters known as Kamajors) (quotation at para. 721(i)); *AFRC* Trial Judgement, *supra* note 497, paras. 1716, 1782 (Brima ordered murder); *Ibid.*, para. 1744 (Brima responsible as a superior); *ibid.*, para. 1916 (Kamara ordered murder); *ibid.*, para. 1928 (Kamara responsible as a superior); *ibid.*, para. 2044 (Kanu responsible as a superior); *ibid.*, para. 2059 (Kanu ordered murder). But see *ibid.*, para. 1709 (Brima physically perpetrated extermination as a crime against humanity); *ibid.*, para. 1755 (Brima physically perpetrated murder). See also *supra* text accompanying notes 4, 95–109 (discussing the need for precision in describing who must fulfil which element of an international crime).

578 *CDF* Trial Judgement, *supra* note 495, paras. 691–694; see also *ibid.*, para. 693 ('[T]he Chamber recalls the admission of the Prosecutor that "the CDF and the Kamajors fought for the restoration of democracy".'); *ibid.*, para. 116 (civilian population 'includes all of those persons who are not members of the armed forces or otherwise recognised as combatants'); *ibid.*, para. 117 (civilian population must be 'predominantly civilian in nature'). The Chamber's discussion of the elements of murder and other inhumane acts as crimes against humanity was thus unnecessary and is presumably *dicta*. See *ibid.*, paras. 143–144, 150–153. All charges against the third *CDF* accused, Samuel Hinga Norman, were dropped following his 22 February 2007 death. *Ibid.*, para. 5.

responsible for extermination, murder, enslavement, and rape as crimes against humanity.[579]

The Trial Chamber also appears to have found that AFRC or AFRC/RUF Junta forces acting at the direction of the accused mutilated or made sexual slaves of vast numbers of civilian victims;[580] both these offences were charged in the indictment as crimes against humanity, the former in Count 7 under Article 2(g) of the SCSL Statute, and the latter in Count 11 as an inhumane act under Article 2(i).[581] The Trial Chamber acquitted the three accused of these crimes against humanity, however,[582] based on a novel procedural rule not present in *ad hoc* jurisprudence. In a concurring opinion appended to an earlier decision of the *AFRC* Trial Chamber, Justice Sebutinde opined that Count 7, which repeats the language of Article 2(g) in charging both 'sexual slavery' and 'any other form of sexual violence', was 'duplex and defective in as far as it does not enable the accused persons to know precisely which of the two crimes (sexual slavery or sexual violence) they should be defending themselves against'.[583] Despite the very different approach in the ICTY,[584] the full Chamber endorsed Judge Sebutinde's position in the Trial Judgement with little explanation or analysis, and took the drastic measure of striking out Count 7 in its entirety as 'bad for duplicity'.[585] The Chamber applied the same rule to Count 11, which it interpreted as 'duplicitous' in charging both 'ill-treatment' as an inhumane act and mutilation as an inhumane act. Yet instead of striking Count 11 in its entirety as it had done with Count 7, and for unexplained reasons, the Trial Chamber held that it would only consider the allegations in the count relating to ill-treatment, and would disregard those relating to mutilations.[586] It is disappointing that no judgement was pronounced on the crimes against humanity of mutilations and sexual

579 *AFRC* Trial Judgement, *supra* note 497, para. 2113 (Brima); *ibid.*, para. 2117 (Kamara); *ibid.*, para. 2121 (Kanu).

580 See, e.g., *ibid.*, para. 1109 (sexual slavery perpetrated against women in Kono District); *ibid.*, para. 1126 (same for Koinadugu District); *ibid.*, para. 1170 (same for Freetown and Western Area); *ibid.*, para. 1187 (same for Port Loko District); *ibid.*, para. 1213 (mutilation of civilians in Kono); *ibid.*, para. 1218 (same for Koinadugu); *ibid.*, para. 1243 (same for Freetown and Western Area).

581 See *Prosecutor* v. *Brima, Kamara, and Kanu*, Case No. SCSL-2004-16-PT, Further Amended Consolidated Indictment, 18 February 2005, paras. 51–57 (Count 7 charging the three accused with sexual slavery 'and any other form of sexual violence' as crimes against humanity for the abduction and use as sex slaves of an unknown number of women and girls in several districts by AFRC and RUF forces); *ibid.* paras. 58–59, 61–64 (Count 11 charging the accused with other inhumane acts as a crime against humanity for the mutilation of civilians by AFRC and RUF forces).

582 *AFRC* Trial Judgement, *supra* note 497, para. 2116 (Brima); *ibid.*, para. 2120 (Kamara); *ibid.*, para. 2123 (Kanu).

583 *AFRC* Rule 98 Decision, *supra* note 575, Separate Concurring Opinion of Hon. Justice Julia Sebutinde, para. 8.

584 See *Prosecutor* v. *Haradinaj, Balaj, and Brahimaj*, Case No. IT-04-84-PT, Decision on Motion to Amend the Indictment and Challenges to the Form of the Amended Indictment, 25 October 2006, para. 13 (holding that manner in which the prosecution chooses to organise its charging instrument is not binding on trial chambers, and that chambers must instead look beneath the counts to the substance of the charges in the indictment to determine how many crimes have actually been charged and in respect of what conduct). See also Chapter 5, note 177 and accompanying text (discussing this notion with respect to the underlying offences of genocide).

585 *AFRC* Trial Judgement, *supra* note 497, para. 94; see also *ibid.*, para. 696.

586 See *ibid.*, para. 726.

slavery, as these are perhaps the two most emblematic atrocities of an exceptionally brutal conflict.[587]

2.3.2.2 East Timor: Special Panels for Serious Crimes (SPSC)

The constitutive document for East Timor's Special Panels for Serious Crimes closely follows the Rome Statute in its definition of crimes against humanity.[588] Section 5 of Regulation No. 2000/15 on the Establishment of Panels with Exclusive Jurisdiction over Serious Criminal Offences, promulgated by the UN Transitional Administration in East Timor ('UNTAET Regulation'),[589] contains the same list of underlying offences and definitions that appears in the Rome Statute,[590] with one exception: 'attack directed against any civilian population' is not defined.[591] Bert Swart has proffered an explanation: 'The omission seems … to find its origin in the fear that the rather controversial definition of the term "attack" contained in the Rome Statute unduly restricts that concept with regard to situations in which an attack against a civilian population is characterized by its widespread, rather than its systematic, nature.'[592]

587 See David Cohen, '"Hybrid" Justice in East Timor, Sierra Leone, and Cambodia: "Lessons Learned" and Prospects for the Future', (2007) 43 *Stanford Journal of International Law* 1, 11 (noting that 'tens of thousands of civilians were murdered, tortured, raped, and mutilated' and that '[t]he systematic amputation of hands, arms, and legs by rebel groups participating in the conflict gained worldwide notoriety').

588 In its January 2000 report, the international commission established to investigate human rights abuses committed prior, during, and after the 1999 popular consultation in East Timor determined that 'patterns of gross violations of human rights and breaches of humanitarian law' had occurred, and recommended the establishment of a tribunal to try those responsible. Report of the International Commission of Inquiry on East Timor to the Secretary-General, UN Doc. A/54/726, S/2000/59, 31 January 2000 ('East Timor Commission of Inquiry Report'), para. 123 (determining that 'patterns of gross violations of human rights and breaches of humanitarian law' had occurred, and that these abuses 'took the form of systematic and widespread intimidation, humiliation and terror, destruction of property, violence against women and displacement of people'); *ibid.*, para. 153 (recommending that a tribunal be set up). Following the Commission's recommendation, in March 2000 the UN Transitional Administration in East Timor instituted the hybrid Special Panels within the District Court of East Timor's capital, Dili. United Nations Transitional Administration in East Timor, Regulation No. 2000/11 on the Organization of Courts in East Timor, UN Doc. UNTAET/REG/2000/11, 6 March 2000, as amended by Regulation No. 2001/25, UN Doc. UNTAET/REG/20001/25, 14 September 2001 ('Regulation No. 2000/11'), Sections 10.1–10.2.

589 United Nations Transitional Administration in East Timor, Regulation No. 2000/15 on the Establishment of Panels with Exclusive Jurisdiction over Serious Criminal Offences, UN Doc. UNTAET/REG/2000/15, 6 June 2000 ('UNTAET Regulation'), Section 5.

590 See *supra* text accompanying note 475 (reproducing much of the crimes against humanity text in the Rome Statute); see also *supra* note 65 (comparing the list of underlying offences in the 1996 ILC Draft Code with those of the international and internationalised courts and tribunals).

591 See Rome Statute, *supra* note 59, Art. 7(2)(a). Nevertheless, at least one Trial Panel has held Article 7(2)(a)'s respective definitions of 'widespread' and 'systematic' to be applicable in the SPSC. See *Prosecutor* v. *Joni Marques, Manuel da Costa, João da Costa, Paulo da Costa, Amélio da Costa, Hilário da Silva, Gonsalo dos Santos, Alarico Fernandes, Mautersa Monis, and Gilberto Fernandes*, Case No. 09/2000, Judgment, 11 December 2001 ('*Los Palos* Trial Judgement'), paras. 636–637.

592 Bert Swart, 'Internationalized Courts and Substantive Criminal Law', in Cesare P. R. Romano, André Nollkaemper, and Jann K. Kleffner (eds.), *Internationalized Criminal Courts and Tribunals: Sierra Leone, East Timor, Kosovo, and Cambodia* (2004), p. 300. See also *supra* text accompanying notes 490–497 (discussing the Rome Statute's definition of 'attack directed against any civilian population' and the difficult debates leading up to it).

The Security Council withdrew UN support for the Special Panels in May 2005, effectively terminating them before they had tried the vast majority of their indictees.[593] Eighty-seven accused were ultimately tried for crimes committed during a campaign of violence that resulted in the mass displacement of large parts of the population, left some 1,300 people dead and many more raped or injured, and caused widespread devastation of property.[594] The charges against these and the accused who remained at large consisted exclusively of crimes against humanity and ordinary crimes under domestic law; no accused was charged with war crimes or genocide.[595] The bulk of those tried were low-level militia fighters, mostly 'illiterate farmers and fishermen caught up in the conflict at the local community level'.[596]

The jurisprudence of the SPSC on crimes against humanity, which varies in quality from seriously flawed to acceptable,[597] has been considered at length else-

593 Security Council Resolution 1543, UN Doc. S/RES/1543 (2004), para. 1. See also David Cohen, 'Indifference and Accountability: The United Nations and the Politics of International Justice in East Timor', in *East-West Center Special Reports* (2006), vol. 9, available at www.isn.ethz.ch/pubs/ph/details.cfm?lng=en&id=21911, p. 91 (when the SPSC was shut down, 'only 572 murders out of 1,400 had been captured in indictments, more than 500 investigative files remained open … numerous cases that were ready to go to trial were not brought forward', and many high-level indictees remained at large in Indonesia); see also *infra* note 596 (more statistics on untried cases). For a brief explanation of the institutional framework of the SPSC, see Report to the Secretary-General of the Commission of Experts to Review the Prosecution of Serious Violations of Human Rights in Timor-Leste (then East Timor) in 1999, UN Doc. S/2005/458, Annex II, 26 May 2005 ('UN East Timor Report'), paras. 37–43.

594 See Caitlin Reiger and Marieke Wierda, *The Serious Crimes Process in Timor-Leste: In Retrospect*, International Centre for Transitional Justice, March 2006, available at www.ictj.org/static/Prosecutions/Timor.study.pdf, p. 6 (describing the violence as a 'well-planned attack' perpetrated by the Indonesian armed forces and Timorese militias in the days following the 30 August 1999 referendum in which a majority of East Timorese voted for independence). See also Cohen, *supra* note 593, p. 11 (noting that the SPSC had a 97.7 per cent conviction rate).

595 Reiger and Wierda, *supra* note 594, p. 23. See also Chapter 3, text accompanying notes 383–384 (positing an explanation for why genocide was never charged).

596 Cohen, *supra* note 593, p. 15. '[L]iterally all' of the intermediate- and high-level indictees – including a number of Indonesian army officers and General Wiranto, a prominent Indonesian politician – remained safely at large in Indonesia for the duration of the Special Panels' existence. *Ibid.*, pp. 13, 15 (quotation at p. 15). See also Reiger and Wierda, *supra* note 594, p. 18:

> At the time of its closure in May 2005, the [Special Crimes Unit] had indicted 391 people in 95 separate indictments. These included 37 Indonesian military officers from the TNI, 4 Indonesian police chiefs, 60 Timorese TNI officers and soldiers, the former civilian Governor of Timor-Leste, and 5 former District Administrators. Out of those indicted, 339 remained at large outside the jurisdiction.

See also UN East Timor Report, *supra* note 593, para. 57 (noting that, in the wake of the Special Panels' termination, there is a 'sense of dissatisfaction' among the East Timorese people that 'stems from the knowledge that the persons who bear the greatest responsibility for planning or ordering serious crimes have not appeared before the Special Panels'); *ibid.*, para. 64 ('It cannot be said that the serious crimes process has achieved accountability for those who bear the greatest responsibility for serious crimes.').

597 Regrettably, most judgements of the Special Panels – especially those of the Court of Appeal – are of exceptionally poor quality, often fail to define the elements of the charged crimes or forms of responsibility, and do not make explicit factual findings or apply the law to the facts in a coherent way. See Cohen, *supra* note 593, pp. 45–46 (noting many judgements' failure to use *ad hoc* jurisprudence as a model, resulting in jurisprudential 'groping in the dark') (quotation at p. 46); *ibid.*, pp. 89–90; Reiger and Wierda, *supra* note 594, pp. 23–24 (noting the judges' failure to comprehend the applicable laws in many judgements, and the 'inaccurate application of the elements of crimes in cases dealing with crimes against humanity') (quotation at p. 23).

where.[598] We focus here on the two most noteworthy cases, beginning with the much criticised *dos Santos* case. Armando dos Santos, a commander in one of the pro-Indonesia militias during the conflict, was charged with committing, planning, ordering, aiding and abetting, and participating in a common purpose to commit murder and other inhumane acts as crimes against humanity; he was alleged to have participated in the killing of several persons in the Liquiçá and Dili Districts, and the severe beating of another.[599] After a confused analysis of the general requirements of crimes against humanity that made occasional reference to *ad hoc* jurisprudence,[600] the Trial Panel found that the evidence did not establish dos Santos's knowledge of the widespread or systematic attack, and acquitted him of all charged crimes against humanity.[601] The Trial Panel did convict him, however, of ordinary murder as defined in the Indonesian Penal Code, even though this crime had not been charged in the indictment,[602] and sentenced him to twenty years.[603]

A 2–1 majority of the Court of Appeal overturned the Trial Panel and substituted new convictions, but not because the Trial Panel had violated dos Santos's rights by convicting him of uncharged crimes. Instead, it took the opportunity to promulgate a new rule that Portuguese law, not Indonesian law, applied to ordinary crimes in the Special Panels.[604] It then held, again for the first time, that to apply crimes against humanity as defined in the UNTAET Regulation would violate *nullum crimen sine lege* in the East Timorese Constitution, since dos Santos's alleged crimes were committed in 1999 and the Regulation was not promulgated until 2000.[605] The

598 For discussions of the jurisprudence, see Cohen, *supra* note 593, pp. 42–90 (discussing twenty-eight cases from 2000 to 2005); *ibid.*, p. 5 n. 2 (citing a number of other reports and articles on the SPSC's judicial work); Judicial System Monitoring Programme, *Digest of the Jurisprudence of the Special Panels for Serious Crimes*, April 2007, pp. 63–89 (crimes against humanity elements); Sylvia de Bertodano, 'East Timor: Justice Denied', (2004) 2 *Journal of International Criminal Justice* 910, 916–922; Judicial System Monitoring Programme, *The Paulino de Jesus Decisions*, April 2005; Judicial System Monitoring Programme, *Overview of the Jurisprudence of the Court of Appeal in Its First Year of Operation Since East Timor's Independence*, August 2004; Judicial System Monitoring Programme, *The Prosecutor* v. *Joni Marques and 9 others (the Los Palos case)*, March 2002 ('*Los Palos* Report'). The JSMP publications are available at http://www.jsmp.minihub.org/Language_English/reports_english.htm. Most SPSC indictments, judgements, and other jurisprudence can be found at http://socrates.berkeley.edu/~warcrime/ET-special-panels-docs.htm or http://www.unotil.org/legal/court-decisions/court-decisions.htm.

599 *Prosecutor* v. *Armando dos Santos*, Case No. LI-07-99-SC, Indictment, 5 June 2001, pp. 7–8.

600 See *Prosecutor* v. *Armando [dos] Santos*, Case No. 16/2001, Sentença Final Proferida em Primeira Instância, 9 September 2002, pp. 13–17 (citing the *Blaškić*, *Akayesu*, and *Kayishema and Ruzindana* Trial Judgements).

601 See *Ibid.*, pp. 19–20.

602 *Ibid.*, pp. 22–25. See also *Ibid.*, p. 20 (noting that the accused's criminal responsibility 'indisputably exists', but that it would have to be analysed under the rubric of ordinary crimes instead of crimes against humanity) (authors' translation).

603 *Ibid.*, pp. 25–26.

604 *Prosecutor* v. *Armando dos Santos*, Case No. 16/2001, Julgamento (Tribunal de Recurso), 15 July 2003 ('*dos Santos* Appeal Judgement'), pp. 6, 8. The two judges in the majority were Portuguese; the Timorese judge dissented without appending a separate opinion, although she elaborated her views in a dissenting opinion in a subsequent case. See *Augustinho da Costa* v. *Prosecutor*, Case No. 7/2000, Julgamento (Tribunal de Recurso), 18 July 2003 ('*da Costa* Appeal Judgement'), Dissenting Opinion of Jacinta Correia da Costa.

605 *Dos Santos* Appeal Judgement, *supra* note 604, pp. 17–18.

Court thus determined that the only applicable body of law in the SPSC was Portuguese law,[606] and found that dos Santos had committed three murders under the Portuguese Penal Code.[607] It also found contra the Trial Panel that he did indeed have knowledge of a widespread and systematic attack in the territory in which he operated, and could therefore bear liability for crimes against humanity provided such crimes existed in Portuguese law.[608] In a perplexing twist, the Court then quoted the definition of genocide from the Portuguese Penal Code, and found in one cursory paragraph that: (1) dos Santos's three murders were carried out against supporters of East Timorese independence; (2) he had the intent to destroy independence supporters; and (3) he was consequently responsible for a 'crime against humanity in the form of genocide'.[609] It entered the corresponding conviction for crimes against humanity, in addition to convictions for the three murders,[610] without explaining how genocide constitutes a crime against humanity in Portuguese law or citing any Portuguese or international authority.

The defects of the *dos Santos* Appeal Judgement are manifold and grave. First and most fundamentally, the Court of Appeal, like the Trial Panel, convicted dos Santos for crimes not charged in the indictment, thus depriving him of his right to present a defence against those crimes. Second, the holding that Portuguese law applies in the SPSC departed from previous appellate jurisprudence and implied that every prior SPSC conviction for ordinary crimes was based on the wrong body of law.[611] Third, at least in so far as Section 5 of the UNTAET Regulation does not itself go beyond customary international law, the Court of Appeal ignored a widely accepted principle in international criminal law: although an accused is alleged to have committed his crime prior to the promulgation of the statute including the crime, conviction is permissible as long as the crime existed in custom or in

[606] *Ibid.*, p. 18. [607] *Ibid.*, pp. 19–20, 28 (citing Article 131 of the Portuguese Penal Code).

[608] *Ibid.*, pp. 22–23. See also *ibid.*, pp. 21–22 (Court of Appeal giving its views on what the general requirements of crimes against humanity are, without citing or discussing any authority).

[609] See *ibid.*, pp. 23–24 (citing Article 239 of the Portuguese Penal Code, which itself closely follows the language of Article II of the 1948 Genocide Convention, *supra* note 50). The Court of Appeal later convicted another accused of 'crimes against humanity in the form of genocide'. See *Prosecutor* v. *Manual Gonçalves Bere Aka*, Case No. 10/2000, Julgamento (Tribunal de Recurso), 16 October 2003 ('*Gonçalves Bere* Appeal Judgement'), p. 12.

[610] *Dos Santos* Appeal Judgement, *supra* note 604, pp. 28–29. The Court of Appeal held that 'the values protected by the criminal law are different' with respect to murder as compared to 'genocide as a crime against humanity', and that the former did not constitute lesser-included offences of the latter. *Ibid.*, p. 24 (authors' translation). This method of comparing crimes to determine whether cumulative convictions are appropriate has been rejected by the Appeals Chambers of the *ad hoc* Tribunals. See Chapter 5, text accompanying notes 32–34 (discussing the *Kupreškić* Trial Chamber's 'further test' in which the values protected by each criminal provision are taken into account); *ibid.*, text accompanying notes 37–44 (ICTY Appeals Chamber implicitly overruling the *Kupreškić* Trial Chamber on this point). The Court of Appeal imposed a new sentence of twenty-two years on dos Santos. *Ibid.*, p. 29.

[611] Cohen, *supra* note 593, p. 84. Cohen suggests that the Court's dual holdings on applicable law were an attempt to stage a 'judicial coup' to clear the path to establish Portuguese law as the only body of law applicable law in the SPSC. See *ibid.*, pp. 84–85 (quotation at p. 85).

conventional international law binding in the territory at the time of the crime's commission.[612] Fourth, 'crimes against humanity in the form of genocide' does not exist in contemporary international law, is almost certainly unknown to Portuguese law, and its application surely violated *nullum crimen sine lege* despite the Court's professed respect for that principle. Finally, even if it could be said that such a crime was applicable in this case, as discussed in Chapter 3, neither customary international law nor the jurisprudence of any international or internationalised court or tribunal recognises genocide liability where the relevant actor intends to destroy a political group;[613] nor, apparently, does Portuguese law, judging from the very provision cited by the Court, which lists only the traditional grounds: national, ethnic, racial, and religious. Fortunately, the *dos Santos* holdings were immediately rejected by trial panels of the SPSC[614] despite their obligation to follow decisions of the Court of Appeal,[615] and the Court's ruling on applicable domestic law was later nullified by an act of the East Timor Parliament that Indonesian law applied in East Timor in 1999.[616]

612 See *Kordić and Čerkez* Appeal Judgement, *supra* note 95, paras. 43–46; see also Chapter 1, notes 18, 24–26 and accompanying text. As explained above, there are a number of aspects of the ICC formulation of the core categories of crimes, on which the UNTAET Regulation was based, that probably did not exist in the customary definition of crimes against humanity at the time of the Rome Statute's finalisation in July 1998. See *supra* text accompanying notes 499–501 (additional discriminatory grounds for persecution); 516–517 (apartheid and enforced disappearance as underlying offences). Neither Indonesia nor Portugal had ratified the Rome Statute by the time of the events in East Timor. See www.icc-cpi.int/asp/statesparties/country&id=79.html (Portugal ratified on 5 February 2002; Indonesia had not ratified as of 1 December 2007). It may therefore be difficult to conclude that these aspects of the definition in Section 5 of the UNTAET Regulation were binding on the territory of East Timor during the period of the Special Panels' temporal jurisdiction, 1 January to 25 October 1999. See UNTAET Regulation, *supra* note 589, Section 2.3. But see de Bertodano, *supra* note 594, p. 919:

> It may be that there is a valid argument that some of the more novel provisions of the Rome Statute did not reflect the state of customary international law in 1999. But in this case, which deals with murder as a crime against humanity, there can be no doubt that this was a pre-existing crime under customary international law.

See also *Prosecutor* v. *Rusdin Maubere*, Case No. 23/2003, Julgamento, 5 July 2004, pp. 14–15, 21–25, 27–28 (discussing, but ultimately acquitting the accused of, enforced disappearance as a crime against humanity because the facts failed to establish the elements of this underlying offence).

613 See Chapter 3, text accompanying notes 52–56 (rejection of political groups in Genocide Convention drafting); *ibid.*, text accompanying notes 326–329 (rejection in Rome Statute drafting).

614 See especially *Prosecutor* v. *João Sarmento and Domingos Mendonça*, Case No. 18a/2001, Decision on the Defense (Domingos Mendonça) Motion for the Court to Order the Public Prosecutor to Amend the Indictment, 24 July 2003, available at www.unotil.org/legal/court-decisions/CD-2001-18a.pdf., para. 27 (crimes against humanity formed part of custom in 1999 and a conviction for them does not violate *nullum crimen sine lege*); *ibid.*, para. 40 (Indonesian law is the applicable subsidiary law for the SPSC); *ibid.*, para. 47 (genocide is a separate crime from crimes against humanity, not an underlying offence thereof). See also de Bertodano, *supra* note 594, p. 922 (noting that other SPSC panels and the lower courts in East Timor simply ignored the mandate of the *dos Santos* Appeal Judgement). The Court of Appeal followed *dos Santos*'s holding on applicable law in at least two subsequent cases. See *Gonçalves Bere* Appeal Judgement, *supra* note 609, p. 9; *da Costa* Appeal Judgement, *supra* note 604, p. 7.

615 Regulation No. 2000/11, *supra* note 588, Section 2.3 ('Judges, notwithstanding their rank or grade within the hierarchy of courts have to respect all decisions made by the Court of Appeal.').

616 Cohen, *supra* note 593, p. 85 ('This made perfect sense … because virtually every Timorese lawyer and judge in the country had been educated in Indonesian law schools and knew nothing about Portuguese law.').

At the other end of the spectrum lies the relatively well-reasoned, but still far from perfect,[617] Trial Judgement in the *Los Palos* case.[618] The prosecution alleged that Joni Marques and nine other members of the pro-Indonesia militia 'Team Alfa' were responsible for murder, torture, deportation or forcible transfer, and persecution as crimes against humanity in respect of a number of alleged atrocities in Los Palos and other towns in East Timor's Lautem District in April and September 1999.[619] The Trial Panel's discussion of the general requirements of crimes against humanity largely follows the definition of these requirements as set forth in a number of early *ad hoc* judgements cited by the Panel.[620] Nonetheless, perhaps understandably given that *Los Palos* was rendered relatively early on in the life of the *ad hoc* Tribunals, the Panel also endorses certain propositions that have since been rejected by the ICTY and ICTR Appeals Chambers; these include the stated requirement that the widespread or systematic attack 'results from a state or *de facto* power by means of the policy of that entity',[621] and the notion that a combatant who has temporarily laid down arms can be the victim of a crime against humanity.[622] With respect to the charged underlying offences, the Panel expressly adopted the definition of their

617 See *Los Palos* Report, *supra* note 598, pp. 29–30 (discussing some of the judgement's shortcomings); see also 'Remarks of Nehal Bhuta', in Steven R. Ratner and James L. Bischoff (eds.), *International War Crimes Trials: Making a Difference?* (2004), pp. 125–132 (discussing a number of endemic problems that plagued the SPSC, and remarking that '[t]hese difficulties were perhaps reflected in the fact that, during the Los Palos case, not a single witness for the defense was actually called, and the judgment itself may have been compromised by the absence of transcripts and the relative paucity of reliance on international legal authority') (quotation at p. 129).

618 *Los Palos* Trial Judgement, *supra* note 591. This Trial Judgement is the first in which international crimes – as opposed to ordinary domestic crimes – were adjudicated at the SPSC. *Los Palos* Report, *supra* note 598, pp. 4, 32. No Appeal Judgement exists in *Los Palos*. The prosecution abandoned its grounds of appeal after the President of East Timor issued a partial pardon to some of the accused that had the effect of reducing their sentences, and the various accused failed to deposit their respective appeals before the deadline. See *Prosecutor* v. *Joni Marques, Manuel da Costa, João da Costa, Paulo da Costa, Amélio da Costa, Hilário da Silva, Gonsalo dos Santos, Alarico Fernandes, Mautersa Monis, and Gilberto Fernandes*, Case No. 18/2004, Acta de Audiência, 16 March 2005, p. 2.

619 See *Los Palos* Trial Judgement, *supra* note 591, paras. 15–40.

620 See, e.g., *ibid.*, paras. 640–641 (relying, *inter alia*, on *Kordić and Čerkez* Trial Judgement, *supra* note 75, paras. 185–187, for the holding that the 'perpetrator' must know his conduct occurs in the context of a widespread or systematic attack). See also *Prosecutor* v. *José Cardoso*, Case No. 04/2001, Judgement, 5 April 2003, para. 306 (endorsing the *Los Palos* Trial Panel's definition of the general requirements); *ibid.*, para. 451 (the court must be 'satisfied that the perpetrator knew there [was] an attack on the civilian population and that his acts comprise[d] part of that attack). The *Cardoso* Trial Judgement appears to be the second longest of the SPSC; *Los Palos* is the longest. Like *Los Palos*, *Cardoso* is relatively complete in its discussion of the law and the evidence, and is relatively well reasoned. See also *Prosecutor* v. *Inácio Oliveira, Gilberto Fernandes, and José da Costa*, Case No. 12a/2002, Judgement, 23 February 2004, p. 12 (underlying offence must be part of the widespread or systematic attack, and cannot come 'out of the blue').

621 *Los Palos* Trial Judgement, *supra* note 591, para. 639 (citing, *inter alia*, *Tadić* Trial Judgement, *supra* note 77, para. 655). See also *supra* text accompanying notes 180–181 (discussing *ad hoc* Appeals Chamber jurisprudence holding that there is no policy requirement); *supra* note 59 and accompanying text (discussing the policy requirement in the 1954 ILC Draft Code, and comparing the respective positions of the different international and internationalised tribunals on whether this is a requirement).

622 *Ibid.*, para. 638 (citing *Blaškić* Trial Judgement, *supra* note 90, para. 214). See also *supra* section 2.2.2.3.1 and note 120 and accompanying text (discussing *ad hoc* jurisprudence holding that combatants, even those who have laid down arms, cannot be the victims of crimes against humanity).

elements from the ICC Elements of Crimes,[623] and cites *ad hoc* jurisprudence as a supplemental source only in respect of murder.[624]

The Trial Panel relied on the findings of the UN International Commission of Inquiry to determine that it was 'beyond reasonable doubt that there was an extensive attack by pro-autonomy armed groups supported by Indonesian authorities targeting the civilian population in the area, namely those linked with political movements for the self-determination of East Timor'.[625] The Panel also found that an armed conflict existed in East Timor between pro-autonomy forces and pro-independence forces; that the crimes of the accused before it 'were closely related to the armed conflict';[626] and that the requirement that crimes against humanity be 'closely related' to an armed conflict was therefore satisfied.[627] This holding is certainly curious, and evinces the Panel's unfamiliarity with longstanding ICTY appellate jurisprudence clarifying that the armed conflict requirement is today unique to the ICTY and does not exist in custom.[628] It also suggests the Panel's unawareness that the armed conflict requirement was considered and expressly rejected by the drafters of the Rome Statute, upon which the analogous provision of the UNTAET Regulation was based.[629] Although the Panel cited no authority for the requirement, the language it uses betrays clear inspiration in ICTY jurisprudence on the armed conflict requirement.[630]

The *Los Palos* Trial Panel went on to find that 'all of the accused had awareness about the accomplishment of a widespread and systematic attack against the civilian population of East Timor'.[631] Each accused was found responsible for at least one of the crimes against humanity with which he was charged.[632] Joni Marques – seemingly the most highly ranked of the ten – was convicted on six of the seven counts in the indictment.[633] Although the Panel was generally unclear with respect to the forms of responsibility pursuant to which it found the various accused liable

[623] See *ibid.*, paras. 643–669 (taking the elements of murder, deportation or forcible transfer, torture, and persecution from the corresponding provisions of ICC Elements of Crimes, *supra* note 158).

[624] See *ibid.*, para. 643 (citing *Rutaganda* Trial Judgement, *supra* note 114, para. 80). See also *Prosecutor* v. *Agostinho Cloe, Agostinho Cab, Lazarus Fuli, and António Lelan*, Case No. 4/2003, Judgement, 16 November 2004, para. 15 (*mens rea* of murder may be fulfilled where perpetrator 'intended to cause grievous bodily harm with the knowledge that it was likely to cause death').

[625] *Los Palos* Trial Judgement, *supra* note 591, para. 685 (citing East Timor Commission of Inquiry Report, *supra* note 588, paras. 123–141). See also *Prosecutor* v. *Marcelino Soares*, Case No. 11/2003, Judgement, 11 December 2003, para. 15 (holding that the widespread or systematic attack may be country-wide, and need not be directed against the civilian population of a particular town).

[626] *Los Palos* Trial Judgement, *supra* note 591, paras. 680–682 (quotation at para. 682).

[627] See *ibid.*, para. 684.

[628] See, e.g., *Tadić* Jurisdiction Appeal Decision, *supra* note 55, paras. 141–142. For a more detailed discussion on the armed conflict requirement, including a comparison of the respective positions of the different international and internationalised courts and tribunals, see *supra* note 55.

[629] See *supra* text accompanying notes 479–482.

[630] See *supra* text accompanying note 55 and section 2.2.1.1 (discussing the ICTY's armed conflict requirement).

[631] *Los Palos* Trial Judgement, *supra* note 591, para. 690.

[632] *Ibid.*, paras. 1123–1132. [633] Ibid, para. 1123.

for each crime,[634] it appears to have found Marques responsible for ordering and physically committing the torture and murder of Evaristo Lopes, a supporter of the pro-independence guerrilla army Forças Armadas de Libertação de Timor-Leste (FALINTIL): Marques physically participated in the beating of Lopes with the intent to obtain information from him on FALINTIL's activities, and asked some of the questions himself;[635] he also ordered and 'engaged deliberately in' the killing of Lopes, knew and intended that death would result, and knew that both the murder and the torture were committed as 'part of a systematic attack against independence supporters'.[636] In addition, the Trial Panel found Marques responsible for 'deportation or forcible transfer' as a crime against humanity for ordering Team Alfa to forcibly remove civilians from the village of Leuro and its environs;[637] Marques knew that forced removal 'would occur in the sequence of events' and knew that the removal 'constituted part of a systematic attack against independence supporters'.[638] It also found Marques liable for persecution – presumably in the form of forcible transfer – for this incident, although it did not make explicit findings on the elements of this crime against humanity;[639] instead, the Panel seems simply to have presumed that Marques had the intent to discriminate against a political group – pro-independence supporters – and that the villagers or some of them were members of this group.[640] Finally, the Panel found Marques responsible for physically

634 See Boas, Bischoff, and Reid, *supra* note 100, pp. 134–135:

> [The *Los Palos* Panel's] conclusions show that it was satisfied that the accused were deeply involved and participated in the crimes charged – by their presence or encouragement, command of others, or actual physical commission – but the discussion of their roles in those crimes betrays a failure to distinguish between the elements of the substantive crime and the elements of one or more of the forms of responsibility.

635 See *Los Palos* Trial Judgement, *supra* note 591, paras. 707–710, 712–715. See also *supra* section 2.2.3.6 (elements of torture in *ad hoc* jurisprudence).

636 See *ibid*., paras. 714–719 (quotation at para. 718); see also *ibid*., para. 756 (finding Marques and three co-accused responsible under Sections 5.1(a) (murder) and Section 5.1(f) (torture) of the UNTAET Regulation). See also *supra* section 2.2.3.1 (elements of murder in *ad hoc* jurisprudence).

637 See *ibid*., paras. 796–798 (finding that the plan was devised by Indonesian military authorities and implemented by Team Alfa, under the command of Marques). In keeping with the ICC Elements of Crimes on which it based its definition of the elements of 'deportation or forcible transfer', the *Los Palos* Trial Panel did not differentiate between deportation and forcible transfer. See *supra* text accompanying notes 540–541 (discussing the lack of differentiation in the ICC Elements of Crimes). A subsequent SPSC Trial Panel adopted the distinction generally adhered to in the *ad hoc* Tribunals: '[D]eportation is the forced removal of people from one country to another, while [forcible] population transfer applies to compulsory movement of people from one area to another within the same state.' *Prosecutor* v. *Benjamin Sarmento and Romeiro Tilman*, Case No. 18/2001, Judgement, 16 July 2003, para. 127. See also *supra* section 2.2.3.4 (deportation in *ad hoc* jurisprudence); text accompanying notes 464–466 (forcible transfer in *ad hoc* jurisprudence).

638 See *Los Palos* Trial Judgement, *supra* note 591, paras. 800–802 (quotations at paras. 800 and 801).

639 See *ibid*., para. 843 (finding Marques and three co-accused responsible under Section 5.1(d) (deportation or forcible transfer) and Section 5.1(h) (persecution) of the UNTAET Regulation). The Panel did, however, find that Marques's co-accused 'knew that his conduct would result in the unlawful displacement of the villagers and deprivation of their fundamental rights.' *Ibid*., para. 816 (Paulo da Costa); *ibid*., para. 825 (same for Alarico Fernandes).

640 See generally *ibid*., paras. 782–802. See also *supra* text accompanying notes 2.2.3.8 (persecution in *ad hoc* jurisprudence).

committing or aiding and abetting the murders of several others[641] – including, notoriously, a group of nuns ambushed on the road to Lautem[642] – although it acquitted him of another murder because there was insufficient evidence linking him to the crime.[643] The Panel sentenced Marques to thirty-three years.[644]

2.3.2.3 The Extraordinary Chambers in the Courts of Cambodia (ECCC)

Article 5 of the Law on the Establishment of the Extraordinary Chambers in the Courts of Cambodia for the Prosecution of Crimes Committed During the Period of Democratic Kampuchea ('ECCC Law') sets forth crimes against humanity in terms nearly identical to those of the ICTR formulation,[645] adding that such crimes 'have no statute of limitations'.[646] Like the ECCC's provision on grave breaches, therefore, Article 5 follows the *ad hoc* formulation in its catalogue of underlying offences.[647]

641 See *ibid.*, para. 896 (Marques physically committed the murder of Alfredo Araújo); *ibid.*, para. 899 (Marques aided and abetted the murder of Kalistu Rodrigues by his presence and support at the scene of the crime); *ibid.*, para. 914 (finding Marques and a co-accused responsible under Section 5.1(a) of the UNTAET Regulation). See also Boas, Bischoff, and Reid, *supra* note 100, pp. 307–310 (discussing aiding and abetting by presence at the scene).

642 *Los Palos* Trial Judgement, *supra* note 591, paras. 924–927 (Marques ordered and physically committed several murders); *ibid.*, para. 977 (finding Marques and six co-accused responsible under Section 5.1(a) of the UNTAET Regulation).

643 *Ibid.*, paras. 871–874, 888, 1123 (Marques not responsible for ordering or physically committing the murder of pro-independence supporter Aléxio Oliveira).

644 *Ibid.*, para. 1123. This sentence was later reduced to twenty-five years. See *supra* note 618.

645 The ICTR's crimes against humanity provision is quoted in full at *supra* text accompanying note 81.

646 Law on the Establishment of the Extraordinary Chambers in the Courts of Cambodia for the Prosecution of Crimes Committed During the Period of Democratic Kampuchea, as amended on 27 October 2004, Doc. No. NS/RKM/1004/006, unofficial translation by the Council of Jurists and the Secretariat of the Task Force, revised on 26 August 2007 ('ECCC Law'), Art. 5, available at www.eccc.gov.kh/english/cabinet/law/4/KR_Law_as_amended_27_Oct_2004_Eng.pdf. The statement that crimes against humanity have no statute of limitations is interesting, considering that Cambodia has not yet ratified the 1968 convention abolishing such limitations for war crimes, genocide, and crimes against humanity. See Convention on Non-Applicability of Statutory Limitations, *supra* note 55, Art. 1. See also www.unhchr.ch/html/menu3/b/treaty6.htm (listing states parties to the Convention). The period '17 April 1975 to 6 January 1979' is also listed in Article 5's *chapeau*; this is the duration of the Khmer Rouge regime. See Report of the Group of Experts for Cambodia Established Pursuant to General Assembly Resolution 52/135, annexed to UN Doc. A/53/850, S/1999/231, 16 March 1999 ('Cambodia Group of Experts Report'), para. 149.

647 This formulation of Article 5 appeared in the original version of the ECCC Law promulgated in August 2001. See Doc. No. NS/RKM/0801/12, available at www.genocidewatch.org/CambodianTribunalLaw.htm. In June 2003, Cambodia and the United Nations entered into an agreement detailing several aspects of their cooperation, along with rules on the structure and jurisdiction of the Extraordinary Chambers. See Agreement Between the United Nations and the Royal Government of Cambodia Concerning the Prosecution Under Cambodian Law of Crimes Committed During the Period of Democratic Kampuchea, 17 March 2003 ('Agreement'), approved by General Assembly Resolution 57/2288 (2003), available at www.eccc.gov.kh/english/cabinet/agreement/5/Agreement_between_UN_and_RGC.pdf; see also www.eccc.gov.kh/english/cabinet/agreement/4/Instrument_of_Ratification_of_Agreement.pdf (Cambodian government's ratification of Agreement). The Agreement obligates Cambodia to implement its provisions through amendment to the ECCC Law including, presumably, through the deletion of inconsistent provisions in the original version of the Law. See Agreement, *supra*, Art. 2(2). It provides that the subject matter of the Chambers shall include, *inter alia*, crimes against humanity as defined in the Rome Statute of the ICC. *Ibid.*, Art. 9. The Cambodian Parliament passed the amended version of the ECCC Law in October 2004, but curiously did not amend any of the original articles setting forth international crimes. See ECCC Law, *supra* note 646, Arts. 4–8. Although the ECCC Law's provision on crimes against humanity fails to conform to that of the ICC in several respects, and would thus appear to be *ultra vires* the Agreement, cases appear to be proceeding on the basis of the October 2004 version of the Law without anyone setting off alarm bells. See, e.g., Report of the Secretary-General on the Khmer

It thus excludes from the list enforced disappearance, apartheid, and the sexual offences other than rape in Article 7(1)(g) of the Rome Statute.[648]

In contrast to the other internationalised tribunals, the ECCC's crimes against humanity provision reintroduces the jurisdictional restriction present in the *chapeau* of the ICTR Statute: the widespread or systematic attack must be 'directed against any civilian population, on national, political, ethnical, racial or religious grounds'.[649] Whatever the reasons for its inclusion,[650] this added requirement corresponds to the notion that the ECCC and the ICTR fall into a special category of international tribunals colloquially referred to as 'genocide tribunals',[651] as opposed to 'war crimes tribunals' such as the ICTY and the SCSL: the *raison d'être* of both the ECCC and the ICTR is to bring to justice persons suspected of involvement in government-sponsored[652] campaigns of persecution of certain minority groups.[653] While both Tribunals also have jurisdiction over a limited number of war crimes,[654] crimes committed in the course of armed conflict constitute a relatively small portion of

Rouge Trials, UN. Doc. A/59/432, 12 October 2004 (discussing the imminent ratification of amendments to the ECCC Law to bring it into conformity with the Agreement, but not acknowledging that even with the envisaged amendments the Law would still not be in full conformity).

648 See Ernestine E. Meijer, 'The Extraordinary Chambers in the Courts of Cambodia for Prosecuting Crimes Committed by the Khmer Rouge: Jurisdiction, Organization, and Procedure of an Internationalized National Tribunal', in Romano, Nollkaemper, and Kleffner (eds.), *supra* note 592, p. 213 (noting that the catalogue of underlying offences is 'somewhat more limited than' that of the ICC). See also *supra* note 65 (comparing the list of underlying offences in the 1996 ILC Draft Code with those of the international and internationalised courts and tribunals).

649 ECCC Law, *supra* note 646, Art. 5. See also Swart, *supra* note 592, p. 299 (calling the reproduction of the ICTR's jurisdictional requirement a 'drawback'). See also *supra* note 60 and accompanying text (comparing the respective positions of the different international and internationalised tribunals on whether there is a requirement of a discriminatory attack for crimes against humanity).

650 See *supra* note 60 (Schabas suggesting that the Statute's drafters may have included it because they believed it to be a requirement for all crimes against humanity).

651 See, e.g., BBC News, 'Senior Khmer Rouge Leader Charged', 19 September 2007, available at news.bbc.co.uk/2/hi/asia-pacific/7002053.stm (labelling the ECCC a 'special genocide tribunal'); 'Africa's Most Wanted', *The Economist*, 4 December 2003, available at www.economist.com/world/africa/displaystory.cfm?story_id=E1_NNGJNVD (labelling the ICTR a 'genocide tribunal'). See also 'How the Mighty are Falling', *The Economist*, 5 July 2007, available at www.economist.com/world/international/displaystory.cfm?story_id=9441341 (referring to the 'long-promised genocide trials of an expected dozen or so Khmer Rouge leaders'). As noted in Chapter 3, although the Extraordinary Chambers have jurisdiction over genocide, it is not expected that many accused will actually be charged with that crime; indeed, none of the accused in custody has been charged with genocide thus far. See Chapter 3, text accompanying notes 396–397; see also Chapter 6, section 6.2 (further discussing the notion that the ICTY and the SCSL are referred to as 'war crimes tribunals', and the ICTR and the ECCC as 'genocide tribunals', and concluding that only the ICTR truly deserves the label given to it).

652 However, while government sponsorship characterised the majority of the atrocities in Rwanda and Cambodia, and crimes against humanity in the ICC and the SICT must be committed as part of a state or organisational policy, government sponsorship is not an element of genocide or crimes against humanity under customary international law. See *supra* notes 59, 495–496, *infra* note 692, and accompanying text.

653 See Cambodia Group of Experts Report, *supra* note 646, para. 69:

> [T]he political viewpoint of the victims is included among the listed motives and this element appears to be satisfied regarding many acts of the regime. These include atrocities against the hundreds of thousands of people, if not more, regarded as political enemies by the regime. The acts against the Cham, Vietnamese and other minorities would [also] qualify as crimes against humanity …

654 See ICTR Statute, *supra* note 60, Art. 4; ECCC Law, *supra* note 646, Arts. 6–7.

the abuses of the respective reigns of terror.[655] For this reason, the Group of Experts for Cambodia recommended against reproducing the ICTY's jurisdictional requirement of a nexus to an armed conflict, arguing that it no longer formed part of the customary definition of crimes against humanity by the time the Khmer Rouge came to power: 'Were that nexus still required as of 1975, the vast majority of the Khmer Rouge's atrocities would not be crimes against humanity; historians have not linked the bulk of the atrocities of the Khmer Rouge to the armed conflicts in which it engaged[,] with Viet Nam or domestic rebels[.]'[656]

As discussed in Chapter 3, because most of the regime's crimes are thought to have been committed against disfavoured political and social groups, there will likely be few, if any, charges of genocide.[657] As Steven Ratner and Jason Abrams observe:

> A far greater scope of atrocities are subject to individual culpability as crimes against humanity than as genocide … Most importantly, the former includes atrocities against the hundreds of thousands of people, if not more, regarded as political enemies by the regime. As for the acts against the Cham, Buddhists, Chinese, and other minorities, they qualify as crimes against humanity even without proof that the Khmer Rouge intended to destroy them (the touchstone of genocide); and the sufficiency of political grounds as a basis for discrimination (to the extent any discriminatory intent is required at all) means that it is not necessary to prove that the Khmer Rouge acted against them based on their religion or ethnicity.[658]

It is thus likely that most of the litigation in the ECCC will centre around charges of crimes against humanity.[659]

Shortly after the judges of the Extraordinary Chambers agreed on a set of internal rules in June 2007,[660] the Co-Prosecutors issued a statement informing the public that they had filed before the Co-Investigating Judges a confidential submission identifying 'twenty-five distinct factual situations of murder, torture, forcible transfer, unlawful detention, forced labor and religious, political and ethnic persecution';[661] and

[655] See Cambodia Group of Experts Report, *supra* note 646, para. 72 (noting that atrocities committed in the course of warfare with other states – especially Vietnam – and with rebel groups 'constituted only a small portion of [the Khmer Rouge's] human rights abuses').

[656] Cambodia Group of Experts Report, *supra* note 646, para. 71. See also Ratner and Abrams, *supra* note 8, p. 288 ('A continued linkage to armed conflict would … insulate many Khmer Rouge acts from international culpability.').

[657] See Chapter 3, text accompanying notes 387–389; see also *ibid*., text accompanying notes 396–397 (no accused yet charged with genocide).

[658] Ratner and Abrams, *supra* note 8, p. 289.

[659] See Cambodia Group of Experts Report, *supra* note 646, para. 150 (noting that genocide and crimes against humanity, but '*especially crimes against humanity*, constituted the bulk of the Khmer Rouge terror') (emphasis added). There are also a number of Cambodian domestic crimes in the Law. See ECCC Law, *supra* note 646, Art. 3 new (setting forth homicide, torture, and religious persecution as defined in the 1956 Cambodian Penal Code, and extending the statute of limitations for these crimes for an extra thirty years). Interestingly, as of 1 December 2007, this thirty-year statute of limitations had already expired for any domestic crime committed in the first two and a half years of the Khmer Rouge's reign: April 1975 to April 1977.

[660] See Extraordinary Chambers in the Courts of Cambodia, Internal Rules, 12 June 2007, available at www.eccc.gov.kh/english/cabinet/files/irs/ECCC_IRs_English_2007_06_12.pdf; *Co-Prosecutors* v. *Kaing*, Investigation No. No. 001/18-07-2007, Order on Provisional Detention, 31 July 2007 ('*Kaing* July 2007 Order'), para. 20 (noting that the Rules entered into force on 22 June 2007).

[661] Extraordinary Chambers in the Courts of Cambodia, Statement of the Co-Prosecutors, 18 July 2007, p. 4.

naming 'five suspects who committed, aided, abetted and/or bore superior responsibility for' this conduct.[662] All five had been arrested by the end of November 2007.[663] The first was Kaing Guek Eav, alias 'Duch',[664] the notorious director of 'Security Prison S-21' from 1975 to 1979,[665] who had already been in the custody of Cambodian military authorities for eight years.[666] On 31 July 2007, the Co-Investigating Judges charged Duch with crimes against humanity for 'countless abuses ... allegedly committed against the civilian population' – including 'arbitrary detention, torture and other inhumane acts, [and] mass executions' – by persons under his authority.[667] The second was Nuon Chea, Pol Pot's second-in-command;[668] Nuon was taken into ECCC custody in September 2007 and charged with every underlying offence in Article 5 of the ECCC Law except rape.[669] The third and fourth suspects were Ieng Sary, the Khmer Rouge foreign minister, and his wife Ieng Thirith, the minister of social action; they were arrested in November 2007 and charged with various crimes against humanity.[670] The fifth was Khieu Samphan, the Khmer Rouge head of state; he was also arrested in November 2007 and charged with crimes against humanity.[671] It is hoped

662 *Ibid.*, p. 5.

663 See Seth Mydans, 'Cambodia Arrests Former Khmer Rouge Head of State', *New York Times*, 20 November 2007, available at www.nytimes.com/2007/11/20/world/asia/20cambo.html?_r=1&oref=slogin (stating that Khieu Samphan, who was arrested on 19 November 2007, was 'the last of five top figures targeted by prosecutors in advance of trials expected [in 2008] for the atrocities of the late 1970s').

664 Duch's name has also been spelled Kaing Khek Iev and Kang Kek Ieu.

665 See 'Better Late than Never', *The Economist*, 4 August 2007, p. 37 (noting that crimes against humanity charges had been brought, and that Duch is alleged to have run Tuol Sleng, 'the [Khmer Rouge] regime's interrogation and torture centre').

666 See BBC News, 'First Khmer Rouge Leader Charged', 31 July 2007, available at www.news.bbc.co.uk/2/hi/asia-pacific/6924371.stm.

667 See *Kaing* July 2007 Order, *supra* note 660, para. 1. See also *ibid.*, p. 2 (noting that the 'judicial investigation' opened against Duch 'charged [him] with Crimes against Humanity, crime(s) set out and punishable under articles 5, 29(new) and 39(new)' of the ECCC Law); *ibid.*, paras. 1–23 (analysing and rejecting the defence claim that Duch's prolonged detention deprived the Extraordinary Chambers of jurisdiction); *ibid.*, para. 23 (considering that 'there is a well-founded belief that' Duch 'committed the crimes with which he is charged' and ordering detention for a period not exceeding one year, but not discussing in detail the grounds for this 'well-founded belief' and not specifying which precise underlying offences of crimes against humanity are charged).

668 See BBC News, 'Senior Khmer Rouge Leader Charged', 19 September 2007, available at www.news.bbc.co.uk/2/hi/asia-pacific/7002053.stm.

669 *Co-Prosecutors* v. *Nuon*, Investigation No. 002/19-09-2007, Order on Provisional Detention, 19 September 2007, paras. 1, 5. Nuon is also charged with a number of grave breaches of the Geneva Conventions. See *ibid.*

670 See *Co-Prosecutors* v. *Ieng Sary*, Investigation No. 002/19–09–2007, Provisional Detention Order, 14 November 2007, para. 1 (charging Ieng Sary with instigating, ordering, aiding and abetting, and failing to prevent and punish murder, extermination, imprisonment, persecution, and other inhumane acts as crimes against humanity, as well as several grave breaches of the Geneva Conventions); *Co-Prosecutors* v. *Ieng Thirith*, Investigation No. 002/19–09–2007, Provisional Detention Order, 14 November 2007, para. 1 (charging Ieng Thirith with instigating, ordering, aiding and abetting, and failing to prevent and punish murder, extermination, imprisonment, persecution, and other inhumane acts). See also 'Khmer Rouge Couple Formally Detained', *New York Times*, 14 November 2007, available at www.nytimes.com/aponline/world/AP-Cambodia.html?pagewanted=print.

671 See *Co-Prosecutors* v. *Khieu*, Investigation No. 002/19-09-2007, Provisional Detention Order, 19 November 2007, paras. 1, 5 (charging Khieu with a number of crimes against humanity and grave breaches of the Geneva Conventions).

that the trial of these suspects will begin without undue delay, particularly given their advanced age.[672]

2.3.2.4 Supreme Iraqi Criminal Tribunal (SICT) (also known as the Iraqi High Tribunal (IHT))

Like its analogue in the UNTAET Regulation, Article 12 of the Statute of the Supreme Iraqi Criminal Tribunal[673] defines crimes against humanity in terms largely identical to those of the ICC formulation, although it features some curious additions and omissions.[674] In the list of underlying offences in Article 12(1), 'wilful murder' appears instead of 'murder', and enforced sterilisation and apartheid do not appear at all.[675] Moreover, the Rome Statute's connection requirement for persecution – which provides that persecution must be committed 'in connection with' another underlying offence of crimes against humanity or another crime in the ICC's jurisdiction[676] – has been replaced with a new connection requirement: persecution must be committed 'in connection with any act referred to as a form of sexual violence of comparable gravity'.[677] As M. Cherif Bassiouni and Michael Wahid Hanna point out, this rendering of the connection requirement was surely a drafting mistake, 'as the language appears to be incorrectly taken from the previous provision dealing with crimes of sexual violence'.[678] Persecution in the SICT Statute retains the ICC's additional discriminatory grounds of nationality, ethnicity, culture, and gender.[679] Furthermore, in the list of definitions in Article 12(2), the definition of apartheid has been omitted; so have the definitions of torture and forced pregnancy, even though both offences still appear in the list of underlying offences in Article 12(1).[680]

[672] Nuon and Ieng Sary are 82, Khieu is 76, Ieng Thirith is 75, and Duch is 64. Two of those thought to be most responsible for the regime's atrocities – Pol Pot and Ta Mok – have already died. Seth Mydans, 'Prosecutors Identify Suspects in Khmer Rouge Trial', *New York Times*, 18 July 2007, available at www.nytimes.com/2007/07/19/world/asia/19cambodia.html.

[673] Also known as the Iraqi High Tribunal (IHT). See Chapter 1, note 2 (discussing the different English translations of the Tribunal's name).

[674] See Law No. 10 (2005), Law of the Iraqi Higher Criminal Court, 18 October 2005 ('SICT Statute'), English translation available at www.law.case.edu/saddamtrial/documents/IST_statute_official_english.pdf, reprinted in Michael P. Scharf and Gregory S. McNeal (eds.), *Saddam on Trial: Understanding and Debating the Iraqi High Tribunal* (2006), pp. 283 *et seq.*, Art. 12.

[675] See *ibid.*, Art. 12(1)(A) (wilful murder); *ibid.*, Art. 12(1)(G) (sexual offences). See also *supra* note 65 (comparing the list of underlying offences in the 1996 ILC Draft Code with those of the international and internationalised courts and tribunals).

[676] Rome Statute, *supra* note 59, Art. 7(1)(h). See also *supra* text accompanying notes 505–507 (discussing the negotiations resulting in the inclusion of the connection requirement in the Rome Statute, and how the *ad hoc* Tribunals have no such requirement).

[677] See SICT Statute, *supra* note 674, Art. 12(1)(H).

[678] M. Cherif Bassiouni and Michael Wahid Hanna, 'Ceding the High Ground: The Iraqi High Criminal Court Statute and the Trial of Saddam Hussein', (2006–07) 39 *Case Western Reserve Journal of International Law* 21, 64.

[679] While 'gender' is listed as a discriminatory ground, the Rome Statute's unique definition of gender has been left out of the SICT Statute. See Rome Statute, *supra* note 59, Art. 7(3); see also *supra* note 499 (discussing this definition).

[680] See *ibid.*, Art. 12(2).

Another way in which the SICT opted to follow the ICC is the existence of a document setting forth the elements of the crimes within the Tribunal's jurisdiction.[681] The crimes against humanity provision in the SICT Elements of Crimes is largely a reproduction of its analogue in the ICC Elements, with two major differences: since apartheid and enforced sterilisation have been left out of the SICT's jurisdiction, the SICT Elements do not include elements for these offences; and the 'strict construction' proviso, discussed above with respect to the ICC Elements,[682] has been omitted.[683] Moreover, in contrast to the ICC Statute – which, as explained above, provides that the Elements 'shall assist the Court in the interpretation and application' of the crimes in the Statute[684] – there is no language in either the previous or current version of the SICT Statute describing the status of the SICT Elements. Nevertheless, the Trial Chamber in the Tribunal's first judgement, in the *Dujail* case, appears to have relied upon the SICT Elements to a large degree.[685]

In the *Dujail* case, Saddam Hussein and seven others were charged with crimes against humanity for their roles in the 1982 detention, torture, murder, and forced removal of hundreds of civilians from the predominantly Shiite town of Dujail, in retaliation for a failed assassination attempt on Hussein.[686] Hussein was charged with wilful murder, deportation or forcible transfer, imprisonment, torture, enforced

681 In an order appended to an earlier version of the SICT Statute from 2003, the administrator of the Coalition Provisional Authority delegated to the Iraqi Governing Council the authority to promulgate elements of crimes. Coalition Provisional Authority Order No. 48: Delegation of Authority Regarding an Iraqi Special Tribunal, 10 December 2003, Sections 1(4), 2 1), available at www.loc.gov/law/public/saddam/document/20031210_CPAORD_48_IST_and_Appendix_A.pdf.

682 See *supra* text accompanying notes 529–531.

683 See generally Iraqi Special Tribunal, Elements of Crimes ('SICT Elements of Crimes'), Section 3, available at www.law.case.edu/saddamtrial/documents/IST_Elements.pdf, reprinted in Scharf and McNeal (eds.), *supra* note 674, pp. 327 *et seq*. Beyond minor linguistic changes, the other main difference with the ICC Elements is the inclusion of elements for the three crimes under Iraqi national law set forth in Article 14 of the Statute: unlawful attempt to manipulate the judiciary; wasting of national resources or squandering of public assets; and misuse of official office to wage an aggressive war against an Arab state. See *ibid*., Section 5.

684 Rome Statute, *supra* note 59, Art. 9(1). See also *supra* text accompanying note 519.

685 Compare, e.g., Case No. 1/9 1st/2005, Judgment, 22 November 2006 ('*Dujail* Trial Judgement'), (English translation issued 4 December 2006), available at www.law.case.edu/saddamtrial/dujail/opinion.asp, Part III, pp. 28–29 (also available at (2006–07) 39 *Case Western Journal of International Law*, Appendix A), with SICT Elements of Crimes, *supra* note 683, Art. 12(a)(4), Elements (a) – (e) (judgement expounding elements for deportation as a crime against humanity probably taken from those in the corresponding provision of the SICT Elements, although not stating explicitly from where the elements were taken); *Dujail* Trial Judgement, *supra*, Part II, p. 8; *ibid*., Part III, p. 13, with SICT Elements of Crimes, *supra* note 683, Art. 12(a)(1), Elements (a) – (c) (same for murder as a crime against humanity); *Dujail* Trial Judgement, *supra*, Part III, p. 32 with SICT Elements of Crimes, *supra* note 683, Art. 12(a)(5), Elements (a)–(e) (same for imprisonment as a crime against humanity, although incorrectly referring to Article 12(1)(H) of the Statute as the provision on imprisonment). The incongruities between the language used in the judgement and that used in the SICT Elements is probably a result of the poor English translation of the latter. It should also be noted that the numeration of the paragraphs and subparagraphs in the SICT Elements correspond with that of the 2003 version of the Statute, and not the operative 2005 version.

686 Michael P. Scharf and Gregory S. McNeal, 'What Are the Specific Charges Against Saddam Hussein?', in Scharf and McNeal (eds.), *supra* note 674, pp. 58–59.

disappearance, and other inhumane acts as crimes against humanity.[687] No accused was charged with genocide or war crimes.

Although the poor English translation of the *Dujail* Trial Judgement makes parts of it almost unintelligible,[688] the Trial Chamber clearly relied to some degree on ICTY case law. It invoked the *Krnojelac* Trial Judgement for its exposition of the law on the five general requirements of crimes against humanity,[689] and for several principles related to these requirements, such as the following: an 'attack' for purposes of crimes against humanity need not be a military attack;[690] and the victims of a crime against humanity must be civilians, but the attack need only be directed against a group of persons predominantly composed of civilians.[691] The Trial Chamber appears to have parted ways with ICTY jurisprudence, however, in at least one significant respect: by the terms of the SICT Statute, the attack on a civilian population must be 'pursuant to or in furtherance of a State or organizational policy to commit such attack'.[692] As noted above, the Chamber generally followed the SICT Elements of Crimes in its exposition of the elements of the charged underlying offences.[693]

The Trial Chamber found that, beginning on 8 July 1982 and over the course of several months, the 'former governing authority' perpetrated a 'systematic wide

[687] See *Saddam Hussein*, Case No. 1/1st Criminal/2005, Accusation Document, 15 May 2006. Two co-accused were also charged with these crimes. See *Barzan Ibrahim Al-Hasan*, Case No. 1/1st Criminal/2005, Accusation Document, 15 May 2006; *Taha Yasin Ramadan*, Case No. 1/1st Criminal/2005, Accusation Document, 15 May 2006. Four others were charged with these crimes, with the exception of deportation or forcible transfer. See *Mizhar Abdullah Ruwayyid*, Case No. 1/1st Criminal/2005, Accusation Document, 15 May 2006; *Ali Dayih Ali*, Case No. 1/1st Criminal/2005, Accusation Document, 15 May 2006; *Mohammed Azawi Ali*, Case No. 1/1st Criminal/2005, Accusation Document, 15 May 2006; *Abdullah Kazim Ruwayyid*, Case No. 1/1st Criminal/2005, Accusation Document, 15 May 2006. One accused was charged only with wilful murder. See *Awad al-Bandar*, Case No. 1/1st Criminal/2005, Accusation Document, 15 May 2006. The *Dujail* indictments are available at www.law.case.edu/saddamtrial/content.asp?t=1&id=9, and are reprinted in Scharf and McNeal (eds.), *supra* note 674, pp. 63–66, 266–282.

[688] For (mostly negative) academic appraisal of the *Dujail* proceedings and Judgement, see especially Michael P. Scharf, 'The Iraqi High Tribunal: A Viable Experiment in International Justice?', (2007) 5 *Journal of International Criminal Justice* 258; Miranda Sissons and Ari S. Bassin, 'Was the Dujail Trial Fair?', (2005) 5 *Journal of International Criminal Justice* 272; Jeremy Peterson, 'Unpacking Show Trials: Situating the Trial of Saddam Hussein', (2007) 48 *Harvard Journal of International Law* 257; Michael P. Scharf, 'Foreword: Lessons from the Saddam Trial', (2006–07) 39 *Case Western Journal of International Law* 1; Bassiouni and Hanna, *supra* note 678. Volume 39 of the *Case Western Journal of International Law* contains several other articles relating to the SICT and the *Dujail* case.

[689] *Dujail* Trial Judgement, *supra* note 685, Part II, pp. 9–10 (relying on *Krnojelac* Trial Judgement, *supra* note 111, para. 53).

[690] *Ibid.*, Part I, p. 14; *ibid.*, Part II, p. 10 (relying on *Krnojelac* Trial Judgement, *supra* note 111, para. 54). See also *supra* note 110 and accompanying text (*ad hoc* jurisprudence on this principle).

[691] *Ibid.*, Part II, p. 10 (relying on *Krnojelac* Trial Judgement, *supra* note 111, para. 56). See also *supra* section 2.2.2.3.1 (*ad hoc* jurisprudence on this principle).

[692] *Ibid.*, Part II, p. 10. See also *supra* text accompanying notes 493–495 (ICC requires policy; *ad hoc* Tribunals do not); notes 532–534 (ICC requires policy); notes 559–560 (SCSL does not require policy); note 621 (SPSC requires policy); *supra* note 59 and accompanying text (discussing the policy requirement in the 1954 ILC Draft Code, and comparing the respective positions of the different international and internationalised tribunals on whether this is a requirement).

[693] See *supra* note 685 and accompanying text. See also *ibid.*, Part III, p. 35 (elements of torture); *ibid.*, Part III, p. 42 (elements of enforced disappearance); *ibid.*, Part III, pp. 43–44 (elements of 'other inhumane acts').

range attack' against the civilian population of Dujail.[694] According to the Chamber, the evidence showed that some 543 persons had been 'imprisoned or killed or displaced'.[695] Specifically with respect to Hussein, the Chamber found that his 'behaviour' – apparently consisting mainly of issuing orders to forcibly remove and detain civilians, approving death sentences handed down by a sham court, and acquiescing in, encouraging, and failing to punish the many atrocities – formed part of the widespread and systematic attack,[696] and that Hussein knew his behaviour formed part of the attack.[697] The Chamber went on to determine that the elements of wilful murder had been established with respect to the 148 persons sentenced to death, as well as many others who died while being tortured in Abu Ghraib and other detention centres.[698] The Chamber's findings seem to indicate that Hussein knew of the murders and shared the intent to kill;[699] that he issued orders to carry out some of the murders;[700] that he participated in a common purpose to commit the murders;[701] and that he had effective control over the perpetrators but made no attempt to punish them.[702] It found Hussein responsible for participating in a common purpose to commit murder, ordering murder, and failing to prevent or punish murder as a superior.[703]

The Trial Chamber performed a similar analysis with respect to the other crimes against humanity with which Hussein was charged,[704] imposing liability for all of them except enforced disappearance.[705] It also convicted six of the other accused of

[694] See *ibid.*, Part II, p. 29; see also *ibid.*, Part III, p. 16. [695] *Ibid.*, Part I, p. 17. [696] See *ibid.*, Part III, p. 17.

[697] *Ibid.*, Part III, pp. 18, 20. See also *ibid.*, Part III, pp. 9–11 (discussing evidence of Hussein's knowledge). As discussed above, in the *ad hoc* jurisprudence it is the behaviour of the physical perpetrator, and not that of the accused, that must form part of the attack. See *supra* section 2.2.2.5 and text accompanying note 108.

[698] See *ibid.*, Part III, pp. 14–15. [699] See *ibid.*, Part III, pp. 15–19. [700] See *ibid.*, Part III, pp. 14, 16–18, 21.

[701] See *ibid.*, Part III, pp. 23–24. [702] See *ibid.*, Part III, pp. 25–27.

[703] See *ibid.*, Part III, p. 28. As discussed in Volume I of this series, the *Dujail* Chamber's findings on how the various accused fulfilled the elements of a given form of responsibility are often troubling, placing inappropriate emphasis on the transgressions of the regime in general, and the positions of the accused in that regime, rather than their precise and particular conduct with regard to the crimes charged. See Boas, Bischoff, and Reid, *supra* note 100, pp. 138–140, 273–274. See also Sissons and Bassin, *supra* note 688, p. 284 ('While evidence on the crime base was strong, there was insufficient evidence to show that many of the accused had the requisite criminal intent or knowledge about the crimes committed.').

[704] See *Dujail* Trial Judgement, *supra* note 685, Part III, pp. 28–32; *ibid.*, Part III, pp. 32–35 (imprisonment); *ibid.*, Part III, pp. 35–41 (torture); *ibid.*, Part III, pp. 43–46 ('other inhumane acts'). The Chamber's findings with respect to 'other inhumane acts' as a crime against humanity deserve brief mention. The Chamber determined that the destruction of Dujail residents' gardens and homes, as well as the confiscation of their property, qualified as inhumane acts, and that Hussein bore responsibility for them. See *ibid.*, Part III, pp. 43–46. This holding is curious in light of the Chamber's own acknowledgement that, to qualify as an inhumane act under the SICT Elements of Crimes, the act must be of a character similar to the other underlying offences of crimes against humanity, and it must cause 'great suffering, or serious injury to body or to mental or to physical health' to the victim. See SICT Elements of Crimes, *supra* note 683, Art. 12(a)(10), Elements (a) – (b). Beyond the single suggestion that these property offences caused 'extreme suffering' to the victims, *Dujail* Trial Judgement, *supra* note 685, Part III, p. 44, the Chamber failed to explain how the offences fulfil these two elements, which also appear in *ad hoc* jurisprudence. See *supra* section 2.2.3.9.1. It may be, then, that Hussein's conviction for these offences violated *nullum crimen sine lege*.

[705] See *Dujail* Trial Judgement, *supra* note 685, Part III, p. 43 (holding that there was insufficient evidence to fulfil certain elements of enforced disappearance).

most of the crimes charged against them, and sentenced Hussein and two co-accused to death.[706] The convictions and death sentences were upheld in a perfunctory Appeal Judgement,[707] and Hussein went to the gallows on 30 December 2006.[708]

The second trial before the SICT began in September 2006 and concerned alleged massacres and forced removals of perhaps 200,000 Kurds in the so-called 'Anfal'[709] campaign carried out by Hussein's regime in 1988.[710] After all charges against Hussein were dropped following his death,[711] the highest-ranking remaining accused was Ali Hassan al-Majid – also known as 'Chemical Ali' – the Secretary General of the Northern Bureau of the Ba'ath Party at the time of the campaign.[712] Perhaps as a result of waning interest in the Tribunal's work in the wake of Hussein's death,[713] as of 1 December 2007 the charging instruments and judgement in the *Anfal* case had not been made publicly available in English, although the Prosecutor's closing argument was available. That argument suggests that the five accused were charged with ordering, inciting, aiding and abetting, and failing as superiors to prevent and punish genocide, various war crimes, and several crimes against humanity, including wilful murder, extermination, deportation or forcible transfer, imprisonment, torture, rape, persecution, and enforced disappearance.[714]

[706] See *ibid.*, Part VI, pp. 51–52; see also *ibid.*, Part VI, p. 53 (acquitting Mohammed Azawi Ali).

[707] See generally *Public Prosecutor* v. *Hussein et al.*, Case No. 29/c/2006, Judgement of the Appeals Commission of the Iraqi High Tribunal dated 26 December 2006 (unofficial English translation), available at www.law.case.edu/saddamtrial/documents/20070103_dujail_appellate_chamber_opinion.pdf, *also* available at (2006–07) 39 *Case Western Reserve University Journal of International Law*, Appendix B.

[708] BBC News, 'Saddam Hussein Executed in Iraq', 30 December 2006, at www.news.bbc.co.uk/2/hi/middle_east/6218485.stm.

[709] 'Al Anfal' means 'spoils of war'. *The Holy Qur-ān: English Translation of the Meanings and Commentary* (1984), p. 467 (Sura 8:1).

[710] See Mark A. Drumbl, 'The Significance of the Anfal Campaign Indictment', in Scharf and McNeal (eds.), *supra* note 674, pp. 224–225 (discussing the history of the Anfal campaign, along with prospects and anticipated difficulties in prosecuting the crimes before the SICT); Scharf and McNeal, *supra* note 686, p. 59.

[711] BBC News, 'Timeline: Anfal Trial', at www.news.bbc.co.uk/2/hi/middle_east/5272224.stm. None of the Dujail accused other than Hussein was also charged in the *Anfal* case. The *ad hoc* Tribunals have also taken the view that, where an accused dies before judgement is rendered, he cannot be tried posthumously and the proceedings must be terminated with respect to him. See, e.g., *Prosecutor* v. *Milošević*, Case No. IT-02-54-T, Order Terminating the Proceedings, 14 March 2006, p. 1 (ICTY Trial Chamber noting the death of the accused and ordering that 'all proceedings in this trial' be terminated); *Prosecutor* v. *Dokmanović*, Case No. IT-95-13a, Order Terminating Proceedings Against Slavko Dokmanović, 15 July 1998, p. 1 (same); see also Decision Terminating *Lukwiya* Proceedings, *supra* note 545, p. 4 (same for ICC).

[712] See 'Prosecutorial Closing Argument in the Anfal Case', available at www.iraq-iht.org/en/doc/ppb.pdf (date unknown, on file with authors), pp. 2–3, 7. The SICT Prosecutor described Majid as 'the one who is most responsible for the acts committed by the military and civilian officials in the North Organizing Office [that is, the North Bureau]', and asserted that he 'was directly responsible for issuing orders to all the military and civilian people who carried out the Anfal campaigns against the Kurdish people'. *Ibid.*, p. 7.

[713] See John F. Burns, 'Hussein's Cousin Sentenced to Die for Kurd Attacks', *New York Times*, 25 June 2007, available at www.select.nytimes.com/search/restricted/article?res=F20E10F8355B0C768EDDAF0894DF404482 (noting that 'Iraqi public interest in the [SICT's] trials has flagged'; that few Iraqi and no Kurdish reporters attended the hearing at which the judges handed down the *Anfal* verdict; and that 'only a handful of Western reporters' were in attendance).

[714] 'Prosecutorial Closing Argument in the Anfal Case', *supra* note 712, pp. 12–15 (discussing the elements of these offences in terms seemingly inspired by the SICT Elements of Crimes, *supra* note 683, and discussing some of the evidence that purportedly fulfilled such elements).

The Prosecutor described the Anfal campaign as consisting of 'widespread and organized attacks' deliberately targeting Kurdish civilians in some 4,000 villages in northern Iraq.[715] According to the Prosecutor, five of the six accused 'knew that their behaviour and their orders were part of the widespread attacks against the civilian population, due to the scope, the systematic nature, the role of each of them in the action against the victims … the maintaining of constant communication between them, and their presence at the scene of the crime.'[716] The Tribunal convicted five of the six on 23 June 2007.[717] Media reports indicate that Majid was convicted of genocide, war crimes, and crimes against humanity, while the other four were convicted only of war crimes and crimes against humanity; Majid and two others were sentenced to death.[718] Other trials before the SICT are apparently being prepared or are underway.[719]

[715] See *ibid.*, pp. 7, 20 (quotation at p. 7).

[716] *Ibid.*, p. 11. The Prosecutor requested that the charges against the sixth accused – Tahir Tawfiq al-Ani – be dropped for lack of evidence linking him to the atrocities. *Ibid.*, p. 24.

[717] See, e.g., Burns, *supra* note 713; BBC News, '"Chemical Ali" Sentenced to Hang', 24 June 2007, at www.news.bbc.co.uk/2/hi/middle_east/6233926.stm.

[718] Majid, Sultan Hashim Ahmed al-Jabouri, and Hussein Rashid al-Tikriti (also known as Hussayn Rashid Muhammad) received death sentences. Farhan Motlak al-Jibouri and Sabir Abdul Aziz Al-Duri received sentences of life imprisonment. At the Prosecutor's request, Tahir Tawfiq al-Ani was acquitted for lack of evidence. Burns, *supra* note 713. The appeals court upheld the Tribunal's convictions. See Damien Cave, 'Death Sentence Upheld for Hussein Henchman', *New York Times*, 4 September 2007, available at www.nytimes.com/2007/09/05/world/middleeast/05iraq.html?_r=1&oref=slogin. As of 30 November 2007, none of the death sentences had been carried out, notwithstanding an Iraqi law requiring that they be carried out within thirty days of being upheld on appeal. The delay is due to discussions concerning whether Sultan Hashim Ahmed's death sentence might somehow be commuted. See Damien Cave, 'Iraq Seeks to Execute 3 Former Officials', *New York Times*, 30 November 2007, available at www.nytimes.com/2007/12/01/world/middleeast/01iraq.html?_r=1&oref=slogin.

[719] See Burns, *supra* note 713; Cave, *supra* note 718.

3

Genocide

Since its first codification in the 1948 Genocide Convention, the international crime of genocide has been almost uniformly defined as the intended destruction, in whole or in part, of a national, ethnic, racial, or religious group, as such, by one of six enumerated means.[1] Article II of the Convention lists these six means in five subparagraphs, and Article III sets forth a number of associated 'punishable acts':

Article II
In the present Convention, genocide means any of the following acts committed with intent to destroy, in whole or in part, a national, ethnical, racial or religious group, as such:

(a) Killing members of the group;
(b) Causing serious bodily or mental harm to members of the group;
(c) Deliberately inflicting on the group conditions of life calculated to bring about its physical destruction in whole or in part;
(d) Imposing measures intended to prevent births within the group;
(e) Forcibly transferring children of the group to another group.

Article III
The following acts shall be punishable:

(a) Genocide;
(b) Conspiracy to commit genocide;

[1] Although Article II contains only five subparagraphs, the *ad hoc* jurisprudence has determined that causing serious bodily harm and causing serious mental harm in subparagraph (b) are two separate underlying offences. See *infra* text accompanying note 208.

(c) Direct and public incitement to commit genocide;
(d) Attempt to commit genocide;
(e) Complicity in genocide.[2]

All subsequent formulations of the crime in the statutes of international and internationalised tribunals – including those of the *ad hoc* Tribunals, the International Criminal Court (ICC), the East Timor Special Panels for Serious Crimes (SPSC), the Extraordinary Chambers in the Courts of Cambodia (ECCC), and the Supreme Iraqi Criminal Tribunal (SICT)[3] – essentially replicate the language of Article II.[4]

An important characteristic of genocide is the targeting of a victim not as an individual or for any reason peculiar to him personally, but because he is a member of a national, ethnic, racial, or religious group.[5] The targeting of the individual, therefore, forms just one part of a much larger offence: the targeting for destruction of the victim group, in whole or in part. The authoritative definition of genocide in Article II of the Genocide Convention incorporates this 'group destruction' element by requiring specific intent or *dolus specialis*. In the *Akayesu* case, the first *ad hoc* trial chamber to define specific intent characterised it generally as the 'specific intention, required as a constitutive element of the crime, which demands that the perpetrator clearly seeks to produce the act charged'.[6] Genocide is not the only specific intent crime in the jurisdiction of modern international criminal tribunals; for example, persecution as a crime against humanity also requires a discriminatory intent to be established.[7] However, it is the *nature* of the specific intent in genocide – the intent to destroy a protected group – that most distinguishes it from other international crimes, such as murder and extermination as crimes against humanity.[8]

[2] See Convention on the Prevention and Punishment of the Crime of Genocide, 9 December 1948, entered into force 12 January 1951, 78 UNTS 277 ('Genocide Convention'), Arts. II–III.

[3] Also known as the Iraqi High Tribunal (IHT). See Chapter 1, note 2 (discussing the different English translations of the Tribunal's name).

[4] See *infra* section 3.2 for a detailed discussion of the elements of the crime of genocide; section 3.6 for a detailed discussion of genocide in the ICC and the internationalised tribunals.

[5] This distinction of the crime of genocide as hierarchically more significant than other crimes, including crimes against humanity, is broadly acknowledged in case law and literature, whether explicitly or in referring to it as a crime that stands apart. See, e.g., *Prosecutor* v. *Kambanda*, Case No. ICTR-97-23-S, Judgement and Sentence, 4 September 1998 ('*Kambanda* Trial Judgement'), para. 16; Robert Cryer, Håkan Friman, Darryl Robinson, and Elizabeth Wilmshurst, *An Introduction to International Criminal Law and Procedure* (2007), pp. 165–168; John Quigley, *The Genocide Convention: An International Law Analysis* (2006), ch. 1.

[6] *Prosecutor* v. *Akayesu*, Case No. ICTR-96-4-T, Judgement, 2 September 1998 ('*Akayesu* Trial Judgement'), para. 498. On the nature of the specific intent required to establish the crime of genocide, the ICJ has also contributed. See *Legality of the Threat or Use of Nuclear Weapons* (Advisory Opinion), (1996) ICJ Rep. 226, para. 26; *Application of the Convention on the Prevention and Punishment of the Crime of Genocide* (Merits) (Bosnia and Herzegovina v. Serbia and Montenegro), 26 February 2007 ('*Bosnia* v. *Serbia* Judgement on Merits'), available at www.icj-cij.org/docket/files/91/13685.pdf (not yet published in the ICJ Reports), paras. 70–71.

[7] See Chapter 2, section 2.2.3.8.1, for a discussion of the specific intent required for persecution as a crime against humanity.

[8] For a discussion of the general distinction between genocide and murder, extermination, and other crimes, see, e.g., Quigley, *supra* note 5, pp. 11–14.

Some chambers of the *ad hoc* Tribunals have labelled genocide the 'crime of crimes' – apparently placing it at the top of a hierarchy of international crimes.[9] The point is well made by Guénaël Mettraux: 'In the mind of the lay person, or even in the minds of lawyers, genocide remains the ultimate crime which alone can express the true gravity of a particular kind of criminal conduct'.[10] Yet this conclusion requires some nuance in reasoning given the reluctance of the *ad hoc* Tribunals' Appeals Chambers to enunciate a hierarchy of crimes; and the fact that genocide can be effected through the commission of various underlying offences, some of which may seem less horrific than other international crimes.

Despite some chambers' labelling of genocide as the crime of crimes,[11] the *ad hoc* Appeals Chambers, in consecutive decisions, have stated that there is in law no distinction between the seriousness of different crimes under their jurisdiction. This point has been made in respect of crimes against humanity and war crimes in the *Tadić*[12] and *Kunurac*[13] cases, and is cited with approval in an important dissenting opinion concerning cumulative convictions in the *Čelebići* case.[14] There are also similar rulings specifically comparing genocide with other crimes within the Statutes of the International Criminal Tribunal for the former Yugoslavia (ICTY) and the International Criminal Tribunal for Rwanda (ICTR). For example, in a recent ruling of the ICTY in the *Trbić* case, in which genocide in and around Srebrenica was charged along with several other crimes, the Referral Bench held:

> The gravity of the crimes cannot be assessed only, or even primarily, by reference to their legal description under Articles 2 to 5 of the Statute. This is true even for the crimes of genocide and conspiracy to commit genocide: the Tribunal has repeatedly held that no inherent hierarchy exists among the crimes over which the Tribunal has jurisdiction; a Chamber must instead look to the underlying conduct allegedly constituting a given crime, as well as the surrounding circumstances, to determine its gravity.[15]

[9] See, e.g., *Prosecutor* v. *Niyitegeka*, Case No. ICTR-96-14-A, Judgement, 9 July 2004 ('*Niyitegeka* Appeal Judgement'), para. 53; *Prosecutor* v. *Krstić*, Case No. IT-98-33-A, Judgement, 19 April 2004 ('*Krstić* Appeal Judgement'), Partial Dissenting Opinion of Judge Shahabuddeen, para. 95; *Prosecutor* v. *Jelisić*, IT-95-10-A, Judgement, 14 December 1999 ('*Jelisić* Appeal Judgement'), Partial Dissenting Opinion of Judge Wald, para. 2; *Prosecutor* v. *Stakić*, Case No. IT-97-24-T, Judgement, 31 July 2003 ('*Stakić* Trial Judgement'), para. 502; *Prosecutor* v. *Musema*, Case No. ICTR-96-13-T, Judgement and Sentence, 27 January 2000 ('*Musema* Trial Judgement'), para. 981; *Prosecutor* v. *Rutaganda*, Case No. ICTR-96-3-T, Judgement and Sentence, 6 December 1999 ('*Rutaganda* Trial Judgement'), para. 451; *Kambanda* Trial Judgement, *supra* note 5, para. 16.

[10] Guénaël Mettraux, *International Crimes and the Ad Hoc Tribunals* (2005), p. 316.

[11] See *supra* note 9.

[12] *Prosecutor* v. *Tadić*, Case No. IT-94-1-A and IT-94-1-A*bis*, Judgement in Sentencing Appeals, 26 January 2000, para. 69.

[13] *Prosecutor* v. *Kunarac, Kovač, and Vuković*, Case No. IT-96-23 and IT-96-23/1-A, Judgement, 12 June 2002, para. 171 (citing *Tadić* with approval).

[14] *Prosecutor* v. *Delalić, Mucić, Delić, and Landžo*, Case No. IT-96-21-A, Judgement, 20 February 2001, Separate and Dissenting Opinion of Judge David Hunt and Judge Mohammed Bennouna, para. 41. Cumulative convictions are discussed in Chapter 5 of this volume.

[15] *Prosecutor* v. *Trbić*, Case No. IT-05-88/1-PT, Decision on Referral of Case Under Rule 11 *bis* with Confidential Annex, 27 April 2007 ('*Trbić* Referral Decision'), para. 19 (footnotes omitted). Accord *Rutaganda* v. *Prosecutor*, Case No. ICTR-96-3-A, Judgement, 26 May 2003, para. 590:

The Bench proceeded to refer the case for trial in Bosnia and Herzegovina, on the grounds that, while the crimes charged in the indictment were 'among the gravest ever charged at [the ICTY],'[16] Milorad Trbić's role and degree of authority were not so high as to mandate trial at the Tribunal.[17] The notion that there is no hierarchy of crimes challenges the expression by other chambers that genocide is the ultimate international crime.[18]

The crucial aspect of the crime of genocide is the specific intention of the accused[19] to destroy an identified human group. It is this idea, crystallised by historical examples such as the Holocaust and the Armenian genocide[20] – that at the heart of the crime of genocide is the obliteration of a human group, its eradication from existence and perhaps human memory – that suggests its particular opprobriousness in the regime of international criminal law. It is important to acknowledge, however, that there are different means by which a genocidal intention can give rise to criminality. Article II of the Genocide Convention (and its analogues in the Statutes of international and internationalised criminal courts and tribunals) provides for the destruction of a group by means other than murder, including the causing of serious bodily and mental harm to members of a group, and prevention of births within and the transfer of children from a protected group. Article III of the Convention and its analogues also criminalise different forms of contribution to the commission of genocide – including unsuccessful attempts to commit the crime. Without detracting from the gravity and significance of the crime of genocide committed by any means proscribed by convention or custom, there are examples of massive-scale crimes against humanity – Pol Pot's reign of terror in Cambodia and recent events in Darfur are but the best known – that could conceivably rival the sheer scale and horror of acts that might technically qualify as acts of genocide.[21]

> The Trial Chamber … found that the crime of genocide constitutes the 'crime of crimes' … The Appeals Chamber recalls that there is no hierarchy of crimes under the Statute, and that all the crimes specified therein are serious violations of international humanitarian law. In the instant case, an analysis of the Trial Chamber's conclusions reveals that the key features of its finding on the seriousness of the offence are based on considerations of the Appellant's conduct and on the fact that genocide is inherently an extremely serious crime. The Appeals Chamber considers such an observation correct in the context of this case.

16 *Trbić* Referral Decision, *supra* note 15, para. 21.

17 *Ibid*., paras. 23, 49. See also *ibid*., para. 19 n. 76 (citing cases holding that genocide is the crime of crimes, and cases holding that there is no hierarchy).

18 See *supra* note 9; see also Chapter 5, section 5.3.2 (discussing gravity of crimes in the context of sentencing).

19 The question of who among the potentially large pool of relevant actors involved in the commission of genocide must have the genocidal intent is complicated and is closely tied to the form of responsibility under analysis. This question is discussed below in section 3.2.1.1. Because it is most often the accused, and not the physical perpetrator when these two are separate individuals, whose genocidal intent is under examination, and for the sake of convenience, we used term 'accused' in this introductory section when referring to the element of genocidal intent.

20 For the Nazi Holocaust, see generally, Raphaël Lemkin, *Axis Rule in Occupied Europe* (1944); for Armenia, see generally Howard Ball, *Prosecuting War Crimes and Genocide* (1999).

21 See, e.g., Report of the International Commission of Inquiry on Darfur to the United Nations Secretary-General Pursuant to Security Council Resolution 1564 of 18 September 2004, 25 January 2005 ('Darfur Commission Report'), para. 514 (determining that the intent of the attackers was not to destroy an ethnic group as such but to murder all those men they considered as rebels, and stating that 'the Government of Sudan has not pursued a policy of genocide' because genocidal intent appears to be absent) (quotation at para. 520). See also Beth van Schaack, 'Darfur and the Rhetoric of Genocide', (2005) 26 *Whittier Law Review* 1101; William A. Schabas, 'Problems of International

Whatever the position taken by the *ad hoc* Tribunals, there is little doubt that genocide is overwhelmingly viewed by the international community as the crime of ultimate evil, such that it was (in the context of international norm-setting) developed, refined, and codified with meteoric speed following the Second World War, and was confirmed with similar speed as a norm of customary international law and *jus cogens*.[22] It is, by dint of the special nature of the intent required to give rise to this crime, one that strikes at the very heart of the preservation of humanity and human existence. Genocide *is* appropriately branded the crime of crimes, and stands at the pinnacle of the hierarchy of international crimes.

This chapter focuses on the definition and other important characteristics of the crime of genocide. It begins by tracing the historical evolution of genocide, focusing on its development following the Second World War and codification in the 1948 Genocide Convention, and touching on the sparse examples of domestic trials, the important work of the International Law Commission (ILC), and recent case law regarding state responsibility for genocide before the International Court of Justice (ICJ). The historic *Akayesu* Trial Judgement before the ICTR resulted in the first conviction of an individual for this crime by an international criminal tribunal; it was issued fifty years after the conclusion of the Genocide Convention and marked the beginning of a jurisprudential revolution in the interpretation and application of genocide before the ICTR and ICTY. Section 3.2 considers the extensive corpus of this jurisprudence. After discussing the physical and mental elements that render a given act or omission genocide, the chapter picks up where Chapter 4 of the first volume in this series left off. There, we concluded that three of the so-called 'punishable acts' associated with genocide in the *ad hoc* Statutes are not forms of responsibility: conspiracy to commit genocide, direct and public incitement to commit genocide, and attempt to commit genocide are instead crimes in their own right.[23] Sections 3.3 to 3.5 examine the elements of these inchoate crimes.[24] Finally,

Codification: Were the Atrocities in Cambodia and Kosovo Genocide?', (2001) 35 *New England Law Review* 287. The possibility of genocide charges for Darfur in the ICC is discussed at text accompanying notes 369–374 *infra*; the possibility of genocide charges for the Khmer Rouge atrocities in the ECCC is discussed at 386–389, 394–397 *infra*.

22 See *infra* text accompanying notes 42–79.

23 See Gideon Boas, James L. Bischoff, and Natalie L. Reid, *Forms of Responsibility in International Criminal Law* (2007), p. 290.

24 In addition to the three genocide-related inchoate crimes, there would appear to be one additional inchoate crime in the ICTR Statute, and one more has been recognised by the ICTY's case law interpreting Article 3 of that Tribunal's Statute. In the ICTR Statute, paragraphs (a) to (g) of Article 4 enumerate a number of war crimes over which that Tribunal has jurisdiction. Article 4(h) makes '[t]hreats to commit any of the foregoing acts' also punishable. Statute of the International Criminal Tribunal for Rwanda, (1994) 33 ILM 1602, as amended by Security Council Resolution 1534 of 26 March 2004 ('ICTR Statute'), Art. 4(h). For the ICTY jurisprudence on terror as a violation of the laws or customs of war, see Chapter 4, section 4.2.2.9.

The Rome Statute of the ICC also appears to have inchoate war crimes, including 'declaring that no quarter be given'. See Rome Statute of the International Criminal Court, 17 July 1998, entered into force 1 July 2002, UN Doc. A/CONF. 183/9 (1998) ('Rome Statute'), Art. 8(2)(b) (xii); *ibid.*, Art. 8(2)(e)(x); see also Michael Cottier, 'Quarter', in Otto Triffterer (ed.), *Commentary on the Rome Statute of the International Criminal Court* (1999), p. 227 ('[T]here is no need that persons *hors de combat* were actually killed by forces acting in furtherance of the declaration, order or threat[.]').

Section 3.6 reviews the treatment of genocide in other international and internationalised tribunals, in particular the ICC, the SPSC, the ECCC, and the SICT.

3.1 Evolution of genocide as an international crime

3.1.1 Development through the Second World War

The early laws regulating the conduct of armed conflict focused on criminalisation of acts committed against those placed *hors de combat* (for example, medical personnel or combatants who had laid down arms).[25] Although some protection was given to the civilian population of an occupied territory, the development of detailed laws prohibiting certain conduct against civilians followed the Second World War with Geneva Convention IV of 1949 – which deals with the protection of civilians during armed conflict – and subsequent codifications and jurisprudential developments.[26]

It was the extermination of a civilian population by its own government before and during the Second World War that ultimately inspired the criminalisation of this previously unsanctioned area of international law. Of course, the Nazi Holocaust was hardly the first time a 'genocide' had been committed by a government against its own (as well as other) people.[27] As William Schabas has explained:

> [A]s a general rule, genocide involves violent crimes against the person, including murder. Because these crimes have been deemed anti-social since time immemorial, in a sense there is nothing new in the prosecution of genocide to the extent that it overlaps with the crimes of homicide and assault. Yet genocide almost invariably escaped prosecution because it was virtually always committed at the behest of and with the complicity of those in power.[28]

While the Holocaust of Jews and Gypsies committed by the Nazis before and during the Second World War is the most infamous occurrence – and that which sparked the development of codified and customary law relating to this crime – there are many

[25] See, e.g., Convention for the Amelioration of the Condition of the Wounded in Armies in the Field, 22 August 1864, entered into force 22 June 1865, 18 *Martens Nouveau Recueil* (ser. 1) 607, 129 Consol. T.S. 361; Hague Convention (II) with Respect to the Laws and Customs of War on Land and Its Annex: Regulations Concerning the Laws and Customs of War on Land, 22 July 1899, entered into force 4 September 1900, 26 *Martens Nouveau Recueil* (ser. 2) 949, 187 Consol. T.S. 429; Hague Convention (IV) Respecting the Laws and Customs of War on Land and Its Annex: Regulation Concerning the Laws and Customs of War on Land, entered into force 26 January 1910, 3 *Martens Nouveau Recueil* (ser. 3) 461, 187 Consol. T.S. 227.

[26] See, e.g., Geneva Convention IV Relative to the Protection of Civilian Persons in Time of War, 12 August 1949, entered into force 21 October 1950, 75 UNTS 287; Protocol I Additional to the Geneva Conventions of 12 August 1949, and Relating to the Protection of Victims of International Armed Conflicts, 8 June 1977, entered into force 7 December 1978, 1125 UNTS 3; Protocol II Additional to the Geneva Conventions of 12 August 1949, and Relating to the Protection of Victims of Non-International Armed Conflicts, 8 June 1977, entered into force 7 December 1978, 1125 UNTS 609.

[27] Jean-Paul Sartre wrote: 'The fact of genocide is as old as humanity itself'. William A. Schabas, *Genocide in International Law* (2000), p. 1 (quoting Sartre).

[28] *Ibid.*, pp. 14–15.

other examples of events in modern history that might be said to constitute genocide, including the extermination of Tasmanian Aboriginals in Australia in the nineteenth century, the forced removal and extermination of American Indians in the United States, and the German extermination of the Herero in Namibia in 1904.[29] Moreover, a mere quarter of a century before the Second World War, the Ottoman leadership slaughtered over one million Armenian Christians with a highly bureaucratic and centralised programme of deportations and executions much like that of the Nazi regime, without any effective international legal response.[30]

Genocide was first conceived by the scholar Raphaël Lemkin in his 1944 book *Axis Rule in Occupied Europe*. He used the term to describe the Nazi plan to exterminate identified groups, including the Jews and Gypsies, and laid the foundation for a definition of what would become the gravest of international crimes.[31] Lemkin wrote that '[n]ew conceptions require new terms'.[32] The word itself is a neologism formed from the Greek word *genos* (meaning tribe, race, or nation) and the Latin suffix *cide* (meaning killing).[33] Within just four years of this first usage of the word 'genocide', the legal concept of genocide had manifested itself in the form of the Genocide Convention, a development described below.[34]

Following the Second World War, the Allied countries prosecuted Hermann Göring and other major Nazi leaders at Nuremberg under the Charter of the International Military Tribunal (IMT) for war crimes, crimes against humanity, and crimes against peace.[35] The IMT Charter made no explicit mention of the then-nascent legal concept of genocide. However, the conduct which the developing crime of genocide would concern was well understood, and the IMT indictment in fact charged the accused with 'deliberate and systematic genocide, viz., the extermination of racial and national groups, against the civilian populations of certain occupied territories in order to destroy particular races and classes of people, and national, racial or religious groups, particularly Jews, Poles, and Gypsies'.[36] The term 'genocide' was employed in closing speeches by the French and British prosecutors, and the Tribunal itself described the Nazis' 'plan to get rid of whole

[29] See Ball, *supra* note 20, p. 26.

[30] *Ibid.*, pp. 26, 28–30. See also Vahakn N. Dadrian, *History of the Armenian Genocide: Ethnic Conflict from the Balkans to Anatolia to the Caucasians* (1997); Richard G. Havannisian (ed.), *The Armenian Genocide: History, Politics, Ethics* (1991).

[31] See Lemkin, *supra* note 20, p. 79. For a discussion of the place of genocide in the hierarchy of international crimes, see *supra* text accompanying notes 9–22; Chapter 5, section 5.3.2.

[32] Lemkin, *supra* note 20, p. 79.

[33] *Ibid.* See also Leo Kuper, *The Prevention of Genocide* (1985), p. 9.

[34] See *infra* text accompanying notes 47–68.

[35] Agreement for the Prosecution and Punishment of Major War Criminals of the European Axis, and Establishing the Charter of the International Military Tribunal, Annex, 8 August 1945, 82 UNTS 279, Art. 6(c).

[36] International Military Tribunal Indictment No. 1, in *Trial of Major War Criminals Before the International Military Tribunal, Nuremberg, 14 November 1945–1 October 1946* (1947), vol. II, pp. 45–46.

native populations by expulsion and annihilation', terminology that is now distinctly recognisable as descriptive of genocide.[37]

Following the trial at Nuremberg, the Allied Powers created a number of tribunals, pursuant to Control Council Law No. 10, for the prosecution of lesser German officials.[38] Genocide was discussed in some of these subsequent trials, particularly by the US military tribunals ('subsequent Nuremberg tribunals').[39] The US military tribunal in the *Justice* case, for example, relied upon General Assembly Resolution 96 (I) (discussed below)[40] to support the proposition that genocide as a crime existed under international law; even though genocide was not one of the listed crimes in Control Council Law No. 10, the *Justice* Tribunal entered convictions for crimes against humanity using language very much descriptive of the crime of genocide.[41]

3.1.2 Post-Second World War development

Frenetic legal activity seeking to define and codify genocide followed soon after the IMT Judgement. On 11 December 1946, a few months into the first year of the United Nations' existence, the General Assembly issued one of the more significant resolutions in its history: Resolution 96(I), on 'The Crime of Genocide'.[42] While the Resolution's definition of genocide differed in significant ways from that which would ultimately be agreed upon in the Genocide Convention,[43] it persuasively

[37] *France, Union of Soviet Socialist Republics, United Kingdom, and United States* v. *Göring, Bormann, Dönitz, Frank, Frick, Fritzsche, Funk, Hess, Jodl, Kaltenbrunner, Keitel, von Bohlen und Halbach, Ley, von Neurath, von Papen, Raeder, von Ribbentrop, Rosenberg, Sauckel, Schacht, von Schirach, Seyss-Inquart, Speer, and Streicher, International Military Tribunal, Judgment and Sentence*, 1 October 1946, in *Trial of the Major War Criminals Before the International Military Tribunal, Nuremberg*, vol. XXII, p. 480. See also Schabas, *supra* note 27, p. 38.

[38] Control Council Law No. 10, Punishment of Persons Guilty of War Crimes, Crimes Against Peace and Against Humanity, *Trials of War Criminals Before the Nuernberg Military Tribunals Under Control Council Law No. 10*, (1950), vol. I, pp. xvi–xix. Control Council Law No 10 was issued by the Allied Control Council on 20 December 1945, and empowered any of the occupying authorities to try suspected war criminals in their respective occupation zones. See also Control Council Law No. 10, in *Official Gazette of the Control Council for Germany*, vol. 3 (1946). For a discussion of the subsequent Nuremberg tribunals and their jurisprudence, see Boas, Bischoff, and Reid, *supra* note 23, pp. 153–157, 162–167, 171–172.

[39] See, e.g., *United States* v. *Greifelt, Creutz, Meyer-Hetling, Schwarzenberger, Huebner, Lorenz, Brueckner, Hofmann, Hildebrandt, Schwalm, Sollmann, Ebner, Tesch, and Viermetz*, U.S. Military Tribunal, Judgement, 10 March 1948, in *Law Reports of Trials of War Criminals* (1948) ('*RuSHA* Judgement'), vol. 12, p. 2; *United States* v. *Ohlendorf, Jost, Naumann, Rasch, Schulz, Six, Blobel, Blume, Sandberger, Seibert, Steimle, Biberstein, Braune, Hänsch, Nosske, Ott, Strauch, Haussmann, Klingelhöfer, Fendler, von Radetzky, Rühl, Schubert, and Graf*, in *Trials of War Criminals Before the Nuernberg Military Tribunals Under Control Council Law No. 10* (1950) ('*Einsatzgruppen* Judgement'), vol. 4, pp. 165–167; *United States* v. *Altstötter, von Ammon, Barnickel, Cuhorst, Engert, Joel, Klemm, Lautz, Mettgenbert, Nebelung, Oeschey, Petersen, Rothaug, Rothenberger, Schlegelberger, and Westphal, Trials of War Criminals Before the Nuernberg Military Tribunals Under Control Council Law No. 10* (1953) ('*Justice* Judgement'), vol. 3, pp. 979, 1128, 1156. See also Raphaël Lemkin, 'Genocide as a Crime in International Law', (1947) 41 *American Journal of International Law* 145.

[40] See *infra* text accompanying notes 42–46, 52. [41] See *Justice* Judgement, *supra* note 39, p. 1156.

[42] General Assembly Resolution 96(I), UN Doc. A/RES/96(I) (1946).

[43] For example, it contradicted the terms of the subsequent Genocide Convention in respect of the inclusion of political groups in the definition of genocide. See *infra* text accompanying notes 52–56.

confirmed genocide as a distinct crime under international law for which individuals and officials may be held responsible;[44] it affirmed the absence of any nexus requirement between genocide and the existence of an armed conflict, an assumption that may well have been made in light of the IMT's treatment of crimes against humanity;[45] and, by confirming the existence of the crime of genocide under international law, it provided that perpetrators could be prosecuted even without a breach of the domestic law in force at the time of the crime.[46]

Resolution 96(I) served as the basis for the Genocide Convention, which was adopted on 9 December 1948 and entered into force relatively quickly thereafter, on 12 January 1951. The Convention gave the term 'genocide' something it had technically lacked in proceedings before the IMT and the subsequent Nuremberg tribunals: international legal significance.[47] Yet despite states' near universal desire to establish an international framework defining the crime and setting forth the consequences for its commission, the preparatory work and negotiations for the Convention revealed some issues of profound discordance in the international community's perception of the contours of the crime, some of which persist today.

One of the major issues debated was the nature of the victim groups to be protected. Lemkin himself had envisioned genocide as extending to the 'disintegration of the political and social institutions, of culture, language, national feelings, religion, and the economic existence of groups'.[48] The UN Secretary-General's draft of 1947[49] and the 1948 draft of the UN Economic and Social Council (ECOSOC)[50] both included references to prohibiting the use of a national language, systematic destruction of books in the national language of the group, and the destruction of historical or religious monuments; these activities amounted to a notion of 'cultural genocide'. Interestingly, although the Convention in its adopted form left such references to social or cultural destruction out of the definition and focused instead on physical or biological destruction, the ICTY Trial Chamber in *Krstić* would, over fifty years later, revive the idea that acts targeting cultural and religious property and symbols have at least evidentiary value in establishing the genocidal intent of the accused.[51]

44 In this respect, it is noteworthy that the U.S. Military Tribunal in the *Justice* case found the Resolution persuasive evidence of the fact that genocide was a crime punishable at the time of the Nazi Holocaust. See *Justice* Judgement, *supra* note 39, pp. 41–43.

45 See Chapter 2, text accompanying notes 32–43.

46 For a detailed discussion of these issues, see Schabas, *supra* note 27, pp. 46–47. See also Quigley, *supra* note 5, p. 7.

47 For a discussion of the drafting of the Genocide Convention, see, e.g., Nehemiah Robinson, *The Genocide Convention: A Commentary* (1960); Pieter N. Drost, *Genocide: United Nations Legislation on International Criminal Law* (1959); Schabas, *supra* note 27, ch. 2; Quigley *supra* note 5.

48 Lemkin, *supra* note 20, p. 79.

49 See Draft Convention on the Crime of Genocide, UN Doc. E/447 (1947), Art. II(3).

50 Report of the *ad hoc* Committee on Genocide, UN ESCOR, 7th Sess., UN Doc. E/794 (1948), *ad hoc* Committee Draft, Art. III.

51 See *Prosecutor* v. *Krstić*, Case No. IT-98-33-T, Judgement, 2 August 2001 ('*Krstić* Trial Judgement'), para. 580. For a detailed discussion of the elements of the crime of genocide, see *infra* section 3.2. This holding of the *Krstić* Trial Chamber is discussed at notes 148–149.

Pre-Convention deliberations also focused on one of the perpetual points of debate over the scope of genocide: whether 'political' groups should be subject to protection. Political groups were listed in both Resolution 96(I) and the ECOSOC draft, only to be removed by the Sixth Committee of the Convention's drafting conference.[52] Lemkin had expressed the view that a group could be defined on the basis of political view, but some delegates viewed the reference to political groups as too variable, impermanent, and incoherent.[53] Despite the suggestion of the ICTR Trial Chamber in *Akayesu* that the crime of genocide applies to *any* 'stable and permanent group',[54] along with some scholarly suggestion that customary international law may have brought other groups within the scope of protection – particularly political groups[55] – the sounder legal view appears to be that the groups enumerated in the Convention are exhaustive, and that customary international law has not altered that position, at least not yet.[56]

Debate surrounding the underlying offences of genocide articulated in Article II of the Convention tended to reveal the particular concerns of delegates with respect to conduct by the Axis Powers during the Second World War, and possibly the treatment of the Christian-Armenian minority by the Ottoman government during the First World War. For example, a defeated Chinese proposal concerning the causing of serious mental harm (Article II(b)) made explicit reference to the use of narcotic drugs by Japan during the Second World War.[57] Reference to the deliberate

[52] Schabas, *supra* note 27, p. 73.

[53] See Quigley, *supra* note 5, p. 10; Schabas, *supra* note 27, pp. 106–114.

[54] *Akayesu* Trial Judgement, *supra* note 6, para. 516. See also Steven R. Ratner and Jason S. Abrams, *Accountability for Human Rights Atrocities in International Law: Beyond the Nuremberg Legacy* (2nd edn 2001), p. 42 (calling this part of *Akayesu* 'a surprising piece of dictum', and concluding that that state practice does not support the *Akayesu* Trial Chamber's assertion). This view is not supported in any other case law, see *infra* text accompanying notes 192–205, and is not consistent with the clear decision taken by delegates in the debates leading up to the adoption of the Convention. See Schabas, *supra* note 27, pp. 153–154.

[55] See Matthew Lippman, 'Genocide', in M. Cherif Bassiouni, *International Criminal Law: Crimes* (1999), p. 603; Beth van Schaack, 'The Crime of Political Genocide: Repairing the Genocide Convention's Blind Spot', (1997) 106 *Yale Journal of International Law* 2259; Lawrence J. LeBlanc, 'The United Nations Genocide Convention and Political Groups: Should the United States Propose an Amendment?', (1988) 13 *Yale Journal of International Law* 268, 288–290.

[56] See Schabas, *supra* note 27, pp. 119–120; Cryer, Friman, Robinson, and Wilmshurst, *supra* note 5, pp. 169–170. See also the clear line of authority of the *ad hoc* Tribunals, discussed in detail at text accompanying note 177, *infra*. Fifty years on, the states parties negotiating the Rome Statute of the ICC also considered and rejected proposals for the inclusion of political groups in the definition of genocide for the jurisdiction of the ICC. See *infra* text accompanying note 326. It is also interesting to note that Lemkin himself, in the UN Secretary-General's commentary on the draft Genocide Convention, expressed the view that political groups should be omitted from the Convention on the basis that they lacked permanency. See Draft Convention on the Crime of Genocide, *supra* note 49, p. 17.

[57] See Schabas, *supra* note 27, pp. 159–160. Nehemiah Robinson clearly picks up on the Chinese proposal as indicative of the use of narcotics being the only form of mental harm contemplated. See Robinson, *supra* note 47, p. ix. Schabas has rejected this interpretation. See Schabas, *supra* note 27, p. 161. The treatment of it in the *ad hoc* jurisprudence also refutes the assertion. See, e.g., *Akayesu* Trial Judgement, *supra* note 6, paras. 732–734 (holding that sexual violence can amount to genocide at a mental and physical level).

infliction of conditions of life calculated to bring about the group's destruction (Article II(c)) appeared to be traceable to some of the techniques used against the Armenians.[58]

Nevertheless, the drafting of Article II appears not to have been as difficult as that of Article III, which sets the framework for the types of conduct that give rise to genocidal responsibility. Differences between the treatment of these activities in common law and civil law traditions made for complexity and disagreement as to their meaning and application.[59] So did the inclusion in that Article of inchoate offences that threatened to clash with developing human rights principles; for example, the notion of a crime of incitement to commit genocide was perceived by some to have a negative impact on the notion of freedom of speech.[60] As will be seen below in the discussion concerning the elements of genocide as interpreted and applied by the *ad hoc* Tribunals, and the application and modification of these provisions in the instruments of the ICC and the internationalised criminal tribunals, these issues have continued to present great complexities in the interpretation of this crime.

An aspect of the Genocide Convention that has attracted surprisingly little literary interest is the evolution of its use as an instrument primarily of individual criminal responsibility to one encapsulating the responsibility of states and governments for their role in the commission of genocide. The Convention was always intended to empower and oblige states to prevent or punish individual offenders, or to make arrangements to extradite them for trial elsewhere.[61] During drafting, however, the United Kingdom argued strongly that the Convention should be, first and foremost, an instrument of accountability for the state's role in the commission of genocide, and be less focused on the criminal culpability of individuals.[62] The United Kingdom almost succeeded in including a draft article referring to the culpability of states and referral to the ICJ, but its proposal was defeated because it appeared to confuse the idea of states' civil responsibility with that of criminal responsibility, which attaches to individuals and not states and state entities.[63] This debate and the vote, however, emphasised the idea that states may be responsible for genocide and held liable for civil damages, a proposition clearly reflected in Article IX of the

[58] See Schabas, *supra* note 27, pp. 167–169; see also *ibid.*, ch. 4 (detailed discussion of the drafting of Article II).

[59] For a detailed discussion of the debates leading up to the adoption of the terms of Article III of the Convention, see *ibid.*, ch. 6.

[60] *Ibid.*, pp. 72–73.

[61] See Genocide Convention, *supra* note 2, Art. I ('The Contracting Parties confirm that genocide, whether committed in time of peace or in time of war, is a crime under international law which they undertake to prevent and to punish.'); *ibid.*, Art. VII ('Genocide and the other acts enumerated in article III shall not be considered as political crimes for the purpose of extradition. The Contracting Parties pledge themselves in such cases to grant extradition in accordance with their laws and treaties in force.'). See also Schabas, *supra* note 27, pp. 71–81.

[62] See Schabas, *supra* note 27, pp. 76, 418–424 (discussing the debates).

[63] See *ibid.*, pp. 421–422.

Convention.[64] As Schabas puts it: 'The statements and the vote [concerning the United Kingdom proposal] indicate widespread opposition to any concept of State responsibility in a criminal law sense but an equally widespread support for State civil liability'.[65] While there has been some interest in and discussion of the idea of states' *criminal* responsibility their role in the commission of genocide,[66] an approach that is more consistent with accepted principles of international law has concerned the idea of 'aggravated' state responsibility for serious breaches by a state of a peremptory norm of international law.[67] Interestingly, it took many years before state responsibility for the commission of genocide was raised in litigation before the ICJ. Recent litigation and, particularly, a recent Court ruling concerning the former Yugoslavia, have entrenched the idea of some form of *civil* accountability for states that play a role in the commission of genocide.[68]

While the status of the crime of genocide may have been uncertain immediately following the Second World War and during the drafting of the Genocide Convention, the ICJ's famous Advisory Opinion on reservations to the Convention soon thereafter took the bold step of declaring that 'the principles underlying the Convention are principles which are recognised by civilized nations as binding on States, even without any conventional obligations'.[69] In his report on the creation of the ICTY some forty years later, the UN Secretary-General invoked this passage to support his view that the substantive principles laid down by the Convention amounted to customary law[70] – a view the Security Council endorsed by virtue of its adoption of the Report in Resolution 827 of 1993, which created the ICTY.[71] The Supreme Court of Israel also adhered to the notion that the Convention's definition of genocide had by

[64] Genocide Convention, *supra* note 2, Art. IX ('Disputes between the Contracting Parties relating to the interpretation, application or fulfilment of the present Convention, including those relating to the responsibility of a State for genocide or for any of the other acts enumerated in article III, shall be submitted to the International Court of Justice at the request of any of the parties to the dispute.').

[65] Schabas, *supra* note 27, pp. 420–421.

[66] See, e.g., Nina Jørgensen, *The Responsibility of States for International Crimes* (2000); Pierre-Marie Dupuy, 'International Criminal Responsibility of the Individual and International Responsibility of the State', in Antonio Cassese, Paola Gaeta, and John R. W. D. Jones (eds.), *The Rome Statute of the International Criminal Court: A Commentary* (2002), vol. I, pp. 1085–1100; Marina Spinedi, 'State Responsibility v. Individual Responsibility for International Crimes: *Tertium Non Datu*', (2002) 13 *European Journal of International Law* 895; Shabtai Rosenne, 'War Crimes and State Responsibility', (1995) 24 *Israel Yearbook on Human Rights* 63; Otto Triffterer, 'Prosecution of States for Crimes of State', (1996) 67 *Revue Internationale de Droit Penal* 341.

[67] See, e.g., André Nollkaemper, 'Concurrence Between Individual Responsibility and State Responsibility in International Law', (2003) 52 *International and Comparative Law Quarterly* 615; Marko Milanović, 'State Responsibility for Genocide' (2006) 17 *European Journal of International Law* 553.

[68] See *infra* text accompanying notes 88–90.

[69] Reservations to the Convention on the Prevention and Punishment of the Crime of Genocide, Advisory Opinion ('*Reservations* Opinion'), (1951) ICJ Rep. 15, 23. For further discussion, see Ratner and Abrams, *supra* note 54, pp. 41–42.

[70] Report of the Secretary-General Pursuant to Paragraph 2 of Security Council Resolution 808 (1993), UN Doc. S/25704 (1993), para. 45.

[71] Security Council Resolution 827, UN Doc. S/RES/827 (1993), para. 1.

1961 become customary international law,[72] and this position was later adopted by the Federal High Court of Germany in the *Jorgić* case in 1999.[73] That the Genocide Convention's definition of the crime constitutes custom is today well entrenched in the extensive case law of the *ad hoc* Tribunals,[74] and is reinforced by the widespread ratification of the Convention.[75]

More significantly, the prohibition against genocide is by now widely considered a *jus cogens* norm. Judge Elihu Lauterpacht has stated that 'genocide has long been regarded as one of the few undoubted examples of *jus cogens*'.[76] Such norms sit at the top of the hierarchy of international law sources and cannot therefore be derogated from by states, either by international agreement or national legislative action.[77] All crimes prohibited under *jus cogens* norms have been said to entail universal jurisdiction; courts and international law scholars have overwhelmingly accepted this position both as a general proposition, and particularly in respect of genocide.[78] The prohibition of genocide also constitutes an obligation *erga omnes* binding on all states in their dealings with the international community, whether with other states or with individuals.[79]

Somewhat paradoxically, despite genocide's rapid induction into the realm of customary international law, *jus cogens*, and obligations *erga omnes* thanks largely to ICJ *dicta*, there was strikingly little substantive development or actual application of the norm by courts in the nearly half century between the conclusion of the Genocide Convention and the creation of the *ad hoc* Tribunals.[80] As Schabas

[72] *Attorney-General of the Government of Israel* v. *Eichmann*, Supreme Court, 12 December 1961 ('*Eichmann* Judgement'), (1961) 36 ILR 5, 296–297.

[73] *Jorgić*, Bundesgerichtshof, Case No. 3 StR 215/98, 30 April 1999, para. 16, cited in Antonio Cassese, *International Criminal* Law (2003), p. 168.

[74] See *infra* note 99 and sources cited therein.

[75] To date, 140 states have ratified the Convention. See http://www.ohchr.org/english/countries/ratification11.htm.

[76] Application of the Convention on the Prevention and Punishment of the Crime of Genocide (*Bosnia and Herzegovina* v. *Yugoslavia*), (1993) ICJ Rep. 325, Separate Opinion of Judge *ad hoc* Elihu Lauterpacht, p. 440.

[77] See Michael Akehurst, 'The Hierarchy of the Sources of International Law', (1974–75) 47 *British Yearbook of International Law* 273; Malcolm N. Shaw, *International Law* (5th edn 2003), pp. 115–119.

[78] Lemkin himself had asserted, probably overly optimistically, that this was the case in 1947, although the fact that a reference to universal jurisdiction was expressly left out of the Convention makes his claim highly unlikely. See Lemkin, *supra* note 39, p. 146. However, genocide has certainly been considered for some years now as entailing universal jurisdiction. See, e.g., Ian Brownlie, *Principles of Public International Law* (5th edn 1998), p. 515; M. Cherif Bassiouni, 'International Crimes: *Jus Cogens* and *Obligatio Erga Omnes*', (1996) 59 *Law and Contemporary Problems* 63; Cassese, *supra* note 73, p. 98; Schabas, *supra* note 27, pp. 444 *et seq.*; Christopher C. Joyner, 'Arresting Impunity: The Case for Universal Jurisdiction in Bringing War Criminals to Accountability', (1996) 59 *Law and Contemporary Problems* 153. See also Case Concerning the Application of the Convention on the Prevention and Punishment of the Crime of Genocide (Preliminary Objections) (*Bosnia-Herzegovina* v. *Yugoslavia*) ('*Bosnia* v. *Yugoslavia* Preliminary Objections Judgement'), (1996) ICJ Rep. 565, para. 31; see also *Eichmann* Judgement, *supra* note 72, para. 15; *In the Matter of the Extradition of John Demjanjuk*, 612 F. Supp. 544, 558 (N.D. Ohio 1985); *Prosecutor* v. *Furundžija*, Case No. IT-95-17/1-T, Judgement, 10 December 1998, para. 156.

[79] *Reservations* Opinion, *supra* note 69, p. 23. See also *Bosnia* v. *Yugoslavia* Preliminary Objections Judgement, *supra* note 78, para. 31; Barcelona Traction, Light and Power Co., Ltd. (*Belgium* v. *Spain*), (1970) ICJ Rep. 3, paras. 33–34; Schabas, *supra* note 27, pp. 445–446; Cassese, *supra* note 73, p. 98.

[80] See, e.g., Antonio Cassese, 'Genocide', in Cassese, Gaeta, and Jones (eds.), *supra* note 66, pp. 336–337 (discussing the case of Sabra and Shatilla).

explains, 'forty years of atrophy did the instrument little good', leaving unresolved or further confused the numerous 'intentional ambiguities left by the drafters'.[81] In the rare cases where it was applied, such as *Eichmann*, there were claims of partiality and legal contortionism.[82] Other attempts at domestic prosecutions occurred more recently in Romania (1989–1990), Bolivia (1993), Ethiopia (1997–2001),[83] Lithuania (1997), Latvia (1999), and Brazil (2001).[84] Genocide was considered at length by the ILC in different versions of its Draft Codes of Crimes Against the Peace and Security of Mankind, the earliest of which dates from 1954 and includes genocide among its listed crimes.[85] Nevertheless, aside from a few issues debated by the Commission – such as questioning whether it was appropriate to include the crime of genocide in the Code, as it was a crime that could be committed in times of peace, and debate over the non-inclusion of political groups in the list of protected groups – the 1954 Code and its successors in 1991 and 1996 really added nothing to the definition set out in the Genocide Convention and ultimately incorporated into the Statutes of the *ad hoc* Tribunals and those of the ICC, the SPSC, the ECCC, and the SICT.

The development of genocide has also occurred in the ICJ beyond that Court's 1951 Advisory Opinion. The central purpose behind the Convention was to attribute individual criminal responsibility for genocide and enable its prosecution by a competent national or international tribunal.[86] Even though the responsibility of states for genocide does not extend to any idea of state criminal responsibility, international law clearly contemplates that civil responsibility or 'aggravated' state responsibility might arise, not just from a failure to prevent or punish acts of genocide, but also from a state's contribution to the commission of genocide.[87] Yet the actual civil responsibility of a state before the ICJ for contributing to the commission of genocide – and not simply for failing to legislate genocide in

[81] Schabas, *supra* note 27, p. 545.

[82] See Quigley, *supra* note 5, pp. 25–26; Schabas, *supra* note 27, p. 548.

[83] In Ethiopia, genocide had been incorporated into domestic legislation and the domestic definition included political groups.

[84] See Quigley, *supra* note 5, ch. 6.

[85] See Draft Code of Crimes Against the Peace and Security of Mankind (1954), in Report of the International Law Commission on the Work of Its Sixth Session, UN Doc. A/2963 (1954), Art. 2(10). See also Draft Code of Crimes Against the Peace and Security of Mankind (1991), in Report of the International Law Commission on the Work of Its Forty-third Session, UN Doc. A/46/10 (1991), Art. 19; Draft Code of Crimes Against the Peace and Security of Mankind (1996), in Report of the International Law Commission on the Work of Its Forty-eighth Session ('ILC 1996 Draft Code with Commentaries'), UN Doc. A/51/10 (1996), Art. 17.

[86] See especially Genocide Convention, *supra* note 2, Art. IV ('Persons committing genocide or any of the other acts enumerated in article III shall be punished, whether they are constitutionally responsible rulers, public officials or private individuals.'); *ibid.*, Art. VI ('Persons charged with genocide … shall be tried by a competent tribunal of the State in the territory of which the act was committed, or by such international penal tribunal as may have jurisdiction with respect to those Contracting Parties which shall have accepted its jurisdiction.'). See also Schabas, *supra* note 27, pp. 74, 418–424.

[87] See *supra* text accompanying notes 61–66.

domestic law, or to prosecute or extradite alleged offenders present in its territory – was not settled by the Court until 1996.

In a preliminary decision in that year on Bosnia's claim that Serbia was responsible for perpetrating genocide against Bosnia's people, the Court held that a claim of state responsibility for genocide under Article IX of the Genocide Convention was admissible.[88] This route has now been travelled on three recent occasions, all concerning the conflicts in the former Yugoslavia.[89] The most significant of these cases resulted in the Court's February 2007 finding that, although genocide had occurred in Bosnia, Serbia had 'not committed genocide, through its organs or persons whose acts engage its responsibility under customary international law, in violation of its obligations under the Convention'. Serbia, however, was responsible for failing to prevent genocide occurring in and around Srebrenica.[90] The Judgement of the ICJ in the *Bosnia* case has established two crucial propositions for the enforcement of the *jus cogens* prohibition of genocide: first, states may sue each other for genocide and the other 'punishable acts' in Article III; second, if a state has become a party to the Genocide Convention, then (absent clear reservation) Article IX opens it up to suit before the ICJ.[91] An interesting tension persists: while the prohibition of genocide constitutes an *erga omnes* norm binding on all states, under which they can theoretically be held to account for perpetrating or failing to prevent or punish genocide, the ICJ can only exercise jurisdiction on a consensual basis,[92] leaving somewhat open the question of how to hold states accountable.

3.1.3 Developments in the ad hoc *Tribunals and beyond*

By far the most significant arena for the consideration and application of genocide has been in the jurisprudence of the *ad hoc* Tribunals, especially the ICTR. The importance of the ICTR for the implementation of the prohibition against genocide in the Genocide Convention and customary international law is clear. The ICTR yielded the first genocide conviction by an international Tribunal: the historic *Akayesu* Trial Judgement of September 1998 provided the first comprehensive treatment of the crime by a competent international criminal tribunal,[93] and set the scene for a flurry of jurisprudential activity in the *ad hoc* Tribunals. The ICTR

[88] *Bosnia* v. *Yugoslavia* Preliminary Objections Judgement, *supra* note 78, p. 616. Only Judge Oda dissented, arguing that the Convention does not provide jurisdiction over a state for the perpetration of genocide, but only for failing to punish individuals responsible. See *ibid.*, Declaration of Judge Oda, para. 4.

[89] See Legality of Use of Force (*Yugoslavia* v. *Belgium*) ('*Yugoslavia* v. *Belgium* Judgement'), (1999) ICJ Rep. 124; *Bosnia* v. *Serbia* Judgement on Merits, *supra* note 6; Application of the Convention on the Prevention and Punishment of the Crime of Genocide (*Croatia* v. *Serbia and Montenegro*), (1999) ICJ Rep. (July 2).

[90] *Bosnia* v. *Serbia* Judgement on Merits, *supra* note 6, p. 168.

[91] See *Yugoslavia* v. *Belgium* Judgement, *supra* note 89, para. 95.

[92] See Statute of the International Court of Justice, 26 June 1945, 59 Stat. 1055, Art. 36(2).

[93] See *Akayesu* Trial Judgement, *supra* note 6.

has since produced a large body of additional jurisprudence imposing genocide liability on a variety of accused through all of the forms of responsibility recognised in its Statute; convicted several accused of the inchoate crimes of conspiracy to commit genocide and direct and public incitement to commit genocide; and produced many statements of law on the definition of genocide, its underlying offences, and the inchoate crimes. The comprehensive exposition of the elements of the underlying offences and inchoate crimes in *Akayesu* has been particularly influential. Nevertheless, it should also be acknowledged that, although voluminous, ICTR jurisprudence on the elements of genocide, its underlying offences, and the inchoate crimes has at times been not particularly well developed.

The importance of the ICTY's case law is necessarily much more limited than that of the ICTR, since ICTY cases arise from a much broader set of events, only some of which involve allegations of genocide. Some of the key contributions of the ICTY have been the Tribunal's affirmation that genocide can occur (and penal sanctions applied) in situations that fall short of country-wide massacres; that for genocide to be committed, it is not necessary to prove the intention to destroy the entire group; and that there is no need for the relevant actor to choose the most effective way to destroy the group, with the result that the other underlying offences short of killing still count as genocide if combined with genocidal intent.

The following section of this chapter will consider these innovations along with problems and limitations in the context of the *ad hoc* Tribunal jurisprudence; the nature of genocide as encompassing a precise and limited number of underlying offences; the elements of these offences; and the elements of the inchoate genocide-related crimes that have been gleaned from Article III of the Convention: conspiracy to commit genocide, direct and public incitement to commit genocide, and attempt to commit genocide.

3.2 Elements of genocide

Unlike war crimes and crimes against humanity, genocide is frequently treated as if it were a single crime – albeit one that can be committed in different ways – instead of a category of offences that rise to the level of a crime under international law if certain requirements are satisfied. It is not uncommon for both scholars and judges, in adopting the former approach, to state that different conduct may constitute the *actus reus* of genocide, but that it has only one *mens rea*, which is termed alternatively specific intent, genocidal intent, special intent, or *dolus specialis*.[94] As this

[94] See, e.g., ILC 1996 Draft Code with Commentaries, *supra* note 85, p. 44 (para. 4 of commentary to Art. 17 on genocide); *Prosecutor* v. *Jelisić*, Case No. IT-95-10-T, Judgement, 14 December 1999 ('*Jelisić* Trial Judgement'), para. 62; *Prosecutor* v. *Muvunyi*, Case No. ICTR-00-55A-T, Judgement, 11 September 2006 ('*Muvunyi* Trial Judgement'), para. 477. On the various terms used for the specific intent required for genocide, see *Jelisić* Appeal Judgement, *supra* note 9, para. 45 & n. 80 (collecting earlier judgements with different terminology for the general mental element requirement).

section of the chapter will demonstrate, however, the offences that can constitute genocide have independent physical and mental elements,[95] and at least one has elements almost identical to the underlying offence for a number of other international crimes.[96] Thus killing and causing serious bodily harm are not simply means of committing genocide in the way that stabbing, shooting, or beating someone are all means of inflicting death or serious physical injury. Rather, each act has its own distinct elements, which are separate from the factors that transform particular conduct into the international crime of genocide.

Accordingly, the 'acts of genocide' listed in the Convention[97] are best understood as underlying offences of the crime of genocide, which are distinguished by their actual or intended results – immediate death, mental injury, prevented births – and which can themselves be committed using different methods. For these reasons, this chapter will apply the same analytical model to genocide as for the crimes discussed in the previous two chapters: analysing first the general requirements that must be satisfied before an offence constitutes genocide, and then the elements of each of the underlying offences.[98]

As a result of the different historical circumstances giving rise to their establishment, the two *ad hoc* Tribunals have had very different experiences dealing with the crime of genocide.[99] As is to be expected for a tribunal created in response to the 1994 genocide in Rwanda, almost all of the ICTR's work is focused on this crime

[95] See *infra* section 3.2.2; *see also Bosnia* v. *Serbia* Judgement on Merits, *supra* note 6, para. 186 ('It is well established that the acts [enumerated in the subparagraphs of Article II of the Genocide Convention] themselves include mental elements.').

[96] See *infra* section 3.2.2.1 (discussing killing as an underlying offence of genocide).

[97] These provisions are reproduced in almost every constituting instrument of an international or hybrid criminal court or tribunal. See *infra* text accompanying notes 103–104, 322, 380, 390, 399; but see text accompanying note 378 (noting that genocide is not within the jurisdiction of the Special Court for Sierra Leone).

[98] The reason that some may think of genocide as a single crime appears to have at least three root causes: first, the popular conception of genocide links it almost exclusively with killing, not the other 'acts'; second, the singular term, when compared to the clearly identified categories of war crimes and crimes against humanity, seems to suggest a monolithic crime; and third, the Convention, which was not intended to be read as a criminal statute, does not fully explain the difference between an 'act of genocide' and a 'punishable act', so it is difficult to determine how Articles II and III should be interpreted.

[99] Notwithstanding these different experiences, chambers of both Tribunals have held that the prohibition against genocide and the ascription of individual criminal responsibility for the breach of this prohibition were firmly entrenched in customary international law at the time of the respective events in the former Yugoslavia and Rwanda. See, e.g., *Krstić* Appeal Judgement, *supra* note 9, Partial Dissenting Opinion of Judge Shahabuddeen, para. 60 (observing that the provisions of Article 4 correspond to Articles II and III of the 1948 Genocide Convention, and that these articles reflect custom); *Prosecutor* v. *Kayishema and Ruzindana*, Case No. ICTR 95-1-T, Judgement, 21 May 1999 ('*Kayishema and Ruzindana* Trial Judgement'), para. 88 ('The [prohibition of the] crime of genocide is considered [...] a norm of *jus cogens*.'). Accord *Prosecutor* v. *Blagojević and Jokić*, Case No. IT-02-60-T, Judgement, 17 January 2005, ('*Blagojević and Jokić* Trial Judgement'), para. 639; *Prosecutor* v. *Brđanin*, Case No. IT-99-36-T, Judgement, 1 September 2004 ('*Brđanin* Trial Judgement'), para. 680; *Stakić* Trial Judgement, *supra* note 9, para. 500; *Prosecutor* v. *Bagilishema*, Case No. ICTR-95-1A-T, Judgement, 7 June 2001 ('*Bagilishema* Trial Judgement'), para. 54; *Rutaganda* Trial Judgement, *supra* note 9, para. 45; *Akayesu* Trial Judgement, *supra* note 6, para. 495.

and its underlying offences.[100] Conversely, since the ICTY's mandate covers the territory and the period of the wars associated with the break-up of Yugoslavia, much more of its work focuses on allegations of war crimes and crimes against humanity.[101] To date, in fact, the prosecution has limited its allegations of genocide to indictments arising out of the conflict in Bosnia, and only one series of events – the massacre in and around Srebrenica and the associated forcible displacement of its Bosnian Muslim inhabitants – has been characterised by ICTY chambers as genocide. As a result, relatively few ICTY cases have specifically discussed and applied the elements of this crime.[102]

3.2.1 General requirements

The provisions on genocide in the Statutes of the ICTY and ICTR reproduce verbatim Articles II and III of the Genocide Convention. Article 4 of the ICTY Statute is virtually identical to Article 2 of the ICTR Statute (collectively, 'Article 4/2'),[103] and both merely add a paragraph affirming the respective Tribunal's jurisdiction over

[100] Almost all of the accused before the ICTR have also been charged with one or more crimes against humanity – such as extermination, murder, or rape as crimes against humanity – but trial chamber statements of the law and factual findings tend to be briefer and more conclusory than their treatments of genocide, its underlying offences, and its related inchoate crimes, at least in part because the crimes against humanity and genocide-related charges tend to arise from the same alleged conduct of the accused and of physical perpetrators. See, e.g., *Prosecutor* v. *Nahimana, Barayagwiza, and Ngeze*, Case No. ICTR-99-52-T, Judgement and Sentence, 3 December 2003 ('*Media* Trial Judgement'), paras. 946–1056, 1057–1088 (spending over a hundred paragraphs on genocide, complicity in genocide, direct and public incitement to commit genocide, and conspiracy to commit genocide; and just over thirty paragraphs on extermination, murder, and 'multiple and different crimes' (including advocating ethnic hatred or inciting violence) as forms of persecution as a crime against humanity) (quotation at para. 1080).

[101] See Chapter 1, text accompanying notes 3–8 (discussing the meaning of 'international humanitarian law', and whether genocide and crimes against humanity can properly be considered as falling within that body of law).

[102] See *Krstić* Trial Judgement, *supra* note 51, paras. 594, 598–599 (concluding that genocide was committed in and around Srebrenica), affirmed in *Krstić* Appeal Judgement, *supra* note 9, paras. 35, 37–38; accord *Blagojević and Jokić* Trial Judgement, *supra* note 99, paras. 671–677; *Prosecutor* v. *Blagojević and Jokić*, Case No. IT-02-60-A, Judgement, 9 May 2007 ('*Blagojević and Jokić* Appeal Judgement'), paras. 119–124 (overturning the Trial Judgement on other grounds, but leaving undisturbed the conclusion that genocide was committed). But see *Jelisić* Trial Judgement, *supra* note 94, para. 108 (holding that 'the Prosecutor has not established beyond all reasonable doubt that genocide was committed in Brčko during the period covered by the indictment.'); *Stakić* Trial Judgement, *supra* note 9, paras. 544–561 (concluding that the Prosecution had not proved that genocide had been committed in the municipality of Prijedor, which became part of the Autonomous Region of Krajina (ARK), a 'Serb-led union of municipalities in Bosnia and Herzegovina', in 1992; nor had it proved that the accused had genocidal intent) (quotation at para. 548); *Brđanin* Trial Judgement, *supra* note 99, paras. 963–991 (concluding that, although the underlying offences had been established with regard to conduct of the Bosnian Serb forces in the ARK, the prosecution had not proved genocidal intent – apparently on the part of either the physical perpetrators or the accused – and thus acquitting the accused of the crime); *Prosecutor* v. *Sikirica, Došen, and Kolundžija*, Case No. IT-95-8-T, Judgement on Defence Motions to Acquit, 3 September 2001, paras. 84–97 (finding that the evidence adduced by the prosecution had not established genocidal intent with regard to the crimes committed at the Keraterm camp in Prijedor); *Prosecutor* v. *Krajišnik*, Case No. IT-00-39-T, Judgement, 27 September 2006 ('*Krajišnik* Trial Judgement'), paras. 867–869 (finding, with regard to allegations of crimes in many different municipalities in Bosnia and Herzegovina, that although 'some of the crimes described earlier … meet the requirements of the *actus reus* of genocide … the Chamber does not find … that any of these acts were committed with the intent to destroy, in part, the Bosnian-Muslim or Bosnian-Croat ethnic group, as such').

[103] The ICTR Statute's provision replaces the phrase 'International Tribunal' with 'International Tribunal for Rwanda'.

'persons committing genocide as defined in paragraph 2 of this article [analogue to Article II] or of committing any of the other acts enumerated in paragraph 3 of this article [analogue to Article III]'.[104]

The general requirements for genocide, as they have been applied in the *ad hoc* Tribunals, are contained in the *chapeau* to subparagraph (2) of Article 4/2, and consist of two requirements: the offences must be committed with the 'intent to destroy, in whole or in part, a national, ethnical, racial or religious group, as such'; and the victims must be subjectively perceived as falling within one of the protected categories, which must in turn be objectively identifiable to some extent. The first general requirement, genocidal intent, has three components: (1) the specific intent to achieve the prohibited result, which is (2) the partial or total material destruction of (3) a distinct group defined on the basis of nationality, ethnicity, race, or religion.

3.2.1.1 Preliminary question: who must have the genocidal intent?

As discussed in detail elsewhere in this series,[105] international crimes frequently involve a large number of individuals who are implicated, to varying degrees, in the design, implementation, and perpetration of the alleged criminal activity. The law on the forms of responsibility, the subject of Volume I of this series, is most directly concerned with defining and distinguishing the different ways in which individuals can participate in the commission of an international crime. Relatively little attention has been paid, however, when discussing the elements of the crimes themselves, to whether all the elements must be satisfied by the conduct of a single actor, or whether a crime may be constituted by the cumulative contributions of more than one actor.

With regard to the crime of genocide, the judgements of the *ad hoc* Tribunals have not been clear in articulating which actor, among the possible culprits, is required to have the specific intent to commit genocide. As a result, the jurisprudence has been inconsistent in its terminology, using at various times the words 'accused',[106] 'perpetrator',[107] 'principal perpetrator',[108] and 'principal

[104] See *supra* text accompanying note 2 for the full text of Articles II and III of the Genocide Convention.

[105] See Chapter 2, section 2.2.2.1; see also Boas, Bischoff, and Reid, *supra* note 23, p. 415.

[106] See, e.g., *Prosecutor* v. *Gacumbitsi*, Case No. ICTR-2001-64-A, Judgement, 7 July 2006 ('*Gacumbitsi* Appeal Judgement'), para. 39 (holding that 'the accused [must have] possessed the specific intent to destroy' the targeted group); *Prosecutor* v. *Stakić*, Case No. IT-97-24-A, Judgement ('*Stakić* Appeal Judgement'), para. 45 ('[I]n genocide cases, the reason why the accused sought to destroy the victim group has no bearing on guilt.'); *Prosecutor* v. *Gacumbitsi*, Case No. ICTR-2001-64-T, Judgement, 14 June 2004 ('*Gacumbitsi* Trial Judgement'), para. 258; *Prosecutor* v. *Semanza*, Case No. ICTR-97-20-T, Judgement and Sentence, 15 May 2003 ('*Semanza* Trial Judgement'), para. 314.

[107] See, e.g., *Krstić* Appeal Judgement, *supra* note 9, para. 12 (holding that 'the alleged perpetrator [must have] intended to destroy' the group); *Prosecutor* v. *Mpambara*, Case No. ICTR-01-65-T, Judgement, 11 September 2006 ('*Mpambara* Trial Judgement'), para. 8; *Prosecutor* v. *Muhimana*, Case No. ICTR-95-1B-T, Judgement and Sentence, 28 April 2005 ('*Muhimana* Trial Judgement'), para. 495; *Prosecutor* v. *Ntagerura, Bagambiki, and Imanishimwe*, Case No. ICTR-99-46-T, Judgement and Sentence, 25 February 2004 ('*Cyangugu* Trial Judgement'), para. 662; *Semanza* Trial Judgement, *supra* note 106, paras. 311–313, 315–316.

[108] See, e.g., *Blagojević and Jokić* Appeal Judgement, *supra* note 102, paras. 122–123.

participant'[109] in the definitions or findings of different chambers. The *Krajišnik* Trial Chamber is one of the few to have grappled with the question, and it concluded that there is no need to focus exclusively (or unthinkingly) on either the physical perpetrator or the accused:

> A peculiarity of the present case, which involves multiple levels of actors, is that a crime committed by a person of low political or military rank without genocidal intent may nevertheless be characterized as an act of genocide if it was procured by a person of higher authority acting with that intent.[110]

On the other hand, the *Media* Appeal Judgement simply asserted, without citation or discussion, that the physical perpetrator must have genocidal intent in order for the underlying offence to constitute genocide.[111]

From the inconsistency in terminology has sprung a predictable inconsistency between the findings of certain trial chambers and their statements of the applicable law. In some cases, after legal definitions of the crime that focused exclusively on the conduct of 'the accused' or 'the perpetrator', the chamber eventually concluded that genocide occurred, found that the accused had genocidal intent, and then convicted him for participation in – not commission of – that crime, even absent an explicit determination that the physical perpetrators of the underlying offences also had genocidal intent.[112]

[109] See, e.g., *Krstić* Appeal Judgement, *supra* note 9, para. 143.

[110] *Krajišnik* Trial Judgement, *supra* note 102, para. 857. The Trial Chamber later added, '[p]roof of genocide is not possible without proof of the *mens rea* at some level of the hierarchy of actors.' *Ibid.*, para. 1094. See also *Prosecutor* v. *Kayishema and Ruzindana*, Case No. ICTR-95-1-A, Judgement (Reasons), 1 June 2001 ('*Kayishema and Ruzindana* Appeal Judgement'), para. 161 ('[G]enocide is not a crime that can only be committed by certain categories of persons. As evidenced by history, it is a crime which has been committed by the low-level executioner and the high-level planner or instigator alike.'); *Krstić* Trial Judgement, *supra* note 51, para. 549 ('The gravity and the scale of … genocide ordinarily presume that several protagonists were involved in its perpetration. … In such cases of joint participation, the intent to destroy … must be discernible in the criminal act itself, apart from the intent of particular perpetrators.'). In other judgements, the trial chamber seems to recognise a distinction between the accused and physical perpetrator at one point, but at others uses the terms interchangeably. Compare, e.g., *Semanza* Trial Judgement, *supra* note 106, para. 319 (for the underlying offence of 'killing members of the group', the 'accused' must have possessed genocidal intent and the 'perpetrator' must have carried out the *actus reus* of killing), with *ibid.*, paras. 311–313, 315–316 (referring to the genocidal intent of the 'perpetrator'); *ibid.*, para. 314 (clearly referring to this same person, but employing the term 'accused').

[111] *Prosecutor* v. *Nahimana, Barayagwiza, and Ngeze*, Case No. ITCR-99-52-A, Judgement, 28 November 2007 ('*Media* Appeal Judgement'), para. 523 (drawing a distinction between the physical perpetrator and the accused, and noting that an accused may also be alleged to be responsible for the crime through one or more forms of responsibility). See also *ibid.* (referring inconsistently to the conclusion that 'the accused' had genocidal intent).

[112] See, e.g., *Muvunyi* Trial Judgement, *supra* note 94, para. 479 ('For an accused person to be found guilty of the crime of genocide, it must be proved that he possessed the requisite *mens rea* in addition to committing any of the genocidal acts listed in Article 2 of the Statute.'); *ibid.*, paras. 494–496, 498 (convicting Muvunyi of aiding and abetting genocide after finding that he had genocidal intent, but without making explicit findings as to whether the physical perpetrators who actually committed the underlying offences also had genocidal intent); *Gacumbitsi* Trial Judgement, *supra* note 106, paras. 252–253 (defining genocide with regard to the conduct and mental state of the perpetrator(s)); *ibid.*, 259–293 (convicting Gacumbitsi of planning, instigating, ordering, and aiding and abetting genocide after finding that he had genocidal intent, but without making explicit findings as to whether the physical perpetrators also had genocidal intent); *Gacumbitsi* Appeal Judgement, *supra* note 106, paras. 59–61 (altering some of the Trial Chamber's findings on Gacumbitsi's contribution to the underlying offences, but not on the basis of the Trial Chamber's failure to explicitly pronounce upon whether the physical perpetrators had genocidal intent).

Conflation of an accused and a physical perpetrator is understandable when courts deal with low-level accused who personally performed the criminal acts in question. In such cases, all the elements of the crime must be satisfied by the conduct and mental state of the accused, or he cannot be found guilty of the crime. In the trial of a high-ranking accused, however, who is rarely if ever personally involved in the commission of the charged crimes, the questions of whether a crime under international law was committed, and whether the accused is somehow responsible for that crime, are theoretically and factually distinct. Such cases are appearing more frequently on the dockets of international and hybrid courts and tribunals, which face increasing pressure to focus on senior political and military leaders.[113] From both the theoretical and practical standpoints, therefore, the indifference to conceptual precision demonstrated by the *ad hoc* Tribunals' jurisprudence leads to needless confusion, and may undermine the soundness of judicial findings.

For these reasons, as we have done with crimes against humanity in the previous chapter of this volume,[114] we will employ the terms 'physical perpetrator' or 'other relevant actor' where appropriate. The phrase 'other relevant actor' is deliberately chosen to be broad enough to encompass the accused, but also any intermediate actor between the accused and the physical perpetrator whose conduct or intent may be relevant, such as an intermediate commander who plans, orders, or instigates a crime.[115]

The relevant portion of the annex to this volume, which combines the elements of the forms of responsibility and the elements of the crimes, will specify which elements must be satisfied by an accused in order to hold him responsible for a particular crime under a particular form of responsibility.

3.2.1.2 Genocidal intent

The physical perpetrator or other relevant actor had the intent to materially destroy all or part of a distinct group defined by nationality, ethnicity, race, or religion.

As ICTY and ICTR chambers have uniformly held since the first judgement on genocide in *Prosecutor* v. *Akayesu*, it is the specific intent to destroy all or part of a group defined by nationality, ethnicity, race, or religion, 'as such', that distinguishes

[113] See Security Council Resolution 1534, UN Doc. S/RES/1534 (2004), 26 March 2004, p. 2, para. 5; Security Council Resolution 1503, UN Doc. S/RES/1503 (2003), 28 August 2003, pp. 1–2; see also, e.g., *Prosecutor* v. *Delić*, Case No. IT-04-83-PT, Decision on Motion for Referral Under Rule 11 bis, 5 July 2007, para. 25 (interpreting the term 'most senior leaders' as envisaged by the Security Council and refusing to order the transfer of the accused 'in view [of his] supreme rank and position … in the Bosnian Muslim military and political hierarchy').

[114] See Chapter 2, text accompanying notes 103–109.

[115] For the reasons outlined in detail in Chapter 2, persons responsible for crimes on the bases of the third category of joint criminal enterprise, aiding and abetting, or superior responsibility should not be able to supply the knowledge or intent element of a crime. See Chapter 2, text accompanying notes 104–106.

genocide from domestic crimes like murder and other international crimes such as torture or rape as crimes against humanity, or murder or forcible transfer as forms of persecution as a crime against humanity. Unless this requirement is satisfied, no act qualifies as genocide.

3.2.1.2.1 Specific intent

The physical perpetrator or other relevant actor had the intent...

Recognising that this specific intent may be difficult, if not impossible, to establish through direct evidence, the trial and appeals chambers of both *ad hoc* Tribunals have concluded that genocidal intent may be inferred from the circumstances surrounding the commission of the alleged offences.[116] Somewhat troublingly, the *Krstić* Appeals Chamber has also held that '[t]he inference that a particular atrocity was motivated by genocidal intent may be drawn ... even where the individuals to whom the intent is attributable are not precisely identified.'[117] Nonetheless, as required for judicial findings on the elements of crimes and the forms of responsibility in general,[118] an inference of genocidal intent must be the only reasonable conclusion from the facts presented at trial, and does not relieve the prosecution of its burden of proof beyond reasonable doubt.[119] Among the factors chambers have considered as circumstantial evidence of genocidal intent are a deliberate or systematic targeting of a particular national, ethnic, racial, or religious group to the exclusion of members of other groups;[120] the scale of the alleged atrocities, including the number of members of the targeted group who are

[116] See, e.g., *Gacumbitsi* Appeal Judgement, *supra* note 106, para. 40 (reaffirming past jurisprudence 'that genocide can be proven through inference from the facts and circumstances of a case', noting that '[b]y its nature, intent is not usually susceptible to direct proof' because '[o]nly the accused himself has first-hand knowledge of his own mental state', and concluding that '[i]ntent thus must usually be inferred'); *Krstić* Appeal Judgement, *supra* note 9, para. 34 ('Where direct evidence of genocidal intent is absent, the intent may still be inferred from the factual circumstances of the crime.'); accord *Media* Appeal Judgement, *supra* note 111, para. 524; *Prosecutor* v. *Simba*, Case No. ICTR-01-76-A, Judgement and Sentence, 27 November 2007 ('*Simba* Appeal Judgement'), para. 264; *Rutaganda* Trial Judgement, *supra* note 9, paras. 61-63; *Musema* Trial Judgement, *supra* note 9, para. 167; *Semanza* Trial Judgement, *supra* note 106, para. 313; *Bagilishema* Trial Judgement, *supra* note 99, para. 63; *Brđanin* Trial Judgement, *supra* note 99, para. 704; *Mpambara* Trial Judgement, *supra* note 107, para. 8; *Prosecutor* v. *Simba*, Case No. ICTR-01-76-T, Judgement and Sentence, 13 December 2005 ('*Simba* Trial Judgement'), para. 413; *Muvunyi* Trial Judgement, *supra* note 94, para. 480; *Muhimana* Trial Judgement, *supra* note 107, para. 496.

[117] *Krstić* Appeal Judgement, *supra* note 9, para. 34 (stating also that '[i]f the evidence supports the inference that the crime was motivated by the intent to destroy, in whole or in part, a protected group' apparently without regard to the person who was so motivated, 'a finding that genocide has occurred may be entered').

[118] See, e.g., *Media* Appeal Judgement, *supra* note 111, para. 896. See also Chapter 2, text accompanying note 209; see also Boas, Bischoff, and Reid, *supra* note 23, pp. 22, 40 n. 184, 54 n. 282, 87.

[119] *Media* Appeal Judgement, *supra* note 111, para. 41; *Brđanin* Trial Judgement, *supra* note 99, para. 970. Cf. *Gacumbitsi* Appeal Judgement, *supra* note 106, para. 41 (emphasising that inferring intent is 'simply a different means of satisfying that burden' of proof beyond reasonable doubt).

[120] *Akayesu* Trial Judgement, *supra* note 6, para. 523; see also *Kayishema and Ruzindana* Trial Judgement, *supra* note 99, paras. 93, 289-291 (citing the methodical way of planning and the systematic manner of killing); *Stakić* Appeal Judgement, *supra* note 106, paras. 53, 55; *Jelisić* Appeal Judgement, *supra* note 9, para. 47; *Muvunyi* Trial Judgement, *supra* note 94, para. 480; *Simba* Trial Judgement, *supra* note 116, para. 413; *Muhimana* Trial Judgement, *supra* note 107, para. 496; *Cyangugu* Trial Judgement, *supra* note 107, para. 663.

affected;[121] the repetition of destructive and discriminatory acts;[122] the weapons employed and the extent of bodily injury;[123] a general context of other offences directed at the same target population, whether committed by the accused, the alleged perpetrators involved in the offences for which he is charged, or others;[124] the use of derogatory language toward or about members of the targeted group;[125] other conduct, which falls short of an underlying offence of genocide, but which violates, or which perpetrators consider to violate, 'the very foundation of the group';[126] and other words and conduct of the perpetrators or the accused.[127]

An early ICTR trial judgement posited that genocidal intent must be formed prior to the commission of the acts alleged,[128] but that interpretation has recently been

[121] *Blagojević and Jokić* Trial Judgement, *supra* note 99, paras. 674–677 (inferring the intent of the Bosnian Serb forces to destroy the Muslim population from Srebrenica from the killing of 7,000 men and boys; the forcible transfer of women, children, and elderly; and the creation of a climate of fear); *Kayishema and Ruzindana* Trial Judgement, *supra* note 99, para 93 (referring to 'the relative proportionate scale of the actual or attempted destruction of a group'); accord *Jelisić* Appeal Judgement, *supra* note 9, para. 47; *Muvunyi* Trial Judgement, *supra* note 94, para. 480; *Muhimana* Trial Judgement, *supra* note 107, para. 496; *Brđanin* Trial Judgement, *supra* note 99, para. 973; *Prosecutor* v. *Ndindabahizi*, Case No. ICTR-2001-71-T, Judgement and Sentence, 15 July 2004 ('*Ndindabahizi* Trial Judgement'), para. 454; *Cyangugu* Trial Judgement, *supra* note 107, para. 663; *Semanza* Trial Judgement, *supra* note 106, paras. 313–314; *Akayesu* Trial Judgement, *supra* note 6, para. 523; *Prosecutor* v. *Milošević*, Case No. IT-02-54-T, Decision on Motion for Judgement of Acquittal, 16 June 2004, para. 125. But see *Brđanin* Trial Judgement, *supra* note 99, para. 974 (finding that the underlying offences in question were limited to thirteen municipalities, targeting only a small proportion of the respective Muslim and Croat groups, and thus did not permit the inference of genocidal intent).

[122] *Akayesu* Trial Judgement, *supra* note 6, para. 524; *Jelisić* Appeal Judgement, *supra* note 9, para. 47; *Simba* Trial Judgement, *supra* note 116, para. 413; *Ndindabahizi* Trial Judgement, *supra* note 121, para. 454 n. 587; *ibid.*, para. 470. But see *Brđanin* Trial Judgement, *supra* note 99, paras. 983–984 (concluding that '[w]hile the general and widespread nature of the atrocities committed is evidence of a campaign of persecutions … in the circumstances of this case, it is not possible to conclude from it that the specific intent required for the crime of genocide is satisfied').

[123] *Kayishema and Ruzindana* Trial Judgement, *supra* note 99, para. 93; *ibid.*, para. 544 (finding that '[a]s a result of Ruzindana's consistent pattern of conduct, thousands of Tutsis were killed or seriously injured; men, women and children alike'); *Gacumbitsi* Trial Judgement, *supra* note 106, paras. 252–253.

[124] *Akayesu* Trial Judgement, *supra* note 6, para. 523; *Jelisić* Appeal Judgement, *supra* note 9, para. 47; *Muhimana* Trial Judgement, *supra* note 107, para. 496; *Gacumbitsi* Trial Judgement, *supra* note 106, paras. 252–253; *Muvunyi* Trial Judgement, *supra* note 94, para. 480; *Prosecutor* v. *Sikirica, Došen, and Kolundžija*, Case No. IT-95-8-T, Sentencing Judgement, 13 November 2001 ('*Sikirica et al.* Sentencing Judgement'), paras. 46, 61.

[125] *Muhimana* Trial Judgement, *supra* note 107, para. 496; *Stakić* Appeal Judgement, *supra* note 106, para. 52; *Prosecutor* v. *Kajelijeli*, Case No. ICTR-98-44A-T, Judgement and Sentence, 1 December 2003 ('*Kajelijeli* Trial Judgement'), para. 806; *Gacumbitsi* Trial Judgement, *supra* note 106, para. 253; *Kayishema and Ruzindana* Trial Judgement, *supra* note 99, para. 93. The *Brđanin* Trial Chamber ultimately held that the prosecution had not proved genocidal intent on the part of the accused. See *Brđanin* Trial Judgement, *supra* note 99, paras. 985–988 (finding that, notwithstanding the accused's utterances, which 'strongly suggest[ed] … discriminatory intent', the use of derogatory language '[did] not allow for the conclusion that [he] harboured the intent to destroy the Bosnian Muslims and Bosnian Croats of the [Autonomous Region of Krajina]') (quotations at para. 987).

[126] *Akayesu* Trial Judgement, *supra* note 6, para 524.

[127] See, e.g., *Bagilishema* Trial Judgement, *supra* note 99, para. 63 (cautioning that 'the use of context to determine the intent of an accused must be counterbalanced with the actual conduct of the Accused', whose 'intent should be determined, above all, from his words and deeds, and should be evident from patterns of purposeful action'); *Gacumbitsi* Trial Judgement, *supra* note 106, paras. 252–253, affirmed in *Gacumbitsi* Appeal Judgement, *supra* note 106, paras. 40–43.

[128] See, e.g., *Kayishema and Ruzindana* Trial Judgement, *supra* note 99, para. 91.

rejected by the ICTR Appeals Chamber.[129] Under the Tribunals' jurisprudence, it is thus clear that the crime need not be premeditated, in the sense of deliberate planning well in advance of committing the offences.[130] Early on, the *Akayesu* Trial Chamber held that it was unnecessary to require the prosecution to establish premeditation as a separate element of genocide – a part of the general mental element requirement for the crime – citing, among other things, parts of the *travaux préparatoires* expressing the belief that all of the underlying offences themselves entail premeditation.[131] As the Tribunals' jurisprudence on both the general requirements and the underlying offences of genocide has evolved, it has become clear that premeditation is not a requirement for all the conduct that may constitute genocide.[132] More recent judgements of both Tribunals now simply assert that proof of premeditation is unnecessary.[133]

Similarly, a specific plan to commit underlying offences is not an element of the crime, but it is strong evidence of genocidal intent.[134] One ICTR Trial Chamber has held that even where there is such a plan, the perpetrator need not know all its details in order for his or her acts to constitute genocide.[135]

Much like the specific discriminatory intent for persecution,[136] chambers have repeatedly cautioned that genocidal intent, as a matter of law, is to be distinguished from any personal motives of the physical perpetrator or other relevant actor, such as revenge or desire for personal economic gain.[137] So long as intent is proved, motive

[129] See *Simba* Appeal Judgement, *supra* note 116, para. 266:

> In [the accused-appellant's] view, for the crime of genocide to occur, the intent to commit genocide must be formed prior to the commission of genocidal acts. The Appeals Chamber finds no merit in this submission. The inquiry is not whether the specific intent was formed prior to the commission of the acts, but whether at the moment of commission the perpetrators possessed the necessary intent. The Trial Chamber correctly considered whether the Appellant and the physical perpetrators possessed genocidal intent at the time of the massacres. The Appellant's argument on this point is therefore without merit.

[130] *Krstić* Trial Judgement, *supra* note 51, para. 572 (holding that 'Article 4 of the Statute does not require that the genocidal acts be premeditated over a long period' and that '[i]t is conceivable that, although the intention at the outset of an operation was not the destruction of a group, it may become the goal at some later point during the implementation of the operation'); *Blagojević and Jokić* Trial Judgement, *supra* note 99, para. 656. Cf. *Jelisić* Appeal Judgement, *supra* note 9, para. 48 ('[T]he existence of a plan or policy is not a legal ingredient of the crime.').

[131] See *Akayesu* Trial Judgement, *supra* note 6, para. 501 (citing to the summary records of the meetings of the Sixth Committee of the General Assembly in 1948).

[132] See, e.g., *Kayishema and Ruzindana* Trial Judgement, *supra* note 99, para. 91 ('The individual acts themselves, however, do not require premeditation; the only consideration is that the act should be done in furtherance of the genocidal intent.').

[133] See, e.g., *Simba* Trial Judgement, *supra* note 116, para. 414; *Muvunyi* Trial Judgement, *supra* note 94, para. 486; *Cyangugu* Trial Judgement, *supra* note 107, para. 664.

[134] *Krstić* Appeal Judgement, *supra* note 9, para. 225 ('[T]he existence of a plan or policy is not a legal ingredient of the crime of genocide. While the existence of such a plan may help to establish that the accused possessed the requisite genocidal intent, it remains only evidence supporting the inference of intent, and does not become a legal ingredient of the offence.'). Accord *Simba* Appeal Judgement, *supra* note 116, para. 260; *Prosecutor* v. *Semanza*, Case No. ICTR-97-20-A, Judgement, 20 May 2005, para. 260; *Jelisić* Appeal Judgement, *supra* note 9, para. 48; *Blagojević and Jokić* Trial Judgement, *supra* note 99, para. 656; *Brđanin* Trial Judgement, *supra* note 99, para. 705; *Kayishema and Ruzindana* Trial Judgement, *supra* note 99, paras. 94, 276.

[135] *Kayishema and Ruzindana* Trial Judgement, *supra* note 99, para. 94.

[136] See Chapter 2, section 2.2.3.8.1.

[137] See, e.g., *Simba* Appeal Judgement, *supra* note 116, para. 269; *Jelisić* Appeal Judgement, *supra* note 9, para. 49.

is legally irrelevant to the question of whether the crime has been committed.[138] ICTR accused have occasionally argued on appeal that their convictions for genocide should be overturned because this general requirement should be interpreted to justify conviction only where genocidal intent is the sole motivation for the conduct charged in the indictment. In *Niyitegeka*, for example, the accused-appellant asserted that his conviction should not stand if the reason for which the victims were attacked was that they were perceived as being the political enemy;[139] in *Ntakirutimana and Ntakirutimana*, one accused-appellant argued that a finding that most of the victims killed in one location were Tutsi refugees did not support the conclusion that they had been attacked because of their ethnicity. Both arguments were rejected by the ICTR Appeals Chamber, which noted in the later judgement that:

> The Appeals Chamber need not consider whether the Trial Chamber erred in finding that the refugees were targeted 'solely' for their Tutsi ethnicity because the definition of the crime of genocide does not contain such a requirement. It is immaterial, as a matter of law, whether the refugees were targeted solely on the basis of their ethnicity or whether they were targeted for their ethnicity in addition to other reasons.[140]

In a recent ruling on genocidal intent, the *Stakić* Appeals Chamber rebuked what it viewed as a compartmentalised approach to evaluating the evidence presented on this general requirement. Instead of 'considering separately whether the [accused] intended to destroy the group through each of the genocidal acts specified in' the statutory provisions on genocide, 'the Trial Chamber should expressly have considered whether all of the evidence, taken together, demonstrated a genocidal mental state'.[141] To the extent that the Appeals Chamber's statement was intended as an instruction to trial chambers *not* to consider whether each alleged underlying offence was committed with genocidal intent, it is inconsistent with *ad hoc* jurisprudence,[142]

[138] See, e.g., *Prosecutor* v. *Krnojelac*, Case No. IT-97-25-A, Judgement, 17 September 2003, para. 102 (ICTY Appeals Chamber recalling its holding in *Jelisić* 'which, with regard to the specific intent required for the crime of genocide, sets out "the necessity to distinguish specific intent from motive"', and declaring that 'this distinction between intent and motive must also be applied to the other crimes laid down in the Statute'); *Prosecutor* v. *Blaškić*, Case No. IT-95-14-A, Judgement, 29 July 2004, para. 694; *Kayishema and Ruzindana* Appeal Judgement, *supra* note 110, para. 161; *Brđanin* Trial Judgement, *supra* note 99, para. 696 (citing the *Tadić* Appeal Judgement's observation on 'the irrelevance and inscrutability of motives in criminal law'). See also *Krajišnik* Trial Judgement, *supra* note 102, para. 856; *Muvunyi* Trial Judgement, *supra* note 94, para. 479; *Simba* Trial Judgement, *supra* note 116, para. 412; *Blagojević and Jokić* Trial Judgement, *supra* note 99, para. 669.

[139] *Niyitegeka* Appeal Judgement, *supra* note 9, para. 47 (quoting the appellant's brief).

[140] *Prosecutor* v. *Ntakirutimana and Ntakirutimana*, Case Nos. ICTR-96-10-A and ICTR-96-17-A, Judgement, 13 December 2004 ('*Ntakirutimana and Ntakirutimana* Appeal Judgement'), para. 304. In addition, the Appeals Chamber held that the Trial Chamber's inference that the refugees were targeted because of their ethnicity was not unreasonable on the evidence before it. *Ibid.* para. 303.

[141] *Stakić* Appeal Judgement, *supra* note 106, para. 55.

[142] See, e.g., *Jelisić* Appeal Judgement, *supra* note 9, para. 46 ('The specific intent requires that the perpetrator, *by one of the prohibited acts* enumerated in Article 4 of the Statute, seeks to achieve the destruction, in whole or in part, of a national, ethnical, racial or religious group, as such.') (emphasis added).

and disregards the theoretical structure of the crime.[143] Without the requisite specific intent, no act may constitute genocide, nor should any such act be considered the factual predicate for a conviction of genocide. The better interpretation of this aspect of the *Stakić* Appeal Judgement, therefore, is that the Chamber was referring to the appropriate method of evaluating the evidence presented at trial, and indicating that genocidal intent is to be considered in light of all the conduct of those participating in the general criminal activity, not just with respect to the particular conduct alleged for a specific underlying offence.

3.2.1.2.2 Material destruction

... to materially destroy ...

The judgements of both *ad hoc* Tribunals have almost uniformly adopted the International Law Commission's interpretation of the term 'destroy' in the Genocide Convention:

> As clearly shown by the preparatory work for the Convention on the Prevention and Punishment of the Crime of Genocide, the destruction in question is the material destruction of a group either by physical or by biological means, not the destruction of the national, linguistic, religious, cultural or other identity of a particular group. The national or religious element and the racial or ethnic element are not taken into consideration in the definition of the word 'destruction', which must be taken only in its material sense, its physical or biological sense.[144]

The ILC clarified that 'physical destruction' referred to the underlying offences in subparagraphs (a) through (c) of Article II of the Convention, while 'biological destruction' referred to the offences in subparagraphs (d) and (e).[145] That is, the terms were intended to distinguish between conduct that would result in the immediate or eventual deaths of the direct victims, and that which would result in the eventual disappearance of the group through the natural deaths of the remaining members.[146]

[143] See *supra* text accompanying notes 94–98 (explaining that genocide is best understood as a group of underlying offences, which must be coupled with genocidal intent in order to constitute the crime of genocide).

[144] ILC 1996 Draft Code with Commentaries, *supra* note 85, pp. 45–46 (para. 12 of commentary on Art. 17 on genocide).

[145] *Ibid*., p. 46 (para. 12 of commentary on Art. 17 on genocide).

[146] Neither the ILC, nor any of the *ad hoc* judgements that employed these terms, sought to explain how serious mental harm – the object of one of the two offences in subparagraph 2(b) – could constitute physical destruction. The closest was the *Akayesu* Trial Chamber's observations that a traumatised rape victim could refuse to procreate, and that a protected group could be induced through threats or trauma not to procreate. See *Akayesu* Trial Judgement, *supra* note 6, para. 508. This result, however, would be biological destruction, not physical destruction, and the Chamber's statements were made in the context of its discussion of the offence in subparagraph (2)(d). In addition, although the Chamber did not tackle the question of specific intent, it seems clear that, in order for this theory to ground a conviction for genocide, the prosecution would have to prove that the perpetrators or other relevant actors knew and intended that the rape, threats, or other trauma would cause the targeted group not to procreate.

Accordingly, almost all judgements of both *ad hoc* Tribunals have limited the definition of destruction, for the purposes of determining genocidal intent, to this concept of 'material destruction', excluding 'cultural' genocide or other conduct that may affect the identity of the targeted group, but not its very existence.[147] Here again, however, the Tribunals' cases distinguish between the factors required to establish an element of the crime, and facts that may constitute evidence of that element. Though evidence of the relevant actor's intent to destroy the group's sociological or cultural identity cannot by itself establish genocidal intent,[148] evidence such as the destruction of cultural or religious institutions or objects belonging to the group or its members may be considered in determining whether the relevant actor had the intent to destroy the group materially.[149]

A minority view, espousing a broader interpretation of the term 'destroy', has been advanced by Judge Shahabuddeen in his partial dissenting opinion to the *Krstić* Appeal Judgement. Noting first that a distinction should be made between the underlying offences enumerated in Article 4 of the ICTY Statute and the intent with which those acts must be committed in order for them to constitute genocide, Judge Shahabuddeen observed:

> From their nature, the listed (or initial) acts must indeed take a physical or biological form, but the accompanying intent, by those acts, to destroy the group in whole or in part need not always lead to a destruction of the same character. [Other than the acts in subparagraphs (2)(c) and (2)(d)], the Statute itself does not require an intent to cause physical or biological destruction of the group in whole or in part.
>
> … The question is whether, to prove genocide, it was necessary to show that the intent with which they were killed was to cause the physical or biological destruction of the Srebrenica part of the Bosnian Muslim group. The stress placed in the literature on the need for physical or biological destruction implies, correctly, that a group can be destroyed in

147 See *Krstić* Trial Judgement, *supra* note 51, para. 580 ('[A]n enterprise attacking only the cultural or sociological characteristics of a human group in order to annihilate these elements which give to that group its own identity distinct from the rest of the community would not fall under the definition of genocide.'), affirmed in *Krstić* Appeal Judgement, *supra* note 9, para. 25. Accord *Muhimana* Trial Judgement, *supra* note 107, para. 497; *Blagojević and Jokić* Trial Judgement, *supra* note 99, para. 657; *Semanza* Trial Judgement, *supra* note 106, para. 315; *Akayesu* Trial Judgement, *supra* note 6, para. 497. But see *Kayishema and Ruzindana* Trial Judgement, *supra* note 99, para. 95 (noting, with reference to sexual violence and the non-killing underlying offences in subparagraph 2, that the concept of destruction includes acts falling short of death); *Musema* Trial Judgement, *supra* note 9, para. 933 (same).

148 *See Krstić* Appeal Judgement, *supra* note 9, para. 25; *Blagojević and Jokić* Trial Judgement, *supra* note 99, para. 657; *Krstić* Trial Judgement, *supra* note 51, para. 580. Examples of conduct that may tend to have a destructive effect on sociological or cultural identity could include such acts as prohibiting the use of a language, or destroying or preventing the use of libraries, museums, places of worship, or other cultural institutions or objects. See, e.g., *Krajišnik* Trial Judgement, *supra* note 102, para. 838 (finding that 'Serb forces destroyed Mosques in order to wipe out traces of the Muslim culture and religion'). Moreover, the intent to destroy the cultural or sociological identity of the targeted group may, depending on the circumstances, provide evidence of discriminatory intent for purposes of proving persecution as a crime against humanity. See Chapter 2, section 2.2.3.8.1 (discussing the discriminatory intent specific requirement for persecution).

149 See, e.g., *Stakić* Appeal Judgement, *supra* note 106, paras. 53, 55 (concluding that the Trial Chamber should have considered, *inter alia*, 'destruction of religious sites and homes' in the totality of circumstantial evidence of genocidal intent); *Krstić* Trial Judgement, *supra* note 51, para. 580.

non-physical or non-biological ways. It is not apparent why an intent to destroy a group in a non-physical or non-biological way should be outside the ordinary reach of the Convention on which the Statute is based, provided that that intent attached to a listed act, this being of a physical or biological nature.[150]

Judge Shahabuddeen hastened to add that he was not advancing an argument for cultural genocide, and recalled that '[t]he destruction of culture may serve evidentially to confirm an intent, to be gathered from other circumstances, to destroy the group as such'.[151]

Nine months later, this reasoning was quoted with approval in the *Blagojević and Jokić* Trial Judgement, as part of its attempt to demonstrate that the concept of destruction in the law on genocide had expanded beyond only physical or biological destruction.[152] In support of its conclusion that forcible displacement is encompassed within the term 'destroy', the Trial Chamber asserted:

[T]he physical or biological destruction of a group is not necessarily the death of the group members. While killing large numbers of a group may be the most direct means of destroying a group, other acts or series of acts, can also lead to the destruction of the group. A group is comprised of its individuals, but also of its history, traditions, the relationship between its members, the relationship with other groups, the relationship with the land. The Trial Chamber finds that the physical or biological destruction of the group is the likely outcome of a forcible transfer of the population when this transfer is conducted in such a way that the group can no longer reconstitute itself – particularly when it involves the separation of its members. In such cases the Trial Chamber finds that the forcible transfer of individuals could lead to the material destruction of the group, since the group ceases to exist as a group, or at least as the group it was.[153]

Here too, the Trial Chamber 'emphasise[d] that its reasoning and conclusion are not an argument for the recognition of cultural genocide, but rather an attempt to clarify the meaning of physical or biological destruction',[154] though this qualification is hard to reconcile with its actual statements. Based on its holding that 'the term "destroy" in the genocide definition can encompass the forcible transfer of a population',[155] the Trial Chamber concluded that the forcible removal of women, children and elderly was 'a manifestation of the specific intent to rid the Srebrenica enclave of its Bosnian Muslim population', and that '[t]he manner in which the transfer was carried out … significantly, through its targeting of literally the entire Bosnian Muslim population of Srebrenica, including the elderly and children – clearly indicates that it was a means to eradicate the Bosnian Muslim population from the territory where they had lived.'[156] Combined with subsequent murders in

[150] *Krstić* Appeal Judgement, *supra* note 9, Partial Dissenting Opinion of Judge Shahabuddeen, paras. 48–49.
[151] *Ibid.*, para. 53. [152] See generally *Blagojević and Jokić* Trial Judgement, *supra* note 99, paras. 658–666.
[153] *Ibid.*, para. 666. [154] *Ibid.*, para. 666. [155] *Ibid.*, para. 665. [156] *Ibid.*, para. 675.

Bratunac, a Bosnian municipality close to Srebrenica where the brigade Blagojević commanded was based, the Trial Chamber found that this forcible transfer and accompanying destruction of property established that Bosnian Serb forces had the intent to destroy the Bosnian Muslim population of Srebrenica, that Blagojević knew of that intent, and that his substantial practical assistance therefore resulted in his responsibility for complicity in genocide.[157]

As could be expected in light of its own recent jurisprudence in *Krstić*, the Appeals Chamber rejected both the Trial Chamber's broadened notion of destruction and its apparent conclusion that forcible displacement can, by itself, constitute evidence of destruction or intent to destroy.[158] In the context of discussing the factors that may be considered in divining genocidal intent, the *Blagojević and Jokić* Appeals Chamber noted that 'the forcible transfer operation, the separations, and the mistreatment and murders in Bratunac town are relevant considerations in assessing whether the principal perpetrators had genocidal intent', but cautioned that it was 'not convinced by the Trial Chamber's reasoning that the forcible transfer operation alone or coupled with the murders and mistreatment in Bratunac town would suffice to demonstrate the principal perpetrators' intent to "destroy" the protected group'.[159] The Appeals Chamber affirmed its earlier observation in *Krstić* that forcible transfer by itself is not an underlying offence of genocide, and noted that Krstić had been found guilty of complicity in genocide because the evidence showed he knew of the mass killings that followed the takeover of Srebrenica, and therefore was aware of the genocidal intent of the 'principal perpetrators'.[160] Without this key evidence of the accused's awareness of the massacres – and because the forcible transfer and 'opportunistic' killings in Bratunac would be, at best, 'part of the overall factual assessment' for determining whether the perpetrators had genocidal intent – the Appeals Chamber concluded that no reasonable trier of fact would have found that Blagojević had the requisite knowledge to be complicit in genocide,[161] and reversed his conviction on this count of the indictment.[162]

[157] *Ibid.*, paras. 676, 784–787.

[158] See *infra*, text accompanying notes 261–262, for a discussion of the jurisprudence on whether forcible displacement can be an underlying offence of genocide.

[159] *Blagojević and Jokić* Appeal Judgement, *supra* note 102, para. 123.

[160] *Ibid.*, paras. 122–123.

[161] As explained in Chapter 4 of Volume I of this series, complicity in genocide is best understood as the combination of a form or forms of responsibility with the crime of genocide. The only version of complicity in genocide actually defined by the Appeals Chamber equates complicity with aiding and abetting, so in order to be found guilty of complicity in genocide, an accused must have knowledge of all the elements of the crime of genocide, including the genocidal intent of the perpetrator or other relevant actor. See generally Boas, Bischoff, and Reid, *supra* note 23, pp. 290–291, 329.

[162] *Blagojević and Jokić* Appeal Judgement, *supra* note 102, paras. 123–124. For more on this issue, see *infra* text accompanying notes 258–265.

3.2.1.2.3 Definitions of the protected group and the targeted group

... all or part of a distinct group defined by nationality, ethnicity, race, or religion.

Since few, if any, individuals could destroy or aid in the destruction of an entire national, ethnic, racial or religious group, perhaps the most important element of the crime of genocide, when it comes to its practical implementation in actual criminal cases, is the proviso that the intent need not be to destroy the entire protected group. The physical perpetrator or other relevant actor need only intend to destroy the group 'in part',[163] though the targeted part must be substantial in proportion to, or of particular importance to, the group.[164] As trial chambers have considered individual incidents of murder and physical abuse as underlying offences of genocide,[165] it is clear that this substantiality criterion is an aggregate requirement: in order for the charged conduct to constitute genocide, the portion of the protected group that is targeted for destruction by *all* of the relevant actors must be 'significant enough to have an impact on the group as a whole'.[166]

This aspect of the specific intent element has been relatively uncontroversial at the ICTR.[167] In the ICTY's Srebrenica cases, however, consideration of the

[163] Invoking the Holocaust, as do so many academic and judicial discussions of genocide, the *Krstić* Appeals Chamber noted that 'Nazi Germany may have intended only to eliminate Jews within Europe alone; that ambition probably did not extend, even at the height of its power, to an undertaking of that enterprise on a global scale.' *Krstić* Appeal Judgement, *supra* note 9, para. 13 (citing Schabas, *supra* note 27, p. 235).

[164] See *ibid*., para. 12; *Krajišnik* Trial Judgement, *supra* note 102, para. 853; *Mpambara* Trial Judgement, *supra* note 107, para. 8; *Blagojević and Jokić* Trial Judgement, *supra* note 99, para. 668; *Brđanin* Trial Judgement, *supra* note 99, para. 701; *Ndindabahizi* Trial Judgement, *supra* note 121, para. 454; *Semanza* Trial Judgement, *supra* note 106, para. 316; *Bagilishema* Trial Judgement, *supra* note 99, para. 64; *Jelisić* Trial Judgement, *supra* note 94, para. 82; *Kayishema and Ruzindana* Trial Judgement, *supra* note 99, para. 97.

[165] See *Ndindabahizi* Trial Judgement, *supra* note 121, para. 471 ('The fact that only a single person was killed on this occasion does not negate the perpetrators' clear intent, which was to destroy the Tutsi population of Kibuye and of Rwanda, in whole or in part. Accordingly, the killers of [the victim] committed genocide.'); *Gacumbitsi* Trial Judgement, *supra* note 106, para. 292 (finding that the rape of eight Tutsi women and girls, instigated by the accused, 'caused serious physical harm to members of the Tutsi ethnic group', and thus concluding that 'as to the specific [offence] of serious bodily harm, Sylvestre Gacumbitsi incurs responsibility for the crime of genocide by instigating the rape of Tutsi women and girls'); see also *Jelisić* Trial Judgement, *supra* note 94, para. 100 ('The murders committed by the accused are sufficient to establish the material element of the crime of genocide and it is *a priori* possible to conceive that the accused harboured the plan to exterminate an entire group without this intent having been supported by any organisation in which other individuals participated.'). See also *Mpambara* Trial Judgement, *supra* note 107, para. 8 ('[T]he commission of even a single instance of one of the prohibited acts is sufficient, provided that the accused genuinely intends by that act to destroy at least a substantial part of the group.') (citing *Ndindabahizi* Trial Judgement, *supra* note 121, para. 471). This statement by the *Mpambara* Trial Chamber might best be interpreted as observing that a single act could be an underlying offence if the person committing the act intends to *contribute toward* the destruction of a substantial part of the group, because the Chamber went on to remark in a footnote that '[t]he perpetrator of a single, isolated act of violence could not possess the requisite intent based on a delusion that, by his action, the [partial or entire] destruction of the group … could be effected.' *Ibid*., para. 8 n. 7.

[166] *Krstić* Appeal Judgement, *supra* note 9, para. 8.

[167] See, e.g., *Muvunyi* Trial Judgement, *supra* note 94, paras. 479, 483; *Simba* Trial Judgement, *supra* note 116, para. 412; *Muhimana* Trial Judgement, *supra* note 107, para. 498 (citing *Gacumbitsi* Trial Judgement, *supra* note 106, para. 253; *Semanza* Trial Judgement, *supra* note 106, para. 316; *Kayishema and Ruzindana* Trial Judgement, *supra* note 99, para. 93):

> [I]t is not necessary for the Prosecution to establish that the perpetrator intended to achieve the complete annihilation of a group. There is no numeric threshold of victims necessary to establish genocide, even though the relative proportionate scale of the actual or attempted destruction of a group … is strong evidence of the intent to destroy a group, in whole or in part.

substantiality criterion has been intertwined with the question of the definition of the protected group itself, leading to an emphasis in that Tribunal's jurisprudence on the significance of the targeted portion to the protected group as a whole, and pragmatic consideration of the opportunities available to the perpetrators. Thus, as part of its guidelines for determining whether the targeted portion was sufficiently substantial, the *Krstić* Appeals Chamber observed:

> The number of individuals targeted should be evaluated not only in absolute terms, but also in relation to the overall size of the entire group. In addition to the numeric size of the targeted portion, its prominence within the group can be a useful consideration. If a specific part of the group is emblematic of the overall group, or is essential to its survival, that may support a finding that the part qualifies as substantial within the meaning of Article 4 ... The historical examples of genocide also suggest that the area of the perpetrators' activity and control, as well as the possible extent of their reach, should be considered.[168]

This geographically limited approach is also followed at the ICTR – although it is rarely articulated in such clear terms – and the cases at that Tribunal tend to focus on specific towns, communes, or prefectures. In *Kamuhanda*, for example, the Trial Chamber concluded that 'the killings occurring in Gikomero Parish Compound, Gikomero *commune*, Kigali-Rural *préfecture*, were systematically directed against Tutsi civilians' and that 'the conduct of the Accused shows clearly that he participated in those killings with the specific intent to destroy the Tutsi ethnic group'.[169] Similarly, the *Akayesu* case focused on Taba commune in Gitarama *préfecture*; the *Ntagerura* case focused on the *préfecture* of Cyangugu; and the allegations in the *Ntakirutimana and Ntakirutimana* case focused on two very specific areas in Kibuye *préfecture*: Mugonero Complex in Gishyita commune, and Bisesero in the Gisovu and Gishyita communes.[170] All the Trial Chambers in these cases returned genocide convictions notwithstanding the limited geographical areas under consideration.[171]

[168] *Krstić* Appeal Judgement, *supra* note 9, paras. 12–13. Accord *Krajišnik* Trial Judgement, *supra* note 102, para. 853; *Blagojević and Jokić* Trial Judgement, *supra* note 99, para. 668; *Brđanin* Trial Judgement, *supra* note 99, para. 702. See also *Sikirica et al.* Sentencing Judgement, *supra* note 124, paras. 68, 76–77 (holding that genocidal intent may be established by evidence of an intent to destroy the group's leadership where such destruction would impact upon the survival of the group, and that an approach focusing on the limited geographical area is supported by Tribunal jurisprudence); *Krstić* Trial Judgement, *supra* note 51, para. 634 ('[A]n intent to destroy only part of the group must nevertheless concern a substantial part thereof, either numerically or qualitatively.'); *Jelisić* Trial Judgement, *supra* note 94, para. 82 ('A targeted part of a group would be classed as substantial either because the intent sought to harm a large majority of the group in question or the most representative members of the targeted community.').

[169] *Prosecutor* v. *Kamuhanda*, Case No. ICTR-99-54A-T, Judgement and Sentence, 22 January 2003 ('*Kamuhanda* Trial Judgement'), para. 645.

[170] See *Akayesu* Trial Judgement, *supra* note 6, para. 23; *Prosecutor* v. *Ntakirutimana and Ntakirutimana*, Case Nos. ICTR-96-10 and ICTR-96-17-T, Judgement and Sentence ('*Ntakirutimana and Ntakirutimana* Trial Judgement'), paras. 13, 15; *Cyangugu* Trial Judgement, *supra* note 107, paras. 41–46, 49–57, 61 (quoting the indictments against each of the accused).

[171] The *Cyangugu* Trial Chamber acquitted two of the three accused before it on unrelated grounds. See *Cyangugu* Trial Judgement, *supra* note 107, para. 829. On appeal, the ICTR Appeals Chamber also set aside the conviction of the third accused on unrelated grounds, holding that he had not been on notice that the prosecution intended to charge him with superior responsibility for the underlying offences of genocide allegedly committed in one specific location. See *ibid.*, paras. 164–165.

On the other hand, unlike the ICTR cases, the ICTY cases in which chambers have concluded that genocide occurred have had to deal with a challenging factual context; instead of the largely indiscriminate massacres of the protected group that characterised the Rwandan genocide,[172] the physical perpetrators of the crimes in Bosnia and Herzegovina did not generally kill the women, children, or elderly. The ICTY Appeals Chamber has firmly stated, however, that a full-fledged massacre of the targeted (part of the) group is not the only situation that may be termed genocide:

> In determining that genocide occurred at Srebrenica, the cardinal question is whether the intent to commit genocide existed. While this intent must be supported by the factual matrix, the offence of genocide does not require proof that the perpetrator chose the most efficient method to accomplish his objective of destroying the targeted part. Even where the method selected will not implement the perpetrator's intent to the fullest, leaving that destruction incomplete, this ineffectiveness alone does not preclude a finding of genocidal intent. The international attention focused on Srebrenica, combined with the presence of the UN troops in the area, prevented those members of the VRS Main Staff who devised the genocidal plan from putting it into action in the most direct and efficient way. Constrained by the circumstances, they adopted the method which would allow them to implement the genocidal design while minimizing the risk of retribution.[173]

The group 'as such' as intended target

In its commentary to the 1996 Draft Code, the ILC explained the import of the phrase 'as such' in the Genocide Convention's description of protected groups:

> [T]he intention must be to destroy the group 'as such', meaning as a separate and distinct entity, and not merely some individuals because of their membership in a particular group. In this regard, the General Assembly distinguished between the crimes of genocide and homicide in describing genocide as the 'denial of the right of existence of entire human groups' and homicide as the 'denial of the right to live of individual human beings' in its resolution 96 (I).[174]

[172] See, e.g., *Kayishema and Ruzindana* Trial Judgement, *supra* note 99, para. 289 (noting '[t]he widespread nature of the attacks and the sheer number of those who perished within just three months'); *ibid.*, para. 531:

> The number of Tutsis killed in the massacres, for which Kayishema is responsible, either individually or as a superior, provides evidence of Kayishema's intent. The Trial Chamber finds that enormous number[s] of Tutsis were killed in each of the four crime sites. In the Complex, the number of Tutsis killed was estimated to be about 8,000; there were between 8,000 and 27,000 Tutsis massacred at the Stadium; and, at Mubuga Church between 4,000 and 5,500 Tutsi were massacred. The number killed in Bisesero is more difficult to estimate, however, evidence suggests that the number of those who perished was well into the tens of thousands.

[173] *Krstić* Appeal Judgement, *supra* note 9, para. 32 (rejecting the defence contention that the charged conduct was 'inconsistent with the indiscriminate approach that has characterized all previously recognized instances of modern genocide') (quotation at para. 30). See also *ibid.*, para. 33 (internal quotation marks and footnotes omitted):

> The fact that the forcible transfer does not constitute in and of itself a genocidal act does not preclude a Trial Chamber from relying on it as evidence of the intentions of members of the VRS Main Staff. The genocidal intent may be inferred, among other facts, from evidence of other culpable acts systematically directed against the same group.

See *supra* text accompanying notes 152–162, *infra* text accompanying notes 258–265, for discussions of whether forcible transfer may constitute an underlying offence of genocide.

[174] ILC 1996 Draft Code with Commentaries, *supra* note 85, p. 45 (para. 7 of commentary to Art. 17 on genocide).

Adopting this interpretation, the judgements of the *ad hoc* Tribunals have uniformly held that the underlying offences 'must be committed against an individual because the individual was a member of a specific group and specifically because he belonged to this group, so that the victim is the group itself, not merely the individual.'[175] In particular, after reviewing the *travaux préparatoires* of the Genocide Convention, the *Niyitegeka* Appeals Chamber emphasised:

> [T]he term 'as such' clarifies the specific intent requirement. It does not prohibit a conviction for genocide in a case in which the perpetrator was also driven by other motivations that are legally irrelevant in this context. Thus the Trial Chamber was correct in interpreting 'as such' to mean that the proscribed acts were committed against the victims *because of* their membership in the protected group, but not *solely* because of such membership.[176]

The jurisprudence of the *ad hoc* Tribunals has treated the bases set forth in the Genocide Convention as an exhaustive listing of the characteristics that may define a protected group.[177] The *Akayesu* Trial Chamber provided simple definitions of each of the bases, describing a national group as 'a collection of people who are perceived to share a legal bond based on common citizenship, coupled with reciprocity of rights and duties'; an ethnic group as one 'whose members share a common language or culture'; a racial group as being 'based on the hereditary physical traits often identified with a geographical region, irrespective of linguistic, cultural, national or religious factors'; and a religious group as comprising individuals who 'share the same religion, denomination or mode of worship'.[178] Subsequent judgements have noted that there is no internationally accepted definition of each of these categories, but have generally followed the approach outlined in *Akayesu*.[179] In rejecting the prosecution's argument

175 *Prosecutor* v. *Niyitegeka*, Case No. ICTR 96-14-T, Judgement and Sentence, 16 May 2003 ('*Niyitegeka* Trial Judgement'), para. 410, affirmed in *Niyitegeka* Appeal Judgement, *supra* note 9, para. 53. Accord *Muvunyi* Trial Judgement, *supra* note 94, para. 485; *Mpambara* Trial Judgement, *supra* note 107, para. 8; *Blagojević and Jokić* Trial Judgement, *supra* note 99, para. 670; *Brđanin* Trial Judgement, *supra* note 99, para. 700; *Stakić* Trial Judgement, *supra* note 9, para. 521; *Krstić* Trial Judgement, *supra* note 51, para. 551; *Bagilishema* Trial Judgement, *supra* note 99, para. 64; *Musema* Trial Judgement, *supra* note 9, para. 165; *Rutaganda* Trial Judgement, *supra* note 9, para. 60. See also *Jelisić* Trial Judgement, *supra* note 94, para. 108:

> [T]he behaviour of the accused appears to indicate that, although he obviously singled out Muslims, he killed arbitrarily rather than with the clear intention to destroy a group. The Trial Chamber therefore concludes that it has not been proved beyond all reasonable doubt that the accused was motivated by the *dolus specialis* of the crime of genocide.

176 *Niyitegeka* Appeal Judgement, *supra* note 9, para. 53 (rejecting the appellant's contention that a motivation to commit the alleged acts against 'the enemy or supporters of the enemy' – see *ibid.*, para. 47 – should preclude criminal liability for genocide). See also *supra*, text accompanying notes 136–138, for a discussion of the legal irrelevance of personal or political motives.

177 See, e.g., *Blagojević and Jokić* Trial Judgement, *supra* note 99, para. 640; *Rutaganda* Trial Judgement, *supra* note 9, para. 48.

178 *Akayesu* Trial Judgement, *supra* note 6, paras. 512–515 (citing no authorities for the definitions, except the *Nottebohm* case before the International Court of Justice, in support of its definition of nationality).

179 See, e.g., *Rutaganda* Trial Judgement, *supra* note 9, para. 56 ('[T]here are no generally and internationally accepted precise definitions [of] national, ethnical, racial and religious groups'; each should 'be assessed in the light of a particular political, social and cultural context.'); accord *Kajelijeli* Trial Judgement, *supra* note 125, para. 811; *Musema* Trial Judgement, *supra* note 9, para. 161.

that a protected group could be defined negatively – all non-Serbs, for example – the Appeals Chamber has held that the Genocide Convention protects 'unique, positively defined groups with particular identities'.[180]

As noted above, consideration of the definition of the targeted group at the ICTY has been linked to the substantiality criterion for destruction and the geographic limitations of the alleged criminal activity. In a challenge to his conviction for committing genocide, the first at the ICTY,[181] Radislav Krstić, a general and corps commander in the Bosnian Serb army, asserted that 'the Trial Chamber's definition of the part of the national group he was found to have intended to destroy was unacceptably narrow.'[182] In reviewing this ground of appeal, the Appeals Chamber noted first that the indictment identified the targeted group as Bosnian Muslims, that this identification had been accepted by the Trial Chamber, and that it was unchallenged on appeal.[183] The precise question, therefore, was 'whether, in finding that … Krstić had genocidal intent, the Trial Chamber defined the relevant part of the Bosnian Muslim group in a way which comports with the requirements of Article 4 and the Genocide Convention'.[184]

Krstić argued that the Trial Chamber had impermissibly concluded that the shared intent of the army and himself had been to destroy the male Bosnian Muslim inhabitants of Srebrenica, a group that would not satisfy the substantiality criterion.[185] After reviewing various sources interpreting the Statute and the Convention, including the Tribunals' jurisprudence, the Appeals Chamber rejected Krstić's assertions and upheld the Trial Judgement's interpretation of the law. Placing particular emphasis on the symbolic importance of Srebrenica to Bosnian Muslims, the Appeals Chamber explained its conclusions thus:

> In this case, having identified the protected group as the national group of Bosnian Muslims, the Trial Chamber concluded that *the part the VRS Main Staff and Radislav Krstić targeted was the Bosnian Muslims of Srebrenica, or the Bosnian Muslims of Eastern Bosnia.*[186] … Although this population constituted only a small percentage of the overall Muslim population of Bosnia and Herzegovina at the time, the importance of the Muslim community of Srebrenica is not captured solely by its size. … Control over the Srebrenica region was … essential to … the continued survival of the Bosnian Muslim people. Because most of the Muslim inhabitants of the region had, by 1995, sought refuge within the Srebrenica enclave,

[180] *Stakić* Appeal Judgement, *supra* note 106, para. 24 (affirming the Trial Chamber's rejection of the approach adopted in the *Jelisić* Trial Judgement, *supra* note 94, para. 71). See also *ibid*., paras. 21, 23 (holding that the targeted group must be a 'group with a particular positive identity' and 'specific distinguishing characteristics').

[181] To date, the *Krstić* Trial Judgement, *supra* note 51, which concluded that the accused had participated in a first-category joint criminal enterprise to commit genocide, is the only instance in which an ICTY accused has been convicted for *committing* this crime. The conviction was overturned by the Appeals Chamber, which substituted a conviction for aiding and abetting genocide. See *Krstić* Appeal Judgement, *supra* note 9, paras. 134–144 & p. 87; see also Boas, Bischoff, and Reid, *supra* note 23, pp. 296–298.

[182] *Krstić* Appeal Judgement, *supra* note 9, para. 5. [183] *Ibid*., para. 6.

[184] *Ibid*., para. 7. [185] See *ibid*., para. 18.

[186] *Ibid*., para. 15 (emphasis added) (explaining that 'the Bosnian Muslim population in Srebrenica prior to its capture by the VRS forces in 1995 … represented not only the Muslim inhabitants of the Srebrenica municipality but also many Muslim refugees from the surrounding region').

> the elimination of that enclave would have accomplished the goal of purifying the entire region of its Muslim population.
>
> In addition, Srebrenica was important due to its prominence in the eyes of both the Bosnian Muslims and the international community … The elimination of the Muslim population of Srebrenica, despite the assurances given by the international community, would serve as a potent example to all Bosnian Muslims of their vulnerability and defenselessness in the face of Serb military forces. The fate of the Bosnian Muslims of Srebrenica would be emblematic of that of all Bosnian Muslims.
>
> Finally, the ambit of the genocidal enterprise in this case was limited to the area of Srebrenica … From the perspective of the Bosnian Serb forces alleged to have had genocidal intent in this case, the Muslims of Srebrenica were the only part of the Bosnian Muslim group within their area of control.[187]

In sum, the Appeals Chamber's response to Krstić's allegation that the group had been defined too narrowly was a series of logical steps: (1) the protected group was Bosnian Muslims; (2) the targeted population, which was an extremely significant portion of the protected group, was the Muslims of Eastern Bosnia, most of whom had gathered in the Srebrenica enclave; and (3) the murders of thousands of men and boys from that population were merely part of the entire genocidal enterprise, the goal of which was the destruction of the specifically targeted part of the Bosnian Muslim population.[188] This explanation is a more cogent justification for the conclusion that genocide was committed at Srebrenica than the reasoning of the Trial Chamber,[189] because it is more faithful to the terms and rationale of the law defining the elements of this crime.[190]

3.2.1.3 Requirement of actual membership in the group?

One of the few areas in which the Tribunals' application of the law on genocide has changed since *Akayesu* is the issue of whether the individual victims must in fact have been members of the protected group, or whether the subjective perception of such membership on the part of the relevant actor is sufficient. In both its statement

[187] *Ibid.*, paras. 15–17. [188] See especially *ibid.*, paras. 18–23.

[189] In so doing, the Appeals Chamber essentially substituted its own reasoning for that of the Trial Chamber, whose focus on the male murder victims undermined the conclusion that the charged offences constituted genocide. See, e.g., *Krstić* Trial Judgement, *supra* note 51, para. 581 (internal quotation marks omitted):

> Since in this case primarily the Bosnian Muslim men of military age were killed, a second issue is whether this group of victims represents a sufficient part of the Bosnian Muslim group so that the intent to destroy them qualifies as an intent to destroy the group in whole or in part[.]

See also *Krstić* Appeal Judgement, *supra* note 9, para. 22 (conceding that 'in portions of its Judgement, the Trial Chamber used imprecise language which lends support to the Defence's argument', but asserting nonetheless that 'the Trial Chamber's overall discussion makes clear that it identified the Bosnian Muslims of Srebrenica as the substantial part in this case'). Accord *Blagojević and Jokić* Trial Judgement, *supra* note 99, para. 673 (concluding that 'the targeted group was the Bosnian Muslims of Srebrenica – a substantial part of the Bosnian Muslim group').

[190] For a trial judgement applying the reasoning of the *Krstić* Appeals Chamber to a case not involving Srebrenica, see *Brđanin* Trial Judgement, *supra* note 99, paras. 731–736 (rejecting the prosecution argument that the protected groups were the Bosnian Muslims and the Bosnian Croats of the Autonomous Region of Krajina (ARK), and concluding instead that 'the protected groups … must be defined, in the present case, as the Bosnian Muslims and Bosnian Croats, as such', and that '[t]he Bosnian Muslims and Bosnian Croats of the ARK would therefore constitute parts of the protected groups').

of the law and its findings of fact, the *Akayesu* Trial Chamber explicitly chose the former approach, holding that offences committed against Hutu individuals could not constitute genocide because they were not members of the targeted group.[191] In addition, relying on the drafting history of the Genocide Convention, the Chamber concluded that the prohibition against genocide was intended to protect '"stable" groups, constituted in a permanent fashion and membership of which is determined by birth, with the exclusion of the more "mobile" groups which one joins through individual voluntary commitment, such as political and economic groups'.[192] Subsequent judgements take a more relaxed approach to the question of membership in the group, and two themes are discernible in these later cases.

The first theme, seeking to respond to observations that the differences between 'Tutsi' and 'Hutu', or 'Bosnian Serb' and 'Bosnian Muslim', are more socially and historically manufactured than the sort of permanent or immutable characteristic that is intended to define the protected groups, emphasises that group identities necessarily have both objective and subjective factors.[193] What matters ultimately, this line of authority holds, is the manner in which a group views itself and is treated by others:[194] if all Rwandans, for example, understood and employed the difference between Hutu and Tutsi,[195] and if people were targeted on this basis, then it would be inconsistent with the purpose of the prohibition to assert that genocide did not occur because the targeted group did not meet a particular definition of ethnicity.

A second, less developed theme in the later cases seems to echo the subjective perception branch of the law on persecution as a crime against humanity.[196] Thus in *Rutaganda*, the Trial Chamber noted that 'membership of a group is, in essence, a subjective rather than an objective concept. The victim is *perceived by the perpetrator of genocide* as belonging to a group slated for destruction. In some instances, the victim may perceive himself/herself as belonging to the said group.'[197] Almost immediately, however, the Chamber qualified its statement by observing that 'a

[191] See, e.g., *Akayesu* Trial Judgement, *supra* note 6, paras. 521, 712, 720–721. Accord, e.g., *Jelisić* Trial Judgement, *supra* note 94, para. 66.

[192] *Akayesu* Trial Judgement, *supra* note 6, para. 511 (also observing that 'a common criterion in the four types of groups protected by the Genocide Convention is that membership in such groups would seem to be normally not challengeable by its members, who belong to it automatically, by birth, in a continuous and often irremediable manner').

[193] See, e.g., *Semanza* Trial Judgement, *supra* note 106, para. 317; *Kajelijeli* Trial Judgement, *supra* note 125, para. 811; *Brđanin* Trial Judgement, *supra* note 99, para. 684.

[194] See, e.g., *Brđanin* Trial Judgement, *supra* note 99, para. 683 (citing, *inter alia*, *Krstić* Trial Judgement, *supra* note 51, paras. 557, 559; *Jelisić* Trial Judgement, *supra* note 94, para. 70; *Rutaganda* Trial Judgement, *supra* note 9, para. 56):

> In accordance with the jurisprudence of the Tribunal, the relevant protected group may be identified by means of the subjective criterion of the stigmatisation of the group, notably by the perpetrators of the crime, on the basis of its perceived national, ethnical, racial or religious characteristics. In some instances, the victim may perceive himself or herself to belong to the aforesaid group.

[195] See, e.g., *Muhimana* Trial Judgement, *supra* note 107, paras. 10–11.

[196] See Chapter 2, text accompanying notes 408–415.

[197] *Rutaganda* Trial Judgement, *supra* note 9, para. 56 (emphasis added). Accord *Jelisić* Trial Judgement, *supra* note 94, para. 70 (noting also that 'to attempt to define a national, ethnical or racial group today using objective

subjective definition alone is not enough to determine victim groups',[198] and ultimately held that 'in assessing whether a particular group may be considered as protected from the crime of genocide, it [would] proceed on a case-by-case basis, taking into account both the relevant evidence proffered and the political, social and cultural context'.[199] This reasoning confuses the questions of (1) how a group can be defined for purposes of determining whether it is protected by the Genocide Convention, and (2) whether a physical perpetrator or other relevant actor targeted an individual because of a belief (mistaken or not) that he or she was a member of the group. Unfortunately, it is this vague, fact-dependent formulation that has been adopted by most of the judgements to date.[200] In one of the most recent statements by either Appeals Chamber on this question, the *Media* Appeal Judgement noted that the jurisprudence of both Tribunals recognises that the subjective perception of those who commit the crime may, in certain circumstances, be taken into account for determining membership of the victim in a protected group.[201]

As such, all that may be drawn from the current jurisprudence is that, in order for any offences against specific individuals to constitute the crime of genocide, the victims must be at least perceived as belonging to the targeted group; which must at least be perceived as forming a distinct national, ethnic, racial, or religious group; and that there must be some objective support for the group to be treated as such.[202]

and scientifically irreproachable criteria would be a perilous exercise whose result would not necessarily correspond to the perception of the persons concerned by such categorisation'); *Semanza* Trial Judgement, *supra* note 106, para. 312; *Bagilishema* Trial Judgement, *supra* note 99, para. 65.

198 *Rutaganda* Trial Judgement, *supra* note 9, para. 57. 199 *Ibid.*, paras. 58, 373.

200 See, e.g., *Brđanin* Trial Judgement, *supra* note 99, para. 684:

> The correct determination of the relevant protected group has to be made on a case-by-case basis, consulting both objective and subjective criteria. This is so because subjective criteria alone may not be sufficient to determine the group targeted for destruction and protected by the Genocide Convention, for the reason that the acts identified in subparagraphs (a) to (e) of Article 4(2) must be in fact directed against 'members of the group'.

Accord *Kajelijeli* Trial Judgement, *supra* note 125, para. 811; *Muvunyi* Trial Judgement, *supra* note 94, para. 484; *Blagojević and Jokić* Trial Judgment, *supra* note 99, para. 36 ('The Trial Chamber finds that the correct determination of the relevant protected group has to be made on a case-by-case basis, consulting both objective and subjective criteria.'); *Musema* Trial Judgement, *supra* note 9, paras. 162–163. A few chambers, however, have placed more emphasis on the subjective aspect of the group's definition. See *Jelisić* Trial Judgement, *supra* note 94, para. 70 ('It is the stigmatisation of a group as a distinct national, ethnical or racial unit by the community which allows it to be determined whether a targeted population constitutes a national, ethnical or racial group in the eyes of the alleged perpetrators.'); *Ndindabahizi* Trial Judgement, *supra* note 121, paras. 468–470 (noting that 'the subjective intentions of the perpetrators are of primary importance'); *Bagilishema* Trial Judgement, *supra* note 99, para. 65:

> Moreover, the perpetrators of genocide may characterize the targeted group in ways that do not fully correspond to conceptions of the group shared generally, or by other segments of society … [I]f a victim was perceived by a perpetrator as belonging to a protected group, the victim should be considered by the Chamber as a member of the protected group, for the purposes of genocide.

201 See *Media* Appeal Judgement, *supra* note 111, para. 496 (observing that 'Hutu political enemies' did not constitute a protected group under the Convention, even under this approach, because neither the Trial Chamber nor the prosecution cited any evidence that the perpetrators considered these Hutu individuals to be equivalent to Tutsi).

202 See, e.g., *Muhimana* Trial Judgement, *supra* note 107, para. 500 ('The Prosecutor also has the burden of proving either that the victim belongs to the targeted ethnic, racial, national, or religious group or that the perpetrator of the crime believed that the victim belonged to the group.').

In the practice of the *ad hoc* Tribunals, this question is largely academic, as the ICTR chambers have universally concluded that the Tutsi victims were part of a distinct ethnic group,[203] and the ICTY chambers have similarly held that the Bosnian Muslims were a separate ethnic or national group.[204] More recent judgements rely on the growing body of jurisprudence, and simply cite to the conclusions of earlier chambers.[205]

In one respect, however, the law on genocide is actually broader in its definition of possible victims than other categories of crimes. Instead of restricting the qualifying targets of the crime to civilians, as the Tribunals have done for crimes against humanity, the Appeals Chamber has clarified that military personnel may be victims of underlying offences of genocide:

> [T]he intent requirement of genocide is not limited to instances where the perpetrator seeks to destroy only civilians. Provided the part intended to be destroyed is substantial, and provided that the perpetrator intends to destroy that part as such, there is nothing in the definition of genocide prohibiting, for example, a conviction where the perpetrator killed detained military personnel belonging to a protected group because of their membership in that group. It may be that, in practice, the perpetrator's genocidal intent will almost invariably encompass civilians, but that is not a legal requirement of the offence of genocide.[206]

3.2.2 Underlying offences

Unlike war crimes and crimes against humanity, the provisions on genocide in the Statutes of the ICTY and ICTR do not include a clearly designated residual category, nor are they open-ended lists. The conduct of the physical perpetrator, though it may vary in its specific details, must constitute one of the acts listed in subparagraphs (2)(a) to (2)(e) of Article 4/2 before it may qualify as an underlying

[203] *Simba* Trial Judgement, *supra* note 116, para. 415 ('It is not disputed in the present case that Tutsi are members of a protected group under the Statute.'); *Cyangugu* Trial Judgment, *supra* note 107, para. 690 (remarking that '[i]t has not been disputed that the Tutsi were considered an ethnic group during the events in 1994'); *Kajelijeli* Trial Judgement, *supra* note 125, paras. 241, 817 (taking judicial notice of the fact that 'between 6 April 1994 and 17 July 1994, citizens of Rwanda were severally identified according to the following ethnic classifications: Tutsi, Hutu and Twa', and finding accordingly 'that it has been established for the purposes of this case that the Tutsi in Rwanda were an ethnic group'); *Kayishema and Ruzindana* Trial Judgement, *supra* note 99, paras. 523–524 (accepting that the Tutsis were an ethnic group in part based on 'evidence that since 1931, Rwandans were required to carry identification cards which indicated the ethnicity of the bearer as Hutu, Tutsi or Twa' and expert testimony that 'identification based on ethnicity was a highly divisive issue in Rwanda'). See especially *Prosecutor* v. *Karemera, Ngirumpatse, and Nzirorera*, Decision on the Prosecutor's Interlocutory Appeal of Decision on Judicial Notice, 16 June 2006, Case No. ICTR-98-44, para. 25 (upholding the *Karemera* Trial Chamber's decision to take judicial notice of 'the existence of the Twa, Tutsi and Hutu as protected groups falling under the Genocide Convention').

[204] See, e.g., *Krajišnik* Trial Judgement, *supra* note 102, para. 855 (observing that '[t]here is no dispute that Bosnian Muslims and Bosnian Croats were national or ethnic groups in the sense of the Genocide Convention'); accord *Blagojević and Jokić* Trial Judgement, *supra* note 99, para. 667; *Krstić* Trial Judgement, *supra* note 51, paras. 559–560.

[205] See, e.g., *Muvunyi* Trial Judgement, *supra* note 94, para. 484.

[206] *Krstić* Appeal Judgement, *supra* note 9, para. 226.

offence of genocide.[207] While there are five subparagraphs, subparagraph (2)(b) contains two separate underlying offences – causing serious bodily harm and causing serious mental harm – so there are actually six underlying offences.[208] Of the underlying offences, four require proof of the result described: killing, causing serious bodily harm, causing serious mental harm, and forcible transfer of children.[209] Although the other two offences must still be combined with genocidal intent in order to constitute the crime of genocide, neither deliberate infliction of conditions calculated to bring about physical destruction, nor imposition of measures intended to prevent births, requires proof that the physical destruction or birth prevention has actually occurred.[210] Instead, and much like the defining general requirement of the crime itself, the offensive nature of the underlying act is in its intent; each offence must be committed in order to cause the eventual material destruction of the group.

As with much of the *ad hoc* Tribunals' jurisprudence on genocide, the definitions of the elements of these underlying offences were first offered by the *Akayesu* Trial Chamber, and have changed little since that 1998 judgement.[211] Developments in this area of the law on genocide have focused, and will likely continue to focus, on whether particular charged conduct meets the already established tests and standards for each underlying offence.[212]

[207] *Akayesu* Trial Judgement, *supra* note 6, para. 499; accord *Media* Appeal Judgement, *supra* note 111, para. 492; *Niyitegeka* Appeal Judgement, *supra* note 9, para. 48; *Jelisić* Appeal Judgement, *supra* note 9, para. 46; *Simba* Trial Judgement, *supra* note 116, para. 412; *Blagojević and Jokić* Trial Judgement, *supra* note 99, paras. 640, 656; *Cyangugu* Trial Judgement, *supra* note 107, para. 662; *Bagilishema* Trial Judgement, *supra* note 99, para. 55; *Musema* Trial Judgement, *supra* note 9, para. 154; *Rutaganda* Trial Judgement, *supra* note 9, para. 59.

[208] Cf. 18 U.S.C. § 1091 (2002) (United States federal statute codifying genocide and listing six underlying offences, including an analogue to causing serious mental harm as distinct from causing serious bodily harm). Most *ad hoc* judgements tend to lump both acts together, perhaps out of a desire to hew closely to the statutory text, and therefore the Genocide Convention. Yet it is clear that causing serious bodily harm and causing serious mental harm have been considered as offences separate and distinct from each other. See, e.g., *Akayesu* Trial Judgement, *supra* note 6, paras. 114–116 (finding that certain evidence of widespread deaths and grave injuries constituted proof of both killing and causing serious bodily harm); *Blagojević and Jokić* Trial Judgement, *supra* note 99, para. 647 (discussing the serious mental harm inflicted on Bosnian Muslim male survivors of the Srebrenica massacre); *ibid.*, paras. 650, 652–654 (finding that the forcible displacement of women, children, and the elderly from Srebrenica constituted serious mental harm). Beyond an unwillingness to undertake the difficult task of enunciating a clear standard for what constitutes serious mental harm, there is thus no legal or theoretical reason to avoid treating 'causing serious mental harm' as a separate offence. There may be a practical reason to avoid such precision in most circumstances, because serious physical harm usually causes or is accompanied by acute mental suffering. See, e.g., *Akayesu* Trial Judgement, *supra* note 6, para. 733 (finding that the practice of raping and mutilating Tutsi women before killing them, along with other acts of bodily and mental harm, was intended to destroy the group while inflicting acute suffering on its members in the process). Nevertheless, because judgements in these cases also serve the purpose of developing the field of international criminal law, it would be preferable for such decisions to distinguish clearly and consistently between the two underlying offences.

[209] See, e.g., *Brđanin* Trial Judgement, *supra* note 99, para. 688 ('The acts in subparagraphs (a) and (b) of Article 4 (2) require proof of a result.'); accord *Stakić* Trial Judgement, *supra* note 9, para. 514.

[210] See, e.g., *Brđanin* Trial Judgement, *supra* note 99, para. 691; *Stakić* Trial Judgement, *supra* note 9, para. 517.

[211] See, e.g., *Kayishema and Ruzindana* Trial Judgement, *supra* note 99, paras. 95, 108, 117–118; *Rutaganda* Trial Judgement, *supra* note 9, para. 47; *Brđanin* Trial Judgement, *supra* note 99, paras. 690–691.

[212] See *infra* note 241 (referring to the debate in the jurisprudence on whether forcible displacement may constitute genocide).

3.2.2.1 Killing

The physical perpetrator(s) intentionally caused the deaths of a member or members of the protected group[213]

3.2.2.1.1 Physical elements Most trial and appeal judgements do not provide a separate definition of the elements of killing as an underlying offence of genocide,[214] emphasising instead the two characteristics that distinguish this act from homicide offences underlying other international crimes. The first, discussed below, is the restriction of the possible *mens rea*. The second, related to the physical act itself, is the requirement that the victims be members of a group defined by one or more of the characteristics identified in the Genocide Convention and reiterated in the Tribunals' Statutes.[215] The clearest statement of the *actus reus* for this underlying offence is thus simply a modification of the definition of the other homicide underlying offences: (1) an individual, a member of a protected group, (2) is dead (3) as a result of (4) the act or omission of the physical perpetrator.[216]

3.2.2.1.2 Mental element Killing, as an underlying offence of genocide, has been consistently defined by *ad hoc* chambers as requiring the specific intent to cause the death of the victim.[217] Grounding its conclusion on a comparative textual analysis of the English and French texts of the ICTR Statute, the Penal Code of Rwanda, and the *travaux préparatoires* of the Genocide Convention, the *Akayesu* Trial Chamber held that:

213 As explained above, there is no minimum or maximum number of victims before qualifying conduct directed at a target group may constitute an underlying offence genocide. See *supra* note 167; see also *Muvunyi* Trial Judgement, *supra* note 94, para. 483; *Semanza* Trial Judgement, *supra* note 106, para. 316. In these restatements of the elements of the underlying offences, the use of singular and plural alternatives for both the perpetrators and the victims is intended to make clear that individual acts may qualify as underlying offences of genocide, even if most cases will include evidence of many different acts by a multiplicity of physical perpetrators and other actors (such as commanders, civilian superiors, or local officials). This approach is also consistent with the demands of complex international criminal trials, where individual witnesses are frequently unable to give direct evidence of mass atrocities, testifying instead to the individual horrors they saw or experienced.

214 See, for example, the following judgements, holding or implying that the elements of killing are the same as those of 'murder' without re-listing them: *Krajišnik* Trial Judgement, *supra* note 102, para. 859; *Blagojević and Jokić* Trial Judgement, *supra* note 99, para. 642; *Brđanin* Trial Judgement, *supra* note 99, para. 689; *Krstić* Trial Judgement, *supra* note 51, para. 543; *Jelisić* Trial Judgement, *supra* note 94, para. 63.

215 See, e.g., *Muvunyi* Trial Judgement, *supra* note 94, para. 486; *Blagojević and Jokić* Trial Judgement, *supra* note 99, para. 638; *Brđanin* Trial Judgement, *supra* note 99, para. 689; *Niyitegeka* Trial Judgement, *supra* note 175, para. 409. See *supra* text accompanying notes 163–190 (discussing definition of the protected group).

216 See Chapter 2, text accompanying note 204; Chapter 4, text accompanying notes 321–322.

217 Although the term 'specific intent' has been used almost exclusively by *ad hoc* chambers to refer to either genocidal or discriminatory intent for persecution as a crime against humanity, it is actually a term of art that has a broader meaning in criminal law. See *Black's Law Dictionary* (8th edn 2004), p. 826 (defining specific intent as 'the intent to accomplish the precise criminal act that one is later charged with'). Genocidal intent is but one example of specific intent. See *Akayesu* Trial Judgement, *supra* note 6, para. 498 (defining the 'special intent' for genocide as 'the specific intention, required as a constitutive element of the crime, which demands that the perpetrator clearly seeks to produce the act [or result] charged').

the term 'killing' used in the English version is too general, since it could very well include both intentional and unintentional homicides, whereas the term '*meurtre*', used in the French version, is more precise ... Given the presumption of innocence of the accused, and pursuant to the general principles of criminal law, the Chamber holds that the version more favourable to the accused should be upheld and finds that Article 2(2)(a) of the Statute must be interpreted in accordance with the definition of murder given in the Penal Code of Rwanda, according to which '*meurtre*' ... is homicide committed with the intent to cause death.[218]

Thus in contrast to the jurisprudence on crimes against humanity and war crimes, where the homicide that is the underlying offence for murder as a crime against humanity or as a form of persecution need not necessarily be committed with the intention to cause death,[219] subsequent chambers from both Tribunals have adopted the *Akayesu* approach without exception.[220] At least one trial judgement has expanded on the usual explanation for the requirement of intent to kill, stating that 'by their very nature the enumerated acts [in Article 4/2] are conscious, intentional, volitional acts that an individual cannot commit by accident or as a result of mere negligence'.[221] Few chambers, however, have truly attempted to explain why an intent to harm with knowledge that death is the likely result is a sufficiently culpable

218 *Akayesu* Trial Judgement, *supra* note 6, paras. 500–501. See also *ibid*., para. 501 (noting that in the drafting of the Genocide Convention, 'the proposal by certain delegations that premeditation be made a necessary condition for there to be genocide, was rejected, because [others] deemed it unnecessary ... in their opinion, by its constitutive physical elements, the very crime of genocide, necessarily entails premeditation'). Although the Chamber did not expand on its reference to the *travaux*, the view that premeditation was necessarily a factor in the 'constitutive physical elements' of genocide – the underlying offences – would explain the exclusion of unintentional homicides. Even though not all intentional homicides are premeditated, by definition no unintentional homicide can be premeditated. Nonetheless, the *ad hoc* jurisprudence makes clear that premeditation is not a requirement for killing as an underlying offence of genocide. See, e.g., *Stakić* Trial Judgement, *supra* note 9, para. 515 ('As regards the underlying acts, the word "killing" is understood to refer to intentional but not necessarily premeditated acts.').

219 See Chapter 2, text accompanying notes 216–220; Chapter 4, text accompanying notes 326, 330 (explaining that murder as an underlying offence is more frequently defined with an alternative mental state of indirect intent, usually described as intent to harm with acceptance of the reasonable likelihood that death will result). But see Chapter 2, text accompanying notes 212–215 (noting that ICTR trial chambers have required premeditation for murder as an underlying offence of crimes against humanity).

220 See, e.g., *Kayishema and Ruzindana* Appeal Judgement, *supra* note 110, para. 151; *Stakić* Trial Judgement, *supra* note 9, para. 515; *Semanza* Trial Judgement, *supra* note 106, para. 319; *Krstić* Trial Judgement, *supra* note 51, para 543; *Jelisić* Trial Judgement, *supra* note 94, para. 63; *Musema* Trial Judgement, *supra* note 9, para. 155; *Blagojević and Jokić* Trial Judgement, *supra* note 99, para. 640 n. 2057:

> In accordance with the general principle of interpretation *in dubio pro reo*, the International Tribunals' case law has opted for the interpretation most favourable to the accused and found that the term 'killings', in the context of a genocide charge, must be interpreted as referring to the definition of murder, i.e. intentional homicide.

Some judgments assert that the underlying offence for the crime of genocide by killing is the same as the homicide underlying offence for other international crimes, without acknowledging this restriction of the satisfactory mental state to the specific intent to kill. See, e.g., *Brđanin* Trial Judgement, *supra* note 99, para. 739 ('The elements of Article 4(2)(a) are identical to those required for wilful killing under Article 5(b) [*sic*] of the Statute, except that the former requires that they be committed against members of the protected groups.'). None, however, has specifically held that the alternative mental state recognised for those other crimes also applies to genocide, and none has explicitly found that a killing committed without the intent to kill may constitute an underlying offence of genocide.

221 *Bagilishema* Trial Judgement, *supra* note 99, para. 58.

mental state for a crime against humanity (including one coupled with persecutory intent), but not for genocide.[222] The most persuasive explanation is that of the *Kayishema and Ruzindana* Trial Chamber, which reasoned that since genocidal intent is a general requirement for the crime, it was inconsistent with this strict standard to expand the qualifying mental states for underlying offences.[223] This explanation may prove insufficient, however, if more chambers and other international courts explicitly adopt the approach that the genocidal intent requirement may be satisfied by an actor other than the physical perpetrator. Moreover, this reasoning does not take account of the multiplicity of underlying offences for genocide. If a physical perpetrator or other relevant actor merely intends to cause serious bodily harm, or to inflict eventually fatal conditions of life, but the conduct instead results in the immediate death of the victim, it would be logical for the underlying offence to be classified as killing, even if the intent was not to cause that death.

Trial chamber findings on killing as an underlying offence of genocide have been relatively straightforward, and in the ICTR, frequently involve consideration of extensive evidence of massacres or systematic murders of Tutsi victims by the accused or those under their effective control.[224] Typically in such cases, there was no question about the causation element, because the physical perpetrators used a weapon to end the life of the victims. In support of its conclusions that the accused in the *Media* case were responsible for genocide, however, the Trial Chamber employed a broader understanding of causation:

> The nature of media is such that causation of killing and other acts of genocide will necessarily be effected by an immediately proximate cause in addition to the communication itself … [T]his does not diminish the causation to be attributed to the media, or the criminal accountability of those responsible for the communication … [T]he killing of Tutsi civilians can be said to have resulted, at least in part, from the message of ethnic targeting for death that was clearly and effectively disseminated through RTLM [radio], *Kangura* [newspaper] and CDR [political party propaganda], before and after 6 April 1994.[225]

[222] See Chapter 2, text accompanying notes 212–222 (discussing the variations in the definition of the *mens rea* element of murder, one of which includes the indirect intent alternative mental state described above); *ibid.*, text accompanying notes 240–247 (similar discussion for extermination). See also Chapter 4, section 4.2.2.4 (discussing this issue in the context of murder as an underlying offence for war crimes).

[223] See *Kayishema and Ruzindana* Trial Judgement, *supra* note 99, paras. 101–104, affirmed in *Kayishema and Ruzindana* Appeal Judgement, *supra* note 110, para. 151 (holding that 'there is virtually no difference' between the terms 'killing' and '*meurtre*' because both are linked to the intent to destroy in whole or in part, and refer to 'intentional but not necessarily premeditated murder').

[224] See, e.g., *Gacumbitsi* Trial Judgement, *supra* note 106, para. 261 (finding that 'a substantial number of Tutsi civilians were killed in Rusumo *commune* between 7 and 18 April 1994'); *Niyitegeka* Trial Judgement, *supra* note 175, paras. 411–420 (outlining findings that the accused was one of the leaders of several 'large-scale attacks' against Tutsi); *Semanza* Trial Judgement, *supra* note 106, paras. 424–435 (grounding its conclusion that genocide occurred on killings that took place at four sites as part of 'a general campaign')

[225] *Media* Trial Judgement, *supra* note 100, paras. 952–953. See also *Media* Appeal Judgement, *supra* note 111, para. 515 (finding that the Trial Chamber's conclusion that RTLM broadcasts substantially contributed to the killings of certain named individuals was reasonable).

Nevertheless, it does not appear that the Chamber intended to expand the permissible scope of the conduct that would qualify as killing as an underlying offence of genocide, as none of the accused was held responsible for physically committing genocide, even though their words and deeds 'caused' the victims' deaths.[226]

3.2.2.2 Causing serious bodily or mental harm[227]

The physical perpetrator(s) intentionally caused harm to the organs, senses, or physical health, or to mental faculties of a member or members of the protected group, and that harm significantly and adversely affected the ability to lead a normal life.

3.2.2.2.1 Physical elements As defined by the *Kayishema and Ruzindana* Trial Chamber, and applied by almost every other chamber since, 'serious bodily harm' means 'harm that seriously injures the health, causes disfigurement or causes any serious injury to the external [or] internal organs or senses'.[228] A clear definition of 'serious mental harm' appeared more elusive, leading the Trial Chamber to assert unhelpfully that the term 'should be interpreted on a case-by-case basis in light of the relevant jurisprudence'.[229] The jurisprudence has clarified that, although the harm need not be 'permanent or irremediable',[230] the requirement of seriousness 'entails more than minor impairment [of] mental or physical faculties',[231] and mandates that the harm result in 'a grave and long-term disadvantage to a person's

[226] See, e.g., *Media* Trial Judgement, *supra* note 100, paras. 973, 977 (finding Barayagwiza responsible for genocide, ostensibly with killing as the underlying offence, on the basis of superior responsibility); *ibid.*, paras. 974–975 (holding Nahimana and Barayagwiza responsible for instigating genocide); *ibid.*, para. 977A (concluding that Ngeze was responsible for instigating, ordering, and aiding and abetting genocide).

[227] As noted above, the disjunctive 'or' in 'causing serious bodily or mental harm' means that this phrase actually describes two different underlying offences. See *supra* note 208. However, since almost all the jurisprudence discusses the acts in subparagraph (b) jointly, they are presented here in the same subsection.

[228] *Kayishema and Ruzindana* Trial Judgement, *supra* note 99, para. 109; accord, e.g., *Muvunyi* Trial Judgement, *supra* note 94, para. 487; *Blagojević and Jokić* Trial Judgement, *supra* note 99, para. 645; *Cyangugu* Trial Judgement, *supra* note 107, para. 664 ('The term causing serious bodily harm refers to serious acts of physical violence falling short of killing that seriously injure the health, cause disfigurement, or cause any serious injury to the external or internal organs or senses.'); *Stakić* Trial Judgement, *supra* note 9, para. 516 (causing serious bodily harm includes 'harm that damages health or causes disfigurement or injury').

[229] *Kayishema and Ruzindana* Trial Judgement, *supra* note 99, para. 113. See also *Blagojević and Jokić* Trial Judgement, *supra* note 99, para. 646 (noting that a case-by-case approach 'with due regard for the particular circumstances of the case' is appropriate).

[230] *Akayesu* Trial Judgement, *supra* note 6, para. 502; accord *Muvunyi* Trial Judgement, *supra* note 94, para. 487; *Muhimana* Trial Judgement, *supra* note 107, para. 502; *Cyangugu* Trial Judgement, *supra* note 107, para. 664; *Kamuhanda* Trial Judgement, *supra* note 169, para. 634; *Stakić* Trial Judgement, *supra* note 9, para. 516; *Semanza* Trial Judgement, *supra* note 106, paras. 320–322; *Krstić* Trial Judgement, *supra* note 51, para. 513; *Bagilishema* Trial Judgement, *supra* note 99, para. 59; *Musema* Trial Judgement, *supra* note 9, para. 156; *Rutaganda* Trial Judgement, *supra* note 9, para. 51; *Kayishema and Ruzindana* Trial Judgement, *supra* note 99, para. 108.

[231] *Bagilishema* Trial Judgement, *supra* note 99, para. 59; accord *Muvunyi* Trial Judgement, *supra* note 94, para. 487; *Muhimana* Trial Judgement, *supra* note 107, para. 502; *Blagojević and Jokić* Trial Judgement, *supra* note 99, para. 645; *Cyangugu* Trial Judgement, *supra* note 107, para. 664; *Semanza* Trial Judgement, *supra* note 106, para. 321; *Krstić* Trial Judgement, *supra* note 51, para. 510.

ability to lead a normal and constructive life'.[232] Chambers have accordingly recognised that conduct rising to the level of serious mental harm includes any inhumane or degrading treatment that would not otherwise constitute physical harm,[233] and acts of mental torture,[234] but no further refinements of the definition have been offered.

Ultimately, whether the conduct alleged causes the requisite level of harm within the meaning of Article 4/2 is a fact-intensive inquiry, which should be considered in light of the evidence presented in a particular case.[235] As such, the factual circumstances underlying *ad hoc* chamber findings have varied widely, and the following have been found to constitute serious bodily or mental harm: severe beatings;[236] torture;[237] inhumane or degrading treatment;[238] sexual violence including rape;[239] death threats during interrogations, either alone or combined with beatings;[240] and

[232] *Krstić* Trial Judgement, *supra* note 51, para. 513 (noting also, in apparent reference to mental harm, that 'serious harm … must involve harm that goes beyond temporary unhappiness, embarrassment or humiliation'); see also *Krajišnik* Trial Judgement, *supra* note 102, para. 862; *Blagojević and Jokić* Trial Judgement, *supra* note 99, para. 645; *Brđanin* Trial Judgement, *supra* note 99, para. 690; *Stakić* Trial Judgement, *supra* note 9, para. 516.

[233] See *Bagilishema* Trial Judgement, *supra* note 99, para. 59; *Musema* Trial Judgement, *supra* note 9, para. 156; *Rutaganda* Trial Judgement, *supra* note 9, para. 51.

[234] *Bagilishema* Trial Judgement, *supra* note 99, para. 59; *Musema* Trial Judgement, *supra* note 9, para. 156; *Rutaganda* Trial Judgement, *supra* note 9, para. 51.

[235] See, e.g., *Krstić* Trial Judgement, *supra* note 51, para. 513 ('The gravity of the suffering must be assessed on a case-by-case basis and with due regard for the particular circumstances.'); accord *Blagojević and Jokić* Trial Judgement, *supra* note 99, para. 646.

[236] See, e.g., *Brđanin* Trial Judgement, *supra* note 99, paras. 745–903 (detailing the evidence establishing beyond a reasonable doubt that serious bodily harm, particularly regular and severe beatings, was intentionally inflicted on Bosnian Muslim and Bosnian Croat victims held in Bosnian Serb detention facilities).

[237] See, e.g., *ibid.*, paras. 746, 751, 772, 776 (finding that Bosnian Muslim and Bosnian Croat detainees were beaten and given electroshocks during interrogation); Chapter 2, section 2.2.3.6.2 (noting that the definition of torture under customary international law and the jurisprudence of the Tribunals includes beatings inflicted for the purpose of gleaning information in interrogations).

[238] See, e.g., *Musema* Trial Judgement, *supra* note 9, paras. 932, 933 (finding that '[c]ertain degrading acts were purposely intended to humiliate [the victims] for being Tutsis', and noting that 'acts of serious bodily and mental harm … were often accompanied by humiliating utterances, which clearly indicated that the intention underlying each specific act was to destroy the Tutsi group as a whole'); *Brđanin* Trial Judgement, *supra* note 99, paras. 823–825 (finding that male and female Bosnian Muslim and Bosnian Croat detainees were 'forced to perform sexual acts with each other, in front of a crowd of cheering men in police and Bosnian Serb military uniforms'; that 'two other male detainees, at least one of whom was a Bosnian Muslim, were forced to perform *fellatio* on each other … whilst being subjected to ethnic slurs'; that one detainee 'was forced to eat his statement, which he had written in the Latin script, and forced to rewrite it in Cyrillic'; and that detainees were 'forced to extend the Serbian three-fingered salute').

[239] See, e.g., *Brđanin* Trial Judgement, *supra* note 99, paras. 835, 847, 852, 856; *Akayesu* Trial Judgement, *supra* note 6, paras. 706–707. See especially *Musema* Trial Judgement, *supra* note 9, para. 933:

> In this context, the acts of rape and sexual violence were an integral part of the plan conceived to destroy the Tutsi group. Such acts targeted Tutsi women, in particular, and specifically contributed to their destruction and therefore that of the Tutsi group as such. Witness N testified before the Chamber that [one victim], who was left for dead by those who raped her, had indeed been killed in a way. Indeed, the Witness specified that 'what they did to her is worse than death'.

For the definition of rape under the jurisprudence of the Tribunals, see Chapter 2, section 2.2.3.7.

[240] *Akayesu* Trial Judgement, *supra* note 6, paras. 711–712. Although not stated explicitly, this holding would support a conclusion that death threats, at least during an interrogation, constitute 'serious mental harm' within the meaning of Article 4 of the ICTY Statute and Article 2 of the ICTR Statute. This interpretation has apparently been adopted by ICTY trial chambers. See *Blagojević and Jokić* Trial Judgement, *supra* note 99, para. 646; *Brđanin* Trial Judgement, *supra* note 99, para. 690.

forcible displacement.[241] Although not clearly and distinctly treated as such in the *Akayesu* Trial Judgement, which was the first judicial decision ever to treat rape as a manifestation of genocide, the Chamber's discussion of this offence is most logically construed as characterising it as serious bodily or mental harm.[242]

3.2.2.2.2 Mental element In discussing the offence of causing serious mental harm, the *Kayishema and Ruzindana* Trial Chamber concluded that liability only arises 'under these circumstances only where, at the time of the act, the accused [or other relevant actor] had the intention to inflict serious mental harm in pursuit of the specific intention to destroy a group in whole or in part'.[243] The same intent requirement has been imposed for causing serious physical harm.[244]

3.2.2.3 Deliberate infliction of eventually destructive conditions of life

The physical perpetrator(s) deliberately inflicted on a member or members of the protected group conditions of life calculated to bring about the partial or total physical destruction of the group.

3.2.2.3.1 Examples of qualifying conduct This underlying offence, although frequently the subject of *obiter dicta* in *ad hoc* Tribunal judgements, has received comparatively less attention in terms of its definition. Most discussions in ICTR and ICTY judgements do little more than recite or invoke the description first outlined by the *Akayesu* Trial Judgement, which noted that this underlying offence entails 'methods of destruction by which the perpetrator does not immediately kill the members of the group, but which, ultimately, seek their physical destruction'.[245] Subsequent ICTY judgements have clarified that this offence entails conduct which, while falling short of

241 See, e.g., *Blagojević and Jokić* Trial Judgement, *supra* note 99, para. 671 (finding that '[t]he forcible transfer out of the enclave of the women, children and elderly, in combination with [the massacre of over 7,000 men], or on its own, caused the survivors to suffer serious mental harm'); *Stakić* Trial Judgement, *supra* note 9, para. 516; *Krstić* Trial Judgement, *supra* note 51, para. 513. But see *supra* text accompanying notes 158–162, *infra* text accompanying notes 258–265 (Appeals Chamber jurisprudence explaining that forcible transfer by itself cannot constitute the actual or eventual destruction that is required for genocide).

242 *Akayesu* Trial Judgement, *supra* note 6, paras. 706–707 (noting that '[n]umerous Tutsi women were forced to endure acts of sexual violence, mutilations and rape, often repeatedly, often publicly and often by more than one assailant; that 'on several occasions, by his presence, his attitude and his utterances, Akayesu encouraged such acts'; and that 'the above-mentioned acts with which Akayesu is charged indeed render him individually criminally responsible for having abetted in [*inter alia*] the infliction of serious bodily and mental harm on members of said group'); see also *ibid.*, paras. 731–733 (finding that rape was part of a 'process of destruction', and was followed in most cases by killing the victim).

243 *Kayishema and Ruzindana* Trial Judgement, *supra* note 99, para. 112.

244 *Blagojević and Jokić* Trial Judgement, *supra* note 99, para. 645 ('[T]he harm must be inflicted intentionally.'). See also *Muvunyi* Trial Judgement, *supra* note 94, para. 487; *Brđanin* Trial Judgement, *supra* note 99, para. 690; *Kayishema and Ruzindana* Trial Judgement, *supra* note 99, para. 112; but see *Cyangugu* Trial Judgment, *supra* note 107, para. 693 (not holding the accused liable for serious bodily harm where there was not sufficient reliable evidence to determine that the physical perpetrators caused it with the requisite genocidal intent).

245 *Akayesu* Trial Judgement, *supra* note 6, para. 505, cited or quoted with approval in, e.g., *Brđanin* Trial Judgement, *supra* note 99, para. 692; *Stakić* Trial Judgement, *supra* note 9, para. 518; *Musema* Trial Judgement, *supra* note 9, para. 157; *Rutaganda* Trial Judgement, *supra* note 9, para. 51.

killing or inflicting serious bodily or mental harm,[246] could reasonably be expected to lead to the partial or total destruction of the targeted group,[247] and which in fact tended to have a destructive effect on the group.[248] Relevant factors for making this assessment include the length of time during which the group members were subjected to such conditions,[249] and the particular vulnerabilities of the victims in question.[250]

ICTR and ICTY Chambers have ruled that qualifying conduct includes 'systematic expulsion from homes', or forcible displacement;[251] and reduction of essential medical services below minimum requirements.[252] Again echoing the *Akayesu* Trial Judgement without commentary or elaboration, most chambers also include the imposition of a subsistence diet; a forced lack of proper housing, clothing, or hygiene; and requiring excessive work or physical exertion as examples of qualifying conduct.[253] Little effort is expended to explain, however, why these latter circumstances would necessarily lead to the eventual physical destruction of the group through the death of its members. It is an unfortunate truth that the lives of millions of people around the world are currently characterised by such conditions, and it is unclear from the jurisprudence whether it is the *imposition* of the conditions,[254] or their severity, or their accumulation[255] that would qualify their infliction as this underlying offence of genocide.[256]

246 *Brđanin* Trial Judgement, *supra* note 99, paras. 691, 905.

247 See, e.g., *ibid*., para. 906 (focusing on 'the objective probability of these conditions leading to the physical destruction of the group in part').

248 *Krajišnik* Trial Judgement, *supra* note 102, paras. 862–863.

249 *See Brđanin* Trial Judgement, *supra* note 99, para. 906; *Kayishema and Ruzindana* Trial Judgement, *supra* note 99, para. 548.

250 *See Brđanin* Trial Judgement, *supra* note 99, para. 906.

251 *Akayesu* Trial Judgement, *supra* note 6, para. 506. Accord *Brđanin* Trial Judgement, *supra* note 99, para. 691; *Musema* Trial Judgement, *supra* note 9, para. 157; *Rutaganda* Trial Judgement, *supra* note 9, para. 51. In fact, even the *Stakić* Trial Chamber echoed earlier chambers in holding that 'systematic expulsion from homes' could qualify as this underlying offence, see *Stakić* Trial Judgement, *supra* note 9, para. 517, notwithstanding its admonition, two paragraphs later, that deportation cannot be genocide. See *infra* text accompanying note 258. No effort was made to reconcile these two statements.

252 *Akayesu* Trial Judgement, *supra* note 6, para. 506; *Kayishema and Ruzindana* Trial Judgement, *supra* note 99, para. 116; see also *Brđanin* Trial Judgement, *supra* note 99, para. 691 (describing this conduct as 'denial of the right to medical services').

253 *Akayesu* Trial Judgement, *supra* note 6, para. 506; see also *Brđanin* Trial Judgement, *supra* note 99, para. 691 (describing these circumstances as 'lead[ing] to a slow death'); *Stakić* Trial Judgement, *supra* note 9, para. 517; *Musema* Trial Judgement, *supra* note 9, para. 157; *Rutaganda* Trial Judgement, *supra* note 9, para. 51; *Kayishema and Ruzindana* Trial Judgement, *supra* note 99, paras. 115–116.

254 See ILC 1996 Draft Code with Commentaries, *supra* note 85, p. 46 (para. 15 n. 124 of commentary to Art. 17 on genocide) (quoting Robinson, *supra* note 47, which noted that '[i]nstances of genocide that could come under subparagraph (c) are such as placing a group of people on a subsistence diet, reducing required medical services below a minimum, withholding sufficient living accommodations, etc., *provided that these restrictions are imposed* with intent to destroy the group in whole or in part') (emphasis added).

255 For example, a subsistence diet is, by definition, enough food to sustain life. See, e.g., *Oxford English Dictionary* (2d edn 1989) (defining the term as 'the minimum amount of food requisite to keep a person in health'). Unless it is combined with other conduct, such as excessive labour, it is difficult to see how it would lead to the physical destruction of the group.

256 It is likely that the drafters of the Genocide Convention, confident that all would remember the deprivations imposed on victims of the Holocaust in ghettoes and labour and concentration camps, felt no need to craft specific standards for this 'act of genocide'. International tribunals trying criminal cases half a century later have a different task, and their rulings should comply with the exigencies of criminal law.

The issue of forcible displacement as the factual basis for an underlying offence of genocide was, until recently, the subject of some controversy at the ICTY.[257] In 2003, the *Stakić* Trial Judgement opined as follows, relying on commentators and the *travaux préparatoires* of the Genocide Convention:

> It does not suffice to deport a group or a part of a group. A clear distinction must be drawn between physical destruction and mere dissolution of a group. The expulsion of a group or part of a group does not in itself suffice for genocide. As Kreß has stated, '[t]his is true even if the expulsion can be characterised as a tendency to the dissolution of the group, taking the form of its fragmentation or assimilation. This is because the dissolution of the group is not to be equated with physical destruction'. In this context the Chamber recalls that a proposal by Syria in the Sixth Committee to include '[i]mposing measures intended to oblige members of a group to abandon their homes in order to escape the threat of subsequent ill-treatment' as a separate sub-paragraph of Article II of the Convention against Genocide was rejected by twenty-nine votes to five, with eight abstentions.[258]

In particular, the *Stakić* Trial Chamber asserted later in the judgement that 'deporting a group or part of a group is insufficient if it is not accompanied by methods seeking the physical destruction of the group'.[259] In 2005, however, while the *Stakić* appeal was pending, the *Blagojević and Jokić* Trial Chamber offered the opposing view.[260]

In 2004, the *Krstić* Appeals Chamber had noted in passing that 'forcible transfer does not constitute in and of itself a genocidal act'.[261] It did also observe, however, that 'forcible transfer could be an additional means by which to ensure the physical destruction of the Bosnian Muslim community in Srebrenica'.[262] The Appeals Chamber did not have occasion to elaborate on or reconcile these statements in either of its judgements in *Stakić*[263] or *Blagojević and Jokić*, though in the latter judgement it did rely on its *Krstić* holding to reject the Trial

[257] See also *supra* text accompanying notes 152–162.

[258] *Stakić* Trial Judgement, *supra* note 9, para. 519 (quoting and citing K. Kreß, *Münchner Kommentar zum StGB*, Rn 57, §6 VStGB, (Munich 2003)).

[259] *Ibid.*, para. 557.

[260] *Blagojević and Jokić* Trial Judgement, *supra* note 99, para. 666 (quoted *supra* p. 166).

[261] *Krstić* Appeal Judgement, *supra* note 9, para. 33 (citing, *inter alia*, the same German commentator and case relied upon in the *Stakić* Trial Judgement, see *supra* note 258).

[262] *Ibid.*, para. 31.

[263] The issue of whether forcible displacement by itself could constitute one of the underlying offences of genocide was raised only obliquely in *Stakić*, in relation to the prosecution's appeal of the Trial Chamber's finding that 'the *dolus specialis* has not been proved in relation to "deliberately inflicting on the group conditions of life calculated to bring about its physical destruction in whole or in part"', which was coupled with a specific reference to deportation. *Stakić* Trial Judgement, *supra* note 9, para. 557, quoted in *Stakić* Appeal Judgement, *supra* note 106, para. 46. The Appeals Chamber's discussion, and subsequent dismissal of the prosecution's appeal on this point, focused on the Trial Chamber's analysis of other evidence in the case, specifically the accused's 'public statements suggest[ing] that his intention was only to displace the Bosnian Muslim population and not to destroy it'. *Stakić* Appeal Judgement, *supra* note 106, para. 47.

Chamber's reasoning that forcible displacement by itself can qualify as the actual or eventual destruction required for genocide.[264] It would seem, however, that even if forcible displacement of part or all of a protected group would not, by itself, constitute any of the underlying offences of genocide, it should qualify as the 'deliberate infliction of conditions of life calculated to bring about physical destruction' if it is conducted under conditions that actually threaten physical survival, or with the knowledge that the displaced persons will be unable to survive. Such circumstances could include, for example, the expulsion of a population in harsh or severe weather conditions without adequate clothing or temporary shelter, or without adequate food or water.[265]

3.2.2.3.2 Mental element? The plain text of the Statute makes clear that the conduct for this underlying offence must be undertaken deliberately, and that the measures imposed must be consciously designed to achieve the genocidal result. To the extent that the person committing the offence is the accused, those minor qualifications add little, if anything, to the general requirement of genocidal intent, because deliberate action to impose these kinds of measures and the conscious design of such measures would be subsumed within the intent to cause the partial or entire destruction of the group. But in a case where the trial chamber distinguishes between the physical perpetrator and the accused or other relevant actors, these textual criteria may lead it to conclude that general intent on the part of the physical perpetrator is required. That is, the physical perpetrator must deliberately undertake the conduct that results in the harm to the victim, but need not have specific genocidal intent, which may be supplied by a different relevant actor.

3.2.2.4 Prevention of births

The physical perpetrator(s) imposed measures intended to prevent births within the protected group.

3.2.2.4.1 Examples of qualifying conduct Mindful of its place in history, the *Akayesu* Trial Chamber attempted to define, or at least give examples of qualifying

[264] *Blagojević and Jokić* Appeal Judgement, *supra* note 102, para. 123 (citing the *Krstić* Appeal Judgement and holding that, while forcible transfer is not 'in and of itself a genocidal act', it is 'a relevant consideration as part of the overall factual assessment' for an inference of genocidal intent). See *supra* text accompanying notes 158–162.

[265] See ILC 1996 Draft Code with Commentaries, *supra* note 85, p. 46 (para. 17 of commentary to Art. 17 on genocide) ('Moreover, the forcible transfer of members of a group, particularly when it involves the separation of family members, could also constitute genocide under subparagraph (c).'). This underlying offence appears to have been charged in the *Popović* case, so it is possible that decisions and judgements of the trial or appeals chambers in this case may shed additional light on its elements. See *Prosecutor* v. *Popović, Beara, Nikolić, Borovčanin, Miletić, Gvero, and Pandurević*, Case No. IT-05-88-T, Indictment, 4 August 2006 ('*Popović et al.* Indictment'), para. 33.

conduct for, each of the underlying offences of genocide.[266] For this offence, it gave several examples of conduct that may constitute the prevention of births: sexual mutilation; sterilisation; forced birth control; separation of the sexes; prohibition of marriages; and deliberate impregnation of women in patriarchal societies where identity is determined patrilineally.[267] The Chamber also noted that the prohibited results could also be accomplished indirectly, by what it referred to as 'mental means': 'For instance, rape can be a measure intended to prevent births when the person raped refuses subsequently to procreate, in the same way that members of a group can be led, through threats or trauma, not to procreate.'[268] These statements appear to have been *obiter dicta*, because the Chamber made no finding that any of the acts charged constituted the prevention of births within the Tutsi population of Rwanda. Similarly, although subsequent ICTR judgements have repeated *Akayesu*'s list of qualifying conduct,[269] none has ever convicted an accused on the basis of this underlying offence, or otherwise found that it was established by the evidence.

None of the ICTY chambers has ever had reason to discuss this underlying offence, as the allegation has never appeared in any indictment before that Tribunal.

3.2.2.4.2 Mental element? As with the underlying offence of deliberate infliction of destructive conditions of life (listed in Article 4/2(2)(c)), there is no indication in either the statutory text or in the limited jurisprudence that this offence has an independent mental element for cases involving accused who are also physical perpetrators. As noted above, however, in a case where the trial chamber distinguishes between the physical perpetrator and the accused or other relevant actors, it may conclude that general intent on the part of the physical perpetrator is required.

3.2.2.5 Forcible transfer of children

The physical perpetrator(s) forcibly transferred children of the protected group to another group.

No *ad hoc* chamber has ever attempted to outline the elements of this underlying offence, even in *obiter dicta*. The *Akayesu* Trial Judgement sought to clarify the

[266] The indictment did not specifically charge Akayesu with all the underlying offences, and it is only at the end of the judgement that the Chamber clearly explains which underlying offence was established by the evidence presented at trial. See *Akayesu* Trial Judgement, *supra* note 6, paras. 698–734 (finding that Akayesu was responsible for killing and causing serious bodily and mental harm as underlying offences of genocide).

[267] *Ibid.*, paras. 507–508. [268] *Ibid.*, para. 508.

[269] See *Musema* Trial Judgement, *supra* note 9, para. 158; *Rutaganda* Trial Judgement, *supra* note 9, para. 53; *Kayishema and Ruzindana* Trial Judgement, *supra* note 99, para. 117.

scope of the prohibition, stating that the statutory text was intended to sanction not only direct forcible transfer, but also 'acts of threats or trauma which would lead to the forcible transfer of children'.[270] Although this assertion has been repeated by later trial chambers,[271] neither *Akayesu* nor any of the later judgements cited to the *travaux préparatoires* of the Genocide Convention or any other authority or source of international law to support this interpretation.

3.2.2.5.1 Mental element? As with the two previous underlying offences, there is no indication in either the statutory text or in the limited jurisprudence that the forcible transfer of children has an independent mental element in cases involving accused who are also physical perpetrators. As noted above, however, in a case where the trial chamber distinguishes between the physical perpetrator and the accused or other relevant actors, it may conclude that general intent on the part of the physical perpetrator is required.

3.3 Elements of conspiracy to commit genocide

An agreement between two or more persons that genocide or any of its underlying offences shall be committed, concluded with the intent to partially or completely destroy a national, ethnic, racial, or religious group.

Conspiracy to commit genocide is one of the three inchoate crimes in the *ad hoc* Tribunal Statutes that are related to the separate crime of genocide.[272] As Volume I of this series explains, international criminal law recognises at least three forms of common-purpose liability, one of which – joint criminal enterprise – has been defined, developed, and applied at the *ad hoc* Tribunals.[273] It is important to keep in mind, however, the distinctions between common-purpose liability and conspiracy: although some of the elements are the same, such as an agreement to commit a crime,[274] common-purpose liability remains a method of participation in a realised crime; a conspiracy to commit a crime, by contrast, need not be successful in order to attract penal sanctions.[275]

[270] *Akayesu* Trial Judgement, *supra* note 6, para. 509.

[271] See *Musema* Trial Judgement, *supra* note 9, para. 159; *Rutaganda* Trial Judgement, *supra* note 9, para. 54; *Kayishema and Ruzindana* Trial Judgement, *supra* note 99, para. 118.

[272] The ICTR Statute has one inchoate war crime, see *supra* note 24, but it appears that it has never been charged in an indictment at that Tribunal.

[273] Boas, Bischoff, and Reid, *supra* note 23, pp. 124–125, 138.

[274] See, e.g., *ibid.*, pp. 37–44, 283 n. 13.

[275] See, e.g., *Niyitegeka* Trial Judgement, *supra* note 175, para. 423 ('[T]he act of conspiracy itself is punishable, even if the substantive offence [genocide] has not actually been perpetrated.'); *Musema* Trial Judgement, *supra* note 9, para. 194 (holding that the 'crime of conspiracy to commit genocide is punishable, even if it fails to produce a result'). Accord *Brđanin* Trial Judgement, *supra* note 99, para. 725; *Kajelijeli* Trial Judgement, *supra* note 125, para. 855; *Semanza* Trial Judgement, *supra* note 106, para. 378.

In the ICTR, the elements of conspiracy to commit genocide have been defined simply, and consistently applied, as 'an agreement between two or more persons to commit the crime of genocide',[276] coupled with 'the intent required for the crime of genocide'.[277] Until relatively recently, conspiracy to commit genocide had not even been alleged at the ICTY, and no chamber of that Tribunal has issued a final judgement discussing this crime in the first fifteen years of the ICTY's existence.[278]

Expanding on the basic definition of the crime, the ICTR Trial Chamber in the *Media* case explained that while the agreement to commit genocide is 'the defining element of the crime of conspiracy',[279] it need not be a formal or express agreement; rather, its existence may be 'inferred from coordinated actions by individuals who have a common purpose and are acting within a unified framework'.[280] Applying a

Cf. *Media* Appeal Judgement, *supra* note 111, para. 723 (similar holding in the context of direct and public incitement to commit genocide). See Chapter 5 for a detailed discussion of the Tribunals' jurisprudence on cumulative convictions.

276 *Musema* Trial Judgement, *supra* note 9, para. 191; accord *Media* Trial Judgement, *supra* note 100, paras. 1041–1042; *Niyitegeka* Trial Judgement, *supra* note 175, para. 423; *Ntakirutimana and Ntakirutimana* Trial Judgement, *supra* note 170, para. 798. See also *Media* Trial Judgement, *supra* note 100, para. 1048 ('[C]onspiracy to commit genocide can be comprised of individuals acting in an institutional capacity as well as or even independently of their personal links with each other. Institutional coordination can form the basis of a conspiracy among those individuals who control the institutions that are engaged in coordinated action.'). This 'institutional' approach to conspiracy to commit genocide was implicitly approved in theory by the Appeals Chamber, even though it reversed the Trial Chamber's conclusion that this theory was borne out by the facts in that case. See *Media* Appeal Judgement, *supra* note 111, paras. 910, 912.

277 *Media* Appeal Judgement, *supra* note 111, para. 894; *Musema* Trial Judgement, *supra* note 9, para. 191. This intent requirement is explained in detail above, see *supra* section 3.2.1.2, so this discussion will not be repeated here. This section therefore focuses on the *actus reus* of conspiracy.

278 The trial judgement in *Popović*, in which a number of high-ranking officers and commanders from the Bosnian Serb military and police are being tried, is likely to be the first at the ICTY to address this crime. See *Popović et al.* Indictment, *supra* note 265, paras. 34–44 (Count 2). A final judgement by the Trial Chamber in this case is expected in 2009. Two accused were severed from this case before trial proceedings began, and their individual indictments also charge conspiracy to commit genocide. See *Prosecutor* v. *Trbić*, Case No. IT-05-88/1-PT, Indictment, 18 August 2006, paras. 25–29; *Prosecutor* v. *Tolimir*, Case No. IT-05-88/2-PT, Indictment, 28 August 2006, paras. 25–29. Trbić's case was subsequently referred to the State Court of Bosnia and Herzegovina pursuant to Rule 11 *bis* of the ICTY Rules of Procedure and Evidence. See *Trbić* Referral Decision, *supra* note 15. As of 1 December 2007, Tolimir was still in pre-trial proceedings. The accused in the *Popović* and *Tolimir* cases are also charged with committing genocide through the form of responsibility known as joint criminal enterprise, so the judgements in those cases may provide useful insight into the interplay of this form of responsibility and genocide on one hand, and the inchoate crime of conspiracy to commit genocide on the other. See Boas, Bischoff, and Reid, *supra* note 23, pp. 202–203 (questioning whether the combination of joint criminal enterprise and conspiracy to commit genocide can withstand scrutiny under the principle of culpability). For a list of the ICTR cases where conspiracy to commit genocide has been charged, see Chapter 5, notes 183–184.

279 *Media* Trial Judgement, *supra* note 100, para. 1042.

280 *Ibid.*, para. 1047, affirmed in *Media* Appeal Judgement, *supra* note 111, paras. 896–898 (reiterating that, as with any finding based on circumstantial evidence, the conclusion must be the only reasonable one to be drawn from the established facts). The remainder of the Trial Judgement's paragraph, however, comes uncomfortably close to mirroring the elements of joint criminal enterprise, with neither an explanation of the source of the proposed elements nor a reasoned effort to support their application to the crime at issue. See *ibid.* ('A coalition, even an informal coalition, can constitute such a framework so long as those acting within the coalition are aware of its existence, their participation in it, and its role in furtherance of their common purpose.').

similar approach to the facts in its case, the *Niyitegeka* Trial Chamber had concluded that the manner in which crimes were committed, when combined with evidence that the accused had outlined a plan to attack Tutsi victims at an earlier meeting, supported the conclusion that he was guilty of conspiracy to commit genocide:

> Bearing in mind that the Accused and others acted together as leaders of attacks against Tutsi … taking into account the organized manner in which the attacks were carried out, which presupposes the existence of a plan, and noting, in particular, that the Accused sketched a plan for an attack in Bisesero at a meeting … to which the people in attendance … agreed, the Chamber finds that the above facts evidence the existence of an agreement between the Accused and others … to commit genocide.[281]

Unsurprisingly, perhaps, given the positions of the three accused before and during the genocide, the *Media* case contains the most detailed consideration of the crime and most expansive factual findings by an *ad hoc* chamber to date. Ferdinand Nahimana was the co-founder and a member of the Steering Committee of Radio Télévision Libre des Milles Collines (RTLM), and a member of the political party Mouvement Révolutionnaire National pour le Développement (MRND); Jean-Bosco Barayagwiza was a founding member of the political party Coalition pour la Défense de la République (CDR) and another RTLM co-founder; and Hassan Ngeze was also a founding CDR member and the founder and editor-in-chief of the *Kangura* newspaper.[282] None of the accused was charged with personally committing any of the underlying offences of genocide. Instead, the Chamber concluded that their criminal responsibility rested on conspiracy to commit genocide; direct and public incitement to commit genocide; and liability for genocide through other forms of responsibility,[283] arising primarily from their positions with, and conduct at, the media outlets they controlled.[284]

After discussing the definitions of conspiracy to commit genocide provided in earlier jurisprudence, and reviewing the personal and institutional links between the accused and their respective media, as well as the common agenda pursued and promoted by all three, the Trial Chamber concluded that:

> As a political institution, CDR provided an ideological framework for genocide, and the two media institutions formed part of the coalition that disseminated the message of CDR that the destruction of the Tutsi was essential to the survival of the Hutu.

281 *Niyitegeka* Trial Judgement, *supra* note 175, para. 428.

282 *Media* Trial Judgement, *supra* note 100, paras. 5–7.

283 See *ibid*., paras. 973–977A (finding Barayagwiza guilty of genocide on the basis of superior responsibility; Ngeze guilty of ordering and aiding and abetting genocide; and all three accused guilty of instigating genocide).

284 See *ibid*., paras. 8–10; cf. *ibid*., para. 979 ('Unlike Akayesu and others [who] engaged in incitement through their own words, the Accused in this case used the print and radio media systematically … for the collective communication of ideas and for the mobilization of the population on a grand scale.').

> This evidence establishes, beyond a reasonable doubt, that Nahimana, Barayagwiza and Ngeze consciously interacted with each other, using the institutions they controlled to promote a joint agenda, which was the targeting of the Tutsi population for destruction. There was public presentation of this shared purpose and coordination of efforts to realize their common goal.[285]

In convicting these accused of conspiracy to commit genocide, the Trial Chamber implicitly confirmed that the agreement in question need not contemplate that the conspirators themselves will commit the crime. Rather, as the Chamber found that Nahimana, Barayagwiza, and Ngeze had intended, the conspirators need merely agree that genocide will be committed by others – in this case the members of CDR, the listeners of RTLM, or the readers of *Kangura*. Since these accused were not charged with physical commission, and since the Trial Chamber did not specifically analyse whether the physical perpetrators had genocidal intent, this judgement appears to stand for the proposition that the crime of conspiracy to commit genocide is established even if the conspirators are the only actors who satisfy the specific intent general requirement.

While the Appeals Chamber ultimately reversed all three accused's convictions for conspiracy to commit genocide, it did so on other grounds – namely, that no reasonable trier of fact could have found that the only reasonable conclusion from the circumstantial evidence adduced at trial was that the accused were guilty of conspiracy to commit genocide.[286] It did not address, and certainly did not reject, the principle that the conspirators need not intend to commit the contemplated crime themselves.

As such, and although no judgement explicitly so states, it would be consistent with both the statutory text and the limited jurisprudence on conspiracy to commit genocide for the definition of the crime to include an agreement that any of the underlying offences of genocide shall be committed,[287] as long as the general requirement of genocidal intent is satisfied by those charged with the conspiracy.

3.4 Elements of direct and public incitement to commit genocide

The public prompting or provocation of others to commit genocide or any of its underlying offences, deliberately undertaken with the intention that the

[285] *Ibid.*, paras. 1053–1054. [286] See, e.g., *Media* Appeal Judgement, *supra* note 111, para. 912.

[287] See, e.g., *Popović et al.* Indictment, *supra* note 265, para. 35 (alleging that five of the seven accused 'entered the agreement' that was the predicate for the charge of conspiracy to commit genocide 'with the intent to kill the Muslim men from Srebrenica and to cause serious bodily or mental harm to the Muslims of Srebrenica').

prompting or provocation result in the partial or total destruction of a protected group.

Much of the work of defining and applying the elements of direct and public incitement to commit genocide, the second genocide-related inchoate crime in the Tribunals' Statutes,[288] has been accomplished by the ICTR trial judgements in *Akayesu* and the *Media* case.[289] As discussed in Volume I of this series, direct and public incitement has much the same relationship to the crime of genocide as instigation as a form of responsibility has to the other crimes in the *ad hoc* Statutes. Nevertheless, it is important to keep in mind that direct and public incitement to commit genocide is an inchoate crime and punishable as such even if it is not successful, while instigation in respect of another international crime may only result in a conviction if that crime is actually committed.[290]

After a cursory review of what it termed 'civil law' and 'common law' approaches to the subject, the *Akayesu* Trial Judgement defined the *actus reus* of direct and public incitement to commit genocide, for the purposes of the Statute, as

> directly provoking the perpetrator(s) to commit genocide, whether through speeches, shouting, or threats uttered in public places or at public gatherings, or through the sale or dissemination, offer for sale or display of written material or printed matter in public places or at public gatherings, or through the public display of placards or posters, or through any other means of audiovisual communication.[291]

[288] See *Akayesu* Trial Judgement, *supra* note 6, paras. 552–554, 561–562 (concluding that, although the drafters of the Genocide Convention did not clarify the status of direct and public incitement, it is clearly an inchoate crime, not a form of responsibility; and holding that 'genocide clearly falls within the category of crimes so serious that direct and public incitement to commit such a crime must be punished as such, even where such incitement failed to produce the result expected by the perpetrator') (quotation at para. 562). Accord *Media* Trial Judgement, *supra* note 100, para. 1017. See also Boas, Bischoff, and Reid, *supra* note 23, pp. 290–291 (analysing the relevant jurisprudence and arriving at the conclusion that conspiracy to commit genocide, direct and public incitement to commit genocide, and attempt to commit genocide are inchoate crimes, while complicity in genocide is a package that 'incorporates both the crime of genocide and either a single form of responsibility or a group of forms of responsibility ordinarily labelled "accomplice liability" in certain domestic jurisdictions') (footnotes removed).

[289] In fact, to date, most ICTY judgements only list the crime, which is not generally charged in indictments before that Tribunal, when they are quoting the statutory provision. It appears that the ICTY Prosecutor has opted for using a form of responsibility combined with the crime of genocide to capture conduct that is also prohibited by this separate crime. See Boas, Bischoff, and Reid, *supra* note 23, pp. 297–302 (discussing the permissibility of charging the crime of genocide through any of the forms of responsibility in the ICTY and ICTR Statutes, and both *ad hoc* Prosecutors' practice of doing so). Cf. *Stakić* Trial Judgement, *supra* note 9, para. 503 (observing that '[i]n respect of genocide, the Trial Chamber regards instigating as the derogated mode of criminal liability insofar as the direct and public incitement to commit genocide punishable under Article 4(3)(c) would take priority (*lex specialis derogat legi generali*)', but declining to consider the inchoate crime because it was not charged in the indictment). For a list of the ICTR cases where direct and public incitement to commit genocide has been charged, see Chapter 5, note 184.

[290] See, e.g., *Media* Appeal Judgement, *supra* note 111, para. 678. See also Boas, Bischoff, and Reid, *supra* note 23, pp. 358–364 (discussing instigation as a form of responsibility).

[291] *Akayesu* Trial Judgement, *supra* note 6, para. 559.

The *mens rea* of the crime, the Chamber continued, is the 'intent to directly prompt or provoke another to commit genocide',[292] which itself requires that the inciter have genocidal intent.[293] The requirement of directness must be considered in light of the factual circumstances presented by each case: although it must rise above 'mere vague or indirect suggestion',[294] the concept must be flexible enough to take account of varying 'cultural and linguistic content', according to which 'a particular speech may be perceived as "direct" in one country, and not so in another, depending on the audience'.[295] The test for directness, therefore, is 'whether the persons for whom the message was intended immediately grasped the implication thereof'.[296] As for the public nature of the incitement, the Trial Chamber relied on the ILC's commentary to its 1996 Draft Code, which had explained that 'public incitement is characterized by a call for criminal action to a number of individuals in a public place or to members of the general public at large by such means as the mass media, for example, radio or television'.[297]

Applying these elements, the accused Jean-Paul Akayesu, the *bourgmestre* or leader of a commune in Rwanda,[298] was found guilty of the crime because he had

[292] *Ibid*., para. 560 (also noting that this definition 'implies desire on the part of the perpetrator to create by his actions a particular state of mind necessary to commit such a crime in the minds of the person(s) he is so engaging').

[293] *Ibid*., paras. 560, 729. Accord *Media* Appeal Judgement, *supra* note 111, para. 677; *Niyitegeka* Trial Judgement, *supra* note 175, para. 431; *Prosecutor* v. *Ruggiu*, Case No. ICTR-97-32-I, Sentencing Judgement, 1 June 2000 ('*Ruggiu* Sentencing Judgement'), para. 14.

[294] *Akayesu* Trial Judgement, *supra* note 6, para. 557. See especially *Media* Appeal Judgement, *supra* note 111, paras. 692–693 (noting that incitement is 'direct' if the communication contains a direct call to commit one or more of the underlying offences of genocide, and holding that an accused cannot be convicted for hate speech that does not satisfy this standard) (citing *Kajelijeli* Trial Judgement, *supra* note 125, para. 852); *ibid*., para. 706 (holding that a communication does not constitute direct and public incitement merely because the author or speaker has a criminal intent).

[295] *Akayesu* Trial Judgement, *supra* note 6, para. 557; accord *Media* Appeal Judgement, *supra* note 111, paras. 697–699.

[296] *Akayesu* Trial Judgement, *supra* note 6, para. 558. See also *Muvunyi* Trial Judgement, *supra* note 94, para. 502 (explicitly following *Akayesu* and holding that '[a]n important consideration … is whether the members of the audience to whom the message was directed immediately understood its implication'). Accord *Media* Appeal Judgement, *supra* note 111, paras. 700–701, 703 (holding as a result that a communication that appears ambiguous on its face may nevertheless constitute direct and public incitement if understood as such by its audience); *Kajelijeli* Trial Judgement, *supra* note 125, para 852; *Niyitegeka* Trial Judgement, *supra* note 175, para. 431.

[297] *Akayesu* Trial Judgement, *supra* note 6, para. 556 (citing ILC 1996 Draft Code with Commentaries, *supra* note 85). Accord *Niyitegeka* Trial Judgement, *supra* note 175, para. 431; *Ruggiu* Sentencing Judgement, *supra* note 293, para. 17. See also *Kajelijeli* Trial Judgement, *supra* note 125, paras. 856–857 (concluding that the accused was guilty of direct and public incitement because he, *inter alia*, 'instructed the *Interahamwe* at Byangabo Market and incited the crowd assembled there to "[k]ill and exterminate all those people in Rwankeri" and to "exterminate the Tutsis"' and 'acted with the requisite intent to destroy the Tutsi ethnic group in whole or in part'); *Muvunyi* Trial Judgement, *supra* note 94, para. 503:

> There is no requirement that the incitement message be addressed to a certain number of people or that it should be carried through a specific medium such as radio, television, or a loudspeaker. However, both the number and the medium may provide evidence in support of a finding that the incitement was public.

[298] As the *Akayesu* indictment explained, 'Rwanda is divided into 11 prefectures, each of which is governed by a prefect. The prefectures are further subdivided into communes which are placed under the authority of *bourgmestres*.' *Akayesu* Trial Judgement, *supra* note 6, para. 6 (reproducing indictment).

intentionally provoked others to commit genocide through speeches he gave, in which he 'clearly urged the population to unite in order to eliminate what he termed the sole enemy: the accomplices of the Inkotanyi [the derogatory name for Tutsis]'.[299] The Trial Chamber considered that he had been 'fully aware of the impact of his speech on the crowd and … that his call to fight against the accomplices of the Inkotanyi would be construed as a call to kill the Tutsi in general', and emphasised the accused's own admission that anyone he named in public as an 'accomplice' would be in danger as a result of his denunciation.[300] The Chamber therefore concluded that, 'by the above-mentioned speeches made in public and in a public place, Akayesu had the intent to directly create a particular state of mind in his audience necessary to lead to the destruction of the Tutsi group, as such',[301] and convicted him of direct and public incitement to commit genocide.[302]

As part of its findings on this crime, the *Akayesu* Chamber had noted that there was a causal relationship between the accused's speeches and subsequent widespread massacres of Tutsi, noting that Akayesu's incitement 'was indeed successful and did lead to the destruction of a great number of Tutsi in the commune of Taba'.[303] Nevertheless, because direct and public incitement to commit genocide is an inchoate crime, there is no requirement that genocide actually occur, and it is therefore unnecessary to prove a causal connection. This point was clarified by the later *Media* Judgement, which held that '[i]t is the potential of the communication to cause genocide that makes it incitement … [W]hen this potential is realized, a crime of genocide as well as incitement to genocide has occurred'.[304]

Five years after the *Akayesu* Judgement, the *Media* Trial Chamber was faced with a case in which almost all the conduct with which the accused were charged could be construed as provocation of others to commit crimes, and in which the Chamber had to tackle the thorny issue of compatibility of this inchoate crime with freedom of expression, itself guaranteed by international human rights law.[305] It is not surprising, therefore, that the Trial Chamber employed a more methodical approach to refining the definition of the crime, and took pains to distinguish

[299] *Ibid.*, para. 673(iii). [300] *Ibid.*, para. 673(iv)–(vi). [301] *Ibid.*, para. 674.

[302] See *ibid.*, paras. 709–710 & section 8 (verdict). See also *Niyitegeka* Trial Judgement, *supra* note 175, paras. 435–437 (concluding that 'the Accused's words, including the call to "work", were understood by his audience as a call to kill the Tutsi, and that the Accused knew his words would be interpreted as such', and finding that 'in urging attackers to work, and to eat meat so that they would be strong to return the next day to continue the "work", the Accused is individually criminally responsible … for inciting attackers to cause the death and serious bodily and mental harm of Tutsi refugees in Bisesero').

[303] *Akayesu* Trial Judgement, *supra* note 6, paras. 673(vii), 675 (quotation at para. 675).

[304] *Media* Trial Judgement, *supra* note 100, para. 1015. See also *ibid.*, para. 1007 ('[I]nternational jurisprudence does not include any specific causation requirement linking the expression at issue with the demonstration of a direct effect.').

[305] See, e.g., Universal Declaration of Human Rights, UN Doc. A/810 (1948), Art. 19; International Covenant on Civil and Political Rights, 16 December 1966, entered into force 23 March 1976, UN Doc. A/6316 (1966), 999 UNTS 171, Art. 19.

conduct that was protected by international law from that which was appropriately punishable.[306]

After reviewing international jurisprudence and authoritative interpretations of regional and international human rights treaties, the Chamber derived 'a number of central principles', which it considered useful in 'in defining elements of "direct and public incitement to genocide" as applied to mass media'.[307] These principles were to be applied in interpreting the Tribunal's existing jurisprudence to ensure, among other things, that the accused were not punished for protected expression, and included: the purpose or intent of the communication;[308] and the importance of context when considering both the intention of the communicator and the potential impact of the communication.[309]

As suggested by these principles, much of the Chamber's consideration of the evidence for this crime was focused on whether it established that the author, broadcaster, or publisher had the requisite intent, and had deliberately set out to inflame tensions and provoke genocidal violence. The Judgement makes a point, for instance, of distinguishing between discussing or promoting 'ethnic consciousness' and fomenting 'ethnic hatred':[310]

> In its review of *Kangura* and RTLM, the Chamber notes that some of the articles and broadcasts highlighted by the Prosecution convey historical information, political analysis, or advocacy of an ethnic consciousness regarding the inequitable distribution of privilege in Rwanda. Barayagwiza's RTLM broadcast of 12 December 1993, for example, is a moving personal account of his experience of discrimination as a Hutu …

[306] See *Media* Trial Judgement, *supra* note 100, paras. 979–980:

> Unlike Akayesu and others found by the Tribunal to have engaged in incitement through their own speech, the Accused in this case used the print and radio media systematically, not only for their own words but for the words of many others, for the collective communication of ideas and for the mobilization of the population on a grand scale … [A] review of international law and jurisprudence on incitement to discrimination and violence is helpful as a guide to the assessment of criminal accountability for direct and public incitement to genocide, in light of the fundamental right of freedom of expression.

[307] *Ibid.*, para. 1000. The Trial Chamber rejected one of the accused's attempts to use United States First Amendment law as the appropriate standard for freedom of expression. See *ibid.*, para. 1010.

[308] *Ibid.*, paras. 1001–1003; see also *ibid.*, para. 1024 (explaining how editors or publishers could escape liability by maintaining a critical distance between the communication and any hate speech or provocation contained therein):

> In cases where the media disseminates views that constitute ethnic hatred and calls to violence for informative or educational purposes, a clear distancing from these is necessary to avoid conveying an endorsement of the message and in fact to convey a counter-message to ensure that no harm results from the broadcast. The positioning of the media with regard to the message indicates the real intent of the message, and to some degree the real message itself.

[309] *Ibid.*, para. 1000–1006. See also *ibid.*, para. 1001 ('The actual language used in the media has often been cited as an indicator of intent.').

[310] On appeal, the ICTR Appeals Chamber emphasised that the crime of direct and public incitement to commit genocide does not penalise all hate speech or propaganda, even that which may tend to lead to genocide; instead, only precise acts that constitute direct and public incitement are criminalised. As such, a 'programme' of hate is insufficient to ground a conviction for this inchoate crime, and a trial chamber must clearly identify the conduct that constitutes direct and public incitement to commit genocide. See, e.g., *Media* Appeal Judgement, *supra* note 111, para. 726.

The Chamber considers that it is critical to distinguish between the discussion of ethnic consciousness and the promotion of ethnic hatred. This broadcast by Barayagwiza is the former but not the latter. While the impact of these words, which are powerful, may well have been to move listeners to want to take action to remedy the discrimination recounted, such impact would be the result, in the Chamber's view, of the reality conveyed by the words rather than the words themselves. A communication such as this broadcast does not constitute incitement. In fact, it falls squarely within the scope of speech that is protected by the right to freedom of expression. Similarly, public discussion of the merits of the Arusha Accords, however critical, constitutes a protected exercise of free speech.

The Chamber considers that speech constituting ethnic hatred results from the stereotyping of ethnicity combined with its denigration.[311]

Notwithstanding this drawing of fine lines, the Chamber ultimately concluded that all the accused were guilty of direct and public incitement to commit genocide.[312] Among the factors the Chamber found persuasive in concluding that each accused had intentionally provoked the underlying offences of genocide which ensued[313] were the fact that the media outlets they controlled 'did not

311 *Media* Trial Judgement, *supra* note 100, paras. 1019–1021. Article 7 of the ICTR Statute limits the Tribunal's temporal jurisdiction to the calendar year 1994, so under a strict reading of this provision, this broadcast would lie outside that jurisdiction. As it did with the crime of conspiracy to commit genocide, however, the Trial Chamber concluded that as an inchoate crime, direct and public incitement to commit genocide has a continuing nature, so acts prior to 1994 that resulted in the commission of genocide during that year fall within the Tribunal's jurisdiction. *Ibid.*, para. 1017. The ICTR Appeals Chamber disagreed with the Trial Chamber on both counts. First, it held that direct and public incitement to commit genocide is not a continuing crime. *Media* Appeal Judgement, *supra* note 111, para. 723. Second, it firmly rejected the Trial Chamber's broad interpretation of temporal jurisdiction, holding, for example, that only issues of *Kangura* first published by Ngeze in 1994 could be considered as falling within the temporal jurisdiction of the ICTR. See *Media* Appeal Judgement, *supra* note 111, para. 517 (excluding, therefore, any past issues that were republished or redistributed); *ibid.*, paras. 723–724 (rejecting the expansive approach to temporal jurisdiction in the context of direct and public incitement). But cf. *ibid.*, paras. 561, 565 (holding that the temporal jurisdiction of the Tribunal does not preclude the admission of evidence from before 1 January 1994 to establish an accused's genocidal intent); *ibid.*, para. 725 (noting that pre-1994 broadcasts may be relevant contextual evidence going to the audience's perception of broadcasts during 1994).

The Appeals Chamber is certainly correct with regard to conduct – no accused should face conviction for conduct that that occurred before or after the temporal jurisdictional limits – but it is less clear that its conclusion is correct in the context of publications, as one could argue that the republication or redistribution of past issues is itself a positive act taken during the relevant period.

312 In so doing, the Chamber rejected the proffered defences of, *inter alia*, reliance on official information and mobilisation of civil defence. See generally *Media* Trial Judgement, *supra* note 100, paras. 1023–1027. Ultimately, the Chamber concluded, 'the truth' the accused claimed to seek and disseminate 'was subservient to their objective of protecting the population from the R[wandan] P[atriotic] F[ront] through the destruction of the Tutsi ethnic group.' *Ibid.*, para. 1027. The Rwandan Patriotic Front was an army of Tutsi exiles, based in Uganda, with whom the Hutu government had been battling for years. See *ibid.*, para. 106 (quoting *Akayesu* Trial Judgement, *supra* note 6, especially paras. 95–97 of that judgement). The Appeals Chamber partially overturned these conclusions, resolving that Nahimana was liable for direct and public incitement solely on the basis of superior responsibility; reversing Barayagwiza's conviction for this crime; and restricting the factual basis for its confirmation of Ngeze's conviction for this crime to the 1994 publications in *Kangura*. See *Media* Appeal Judgement, *supra* note 111, pp. 422–423.

313 Although causation is not a requirement for incitement, the Chamber considered that subsequent crimes could be indicative that the incitement was intentional. See *Media* Trial Judgement, *supra* note 100, para. 1029 ('In determining whether communications represent an intent to cause genocide and thereby constitute incitement, the Chamber considers it significant that in fact genocide occurred. That the media intended to have this effect is evidenced in part by the fact that it did have this effect.')

distance themselves from the message of ethnic hatred' but rather 'purveyed the message';[314] the identification of the entire Tutsi population as a threat in the publications and radio broadcasts at issue;[315] the publication of the names of Tutsi 'suspects' with explicit or implicit encouragement to the listeners or readers to protect themselves against the suspects;[316] the 'denigration of Tutsi ethnicity', which 'was augmented by the visceral scorn coming out of the airwaves' in radio broadcasts;[317] and the explicit call for extermination of 'the enemy' (perennially identified as the Tutsi population) in communications by the party founded and led by the accused Barayagwiza,[318] and in the publication founded, owned, and edited by his co-accused Ngeze.[319] In addition, the Chamber specifically noted the personal actions of Ngeze, who 'often drove around with a megaphone in his vehicle, mobilizing the Hutu population to come to CDR meetings and spreading the message that the Inyenzi would be exterminated, Inyenzi meaning, and being understood to mean, the Tutsi ethnic minority'.[320]

For the same reasons discussed above in relation to the crime of conspiracy to commit genocide, the findings of the *Media* Trial Chamber support a definition of direct and public incitement that includes prompting others to commit any of the underlying offences of genocide, as long as the inciters themselves have genocidal intent. That is, by focusing almost exclusively on the intent of the three accused, who were not physical perpetrators, the Chamber appears to have concluded that the question of whether the perpetrators had genocidal intent was either irrelevant to the fundamental question of whether the crime of incitement had been committed, or secondary to an examination of the inciters' intent.

3.5 Elements of attempt to commit genocide

No chamber in either Tribunal has defined this inchoate crime. The best approximation of such elements may be found in the Statute and Elements of Crimes of the International Criminal Court, by combining the detailed provisions on attempt in the Statute with the elements of genocide outlined in the Elements, the subsidiary document defining the crimes within the jurisdiction of the Court.[321]

314 *Ibid.*, para. 1024. 315 *Ibid.*, para. 1025. 316 *Ibid.*, para. 1028.
317 *Ibid.*, para. 1031. 318 *Ibid.*, para. 1035. 319 *Ibid.*, para. 1036.
320 *Ibid.*, para. 1039. See also *Muvunyi* Trial Judgement, *supra* note 94, para. 507 (concluding that 'when considered in the context of the language and culture of Rwanda, [the accused's speech] equating Tutsis to snakes was … synonymous with condemning members of this ethnic group to death', and finding that Muvunyi was guilty of this crime because he 'knew that his audience immediately understood the genocidal implication of his words').
321 See *infra* text accompanying notes 367–368.

3.6 Genocide in the International Criminal Court and Internationalised Tribunals

3.6.1 The International Criminal Court

3.6.1.1 The Rome Statute

Article 6 of the Rome Statute of the ICC includes the crime of genocide in terms virtually identical to those of Article II of the Genocide Convention, listing the same six underlying offences and four protected groups.[322] At the various drafting meetings convened between 1995 and 1998, there appears to have been sustained majority support for leaving the Convention's definition of the crime untouched.[323] Some delegations pointed out that the International Court of Justice had opined as early as 1951 that this definition reflected customary international law, and that it had been widely accepted by states and incorporated into national law.[324] Certain delegations also expressed the view that maintaining the Convention's formulation would promote uniform jurisprudence across international judicial bodies.[325]

Other delegations made suggestions for modifications to this definition, however, the most salient of which was the proposed inclusion of social and political groups as potential targets of genocide.[326] Another proposal was to clarify, either in the definition of genocide or in the provisions of the Statute concerning general principles of criminal law, whether the perpetrator of an underlying offence of genocide would be required to have genocidal intent, or whether he would merely need the general intent required for the underlying offence (for example, the intent

[322] Rome Statute, *supra* note 24, Art. 6. See *supra*, text accompanying note 2, for the complete text of Article II of the Convention.

[323] See Valerie Oosterveld, 'The Elements of Genocide: Introduction', in Roy S. Lee (ed.), *The International Criminal Court: Elements of Crimes and Rules of Procedure and Evidence* (2001), p. 41.

[324] See Report of the Preparatory Committee on the Establishment of an International Criminal Court, UN Doc. A/51/22, 13 September 1996 ('1996 Preparatory Committee Report'), vol. I, para. 59; Report of the *ad hoc* Committee on the Establishment of an International Criminal Court, UN Doc. A/50/22, 6 September 1995 ('1995 *ad hoc* Committee Report'), paras. 60–61. See also *Reservations* Opinion, *supra* note 69, p. 23 (holding that the 'principles underlying the [Genocide] Convention are principles which are recognized by civilized nations as binding on States, even without any conventional obligation'); *Bosnia* v. *Yugoslavia* Preliminary Objections Judgement, *supra* note 78, p. 616 (observing that 'the rights and obligations enshrined by the [Genocide] Convention are rights and obligations *erga omnes*').

[325] See 1995 *Ad Hoc* Committee Report, *supra* note 324, para. 61 (noting that some delegations were concerned that any deviations might result in inconsistent holdings from the ICJ and the ICC); 1996 Preparatory Committee Report, *supra* note 324, para. 59.

[326] See Report of the Preparatory Committee on the Establishment of an International Criminal Court, UN Doc. A/CONF.183/2/Add.1, 14 April 1998 ('1998 Preparatory Committee Report'), p. 11 n. 2; Decisions Taken by the Preparatory Committee at Its Session Held from 11 to 21 February 1997, UN Doc. A/AC.249/1997/L.5, 12 March 1997 ('1997 Preparatory Committee Report'), Annex I, p. 3 n. 2; 1996 Preparatory Committee Report, *supra* note 324, para. 60. One counterargument to this proposal was that crimes against social and political groups would fall under the Statute's provision on crimes against humanity in any event. See 1995 *ad hoc* Committee Report, *supra* note 324, para. 61. See also Herman von Hebel and Darryl Robinson, 'Crimes with the Jurisdiction of the Court', in Roy S. Lee (ed.), *The International Criminal Court: The Making of the Rome Statute* (1999), p. 89 n. 37 (Egypt submitted the original proposal to include social and political groups).

to kill), provided 'the responsible decision makers or planners' had genocidal intent.[327] This imaginative proposal evinces some appreciation of the very complicated question of distribution of genocidal intent, discussed in Section 3.2.1.1 above.[328] Ultimately, the majority remained in favour of replicating the unaltered text of Article II in the Rome Statute.[329]

Unlike the *ad hoc* Statutes, the Rome Statute does not contain a verbatim reproduction of Article III of the Genocide Convention, which lists five so-called 'punishable acts':[330] the crime of genocide itself; the inchoate crimes of conspiracy to commit genocide, direct and public incitement to commit genocide, and attempt to commit genocide; and a hybrid of a crime and a form or forms of accomplice liability labelled 'complicity in genocide'.[331] As the relevant *travaux* demonstrate, the Statute's drafters ultimately decided to omit Article III in the belief that the modes of participation in the offences which may constitute genocide were adequately captured in the provisions set forth in Article 25 of the Statute.[332]

Although the Rome Statute consequently avoids the redundancy of the *ad hoc* Statutes, which contain both a provision on complicity in genocide and a provision

327 1995 *ad hoc* Committee Report, *supra* note 324, para. 62. Accord 1997 Preparatory Committee Report, *supra* note 326, Annex I, p. 3 n. 3; 1996 Preparatory Committee Report, *supra* note 324, para. 60.

328 See *supra* section 3.2.1.1.

329 William A. Schabas, 'Genocide', in Triffterer (ed.), *supra* note 24, p. 108; *ibid.*, p. 100 (stating that Cuba made a final plea in the Committee of the Whole for the inclusion of political and social groups, and Ireland responded that, as the delegates were not drafting a new Genocide Convention, 'it was better to stick with the existing definition'). See also Committee of the Whole, Bureau, Discussion Paper, UN Doc. A/CONF.183/C.1/L.53, 6 July 1998, Part 2, p. 1 ('The definition of the crime of genocide is literally taken from the 1948 Genocide Convention.'). For academic commentary approving of the unaltered reproduction of Article II of the Genocide Convention, see Jordan J. Paust, 'Commentary on Parts 1 and 2 of the Zutphen Intersessional Draft', (1998) 13*bis Nouvelles Etudes Pénales* 27; L. Sadat Wexler, 'First Committee Report on Jurisdiction, Definition of Crimes and Complementarity', (1997) 13 *Nouvelles Etudes Pénales* 169. For commentary disapproving, see M. Cherif Bassiouni, *The Legislative History of the International Criminal Court* (2005), vol. I, p. 149.

330 Genocide Convention, *supra* note 2, Art. III(a)–(e). See also Statute of the International Criminal Tribunal for the Prosecution of Persons Responsible for Serious Violations of International Humanitarian Law Committed in the Territory of the former Yugoslavia since 1991, (1993) 32 ILM 1159, *as amended by* Security Council Resolution 1660 of 28 February 2006, Art. 4(3)(a)–(e) (identical language); ICTR Statute, *supra* note 24, Art. 2 (3)(a)–(e) (identical language).

331 See Boas, Bischoff, and Reid, *supra* note 23, pp. 290–291 (examining *ad hoc* jurisprudence on the 'punishable acts' in Article III indicating that conspiracy, incitement, and attempt are inchoate crimes, and concluding that complicity in genocide 'incorporates both the crime of genocide and either a single form of responsibility or a group of forms of responsibility ordinarily labelled "accomplice liability" in certain domestic jurisdictions').

332 See Committee of the Whole, Summary Record of the 3rd Meeting, held on 17 June 1998, UN Doc. A/CONF.183/C.1/SR.3, 20 November 1998, para. 174 (noting that the proposed text of the article on genocide would be referred to the Drafting Committee without the text of Article III, at least until further work had been done on the article on individual criminal responsibility); Report of the Working Group on General Principles of Criminal Law, UN Doc. A/CONF.183/C.1/WGGP/L.4, 18 June 1998, p. 3 (recommending, in a footnote to the provision on direct and public incitement in what would eventually become Article 25, that '[t]he second paragraph of the definition of the crime of genocide in article 5 [reproducing Article III of the Convention] which appears between square brackets should be deleted'); Report of the Drafting Committee to the Committee of the Whole, UN Doc. A/CONF.183/C.1/L.91, 16 July 1998, p. 2 (adopting this recommendation, and limiting the text of then-Article 5 – now Article 6 – to reproducing Article II of the Convention). See also Schabas, *supra* note 329, p. 115 (discussing the decision to omit Article III).

on accomplice liability applicable to all crimes, including genocide,[333] it also awkwardly refers to inchoate crimes in an article otherwise dedicated to forms of responsibility.[334] The first of these is attempt,[335] which the drafters were willing to extend not only to genocide, but to all crimes in the Court's jurisdiction.[336] The second inchoate crime is incitement,[337] although the approach taken here was much more limited: the drafters could only reach consensus as to this crime's application to genocide, and only then with the qualifiers 'direct and public'.[338] Article III's other inchoate crime, conspiracy to commit genocide, does not appear in the Rome Statute, despite the existence of such a crime in international law since the 1948 adoption of the Genocide Convention, its possible existence in customary international law,[339] and its actual application in several judgments of the ICTR.[340] Some commentators have remarked that the absence of conspiracy in the Statute – in relation to genocide or any other crime – is a result of a broader and long-standing disagreement concerning the disparate treatment of conspiracy in common-law and

333 See Payam Akhavan, 'The Crime of Genocide in the ICTR Jurisprudence', (2005) 3 *Journal of International Criminal Justice* 989, 994 (referring to this coexistence in the ICTY Statute as a 'normative redundancy'); Boas, Bischoff, and Reid, *supra* note 23, pp. 293–302 (discussing in detail the *ad hoc* Tribunals' attempts to address this redundancy).

334 See Albin Eser, 'Individual Criminal Responsibility', in Cassese, Gaeta, and Jones (eds.), *supra* note 66, p. 771 ('[O]ne may wonder why attempt is regulated in the direct neighbourhood of participation [– that is, forms of responsibility –] as if it were just another type of it, instead of regulating attempt in its own independent provision[.]'); *ibid*., p. 804 (making the same observation with respect to incitement to commit genocide, and suggesting that it would have been better placed in Article 6 of the Statute along with genocide).

335 Rome Statute, *supra* note 24, Art. 25(3)(f).

336 See Per Saland, 'International Criminal Law Principles', in Lee (ed.), *supra* note 326, p. 198; Kai Ambos, 'Individual Criminal Responsibility', in Triffterer (ed.), *supra* note 24, p. 488 (observing that the Rome Statute follows one particular legislative approach to criminalising attempt, but does not limit it to any particular crime within the jurisdiction of the Court); Boas, Bischoff, and Reid, *supra* note 23, pp. 332–333.

337 Rome Statute, *supra* note 24, Art. 25(3)(e). Despite the placement of this provision in the article devoted to forms of responsibility, the drafting history and commentary on Article 25(3)(e) make it clear that it is intended to be treated in the same manner as it is in the *ad hoc* Tribunals – that is, as an inchoate crime, not as a true form of responsibility. See Kai Ambos, 'General Principles of Criminal Law in the Rome Statute', (1999) 10 *Criminal Law Forum* 11, 14; Ambos, *supra* note 336, p. 487 ('[T]he act of incitement [to genocide] is as such sufficiently dangerous and blameworthy to be punished.'); Elies van Sliedregt, *The Criminal Responsibility of Individuals for Violations of International Humanitarian Law* (2003), p. 110 ('[I]ncitement to commit genocide is an inchoate crime and … not a mode of criminal participation[.]').

338 See Saland, *supra* note 336, p. 200; Schabas, *supra* note 329, p. 115 (also recalling that 'direct and public' was included in Article III to 'appease [s]tates that were concerned about threats to freedom of expression'). See also Ambos, *supra* note 336, p. 486 (opining that conduct constituting incitement to commit the other crimes in the Statute is probably captured by the forms of responsibility 'soliciting' and 'inducing' in Article 25(3)(b)).

339 See Antonio Cassese, *supra* note 80, p. 347 (arguing that customary international law 'prohibits and makes punishable "conspiracy to commit genocide"; that is, an inchoate crime consisting of the planning and organizing of genocide not necessarily followed by the perpetration of the crime'). See also *Hamdan* v. *Rumsfeld*, 126 S. Ct. 2749, 2784 (2006) (observing that 'the only "conspiracy" crimes that have been recognized by international war crimes tribunals … are conspiracy to commit genocide and common plan to wage aggressive war').

340 See, e.g., *Media* Trial Judgement, *supra* note 100, paras. 1040–1055, 1092–1094 (convicting all three accused of conspiracy to commit genocide); *Musema* Trial Judgement, *supra* note 9, paras. 184–198, 937–941 (finding that the prosecution had failed to prove that *Musema* had conspired with others to commit genocide); *Kambanda* Trial Judgement, *supra* note 5, para. 40 & p. 27 (convicting Kambanda of conspiracy to commit genocide).

civil-law jurisdictions.[341] The true effect of the exclusion of a conspiracy provision is still unclear, however, and likely depends on the Court's eventual interpretation of the provision on common-purpose liability in Article 25(3)(d).[342]

3.6.1.2 The Elements of Crimes

As discussed in Chapter 2,[343] the Rome Statute provides for recourse by the Court to an instrument setting forth non-binding elements of crimes to 'assist … in the interpretation and application of articles 6, 7 and 8' – that is, the respective articles on genocide, crimes against humanity, and war crimes.[344] The genocide provision of the Elements of Crimes contains an introductory section with definitions and clarifications, a discrete list of elements for each of the five underlying offences of genocide, and a number of explanatory footnotes.[345] As the negotiations resulting in the precise structure and language of this provision have been addressed at length elsewhere,[346] we focus on a few of the more salient features.

Each of the six underlying offences in the Elements contains an element by which the victim must have 'belonged to a particular national, ethnical, racial or religious group'.[347] This requirement would appear to preclude liability for genocide where the victim was not in fact a member of one of the enumerated groups, even if the physical perpetrator or the accused believed he was a group member. As noted above, many chambers of the *ad hoc* Tribunals have adopted a mixed approach to this question, in which the victims must be at least perceived as belonging to a

[341] See Eser, *supra* note 334, p. 802 (noting that a compromise provision was proposed that would have allowed for non-inchoate conspiracy liability, but that it was ultimately rejected); Cassese, *supra* note 80, p. 347. See also 1998 Preparatory Committee Report, *supra* note 326, Art. 23(e)(ii) (containing a draft conspiracy provision applicable to all crimes, with bracketed draft language that the crime must actually be committed); *ibid.*, p. 50 n. 6 (noting that '[t]he inclusion of this subparagraph gave rise to divergent views'). This debate over the role and definition of conspiracy in international criminal law has gone on for at least sixty years. See, e.g., Telford Taylor, *Anatomy of the Nuremberg Trials: A Personal Memoir* (1992), p. 36 (explaining that the judges at Nuremberg refused to recognise the crime of conspiracy to commit war crimes because '[t]he Anglo-American concept of conspiracy was not part of European legal systems and arguably not an element of the internationally recognized laws of war').

[342] Rome Statute, *supra* note 24, Art. 25(3)(d). See also Ambos, *supra* note 336, p. 483 (noting that conspiracy had been controversial since Nuremberg, and Article 25(3)(d) represents the compromise over proposed conspiracy provisions from earlier drafts of the Rome Statute). See also Boas, Bischoff, and Reid, *supra* note 23, pp. 124–128 (discussing the Rome Statute's approach to common-purpose liability in detail).

[343] See Chapter 2, text accompanying note 519.

[344] Rome Statute, *supra* note 24, Art. 9(1).

[345] See Assembly of States Parties to the Rome Statute of the International Criminal Court, First Session: Official Records, Part II(B): Elements of Crimes, UN Doc. ICC-ASP/1/3 (2002) ('ICC Elements of Crimes'), pp. 113–115.

[346] See, e.g., Cassese, *supra* note 80, pp. 348–350; Bassiouni, *supra* note 329, pp. 153–154; Philippe Kirsch, 'The Work of the Preparatory Commission', in Lee (ed.), *supra* note 323, pp. xlvii–xlix; Maria Kelt and Herman von Hebel, 'The Making of the Elements of Crimes', in Lee (ed.), *supra* note 323, pp. 3–18; Oosterveld, *supra* note 323, pp. 41–44; Valerie Oosterveld, 'The Elements of Genocide: The Context of Genocide', in Lee (ed.), *supra* note 323, pp. 44–49; Charles Garraway, 'The Elements of Genocide: Elements of the Specific Forms of Genocide', in Lee (ed.), *supra* note 323, pp. 49–55; Von Hebel and Robinson, *supra* note 326, pp. 87–88.

[347] ICC Elements of Crimes, *supra* note 345, Art. 6(a), Element 2; *ibid.*, Art. 6(b), Element 2; *ibid.*, Art. 6(c), Element 2; *ibid.*, Art. 6(d), Element 2; *ibid.*, Art. 6(e), Element 2.

national, ethnic, racial, or religious group, and there must be some objective support for the group to be treated as such.[348]

In addition, each underlying offence in the ICC Elements requires that '[t]he conduct took place in the context of a manifest pattern of similar conduct directed against [the targeted] group or was conduct that could itself effect [the group's] destruction'.[349] Valerie Oosterveld explains that this element was inserted at the prompting of delegates of the United States and others who 'were concerned about trivializing genocide by defining it in such a way as to include an isolated hate crime – for example, where a single crazed individual formed the necessary genocidal intent in his or her own mind, and committed an isolated murder'.[350] According to Oosterveld, the delegations based the compromise formulation on passages from the then-recent *Akayesu* Trial Judgement,[351] although on close inspection it would appear that neither *Akayesu* nor its *ad hoc* progeny set forth a contextual element that must be established for genocide liability to ensue. Instead, these judgements merely make reference to contextual facts – such as the deliberate and systematic targeting of the group – as criteria that may be taken into account by a chamber as support for the inference that the person in question possessed genocidal intent.[352] In this sense, the genocide provision of the ICC Elements goes beyond what has been required thus far in the *ad hoc* Tribunals.[353]

Another potentially problematic aspect of the genocide provision in the Elements of Crimes is the question of which of the participants in the crime must fulfil which of the requisite mental elements. The first two underlying offences – 'genocide by killing' and 'genocide by causing serious bodily or mental harm' – have only one mental element each: that a person labelled the 'perpetrator' possessed genocidal intent.[354] It is also the 'perpetrator' who must carry out the *actus reus*.[355]

[348] See *supra* text accompanying notes 193–199.

[349] ICC Elements of Crimes, *supra* note 345, Art. 6(a), Element 4; *ibid.*, Art. 6(b), Element 4; *ibid.*, Art. 6(c), Element 5; *ibid.*, Art. 6(d), Element 5; *ibid.*, Art. 6(e), Element 7.

[350] Oosterveld, *supra* note 323, p. 45. This element's ultimate formulation resulted from negotiations that ensued in the working group over a US draft that would have imported into each underlying offence a requirement of a widespread or systematic policy or practice aimed at destroying the group. *Ibid.* See also Preparatory Commission for the International Criminal Court, Proposal Submitted by the United States of America: Draft Elements of Crimes, UN Doc. PCNICC/1999/DP.4 (1999), pp. 5–6.

[351] Oosterveld, *supra* note 323, p. 46. Oosterveld explains the concern of some delegations that the inclusion of this contextual element would allow the first few persons involved in genocidal activities to escape liability, as the requisite 'manifest pattern' would not yet have formed. *Ibid.* The compromise was the inclusion of a definition of 'in the context of' to 'include the initial acts in an emerging pattern'. ICC Elements of Crimes, *supra* note 345, p. 113.

[352] See *supra* text accompanying notes 120–127.

[353] Antonio Cassese argues that the 'manifest pattern of similar conduct' alternative is also unnecessarily more stringent than what is required by customary international law. Cassese, *supra* note 339, pp. 349–350 ('Admittedly, in fact genocidal acts are seldom isolated or sporadic events … . These circumstances remain however factual events, not provided for as legal requirements of the crime.').

[354] ICC Elements of Crimes, *supra* note 345, Art. 6(a), Element 3; *ibid.*, Art. 6(b), Element 3 ('The perpetrator intended to destroy, in whole or in part, that national, ethnical, racial or religious group, as such.').

[355] *Ibid.*, Art. 6(a), Element 1; *ibid.*, Art. 6(b), Element 1.

The fifth – 'genocide by forcibly transferring children' – has two mental elements: that the 'perpetrator' possessed genocidal intent, and that '[t]he perpetrator knew, or should have known, that the person or persons were under the age of 18 years'.[356] Again, the 'perpetrator' must also fulfil the *actus reus*.[357] The use of the term 'perpetrator' in all these positions suggests, on a plain reading of the text, that the person who must fulfil the mental elements is also the one performing the *actus reus* – in our terminology, the physical perpetrator.

Nevertheless, it would appear that the delegates did not intend to allow an accused to escape liability for genocide where he possesses genocidal intent but the foot-soldier acting at his direction does not. The weight of the *ad hoc* jurisprudence indicates that such an accused would bear liability.[358] As discussed in Chapter 2,[359] the delegates did have some appreciation for the general notion that the elements of an international crime may be fulfilled by different actors.[360] They included an explicit provision in the General Introduction to the Elements defining 'perpetrator' as a term of art:

> As used in the Elements of Crimes, the term 'perpetrator' is neutral as to guilt or innocence. The elements, including the appropriate mental elements, apply *mutatis mutandis* to all those whose criminal responsibility may fall under articles 25 and 28 of the Statute [setting forth the forms of responsibility].[361]

Also interesting in this regard is the rare understanding evinced by some delegations as early as the 1995 *ad hoc* Committee, described above,[362] that different participants in the crime of genocide may fulfil different intent elements, and that it is more important that those at higher levels have the genocidal intent:

> There was a further suggestion [in the *ad hoc* Committee] to clarify the intent requirement for the crime of genocide by distinguishing between a specific intent requirement for the

[356] *Ibid.*, Art. 6(e), Elements 3, 6. [357] *Ibid.*, Art. 6(e), Element 1.
[358] See *supra* section 3.2.1.1. [359] See Chapter 2, text accompanying notes 522–528.
[360] See Kelt and Von Hebel, *supra* note 346, pp. 17–18 (discussing the debate over what term should be used in this position; that delegates rejected 'accused' because the accused is not always the physical perpetrator; and that they rejected 'actor' as too vague a term). See also, e.g., Preparatory Commission for the International Criminal Court, Proceedings of the Preparatory Commission at Its Fourth Session (13–31 March 2000), Annex III: Elements of Crimes, UN Doc. PCNICC/2000/L.1/Rev.1/Add.2 (2000), pp. 6–7 (using 'accused' where the final Elements uses 'perpetrator'); Preparatory Commission for the International Criminal Court, Proceedings of the Preparatory Commission at Its First Session (16–26 February 1999), Annex II: Elements of Crimes, UN Doc. PCNICC/1999/L.3/Rev.1 (1999), pp. 20–21 (same). Indeed, as we have stated repeatedly in this and in the first volume of this series, the practice of the *ad hoc* Tribunals – and especially the ICTY – for the last several years has been focused on those alleged to be more responsible for the crimes within the Tribunal's jurisdiction. As a result, the accused and the physical perpetrator are seldom one and the same person. See Chapter 2, section 2.2.2.1; *supra* section 3.2.1.1; Chapter 4, text accompanying note 122; Boas, Bischoff, and Reid, *supra* note 23, pp. 9, 93, 140–141, 416, 420–423.
[361] ICC Elements of Crimes, *supra* note 345, General Introduction, para. 8.
[362] See *supra* text accompanying note 327.

responsible decision makers or planners and a general-intent or knowledge requirement for the actual perpetrators of genocidal acts. Some delegations felt that it might be useful to elaborate on various aspects of the intent requirement without amending the Convention, including the intent required for the various categories of responsible individuals[.][363]

When faced with an accused who did not physically perpetrate the underlying offences of genocide with which he is charged, the Court will likely have to adopt a broad and varying interpretation of the term 'perpetrator': while it is indeed the physical perpetrator who must fulfil the *actus reus* of the underlying offence, the requirement of genocidal intent may be fulfilled by the accused or another relevant actor, depending on the form of responsibility charged.[364]

As a final point on the Elements' genocide provisions, it is noteworthy that the document omits any mention of the related inchoate crimes: direct and public incitement to commit genocide and attempt to commit genocide. The United States suggested that such elements be explored by the working group, but the group declined to do so.[365] As a consequence, the Court will presumably have a freer hand to divine the elements of direct and public incitement to commit genocide, and can perhaps be expected to rely to a greater degree on the jurisprudence of the *ad hoc* Tribunals for the definition of this crime than it may with respect to the underlying offences of genocide itself, whose elements have been expressly laid out in the Elements of Crimes.[366] On the other hand, the Court will have considerably less freedom to define attempt, notwithstanding that crime's absence from the Elements of Crimes and the lack of any real discussion of it in *ad hoc*

363 1995 *Ad Hoc* Committee Report, *supra* note 324, para. 62.

364 See *supra* section 3.2.1.1 (discussing, in the context of the *ad hoc* jurisprudence, who must have genocidal intent among the potentially many persons involved in the commission of genocide). The Elements' exposition of the third and fourth underlying offences of genocide – 'genocide by deliberately inflicting conditions of life calculated to bring about physical destruction' and 'genocide by imposing measures intended to prevent births' – is also somewhat confusing. These offences contain two mental elements each: for the former, that the 'perpetrator' had genocidal intent, and that '[t]he conditions of life were calculated to bring about the physical destruction of that group, in whole or in part', ICC Elements of Crimes, *supra* note 345, Art. 6(c), Elements 3, 4; for the latter, that the 'perpetrator' had genocidal intent, and that '[t]he measures imposed were intended to prevent births within that group', *ibid.*, Art. 6(b), Elements 3, 4. At first glance, the second mental element for each of these offences would seem to be redundant in most real-world scenarios: the intent of the 'perpetrator' to destroy the targeted group as such probably subsumes any calculation to destroy the group through the imposition of intolerable conditions of life, or the intent to prevent births within the group. Yet the use of the passive voice leaves the door open for other interpretations, including that two separate persons may satisfy these elements. Maria Kelt and Herman von Hebel observe with respect to these elements that '[i]t is not clear whose calculations and whose intentions are considered here'. Maria Kelt and Herman von Hebel, 'General Principles of Criminal Law and the Elements of Crimes', in Lee (ed.), *supra* note 323, p. 27. They contend that the elements 'do not seem to refer to the calculation or the intention in the perpetrator's mind, but rather describe the character of those conditions or measures', and thus constitute objective 'material' elements instead of mental elements. *Ibid.*

365 Von Hebel and Kelt, *supra* note 346, p. 18.

366 For direct and public incitement to commit genocide, this jurisprudence is exclusively that of the ICTR, as this crime has never been charged at the ICTY. See *supra* section 3.4.

jurisprudence.[367] This is because the Rome Statute itself contains an unusually detailed provision on attempt, and unlike the Elements of Crimes, the elements set forth in that provision are binding on the chambers of the Court.[368]

The ICC Prosecutor has not yet sought to charge genocide against any of the persons publicly implicated in proceedings before the Court.[369] Moreover, while the US government has used the term 'genocide' when referring to the situation in Darfur, Sudan,[370] the Prosecutor has not yet sought to charge genocide against the two suspects in that case for whom arrest warrants have been issued.[371] This forbearance may be prompted by conclusions in the UN Commission of Inquiry January 2005 report that led to the Security Council's referral of the situation to the Court.[372] The Commission's conclusion that, while 'genocidal acts' had occurred in Darfur, there was insufficient evidence of a systematic policy of genocide,[373] has drawn sharp criticism.[374]

[367] See *supra* section 3.5 (noting that the *ad hoc* Tribunals have not developed elements for the only 'attempt' crime in their Statutes – attempt to commit genocide – because no accused before them has yet been charged with this crime).

[368] See Rome Statute, *supra* note 24, Art. 25(3)(f).

[369] See Chapter 2, text accompanying notes 544–550 (arrest warrants issued for five members of the Ugandan Lord's Resistance Army for crimes against humanity and war crimes); *ibid.*, text accompanying note 555 (arrest warrant issued against Germain Katanga for crimes against humanity and war crimes in the Democratic Republic of the Congo (DRC)); *ibid.*, text accompanying note 554 (charges confirmed against Thomas Lubanga for war crimes in the DRC). Chapter 4, text accompanying notes 505–517, discusses the war crimes charges against these suspects and accused.

[370] Colin L. Powell, Testimony Before the Senate Foreign Relations Committee, 9 September 2004, available at www.state.gov/secretary/former/powell/remarks/36042.htm. See also 'Powell Declares Genocide in Sudan', BBC News, 9 September 2004, available at www.news.bbc.co.uk/2/hi/africa/3641820.stm. See also H. R. Con. Res. 467, 108th Cong. § 1 (2004) (US House of Representatives declaring that the 'atrocities unfolding in Darfur, Sudan are genocide').

[371] These are Ali Kushayb and Ahmad Harun. See Chapter 2, text accompanying notes 551–552 (discussing the arrest warrants against these accused for crimes against humanity).

[372] See Security Council Resolution 1593, UN Doc. S/RES/1593 (2005), preambular para. 1 ('taking note of the report of the International Commission of Inquiry on violations of international humanitarian law and human rights law in Darfur'); *ibid.*, para. 1 (deciding 'to refer the situation in Darfur since 1 July 2002 to the Prosecutor of the International Criminal Court').

[373] See Darfur Commission Report, *supra* note 21, para. 514 ('This case clearly shows that the intent of the attackers was not to destroy an ethnic group as such … Instead, the intention was to murder all those men they considered as rebels[.]'); *ibid.*, para. 518 (concluding that 'the Government of Sudan has not pursued a policy of genocide' because genocidal intent appears to be absent); *ibid.*, para. 520 (allowing for the possibility that '*single individuals*, including Government officials, may entertain a genocidal intent') (emphasis in original).

[374] See, e.g., Nsongurua J. Udombana, 'An Escape from Reason: Genocide and the International Commission of Inquiry on Darfur', (2006) 40 *International Lawyer* 41, 41 (levelling the accusation that the Commission's reasoning hides a state's political motive to avoid having obligations triggered under the Genocide Convention); David Luban, 'Calling Genocide by Its Rightful Name: Lemkin's Word, Darfur, and the UN Report', (2006) 7 *Chicago Journal of International Law* 303, 306; Jamie A. Mathew, 'The Darfur Debate: Whether the ICC Should Determine that the Atrocities in Darfur Constitute Genocide', (2006) 18 *Florida Journal of International Law* 517, 547; van Schaack, *supra* note 21, pp. 1130–1134.

3.6.2 The Internationalised Tribunals

3.6.2.1 Special Court for Sierra Leone (SCSL)

In its resolution delineating the political and legal parameters of the SCSL, the Security Council noted that the crimes in question were perpetrated 'against the people of Sierra Leone and United Nations and associated personnel'.[375] It recommended that the subject-matter jurisdiction of the Special Court include 'notably crimes against humanity, war crimes and other serious violations of international humanitarian law, as well as crimes under relevant Sierra Leonean law'.[376] In his subsequent report on the establishment of the Special Court, the Secretary-General stated that:

> [b]ecause of the lack of any evidence that the massive, large-scale killing in Sierra Leone was at any time perpetrated against an identified national, ethnic, racial or religious group with an intent to annihilate the group as such, the Security Council did not include the crime of genocide in its recommendation, nor was it considered appropriate by the Secretary-General to include it in the list of international crimes falling within the jurisdiction of the Court.[377]

Consequently, there is no provision of the Special Court's governing law, nor any aspect of its jurisprudence, that concerns genocide.[378]

3.6.2.2 East Timor: Special Panels for Serious Crimes (SPSC)

Although the International Commission of Inquiry established to investigate human rights abuses committed prior to, during, and after the 1999 popular consultation in East Timor did not explicitly mention genocide among the atrocities committed,[379] genocide was included in the constitutive document for East Timor's Special Panels for Serious Crimes. Section 4 of Regulation No. 2000/15 on the Establishment of

[375] Security Council Resolution 1315, UN Doc. S/RES/1315 (2000), 14 August 2000, preamble.

[376] *Ibid.*, para. 2.

[377] Report of the Secretary-General on the Establishment of a Special Court for Sierra Leone, UN Doc. S/2000/915, 4 October 2000, para. 13. See also Daphna Shraga, 'The Second Generation UN-Based Tribunals: A Diversity of Mixed Jurisdictions', in Cesare P.R. Romano, André Nollkaemper, and Jann K. Kleffner (eds.), *Internationalized Criminal Courts and Tribunals: Sierra Leone, East Timor, Kosovo, and Cambodia* (2004), p. 23 (observing that, 'for all their brutality … the killings and mass executions [in Sierra Leone] were not committed on ethnic, religious, or racial grounds with an intent to annihilate the group distinguished on any of these grounds, as such'). Accord Sarah Williams, 'Amnesties in International Law: The Experience of the Special Court for Sierra Leone', (2005) 5 *Human Rights Law Review* 271, 292 n. 93.

[378] See Statute of the Special Court for Sierra Leone, 2178 UNTS 138, UN Doc. S/2002/246, 16 January 2002, Appendix II ('SCSL Statute'), Arts. 2–5 (setting forth the Special Court's jurisdiction over certain crimes against humanity, war crimes, and crimes under Sierra Leonean law, but excluding any provision on genocide). As of 1 December 2007, Sierra Leone had not yet ratified the Genocide Convention. See www.unhchr.ch/html/menu3/b/treaty1gen.htm. The only domestic Sierra Leonean crimes in the jurisdiction of the Special Court, moreover, are those specifically enumerated in the Court's Statute: '[o]ffences relating to the abuse of girls' and '[o]ffences relating to the wanton destruction of property'. See SCSL Statute, *supra*, Art. 5. Prosecutions before the Court for genocide as codified in domestic law would therefore be impermissible in any event absent an amendment to the Statute.

[379] See Chapter 2, note 588 (discussing the report and the establishment of the Special Panels).

Panels with Exclusive Jurisdiction over Serious Criminal Offences, promulgated by the UN Transitional Administration in East Timor ('UNTAET Regulation'), was virtually identical to Article II of the Genocide Convention.[380] As concerns the list of 'punishable acts' in Article III of the Genocide Convention, the Regulation followed the model used for the ICC ('ICC model'). Section 4 of the Regulation omitted any reference to these acts. Direct and public incitement to commit genocide, along with a general provision on attempt which applied to all of the crimes in the Special Panels' jurisdiction, were incorporated into the section of the Regulation dealing with individual criminal responsibility.[381]

As noted in Chapter 2, the Security Council withdrew UN support for the Special Panels in May 2005, effectively terminating them before they had tried the vast majority of their indictees.[382] No accused was ever charged with genocide or a related inchoate crime.[383] This absence may well be due to the General Prosecutor's determination that none of the crimes in question was committed with genocidal intent, or that such intent would be too difficult to prove. Nevertheless, the SPSC Court of Appeal discussed genocide in two aberrant cases in which it convicted the accused of a crime it labelled 'crimes against humanity in the form of genocide'.[384] These cases and the concerns raised by their flawed reasoning are examined in Chapter 2.[385]

3.6.2.3 The Extraordinary Chambers in the Courts of Cambodia (ECCC)

As several commentators have acknowledged,[386] most of the atrocities that characterised the Khmer Rouge regime in Cambodia cannot be legally qualified as 'genocide', despite frequent references to this crime in news reports and other

[380] United Nations Transitional Administration in East Timor, Regulation No. 2000/15 on the Establishment of Panels with Exclusive Jurisdiction over Serious Criminal Offences, UN Doc. UNTAET/REG/2000/15, 6 June 2000, Section 4. See *supra*, text accompanying note 2, for the complete text of Article II of the Convention.

[381] *Ibid.*, Section 14(e) (direct and public incitement to commit genocide); *ibid.*, Section 14(f) (attempt). As a result, like the ICC and unlike the *ad hoc* Tribunals, the Special Panels did not have, at least explicitly, jurisdiction over conspiracy to commit genocide.

[382] See Chapter 2, text accompanying notes 593–596.

[383] Caitlin Reiger and Marieke Wierda, *The Serious Crimes Process in Timor-Leste: In Retrospect*, International Centre for Transitional Justice, March 2006, available at www.ictj.org/static/Prosecutions/Timor.study.pdf, p. 23.

[384] See *Prosecutor* v. *Armando dos Santos*, Case No. 16/2001, Julgamento (Tribunal de Recurso), 15 July 2003, pp. 23–24; *Prosecutor* v. *Manual Gonçalves Bere Aka*, Case No. 10/2000, Julgamento (Tribunal de Recurso), 16 October 2003, p. 12.

[385] See Chapter 2, text accompanying notes 599–616.

[386] See Bassiouni, *supra* note 329, p. 149 (stating that, under the Genocide Convention's restrictive definition of genocide excluding political and social groups as potential targets, 'the Khmer Rouge massacre of over one million Cambodians, 40% of the population, does not qualify as genocide ... because the extermination was of Khmer by Khmer'); Shraga, *supra* note 377, p. 22; Ratner and Abrams, *supra* note 54, pp. 286–287 (stating that, even though the Khmer people 'clearly constitute a national group', the facts suggest that the Khmer Rouge targeted their Khmer victims on economic, social, or political grounds, and not as members of the Khmer nation as such) (quotation at p. 287).

general literature.[387] The massacres were not, in most cases, carried out with the intent to destroy a national, ethnic, racial, or religious group as such, and the definition of genocide in customary international law almost certainly excludes acts targeting groups that are only political or social in nature.[388] Nevertheless, the Group of Experts for Cambodia recommended that genocide be included within the jurisdiction of an *ad hoc* international criminal tribunal to allow for the imposition of liability for a limited range of the regime's activities:

> In the view of the Group of Experts, the existing historical research justifies including genocide within the jurisdiction of a tribunal to prosecute Khmer Rouge leaders. In particular, evidence suggests the need for prosecutors to investigate the commission of genocide against the Cham, Vietnamese and other minority groups, and the Buddhist monkhood. The Khmer Rouge subjected these groups to an especially harsh and extensive measure of the acts enumerated in the Convention. The requisite intent has support in direct and indirect evidence, including Khmer Rouge statements, eyewitness accounts and the nature and number of victims in each group, both in absolute terms and in proportion to each group's total population. These groups qualify as protected groups under the Convention: the Muslim Cham as an ethnic and religious group; the Vietnamese communities as an ethnic and, perhaps, a racial group; and the Buddhist monkhood as a religious group.[389]

In accordance with this recommendation, Article 4 of the Cambodian law establishing the hybrid Extraordinary Chambers ('ECCC Law') gives them jurisdiction over genocide:

> The Extraordinary Chambers shall have the power to bring to trial all Suspects who committed the crimes of genocide as defined in the Convention on the Prevention and Punishment of the Crime of Genocide of 1948, and which were committed during the period from 17 April 1975 to 6 January 1979.

[387] See, e.g., Bruce Zagaris, 'Legal Requirements Met to Establish Cambodia Tribunals', *International Enforcement Law Reporter*, July 2005, p. 269 (referring to 'Cambodia's genocide'); David J. Scheffer, 'International Judicial Intervention', (1996) 102 *Foreign Policy* 34, 34 (referring to 'the unforgettable genocide in Cambodia'); Winston P. Nagan and Vivile F. Rodin, 'Racism, Genocide, and Mass Murder: Toward a Legal Theory About Group Deprivations', (2003–2004) 17 *National Black Law Journal* 133, 177 (dubiously labelling as genocide, along with the acts of the Khmer Rouge, abuses against the Ibo in Nigeria, the East Timorese, the Croatians in Bosnia, and the Arabs in Zanzibar). See also Ratner and Abrams, *supra* note 54, p. 288 (stating that the Cambodian government has for many years used the term genocide 'as a blanket label for the full gamut of the Khmer Rouge's atrocities'); see also www.law.case.edu/saddamtrial/ ('International War Crimes Blog' labelling the ECCC trials the 'Khmer Rouge Genocide Trials').

[388] See *supra* note 386. See also Ratner and Abrams, *supra* note 54, p. 287 (arguing that 'the definition of genocide under customary international law likely coincides with that under the [Genocide] Convention').

[389] Report of the Group of Experts for Cambodia Established Pursuant to General Assembly Resolution 52/135, annexed to UN Doc. A/53/850, S/1999/231, 16 March 1999 ('Cambodia Group of Experts Report'), para. 63. See also *ibid.*, para. 150 ('[T]he abuses of the period of Democratic Kampuchea are such as to suggest that a court could have jurisdiction over … genocide …. The Group believes that a United Nations tribunal must have jurisdiction over crimes against humanity and genocide. These two crimes … constituted the bulk of the Khmer Rouge terror.'). See also Ball, *supra* note 20, pp. 109–112 (giving a detailed breakdown of the quantitative extermination of ethnic minorities, and arguing that Pol Pot's regime conducted a campaign of eradication of these groups for ideological reasons). Although Ball fails to undertake a legal analysis of the commission of these crimes in terms of the elements required to establish the crime of genocide, he clearly expresses the view that the killings were undertaken with genocidal intent.

The acts of genocide, which have no statute of limitations, mean any acts committed with the intent to destroy, in whole or in part, a national, ethnical, racial or religious group, such as:

- killing members of the group;
- causing serious bodily or mental harm to members of the group;
- deliberately inflicting on the group conditions of life calculated to bring about its physical destruction in whole or in part;
- imposing measures intended to prevent births within the group;
- forcibly transferring children from one group to another group.

The following acts shall be punishable under this Article:

- attempts to commit acts of genocide;
- conspiracy to commit acts of genocide;
- participation in acts of genocide.[390]

In a manner identical to that of the *ad hoc* Statutes, the Rome Statute, and the UNTAET Regulation (which, as mentioned above,[391] follows the ICC model in its genocide provision) the first bulleted acts in Article 4 and the *chapeau* introducing them essentially reproduce Article II of the Genocide Convention. Interestingly, however, the second set of bulleted acts replicates Article III of the Genocide Convention only partially,[392] and the ECCC Law differs in certain respects from the analogous provisions in the *ad hoc* Statutes, the Rome Statute, and the UNTAET Regulation. Like its predecessors, the Cambodian law grants the Extraordinary Chambers jurisdiction over the inchoate crime of attempt to commit genocide; unlike all the earlier instruments, it curiously omits direct and public incitement to commit genocide. Moreover, like the Genocide Convention and the *ad hoc* Statutes and unlike the Rome Statute and the UNTAET Regulation, the Cambodian law covers conspiracy to commit genocide. As discussed in Volume I of this series, the reference to 'complicity in genocide' in the Genocide Convention and the *ad hoc* Statutes appears to have been replaced by a potentially broader category labelled 'participation'.[393]

As noted in Chapter 2, on 18 July 2007, the ECCC Co-Prosecutors released a brief statement informing the public that they had filed before the Co-Investigating

390 The Law on the Establishment of the Extraordinary Chambers in the Courts of Cambodia for the Prosecution of Crimes Committed During the Period of Democratic Kampuchea, as amended on 27 October 2004, Doc. No. NS/RKM/1004/006, unofficial translation by the Council of Jurists and the Secretariat of the Task Force, revised on 26 August 2007, Art. 4, available at www.eccc.gov.kh/english/cabinet/law/4/KR_Law_as_amended_27_Oct_2004_Eng.pdf.

391 See *supra* text accompanying note 381.

392 This partial reproduction of Article III of the Genocide Convention may be *ultra vires* the cooperation agreement reached between Cambodia and the United Nations, which requires that the definition of genocide in the ECCC Law be that of the Convention. See Agreement Between the United Nations and the Royal Government of Cambodia Concerning the Prosecution Under Cambodian Law of Crimes Committed During the Period of Democratic Kampuchea, 17 March 2003, Arts. 2(2), 9, approved by General Assembly Resolution 57/2288 (2003), available at www.eccc.gov.kh/english/cabinet/agreement/5/Agreement_between_UN_and_RGC.pdf. See also Chapter 2, note 647 (discussing this possibility in more detail with respect to crimes against humanity).

393 Boas, Bischoff, and Reid, *supra* note 23, pp. 338–339.

Judges an 'Introductory Submission' identifying five suspects thought to have committed 'crimes against humanity, genocide, grave breaches of the Geneva Conventions, homicide, torture and religious persecution'.[394] All five had been arrested by the end of November 2007.[395] While all have been charged with crimes against humanity and three with war crimes, none has yet been charged with genocide or a related inchoate crime, despite the Co-Prosecutors' July 2007 statement.[396] The absence of genocide charges is unsurprising: the Co-Prosecutors and Co-Investigating Judges can be expected to focus on crimes against humanity committed by Khmers against Khmers to the exclusion of the relatively small number of crimes perpetrated against victims of other ethnic and religious groups.[397]

3.6.2.4 Supreme Iraqi Criminal Tribunal (SICT) (also known as the Iraqi High Tribunal (IHT))

Article 11 of the Statute of the Supreme Iraqi Criminal Tribunal[398] reproduces both Articles II and III of the Genocide Convention, with one minor addition: the *chapeau* of the provision corresponding to Article II makes express mention of Iraq's 20 January 1959 ratification of the Convention.[399] The result is a provision that is almost identical to its analogue in the *ad hoc* Tribunals' Statutes ('*ad hoc* model'); this is curious, since the ICC model is followed in the SICT Statute's provisions on crimes against humanity,[400] war crimes,[401] and individual criminal responsibility.[402] The strict adherence to the language of Articles II and III of the

394 Extraordinary Chambers in the Courts of Cambodia, Statement of the Co-Prosecutors, 18 July 2007, p. 4. See Chapter 2, text accompanying notes 661–666.

395 See Seth Mydans, 'Cambodia Arrests Former Khmer Rouge Head of State', *New York Times*, 20 November 2007, available at www.nytimes.com/2007/11/20/world/asia/20cambo.html?_r=1&oref=slogin (stating that Khieu Samphan, who was arrested on 19 November 2007, was 'the last of five top figures targeted by prosecutors in advance of trials expected [in 2008] for the atrocities of the late 1970s').

396 See Chapter 2, notes 667–671 and accompanying text (discussing the crimes against humanity charges against Kaing Guek Eav, Nuon Chea, Ieng Sary, Ieng Thirith, and Khieu Samphan); Chapter 4, notes 586–590 and accompanying text (discussing the war crimes charges against Nuon, Ieng Sary, and Khieu).

397 See Cambodia Group of Experts Report, *supra* note 389, para. 150 (noting that genocide and crimes against humanity, but '*especially crimes against humanity*, constituted the bulk of the Khmer Rouge terror') (emphasis added). Some commentators have given these Khmer on Khmer crimes the strange and oxymoronic label of 'auto-genocide'. See, e.g., Steven Feldstein, 'Applying the Rome Statute of the International Criminal Court: A Case Study of Henry Kissinger', (2004) 92 *California Law Review* 1663, 1667; Shraga, *supra* note 377, p. 22 (referring to the 'so-called "auto-genocide"').

398 See Chapter 1, note 2 (discussing the different English translations of the Tribunal's name).

399 See Law No. 10 (2005), Law of the Iraqi Higher Criminal Court, 18 October 2005 ('SICT Statute'), English translation available at www.law.case.edu/saddamtrial/documents/IST_statute_official_english.pdf *reprinted* in Michael P. Scharf and Gregory S. McNeal (eds.), *Saddam on Trial: Understanding and Debating the Iraqi High Tribunal* (2006), pp. 283 *et seq*., Art. 11(1). Article 11 defines genocidal intent as the intent to 'abolish' (instead of 'destroy')[0] one of the protected groups. This deviation from the usual terminology surely makes no difference in real terms.

400 See *ibid*., Art. 12. 401 See *ibid*., Art. 13.

402 See *ibid*., Art. 15. See also Boas, Bischoff, and Reid, *supra* note 23, pp. 137–140, 272–274, 378–379, 339–340 (discussing the SICT's approach to forms of responsibility in detail).

Genocide Convention may have been intended to pre-empt questions over whether individuals in Iraq could be held liable for genocide as defined in the Statute for deeds committed as early as 17 July 1968, the start date of the Tribunal's temporal jurisdiction.[403] Perhaps for this reason as well, Article 11 makes explicit reference to the respective dates of the Genocide Convention's adoption by the UN General Assembly and Iraq's ratification of the Convention.[404] Furthermore, a bizarre (and almost certainly unintended) consequence of the SICT's reliance on the *ad hoc* model in its genocide provision and on the ICC model in its provision on individual criminal responsibility is that the Statute lists two of the inchoate crimes twice: direct and public incitement to commit genocide appears at Articles 11(2)(C) and Article 15(2)(E); attempt to commit genocide is enshrined in Article 11(2)(D); and a general provision on attempt applicable to all crimes in the Statute appears at Article 15(2)(F). As discussed in Chapter 2, the SICT also has recourse to a document setting forth the elements of the crimes within its jurisdiction.[405] The elements of genocide are essentially identical to those of the ICC Elements of Crimes;[406] like the ICC Elements, the SICT Elements of Crimes lack any exposition of the elements of the genocide-related inchoate crimes in the Tribunal's jurisdiction.

In the *Dujail* case – the Tribunal's first – Saddam Hussein and his seven co-accused were charged with crimes against humanity only; as a result, neither the Trial nor Appeal Judgement in that case deals in any way with genocide or its related inchoate crimes.[407] The second trial before the SICT began in September 2006 and concerned alleged massacres and forced removals involving perhaps 200,000 Kurds in the 'Anfal' campaign carried out by Hussein's regime in 1988.[408] Perhaps as a result of waning interest in the Tribunal's work in the wake of Hussein's execution,[409] as of

403 SICT Statute, *supra* note 399, Art. 1(2) (granting temporal jurisdiction from 17 July 1968 to 1 May 2003).

404 *Ibid*., Art. 11(1) (referring to the Convention's adoption on 9 December 1948, and Iraq's ratification of it on 20 January 1959).

405 See Chapter 2, notes 681–685 and accompanying text (also discussing the status of the SICT Elements and the reliance on them by the Trial Chamber in the *Dujail* case).

406 See Iraqi Special Tribunal, Elements of Crimes, Section 2 ('SICT Elements of Crimes'), available at www.law.case.edu/saddamtrial/documents/IST_Elements.pdf, reprinted in Scharf and McNeal (eds.), *supra* note 399, pp. 327 *et seq*. (differing from the language of the ICC Elements of Crimes only by moving footnotes 3 to 5 of the ICC Elements – which elaborate on aspects of three of the elements – into the main text).

407 See Chapter 2, text accompanying notes 686–708 (discussing the *Dujail* charges and judgements in detail).

408 See Michael P. Scharf and Gregory S. McNeal, 'What Are the Specific Charges Against Saddam Hussein?', in Scharf and McNeal (eds.), *supra* note 399, p. 59; Michael A. Newton, 'The Significance of the Anfal Campaign Indictment', in Scharf and McNeal (eds.), *supra* note 399, pp. 220–222; Michael P. Scharf, 'The Significance of the Anfal Campaign Indictment', in Scharf and McNeal (eds.), *supra* note 399, pp. 222–224; Mark A. Drumbl, 'The Significance of the Anfal Campaign Indictment', in Scharf and McNeal (eds.), *supra* note 399, pp. 224–225 (discussing the history of the Anfal campaign, along with prospects and anticipated difficulties in prosecuting the crimes before the SICT).

409 See John F. Burns, 'Hussein's Cousin Sentenced to Die for Kurd Attacks', *New York Times*, 25 June 2007, available at www.select.nytimes.com/search/restricted/article?res=F20E10F8355B0C768EDDAF0894DF404482 (noting that 'Iraqi public interest in the [SICT's] trials has flagged'; that few Iraqi and no Kurdish reporters attended the hearing at which the judges handed down the *Anfal* verdict; and that 'only a handful of Western reporters' were in attendance).

1 December 2007 the charging instruments and judgements in the *Anfal* case had not been made publicly available in English, although the Prosecutor's closing argument was available. It appears to show that the five accused – the highest-ranked of whom was Ali Hassan al-Majid, also known as 'Chemical Ali'[410] – were charged with ordering, inciting, aiding and abetting, and failing as superiors to prevent and punish various war crimes and crimes against humanity, as well as genocide through four underlying offences: killing members of the Kurdish group, inflicting serious physical harm on them, inflicting serious mental harm on them, and inflicting on them eventually destructive conditions of life.[411] The Prosecutor argued that the Kurds qualified as national, ethnic, and racial group by virtue of their shared language, physical features, and origins in the geographical region of Kurdistan.[412] The 'figure-heads' of Hussein's regime 'were the instrument of evil which endeavored to harm and kill the Kurds as a group':[413]

> Since it fell entirely upon the Kurdish villagers, and they were attacked with chemical and other types of weapons, and those who survived this bombardment were detained in special, pre-prepared camps, and then children, women, and young people were put into mass graves, this is clear proof of the fulfillment of the specific definition of the destruction of this nation, in whole or in part, because it was solely [*sic*] the Kurds.[414]

According to the Prosecutor, the accused and other officials of the Hussein regime achieved their goal: 'thousands of Kurdish villages' were destroyed, 'including schools and places of worship'.[415] The Tribunal convicted five of the six on 23 June 2007.[416] Media reports indicate that Majid was convicted of genocide, war crimes, and crimes against humanity, while the other four were convicted only of war crimes and crimes against humanity.[417]

[410] See 'Prosecutorial Closing Argument in the Anfal Case', available at www.iraq-iht.org/en/doc/ppb.pdf (date unknown, on file with authors), pp. 2–3, 7. All charges against Saddam Hussein in the *Anfal* case were dropped following his execution by hanging. See Chapter 2, note 711 and accompanying text.

[411] *Ibid.*, pp. 8–11 (discussing the elements of these underlying offences in terms seemingly inspired by both the SICT Elements of Crimes, *supra* note 406, and *ad hoc* jurisprudence, and discussing some of the evidence that purportedly fulfilled such elements).

[412] See *ibid.*, p. 9. [413] *Ibid.*, p. 1. [414] *Ibid.*, p. 8. [415] *Ibid.*, p. 1.

[416] See, e.g., Burns, *supra* note 409; BBC News, '"Chemical Ali" Sentenced to Hang', 24 June 2007, at www.news.bbc.co.uk/2/hi/middle_east/6233926.stm.

[417] Majid and two others were sentenced to death; the death sentences had yet to be carried out as of 1 December 2007. A sixth accused was acquitted. Other trials before the SICT are apparently being prepared or are underway. See Chapter 2, notes 718–719 and accompanying text.

4

War crimes

A war crime is a breach of the international law of armed conflict that is regarded as so serious that it entails not just state responsibility, but individual criminal responsibility. Unlike crimes against humanity, there is no general requirement that a war crime take place in the context of widespread, massive, or systematised criminality; instead, such a crime may be a single, isolated incident, so long as it occurs in the context of an armed conflict.[1] Articles 2 and 3 of the Statute of the International Criminal Tribunal for the former Yugoslavia (ICTY) set forth two classic categories of war crimes. Article 2 lists the 'grave breaches' of the 1949 Geneva Conventions, punishable only when committed in international armed conflict:

Article 2: **Grave breaches of the Geneva Conventions of 1949**
The International Tribunal shall have the power to prosecute persons committing or ordering to be committed grave breaches of the Geneva Conventions of 12 August 1949, namely the

[1] The notion that a war crime can be an isolated incident has been widely accepted. See *infra* note 443 (citing ICTY jurisprudence). At the insistence of certain states, however, a jurisdictional restriction was incorporated into the war crimes provision of the Rome Statute of the International Criminal Court: 'The Court shall have jurisdiction in respect of war crimes *in particular* when committed as part of a plan or policy or as part of a large-scale commission of such crimes.' Rome Statute of the International Criminal Court, 17 July 1998, entered into force 1 July 2002, UN Doc. A/CONF. 183/9 (1998) ('Rome Statute'), Art. 8(1) (emphasis added). See also *infra* text accompanying notes 443–444 (discussing the negotiations resulting in this restriction); *infra* section 4.2 (detailed discussion of the elements of war crimes).

following acts against persons or property protected under the provisions of the relevant Geneva Convention:

(a) wilful killing;
(b) torture or inhuman treatment, including biological experiments;
(c) wilfully causing great suffering or serious injury to body or health;
(d) extensive destruction and appropriation of property, not justified by military necessity and carried out unlawfully and wantonly;
(e) compelling a prisoner of war or a civilian to serve in the forces of a hostile power;
(f) wilfully depriving a prisoner of war or a civilian of the rights of fair and regular trial;
(g) unlawful deportation or transfer or unlawful confinement of a civilian;
(h) taking civilians as hostages.[2]

This list of grave breaches is taken from Article 50 of Geneva Convention I (protecting the wounded and sick in the field), Article 51 of Geneva Convention II (protecting the wounded, sick, and shipwrecked at sea), Article 130 of Geneva Convention III (protecting prisoners of war), and Article 147 of Geneva Convention IV (protecting civilians).[3]

Article 3 of the ICTY Statute sets forth other 'violations of the laws or customs of war' which, as the Appeals Chamber controversially held in the October 1995 *Tadić* Jurisdiction Decision,[4] are punishable whether committed in international or non-international armed conflict:

[2] Statute of the International Criminal Tribunal for the Prosecution of Persons Responsible for Serious Violations of International Humanitarian Law Committed in the Territory of the former Yugoslavia since 1991, (1993) 32 ILM 1159, *as amended by* Security Council Resolution 1660 of 28 February 2006 ('ICTY Statute'), Art. 2.

[3] The four Geneva Conventions of 12 August 1949, which entered into force on 21 October 1950, are: (1) Geneva Convention for the Amelioration of the Condition of the Wounded and Sick in Armed Forces in the Field, 75 UNTS 31 ('Geneva Convention I'); (2) Geneva Convention for the Amelioration of the Condition of Wounded, Sick and Shipwrecked Members of Armed Forces at Sea, 75 UNTS 85 ('Geneva Convention II'); (3) Geneva Convention relative to the Treatment of Prisoners of War, 75 UNTS 135 ('Geneva Convention III'); (4) Geneva Convention relative to the Protection of Civilian Persons in Time of War, 75 UNTS 287 ('Geneva Convention IV'). The four Geneva Conventions expressly apply – with the very important exception of Article 3, which is identical in all four conventions – only to international armed conflicts. See Geneva Convention I, *supra*, Art. 2 (same in the other three conventions). Article 3 of the four conventions will hereinafter be referred to as 'Common Article 3'. In 1977, two additional protocols were adopted: Protocol I Additional to the Geneva Conventions of 12 August 1949, and Relating to the Protection of Victims of International Armed Conflicts, entered into force 7 December 1978, 1125 UNTS 3 ('Additional Protocol I'); Protocol II Additional to the Geneva Conventions of 12 August 1949, and Relating to the Protection of Victims of Non-International Armed Conflicts, entered into force 7 December 1978, 1125 UNTS 609 ('Additional Protocol II').

[4] See *Prosecutor* v. *Tadić*, Case No. IT-94-1-A, Decision on the Defence Motion for Interlocutory Appeal on Jurisdiction, 2 October 1995 ('*Tadić* Jurisdiction Appeal Decision'), para. 94. The Appeals Chamber opined that it was the intention of the Security Council to leave open the legal resolution of the character of the armed conflict or conflicts in the former Yugoslavia, and that Article 3 was therefore intended to apply to any type of armed conflict:

> [T]he conflicts in the former Yugoslavia have both internal and international aspects[.] … [T]he members of the Security Council clearly had both aspects of the conflicts in mind when they adopted the Statute of the International Tribunal, and … they intended to empower the International Tribunal to adjudicate violations of humanitarian law that occurred in either context. To the extent possible under existing international law, the Statute should therefore be construed to give effect to that purpose.

Ibid., para. 77. But see William A. Schabas, *The UN International Criminal Tribunals: The Former Yugoslavia, Rwanda and Sierra Leone* (2006), pp. 232–236 (discussing some of the flaws in the *Tadić* Appeals Chamber's reasoning leading to this conclusion, and suggesting that the Statute was not, in fact, intended to confer jurisdiction over war crimes committed in non-international armed conflict).

Article 3: Violations of the laws or customs of war
The International Tribunal shall have the power to prosecute persons violating the laws or customs of war. Such violations shall include, but not be limited to:

(a) employment of poisonous weapons or other weapons calculated to cause unnecessary suffering;
(b) wanton destruction of cities, towns or villages, or devastation not justified by military necessity;
(c) attack, or bombardment, by whatever means, of undefended towns, villages, dwellings, or buildings;
(d) seizure of, destruction or wilful damage done to institutions dedicated to religion, charity and education, the arts and sciences, historic monuments and works of art and science;
(e) plunder of public or private property.[5]

This open catalogue of crimes was largely inspired by an instrument that, despite its centenarian status, still retains great relevance in modern international humanitarian law (IHL): Hague Convention IV of 1907 and its annexed Regulations, which together govern the means and methods of land warfare.[6] The *Tadić* Appeals Chamber established the now widely accepted rule that, even though it does not qualify as one of the grave breaches of the Geneva Conventions, a violation of IHL may still be punished as a war crime – in the ICTY through the vehicle of Article 3 – if it fulfils certain criteria.[7] The development and application of these criteria in the *ad hoc* Tribunals will be explored in detail in the next section of the chapter.[8] What is significant to stress at this point is the indisputable notion, as Antonio Cassese puts it, that this category of crimes outside of the grave breaches regime 'must now also be regarded as amounting to war crimes proper'.[9]

In contrast to the ICTY Statute, the Statute of the International Criminal Tribunal for Rwanda (ICTR) was drafted with the intention to invest that Tribunal with jurisdiction over war crimes only when they are committed in non-international armed conflict.[10] Accordingly, Article 4 incorporates certain provisions from the two main texts governing the conduct of hostilities in non-international armed

[5] ICTY Statute, *supra* note 2, Art. 3.

[6] Compare, respectively, Hague Convention (IV) Respecting the Laws and Customs of War on Land and Its Annex: Regulation Concerning the Laws and Customs of War on Land, 18 October 1907, entered into force 26 January 1910, 3 *Martens Nouveau Recueil* (ser. 3) 461, 187 Consol. T.S. 227, Annex ('1907 Hague Regulations'), Arts. 23(a), 25, 27 with ICTY Statute, *supra* note 2, Arts. 3(a), 3(c), 3(d).

[7] *Tadić* Jurisdiction Appeal Decision, *supra* note 4, para. 94.

[8] See *infra* section 4.2.1.5.

[9] Antonio Cassese, *International Criminal Law* (2003), p. 47. But see Alexander Zahar and Göran Sluiter, *International Criminal Law: A Critical Introduction* (2007), pp. 113–117 (arguing that the *ad hoc* Tribunals have dealt unsatisfactorily with the question of whether and when the so-called 'Common Article 3 war crimes' punishable in the ICTY under Article 3 of the Tribunal's Statute gave rise to individual criminal responsibility).

[10] See Report of the Secretary-General Pursuant to Paragraph 5 of Security Council Resolution 955 (1994), UN Doc. S/1995/134, 13 February 1995, para. 11.

conflict – Common Article 3 of the 1949 Geneva Conventions,[11] and Additional Protocol II to the Geneva Conventions[12] – in a non-exhaustive list:

Article 4: Violations of Article 3 Common to the Geneva Conventions and of Additional Protocol II

The International Tribunal for Rwanda shall have the power to prosecute persons committing or ordering to be committed serious violations of Article 3 common to the Geneva Conventions of 12 August 1949 for the Protection of War Victims, and of Additional Protocol II thereto of 8 June 1977. These violations shall include, but shall not be limited to:

(a) Violence to life, health and physical or mental well-being of persons, in particular murder as well as cruel treatment such as torture, mutilation or any form of corporal punishment;
(b) Collective punishments;
(c) Taking of hostages;
(d) Acts of terrorism;
(e) Outrages upon personal dignity, in particular humiliating and degrading treatment, rape, enforced prostitution and any form of indecent assault;
(f) Pillage;
(g) The passing of sentences and the carrying out of executions without previous judgement pronounced by a regularly constituted court, affording all the judicial guarantees which are recognized as indispensable by civilised peoples;
(h) Threats to commit any of the foregoing acts.[13]

War crimes are by far the most ancient of the three core categories of international crimes treated in this volume, tracing their origins centuries or even millennia into the past. Section 4.1 discusses the historical development of war crimes and their early notions in different cultures, religions, and military doctrine, through to the prolific treaty and customary evolution in the nineteenth and twentieth centuries leading up to the creation of the ICTY and the ICTR. Section 4.2 considers the important contribution of the *ad hoc* Tribunals to the development and understanding of war crimes. The general requirements for all war crimes are considered first, followed by the additional general requirements that must be fulfilled for an offence to rise to the level of a grave breach under Article 2 of the ICTY Statute; a violation of the laws or customs of war under Article 3 of the ICTY Statute; or a violation of Common Article 3 or Additional Protocol II under Article 4 of the ICTR Statute. This section of the chapter also discusses the jurisprudence on the elements of the underlying offences that are explicitly listed in the subparagraphs of these three provisions, as well as those that do not expressly appear in the Statutes, but have been determined by the Tribunals to fall within their residual jurisdiction. Finally,

[11] See Common Article 3, *supra* note 3 (all subparagraphs).
[12] See Additional Protocol II, *supra* note 3, Arts. 4(1)(a)–(e), (g)–(h), 6(2).
[13] Statute of the International Criminal Tribunal for Rwanda, (1994) 33 ILM 1602, as amended by Security Council Resolution 1534 of 26 March 2004 ('ICTR Statute'), Art. 4.

Section 4.3 looks at war crimes as defined and applied in the International Criminal Court (ICC) and the various internationalised criminal tribunals: the Special Court for Sierra Leone (SCSL), the Special Panels for Serious Crimes in East Timor (SPSC), the Extraordinary Chambers in the Courts of Cambodia (ECCC), and the Supreme Iraqi Criminal Tribunal (SICT).[14]

4.1 Evolution of war crimes

4.1.1 Ancient to modern conceptions of war crimes

As discussed in Chapter 1, particularly with the advent of the *ad hoc* Tribunals, the notion has arisen in some quarters that genocide and crimes against humanity can today be considered as falling under the umbrella of 'international humanitarian law'.[15] Whatever the proper characterisation of those two core categories of crimes, war crimes are incontrovertibly the domain of IHL.[16] Indeed, the development of IHL – one of the more complex areas of public international law – is inextricably linked to the evolution of the law relating to war crimes, which has ancient roots.

International humanitarian law has somewhat chauvinistically been perceived as Eurocentric in philosophical and geographical origin.[17] There exists considerable evidence that this is not the case. Leslie Green notes that the Old Testament speaks of God imposing rules and restraints on the conduct of war, including the sparing of women and children, respect for prisoners of war, and precautions against the killing of flora and fauna on enemy territory unless military necessity dictated their destruction.[18] More concrete examples also exist. In *The Art of War*, Sun Tzu, a

[14] Also known as the Iraqi High Tribunal (IHT). See Chapter 1, note 2 (discussing the different English translations of the Tribunal's name).

[15] See Chapter 1, text accompanying notes 3–8 (discussing whether crimes against humanity and genocide pertain to international humanitarian law). For a discussion of the historical development of crimes against humanity, see Chapter 2, section 2.2; for a discussion of the development of genocide, see Chapter 3, section 3.2.

[16] International humanitarian law regulates the way in which armed force may be used and is referred to by a number of different names: 'IHL', '*jus in bello*', the 'law of war', the 'law of armed conflict', and 'international humanitarian law applicable in armed conflict'. See UK Ministry of Defence, *The Manual of the Law of Armed Conflict* (2004), para. 1.2; Michel Veuthey, 'Non-International Armed Conflict and Guerrilla Warfare', in M. Cherif Bassiouni (ed.), *International Criminal Law* (2nd edn 1999), pp. 417–420; Christopher Greenwood, 'Historical Development and Legal Basis', in Dieter Fleck (ed.), *The Handbook of Humanitarian Law in Armed Conflicts* (1995), paras. 101–104; Hilaire McCoubrey and Nigel White, *International Law and Armed Conflict* (1992), pp. 209–224.

[17] Scholarly work on this issue reveals that such a view is not historically accurate. See Leslie C. Green, 'International Regulation of Armed Conflicts', in Bassiouni (ed.), *supra* note 16, p. 355. See also Greenwood, *supra* note 16, para. 107; Marco Sassòli and Antoine Bouvier, *How Does Law Protect in War?* (1999), pp. 97–104; Jean Pictet, *Development and Principles of International Humanitarian Law* (1985), p. 6; see also generally Hirad Abtahi, 'Reflections on the Ambiguous Universality of Human Rights: Cyrus the Great's Proclamation as a Challenge to the Athenian Democracy's Perceived Monopoly on Human Rights', in Hirad Abtahi and Gideon Boas (eds.), *The Dynamics of International Criminal Justice: Essays in Honour of Sir Richard May* (2005), pp. 1 *et seq.*; Leslie C. Green, *Essays on the Modern Law of War* (1985); Majid Khadduri, *War and Peace in the Law of Islam* (1955).

[18] Green, *supra* note 17, p. 356. See also Howard S. Levie, *Terrorism in War: The Law of War Crimes* (1993), p. 9.

Chinese warrior in the sixth century B.C., discusses the restraint required of leaders and military commanders in the waging of war, including the sparing of prisoners of war: 'When troops flee, are insubordinate, distressed, collapse in disorder or are routed, it is the fault of the general. None of these disorders can be attributed to natural causes.'[19] Timothy McCormack explains that 'nothing in Tzu's writing [suggests] a conviction on his part that the limitations he prescribed formed part of a body of law or morality binding on those engaged in armed conflict'.[20] Rather, the concern is a self-interested desire to achieve most effectively a favourable outcome of hostilities.[21]

Christopher Greenwood and other scholars point to numerous other ancient examples of restraint in the waging of war and the condemnation of conduct that, under modern IHL, would amount to war crimes. In Sumer, one of the early civilizations of the Ancient Near East in what is today south-eastern Iraq, evidence exists that war was regulated, including the provision of immunity for enemy negotiators.[22] The Code of Hammurabi, dating from 1728 to 1686 B.C., provided for the protection of the weak against oppression by the strong, the release of hostages on payment of ransom, and a catalogue of sanctions aimed at repairing the prejudices caused to both victims and society.[23] The Law of Hittites required respect for the inhabitants of an enemy city that had capitulated.[24] In the sixth century B.C., Cyrus the Great of Persia prescribed the treatment of enemy soldiers as though they were his own. The Proclamation of Cyrus was divided into three parts: the first two parts explained why Cyrus conquered Babylon, while the third part was recited as a factual account of what he did upon seizing Babylon. This part reveals some extraordinary core principles of present-day international humanitarian law and human rights law, including the freedom of thought, conscience, and religion, and the protection of civilians and property.[25]

[19] Sun Tzu, *The Art of War*, p. 125, cited in William H. Parks, 'Command Responsibility for War Crimes', (1973) 62 *Military Law Review* 1, 3. See also Elies van Sliedregt, *The Criminal Responsibility of Individuals for Violations of International Humanitarian Law* (2003), p. 119 n. 5; Green, *supra* note 17, p. 356.

[20] Timothy L. H. McCormack, 'From Sun Tzu to the Sixth Committee: the Evolution of an International Criminal Regime', in Timothy L. H. McCormack and Gerry J. Simpson (eds.), *The Law of War Crimes: National and International Approaches* (1997), 33.

[21] See *ibid.* [22] See Greenwood, *supra* note 16, para. 107. [23] See *ibid.*

[24] *ibid.* The Hittites were an ancient people who established a kingdom centred at Hattusa in north-central Anatolia from the eighteenth century B.C.

[25] See Abtahi, *supra* note 17, pp. 14–21; Tristan Gilbertson, 'War Crimes', (1995) 25 *Victoria University Wellington Law Review* 315, 317–318; Hilaire McCoubrey, *International Humanitarian Law: The Regulation of Armed Conflict* (1990), pp. 6–11; Pictet, *supra* note 17, pp. 5–18; Hirsch Lauterpacht, *Oppenheim's International Law* (8th edn 1955), vol. 2, pp. 202–209. Greenwood cites many other examples, including (1) the Laws of Manu, an important work of ancient Hindu law, in part prohibited the killing of a surrendering adversary no longer capable of fighting, forbade certain means of combat (such as poisoned or burning arrows), and provided for the protection of enemy property and prisoners of war; (2) Alexander the Great, in his war with Persia, required the Greeks to respect the life and dignity of war victims, respect temples, priests, embassies, and diplomatic envoys, and exchange prisoners of war; and (3) the Romans respected the right to life of prisoners of war. See Greenwood, *supra* note 16, para. 107.

Other examples of rules reflecting current IHL principles appeared in the middle ages, including the espousal by St. Augustine of the popular (but not always or often respected) principle of protecting women, children, and the elderly from hostilities; Augustine also developed the theory of the 'just war', giving divine justification to Christians to fight in a war justified by lawful authority, just cause, and rightful intention.[26] The Code of Chivalry, originally designed to regulate the conduct of warfare among knights, had the more general effect of developing humane treatment for non-combatants in armed conflict.[27] Richard II of England, in the fourteenth century, issued rules for the conduct of war known as the 'Articles of War', which included a prohibition on the taking of booty, robbery, and pillage, as well as the 'forcing' of women.[28] And in Japan, Bushi-Do, the Japanese medieval Code of Honour, espoused the principle of humanity in war, which extended to prisoners of war.[29]

Evincing the application of the chivalrous principles developed in the middle ages in Europe, the first recorded international war crimes trial appears to have taken place in 1474, when the knight Peter Hagenbach was put on trial by the Archduke of Austria before an international tribunal composed of twenty-eight judges from the allied states of the Holy Roman Empire. He was convicted of murder, which the tribunal held he should have prevented because, as a knight, he had a duty and was in a position to prevent such crimes.[30] In 1625, Hugo Grotius recorded his horror at the barbarous conduct of war and the crimes committed by men in war.[31] Soon thereafter, in 1649, Charles I of England was famously indicted on 'A Charge of High Treason and Other Charges', tried, and executed for having mounted a civil

[26] See Greenwood, *supra* note 16, para. 109; see also Green, *supra* note 17, p. 359. A just war required four conditions to be met: (1) a war could only be waged by a legitimate public authority; (2) a just cause was required, meaning that the cause had to be just, and damage caused by war had to be justified; (3) the war had to be necessary, meaning that there had to be no other means by which justice could be achieved; and (4) the war had to be conducted in a manner appropriate for the renewed restoration of order and peace.

[27] See generally Gerald Draper, 'The Interaction of Christianity and Chivalry in the Historical Development of the Law of War', (1965) 46 *International Review of the Red Cross* 3. See also Greenwood, *supra* note 16, para. 109; Green, *supra* note 17, pp. 358–359.

[28] See Green, *supra* note 17, p. 360.

[29] See Greenwood, *supra* note 16, para. 109. See also McCormack, *supra* note 20, p. 37; M. Cherif Bassiouni, 'Crimes Against Humanity', in Bassiouni (ed.), *supra* note 17, pp. 196–197. See also generally Theodor Meron, 'Shakespeare's Henry the Fifth and the Law of War', (1992) 86 *American Journal of International Law* 1.

[30] Parks, *supra* note 19, p. 4; see also van Sliedregt, *supra* note 19, p. 120; Georg Schwarzenberger, *International Law: The Law of Armed Conflict* (1968), pp. 329–330 (noting some other ancient examples of punishment of war crimes, including Conradin von Hohenstafen in 1268 and Sir William Wallace in 1305). See also Gideon Boas, James L. Bischoff, and Natalie L. Reid, *Forms of Responsibility in International Criminal Law* (2007), pp. 152–174 (giving an account of the historical development of the doctrine of superior responsibility in international humanitarian law); *ibid.*, p. 145 (discussing the Hagenbach trial in this context).

[31] Hugo Grotius, *De jure belli ac pacis: libri tres* (1625), translated in F. W. Kelsey, *The Classics of International Law* (J. B. Scott, ed. 1925), p. 28. See also G. I. A. D. Draper, 'The Development of International Humanitarian Law', in Henri-Dunant Institute and UNESCO (eds.), *International Dimensions of Humanitarian Law* (1988), pp. 67–68.

war against some of his own people, the conduct of which was characterised by what are now well-recognised violations of the laws or customs of war.[32]

The Age of Enlightenment spelled the beginning of a new era in the development of IHL and the conceptualisation of rules regulating the conduct of war that led, ultimately, to concrete proscriptions for behaviour that became known as war crimes.[33] Of crucial importance to this philosophical revolution was the work of Jean-Jacques Rousseau. In 1772, he wrote:

> War then is a relation, not between man and man, but between State and State, and individuals are enemies only accidentally, not as men, nor even as citizens, but as soldiers; not as members of their country, but as its defenders … The object of the war being the destruction of the hostile State, the other side has a right to kill its defenders while they are bearing arms; but as soon as they lay them down and surrender, they cease to be enemies or instruments of the enemy, and become once more merely men, whose life no one has any right to take.[34]

This idea of war as depersonalised, as an effectuation of a pragmatic political struggle that necessitated the strict adherence to restraint and humanitarian values, contrasted sharply with the later contemporary work of the Prussian General Carl Philipp Gottlieb von Clausewitz, who advocated the idea of total war. In *On War*, in 1832, von Clausewitz wrote:

> Now, philanthropists may easily imagine there is a skilful method of disarming and overcoming an enemy without causing great bloodshed, and that this is the proper tendency of the Art of War. However plausible this may appear, still it is an error which must be extirpated; for in such dangerous things as war, the errors which proceed from a spirit of benevolence are just the worst. As the use of physical power to the utmost extent by no means excludes the co-operation of the intelligence, it follows that he who uses force unsparingly, without reference to the quantity of bloodshed, must obtain a superiority if his adversary does not act likewise. By such means the former dictates the law to the latter, and both proceed to extremities, to which the only limitations are those imposed by the amount of counteracting force on each side.[35]

While it was the enlightened and more compassionate views of Rousseau that would ultimately set the framework for the development of international humanitarian law,[36] the vast majority of armed conflicts that have taken place since von

[32] The title of the indictment is quoted in Robert Partridge, '*O Horrible Murder*': *The Trial, Execution and Burial of Charles I* (1998), p. 48, cited in Geoffrey Robertson, *The Tyrannicide Brief* (2007), p. 147 n. 17. See especially Robertson's account in *ibid.*, ch. 10 (entitled 'The King's Trial').

[33] See Green, *supra* note 17, pp. 84–85; Gilbertson, *supra* note 25, pp. 318–319.

[34] Jean-Jacques Rousseau, *On the Social Contract* (1772) (trans., G. D. H. Cole (1993)), p. 6. See also Greenwood, *supra* note 16, para. 113; Judith Gardam, *Non-Combatant Immunity as a Norm of International Humanitarian Law* (1993), p. 16; Edward K. Kwakwa, *The International Law of Armed Conflict: Personal and Material Fields of Application* (1992), pp. 10–11; Draper, *supra* note 31, p. 69.

[35] Carl Philipp Gottlieb von Clausewitz, *Total War* (1832) (trans. J. J. Graham (1873)), p. 3. This work was published posthumously.

[36] See Kwakwa, *supra* note 34, pp. 11–16.

Clausewitz and the Napoleonic period have been characterised by this experience of total war.[37]

4.1.2 The birth of modern international humanitarian law sanctioning war crimes

The first modern codification of international humanitarian law was the so-called 'Lieber Code',[38] prepared by Professor Francis Lieber of Columbia University for President Abraham Lincoln as a manual for the Union Army's use during the American Civil War. The Code contained 157 articles of 'Rousseauesque' conception prescribing, *inter alia*, that only armed enemies should be attacked; that unarmed civilians and their property, including cultural property, should be respected; and that prisoners of war and the wounded should be humanely treated.[39]

A profusion of international treaties with norms similar to those contained in the Lieber Code followed shortly thereafter. The well-documented plight of Henri Dunant at the 1859 Battle of Solferino led to the creation of the International Committee of the Red Cross (ICRC) and the first Geneva Convention in 1864, on the amelioration of the condition of the wounded in armies in the field.[40] In 1868, the Declaration of St. Petersburg became the first modern treaty to introduce limitations on the use of weapons of war that cause unnecessary suffering,

[37] See Cassese, *supra* note 9, p. 400. But see Gilbertson, *supra* note 25, pp. 319–320 (suggesting a greater humanising effect of these rules on the conduct of war).

[38] See Francis Lieber, *Instructions for the Government of Armies of the United States in the Field*, reprinted in Daniel C. Gilman (ed.), *The Miscellaneous Writings of Francis Lieber* (1881) ('Lieber Code'). The Lieber Code is also known as the 'Lieber Instructions'. For a discussion of this and other international law instruments adopted at the time, see generally Geoffrey Best, *Humanity in Warfare: The Modern History of the International Law of Armed Conflict* (1983).

[39] See generally Burrus M. Carnahan, 'Lincoln, Lieber and the Laws of War: The Origins and Limits of the Principle of Military Necessity', (1998) 92 *American Journal of International Law* 213. See also, e.g., Lieber Code, *supra* note 38, Art. 16:

> Military necessity does not admit of cruelty – that is, the infliction of suffering for the sake of suffering or for revenge, nor of maiming or wounding except in fight, nor of torture to extort confessions. It does not admit of the use of poison in any way, nor of the wanton devastation of a district. It admits of deception, but disclaims acts of perfidy; and, in general, military necessity does not include any act of hostility which makes the return to peace unnecessarily difficult.

See also *ibid.*, Art. 23 ('Private citizens are no longer murdered, enslaved, or carried off to distant parts[.]'); *ibid.*, Art. 35 ('Classical works of art, libraries, scientific collections … as astronomical telescopes, [and] hospitals, must be secured against all avoidable injury[.]'); *ibid.*, Art. 75 ('Prisoners of war are subject to confinement or imprisonment such as may be deemed necessary on account of safety, but they are to be subjected to no other intentional suffering or indignity.'); *ibid.*, Art. 60 ('It is against the usage of modern war to resolve, in hatred and revenge, to give no quarter.').

[40] See Convention for the Amelioration of the Condition of the Wounded in Armies in the Field, 22 August 1864, entered into force 22 June 1865, 18 *Martens Nouveau Recueil* (ser. 1) 607, 129 Consol. T.S. 361 ('1864 Geneva Convention') (providing for the collection and care of enemy wounded on an equal basis, and for the protection of medical officers). See also Henri Dunant, *Un Souvenir de Solférino* (1862).

specifically banning projectiles weighing less than 400 grams that explode on impact.[41] Although it was never ratified, another important international instrument of this era, the 1874 Brussels Declaration, inspired some of the provisions of later conventions.[42]

All of this early treaty activity, much of it aspirational and often general in nature, set the foundation for the development of concrete and binding provisions in the influential Hague Conventions of 1899 and 1907 and, even more importantly, the Geneva Conventions of 1949 and their Additional Protocols of 1977. The vast corpus of proscriptions that make up modern war crimes law derives from two historically distinct bodies of law: 'Hague Law', emerging out of the Hague Conventions of 1899 and 1907, seeks to regulate the means and methods of warfare, with the purpose of reducing unnecessary suffering and destruction; and 'Geneva Law', emerging mainly out of the 1949 Conventions and the 1977 Additional Protocols[43] but with foundations in earlier treaties,[44] seeks to protect and ameliorate the suffering of civilians and others not engaged in active hostilities, such as the wounded, sick, shipwrecked, prisoners of war, and medical personnel.[45]

An international peace conference held at The Hague in 1899 produced a number of conventions and declarations that form part of Hague Law. Hague Declaration III rendered illegal the use of 'dumdum' bullets,[46] while Hague Declaration II banned

[41] See Declaration Renouncing the Use, in Time of War, of Explosive Projectiles Under 400 Grammes Weight, 11 December 1868, entered into force 11 December 1868, reprinted in (1907) 1 *AJIL Supp*. 95 ('St. Petersburg Declaration').

[42] See International Declaration Concerning the Laws and Customs of War, 27 August 1874, reprinted in Dietrich Schindler and Jirí Toman (eds.), *The Laws of Armed Conflicts* (3d edn 1988), pp. 22–34. See also UK Ministry of Defence, *supra* note 16, paras. 1.23–1.24.

[43] See generally *supra* note 3.

[44] See, e.g., Convention Relative to the Treatment of Prisoners of War, 27 July 1929, entered into force 19 June 1931, 47 Stat. 2055, 118 LNTS 303 ('1929 Geneva POW Convention'); Convention for the Amelioration of the Condition of the Wounded in Armies in the Field, 6 July 1906, entered into force 9 August 1907 (no longer in force), 2 *Martens Nouveau Recueil* (ser. 3) 620, 35 Stat. 1885, 1 Bevans 516 ('1906 Geneva Convention').

[45] For a general discussion of the distinction, see, e.g., Robert Cryer, Håkan Friman, Darryl Robinson, and Elizabeth Wilmshurst, *An Introduction to International Criminal Law and Procedure* (2007), p. 222; UK Ministry of Defence, *supra* note 16, para. 1.9; Vincent Chetail, 'The Contribution of the International Court of Justice to International Humanitarian Law', (2003) 85 *International Review of the Red Cross* 235, 238; François Bugnion, 'Law of Geneva and Law of The Hague', (2001) 83 *International Review of the Red Cross* 901. The distinction between Hague Law and Geneva Law has taken on less importance since the adoption of Additional Protocol I, *supra* note 3, as it combined rules on the protection of civilians, prisoners of war, and persons *hors de combat* with rules on the means and methods of warfare. 'International humanitarian law' has been the term generally used thereafter to describe both sets of laws together. But see John B. Bellinger III and William Haynes, 'U.S. Initial Reactions to ICRC Study on Customary International Law', 3 November 2006, available at www.state.gov/s/l/rls/82630.htm ('Although the Study uses the term "international humanitarian law," we [the Legal Adviser of the United States Department of State and General Counsel of the Department of Defence] prefer the "law of war" or the "laws and customs of war."').

[46] See Declaration (IV, 3) Concerning Expanding Bullets, 29 July 1899, entered into force 4 September 1900, 26 *Martens Nouveau Recueil* (ser. 2) 1002, 187 Consol. T.S. 459. This prohibition was later reproduced as a war crime in the Rome Statute of the ICC. See *infra* note 436.

the use of asphyxiating gases[47] – a provision that presaged the conduct of hostilities during the First World War (although, sadly, was largely ignored). Hague Convention II was the first successful effort on the part of states to set forth a relatively comprehensive multilateral treaty governing the conduct of hostilities on land.[48] The follow-up conference at The Hague in 1907 spawned thirteen additional conventions and one declaration. The Regulations annexed to Hague Convention IV, in particular, were an important early recognition that the means a belligerent may adopt to injure the enemy are not unlimited.[49] Hague Convention IV of 1907, with its annexed Regulations, is still regarded as one of the most important international treaties regulating the means and methods of warfare, and several international courts – including the Nuremberg Tribunal[50] and the ICTY Appeals Chamber[51] – have held that its provisions constitute customary international law.

Unlike certain provisions of the 1949 Geneva Conventions and Additional Protocol I of 1977,[52] the 1899 and 1907 conventions and declarations do not expressly provide for individual criminal responsibility for breaches of any of their provisions. Such breaches were intended to give rise to state responsibility only. The notion that individuals may be held criminally liable for contravening the Regulations annexed to Hague Convention IV of 1907 appears to have arisen for the first time during the Nuremberg trial.[53] Several of the Regulations' articles appear under the headings 'war crimes' and 'violations of the laws or customs of war' in the Nuremberg Charter, the relevant portion of which reads as follows:

> The following acts … are crimes coming within the jurisdiction of the Tribunal for which there shall be individual responsibility: … War Crimes: namely, violations of the laws or

47 See Declaration (IV, 2) on the Use of Projectiles the Object of Which is the Diffusion of Asphyxiating or Deleterious Gases, 29 July 1899, entered into force 4 September 1900, 26 *Martens Nouveau Recueil* (ser. 2) 1002, 187 Consol. T.S. 453.

48 See Regulations Respecting the Laws and Customs of War on Land, annexed to Hague Convention (II) Respecting the Laws and Customs of War on Land, 29 July 1899, entered into force 4 September 1900, 187 Consol. T.S. 429, 32 Stat. 1803 ('1899 Hague Regulations'). See also Adam Roberts and Richard Guelff (eds.), *Documents on the Laws of War* (3d edn 2000), p. 68.

49 See, e.g., 1907 Hague Regulations, *supra* note 6, Art. 23(a) (no poisoned weapons); *ibid.*, Art. 23(d) (no declaring that no quarter be given); *ibid.*, Art. 23(e) (no employing weapons calculated to cause unnecessary suffering); *ibid.*, Art. 25 (no attacking undefended towns or villages); *ibid.*, Art. 28 (no pillage).

50 See *France, Union of Soviet Socialist Republics, United Kingdom, and United States* v. *Göring, Bormann, Dönitz, Frank, Frick, Fritzsche, Funk, Hess, Jodl, Kaltenbrunner, Keitel, von Bohlen und Halbach, Ley, von Neurath, von Papen, Raeder, von Ribbentrop, Rosenberg, Sauckel, Schacht, von Schirach, Seyss-Inquart, Speer, and Streicher*, International Military Tribunal, Judgment and Sentence, 1 October 1946, in *Trial of the Major War Criminals Before the International Military Tribunal, Nuremberg* ('Nuremberg Judgement'), vol. I, pp. 84–92.

51 See *Tadić* Jurisdiction Appeal Decision, *supra* note 4, paras. 87, 89, 94. Accord *Prosecutor* v. *Strugar*, Case No. IT-01-42-T, Judgement, 31 January 2005 ('*Strugar* Trial Judgement'), para. 227 ('Both [t]he Hague Convention (IV) of 1907 and [t]he Hague Regulations [annexed thereto] are rules of international humanitarian law and they have become part of customary international law.'). See also *infra* note 62 and accompanying text.

52 See *infra* note 58 and accompanying text.

53 See Yves Sandoz, 'Penal Aspects of International Humanitarian Law', in Bassiouni (ed.), *supra* note 16, pp. 395–399; Steven R. Ratner and Jason S. Abrams, *Accountability for Human Rights Atrocities in International Law: Beyond the Nuremberg Legacy* (2nd edn 2001), p. 81.

customs of war. Such violations shall include, but not be limited to, murder, ill-treatment or deportation to slave labor or for any other purpose of civilian population of or in occupied territory, murder or ill-treatment of prisoners of war or persons on the seas, killing of hostages, plunder of public or private property, wanton destruction of cities, towns or villages, or devastation not justified by military necessity ...[54]

The International Military Tribunal (IMT) at Nuremberg acknowledged that this provision incorporates several of the proscriptions in the Regulations annexed to Hague Convention IV, along with certain rules from the 1929 Geneva Convention on Prisoners of War.[55] The IMT confirmed that individuals may be held criminally responsible for engaging in these acts despite the absence of express language in the Hague Regulations making such conduct criminal,[56] a point now well-entrenched in the jurisprudence of the ICTY.[57] The IMT tried twenty-four of the most senior captured leaders of Nazi Germany and ultimately found nineteen of them responsible for war crimes.

Yet it was the Geneva Conventions of 1949 that gave much greater depth and clarity to international humanitarian law, and that incorporated a set of provisions that was intended from its very inception to prescribe individual criminal responsibility: the grave breaches.[58] These provisions reflect a broad range of 'serious' violations of international humanitarian law; as early as 1949, states were prepared to oblige themselves to prosecute alleged perpetrators of these breaches, or to surrender them to another state that would conduct such prosecutions. The so-called '*aut dedere aut judicare*' obligation with respect to the grave breaches is one of the earliest clear examples of the operation of the powerful principle of universal

[54] Agreement for the Prosecution and Punishment of Major War Criminals of the European Axis, and Establishing the Charter of the International Military Tribunal, Annex, 8 August 1945, 82 UNTS 279, Art. 6(b).

[55] See Nuremberg Judgement, *supra* note 50, vol. I, pp. 68, 83, 84–92, 138–140. See also 1907 Hague Regulations, *supra* note 6, Arts. 4, 25, 28, 46, 47, 56; 1929 Geneva POW Convention, *supra* note 44, Art. 2.

[56] See Nuremberg Judgement, *supra* note 50, vol. I, p. 50. Interestingly, although no international treaty providing for individual criminal responsibility arose until the flawed 1919 Treaty of Versailles, see Treaty of Peace Between the Allied and Associated Powers and Germany, 28 June 1919, 226 Consol. T.S. 188, Arts. 227–230, many of the early treaties provide some basis for the evolution of such responsibility later. See Sandoz, *supra* note 53, pp. 393–401 (referring to the 1864 Geneva Convention, *supra* note 40, the St. Petersburg Declaration, *supra* note 41, the 1906 Geneva Convention, *supra* note 44, and the Oxford Manuals of 1880 and 1913).

[57] See, e.g., *Strugar* Trial Judgement, *supra* note 51, para. 227 ('Article 3(b) [of the ICTY Statute] is based on Article 23 of the Hague Convention (IV) of 1907 and the annexed Regulations'); *Prosecutor* v. *Hadžihasanović and Kubura*, Case No. IT-01-47-AR73.3, Decision on Joint Defence Interlocutory Appeal of Trial Chamber Decision on Rule 98*bis* Motions for Acquittal, 11 March 2005, paras. 30 (Article 3(b)); *ibid.*, para. 37 (Article 3 (e)); *ibid.*, para. 45 (Article 3(d)); *Prosecutor* v. *Orić*, Case No. IT-03-68-T, Judgement, 30 June 2006 ('*Orić* Trial Judgement'), paras. 579–589 (Article 3(b)); *Prosecutor* v. *Hadžihasanović and Kubura*, Case No. IT-01-47-T, Judgement, 15 March 2006 ('*Hadžihasanović and Kubura* Trial Judgement'), paras. 39–64 (Articles 3(b), 3(d), and 3(e)); *Prosecutor* v. *Naletilić and Martinović*, Case No. IT-98-34-T, Judgement, 31 March 2003 ('*Naletilić and Martinović* Trial Judgement'), para. 602 (Article 3(d)); *Prosecutor* v. *Kordić and Čerkez*, Case No. IT-95-14/2-T, Judgement, 26 February 2001 ('*Kordić and Čerkez* Trial Judgement'), para. 346 (Article 3(b)); *Prosecutor* v. *Blaškić*, Case No. IT-95-14-T, Judgement, 3 March 2000 ('*Blaškić* Trial Judgement'), para. 185 (Article 3(d)).

[58] See Geneva Convention I, *supra* note 3, Art. 50; Geneva Convention II, *supra* note 3, Art. 51; Geneva Convention III, *supra* note 3, Art. 130; Geneva Convention IV, *supra* note 3, Art. 147. See also *infra*, section 4.2.1.3.

jurisdiction outside of the international crime of piracy.[59] Additional Protocol I of 1977 expanded this list of grave breaches.[60]

As with Hague Convention IV and its annexed Regulations,[61] it is now well accepted that much of the content of the 1949 Geneva Conventions and their Additional Protocols constitutes customary international law, thus binding on all parties to a conflict regardless of whether they have joined the relevant convention.[62] This notion extends significantly to the operation of Common Article 3 to the Geneva Conventions, as well as certain provisions of Additional Protocol II.[63] Nevertheless, in spite of the remarkable development of IHL and war crimes law in these treaties, one of their greatest failings is the persistent legal distinction between international and non-international armed conflicts, a matter to which we now briefly turn.

4.1.3 The distinction between international and non-international armed conflict in war crimes law

In 1995, the *Tadić* Appeals Chamber wrote:

> Gradually the maxim of Roman law *hominum causa omne jus constitutum est* (all law is created for the benefit of human beings) has gained a firm foothold in the international community ... It follows that in the area of armed conflict the distinction between interstate wars and civil wars is losing its value as far as human beings are concerned. Why protect civilians from belligerent violence, or ban rape, torture or the wanton destruction of hospitals, churches, museums or private property, as well as proscribe weapons causing unnecessary suffering when two sovereign States are engaged in war, and yet refrain from enacting the same bans or providing the same protection when armed violence has erupted 'only' within the territory of a sovereign State? If international law, while of course duly safeguarding the legitimate interests of States, must gradually turn to the protection of

[59] For an interesting account of the contemporary legal views surrounding the application of the universal jurisdiction doctrine to the 1949 Geneva Conventions, see Frits Kalshoven, 'From International Humanitarian Law to International Criminal Law', (2004) 3 *Chinese Journal of International Law* 151, 151–152.

[60] See Additional Protocol I, *supra* note 3, Art. 85.

[61] See *supra* text accompanying notes 50–51.

[62] See Final Report of the Commission of Experts Established Pursuant to Security Council Resolution 780, UN Doc. S/1994/674, Annex, 27 May 1994, paras. 42, 52–54; Report of the Secretary-General Pursuant to paragraph 2 of Security Council Resolution 808, UN Doc. S/25704, 3 May 1993, paras. 41–44; Military and Paramilitary Activities in and Against Nicaragua (*Nicaragua* v. *United States*), 1986 ICJ Rep. 14, para. 218 (stating that Common Article 3 of the Geneva Conventions was declaratory of customary international law and acted as a 'minimum yardstick' for international and non-international armed conflicts); Theodor Meron, *Human Rights and Humanitarian Norms as Customary Law* (1999), pp. 41–62; Theodor Meron, 'The Geneva Conventions as Customary international Law', (1987) 81 *American Journal of International Law* 348. See also generally Jean-Marie Henckaerts and Louise Doswald-Beck (eds.), *Customary International Humanitarian Law* (2005), vol. I.

[63] As discussed in greater detail elsewhere in this chapter, one of the most important contributions the *ad hoc* Tribunals have made to war crimes law is the development and application of war crimes punishable when committed in non-international armed conflict, through Article 3 of the ICTY Statute and Article 4 of the ICTR Statute. See *supra* text accompanying notes 4–13; *infra* sections 4.1.4, 4.2.1.4, 4.2.1.5.

human beings, it is only natural that the aforementioned dichotomy should gradually lose its weight.[64]

This optimistic statement reveals a teleological approach to international humanitarian law that is consistent with its fundamental purpose: the extension of the greatest protection possible to those not taking active part in the hostilities.[65] It has inspired the view that the 'two-legged edifice of the laws of armed conflict' has gradually begun to give way to a holistic set of protections for (in particular) civilians in armed conflict, that is, towards a single law of armed conflict.[66]

Nevertheless, despite some whittling down of this dichotomy by the *ad hoc* Tribunals in respect of particular offences,[67] the distinction between the war crimes regime applicable in the different conflicts remains striking. As James G. Stewart has noted, the 1949 Geneva Conventions and their Additional Protocols contain 'close to 600 articles, of which only Article 3 common … and the 28 articles of Additional Protocol II apply to internal conflicts'.[68] Comparing the sparse provisions of Common Article 3 and Additional Protocol II against the full body of provisions in the Geneva Conventions and Additional Protocol I – along with the many other IHL treaties meant to apply only in international armed conflict, such as Hague Convention IV of 1907 – it is clear that there are significant shortfalls in the regulation of combat and protection of civilians; a lack of explicit reference to the principle of proportionality,[69] the prohibitions on indiscriminate attack,[70] or the

[64] *Tadić* Jurisdiction Appeal Decision, *supra* note 4, para. 97. See also *ibid.*, para. 83 (suggesting that customary international law may be evolving toward the application of grave breaches provisions regardless of the character of the armed conflict).

[65] See Zahar and Sluiter, *supra* note 9, pp. 110–113; Henckaerts and Doswald-Beck, *supra* note 62, p. xxix.

[66] See Sonja Boelaert-Suominen, 'Grave Breaches, Universal Jurisdiction and Internal Armed Conflict: Is Customary Law Moving Towards a Uniform Enforcement Mechanism for All Armed Conflicts?', (2000) 5 *Journal of Conflict and Security Law* 63, 102. See also James G. Stewart, 'Towards a Single Definition of Armed Conflict in International Humanitarian Law: A Critique of Internationalized Armed Conflict', (2003) 85 *International Review of the Red Cross* 313, 322.

[67] For example, trial chambers have held that the elements of 'wilful killing' as a grave breach and 'murder' as a violation of Common Article 3, punishable through Article 3 of the ICTY Statute and Article 4 of the ICTR Statute, are the same. See, e.g., *Prosecutor* v. *Delalić, Mucić, Delić and Landžo*, Case No. IT-96–21, Judgement, 16 November 1998 ('*Čelebići* Trial Judgement'), paras. 421–423; *Prosecutor* v. *Akayesu*, Case No. ICTR-96-4-T, Judgement and Sentence, 2 September 1998 ('*Akayesu* Trial Judgement'), paras. 589–590. The same is true for the war crime of torture. See, e.g., *Čelebići* Trial Judgement, *supra* note 67, paras. 452–459; *Prosecutor* v. *Furundžija*, Case No. IT-95–17/1-T, Judgement, 10 December 1998 ('*Furundžija* Trial Judgement'), paras. 143–162.

[68] Stewart, *supra* note 66, p. 320. See also Asbjørn Eide, 'The New Humanitarian Law in Non-International Armed Conflict', in Antonio Cassese (ed.), *The New Humanitarian Law of Armed Conflict* (1979), p. 290 (lamenting that the final text of Additional Protocol II was 'a depressingly meager result of long and hard negotiations'). Leslie Green has also criticised the relative laxity of the rules governing non-international armed conflict, and points to a disturbing contradiction: 'Perhaps it is more necessary in non-international armed conflict to provide for the protection of [persons taking no active part in the hostilities] than in international conflict because ideologies and emotions are not normally so important.' Leslie C. Green, *The Contemporary Law of Armed Conflict* (2nd edn 2000), p. 327.

[69] In international armed conflict, this principle is reflected in Additional Protocol I, *supra* note 3, Arts. 51(5)(b), 57 (2)(iii) and 85(3).

[70] In international armed conflict, this norm is reflected in *ibid.*, Art. 51.

means and methods of warfare;[71] and absolutely no recognition of prisoner of war status for fighters[72] in non-international armed conflicts.[73] Therefore, despite acknowledgement by the *Tadić* Appeals Chamber that customary rules have developed to govern internal strife,[74] the emergence of these rules:

> does not imply that internal strife is regulated by general international law in all its aspects. Two particular limitations may be noted: (i) only a number of rules and principles governing international armed conflicts have gradually been extended to apply to internal conflicts; and (ii) this extension has not taken place in the form of a full and mechanical transplant of those rules to internal conflicts; rather, the general essence of those rules, and not the detailed regulation they may contain, has become applicable to internal conflicts.[75]

These facts emphasise the dichotomy between crimes committed in the context of an international armed conflict ('international armed conflict war crimes') and those committed in a non-international armed conflict ('non-international armed conflict war crimes' or 'internal armed conflict war crimes') as probably the single greatest thorn in the side of the *Tadić* Chamber's teleological view of international humanitarian law.[76] As will be discussed below, the structure of the Rome Statute of the ICC reveals that, while a significant number of states believe that war crimes

[71] In international armed conflict, these norms are reflected, for example, in Additional Protocol I, *supra* note 3, Art. 35(2) ('It is prohibited to employ weapons, projectiles and material and methods of warfare of a nature to cause superfluous injury or unnecessary suffering.'), and 1907 Hague Regulations, *supra* note 6, Art. 23.

[72] See, e.g., *Mrkšić* Trial Judgement, para. 457 (explaining that 'fighters' is a more appropriate term than 'combatants' for those participating in non-international armed conflicts).

[73] See generally Henckaerts and Doswald-Beck (eds.), *supra* note 62, pp. 384–395. Governments may therefore try and execute captured insurgent fighters for treason or other violations of national law even before the close of hostilities. See Laura Lopez, 'Uncivil Wars: The Challenge of Applying International Humanitarian Law to Internal Armed Conflicts', (1994) 69 *New York University Law Review* 916, 934; Waldemar A. Solf, 'Comment', (1982) 31 *American University Law Review* 927, 928 (discussing states' unwillingness to immunise insurgent fighters suspected of committing national crimes); Lieber Code, *supra* note 38, Art. 154 ('Treating ... the rebellious enemy according to the law and usages of war [ ] has never prevented the legitimate government from trying the ... chief rebels for high treason ... unless they are included in a general amnesty.'). See also *infra* note 438 (discussing states' concerns at the drafting meetings of the Rome Statute of the ICC concerning war crimes in non-international armed conflict, and the appropriate threshold for their applicability).

[74] *Tadić* Jurisdiction Appeal Decision, *supra* note 4, para. 127:

> These rules, as specifically identified in the preceding discussion, cover such areas as protection of civilians from hostilities, in particular from indiscriminate attacks, protection of civilian objects, in particular cultural property, protection of all those who do not (or no longer) take active part in hostilities, as well as prohibition of means of warfare proscribed in international armed conflicts and ban of certain methods of conducting hostilities.

[75] *Ibid.*, para. 126.

[76] There is extensive literature discussing this issue. See, e.g., Emily Crawford, 'Unequal Before the Law: The Case for the Elimination of the Distinction Between International and Non-International Armed Conflicts', (2007) 20 *Leiden Journal of International Law* 441; Diedre Willmott, 'Removing the Distinction Between International and Non-International Armed Conflict in the Rome Statute of the International Criminal Court', (2004) 5 *Melbourne Journal of International Law* 196; Stewart, *supra* note 66; Ingrid Detter, *The Law of War* (3rd edn 2000), p. 49; Boelaert-Suominen, *supra* note 66; Theodor Meron, W. Michael Reisman, Luigi Condorelli, George H. Aldrich, Rene Kosirnik, J. Ashley Roach, and Peter Lipperman, 'Application of Humanitarian Law in Non-International Armed Conflicts: A Panel', (1991) 85 *American Society of International Law Proceedings* 83; Veuthey, *supra* note 16; Waldemar A. Solf, 'The Status of Combatants in Non-International Armed Conflicts Under Domestic Law and Practice', (1983) 33 *American University Law Review* 53. See also *Tadić* Jurisdiction Appeal Decision, *supra* note 4, paras. 65–137.

provisions applicable to international armed conflicts should be equally applicable to non-international armed conflicts, the Statute also clearly reinforces this distinction.[77]

More than fifty years ago, Hersch Lauterpacht wrote: 'If international law is, in some ways, at the vanishing point of law, the law of war is, perhaps even more conspicuously, at the vanishing point of international law.'[78] Much has been achieved in the development of the war crimes which are prosecuted in the international and internationalised criminal courts and tribunals. One profound development that will serve to bring the law of war, and international criminal law, out of the shadows of international law will be the evolution beyond the short-sighted preoccupations of states with seeking to assure the protection of their governments and military forces for wrongdoing, and the creation of a single and robust legal regime applicable in armed conflicts of all kinds.

4.1.4 Contribution of the ad hoc *Tribunals to the development of war crimes law*

The contribution of the *ad hoc* Tribunals to the development of war crimes law, in particular that of the ICTY, is difficult to overestimate. Some of the important developments in these Tribunals have been discussed above. For example, the work of these Tribunals has contributed considerably to the clear incorporation of violations of the laws and customs of war not constituting 'grave breaches' into war crimes law,[79] giving international criminal law greater reach in the prosecution of violations of IHL.

Probably the most significant contribution to war crimes law, however, was the *Tadić* Appeals Chamber's holding that individual criminal responsibility may attach for certain IHL violations committed in non-international armed conflict.[80] This was a bold move for what was then a young Tribunal, as it is unlikely that the drafters of the ICTY Statute, or the Security Council that promulgated the Statute, contemplated that such violations would be tried in the ICTY, for at least three reasons. First and most significantly, the notion of *criminal* responsibility for violations of the rules governing non-international armed conflict was not well developed prior to the October 1995 *Tadić* Jurisdiction Decision, as noted by

[77] See *infra* text accompanying notes 434–438 (discussing the dichotomy in the Rome Statute of the ICC). See also Boelaert-Suominen, *supra* note 66, p. 102; see also generally Heike Spieker, 'The International Criminal Court and Non-International Armed Conflicts', (2000) 13 *Leiden Journal of International Law* 417.

[78] Hersch Lauterpacht, 'The Problem of the Revision of the Law of War', (1952) 29 *British Yearbook of International Law* 360, 382.

[79] See *supra* text accompanying notes 4–9; *infra* text accompanying notes 94–95, sections 4.2.1.4, 4.2.1.5.

[80] See *supra* note 4 and accompanying text. The *Tadić* Jurisdiction Decision and the treatment of these issues by the *ad hoc* Tribunals is discussed in detail in the following section of this chapter. The impact on other international and internationalised criminal courts and tribunals will be discussed in detail in section 4.3.

commentators and experts studying the atrocities in Cambodia and Iraq in the 1970s and 1980s.[81] Second, the norms enumerated in the ICTY Statute were taken from the grave breaches of the Geneva Conventions,[82] the Regulations annexed to Hague Convention IV of 1907,[83] and the Nuremberg Charter,[84] and not from instruments dealing with non-international armed conflict such as, most notably, Common Article 3 and Additional Protocol II. Third, many of these non-international armed conflict norms from Common Article 3 and Additional Protocol II were explicitly inserted into the ICTR Statute less than a year later but before the issuance of the *Tadić* Jurisdiction Decision,[85] suggesting that, had the drafters of the ICTY Statute contemplated the adjudication of these crimes by the ICTY, they would have put them in the ICTY Statute as well. The *Tadić* Jurisdiction Decision's extension of war crimes law to non-international armed conflict can therefore be seen as truly revolutionary, and *Tadić* has greatly influenced the definition and application of war crimes law in subsequent international and internationalised criminal courts and tribunals, most notably the ICC.[86] Yet notwithstanding this laudable contribution, as discussed above,[87] it is perhaps regrettable that the *Tadić* Appeals Chamber, despite a clear opportunity to further expand the law, chose to maintain the general international/non-international dichotomy by reserving the grave breaches in Article 2 of the Statute for international armed conflict. Although the occasional dissenting judge has sought to render irrelevant the distinction in the application of the grave breaches regime to the particular type of conflict, the distinction remains.[88]

In a situation that is the converse of that discussed in Chapter 3 with respect to genocide,[89] of the two *ad hoc* Tribunals it is the ICTY that has contributed the bulk of jurisprudence on war crimes, developing and applying the law to a considerable degree and entering many convictions, including for a number of war crimes not explicitly listed in the ICTY Statute.[90] By contrast, war crimes convictions in the ICTR are rare, for two reasons: first, war crimes are simply charged less frequently than in ICTY indictments;[91] second, in the early cases, trial chambers concluded that the prosecution had not established the required nexus between the acts with which

[81] See *infra* text accompanying notes 573, 600. [82] See *supra* text accompanying notes 2–3.

[83] See *supra* note 51 and accompanying text. [84] See *supra* notes 50, 54 and accompanying text.

[85] See *supra* text accompanying notes 11–13.

[86] See *infra* text accompanying notes 434–438 (discussing the dichotomy in the Rome Statute of the ICC).

[87] See *supra* text accompanying notes 75–76.

[88] See, e.g., *Tadić* Jurisdiction Appeal Decision, *supra* note 4, Separate Opinion of Judge Abi-Saab on the Defence Motion for Interlocutory Appeal on Jurisdiction; *Prosecutor* v. *Aleksovski*, Case No. IT-95-14/1-T, Judgement, 25 June 1999 ('*Aleksovski* Trial Judgement'), Dissenting Opinion of Judge Rodrigues, Presiding Judge of the Trial Chamber.

[89] See Chapter 3, text accompanying notes 99–102.

[90] Examples include (1) 'acts or threats of violence the primary purpose of which is to spread terror', see *Prosecutor* v. *Galić*, Case No. IT-98-29-A, Judgement, 30 November 2006 ('*Galić* Appeal Judgement'), paras. 81–109; (2) attacks on cultural property, see *Strugar* Trial Judgement, *supra* note 51, paras. 227–233, 446, 478; and (3) forced labour, see *Naletilić and Martinović* Trial Judgement, *supra* note 57, paras. 250–261, 333–334).

[91] See *infra* note 95 (listing the thirteen ICTR cases in which war crimes have been charged).

the accused were charged, on the one hand, and the armed conflict between the Rwandan Armed Forces and the rebel Rwandan Patriotic Front, on the other. Indeed, the first conviction for war crimes was entered by the Appeals Chamber, and only in 2003, some eight years into the life of the Tribunal.[92] The following section of this chapter discusses in detail the elements of war crimes as developed in the *ad hoc* Tribunals.

4.2 Elements of war crimes

Three Articles in the Statutes of the ICTY and ICTR grant these Tribunals jurisdiction over violations of international humanitarian law for which individual criminal responsibility may be imposed: Article 2 of the ICTY Statute covers grave breaches of the Geneva Conventions;[93] Article 3 of that Statute covers other war crimes by granting jurisdiction over 'violations of the laws or customs of war';[94] and Article 4 of the ICTR Statute restricts the applicable substantive rules to violations of Common Article 3 of the Geneva Conventions and Additional Protocol II.[95] The crimes covered by these provisions share two general requirements, and each subcategory of war crimes also has its own additional general requirements.

4.2.1 General requirements for war crimes

In order for a particular underlying offence to qualify as a war crime, it must take place in the context of an armed conflict. That is, the existence of an armed conflict and the connection between that conflict and the underlying offence are elements of the crime itself; otherwise, although the offence may be another international crime or a domestic crime, it cannot be said to violate the rules of international humanitarian

92 See *Prosecutor* v. *Rutaganda*, Case No. ICTR 96-3-A, Judgment, 26 May 2003 ('*Rutaganda* Appeal Judgement'), para. 584, p. 168. See also Jamie A. Williamson, 'The Jurisprudence of the International Criminal Tribunal for Rwanda on War Crimes', (2005) 12 *New England Journal of International and Comparative Law* 51, 64–66.

93 See *supra* text accompanying note 2 for the full text of Article 2 of the ICTY Statute.

94 See *supra* text accompanying note 5 for the full text of Article 3 of the ICTY Statute.

95 See *supra* text accompanying note 13 for the full text of Article 4 of the ICTR Statute. War crimes have been charged in thirteen cases before the ICTR: *Akayesu*, *Kayishema and Ruzindana*, *Rutaganda*, *Musema*, *Bagilishema*, *Ntakirutimana and Ntakirutimana*, *Semanza*, *Niyitegeka*, *Kajelijeli*, *Kamuhanda*, *Ntagerura et al.* (*Cyangugu*), *Bagosora et al.* (*Military I*), and *Bizimungu et al.* (*Military II*). In *Niyitegeka*, however, the prosecution withdrew the war crimes charges in its closing brief. See *Prosecutor* v. *Niyitegeka*, Case No. ICTR-96-14-T, Judgement, 16 May 2003, paras. 468–469. Similarly, at the midpoint of the *Kajelijeli* case, the prosecution conceded that it had presented insufficient evidence in support of its war crimes allegations, and the Trial Chamber entered a partial acquittal on those counts. See *Prosecutor* v. *Kajelijeli*, Case No. ICTR-98-44A-T, Decision on Kajelijeli's Motion for Partial Acquittal Pursuant to Rule 98 *bis*, 13 September 2002, paras. 8, 10–11.

law, which apply only in times of armed conflict.[96] Thus these two elements are general requirements for all the war crimes within the Tribunals' jurisdiction.

4.2.1.1 Existence of an armed conflict

A resort to armed force between states, or protracted armed violence between organised armed groups within a state.

As it is the key characteristic of a war crime, the prosecution must establish beyond a reasonable doubt that an armed conflict existed at the time the alleged underlying offence was committed. In one of the earliest and most important interlocutory decisions in the ICTY, the *Tadić* Appeals Chamber set forth the definition that is still applied by chambers of both Tribunals, holding that 'an armed conflict exists whenever there is a resort to armed force between States or protracted armed violence between governmental authorities and organized armed groups or between such groups within a State'.[97] Rejecting an argument that advanced a 'concept of armed conflict covering only the precise time and place of actual hostilities',[98] the Appeals Chamber further declared:

> International humanitarian law applies from the initiation of such armed conflicts and extends beyond the cessation of hostilities until a general conclusion of peace is reached; or, in the case of internal conflicts, a peaceful settlement is achieved. Until that moment, international humanitarian law continues to apply in the whole territory of the warring States or, in the case of internal conflicts, the whole territory under the control of a party, whether or not actual combat takes place there.[99]

[96] Until relatively recently, however, chambers of the *ad hoc* Tribunals often referred to these general requirements as 'jurisdictional prerequisites' or 'preconditions to the applicability' of the relevant article of the Statute. See, e.g., *Prosecutor* v. *Blaškić*, Case No. IT-95-14-A, Judgement, 29 July 2004 ('*Blaškić* Appeal Judgement'), para. 170; *Prosecutor* v. *Simić, Tadić, and Zarić*, Case No. IT-95-9-T, Judgement, 17 October 2003 ('*Simić et al.* Trial Judgement'), para. 105. This terminology is potentially misleading, because it suggests that these requirements are not elements of the crime, but akin to the jurisdictional requirements for crimes against humanity that appear in the Tribunals' Statutes, but are not part of customary international law. See Chapter 2, sections 2.2.1.1, 2.2.1.2. As the ICTY Appeals Chamber recently confirmed with regard to Article 2 of its Statute, however, '[i]f certain conduct becomes a crime under the Statute only if it occurs in the context of an international armed conflict, the existence of such a conflict is not merely a jurisdictional prerequisite: it is a substantive element of the crime charged.' *Prosecutor* v. *Naletilić and Martinović*, Case No. IT-98-34-A, Judgement, 3 May 2006 ('*Naletilić and Martinović* Appeal Judgement'), para. 116; accord *Galić* Appeal Judgement, *supra* note 90, para. 84. See also *infra*, text accompanying notes 116–120, 172–173 (discussing the *Naletilić and Martinović* Appeals Chamber's holdings with regard to the requirements associated with crimes committed in an international armed conflict).

[97] *Tadić* Jurisdiction Appeal Decision, *supra* note 4, para. 70; accord, e.g., *Prosecutor* v. *Kunarac, Kovač, and Vuković*, Case Nos. IT-96-23-A & IT-96-23/1-A, 12 June 2002 ('*Kunarac et al.* Appeal Judgement'), para. 56; *Hadžihasanović and Kubura* Trial Judgement, *supra* note 57, para. 14; *Prosecutor* v. *Blagojević and Jokić*, Case No. IT-02-60-T, Judgement, 17 January 2005 ('*Blagojević and Jokić* Trial Judgement'), para. 536; *Prosecutor* v. *Stakić*, Case No. IT-97-24-T, Judgement, 29 October 2003 ('*Stakić* Trial Judgement'), para. 568; *Prosecutor* v. *Semanza*, Case No. ICTR-97-20-T, Judgement and Sentence, 15 May 2003 ('*Semanza* Trial Judgement'), paras. 355–356; *Prosecutor* v. *Krstić*, Case No. IT-98-33-T, Judgement, 2 August 2001 ('*Krstić* Trial Judgement'), para. 481; *Prosecutor* v. *Musema*, Case No. ICTR-96-13-T, Judgement and Sentence, 27 January 2000 ('*Musema* Trial Judgement'), paras. 247–248; *Čelebići* Trial Judgement, *supra* note 67, para. 183; *Akayesu* Trial Judgement, *supra* note 67, para. 619.

[98] *Tadić* Jurisdiction Appeal Decision, *supra* note 4, para. 66.

[99] *Ibid.*, para. 70.

A 'resort to armed force between [s]tates' is an international armed conflict; and protracted armed violence between organised armed groups within a state, which may include the formal armed forces of that state, describes a non-international, or internal, armed conflict.[100] The ICTY Appeals Chamber explained in a later judgement that the purpose of the 'protracted armed violence' requirement for internal armed conflicts is to exclude 'mere cases of civil unrest or single acts of terrorism'.[101] A similar reason may be divined from the *Tadić* Appeals Chamber's reference to 'organized armed groups' – a description likely drawn from the terms of Additional Protocol II – which would rule out mobs or spontaneous unorganised violence.[102] Chambers at both Tribunals have emphasised that since an armed conflict 'suggests the existence of hostilities between armed forces organized to a greater or lesser extent', it is 'necessary to evaluate both the intensity of the conflict and organization of the parties' in order to determine whether the situation qualifies as an internal armed conflict.[103]

The *Mrkšić* Trial Chamber recently summarised the factors that are to be assessed, in light of the facts in each case,[104] to determine whether the intensity of the conflict and the organisation of the parties lead to the conclusion that an armed conflict existed:

Relevant for establishing the intensity of a conflict are, *inter alia*, the seriousness of attacks and potential increase in armed clashes, their spread over territory and over a period of time, the increase in the number of government forces, the mobilisation and the distribution of weapons among both parties to the conflict, as well as whether the conflict has attracted the attention of the United Nations Security Council, and if so whether any resolutions on the matter have been passed. While some degree of organisation by the parties will suffice to establish the existence of an armed conflict, this degree need not be the same as that required

[100] Most scholars, commentators, and international tribunals treat 'non-international' and 'internal' as interchangeable terms to describe the category of armed conflicts that do not qualify as international.

[101] *Prosecutor* v. *Kordić and Čerkez*, Case No. IT-95-14/2-A, Judgement, 17 December 2004 ('*Kordić and Čerkez* Appeal Judgement'), para. 341.

[102] See Additional Protocol II, *supra* note 3, Art. 1 (defining the Protocol's scope of application as 'all armed conflicts which are not covered by Article 1 of [Additional Protocol I] and which take place in the territory of a High Contracting Party between its armed forces and dissident armed forces or other organized armed groups', and providing that the Protocol 'shall not apply to situations of internal disturbances and tensions, such as riots, isolated and sporadic acts of violence and other acts of a similar nature, as not being armed conflicts').

[103] *Akayesu* Trial Judgement, *supra* note 67, para. 620 (relying on, but not citing, *Prosecutor* v. *Tadić*, Case IT-94-1-T, Judgement, 7 May 1997 ('*Tadić* Trial Judgement'), para. 562); accord *Prosecutor* v. *Rutaganda*, Case No. ICTR-96-3-T, Judgement and Sentence, 6 December 1999 ('*Rutaganda* Trial Judgement'), para. 92 (ruling out, *inter alia*, 'mere acts of banditry … and unorganized and short-lived insurrections'); *Prosecutor* v. *Kayishema and Ruzindana*, Case No. ICTR-95-1-T, Judgement and Sentence, 21 May 1999 ('*Kayishema and Ruzindana* Trial Judgement'), para. 171 (qualifying the excluded situations as 'internal conflicts … fall[ing] below a certain threshold'); *Prosecutor* v. *Mrkšić, Radić, and Šljivančanin*, Case No. IT-95-13/1-T, Judgement, 27 September 2007 ('*Mrkšić et al.* Trial Judgement'), para. 407; *Prosecutor* v. *Limaj, Bala, and Musliu*, Case No. IT-03-66-T, Judgement, 30 November 2005 ('*Limaj et al.* Trial Judgement'), para. 84; *Musema* Trial Judgement, *supra* note 97, para. 248.

[104] See, e.g., *Rutaganda* Trial Judgement, *supra* note 103, para. 93 (noting that the determination of whether an armed conflict existed is a case-by-case factual assessment of the evidence adduced at trial); accord *Limaj et al.* Trial Judgement, *supra* note 103, para. 90; *Mrkšić et al.* Trial Judgement, *supra* note 103, para. 407.

for establishing the responsibility of superiors for the acts of their subordinates within the organisation, as no determination of individual criminal responsibility is intended under this provision of the Statute.[105]

Although most of the ICTY jurisprudence on these issues has come in the context of Article 3 of that Tribunal's Statute, where the international or internal character of the armed conflict is irrelevant,[106] these factors are most useful when trying to determine whether a particular struggle within a state qualifies as an armed conflict. Applying these guidelines, the *Limaj* Trial Chamber concluded that, in 1998, an armed conflict existed in Kosovo between the forces of the Republic of Serbia and the Kosovo Liberation Army (KLA). Not only were KLA units 'constantly engaged in armed clashes with substantial Serbian forces' across the province,[107] but by the end of May 1998:

the KLA had a General Staff, which appointed zone commanders, gave directions to the various units formed or in the process of being formed, and issued public statements on behalf of the organisation. Unit commanders gave combat orders and subordinate units and soldiers generally acted in accordance with these orders. Steps ha[d] been established to introduce disciplinary rules and military police, as well as to recruit, train and equip new members. Although generally inferior to the VJ and MUP's equipment, the KLA soldiers had weapons, which included artillery mortars and rocket launchers.[108]

The ICTR Appeals Chamber has confirmed that trial chambers at that Tribunal may take judicial notice of the existence of a non-international armed conflict in Rwanda in 1994.[109] In addition, as one of the chambers trying former officers in the Forces Armées Rwandaises noted in its decision on the accused's motions for acquittal, it is now 'beyond dispute that large-scale violations of international humanitarian law, potentially amounting to war crimes, were committed during the conflict, resulting in the death of large numbers of civilians'.[110] ICTY chambers

[105] *Mrkšic et al.* Trial Judgement, *supra* note 103, para. 407 (citing *Limaj et al.* Trial Judgement, *supra* note 103, para. 90; *Čelebići* Trial Judgement, *supra* note 67, paras. 188–190; *Tadić* Trial Judgement, *supra* note 103, paras. 565–567; *Prosecutor* v. *Slobodan Milošević*, Case No. IT-02-54-T, Decision on Motion for Judgement of Acquittal, 16 June 2004, paras. 28–31).

[106] See *infra* note 231 and accompanying text (discussing this aspect of the ICTY's Article 3 jurisprudence).

[107] *Limaj et al.* Trial Judgement, *supra* note 103, para. 172.

[108] *Ibid.*, para. 171 (noting also that by July 1998, 'the KLA had gained acceptance as a necessary and valid participant in negotiations with international governments and bodies to determine a solution for the Kosovo's crisis, and to lay down conditions in these negotiations for refraining from military action').

[109] See *Prosecutor* v. *Semanza*, Case No. ICTR-97-20-A, Judgement, 20 May 2005 ('*Semanza* Appeal Judgement'), para. 192; accord *Prosecutor* v. *Karemera, Ngirumpatse, and Nzirorera*, Case No. ICTR-98-44-AR73(C), Decision on Prosecutor's Interlocutory Appeal of Decision on Judicial Notice, 16 June 2006, paras. 28–29; see also *Prosecutor* v. *Ndindiliyimana, Bizimungu, Nzuwonemeye, and Sagahutu*, Case No. ICTR-00-56-T, [Corrected] Decision on Defence Motions Pursuant to Rule 98 *bis*, 18 June 2007 ('*Military II* 98 *bis* Decision'), para. 39 (holding that '[t]he fact that a non-international armed conflict prevailed in Rwanda from April to June 1994 is no longer subject to dispute'); accord *Prosecutor* v. *Muvunyi*, Case No. ICTR-00-55-T, Judgement and Sentence, 12 September 2006, para. 16; *Prosecutor* v. *Ntagerura, Bagambiki, and Imanishimwe*, Case No. ICTR-99-46-T, Judgement and Sentence, 25 February 2004 ('*Cyangugu* Trial Judgement'), para. 74.

[110] *Military II* 98 *bis* Decision, *supra* note 109, para. 39.

have concluded that armed conflicts existed throughout the former Yugoslavia between 1991 and 1998,[111] but so far no judgement has taken judicial notice of the existence of an armed conflict.

As indicated by the *Tadić* definition and affirmed by later jurisprudence, international humanitarian law does not require that the entire territory of a state be involved in a non-international armed conflict, and the existence of a conflict can be established by evidence of localised areas in which 'serious fighting for an extended period of time' occurred.[112] Thus the *Kordić and Čerkez* Appeals Chamber upheld the Trial Chamber's conclusion in that case that an armed conflict existed at all times relevant to the indictment, in light of the evidence that significant fighting of varying intensity took place in at least four municipalities in central Bosnia between October 1992 and April 1993.[113]

4.2.1.1.1 Is knowledge of the existence of the armed conflict an element of war crimes? Judgements from both Tribunals have stated that the existence of an armed conflict is to be determined from an objective assessment of the evidence, and is not dependent on the views of the parties to the conflict.[114] The purpose of this rule is to prevent the participants in the hostilities, and thus the likely alleged perpetrators of the crimes at issue, from determining for themselves whether international humanitarian law applies to regulate and restrain their conduct.[115] Yet is there a subjective aspect to the armed conflict requirement, in that the prosecution must also establish that someone involved in the commission of the crime was in fact aware of the existence of the armed conflict?

[111] See, e.g., *Limaj et al.* Trial Judgement, *supra* note 103, paras. 171–173 (Kosovo in 1998); *Blagojević and Jokić* Trial Judgement, *supra* note 97, para. 549 (eastern Bosnia and Herzegovina in 1995); *Prosecutor* v. *Brđanin*, Case No. IT-99-36-T, Judgement, 1 September 2004 ('*Brđanin* Trial Judgement'), paras. 140–142 (Autonomous Region of the Krajina in Bosnia and Herzegovina in 1992); *Stakić* Trial Judgement, *supra* note 97, paras. 571–574 (municipality of Prijedor in Bosnia and Herzegovina in 1992); *Mrkšić et al.* Trial Judgement, *supra* note 103, paras. 409, 418, 422 (Vukovar municipality in Croatia in 1991).

[112] See *Kordić and Čerkez* Appeal Judgement, *supra* note 101, paras. 336, 341 (quotation at para. 341). Accord, e.g., *Prosecutor* v. *Tadić*, Case No. IT-94-1-A, Judgement, 15 July 1999 ('*Tadić* Appeal Judgement'), para. 70; *Hadžihasanović and Kubura* Trial Judgement, *supra* note 57, para. 14; *Naletilić and Martinović* Trial Judgement, *supra* note 57, para. 177; *Semanza* Trial Judgement, *supra* note 97, para. 367; *Kordić and Čerkez* Trial Judgement, *supra* note 57, paras. 27, 31; *Blaškić* Trial Judgement, *supra* note 57, para. 64; *Rutaganda* Trial Judgement, *supra* note 103, paras. 102–103.

[113] *Kordić and Čerkez* Appeal Judgement, *supra* note 101, paras. 333–341 (rejecting the accused's implied argument that the Trial Chamber's statement that no 'generalised state of armed conflict' existed until April 1993 precluded the applicability of Article 3 of the ICTY Statute).

[114] See, e.g., *ibid.*, para. 373 (noting, in the context of grave breaches charges, that '[t]he purpose of Geneva Convention IV, i.e., safeguarding the protected persons, would be endangered if States were permitted to escape from their obligations by denying a state of armed conflict'); accord *Akayesu* Trial Judgment, *supra* note 67, paras. 603, 624; *Semanza* Trial Judgement, *supra* note 97, para. 357.

[115] See, e.g., *Kordić and Čerkez* Appeal Judgement, *supra* note 101, para. 373 (recalling the warning in the commentary to Geneva Convention IV that 'the Conventions have been drawn up first and foremost to protect individuals, and not to serve State interests'); *Akayesu* Trial Judgment, *supra* note 67, para. 603 ('If the application of international humanitarian law depended solely on the discretionary judgment of the parties to the conflict, in most cases there would be a tendency for the conflict to be minimized by the parties thereto.').

In a recent holding on the elements of grave breaches of the Geneva Conventions under Article 2 of the ICTY Statute, the *Naletilić and Martinović* Appeals Chamber offered the following rationale for including knowledge of the *nature* of the conflict as an element of these crimes:[116]

> The principle of individual guilt requires that an accused can only be convicted for a crime if his *mens rea* comprises the *actus reus* of the crime. To convict him without proving that he knew of the facts that were necessary to make his conduct a crime is to deny him his entitlement to the presumption of innocence. The specific required mental state will vary, of course, depending on the crime and the mode of liability. But the core principle is the same: for a conduct to entail criminal liability, it must be possible for an individual to determine *ex ante*, based on the facts available to him, that the conduct is criminal. At a minimum, then, to convict an accused of a crime, he must have had knowledge of the facts that made his or her conduct criminal.[117]

The Chamber ultimately confirmed that knowledge of the facts that establish the international character of an armed conflict is an element of the crime that must be proved beyond reasonable doubt by the prosecution. Almost in passing, the Appeals Chamber also noted that knowledge of the *existence* of an armed conflict is required:

> The perpetrator only needs to be aware of factual circumstances on which the judge finally determines *the existence of the armed conflict* and the international (or internal) character thereof. It is a general principle of criminal law that the correct legal classification of … conduct by the perpetrator is not required. The principle of individual guilt, however, demands sufficient awareness of factual circumstances *establishing the armed conflict* and its (international or internal) character.[118]

Although the ICTY Appeals Chamber has since confirmed that this section of the judgement means that knowledge of the existence of an armed conflict is a requirement for war crimes,[119] subsequent trial judgements do not appear explicitly to have implemented this holding, or heeded the Appeals Chamber's reminder that

[116] The specifics of this holding are discussed below, at text accompanying notes 172–173.

[117] *Naletilić and Martinović* Appeal Judgement, *supra* note 96, para. 114.

[118] *Ibid.*, para. 119 (emphases added). See also *ibid.*, para. 120 (noting that in the drafting of the Rome Statute, there was disagreement about whether the knowledge of both the existence and nature of an armed conflict was required, and holding that 'the *existence* of an armed conflict or its character has to be regarded, in accordance with the principle of *in dubio pro reo*' – in case of doubt, favour the accused – 'as ordinary elements of a crime under customary international law') (emphasis added); *ibid.*, para. 118 (analogising this requirement to the general requirement for crimes against humanity, where some actor involved in the underlying offence must know that it forms part of a widespread or systematic attack on a civilian population); Chapter 2, section 2.2.2.6 (discussing this general requirement for crimes against humanity).

[119] See *Prosecutor* v. *Limaj, Bala, and Musliu*, Case No. IT-03-66-A, Judgement, 27 September 2007 ('*Limaj et al.* Appeal Judgement'), para. 21 (asserting that '[i]n *Naletilić and Martinović*, the Appeals Chamber recognized the applicability of this principle [*in dubio pro reo*] to the *mens rea* requirement of knowledge of the existence of an armed conflict').

the existence and nature of an armed conflict are not merely jurisdictional prerequisites.[120]

The *Naletilić and Martinović* Appeals Chamber's interchangeable use of the terms 'accused' and 'perpetrator' raises a point that occurs repeatedly in this area of international criminal law: whose mental state is relevant to the factors that make an underlying offence a crime of international concern? As we have argued with regard to crimes against humanity and genocide in the preceding chapters of this volume,[121] focusing exclusively on either the accused or the physical perpetrator would be inconsistent with both the structure of international crimes and the types of circumstances in which they typically occur. On one hand, assuming that the person on trial is the one who committed the underlying offences, as is suggested by the first quotation from the *Naletilić and Martinović* Appeal Judgement, ignores the fact that most of the conduct that is alleged to constitute war crimes is inevitably committed by low-ranking combatants or fighters, who are increasingly infrequently prosecuted in international tribunals. On the other hand, framing the element in terms of the knowledge or mental state of only the physical perpetrator, as it appears in the second quotation, poses at least three separate problems. First, it risks being underinclusive, because there might be situations in which a civilian or military superior knows of the existence (or the nature) of an armed conflict before that information filters through the ranks. Second, it would be out of step with the current focus of international and internationalised courts and tribunals on charging and trying the most senior accused – high-ranking civilian officials or military commanders – who rarely if ever personally physically commit the crimes with which they are charged.[122] Third, it could place an unrealistic burden on the

[120] See, e.g., *Orić* Trial Judgement, *supra* note 57, para. 253 (holding that the elements of an armed conflict and nexus between the offence and the conflict are 'two preliminary requirements' that must be satisfied '[i]n order for the Tribunal to have jurisdiction'); *Prosecutor* v. *Krajišnik*, Case No. IT-00-39&40-T, Judgement, 27 September 2006 ('*Krajišnik* Trial Judgement'), para. 844 (referring to the two elements as 'two general conditions that must be met for the applicability of Article 3', but treating them as distinct from jurisdictional considerations); *Prosecutor* v. *Martić*, Case No. IT-95-11-T, Judgement, 12 June 2007 ('*Martić* Trial Judgement'), para. 40 (holding that '[t]he application of Article 3 requires' the determination that these two elements have been established, but not explicitly treating them as elements to be proved beyond a reasonable doubt); *Mrkšić et al.* Trial Judgement, *supra* note 103, paras. 405, 423 (treating these two elements as 'preliminary requirements' that must be satisfied for jurisdictional purposes, although specifically noting that the nexus requirement must be established by the prosecution). All these trial judgements cite only pre-*Naletilić and Martinović* jurisprudence of the ICTY Appeals Chamber in support of their discussions of these requirements, and none made any findings as to knowledge of the existence or nature of the armed conflict. It is possible, of course, that these chambers considered that it was the prosecution's duty to establish that these general requirements had been met, but their statements of the law do not reflect a conscious adoption of the Appeals Chamber's more precise treatment of these requirements as elements of the crime. It should be noted that the Appeals Chamber is itself not careful about the terminology it uses. See, e.g., *Prosecutor* v. *Brđanin*, Case No. IT-99-36-A, Judgement, 3 April 2007 ('*Brđanin* Appeal Judgement'), para. 256 (referring to the nexus requirement as one of the 'jurisdictional prerequisites for the application of Article 2 of the Statute').

[121] See Chapter 2, section 2.2.2.1; Chapter 3, section 3.2.1.1.

[122] See Boas, Bischoff, and Reid, *supra* note 30, p. 140 n. 798 (discussing the Security Council resolutions instituting the completion strategies for the *ad hoc* Tribunals, which include focusing remaining cases on the

prosecution to prove, and trial chambers to evaluate, the mental state of a potentially huge number of physical perpetrators who are not accused in the case.

Accordingly, and for the reasons discussed in detail in Chapter 2, the best restatement of this element would be that in order for an underlying offence to qualify as a war crime, the physical perpetrator or other relevant actor involved in the commission of the offence must know of the existence of an armed conflict.[123] It is also possible that, in line with the *Naletilić and Martinović* Appeals Chamber's reasoning and consonant with the requirements for crimes against humanity, the physical perpetrator or other relevant actor must also have knowledge of the next general requirement for war crimes: the connection between the underlying offence and the armed conflict.[124]

4.2.1.2 Nexus between the underlying offence and the armed conflict

The underlying offence is closely related to the armed conflict.

Even if an offence is committed during an armed conflict, it cannot be considered a war crime unless there is a connection between the offence and the conflict; otherwise, depending on the circumstances, it could be an ordinary crime falling within the domestic jurisdiction of a state, not an international court.[125] Under the Tribunals' war crimes case law, however, the prosecution need not prove that actual combat took place in the location where the underlying offence is alleged to have occurred. Instead, the *Tadić* precedent established that all that is required is that the

most senior accused); *infra* notes 507–509 (citing the cases of the persons publicly implicated in proceedings before the ICC, many of whom held or hold high political office, such as Thomas Lubanga and Ahmad Harun, or are militia leaders, such as Joseph Kony and Ali Kushayb); *infra* notes 527–530 (citing the cases of the ten accused before the SCSL, all of whom were mid- or high-level military, militia, or political leaders); *infra* notes 588–589 (citing the cases of the five accused before the ECCC, all of whom held senior positions in the Khmer Rouge government); Chapter 2, notes 690, 715 (citing the *Dujail* and *Anfal* cases in the SICT, which concerned Saddam Hussein and other mid- and high-ranking Ba'ath Party officials); but see *ibid*., note 599 (East Timor SPSC tried only low-ranking accused; mid- and high-ranking accused remained at large until the Panels were shut down).

[123] See Chapter 2, section 2.2.2.1. As we note in Chapter 2, the phrase 'other relevant actor' is deliberately broad enough to include the accused, but should not be read to encompass all persons who could bear criminal responsibility with regard to the underlying offence. If the relationship of a person to the crime can only be captured by the forms of responsibility of aiding and abetting, superior responsibility, or the third category of joint criminal enterprise (JCE), his mental state is irrelevant to the question of whether an international crime was committed, because persons in these positions are incidental to the crime. On the other hand, persons whose responsibility can be described as planners, instigators, orderers, and first-category JCE participants are often the real authors of a crime, and the physical perpetrators merely the tools with which they accomplish that crime.

[124] See, e.g., *Naletilić and Martinović* Appeal Judgement, *supra* note 96, para. 118 (observing, again in passing, that if one were to apply the reasoning of the crimes against humanity general requirements to grave breaches, 'the Prosecution has to show that the accused *knew* that his crimes had a nexus to an international armed conflict' as well as knew of the nature of the conflict). Unlike the Chamber's holdings with regard to knowledge of the existence and nature of an armed conflict, this statement was not supported by citations to earlier judgements, and does not appear to have been reprised in later appeal or trial judgements.

[125] See, e.g., *Mrkšić et al*. Trial Judgement, *supra* note 103, para. 423 ('The nexus requirement serves to distinguish war crimes from purely domestic crimes and also prevents purely random or isolated criminal occurrences from being characterized as war crimes.').

offence be 'closely related to the hostilities occurring in other parts of the territories controlled by the parties to the conflict'.[126]

Although the underlying offence does not have to be 'part of a policy or … practice officially endorsed or tolerated by one of the parties to the conflict, or … be in actual furtherance of a policy associated with the conduct of war',[127] or even have been planned,[128] the *Kunarac* Appeal Judgement explained that '[w]hat ultimately distinguishes a war crime from a purely domestic offence is that a war crime is shaped by or dependent upon the environment – the armed conflict – in which it is committed.'[129] While that environment need not have caused the crime:

> the existence of an armed conflict must, at a minimum, have played a substantial part in the perpetrator's ability to commit it, his decision to commit it, the manner in which it was committed or the purpose for which it was committed. Hence, if it can be established … that the perpetrator acted in furtherance of or under the guise of the armed conflict, it would be sufficient to conclude that his acts were closely related to the armed conflict.[130]

In order to determine whether the underlying offence is 'closely related' to the armed conflict, in that the conflict played a 'substantial part' in the commission of the offence, the *Kunarac* Appeals Chamber instructed trial chambers to consider at least five factors: (1) whether the physical perpetrator is a combatant; (2) whether the victim is a non-combatant; (3) whether the victim is a member of the opposing party; (4) whether the offence serves the ultimate goal of a military campaign; and (5) whether the offence was committed as part of, or in the context of, the physical perpetrator's official duties.[131]

Since the requirement of a nexus to the armed conflict is an element common to war crimes committed in both international and non-international armed conflicts,

[126] *Tadić* Jurisdiction Appeal Decision, *supra* note 4, para. 70; accord, e.g., *Prosecutor* v. *Stakić*, Case No. IT-97-24-A, Judgement, 22 March 2006 ('*Stakić* Appeal Judgement'), para. 342 (noting that '[i]t is essential, however, that a Trial Chamber establish the existence of a geographical and temporal linkage between the crimes ascribed to the accused and the armed conflict'); *Semanza* Appeal Judgement, *supra* note 109, para. 369; *Rutaganda* Appeal Judgement, *supra* note 92, paras. 569–571; *Kunarac et al.* Appeal Judgement, *supra* note 97, para. 55; *Prosecutor* v. *Akayesu*, Case No. ICTR-96-4-A, Judgement, 1 June 2001 ('*Akayesu* Appeal Judgement'), para. 438 n. 807; *Hadžihasanović and Kubura* Trial Judgement, *supra* note 57, para. 15; *Brđanin* Trial Judgement, *supra* note 111, para. 123; *Semanza* Trial Judgement, *supra* note 97, paras. 368–369; *Naletilić and Martinović* Trial Judgement, *supra* note 57, para. 177; *Kayishema and Ruzindana* Trial Judgement, *supra* note 103, paras. 185–186; *Čelebići* Trial Judgement, *supra* note 67, paras. 185, 193–195.

[127] *Blaškić* Trial Judgement, *supra* note 57, para. 70 (citing and quoting *Tadić* Trial Judgement, *supra* note 103, para. 573); accord, e.g., *Kunarac et al.* Appeal Judgement, *supra* note 97, para. 58; *Martić* Trial Judgement, *supra* note 120, para. 43.

[128] *Kunarac et al.* Appeal Judgement, *supra* note 97, para. 58. Note, however, that proof of a plan or policy may be strong evidence that the underlying offences are in fact war crimes, as opposed to isolated domestic crimes. See *ibid.*; *Tadić* Trial Judgement, *supra* note 103, para. 573; *Čelebići* Trial Judgement, *supra* note 67, paras. 194–195.

[129] *Kunarac et al.* Appeal Judgement, *supra* note 97, para. 58.

[130] *Ibid.* Accord *Stakić* Appeal Judgement, *supra* note 126, para. 342; *Mrkšić et al.* Trial Judgement, *supra* note 103, para. 423; *Hadžihasanović and Kubura* Trial Judgement, *supra* note 57, para. 16; *Limaj et al.* Trial Judgement, *supra* note 103, para. 91; *Strugar* Trial Judgement, *supra* note 51, para. 215.

[131] *Kunarac et al.* Appeal Judgement, *supra* note 97, para. 59.

however, the focus in the first two factors on 'combatant' status appears misplaced.[132] Moreover, as the *Blaškić* Trial Chamber noted, a particular underlying offence could be seen as contrary to the ultimate goal of the military campaign – for example, because it would distract the troops or increase the resistance of the civilian population – and yet still undeniably be a war crime.[133] Nevertheless, subsequent *ad hoc* chambers have repeated this list of factors in the course of their statements of the law on war crimes,[134] though it is unclear how closely they have followed it in their factual findings.

The *Mrkšić* Trial Chamber recently presented one of the clearer applications of some of the *Kunarac* factors. In the Trial Judgement, the Chamber concluded that the offences were closely related to the armed conflict between Serb and Croat forces in Croatia in 1991 because 'the victims … were selected by members of the Serb forces having regard, *inter alia*, to their ethnicity and their known or believed involvement in the Croat forces in the conflict', and moreover, 'the primary motive for the offences was revenge or punishment because the victims were known or believed to have been in the Croat forces'.[135] The findings in the *Naletilić and Martinović* Trial Judgement are more typical of the conclusory manner in which trial chambers have tended to present their findings on the nexus requirement:

> The Chamber is satisfied that the acts with which Mladen Naletilić and Vinko Martinović are charged were committed in the course, and as a consequence, of the armed conflict between the HVO [Bosnian Croat forces] and the ABiH [official armed forces of Bosnia and Herzegovina]. The victims of this conflict were living within the relevant territory in the relevant period. Further, both accused were members of the armed forces taking part in the hostilities. The Chamber is thus satisfied that the nexus requirement has been met in the present case.[136]

[132] See *supra* note 72 (noting that for non-international armed conflicts, the more appropriate term for persons participating in hostilities is 'fighters').

[133] See *Blaškić* Trial Judgement, *supra* note 57, para. 70 (holding that the offence need not be in 'the actual interest of a party to the conflict').

[134] See, e.g., *Mrkšić et al.* Trial Judgement, *supra* note 103, para. 423; *Limaj et al.* Trial Judgement, *supra* note 103, para. 91.

[135] *Mrkšić et al.* Trial Judgement, *supra* note 103, para. 424. Other trial judgements in cases involving crimes committed during or in preparation for active combat have also been clear in explaining that the nexus requirement was satisfied, but they did not have to consider the *Kunarac* factors in order to do so, because the connection was evident. See, e.g., *Prosecutor* v. *Halilović*, Case No. IT-01-48-T, Judgement, 16 November 2005 ('*Halilović* Trial Judgement'), para. 727 (discussing crimes committed in Grabovica and Uzdol in Bosnia and Herzegovina in preparation for, and during, an attack on Uzdol); *Strugar* Trial Judgement, *supra* note 51, para. 217 (discussing crimes committed during the shelling of the Old Town of Dubrovnik in Croatia).

[136] *Naletilić and Martinović* Trial Judgement, *supra* note 57, para. 180. See also *Prosecutor* v. *Vasiljević*, Case No. IT-98-32-T, Judgement, 29 November 2002 ('*Vasiljević* Trial Judgement'), para. 57 (concluding that the acts of the accused were closely related to the conflict because he 'was closely associated with Serb paramilitaries, his acts were all committed in furtherance of the armed conflict, and he acted under the guise of the armed conflict'); *Blagojević and Jokić* Trial Judgement, *supra* note 97, para. 549 (finding '[b]ased on all the evidence' that the underlying offences were closely related because they were 'committed as a result of the hostilities').

While the *Kunarac* factors are intended to assist trial chambers in their assessments of the evidence, they are not prerequisites to a conclusion that the underlying offences are closely related to the armed conflict. For example, in early judgements from both Tribunals, there was some question as to whether the physical perpetrator had to be associated with one of the parties to the conflict in order for the offence to constitute a war crime. At the ICTR, the *Akayesu* Trial Chamber had held in 1998 that only members of the armed forces 'under the military command of either of the belligerent parties', or 'public officials or agents or persons otherwise holding public authority or *de facto* representing the government', could be held responsible for war crimes.[137] At the ICTY, in the February 2001 *Kunarac* Trial Judgement, the Chamber noted that Common Article 3 might require some relationship between the perpetrator and a party to the conflict.[138] The question was definitively settled by the *Akayesu* Appeal Judgement, which in June 2001 reversed the Trial Chamber's restrictive interpretation. Even though the nexus requirement means that physical perpetrators 'will probably have a special relationship with one party to the conflict,' the ICTR Appeals Chamber observed, 'such a relationship is not a condition precedent' to the application of the relevant rules of international humanitarian law.[139]

Although ICTR trial chambers consistently agreed with the ICTY that a nexus between the underlying offence and the armed conflict was a requirement for war crimes,[140] the early judgements generally concluded that this nexus requirement had not been satisfied on the evidence before the chambers.[141] Jamie Williamson posits that these conclusions were the result of two errors on the part of these trial chambers. The first error, one of logic, was the use of a 'cumbersome' two-step analysis, in which the trial chamber first analysed whether the genocide that occurred in Rwanda was connected to the armed conflict, and only then whether the underlying offences with which the accused were charged constituted war crimes in addition to genocide. The second error, which he asserts was a fundamental misapprehension of the evidence adduced at trial, was the conclusion by some chambers that the genocide was a distinct event that was unconnected to the

[137] Accord *Kayishema and Ruzindana* Trial Judgement, *supra* note 103, para. 174 (holding that a civilian could only be responsible for war crimes if he is associated with the armed forces of one of the parties to the conflict).

[138] *Prosecutor* v. *Kunarac, Kovač, and Vuković*, Case No. IT-96-23 & 23/1-T, Judgement, 22 February 2001 ('*Kunarac et al.* Trial Judgement'), para. 407. The Chamber concluded that it did not need to reach the question: even if there were such a requirement, the evidence established that the three accused had fought on behalf of the Serb forces, one of the parties to the conflict. *Ibid.*

[139] *Akayesu* Appeal Judgement, *supra* note 126, para. 444. Accord *Semanza* Trial Judgement, *supra* note 97, paras. 361–362.

[140] See *supra* note 126 for an illustrative listing of ICTY and ICTR judgements including this requirement.

[141] See Williamson, *supra* note 92, p. 60 (explaining that notwithstanding agreement on the test to be applied, 'in many of the cases the ICTR struggled in assessing whether such a nexus had been factually established'); *Akayesu* Trial Judgement, *supra* note 67, paras. 642–643; *Kayishema and Ruzindana* Trial Judgement, *supra* note 103, paras. 619–621; *Rutaganda* Trial Judgement, *supra* note 103, paras. 438–443.

armed conflict between the Forces Armées Rwandaises and the Rwandan Patriotic Front.[142]

Both erroneous practices were rejected by the ICTR Appeals Chamber in its 2003 judgement in *Rutaganda*. Adopting the approach of the *Kunarac* Appeals Chamber,[143] the *Rutaganda* Appeals Chamber further elaborated on the terms in which the ICTY test was framed:

> First, the expression 'under the guise of the armed conflict' does not mean simply 'at the same time as an armed conflict' and/or 'in any circumstances created in part by the armed conflict'. For example, if a non-combatant takes advantage of the lessened effectiveness of the police in conditions of disorder created by an armed conflict to murder a neighbour he has hated for years, that would not, without more, constitute a war crime … By contrast, the accused in *Kunarac*, for example, were combatants who took advantage of their positions of military authority to rape individuals whose displacement was an express goal of the military campaign in which they took part.[144]

In addition, the ICTR Appeals Chamber followed the single-step test applied at the ICTY, and examined simply whether the underlying offences were closely related to the armed conflict.[145] Applying the appellate standard of review, it concluded that 'no reasonable trier of fact could have failed to find … that [there was a] nexus between Rutaganda's acts and the armed conflict, in relation to the forced diversion of refugees to Nyanza and the attack that took place there'.[146] It therefore reversed the accused's acquittal on two counts of murder as a violation of Common Article 3.[147]

4.2.1.3 Additional general requirements for grave breaches of the Geneva conventions: war crimes committed in international armed conflict

Of the two *ad hoc* Tribunals, only the ICTY has jurisdiction over grave breaches of the Geneva Conventions,[148] and the jurisprudence of that Tribunal has consistently

142 Williamson, *supra* note 92, pp. 60–62; see especially *ibid*., p. 63 (referring to the *Kayishema and Ruzindana* Trial Judgement, which 'conceded that the atrocities had occurred during the armed conflict, [but] held that the crimes formed "part of a distinct policy of genocide; they were committed parallel to, and not as a result of, the armed conflict."'). But see *Rutaganda* Trial Judgement, *supra* note 103, para. 443 (concluding that there was a link between the genocide and the armed conflict).

143 See *supra* text accompanying note 130 for the *Kunarac* explication of the *Tadić* 'closely related' test.

144 *Rutaganda* Appeal Judgement, *supra* note 92, para. 570.

145 See, e.g., *Tadić* Trial Judgement, *supra* note 103, para. 573 ('The only question, to be determined in the circumstances of each individual case, is whether the offences were closely related to the armed conflict as a whole.').

146 *Rutaganda* Appeal Judgement, *supra* note 92, para. 579 (listing several supporting facts, including 'that the RAF soldiers told the *Interahamwe*' – the physical perpetrators, who were not soldiers – 'to kill and look for those who were not dead and finish them off').

147 *Ibid*., para. 583. Compare *Prosecutor* v. *Kamuhanda*, Case No. ICTR-99-54-T, Judgement, 22 January 2004 ('*Kamuhanda* Trial Judgement'), para. 743:

> In the present case, as distinguished from *Rutaganda*, insufficient evidence has been established to enable a finding that there is a nexus between any crimes committed by the Accused and any conflict – either a conflict generally raging in Rwanda or one specifically affecting the material regions indicated in the Indictment.

148 See *supra* text accompanying notes 2, 5, 13 (setting forth the respective relevant provisions of the ICTY and ICTR Statutes).

interpreted the Geneva Conventions as imposing two additional general requirements for these crimes: the armed conflict to which the offence is closely related must be of an international character, and the persons or property that are the object of the offence must be protected under those Conventions. ICTY jurisprudence has treated the subparagraphs of Article 2 as an exhaustive list of qualifying underlying offences.[149]

4.2.1.3.1 The requirement of an international armed conflict

The armed conflict to which the underlying offence is closely related is international in character.

Referring to the *travaux préparatoires* of the ICTY Statute and widely held understandings of the Geneva Conventions, and rejecting arguments to the contrary by an *amicus curiae* in the case, the *Tadić* interlocutory appeal decision on jurisdiction held that grave breaches of the Geneva Conventions can only occur in the context of international armed conflicts.[150] This precedent has been uniformly applied in subsequent judgements.[151] The Appeal Judgement in *Tadić* further explained that there are three circumstances in which an armed conflict may be considered to be international in nature: (1) the conflict takes place between two or more states; (2) another state intervenes in an internal armed conflict through its troops; or (3) some of the participants in an internal armed conflict act on behalf of another state, which exerts a certain degree of control over their activities (collectively, 'international armed conflict tests').[152]

For the third option, *Tadić* and its progeny apply three different tests derived from the law of state responsibility to determine whether the degree of control is sufficient to conclude that participants in an internal conflict were acting on behalf of a state – that is, to deem them *de facto* state organs (collectively, 'degree of control tests'). Each degree of control test is specifically pegged to the circumstances of the conflict

149 See, e.g., *Kunarac et al.* Appeal Judgement, *supra* note 97, para. 187 ('Alone among the Articles of the Statute, Article 3 is illustrative, serving as a residual clause.'). See also *infra* text accompanying note 232 (citing cases holding that Article 3 is a residual provision capturing conduct not specifically mentioned in Article 2).

150 See *Tadić* Interlocutory Appeal Decision, *supra* note 4, paras. 71, 81–84.

151 See, e.g., *Brđanin* Appeal Judgement, *supra* note 120, para. 256; *Blaškić* Appeal Judgement, *supra* note 96, para. 170; *Prosecutor* v. *Aleksovski*, Case No. IT-95-14/1-A, Judgement, 24 March 2000 ('*Aleksovski* Appeal Judgement'), para. 113; *Tadić* Appeal Judgement, *supra* note 112, para. 80. See also *supra* section 4.1.3 (arguing that this distinction is of decreasing importance in contemporary international criminal law). But cf. Guénaël Mettraux, *International Crimes and the Ad Hoc Tribunals* (2005), p. 62 (noting that there are at least three reasons a prosecutor would prefer to have a situation deemed an occupation to which the grave breaches regime would apply, including the greater protection of more detailed rules of international humanitarian law).

152 *Tadić* Appeal Judgement, *supra* note 112, para. 84 (noting also that the conflict may, 'depending on the circumstances, be international in character alongside an internal armed conflict'); accord, e.g., *Brđanin* Trial Judgement, *supra* note 111, para. 124; *Kordić and Čerkez* Trial Judgement, *supra* note 57, para. 66. As the *Tadić* Appeals Chamber's later discussion of the rules of attribution under the law of superior responsibility demonstrates, its reasoning proceeded from the fundamental premise that although an international conflict must involve at least two different states, the requirement can be satisfied by the indirect participation of one state in an internal armed conflict through control exerted over a non-state party to the conflict. See, e.g., *Tadić* Appeal Judgement, *supra* note 112, paras. 96–97.

and the persons alleged to be acting on behalf of the intervening state.[153] For unorganised groups of individuals or most private individuals, the traditional state responsibility tests of imputation or adoption apply, and the prosecution must establish that the state either issued specific instructions concerning the commission of the particular act, or subsequently publicly endorsed or approved the unlawful act.[154] For armed forces, militias or paramilitary units – any 'organised and hierarchically structured group' – the *Tadić* Appeals Chamber disagreed with the high standard of effective control set by the International Court of Justice in the *Nicaragua* case, and held that it is sufficient to establish the overall character of the control by the state, by proving that it (1) financed, equipped, trained, or provided operational support to the group, *and* (2) coordinated, directed, or assisted in the general planning of the group's military activities[155] (the 'overall control test'). Finally, private individuals who are assimilated to state organs because of their actual behaviour within the structure of the state may be regarded as *de facto* state organs, regardless of the presence or absence of specific instructions.[156]

Trial judgements at the ICTY have focused on whether the second or third type of international conflict has been established, that is, whether a foreign state's troops have intervened in an internal conflict, or whether any of the three degree of control tests has been satisfied. For example, in assessing whether alleged crimes in Central Bosnia were committed in the context of an international armed conflict, the *Kordić and Čerkez* Trial Chamber held that it could rely on evidence of the presence of Croatian Army (HV) troops in areas outside of Central Bosnia 'if the location of those areas is of strategic significance to the conflict', reasoning that the inquiry is focused on the intervention of a state in the conflict itself, which was not geographically

[153] See *Tadić* Appeal Judgement, *supra* note 112, para. 117 (holding that, although international law requires that a state exercise control over individuals in order for their conduct to be attributed to the state, '[t]he degree of control may … vary according to the factual circumstances of each case', and explaining that it 'fails to see why in each and every circumstance international law should require a high threshold for the test of control').

[154] *Ibid.*, paras. 118, 124, 132–137. These tests generally correspond to the tests elucidated in two judgements of the International Court of Justice: the *Nicaragua* 'effective control' test, and the *ex post facto* approval or endorsement test from the *Tehran Hostages* case. See *Military and Paramilitary Activities in and Against Nicaragua* (Merits) (*Nicaragua* v. *United States*), Judgement, 27 June 1986, (1986) ICJ Rep. 14, paras. 75–80; *United States Diplomatic and Consular Staff in Tehran* (Merits) (*United States* v. *Iran*), Judgement, 24 May 1980, (1980) ICJ Rep. 3, para. 74. This first *Tadić* control test also includes private individuals or unorganised groups who are entrusted with a specific lawful task by a state, but breach an international obligation of the state in the course of discharging the task. *Tadić* Appeal Judgement, *supra* note 112, para. 119 (noting that this holding is 'by analogy with the rules of State responsibility for acts of State officials acting *ultra vires*'). See also *Brđanin* Trial Judgement, *supra* note 111, para. 124 n. 319.

[155] *Tadić* Appeal Judgement, *supra* note 112, paras. 120, 125–131, 137–138 (quotation at para. 120). See also *Brđanin* Trial Judgement, *supra* note 111, para. 124 & n. 319 (phrasing the second factor used to prove overall control as 'a State … has a role in … organising, coordinating or planning the military actions of the military group'). This paragraph of the *Brđanin* Trial Judgement erroneously uses the term 'Party to the conflict' as a synonym for 'State' in an apparent importation of the Geneva Conventions' terminology into the test for state responsibility. In the context of the test for whether the actions of a non-state group may be attributed to a state, it is evident that the former (and not the latter) is the party to the conflict.

[156] *Tadić* Appeal Judgement, *supra* note 112, paras. 141–144.

limited to the crime base locations.[157] The Trial Chamber concluded that 'the conflict between the Bosnian Croats and the Bosnian Muslims in Bosnia and Herzegovina was internationalised by the intervention of Croatia in that conflict through its troops'.[158] Similarly, the *Blaškić* Trial Chamber also concluded that the evidence adduced at trial established the presence of the HV in areas both outside and within the geographic region under the command of the accused; found that 'the presence of the HV in the areas outside [Central Bosnia] inevitably also had an impact on the conduct of the conflict in that zone'; and therefore held that Croatia's direct intervention in Bosnia and Herzegovina rendered the conflict international.[159]

Notwithstanding the three different degree of control tests, most judgements to consider the issue have focused on whether the state exercised overall control over the party to the internal conflict. In *Tadić* itself, the Appeals Chamber applied the overall control test to the factual findings made by the Trial Chamber, and concluded that the Yugoslav Army (VJ) exercised the degree of control over the Bosnian Serb Army (VRS) required to render the conflict international. In particular, the Appeals Chamber relied on three factors or categories of evidence: (1) the transfer to VRS units of former officers in the defunct armed forces of the Socialist Federal Republic of Yugoslavia who were not of Bosnian Serb extraction; (2) the continuing payment of salaries to Bosnian Serb and non-Bosnian Serb officers in the VRS by the government of Federal Republic of Yugoslavia (FRY); and (3) evidence demonstrating 'that the VRS and the VJ did not, after May 1992, comprise two separate armies in any genuine sense'.[160]

The Chamber cautioned, however, against reaching hasty conclusions about the nature of a state's involvement in an armed conflict in chaotic conditions similar to those then prevailing in the former Yugoslavia. It noted that substantial evidence of overall control is required where either the allegedly controlling state 'is not the

157 *Kordić and Čerkez* Trial Judgement, *supra* note 57, paras. 27, 70–72. Accord *Naletilić and Martinović* Trial Judgement, *supra* note 57, para. 194:

> There is no requirement to prove that HV troops were present in every single area where crimes were allegedly committed. On the contrary, the conflict between the ABiH and the HVO must be looked upon as a whole and, if it is found to be international in character through the participation of HV troops, then Article 2 of the Statute will apply to the entire territory of the conflict.

158 *Kordić and Čerkez* Trial Judgement, *supra* note 57, para. 109. Although the Appeals Chamber affirmed the legal principle that foreign troops need not be present in the crime base locations, it overturned the Trial Chamber's finding that Croatia had directly intervened in the conflict, because no reasonable trier of fact could have found that the vague, conflicting, or inconclusive evidence presented at trial established that Croatian troops were sent to Bosnia. *Kordić and Čerkez* Appeal Judgement, *supra* note 101, paras. 314–321, 355–360.

159 *Blaškić* Trial Judgement, *supra* note 57, paras. 83–94 (quotation at para. 94).

160 See *generally Tadić* Appeal Judgement, *supra* note 112, paras. 150–152; see also *ibid.*, para. 153 (overturning the Trial Chamber's finding on the absence of specific orders circumventing or overriding local superiors and concluding that proof of such orders was unnecessary, not only because it applied the wrong legal test, but also because '[a] distinguishing feature of the VJ and the VRS was that they possessed *shared* military objectives') (emphasis in original); *ibid.*, paras. 157–161 (noting, and apparently relying on, *ex post facto* confirmation of FRY control of the Republika Srpska in the processes of negotiation and conclusion of the Dayton-Paris Accord).

territorial State where the armed clashes occur', or even if that state is the location of the conflict, where 'the general situation is one of turmoil, civil strife and weakened State authority'.[161] In contrast with those situations, however, '[w]here the controlling State in question is an adjacent State with territorial ambitions on the State where the conflict is taking place, and the controlling State is attempting to achieve its territorial enlargement through the armed forces which it controls, it may be easier to establish the threshold' necessary to show foreign involvement sufficient to internationalise an otherwise internal conflict.[162] Based on this holding, the *Čelebići* Appeals Chamber noted that '[t]he "overall control" test could thus be fulfilled even if the armed forces acting on behalf of the "controlling State" had autonomous choices of means and tactics although participating in a common strategy along with the "controlling State"'.[163]

Chambers have also applied different international armed conflict tests to different phases of the same conflict. In *Brđanin*, for example, the Trial Chamber concluded easily that the first test was satisfied by the direct intervention of troops of the FRY in the Bosnian conflict between April and May 1992.[164] More difficult, however, was the question of whether the conflict remained international in character for the remaining seven months of that year, the rest of the period at issue in the indictment. The Chamber found that both prongs of the second test – overall control – had been satisfied, because the FRY 'provided considerable quantities of military equipment, fuel and ammunition to the VRS', and furnished other support through paying salaries and pensions, and training VRS military personnel;[165] and because the civilian and military authorities of the FRY continued to exert decisive influence over the planning, coordination, and execution of the strategy to expand the territory that would be occupied by Serbs and prevent it from being incorporated

[161] *Tadić* Appeal Judgement, *supra* note 112, paras. 138, 139.

[162] *Ibid*., para. 140. For other applications of the 'overall control' test, see, e.g., *Kordić and Čerkez* Trial Judgement, *supra* note 57, paras. 111–145 (relying on evidence that Croatia had provided training and logistical support to the Croatian Defence Council (HVO) since 1992, including shipments of military equipment; and that the commander of all Croatian army units on the southern frontier with Bosnia and Herzegovina had appointed officers to the defence command of Tomislavgrad for the purpose of achieving 'effective, operational and secure command' in HVO units, had appointed an officer as commander with the authorities of co-ordinating and commanding forces in the Central Bosnia region, had established command posts in Bosnia and Herzegovina, and generally exerted leadership and influence throughout the conflict), affirmed in *Kordić and Čerkez* Appeal Judgement, *supra* note 101, paras. 313, 361–374; *Prosecutor* v. *Delalić, Mucić, Delić, and Landžo*, Case No. IT-96-21-A *bis*, Judgement, 20 February 2001 ('*Čelebići* Appeal Judgement'), para. 26; *Aleksovski* Appeal Judgement, *supra* note 151, paras. 131–134.

[163] *Čelebići* Appeal Judgement, *supra* note 162, para. 47. See also *Kordić and Čerkez* Trial Judgement, *supra* note 57, paras. 133–144 (discussing Croatian President Tuđman's territorial aspirations and the ties between him and the leadership of the Bosnian Croats, factors which it found lent credibility to the Prosecution's theory of Croatian involvement and intervention in the conflict), affirmed in *Kordić and Čerkez* Appeal Judgement, *supra* note 101, paras. 361–374.

[164] *Brđanin* Trial Judgement, *supra* note 111, para. 144 & nn. 372–374 (noting that the FRY formally came into existence as a state in late April 1992, and indirectly noting that Bosnia and Herzegovina was independent by then).

[165] *Ibid*., paras. 145–147.

into an independent Bosnia and Herzegovina.[166] Consequently, the Trial Chamber concluded that the armed conflict that took place in the Autonomous Region of the Krajina in Bosnia and Herzegovina was international in nature throughout the entire indictment period.[167]

Knowledge of the nature of the armed conflict

The physical perpetrator or other relevant actor knew of the factual circumstances that rendered the armed conflict international in character.

Although the ICTY's jurisprudence on the elements of international armed conflict war crimes dates from the earliest decisions of the Tribunal, it was not until late 2004 that any chamber specifically addressed the question of whether knowledge of the nature of the armed conflict is also a general requirement for grave breaches under Article 2 of the ICTY Statute. This lag is somewhat surprising, given that a similar requirement of the context in which the alleged offence occurs has been a general requirement for crimes against humanity, another category of international crimes within the jurisdiction of the Tribunal, since the first trial judgement on the merits.[168]

The first mention of a similar knowledge requirement for war crimes appeared in the *Kordić and Čerkez* Appeal Judgement. On appeal, the accused Kordić argued that he should not have been convicted for grave breaches of the Geneva Conventions on the basis of the *Tadić* overall control test, because 'the *Tadić* Appeal Judgement was rendered five years after the relevant events in this case and … at that time he could not have known that the conflict would later be deemed to be of an international character'.[169] Rejecting this argument, the Appeals Chamber held that international criminal law 'does not require that an accused knew the specific *legal* definition of each element of a crime he committed'; instead, '[i]t suffices that he was aware of the

[166] See *ibid*., paras. 150–154 (describing the evidence that supported its conclusion, including the shared military objective, coordination on strategic policy, and the lack of any real distinction between the VRS and the troops of the FRY. See also *Blaškić* Trial Judgement, *supra* note 57, paras. 108–110 (similar finding of shared goals between the HVO and Croatia); *ibid*., paras. 114–119 (relying on shared personnel between HV and HVO, coordination between Bosnian Croats and Croatian government, and the influence of the Croatian government over the membership of Bosnian Croat leadership and its policies).

[167] *Brđanin* Trial Judgement, *supra* note 111, para. 154, affirmed in *Brđanin* Appeal Judgement, *supra* note 120, para. 256. See also *Čelebići* Trial Judgement, *supra* note 67, paras. 224, 227, 231 (holding that, as the factual situation under consideration was 'characterised by the breakdown of previous state boundaries and the creation of new ones … the question which [arose was] one of continuity of control of particular forces' and finding that, despite the purported withdrawal of its troops, '[t]he FRY maintained its support of the Bosnian Serbs and their army and exerted substantial influence over their operations'), affirmed in *Čelebići* Appeal Judgement, *supra* note 162, para. 48 (upholding the Trial Chamber's application of a 'continuity of control' test as 'entirely consistent with the previous jurisprudence of the Tribunal' on overall control).

[168] See *Tadić* Trial Judgement, *supra* note 103, para. 659 (holding that 'the perpetrator must know that there is an attack on the civilian population, [and] know that his act fits in with the attack' in order for his offence to constitute a crime against humanity). For more on these and the other general requirements for crimes against humanity, see generally Chapter 2, section 2.2.2.

[169] *Kordić and Čerkez* Appeal Judgement, *supra* note 101, para. 303 (citing Kordić's appeal brief).

factual circumstances, *e.g.* that a foreign state was involved in the armed conflict. It is thus not required that Kordić could make a correct legal evaluation as to the international character of the armed conflict.'[170]

As discussed above,[171] this holding was reinforced eighteen months later in the *Naletilić and Martinović* Appeal Judgement, in which the Appeals Chamber concluded that fundamental principles of international criminal law required that the prosecution prove knowledge of the nature of the armed conflict in order for a trial chamber to conclude that an international armed conflict war crime was committed:

> The principle of individual guilt … requires that fundamental characteristics of a war crime be mirrored in the perpetrator's mind. In this context, it is useful to remark that, in the case of crimes falling under Article 2 of the Statute, there has to be a nexus between the act of the accused and the international armed conflict. It is illogical to say that there is such a nexus unless it is proved that the accused has been aware of the factual circumstances concerning the nature of the hostilities.[172]

Drawing the parallel to the similar requirement for crimes against humanity, the Chamber instructed that 'the Prosecution has to show that the accused *knew* that his crimes had a nexus to an international armed conflict, or at least that he had knowledge of the factual circumstances later bringing the Judges to the conclusion that the armed conflict was an international one'.[173]

Here again,[174] the Appeals Chamber's interchangeable use of the terms 'accused' and 'perpetrator' is misleading, and incorrectly assumes that as a general rule, the accused and the physical perpetrator are one and the same person. From the jurisprudence on the nexus requirement, however, it is clear that the connection must exist between the underlying offence – that is, the conduct of the physical perpetrator, regardless of whether that person is also the accused on trial – and the armed conflict.[175] Moreover, although the perpetrator's knowledge that the underlying offence had this nexus, and of the factual circumstances establishing the international nature of the armed conflict, would be *sufficient* to render the offence

[170] *Ibid.*, para. 311 (emphasis in original). [171] See *supra* text accompanying notes 117–118.

[172] *Naletilić and Martinović* Appeal Judgement, *supra* note 96, para. 118. See also *infra* text accompanying notes 473–482 (discussing the rejection of this particular aspect of the knowledge requirement by the drafters of the ICC Elements of Crimes).

[173] *Ibid.* But see *supra* note 124 (noting that no subsequent trial or appeal judgement has since applied or reprised the holding that knowledge that the underlying offence has a nexus to the armed conflict is an element of the crime). Unlike violations of the laws or customs of war under Article 3 of the ICTY Statute, see *infra* section 4.2.1.5.4, it appears that no ICTY judgement has explicitly held that knowledge of the protected status of the victims or property is an element of grave breaches. If the jurisprudence were extended in this manner, it would be consistent with the ICTY Appeals Chamber's recent emphasis on knowledge of the factual circumstances defining a war crime as an element of the crime itself.

[174] See *supra* text accompanying notes 121–123 (discussing this confusion in the context of the requirement that someone have knowledge of the existence of the armed conflict).

[175] See generally *supra* section 4.2.1.2.

an international armed conflict war crime if the other requirements for this category are satisfied, such knowledge should not be *necessary*. There are clearly circumstances in which the physical perpetrator would not be aware of the factual circumstances that render the armed conflict international in character, but another relevant actor[176] involved in the commission of the crime has this knowledge, especially if the other relevant actor were of higher rank than the foot soldier who physically commits the underlying offence.[177] If that knowledgeable relevant actor is the actual author of the crime, it would be illogical and inconsistent with the purposes of international criminal law to hold that no grave breach has occurred simply because the foot soldier was ignorant of the involvement of a foreign state in the conflict.

4.2.1.3.2 The protected persons or property requirement

The individuals or property targeted in the underlying offences are protected under the Geneva Conventions of 1949.

One of the additional general requirements for grave breaches of the Geneva Conventions is that the targets of the underlying offences must be accorded protected status under those treaties. Each of the four Geneva Conventions identifies the conditions under which a person or object is protected by its provisions.[178] Broadly speaking, three of the four Conventions define protected persons by focusing on the subset of the individuals in the armed forces that corresponds to the purpose of that particular Convention.[179] The fourth Convention protects

[176] See *supra* note 123 for an explanation of this term of art.

[177] See, e.g., *Naletilić and Martinović* Appeal Judgement, *supra* note 96, para. 122 (concluding that, 'in light of… Naletilić's and Martinović's *status as military commanders* and their active involvement in the conflict in the Mostar area, it would not have been reasonable to conclude that they were unaware of the participation of Croatian troops in that conflict') (emphasis added).

[178] See *generally Tadić* Jurisdiction Appeal Decision, *supra* note 4, para. 81; see also *Brđanin* Trial Judgement, *supra* note 111, para. 125 & n. 322.

[179] These groups of individuals are defined in all three Conventions as:

(1) Members of the armed forces of a Party to the conflict as well as members of militias or volunteer corps forming part of such armed forces.

(2) Members of other militias and members of other volunteer corps, including those of organized resistance movements, belonging to a Party to the conflict and operating in or outside their own territory, even if this territory is occupied, provided that such militias or volunteer corps, including such organized resistance movements, fulfil the following conditions:

(a) that of being commanded by a person responsible for his subordinates;
(b) that of having a fixed distinctive sign recognizable at a distance;
(c) that of carrying arms openly;
(d) that of conducting their operations in accordance with the laws and customs of war.

(3) Members of regular armed forces who profess allegiance to a Government or an authority not recognized by the Detaining Power.

(4) Persons who accompany the armed forces without actually being members thereof, such as civil members of military aircraft crews, war correspondents, supply contractors, members of labour units or of services responsible for the welfare of the armed forces, provided that they have received authorization from the armed forces which they accompany.

civilian persons.[180] For all four Conventions, protected property is generally restricted to the real and personal property belonging to that Convention's protected persons or which is necessary to their tasks.

For example, under Geneva Convention I – which focuses on the care of ill and injured members of the armed forces in the field – protected persons are defined as the wounded and sick in the categories of persons belonging to the armed forces,[181] and personnel treating or assisting those wounded and sick;[182] while protected property is restricted to fixed medical establishments and mobile medical units; buildings and material related to those establishments or units; the real and personal property of aid societies; and medical transports.[183] For Geneva Convention II, which focuses on ill, injured, or shipwrecked members of the armed forces at sea, protected persons are defined as 'the wounded, sick and shipwrecked *at sea* belonging to' the same categories,[184] and religious, medical, and hospital personnel of hospital ships and their crews, or who are otherwise assigned to the medical or spiritual care of those wounded, sick, or shipwrecked persons.[185] Property protected under this Convention includes hospital ships, lifeboats, and small craft used for coastal rescue operations, as well as their fixed coastal installations.[186] Geneva Convention III protects prisoners of war, defined as persons belonging to one of the enumerated categories who have fallen into the power of the enemy;[187] it does not specifically protect any real or personal property.

As the official commentaries to the Geneva Conventions make clear, however, the enumeration of persons belonging to the armed forces – the broad categories with reference to which protected persons are defined – is of varying importance in the first three Conventions. In Geneva Conventions I and II, this listing in each treaty's Article 13 'is of purely theoretical value', because 'Article 13 has its origin, and finds its real significance, in the Convention relative to the Treatment of Prisoners of War'.[188] In the latter treaty, Geneva Convention III, the listing 'is constitutive in character; and the enumeration which it gives is comprehensive'; as a

(5) Members of crews, including masters, pilots and apprentices of the merchant marine and the crews of civil aircraft of the Parties to the conflict, who do not benefit by more favourable treatment under any other provisions in international law.
(6) Inhabitants of a non-occupied territory who on the approach of the enemy spontaneously take up arms to resist the invading forces, without having had time to form themselves into regular armed units, provided they carry arms openly and respect the laws and customs of war.

See Geneva Convention I, *supra* note 3, Art. 13; Geneva Convention II, *supra* note 3, Art. 13; Geneva Convention III, *supra* note 3, Art. 4.

[180] Indeed, its full title is the Convention Relative to the Protection of Civilian Persons in Time of War. See *supra* note 3.

[181] See Geneva Convention I, *supra* note 3, Art. 13. [182] *Ibid*., Arts. 24–26. [183] *Ibid*., Arts. 19, 33–35.

[184] See Geneva Convention II, *supra* note 3, Art. 13. [185] *Ibid*., Arts. 36–37. [186] *Ibid*., Arts. 22, 24–27.

[187] See Geneva Convention III, *supra* note 3, Art. 4.

[188] See Jean Pictet (ed.), *Commentary I Geneva Convention for the Amelioration of the Condition of the Wounded and Sick in Armed Forces in the Field* (1952) ('ICRC Commentary to Geneva Convention I'), pp. 145, 146; Jean Pictet (ed.), *Commentary II Geneva Convention for the Amelioration of the Condition of the Wounded, Sick and Shipwrecked Members of Armed Forces at Sea* (1960) ('ICRC Commentary to Geneva Convention II'), pp. 95, 97.

result, '[i]f an individual not belonging to one of the categories specified is captured after committing hostile acts, he may find himself denied the right to be treated as a prisoner of war, not to mention the punishments which may be inflicted on him'.[189] In contrast, reference to these categories in the first two Conventions is merely illustrative, and a belligerent cannot 'refrain from respecting a wounded person, or … deny him the requisite treatment, even where he does not belong to one of the categories specified in the Article. Any wounded person, whoever he may be, must be treated by the enemy in accordance with the Geneva Convention'.[190]

ICTY chambers have long accepted these definitions of protected persons and property,[191] but the Tribunal's decisions and judgements have departed slightly from the terms of the treaties and their commentaries when it comes to the persons protected by Geneva Convention IV, which is focused on the protection of civilians during armed conflict. Consistent with the Convention, ICTY trial and appeal chambers have held that persons protected by this treaty are those who, while not protected under any of the other three Conventions, 'find themselves, in case of a conflict or occupation, in the hands of a Party to the conflict or Occupying Power of which they are not nationals',[192] or who are 'regularly and solely engaged in the operation and administration of civilian hospitals'.[193] Under ICTY jurisprudence, however, protected persons are not defined with reference to the strict requirement of nationality, but rather 'the more realistic bonds demonstrating effective allegiance to a party to a conflict, such as ethnicity'.[194] The *Tadić* Appeals Chamber affirmed that a legal approach 'hinging on substantial relations more than on formal bonds, becomes all the more important in present-day international armed conflicts', in which 'ethnicity rather than nationality may become the grounds for allegiance'; accordingly, 'not only the text and the drafting history of the Convention but also, and more importantly, the Convention's object and purpose suggest that allegiance to a Party to the conflict and, correspondingly, control by this Party over persons

[189] ICRC Commentary to Geneva Convention I, *supra* note 188, p. 145; ICRC Commentary to Geneva Convention II, *supra* note 188, pp. 95–96.

[190] ICRC Commentary to Geneva Convention I, *supra* note 188, p. 145; ICRC Commentary to Geneva Convention II, *supra* note 188, p. 96.

[191] See *Tadić* Jurisdiction Appeal Decision, *supra* note 4, para. 81 (concluding that the concept of protected persons under the first three Geneva Conventions must cover the persons mentioned in the articles specified above, and must extend to at least the property mentioned in the respective articles listed above). Accord, e.g., *Blaškić* Appeal Judgement, *supra* note 96, para. 172; *Brđanin* Trial Judgement, *supra* note 111, para. 121; *Simić et al.* Trial Judgement, *supra* note 96, para. 105; *Naletilić and Martinović* Trial Judgement, *supra* note 57, para. 176.

[192] Geneva Convention IV, *supra* note 3, Art. 4.

[193] *Ibid.*, Art. 20. See, e.g., *Tadić* Jurisdiction Appeal Decision, *supra* note 4, para. 81 (concluding that Articles 4 and 20 of Geneva Convention IV describe the persons protected under that treaty); *Naletilić and Martinović* Trial Judgement, *supra* note 57, para. 203 (focusing on Article 4 because the prosecution apparently relied solely on that provision).

[194] *Brđanin* Trial Judgement, *supra* note 111, para. 125; accord *Kordić and Čerkez* Appeal Judgement, *supra* note 101, paras. 328–331; *Blaškić* Appeal Judgement, *supra* note 96, paras. 172–176; *Čelebići* Appeal Judgement, *supra* note 162, paras. 83, 98; *Naletilić and Martinović* Trial Judgement, *supra* note 57, para. 207; *Blaškić* Trial Judgement, *supra* note 57, paras. 125–133.

in a given territory, may be regarded as the crucial test'.[195] Under this allegiance test, the *Aleksovski* Appeals Chamber noted, 'Article 4 [of Geneva Convention IV] may be given a wider construction so that a person may be accorded protected status, notwithstanding the fact that he is of the same nationality as his captors'.[196]

Article 4(2) of Geneva Convention IV contains exceptions to the category of persons protected by the Convention's provisions. Among those exceptions is the provision that 'nationals of a co-belligerent State … shall not be regarded as protected persons while the State of which they are nationals has normal diplomatic representation in the State in whose hands they are'. In *Kordić and Čerkez*, the accused argued that, by reason of this exception, the Bosnian Muslim victims were not protected persons because Croatia and Bosnia and Herzegovina were co-belligerents in a conflict with the Serbs. The Trial Chamber rejected the argument, noting that the indictment was concerned with a conflict between Bosnian Croats and Bosnian Muslims within Bosnia and Herzegovina, and concluding that 'in respect of that conflict, Bosnia and Herzegovina and Croatia were plainly not co-belligerents'.[197] The Appeals Chamber took a different approach, relying instead on the Trial Chamber's conclusion that the conflict was internationalised due to Croatia's overall control over the Bosnian Croat armed forces (HVO). According to that reasoning, 'Croatia and Bosnia and Herzegovina could therefore be considered belligerents pursuant to Article 4(2) of Geneva Convention IV. This, in itself, establishes that they were not in alliance as co-belligerents within the meaning of Article 4(2) for the purpose of crimes arising out of the conflict in Central Bosnia.'[198]

The protections extended by Geneva Convention IV to property include the prohibitions against pillage and reprisals against the property of protected persons.[199] They cover civilian hospitals and their material and stores;[200] medical

[195] *Tadić* Appeal Judgement, *supra* note 112, para. 166.

[196] *Aleksovski* Appeal Judgement, *supra* note 151, paras. 151–152. Accord *Čelebići* Trial Judgement, *supra* note 67, paras. 263, 262 (concluding that '[t]he provisions of domestic legislation on citizenship in a situation of violent State succession cannot be determinative of the protected status of persons caught up in conflicts which ensue from such events', and holding that the Bosnian Serb victims in the camp had a different nationality from their captors for the purposes of international humanitarian law because '[it was] possible to regard the Bosnian Serbs as acting on behalf of the FRY in its continuing armed conflict against the authorities of Bosnia and Herzegovina'), affirmed in *Čelebići* Appeal Judgement, *supra* note 162, para. 97 (upholding the Trial Chamber's 'broad[,] … purposive, and ultimately realistic' approach as consistent with the *Tadić* reasoning, and noting that the Trial Chamber 'rejected an approach based upon formal national bonds in favour of an approach which accords due emphasis to the object and purpose of the Geneva Conventions').

[197] *Kordić and Čerkez* Trial Judgement, *supra* note 57, para. 157.

[198] *Kordić and Čerkez* Appeal Judgement, *supra* note 101, para. 376. Similar reasoning underlay the *Blaškić* Trial Chamber's conclusion that Croatia and Bosnia and Herzegovina were not co-belligerents with regard to the conflict in central Bosnia, although that Chamber went further, noting that 'it seems obvious if only from the number of casualties they inflicted on each other that the ABiH and the HVO did not act towards each other within the CBOZ [Central Bosnia conflict zone] in the manner that co-belligerent States should'. *Blaškić* Trial Judgement, *supra* note 57, para. 142, affirmed in *Blaškić* Appeal Judgement, *supra* note 96, paras. 183–189. See also *Blaškić* Appeal Judgement, *supra* note 96, paras. 175–177 (rejecting Blaškić's argument that the Bosnian Muslim victims were not protected persons on the ground, *inter alia*, that the HVO, in whose hands the victims found themselves, were *de facto* armed forces of Croatia).

[199] Geneva Convention IV, *supra* note 3, Art. 33. [200] *Ibid.*, Arts. 18, 57.

transports on land and sea for wounded and sick civilians;[201] aircraft used for medical transport of civilians and related material;[202] consignments of medical and hospital stores, objects necessary for religious worship intended only for civilians, and consignments of essential foodstuffs, clothing and tonics intended for children under fifteen, expectant mothers, and maternity cases;[203] real or personal property belonging individually or collectively to private persons, or to the state, or to other public authorities, or to social or cooperative organisations ('Article 53 property');[204] and humanitarian aid, such as consignments of foodstuffs, medical supplies, and clothing.[205]

The official commentary to Geneva Convention IV states that the protection extended to Article 53 property is restricted to objects located within occupied territories.[206] Noting this restriction, the *Blaškić* Trial Chamber concluded that the property of Bosnian Muslims located within the enclaves dominated by the HVO was protected because, by virtue of the conclusion that the conflict was internationalised,[207] Croatia's overall control over the HVO meant that it was an occupying power within the meaning of the Convention.[208] This holding was firmly rejected, however, by the *Naletilić and Martinović* Trial Chamber, which was the first *ad hoc* chamber to present a detailed consideration of the elements that characterised a state of occupation under international law. The Trial Judgement held that:

> there is an essential distinction between the determination of a state of occupation and that of the existence of an international armed conflict. ... A further degree of control is required to establish occupation[, which] is defined as a transitional period following invasion and preceding the agreement on the cessation of hostilities. This distinction imposes more onerous duties on an occupying power than on a party to an international armed conflict.[209]

Citing the commentary to Geneva Convention IV, the *Naletilić and Martinović* Trial Chamber concluded that in the absence of a definition of the term 'occupied territories' in that Convention, the controlling law on the definition of occupation

201 *Ibid.*, Art. 21. 202 *Ibid.*, Art. 22. 203 *Ibid.*, Art. 23. 204 *Ibid.*, Art. 53. 205 *Ibid.*, Art. 59.

206 See generally Jean Pictet (ed.), *Commentary IV Geneva Convention Relative to the Protection of Civilian Persons in Time of War* (1958) ('ICRC Commentary on Geneva Convention IV'), p. 301.

207 See *supra* text accompanying note 159.

208 *Blaškić* Trial Judgement, *supra* note 57, paras. 148–150. This particular holding was not reviewed in the Appeal Judgment in this case, though the Appeals Chamber did affirm the Trial Chamber's conclusion that the Bosnian Muslims were protected persons within the meaning of the Convention because they 'were held captive by the HVO... [which] was operating *de facto* as Croatia's armed forces, [and so the] victims found themselves in the hands of a Party to the conflict of which they were not nationals.' *Blaškić* Appeal Judgement, *supra* note 96, para. 175.

209 *Naletilić and Martinović* Trial Judgement, *supra* note 57, para. 214. See also *Kordić and Čerkez* Trial Judgement, *supra* note 57, para. 337. The affirmation of at least part of the *Blaškić* Trial Chamber's rationale in the *Blaškić* Appeal Judgement, see *supra* note 208, does not resolve the *Blaškić–Naletilić and Martinović* dispute, however, because the latter Trial Chamber specifically distinguished between the rules applicable to protected property and the rules applicable to protected persons. See *infra* notes 213–217.

was contained in the Regulations annexed to Hague Convention IV of 1907.[210] The 1907 Hague Regulations define occupied territory as that which 'is actually placed under the authority of the hostile army', and clarify that '[t]he occupation extends only to the territory where such authority had been established and can be exercised'.[211] In adopting this definition for the purposes of evaluating whether particular property is protected under Geneva Convention IV, the *Naletilić and Martinović* Trial Judgement also held:

> The law of occupation only applies to those areas actually controlled by the occupying power and ceases to apply where the occupying power no longer exercises an actual authority over the occupied area. As a result, the Chamber finds that it must determine on a case by case basis whether this degree of control was established at the relevant times and in the relevant places. There is no requirement that an entire territory be occupied, provided that the isolated areas in which the authority of the occupied power is still functioning are effectively cut off from the rest of the occupied territory.[212]

The Trial Chamber concluded, however, that the application of the law of occupation to a civilian population was different than its application to property.[213] Quoting extensively from and relying heavily on the official commentary to the treaty, the *Naletilić and Martinović* Chamber held that 'the application of the law of occupation as it [a]ffects "individuals" as civilians protected under Geneva Convention IV does not require that the occupying power have actual authority. For the purposes of those individuals' rights,' the protections arising from the law of occupation apply immediately 'upon their falling into "the hands of the occupying power"'.[214] Consequently, where the charges against the accused concerned civilians, the Chamber considered that the victims were protected by the Convention 'from the moment they fell into the hands of the opposing power, regardless of the stage of the hostilities'; the opposing power in this context being defined as a party to the conflict to whom the civilians in question owed no allegiance.[215] The Chamber also noted that, for civilians in an international armed conflict, 'in the hands of' includes 'finding themselves on the territory controlled by that party'.[216] Where the charges concerned the alleged destruction of property, however, the Chamber applied the actual authority test of the Hague Regulations.[217]

[210] *Naletilić and Martinović* Trial Judgement, *supra* note 57, para. 215 (noting that these Regulations were set forth in annexes to the Hague Conventions of 1899 and 1907 concerning the laws and customs of war on land, and have attained the status of customary international law). Accord *Brđanin* Trial Judgement, *supra* note 111, para. 638 & n. 1632; *Kordić and Čerkez* Trial Judgement, *supra* note 57, paras. 337–339. See also *supra* text accompanying notes 50–51 (discussing the content and status of the Regulations).

[211] 1907 Hague Regulations, *supra* note 6, Article 42, quoted in *Naletilić and Martinović* Trial Judgement, *supra* note 57, para. 216.

[212] *Naletilić and Martinović* Trial Judgement, *supra* note 57, para. 216. See also *ibid.*, para. 217 (outlining certain guidelines, based on the Hague Regulations, to assist the determination of whether the authority of the occupying power has been established).

[213] *Ibid.*, para. 219. [214] *Ibid.*, paras. 219–221 (quotation at para. 221).

[215] *Ibid.*, paras. 207, 222 (quotation at para. 222). [216] See *ibid*, para. 208. [217] *Ibid.*, para. 222.

The conflict between the interpretations of the *Blaškić* and *Naletilić and Martinović* Trial Judgements was neither discussed nor resolved by the ICTY Appeals Chamber in the appeal judgement in either case,[218] and it does not appear that any subsequent jurisprudence has attempted to reconcile the disparate approaches.

4.2.1.4 Additional general requirement for violations of Common Article 3 and Additional Protocol II under Article 4 of the ICTR Statute: war crimes committed in non-international armed conflict

The victim was not actively participating in the hostilities at the time of the underlying offence.

Any crimes prosecuted under Article 4 of the ICTR Statute must meet the two common general requirements for war crimes described above: the existence of an armed conflict and a nexus between the underlying offence and the armed conflict.[219] In addition, by virtue of the invocation of Common Article 3 and Additional Protocol II, in order to constitute a crime punishable under this ICTR provision, an underlying offence must be committed against persons taking no active part in the hostilities, including former fighters and persons *hors de combat*.[220] As the *Semanza* Trial Chamber explained, '[t]o take a direct part in hostilities means … to engage in acts of war that strike at personnel or equipment of the enemy armed forces'.[221] Finally, even though ICTY jurisprudence has long established

[218] See *Blaškić* Appeal Judgement, *supra* note 96, paras. 167–189 (discussing the grounds of appeal raised in connection with the grave breaches convictions, which did not include a challenge to the interpretation of occupied territory); *Naletilić and Martinović* Appeal Judgement, *supra* note 96, paras. 106–122 (same).

[219] See *supra* sections 4.2.1.1–4.2.1.2; see also *Rutaganda* Trial Judgement, *supra* note 103, para. 94 (observing that 'conflicts covered by Additional Protocol II have a higher intensity threshold than Common Article 3' and that, as a result, '[i]f an internal armed conflict meets the material conditions of Additional Protocol II, it then also automatically satisfies the threshold requirements of the broader Common Article 3').

[220] See, e.g., Common Article 3, *supra* note 3 (protecting 'persons taking no active part in the hostilities, including members of armed forces who have laid down their arms and those placed *hors de combat* by sickness, wounds, detention, or any other cause'); Additional Protocol II, *supra* note 3, Art. 4 (protecting 'all persons who do not take a direct part or who have ceased to take part in hostilities'); *Akayesu* Trial Judgement, *supra* note 67, para. 629 (holding that the terms in Common Article 3 and Article 4 of Additional Protocol II 'are so similar that … they may be treated as synonymous'); *Prosecutor* v. *Bagosora, Kabiligi, Nsengiyumva, and Ntabakuze*, Case No. ICTR-98-41-T, Decision on Motions for Judgement of Acquittal, 27 February 2005 ('*Military I* 98 *bis* Decision'), para. 36 (noting that there are 'three prerequisites for the applicability of the crimes enumerated in Article 4(1)', including the two common general requirements discussed in sections 4.2.1.1–4.2.1.2 *supra*, and that 'the victims were not directly taking part in the hostilities at the time of the alleged violation'); accord, e.g., *Kamuhanda* Trial Judgement, *supra* note 147, para. 730; *Semanza* Trial Judgement, *supra* note 97, para. 366 (concurring with ICTY precedent that these provisions cover '*any* individual not taking part in the hostilities') (emphasis in original); *Cyangugu* Trial Judgement, *supra* note 109, para. 766; *Prosecutor* v. *Bagilishema*, Case No. ICTR-95-1A-T, Judgement, 7 June 2001, paras. 103–104; *Musema* Trial Judgement, *supra* note 97, para. 280; *Rutaganda* Trial Judgement, *supra* note 103, para. 101; *Kayishema and Ruzindana* Trial Judgment, *supra* note 103, para. 179; *Military II* 98 *bis* Decision, *supra* note 109, para. 38. ICTY chambers have also held that for any charge based on Common Article 3, the prosecution must establish that the victims satisfied this requirement. See, e.g., *Čelebići* Appeal Judgement, *supra* note 162, para. 420; *Krajišnik* Trial Judgement, *supra* note 120, para. 847.

[221] *Semanza* Trial Judgement, *supra* note 97, para. 366. Accord, e.g., *Rutaganda* Trial Judgement, *supra* note 103, para. 99 (similar definition, though describing the 'acts of war' as those 'which by their nature and purpose are likely to cause actual harm').

that Common Article 3, at least, applies to both international and non-international armed conflicts,[222] ICTR chambers have consistently held that their jurisdiction over war crimes is limited to those committed in non-international armed conflicts.[223]

Applying these requirements to the evidence presented at trial, the *Cyangugu* Trial Chamber took judicial notice of the existence of an internal armed conflict in Rwanda between 1 January and 17 July 1994;[224] found that there was a nexus between that armed conflict and at least some of the underlying offences charged;[225] and concluded that the accused Samuel Imanishimwe was guilty of violence to life, health, and physical or mental well-being under Article 4(a) of the ICTR Statute for the murder, torture, and cruel treatment of Tutsi civilian refugees who were not actively participating in the hostilities.[226] These convictions were partially set aside on appeal after the ICTR Appeals Chamber concluded that Imanishimwe 'was not informed that he had to defend himself against a charge alleging responsibility as a superior for the Gashirabwoba massacre' – a crucial incident underlying these convictions – because this circumstance 'rendered the proceedings unfair'.[227]

Although Article 4 is, by its terms, a non-exhaustive list of qualifying underlying offences, it has not been treated as such by the ICTR Prosecutors or its chambers; none of the approximately dozen cases in which war crimes charges have been brought has involved allegations of any conduct that is not alleged to fall within the underlying offences specifically enumerated in the subparagraphs of Article 4.[228]

222 See *infra* text accompanying notes 242–244. ICTY chambers have also implicitly adopted this additional general requirement of the status of the victims for all underlying offences alleged to arise from violations of Common Article 3. See *infra* text accompanying note 260.

223 See, e.g., *Rutaganda* Trial Judgement, *supra* note 103, para. 90 ('Offences alleged to be covered by Article 4 of the Statute must, as a preliminary matter, have been committed in the context of a conflict of a non-international character satisfying the requirements of Common Article 3 [or] Additional Protocol II[.]'); accord *Cyangugu* Trial Judgement, *supra* note 109, para. 766; *Semanza* Trial Judgement, *supra* note 97, para. 354; *Military II* 98 *bis* Decision, *supra* note 109, para. 38. See also *supra* text accompanying note 10 (noting that the ICTR's jurisdiction is interpreted as being limited in such a manner); Chapter 6, text accompanying note 11 (same). But see *Akayesu* Trial Judgement, *supra* note 67, para. 604 (acknowledging that '[t]he Security Council, when delimiting the subject-matter jurisdiction of the ICTR, incorporated violations of international humanitarian law which may be committed in the context of both an international and an internal armed conflict' but noting that 'when the Security Council added Additional Protocol II to the subject matter jurisdiction of the ICTR, this could suggest that the Security Council deemed the conflict in Rwanda as an Additional Protocol II conflict', that is, non-international in character).

224 See *Cyangugu* Trial Judgement, *supra* note 109, para. 767.

225 See *ibid.*, para. 793 (discussing Count 13 of the indictment, and concluding that the nexus requirement was satisfied because, *inter alia*, 'the soldiers' actions were motivated by their search for enemy combatants and those associated with them or, at least, that their actions were carried out under the pretext of such a search', and a notorious massacre of refugees by soldiers and others was also committed under the guise of the armed conflict).

226 *Ibid.*, paras. 794–802.

227 See *Prosecutor* v. *Ntagerura, Bagambiki, and Imanishimwe*, Case No. ICTR-99-46-A, Judgement and Sentence, 7 July 2006, para. 164. See also *ibid.*, para. 444 (otherwise upholding Imanishimwe's conviction and sentence for crimes falling under Article 4(a) of the ICTR Statute).

228 See *Prosecutor* v. *Akayesu*, Case No. ICTR-96-4-I, Amended Indictment, June 1997, Counts 6, 8, 10, 12, 15 (alleging murder, cruel treatment and outrages upon personal dignity as violations falling under subparagraphs (a) and (e)); *Prosecutor* v. *Kayishema and Ruzindana*, Case No. ICTR-95-1-I, Indictment, 11 April 1997,

4.2.1.5 Additional general requirements for violations of the laws or customs of war under Article 3 of the ICTY Statute: war crimes committed in any armed conflict

The introductory paragraph to Article 3 of the ICTY Statute provides that '[t]he International Tribunal shall have the power to prosecute persons violating the laws or customs of war',[229] and the remainder of the Article is a non-exhaustive list of offences that qualify as such violations.[230] Article 3 of the ICTY Statute differs from Article 2 of the ICTY Statute and Article 4 of the ICTR Statute in at least two significant respects: Article 3 covers offences committed in both international and non-international armed conflict,[231] and it is treated as a residual provision in the

Counts 5, 6, 11, 12, 17, 18, 23, 24 (alleging murder and serious physical injuries as violations falling under subparagraph (a)); *Prosecutor* v. *Rutaganda*, Case No. ICTR-96-3-I, Indictment, 12 February 1996, Counts 4, 6, 8 (alleging murder under subparagraph (a)); *Prosecutor* v. *Musema*, Case No. ICTR-96-13-I, Amended Indictment, 6 May 1999, Counts 8, 9 (alleging murder and rape as violations falling under subparagraphs (a) and (e)); *Prosecutor* v. *Bagilishema*, Case No. ICTR-95-1A-I, Amended Indictment, 17 September 1999, Counts 6–7 (alleging violence to life, health and physical or mental well-being of persons and outrages upon personal dignity of women as violations falling under subparagraphs (a) and (e)); *Prosecutor* v. *Ntakirutimana and Ntakirutimana*, Case No. ICTR-96-7-I, Indictment, 7 July 1998 ('Bisesero Indictment'), Count 7 (alleging violence to life, health and physical or mental well-being of persons under subparagraph (a)); *Prosecutor* v. *Semanza*, Case No. ICTR-97-20-I, Third Amended Indictment, 12 October 1999, Counts 7, 9 (alleging violence to life, health and physical or mental well-being of persons and outrages upon personal dignity as violations falling under subparagraphs (a) and (e)); *Prosecutor* v. *Niyitegeka*, Case No. ICTR-96-14-I, Amended Indictment, 28 February 2001, Counts 9–10 (same); *Prosecutor* v. *Kajelijeli*, Case No. ICTR-98-44A-I, Amended Indictment, 25 January 2001, Counts 10, 11 (same); *Prosecutor* v. *Kamuhanda*, Case No. ICTR-99-54-I, Indictment, 15 November 2000, Counts 8–9 (same); *Prosecutor* v. *Ntagerura*, Case No. ICTR-96-10-I, Indictment, 29 January 1998, Count 5 (alleging violence to life, health and physical or mental well-being of persons under subparagraph (a)); *Prosecutor* v. *Bagambiki and Imanishimwe*, Case No. ICTR-97-36-I, Indictment, 10 October 1997, Counts 6, 13 (same); *Prosecutor* v. *Bagosora*, Case No. ICTR-96-7-I, Indictment, 12 August 1999, Counts 10–12 (alleging murder, violence to health and to physical or mental well-being, and outrages upon personal dignity under subparagraphs (a) and (e)); *Prosecutor* v. *Ntabakuze and Kabiligi*, Case Nos. ICTR-97-34-I & ICTR-97-30-I, Amended Indictment, 13 August 1999, Counts 9–10 (alleging violence to life, health, and physical or mental well-being of persons and outrages upon personal dignity as violations falling under subparagraphs (a) and (e)); *Prosecutor* v. *Nsengiyumva*, Case No. ICTR-96-12-I, Indictment, 12 August 1999, Counts 10–11 (same); *Prosecutor* v. *Bizimungu, Ndindiliyimana, Nzuwonemeye, and Sagahutu*, Case No. ICTR-2000-56-I, Amended Indictment (Joinder), 23 August 2004, Counts 7–8 (alleging rape and humiliating and degrading treatment, all listed as instances of outrages upon personal dignity in Article 4(e)). See also Mettraux, *supra* note 151, p. 28 (noting that, in contrast to the ICTY, the ICTR 'would appear to have limited the scope of its war crimes jurisdiction to those expressly provided in the statute').

In a few of the cases, more than one accused were jointly tried under separate indictments. For a list of the cases in which war crimes have been charged at the ICTR, see *supra* note 95.

229 See *Tadić* Jurisdiction Appeal Decision, *supra* note 4, para. 87 (explaining that Article 3's 'old-fashioned' reference to 'the laws or customs of war' was intended to invoke Hague Convention IV of 1907 and the Regulations annexed thereto, but that 'the traditional laws of warfare are now more correctly termed "international humanitarian law"'). But see *supra* note 45 (noting that the United States has recently expressed a preference for the older terminology).

230 See *ibid.* ('A literal interpretation of Article 3 shows that … the enumeration of some of these violations provided in Article 3 is merely illustrative, not exhaustive.'); accord, e.g., *Kunarac et al.* Appeal Judgement, *supra* note 97, para. 187; *Aleksovski* Trial Judgement, *supra* note 88, para. 48; *Furundžija* Trial Judgement, *supra* note 67, para. 133.

231 See *Tadić* Jurisdiction Appeal Decision, *supra* note 4, para. 137; accord, e.g., *Limaj et al.* Trial Judgement, *supra* note 103, paras. 83, 92; *Halilović* Trial Judgement, *supra* note 135, para. 25; *Strugar* Trial Judgement, *supra* note 51, para. 216; *Blagojević and Jokić* Trial Judgement, *supra* note 97, para. 536; *Brđanin* Trial Judgement, *supra* note 111, para. 127.

ICTY Statute, covering all violations of international humanitarian law that do not fall within the ambit of the other articles that grant jurisdiction over crimes.[232]

There are five general requirements that must be satisfied for an offence to qualify as a violation of the laws or customs of war under Article 3.[233] Two of these general requirements, the armed conflict and nexus requirements, are common to all war crimes, and have been discussed above.[234] The remaining three requirements were first set forth in the *Tadić* interlocutory appeal decision on jurisdiction, and are therefore referred to as the *Tadić* criteria: (1) the alleged underlying offence must infringe a rule of international humanitarian law, whether customary or conventional in nature;[235] (2) the violation must be 'serious' (the 'gravity requirement');[236] and (3) the breach must give rise to individual criminal responsibility under customary or conventional international law.[237] Each of the three criteria is discussed below.

It is somewhat unclear if these criteria are merely jurisdictional prerequisites or actually elements of the crime. One requirement, that the violation must be 'serious', is intended to reflect the restriction of the ICTY's jurisdiction to the most serious breaches of international humanitarian law,[238] so this criterion appears to be more

[232] See *Tadić* Jurisdiction Appeal Decision, *supra* note 4, para. 91 ('Article 3 thus confers … jurisdiction over *any* serious offence against international humanitarian law not covered by Article[s] 2, 4 or 5 … [It] functions as a residual clause designed to ensure that no serious violation of international humanitarian law is taken away from the jurisdiction of the International Tribunal.') (emphasis in original); accord *Kunarac et al.* Appeal Judgement, *supra* note 97, para. 68; *Krajišnik* Trial Judgement, *supra* note 120, para. 842; *Hadžihasanović and Kubura* Trial Judgement, *supra* note 57, para. 17; *Halilović* Trial Judgement, *supra* note 135, para. 23; *Strugar* Trial Judgement, *supra* note 51, para. 218; *Prosecutor* v. *Galić*, Case No. IT-98-29-T, Judgement, 5 December 2003 ('*Galić* Trial Judgement'), para. 10. Compare text accompanying notes 149, 228 (noting that Article 2 of the ICTY Statute and Article 4 of the ICTR Statute have been treated as exhaustive listings, notwithstanding the terms of the latter provision).

[233] Other judgements have characterised these requirements differently, making a distinction between the two prerequisites for the applicability of Article 3 and the three or four criteria an underlying offence must fulfil to constitute a violation of international humanitarian law that is, in turn, subject to Article 3 ('*Tadić* jurisdictional criteria'). See, e.g., *Tadić* Jurisdiction Appeal Decision, *supra* note 4, para. 94; *Strugar* Trial Judgement, *supra* note 51, para. 215; see also *infra* note 235 (discussing whether there are three or four *Tadić* jurisdictional criteria).

In addition, although it would seem logical for the *Tadić* criteria to be applied only to alleged underlying offences that are not specifically enumerated in the subparagraphs of Article 3, ICTY chambers have applied the test, or specifically noted that the requirements are satisfied, with regard to all underlying offences alleged to arise under Article 3. See, e.g., *Martić* Trial Judgement, *supra* note 120, para. 46 ('Concerning the crimes of wanton destruction of villages, or devastation, and destruction or wilful damage done to institutions dedicated to education or religion, it is established in the jurisprudence of the Tribunal that the crimes meet the four *Tadić* conditions.').

[234] See *supra* sections 4.2.1.1, 4.2.1.2.

[235] *Tadić* Jurisdiction Appeal Decision, *supra* note 4, para. 94(i)–(ii). This requirement is usually expressed as two separate criteria: (1) the offence must violate a prohibition of international humanitarian law; and (2) the prohibition may be derived from either customary or conventional international law, as long as the treaties satisfy certain conditions. The first part of the second criterion simply clarifies that the source of the prohibition may be either customary or conventional international law, so this restatement treats these aspects of the *Tadić* test as two parts of a single requirement.

[236] *Ibid.*, para. 94(iii). [237] *Ibid.*, para. 94(iv).

[238] See *ibid.*, para. 90 (explaining that it is 'appropriate to take the expression "violations of the laws or customs of war" to cover serious violations of international humanitarian law' because 'various provisions, in spelling out the purpose and tasks of the International Tribunal or in defining its functions, refer to "*serious violations*" of international humanitarian law') (emphasis in original).

a jurisdictional requirement than an element of the crime.[239] The remaining two criteria, however, are clearly intended to ensure that the conduct in question is actually a crime under international law: the requirement that the conduct breach a rule of international humanitarian law ensures that the principle of *nullum crimen sine lege* is not violated, because the conduct was clearly prohibited at the time it was committed; while the requirement that the violation be subject to penal sanctions for individuals ensures that the corollary principle of *nulla poena sine lege* is similarly observed.[240] Although these criteria are questions of law, rather than the questions of fact that underlie most elements of international crimes, similar legal requirements for other crimes are treated as elements, such as the equal or similar gravity requirements for persecution or inhumane acts as crimes against humanity.[241] Accordingly, though it does not appear that any ICTY chamber has expressed it in these terms, it would be consistent with the Tribunal's general approach to the elements of crimes to require the prosecution to prove these remaining two criteria for violations of the laws or customs of war beyond reasonable doubt.

4.2.1.5.1 The alleged underlying offence infringes a rule of customary or conventional international humanitarian law ICTY prosecutors have relied heavily on Common Article 3 of the Geneva Conventions as the legal basis for violations alleged to be punishable under Article 3 of the Statute, even though the conduct charged is not specifically listed as underlying offences in the Article's subparagraphs.[242] Indeed, ICTY chambers have recognised that Common Article 3 is the core of customary international humanitarian law,[243] and that breaches of this provision that satisfy the

[239] See Mettraux, *supra* note 151, p. 50 n. 99 (noting that 'this requirement is jurisdictional only, not substantive', so it is possible that conduct not falling within the Tribunal's jurisdiction may nevertheless be a war crime).

[240] See, e.g., *Čelebići* Appeal Judgement, *supra* note 162, paras. 179–180 (affirming the *Čelebići* Trial Chamber's holding that imposing criminal responsibility for violations of Common Article 3 does not violate the principle of legality, or *nullum crimen sine lege*).

[241] See Chapter 2, text accompanying notes 398–404, 456–461 (discussing these specific requirements for these subcategories of underlying offences, that is, the elements that all offences alleged to be persecution or inhumane acts as crimes against humanity must satisfy).

[242] See, e.g., *Prosecutor* v. *Mrkšić, Radić, and Šljivančanin*, Case No. IT-95-13/1-PT, Third Amended Indictment, 15 November 2004, Counts 4, 7, 8 (alleging murder, torture, and cruel treatment as violations of the laws or customs of war); *Prosecutor* v. *Orić*, Case No. IT-03-68-PT, Third Amended Indictment, 30 June 2005, Counts 1–2 (alleging murder and cruel treatment as violations of the laws or customs of war); *Prosecutor* v. *Hadžihasanović and Kubura*, Case No. IT-01-47-PT, Third Amended Indictment, 26 September 2003, Counts 1–4 (same); *Prosecutor* v. *Halilović*, Case No. IT-01-48-PT, Indictment, 10 September 2001 (containing a single count of murder as a violation of the laws or customs of war); *Prosecutor* v. *Strugar*, Case No. IT-01-42-PT, Third Amended Indictment, 10 December 2003, Counts 1–2 (alleging murder and cruel treatment as violations of the laws or customs of war). See *supra* notes 230–232 and accompanying text (noting that the listing in Article 3's subparagraphs is not intended to be exhaustive, and that the Article is a general residual provision in the Statute, covering all serious violations of international humanitarian law not falling within other articles).

[243] See, e.g., *Čelebići* Appeal Judgement, *supra* note 162, para. 143:

> It is indisputable that common Article 3, which sets forth a minimum core of mandatory rules, reflects the fundamental humanitarian principles which underlie international humanitarian law as a whole, and upon which the Geneva Conventions in their entirety are based. These principles … had already become customary

gravity requirement automatically qualify as crimes within the jurisdiction of Article 3 of the ICTY Statute.[244]

Additional customary rules of international humanitarian law are found in other provisions of the Geneva Conventions;[245] the provisions of Hague law on international conflicts, especially Hague Convention IV and its annexed Regulations;[246] and many of the provisions of Additional Protocol II that can now be regarded as having attained customary status, because they codified existing rules, crystallised emerging rules, or were instrumental in their evolution as general principles.[247]

Rules regulating, restraining, or prohibiting certain conduct by the parties to an armed conflict may also be found in international treaties or agreements that do not represent custom.[248] For these rules, however, two additional conditions must be

> law [by 1949] … [and] were codified in common Article 3 to constitute the minimum core applicable to internal conflicts, but are so fundamental that they are regarded as governing both internal and international conflicts … These rules may thus be considered as the 'quintessence' of the humanitarian rules found in the Geneva Conventions as a whole.

Accord, e.g., *Tadić* Jurisdiction Appeal Decision, *supra* note 4, paras. 89, 134; *Blagojević and Jokić* Trial Judgement, *supra* note 97, para. 539.

244 See, e.g., *Kunarac et al.* Appeal Judgement, *supra* note 97, para. 68.

245 Note, however, that violations of certain provisions of the Geneva Conventions which have not been included in the grave breaches regime may not meet the threshold of 'seriousness' for Article 3. See, e.g., *Tadić* Jurisdiction Appeal Decision, *supra* note 4, para. 94(iii):

> Thus, for instance, the fact of a combatant simply appropriating a loaf of bread in an occupied village would not amount to a 'serious violation of international humanitarian law' although it may be regarded as falling foul of the basic principle laid down in Article 46, paragraph 1, of the Hague Regulations (and the corresponding rule of customary international law) whereby 'private property must be respected' by any army occupying an enemy territory[.]

Accord *Prosecutor* v. *Kvočka, Kos, Radić, Žigić, and Prcać*, Case No. IT-98-30-PT, Decision on Preliminary Motions filed by Mlado Radić and Miroslav Kvočka et al. Challenging Jurisdiction, 1 April 1999, paras. 9–11.

246 The offences specifically listed in Article 3 are derived from the 1907 Hague Regulations. *Tadić* Jurisdiction Appeal Decision, *supra* note 4, paras. 86–87. See also *supra* text accompanying notes 43–53, 61 (discussing Hague law).

247 See *Tadić* Jurisdiction Appeal Decision, *supra* note 4, paras. 117, 127 (the customary prohibition of means of warfare proscribed in international armed conflicts and the ban on certain methods of conducting hostilities have developed to apply also to internal conflicts); *Prosecutor* v. *Kordić and Čerkez*, Case No. IT-95-14/2-PT, Decision on the Joint Defence Motion to Dismiss the Amended Indictment for Lack of Jurisdiction Based on the Limited Jurisdictional Reach of Articles 2 and 3, 2 March 1999, paras. 30–31 (holding that although Additional Protocols I and II 'have not yet achieved the near universal participation enjoyed by the Geneva Conventions, it is not controversial that major parts of both Protocols reflect customary law' and affirming that Articles 51(2) and 52(1) of Additional Protocol I and Article 13(2) of Additional Protocol II, relating to unlawful attacks on civilians or civilian objects, have customary status); accord *Blaškić* Appeal Judgement, *supra* note 96, paras. 157–158; *Prosecutor* v. *Strugar, Jokić, and Others*, Case No. IT-01-42-AR72, Decision on Interlocutory Appeal, 22 November 2002, para. 9; *Martić* Trial Judgement, *supra* note 120, para. 45. See also *Akayesu* Trial Judgement, *supra* note 67, paras. 609–610 (holding that the 'Fundamental Guarantees' of Additional Protocol II enumerated in Article 4 of the ICTR Statute formed part of customary international law at the relevant time); *Furundžija* Trial Judgement, *supra* note 67, para. 137 (considering an argument that the entirety of the Geneva Conventions and Additional Protocols were customary international law, and concluding that it was more plausible that 'only the most important provisions of those treaties have acquired the status of general international law').

248 But see *Galić* Appeal Judgement, *supra* note 90, para. 85 (rejecting the accused-appellant's argument that a conviction under Article 3 can only be based on customary international law, but noting that 'while binding conventional international law that prohibits conduct and provides for individual criminal responsibility could provide the basis for the [ICTY's] jurisdiction, in practice the [ICTY] always ascertains that the treaty provision in question is also declaratory of custom').

satisfied for their breach to be punishable under Article 3: the agreement must have been 'unquestionably binding on the parties [to the conflict] at the time of the alleged offence', and the agreement cannot be 'in conflict with or derogate from peremptory norms of international law'.[249]

4.2.1.5.2 The violation is 'serious' The ICTY Statute restricts the Tribunal's jurisdiction to 'serious violations of international humanitarian law'.[250] Accordingly, the last criterion identified by the *Tadić* interlocutory decision is that the alleged underlying offence must breach a rule protecting important values, and the breach must involve grave consequences for the victim.[251] The alleged underlying offences that have been held to satisfy the *Tadić* criteria – including this gravity requirement – include murder;[252] cruel treatment;[253] attacks on civilians or civilian objects;[254] destruction and devastation of property, including cultural or religious property;[255] and terror.[256] The elements of these and other underlying offences are discussed below in section 4.2.2.

4.2.1.5.3 The violation of the rule entails the individual criminal responsibility of the person breaching the rule In order for the ICTY to exercise jurisdiction over an accused for an alleged breach of a rule of international humanitarian law, violation of that particular rule must give rise to individual criminal responsibility.[257] None of the additional general requirements for Article 3 is dependent upon the mental state of any

[249] *Kunarac et al.* Appeal Judgement, *supra* note 97, para. 66; accord *Tadić* Jurisdiction Appeal Decision, *supra* note 4, para. 143; *Kordić and Čerkez* Appeal Judgement, *supra* note 101, paras. 41–42; *Čelebići* Appeal Judgement, *supra* note 162, para. 111.

[250] ICTY Statute, *supra* note 2, Art. 1. See especially *Galić* Trial Judgement, *supra* note 232, para. 107:

> [T]his third condition, correctly interpreted, is not that the *rule* must be inherently 'serious', which would mean that every violation of it would also be serious, but that the alleged *violation* of the rule – that is, of a recognised humanitarian rule – must be serious for the violation to come within the jurisdiction of the Tribunal.

[251] *Tadić* Jurisdiction Appeal Decision, *supra* note 4, para. 90 (referring to the preamble of the Statute, as well as Articles 1, 9(1), 10(1), 10(2), 23(1), and 29(1)). This explanation of the gravity requirement is one of the few circumstances in which the Tribunal's jurisprudence has attempted to give substance or independent weight to the term 'serious'. Compare Chapter 2, text accompanying notes 398–400, 456–461 (discussing the equal gravity requirement and similar gravity requirement, respectively, for persecution and inhumane acts as crimes against humanity). The use of the qualifiers 'important' and 'grave' may be similarly vague, but are likely intended to give chambers the flexibility required to apply the standard to a variety of factual circumstances.

[252] See, e.g., *Hadžihasanović and Kubura* Trial Judgement, *supra* note 57, para. 29; *Halilović* Trial Judgement, *supra* note 135, para. 31; *Strugar* Trial Judgement, *supra* note 51, para. 219.

[253] See, e.g., *Hadžihasanović and Kubura* Trial Judgement, *supra* note 57, para. 29; *Strugar* Trial Judgement, *supra* note 51, para. 219.

[254] See, e.g., *Strugar* Trial Judgement, *supra* note 51, paras. 220–222, 224–226; *Galić* Trial Judgement, *supra* note 232, paras. 16, 25, 27, 29–32.

[255] See, e.g., *Hadžihasanović and Kubura* Trial Judgement, *supra* note 57, para. 38; *Strugar* Trial Judgement, *supra* note 51, paras. 227–233; *Brđanin* Trial Judgement, *supra* note 111, paras. 157–158.

[256] See *Galić* Trial Judgement, *supra* note 232, paras. 95–130, 138, affirmed on different grounds in *Galić* Appeal Judgement, *supra* note 90, paras. 86–98. For a discussion of the elements of this underlying offence as elaborated by the *Galić* Trial and Appeals Chambers, see *infra* section 4.2.2.9.

[257] *Tadić* Jurisdiction Appeal Decision, *supra* note 4, para. 94(iv). Accord, e.g., *Kunarac et al.* Appeal Judgement, *supra* note 97, para. 66; *Limaj et al.* Trial Judgement, *supra* note 103, para. 175; *Strugar* Trial Judgement, *supra* note 51, para. 218; *Galić* Trial Judgement, *supra* note 232, paras. 11, 89.

actor involved in the crime;[258] the crime is thus complete once a qualifying underlying offence has occurred in circumstances that satisfy the general requirements. The *Tadić* criteria are used to determine whether the alleged underlying offence could qualify as a crime within the ICTY's jurisdiction, and the focus of this particular general requirement is on the type of breach – one attracting criminal liability – rather than the actor committing the breach. Not all breaches of international humanitarian law are sufficiently serious to warrant criminalisation and the imposition of individual responsibility, and it is only where the breach of a particular prohibition has been made subject to individual penal sanctions that it may be prosecuted as a crime under Article 3.[259]

4.2.1.5.4 Knowledge of status of targets of underlying offences At least four ICTY trial chambers have held that, where the underlying offence arises from a breach of Common Article 3 or Additional Protocol II, the prosecution must prove that 'the perpetrator was aware or should have been aware' that the victim was not actively participating in the hostilities,[260] an approach which should apply equally to the status of objects that are protected by international humanitarian law. A requirement that an actor involved in the realisation of the crime have knowledge of the factual circumstances that render the physical perpetrator's conduct criminal under international law is consistent with the ICTY Appeals Chamber's recent approach to the general requirements for war crimes,[261] and is thus likely to be applied at the ICTR as well if the issue is squarely presented. There is no reason, however, to require that the physical perpetrator be the actor with that knowledge.[262] For example, if he is ordered to kill a number of individuals who are described to him as fighters, but the person giving those orders in fact knows that they are civilians, the physical perpetrator's ignorance may shield him from liability, but the killings should still qualify as murder under international humanitarian law and international criminal law.

4.2.2 *Underlying offences*

Several of the underlying offences of the war crimes subcategories discussed above are similar or identical to the underlying offences for the other categories of crimes

[258] Compare *supra* section 4.2.1.1.1 (knowledge of existence of armed conflict required); *supra* text accompanying notes 168–176 (knowledge of factual circumstances establishing international character of armed conflict required for grave breaches); cf. Chapter 2, section 2.2.2.6 (knowledge of context as general requirement for crimes against humanity); Chapter 2, section 2.2.3.8.1 (discriminatory intent as specific requirement for persecution as a crime against humanity).

[259] See *Tadić* Jurisdiction Appeal Decision, *supra* note 4, paras. 94(ii), 129–130.

[260] See *Halilović* Trial Judgement, *supra* note 135, para. 36; *Galić* Trial Judgement, *supra* note 232, para. 55 (noting also that in case of doubt, IHL requires fighters to consider the persons as civilians); accord *Martić* Trial Judgement, *supra* note 120, para. 47; *Krajišnik* Trial Judgement, *supra* note 120, para. 847.

[261] See *supra* section 4.2.1.1.1; text accompanying notes 168–176.

[262] See *supra* text accompanying notes 123, 174–176 (similar discussion with regard to the relevant actor for knowledge of existence and nature of armed conflict).

punishable under the Tribunals' Statutes. Where relevant, therefore, we refer the reader to discussions of those underlying offences in other chapters.

4.2.2.1 Destruction of property

Four underlying offences of war crimes in the ICTY Statute deal explicitly with destruction of property: (1) 'extensive destruction … of property, not justified by military necessity and carried out unlawfully and wantonly' in Article 2(d),[263] (2) 'wanton destruction of cities, towns or villages, or [(3)] devastation not justified by military necessity' in Article 3(b),[264] and (4) 'seizure of, destruction or wilful damage done to institutions dedicated to religion, charity and education, the arts and sciences, historic monuments and works of art and science' in Article 3(d).[265] Article 4 of the ICTR Statute does not contain an underlying offence that is expressly geared toward destruction of property,[266] and it does not appear that any such charge has been brought in a case before that Tribunal. As explained below, although definitions of these underlying offences typically include one or more aspects that are dictated by the subcategory of war crimes that is charged, they share roughly similar elements.[267]

4.2.2.1.1 Extensive destruction under Article 2(d) of ICTY Statute

The physical perpetrator(s) either intentionally caused extensive destruction of property protected under the Geneva Conventions, or acted in reckless disregard of the likelihood of such destruction.

The elements of the underlying offence in Article 2(d) are generally summarised as extensive destruction of property with either the intent to destroy or reckless disregard of the likelihood of destruction.[268] Since this underlying offence arises out of the grave breaches provisions of the Geneva Conventions, the property in question must be protected under those treaties.[269] Most of the protected property has that status regardless of its location, and its destruction is prohibited under all circumstances, but the destruction of property mentioned in Article 53 of Geneva Convention IV, which protects certain real and personal property in occupied territories,[270] is a crime only

263 Extensive appropriation of property, an underlying offence also listed in Article 2(d), is discussed in section 4.2.2.6 below.

264 This provision includes two underlying offences. See *infra* text accompanying note 280.

265 See *supra* text accompanying notes 2, 5 for the full text of Articles 2 and 3 of the ICTY Statute.

266 See *supra* text accompanying note 13 for the full text of Article 4 of the ICTR Statute.

267 See, e.g., *Hadžihasanović and Kubura* Trial Judgement, *supra* note 57, para. 41 (noting that 'the offence stipulated in Article 3(b) of the Statute is similar to that stipulated by Article 2(d) of the Statute', and that once the general requirements are set aside, 'the elements of the crimes of destruction under Articles 2(d) and 3(b) of the Statute are identical'). But see *Strugar* Trial Judgement, *supra* note 51, para. 294 (declining to reach the question of whether 'extensive' destruction under Article 2(d) is identical to 'large scale' destruction under Article 3(b)).

268 See, e.g., *Brđanin* Trial Judgement, *supra* note 111, para. 587; *Naletilić and Martinović* Trial Judgement, *supra* note 57, para. 577; *Kordić and Čerkez* Trial Judgement, *supra* note 57, para. 341; *Blaškić* Trial Judgement, *supra* note 57, para. 157.

269 See *supra* section 4.2.1.3.2.

270 See *supra* text accompanying note 204.

when not justified by military necessity.[271] The terms trial chambers use to define and describe this underlying offence are dictated by the language of Article 147 of Geneva Convention IV,[272] and judgements have relied heavily on the commentary to this Article when interpreting the scope of the protection afforded to property.[273] Although trial judgements are not very clear on this point, it appears that the requirement of 'extensive' destruction refers to the aggregate nature of the destruction of a number of different structures, not the extent of the destruction of a particular building.[274] Both the commentaries and ICTY jurisprudence are clear, however, that in certain unique circumstances, the destruction of a single building would nevertheless qualify as a grave breach.[275]

The findings in the *Brđanin* case illustrate the importance of the general requirements that characterise the different subcategories of war crimes. After reviewing the extensive evidence of destruction and appropriation of property in municipalities across Bosnia and Herzegovina, and concluding that 'Bosnian Serb forces extensively destroyed and appropriated property belonging to Bosnian Muslims and Bosnian Croats in the[se] municipalities',[276] the Trial Chamber nevertheless held that the elements of the grave breaches of extensive destruction or extensive appropriation had not been established. The Chamber first noted that '[t]he evidence shows that the property destroyed or appropriated consisted mostly of houses, business premises, vehicles, money and other valuables … [which are] not generally protected by the Geneva Conventions'; it then considered whether the destroyed or appropriated property was protected because it was situated in occupied territory.[277]

271 See, e.g., *Brđanin* Trial Judgement, *supra* note 111, para. 588; *Blaškić* Trial Judgement, *supra* note 57, para. 157. For definitions of military necessity, see *Kordić and Čerkez* Appeal Judgement, *supra* note 101, para. 686 (defining it, with reference to the Lieber Code, as 'lawful' measures 'which are indispensable for securing the ends of war'); *Strugar* Trial Judgement, *supra* note 51, para. 295 (invoking Additional Protocol I, *supra* note 3, Art. 52, and ostensibly interpreting military necessity as actions targeted at military objectives as defined by that provision); accord *Galić* Trial Judgment, *supra* note 232, para. 51.

272 See *Brđanin* Trial Judgement, *supra* note 111, para. 585. See also *ibid.* n. 1488 (referring also to Geneva Convention I, *supra* note 3, Art. 50; Geneva Convention II, *supra* note 3, Art. 51; and Geneva Convention III, *supra* note 3, Art. 130). Article 147 of Geneva Convention IV, *supra* note 3, lists the grave breaches for that Convention, including 'extensive destruction and appropriation of property, not justified by military necessity and carried out unlawfully and wantonly'.

273 See, e.g., *Brđanin* Trial Judgement, *supra* note 111, para. 587 (citing the example of the destruction of a civilian hospital as an instance where an isolated incident would qualify as extensive destruction, and relying on the commentary to Article 147, which used that example); *Naletilić and Martinović* Trial Judgement, *supra* note 57, para. 576 (same); *Blaškić* Trial Judgement, *supra* note 57, para. 157 (same).

274 See *supra* note 273 (all judgements cited therein using the example of the destruction of a civilian hospital as an exceptional circumstance in which destruction of a single building would satisfy the requirement of extensiveness).

275 See *supra* note 273. It is possible that this exception applies to all buildings with similar status to civilian hospitals, or all buildings afforded general protection under the Geneva Conventions regardless of their location. See, e.g., *Kordić and Čerkez* Trial Judgement, *supra* note 57, para. 341 (not requiring extensive destruction for this latter category of structures). ICTY jurisprudence has not included any other examples, however.

276 *Brđanin* Trial Judgement, *supra* note 111, para. 636.

277 *Ibid.*, para. 637.

After applying the actual authority test of occupation as set out in the *Naletilić and Martinović* Trial Judgement,[278] the *Brđanin* Trial Chamber concluded:

The evidence on the degree of authority exercised by the Bosnian [*sic*] armed forces over the Bosnian Krajina is, in the view of the Trial Chamber insufficient to lead it to the conclusion that a state of occupation had already been reached at the time the destruction and appropriation mentioned came to being. The Trial Chamber, therefore, cannot come to the conclusion that the property destroyed and appropriated was located in occupied territory. Consequently, there cannot be a violation of Article 2 (d) of the Statute.[279]

4.2.2.1.2 Wanton destruction and unjustified devastation under Article 3(b) of the ICTY Statute

The physical perpetrator(s) either intentionally caused destruction on a large scale, not justified by military necessity, or acted in reckless disregard of the likelihood of such destruction. For 'devastation', the result of the physical perpetrators' conduct also includes damage falling short of destruction.

Article 3(b) contains two underlying offences: 'wanton destruction' and 'unjustified devastation'.[280] The former has been defined as destruction on a large scale, not justified by military necessity, accompanied with the intent to cause such destruction or reckless disregard of the likelihood of destruction.[281] At least two trial judgements, however, have phrased the indirect intent alternative for the *mens rea* of this underlying offence as knowledge of the likelihood of the destruction, omitting any reference to recklessness.[282]

Two features of this underlying offence distinguish it from the Article 2(d) offence of extensive destruction; both stem from the application of the additional general requirements for the subcategories of war crimes, and are therefore not elements of the underlying offence as such. First, the property in question need not be specifically protected by the Geneva Conventions; instead, the fundamental principle of distinction, a cornerstone of international humanitarian law, requires only that the destruction of the property not be required by military necessity.[283] Second, unlike the real and

278 See *supra* text accompanying notes 209–217 (the *Naletilić and Martinović* Trial Judgement imposing a strict actual authority test applicable to property in occupied territory, but not persons).

279 *Brđanin* Trial Judgement, *supra* note 111, para. 638. The reference to 'Bosnian armed forces' appears to be an error, as the Chamber noted earlier in the paragraph that '[t]he question is therefore whether the relevant municipalities in the ARK [Autonomous Region of Krajina] were occupied by the FRY [Federal Republic of Yugoslavia] when the destruction and appropriation of property took place'. The Trial Chamber's holding was not challenged on appeal.

280 See *Strugar* Trial Judgement, *supra* note 51, para. 292. For cases holding that these offences satisfy the additional general requirements for Article 3 crimes under the ICTY Statute, see *supra* note 255.

281 *Kordić and Čerkez* Trial Judgement, *supra* note 57, para. 346, affirmed in *Kordić and Čerkez* Appeal Judgement, *supra* note 101, para. 74. Accord, e.g., *Hadžihasanović and Kubura* Trial Judgement, *supra* note 57, para. 39; *Strugar* Trial Judgement, *supra* note 51, para. 292; *Stakić* Trial Judgement, *supra* note 97, para. 761; *Naletilić and Martinović* Trial Judgement, *supra* note 57, para 579.

282 See *Blaškić* Trial Judgement, *supra* note 57, para. 183; *Strugar* Trial Judgement, *supra* note 51, para. 296.

283 For more on this principle, see *infra* section 4.2.2.11 on unlawful attacks on civilians and civilian objects.

personal property that only attains protection under Article 53 of Geneva Convention IV once it falls within occupied territory, the property protected by this norm of international humanitarian law may be located on enemy territory.[284]

It appears that the only judgement to discuss the elements of the underlying offence of devastation is the 2005 *Strugar* Trial Judgement. Noting that this offence had scarcely been mentioned in previous ICTY jurisprudence, and that no definition had been offered,[285] the *Strugar* Trial Chamber adapted the definition of wanton destruction under Article 3(b) by substituting the term 'devastation' for 'destruction', although it remarked that devastation could have broader application outside of the facts of the case before it.[286] The *Strugar* definition of devastation also included damage to buildings that falls short of total destruction:

> In sum, the elements of the crime of 'devastation not justified by military necessity', at least in the present context, may be stated as: (a) destruction or damage of property on a large scale; (b) the destruction or damage was not justified by military necessity; and (c) the perpetrator acted with the intent to destroy or damage the property or in the knowledge that such destruction or damage was a probable consequence of his acts.[287]

Applying this definition to the facts before it, the Trial Chamber concluded that the shelling of the Old Town of Dubrovnik in Croatia on 6 November 1991 by forces under Strugar's command constituted the devastation not justified by military necessity.[288] Recalling that its decision on the accused's motion for acquittal at the midpoint of the case had reduced the number of buildings underlying the devastation charges from 450 to 116,[289] the Chamber concluded that fifty-two of the 116 structures were destroyed or damaged during the shelling, only six of which were completely destroyed in the 6 November 1991 attack.[290]

In discussing the extent of destruction required to qualify as the offence of wanton destruction punishable under Article 3 of the ICTY Statute, the *Hadžihasanović and Kubura* Trial Chamber relied on jurisprudence on the similar underlying offence of extensive destruction, *Strugar*'s discussion of devastation, and domestic practice to conclude that the elements of the offence would be established in any of three

[284] See, e.g., *Brđanin* Trial Judgement, *supra* note 111, para. 592; *Kordić and Čerkez* Trial Judgement, *supra* note 57, para. 347.

[285] *Strugar* Trial Judgement, *supra* note 51, para. 292 & n. 935.

[286] *Ibid.*, paras. 293, 297; see also *ibid.*, para. 291:

> At least in the context of this case, which is concerned with the destruction of buildings in the Old Town of Dubrovnik, the Chamber considers it appropriate to equate the two crimes, while recognising that in other contexts, e.g. laying waste to crops or forests, the crime of devastation may have a wider application.

[287] *Ibid.*, para. 297. See also *ibid.*, para. 294 (holding that 'while this element [of 'large-scale damage'] requires a showing that a considerable number of objects were damaged or destroyed, it does not require destruction in its entirety of a city, town or village').

[288] *Ibid.*, paras. 329, 330. [289] *Ibid.*, para. 313 & n. 959.

[290] *Ibid.*, paras. 319, 326 (noting that the extent of the damage varied significantly from building to building, ranging from the total destruction of the six structures to more minor damage to parts of buildings and structures throughout the Old Town).

circumstances: the partial or total destruction of a large quantity of property, or the destruction of a single object of sufficiently high value.[291] Notwithstanding this flexible standard for the extensiveness of the damage, the Trial Chamber concluded that the prosecution had established wanton destruction in only one of the several incidents charged in the indictment, where soldiers of the 7th Brigade, under the control of the accused Amir Kubura, shattered the windows of 'practically all of the shops' in the Bosnian town of Vareš, and destroyed doors and windows throughout the town in order to commit plunder.[292]

4.2.2.1.3 Destruction or wilful damage to institutions dedicated to religion, charity and education, the arts and sciences, historic monuments and works of art and science under Article 3(d)

The physical perpetrators intentionally caused damage to, or destruction of, real property dedicated to religion, charity and education, or the arts and sciences, or historic monuments or works of art or science, where such property has not been used for military purposes.

Unlike the underlying offences in Articles 2(d) and 3(b), which have been defined in strikingly similar fashion,[293] the case law on the underlying offence in Article 3(d) of the ICTY Statute has used different terms to describe analogous concepts. As it has been defined by ICTY chambers, there are four elements to this underlying offence: (1) damage to, or destruction of, real property (2) falling within the descriptions of the subparagraph, that is, 'dedicated to religion, charity and education, the arts and sciences, historic monuments and works of art and science', (3) where such property has not been used for military purposes, and (4) the damage or destruction was intentional, in that the acts resulting in the destruction were directed against the protected property.[294] When evaluating the second element, ICTY chambers have concluded that the property listed in Article 3(d) is protected by both customary and conventional international humanitarian law;[295] when examining the third element, chambers have reaffirmed the military purposes exception,

291 *Hadžihasanović and Kubura* Trial Judgement, *supra* note 57, paras. 43–44. For a similar holding on partial destruction under Article 3(b), see *Naletilić and Martinović* Trial Judgement, *supra* note 57, paras. 584, 596 (convicting the accused Naletilić for wanton destruction for incidents in the village of Doljani in Bosnia and Herzegovina, where half of the houses had been destroyed).

292 *Hadžihasanović and Kubura* Trial Judgement, *supra* note 57, para. 1845. See also *ibid.*, paras. 1786–1835 (concluding that the offence had not been established in respect of other allegations); *ibid.*, paras. 1836–1846 (concluding that the incidents in Vareš constituted wanton destruction under Article 3(b) of the ICTY Statute). See *infra* section 4.2.2.6 for the elements of plunder as an underlying offence for war crimes.

293 See *supra* note 267.

294 See, e.g., *Strugar* Trial Judgement, *supra* note 51, paras. 310–312; *Naletilić and Martinović* Trial Judgement, *supra* note 57, para. 605; *Blaškić* Trial Judgement, *supra* note 57, para. 185. Accord *Hadžihasanović and Kubura* Trial Judgement, *supra* note 57, para. 58 (focusing on religious property).

295 See, e.g., *Kordić and Čerkez* Appeal Judgement, *supra* note 101, paras. 89–92 (citing Additional Protocol I, *supra* note 3, Arts. 52–53; Convention for the Protection of Cultural Property in the Event of Armed Conflict, 14 May 1954, entered into force 7 August 1956, 249 UNTS 240 ('1954 Hague Cultural Property Convention'); and 1907 Hague Regulations, *supra* note 6, and noting that the latter instrument had attained the status of

and generally concluded that it is the use of the property, and not its location or proximity to military objectives, that is determinative of its protected status.[296]

While trial chambers seem to agree that Article 3(d) may be viewed as the *lex specialis* of the offence of attacks on civilian objects,[297] there is a small disagreement on whether that fact should have an effect on the definition of the Article 3(d) offence. The *Brđanin* Trial Chamber believed that this property should have at least the level of protection afforded to regular civilian objects, and thus included the alternative *mens rea* of 'reckless disregard of the likelihood of destruction';[298] while the *Strugar* Trial Chamber merely noted that the standard definition does not include an indirect intent alternative, and concluded that there was no need to reach the question on the facts before it.[299] The definition of this underlying offence was not challenged on appeal in *Brđanin*, and the ICTY Appeals Chamber did not offer an opinion on the issue;[300] in *Strugar*, the prosecution has asserted on appeal that recent jurisprudence establishes that indirect intent is an alternative *mens rea* element for both attacks on civilians and destruction of cultural property.[301]

Applying the standard definition of this underlying offence to the evidence adduced at trial, the *Strugar* Trial Chamber concluded that the shelling attack on the historic Old Town in Dubrovnik, Croatia, qualified as destruction or wilful damage to cultural property as a violation of the laws or customs of war:

> [T]here is no evidence to suggest that any of the 52 buildings and structures in the Old Town which the Chamber has found to have been destroyed or damaged on 6 December 1991, were being used for military purposes at that time. Therefore, the buildings were protected as cultural property under Article 3(d) of the Statute at the time they incurred damage. As discussed earlier, military necessity can, in certain cases, be a justification for damaging or destroying property. In this respect, the Chamber affirms that in its finding there were no military objectives in the immediate vicinity of the 52 buildings and structures which the

customary international law); accord *Strugar* Trial Judgement, *supra* note 51, paras. 303–309 (also referring to Additional Protocol II). For cases holding that this offence satisfies the additional general requirements for Article 3 crimes under the ICTY Statute, see *supra* note 255.

296 See *Strugar* Trial Judgement, *supra* note 51, paras. 300–301, 310, and *Naletilić and Martinović* Trial Judgement, *supra* note 57, para. 604, both disagreeing with *Blaškić* Trial Judgement, *supra* note 57, para. 185 (requiring that the property not be in the vicinity of legitimate military objectives). See also *Brđanin* Appeal Judgement, *supra* note 120, para. 337 (holding that '[d]etermining whether destruction occurred pursuant to military necessity involves a determination of what constitutes a military objective' and whether the alleged targets were military objectives, and referring to Additional Protocol I, *supra* note 3, Art. 52 for the definition of military objectives).

297 See, e.g., *Strugar* Trial Judgement, *supra* note 51, para. 302; *Brđanin* Trial Judgement, *supra* note 111, para. 596; *Kordić and Čerkez* Trial Judgement, *supra* note 57, para. 361.

298 *Brđanin* Trial Judgement, *supra* note 111, para. 599. Accord *Hadžihasanović and Kubura* Trial Judgement, *supra* note 57, para. 59; *Krajišnik* Trial Judgement, *supra* note 120, para. 782 (discussing the underlying offence as a form of persecution as a crime against humanity).

299 *Strugar* Trial Judgement, *supra* note 51, para. 311.

300 See *Brđanin* Appeal Judgement, *supra* note 120, paras. 331–343 (discussing Brđanin's challenge to his conviction for this underlying offence, which did not raise the issue of its definition).

301 See *Prosecutor* v. *Strugar*, Case No. IT-01–42-A, Prosecution's Addendum on Recent Case-Law Pursuant to Order of 23 August 2007, 1 October 2007, p. 13 (supporting its assertion with regard to destruction of cultural property by citing the *Hadžihasanović and Kubura* and *Krajišnik* Trial Judgements Trial Judgement, see *supra* note 298).

Chamber has found to have been damaged on 6 December 1991, or in the Old Town or in its immediate vicinity. In the Chamber's finding, the destruction or damage of property in the Old Town on 6 December 1991 was not justified by military necessity.

As to the *mens rea* element … the Chamber makes the following observations … [T]he direct perpetrators' intent to deliberately destroy cultural property is inferred by the Chamber from the evidence of the deliberate attack on the Old Town, the unique cultural and historical character of which was a matter of renown, as was the Old Town's status as a UNESCO World Heritage site. As a further evidentiary issue regarding this last factor, the Chamber accepts the evidence that protective UNESCO emblems were visible, from the JNA positions at Žarkovica and elsewhere, above the Old Town on 6 December 1991.[302]

4.2.2.2 Hostage-taking

The physical perpetrator(s) seized or detained an individual (the 'victim'), and threatened to kill, injure, or continue to detain the victim, in order to compel a third party to do or to abstain from doing something as a condition for the release of the victim.

The underlying offence of hostage-taking, which may be a grave breach under Article 2(h) or a violation of the laws or customs of war under Article 3 of the ICTY Statute if the appropriate general requirements are fulfilled, is prohibited by Common Article 3, Geneva Convention IV, and Additional Protocol I.[303] The elements of this underlying offence are (1) the seizure or detention of a person (the 'victim'), accompanied by (2) threats to kill, injure, or continue to detain the victim, in order to (3) compel a third party to do or to abstain from doing something as a condition for the release of the victim.[304] It is unclear whether hostage-taking must be committed intentionally or wilfully: no judgement appears explicitly to define the *mens rea* of this offence; the prosecution's submissions in at least one case suggest that it views the offence as requiring intentional action;[305] and the ICTY Appeals Chamber has upheld a trial chamber's conclusion that the elements of the

[302] *Strugar* Trial Judgement, *supra* note 51, paras. 328–329.

[303] See *Blaškić* Appeal Judgement, *supra* note 96, para. 639 (citing Geneva Convention IV, *supra* note 3, Arts. 34, 147; Additional Protocol I, *supra* note 3, Art. 75(2)(c)); accord, e.g., *Kordić and Čerkez* Trial Judgement, *supra* note 57, paras. 319–320 (noting that the elements of the underlying offence are the same for both war crimes); *Blaškić* Trial Judgement, *supra* note 57, para. 187 ('The definition of hostages [for Article 3 purposes] must be understood as being similar to that of civilians taken as hostages within the meaning of grave breaches under Article 2 of the Statute[.]'). Hostage-taking is not specifically enumerated as an underlying offence in the subparagraphs of Article 3 of the ICTY Statute, but is considered to fall within the residual jurisdiction of this open-ended provision.

[304] *Blaškić* Appeal Judgement, *supra* note 96, para. 639 (relying on, *inter alia*, International Convention Against the Taking of Hostages, 18 December 1979, entered into force 3 June 1983, 1316 UNTS 205, Art. 1 for the definition; and holding that 'the essential element in the crime of hostage-taking is the use of a threat concerning detainees so as to obtain a concession or gain an advantage'). Accord *Kordić and Čerkez* Trial Judgement, *supra* note 57, paras. 311–313; *Blaškić* Trial Judgement, *supra* note 57, para. 158.

[305] See *Kordić and Čerkez* Trial Judgement, *supra* note 57, para. 305 (noting that the prosecution submitted that one of the elements of hostage-taking is 'the detained civilians were *wilfully* used for the purpose of obtaining some advantage or securing some commitment from a Party to the conflict, or other person or group of persons') (emphasis added).

underlying offence had been established because the accused 'deliberately ran the risk that many detainees might be taken hostage'.[306]

To date, the only cases in which ICTY chambers have considered and applied the underlying offence of hostage-taking are *Kordić and Čerkez* and *Blaškić*. In both cases, however, the Appeals Chamber overturned the Trial Chamber's convictions for this offence. In *Kordić and Čerkez*, the accused were charged with hostage-taking under Articles 2 and 3 of the ICTY Statute, and the Trial Chamber concluded that the evidence given at trial that Muslim civilian prisoners were used as hostages by the Bosnian Croat armed forces (HVO) against the Bosnian army (ABiH) established the elements of the crimes.[307] It convicted the accused Mario Čerkez for, *inter alia*, taking civilians as hostages as a grave breach of the Geneva Conventions.[308] On appeal, the ICTY Appeals Chamber reversed the conviction, noting that one of the incidents relied upon by the Trial Chamber had not been charged in the indictment; that Čerkez had been acquitted by the Trial Chamber itself in relation to another incident; and that no reasonable trier of fact could have concluded that Čerkez issued the threats in the remaining incident, or that he was responsible for the conduct of those who had been present.[309] Similarly, in *Blaškić*, the ICTY Appeals Chamber did not reverse the Trial Chamber's finding that hostage-taking had been committed;[310] instead, it rejected the lower chamber's conclusion that the accused was responsible for the crime.[311]

4.2.2.3 *Inhuman treatment or cruel treatment*

Like inhumane acts as crimes against humanity, inhuman treatment as a grave breach under Article 2(b) of the ICTY Statute, cruel treatment as a violation of the laws or customs of war under Article 3 of the ICTY Statute,[312] and cruel treatment

[306] *Blaškić* Trial Judgement, *supra* note 57, para. 741, affirmed in *Blaškić* Appeal Judgement, *supra* note 96, para. 637. Both the Trial and Appeals Chambers' reasoning is far from clear. Blaškić did not contest that hostages had been taken, but challenged his conviction for the offence on the ground that the Trial Chamber's findings on his individual responsibility were 'extremely vague', and argued that he could only assume that the basis for the conviction was superior responsibility. *Blaškić* Appeal Judgement, *supra* note 96, paras. 636–637. The Appeals Chamber demurred, noted that Blaškić had 'ordered the defence of Vitez', a town in central Bosnia and Herzegovina, and quoted the Trial Chamber's remarks about Blaškić deliberately running the risk of hostage-taking. See *ibid.* Although it emphasised that Blaškić had not been convicted for ordering hostage-taking, the Appeals Chamber concluded that the basis for his conviction was 'Article 7(1) of the Statute', *ibid.*, and seemed to clarify several paragraphs later that it was referring to the mental state for ordering as a form of responsibility, not the *mens rea* for hostage-taking as an underlying offence for war crimes. See *ibid.*, para. 645; see also Boas, Bischoff, and Reid, *supra* note 30, pp. 349–351 (discussing the *Blaškić* Appeals Chamber's holding on the mental element for ordering).

[307] *Kordić and Čerkez* Trial Judgement, *supra* note 57, para. 784. See also *ibid.*, para. 800 (concluding that 'the underlying offences in Counts 21–36', including the hostage-taking charges, 'are made out').

[308] *Ibid.*, paras. 836, 843.

[309] See *Kordić and Čerkez* Appeal Judgement, *supra* note 101, paras. 933–939.

[310] See *Blaškić* Appeal Judgement, *supra* note 96, para. 642 (noting that Blaškić did not challenge the conclusion that Muslim detainees 'were "threatened with death" in order to prevent the ABiH advance on Vitez').

[311] *Ibid.*, para. 646.

[312] Cruel treatment is not specifically enumerated in the subparagraphs of Article 3 of the ICTY Statute, but is considered to fall within the residual jurisdiction of that open-ended provision.

as a violation of Common Article 3 under Article 4(a) of the ICTR Statute encompass certain serious transgressions against human dignity not specifically enumerated in the *ad hoc* Statutes, but which are nonetheless recognised by customary international law as entailing individual criminal responsibility, and which may qualify as crimes against humanity or war crimes if the respective general requirements are met. Inhuman treatment and cruel treatment also function as subcategories or residual provisions covering a range of potentially criminal conduct, and are characterised by the same specific requirements as inhumane acts.

These requirements, which are discussed in detail in Chapter 2,[313] are (1) the physical perpetrator's conduct must cause serious mental or physical suffering to the victim or constitute a serious attack on human dignity; (2) such suffering or attack must be of similar gravity to the enumerated underlying offences in the respective Article of the ICTY Statute;[314] and (3) the physical perpetrator's conduct must be performed with the intent to inflict serious physical or mental harm upon the victim or commit a serious attack on human dignity, or with the knowledge that it would probably have that effect.[315] The *Naletilić and Martinović* Trial Chamber observed that '[t]he degree of physical or mental suffering required to prove either [inhuman or cruel treatment] is lower than the one required for torture, though at the same level as the one required to prove a charge of "wilfully causing great suffering or serious injury to body or health"'.[316]

Conduct that has been held to constitute inhuman or cruel treatment includes the use of human shields, which is a breach of international humanitarian law

313 See Chapter 2, section 2.2.3.9.

314 ICTR chambers have rarely tried to define 'cruel treatment' as an underlying offence for war crimes under Article 4 of that Tribunal's Statute, but are likely to adopt the ICTY's definition and the standards applied therein. See, e.g., *Cyangugu* Trial Judgement, *supra* note 109, para. 765 (citing ICTY judgements):

> Cruel treatment has been defined as an intentional act or omission causing serious mental or physical suffering or injury or constituting a serious attack on human dignity. … The Chamber notes and accepts that cruel treatment is treatment causing serious mental or physical suffering, including that which may be short of the severe suffering required for a finding of torture.

See also *ibid*., n. 1659 ('Cruel treatment as a violation of Common Article 3 is equivalent to inhuman treatment as a grave breach under the 1949 Geneva Conventions. ')

315 See, e.g., *Kordić and Čerkez* Appeal Judgement, *supra* note 101, para. 39; *Simić et al.* Trial Judgement, *supra* note 96, para. 74; *Naletilić and Martinović* Trial Judgement, *supra* note 57, paras. 246, 340–341; *Vasiljević* Trial Judgement, *supra* note 136, para. 234; *Prosecutor* v. *Krnojelac*, Case No. IT-97-25-T, Judgement, 15 March 2002 ('*Krnojelac* Trial Judgement'), paras. 130, 132. See also *Kordić and Čerkez* Trial Judgement, *supra* note 57, para. 265 (holding that inhuman treatment and cruel treatment have the same elements, and that it is the general requirements for the subcategories of war crimes that distinguish the two crimes); accord *Blaškić* Trial Judgement, *supra* note 57, para. 186; *Blaškić* Appeal Judgement, *supra* note 96, para. 665 (stating that the two crimes are distinct, but citing only the protected persons requirement for grave breaches as the difference between the two). See also *Mrkšić et al.* Trial Judgement, *supra* note 103, para. 517 (holding that 'the failure to provide adequate medicine or medical treatment would constitute the offence of "cruel treatment" if, in the specific circumstances, it causes serious mental or physical suffering or injury, or constitutes a serious attack on human dignity and if it is carried out with the requisite *mens rea*').

316 *Naletilić and Martinović* Trial Judgement, *supra* note 57, para. 246 (citing *Prosecutor* v. *Kvočka, Kos, Radić, Zigić, and Prcać*, Case No. IT-98-30-T, Judgement, 2 November 2001 ('*Kvočka et al.* Trial Judgement'), para 161).

and sufficiently serious to qualify for criminal sanctions even if the victims are not physically harmed;[317] forced labour, in certain circumstances;[318] detention in deplorable conditions;[319] and shelling or bombardment of civilians or civilian objects when it results in injury to persons.[320]

4.2.2.4 Murder or wilful killing

ICTY Chambers have routinely remarked that the elements of murder are the same, regardless of the category or subcategory of crimes that has been charged in the indictment; that is, the elements of the underlying offence do not change, even if the crime charged is wilful killing as a grave breach under Article 2(a), murder as a violation of the laws or customs of war under Article 3, murder as a crime against humanity under Article 5(a); extermination as a crime against humanity under Article 5(b); or murder as a form of persecution as a crime against humanity under Article 5(h).[321] Under this approach, the only distinction between the crimes

317 See, e.g., *Blaškić* Appeal Judgement, *supra* note 96, paras. 653–664, 669.

318 See, e.g., *ibid*., para. 597 (holding that 'the use of persons taking no active part in hostilities to prepare military fortifications for use in operations and against the forces with whom those persons identify or sympathise is a serious attack on human dignity and causes serious mental (and depending on the circumstances physical) suffering or injury', and thus that '[a]ny order to compel protected persons to dig trenches or to prepare other forms of military installations, in particular when such persons are ordered to do so against their own forces in an armed conflict, constitutes cruel treatment').

319 See *Limaj et al.* Trial Judgement, *supra* note 103, paras. 288–289. Notwithstanding this conclusion, neither the Trial Chamber nor the Appeals Chamber found that the prosecution had established a common plan to commit cruel treatment in the Llapushnik/Lapušnik prison camp, the main location of the crimes alleged in the indictment. See *Limaj et al.* Appeal Judgement, *supra* note 119, para. 103 (upholding *Limaj et al.* Trial Judgement, *supra* note 103, para. 666). See also *Mrkšić et al.* Trial Judgement, *supra* note 103, paras. 524–525, 537 (holding that the mere fact of imprisonment was insufficient to constitute cruel treatment as a violation of the laws or customs of war, but that the conditions in which detainees were held, characterised by the detainees' vulnerability to physical assault, their constant fear, and the deprivation of food and water, 'were such as to cause serious mental or physical suffering') (quotation at para. 525); *Hadžihasanović and Kubura* Trial Judgement, *supra* note 57, paras. 35–36 (noting that under IHL, detained persons are to be provided with the same basic sustenance and care as the local population, and that continued detention of such persons without provision of food, water, sanitation, and protection of their health and against the dangers of armed conflict at the same levels as the local population could result in criminal liability for those responsible).

320 See *Strugar* Trial Judgement, *supra* note 51, paras. 268–270, 273–276.

321 See, e.g., *Čelebići* Appeal Judgement, *supra* note 162, paras. 422–423 (applying the same elements for murder under Articles 2(a) and 3); *Blagojević and Jokić* Trial Judgement, *supra* note 97, para. 556 (concerning Articles 3 and 5(a)); *Strugar* Trial Judgement, *supra* note 51, para. 236 (concerning Article 3, but considering Articles 2 (a), 3, and 5(a)); *Brđanin* Trial Judgement, *supra* note 111, paras. 381, 382, 385, 388 (concerning Article 2(a), 3, 5(a), 5(b), and 5(h)); *Stakić* Trial Judgement, *supra* note 97, paras. 584–587, 631, 638–641, 774 (concerning Articles 3, 5(a), 5(b), and 5(h)); *Naletilić and Martinović* Trial Judgement, *supra* note 57, para. 248 (concerning Articles 2(a), 3, 5(a), and 5(h)); *Vasiljević* Trial Judgement, *supra* note 136, para. 205 (concerning Articles 3, 5 (a), 5(b), and 5(h)); *Krnojelac* Trial Judgement, *supra* note 315, paras. 324, 326 (concerning Articles 3, 5(a), and 5(h)); *Kvočka et al.* Trial Judgement, *supra* note 316, para. 132 (concerning Articles 3, 5(a), and 5(h)); *Kordić and Čerkez* Trial Judgement, *supra* note 57, paras. 229, 233, 236 (concerning Articles 2(a), 3, and 5); *Krstić* Trial Judgement, *supra* note 97, paras. 485, 495, 535 (concerning Articles 3, 5(a), 5(b), and 5(h)); *Blaškić* Trial Judgement, *supra* note 57, paras. 153, 181, 217 (concerning Articles 2(a), 3, 5(a), and 5(h)); *Prosecutor* v. *Kupreškić, Kupreškić, Kupreškić, Papić, and Santić*, Case No. IT-95-16-T, Judgement, 14 January 2000 ('*Kupreškić et al.* Trial Judgement'), paras. 560–561, 605 (concerning Articles 5(a) and 5(h)); *Prosecutor* v. *Jelisić*, Case No. IT-95-10-T, Judgement, 14 December 1999, paras. 35, 51 (concerning Articles 3 and 5(a)); *Čelebići* Trial Judgement, *supra* note 67, para. 424, 439 (concerning Articles 2(a) and 3).

arises from the general or specific requirements that must be fulfilled in order to turn the simple underlying offence into an international crime.[322]

As noted in the discussion of this underlying offence in Chapter 2,[323] however, the repetition of this observation and the apparent inattention of the Appeals Chambers have masked a split between the ICTY and ICTR on the definition of murder as an underlying offence of different international crimes.[324] While the ICTY and ICTR definitions generally agree on the *actus reus* of the offence – the death of an individual caused by the conduct of the physical perpetrator[325] – ICTY judgements usually hold that there are two alternative mental states that will suffice to render this conduct murder: either the physical perpetrator intended to cause the victim's death, or he intended to harm the victim in the knowledge that death was likely to ensue.[326] When murder is charged as killing, an underlying offence of genocide, ICTR Chambers require that the conduct resulting in death be committed with the intent to kill the victim, but it need not be premeditated.[327] When it is charged as a crime against humanity, or as extermination as a crime against humanity, there is no consistent ICTR standard: most trial judgements require premeditation for murder as a crime against humanity,[328] but none appears to have extended the requirement to extermination; indeed, for extermination, at least one early judgement espoused three alternative mental states, and a more recent judgement restricted possible mental states to intentional conduct only.[329]

Similar discord can be noted in the definition of murder as a form of the underlying offence of 'violence to life, health and physical or mental well-being of

322 See, e.g., *Kordić and Čerkez* Appeal Judgement, *supra* note 101, para. 38 (noting, in the context of a cumulative convictions discussion, that the material element distinguishing wilful killing under Article 2(a) of the ICTY Statute from murder under Article 3 is the requirement that the victim of wilful killing be a protected person under the Geneva Conventions). The discussions of murder as an underlying offence of war crimes repeat all the points of the jurisprudence discussed in Chapter 2. For details on the other aspects of the definition of murder as an underlying offence, see generally Chapter 2, section 2.2.3.1 (discussing murder as an underlying offence of crimes against humanity).

323 See Chapter 2, section 2.2.3.1.

324 See *ibid.*, text accompanying notes 214–225, 243–250 (noting this split and other variations in the definitions of murder and extermination as underlying offences of crimes against humanity). But see *Brđanin* Trial Judgement, *supra* note 111, para. 386 (noting that ICTR cases have required premeditation for murder and declining to follow their lead).

325 See, e.g., *Brđanin* Trial Judgement, *supra* note 111, paras. 382, 388; *Prosecutor* v. *Ndindabahizi*, Case No. ICTR-01-71-T, Judgement and Sentence, 15 July 2004, para. 487; *Kordić and Čerkez* Trial Judgement, *supra* note 57, paras. 229, 236; *Musema* Trial Judgement, *supra* note 97, para. 215.

326 See, e.g., *Prosecutor* v. *Kvočka, Kos, Radić, Zigić, and Prcać*, Case No. IT-98-30-A, Judgement, 28 February 2005 ('*Kvočka et al.* Appeal Judgement'), para. 261; *Kordić and Čerkez* Appeal Judgement, *supra* note 101, para. 36; *Hadžihasanović and Kubura* Trial Judgement, *supra* note 57, para. 31; *Blagojević and Jokić* Trial Judgement, *supra* note 97, para. 556; *Brđanin* Trial Judgement, *supra* note 111, para. 381; *Galić* Trial Judgement, *supra* note 232, para. 150; *Stakić* Trial Judgement, *supra* note 97, paras. 584–587, 631, 638–641, 774; *Krstić* Trial Judgement, *supra* note 97, para. 485.

327 See Chapter 3, section 3.2.2.1.2 (discussing the mental element of killing as an underlying offence of genocide).

328 See Chapter 2, text accompanying notes 215–218.

329 Compare *Kayishema and Ruzindana* Trial Judgement, *supra* note 103, para. 144 (intentional conduct, recklessness, or gross negligence) with *Semanza* Trial Judgement, *supra* note 97, para. 341 (solely intentional conduct).

persons' under Article 4(a) of the ICTR Statute. The 2000 *Musema* Trial Judgement followed the ICTY model, presenting two alternative mental states, although it phrased the indirect intent alternative as 'the intention … to inflict grievous bodily harm on the deceased having known that such bodily harm is likely to cause the victim's death, and is reckless as to whether or not death [ensues]'.[330] The 2003 *Semanza* Trial Judgement, on the other hand, held that the killing must be intentional, although it did not require premeditation.[331] Another, more recent, restatement of the elements in one of the '*Military*' cases is closer to *Musema*, but more explicit in stating that recklessness is a third alternative mental state.[332]

In practice, the variation in the alternative mental states will not make a significant difference, as most of the offences are alleged, and found, to be incidents of intentional killing. Nevertheless, it is hoped that the Appeals Chamber of either Tribunal will endeavour to clarify the law on the mental states for this underlying offence.

4.2.2.5 Outrages upon personal dignity

The physical perpetrator treated an individual ('the victim') in a manner that would be generally considered to cause serious humiliation, degradation, or otherwise be a serious attack on the human dignity of the victim, in the knowledge that his conduct could have that effect.

Outrages upon personal dignity fall within the jurisdiction of the ICTR under Article 4(e) of that Tribunal's Statute. This subparagraph, which is a verbatim reproduction of Article 4(2)(e) of Additional Protocol II, goes on to specify that the provision covers '*in particular* humiliating and degrading treatment, rape, enforced prostitution and any form of indecent assault'.[333] At the ICTY, where the Statute does not specifically include this text, trial and appeal chambers have concluded that outrages upon personal dignity can qualify as violations of the laws or customs of war falling within Article 3 of the ICTY Statute.[334]

330 *Musema* Trial Judgement, *supra* note 97, para. 215 (murder under Article 4(a) of the ICTR Statute). Some ICTY judgements have also referred to recklessness as an acceptable mental state for murder. See, e.g., *Krstić* Trial Judgement, *supra* note 97, para. 495; *Kordić and Čerkez* Trial Judgement, *supra* note 57, paras. 229, 233; *Kupreškić et al.* Trial Judgement, *supra* note 321, para. 561; *Čelebići* Trial Judgement, *supra* note 67, para. 439. The most recent restatement of the elements of murder as an underlying offence by the ICTY Appeals Chamber, however, included only the two alternatives described above. See *Kvočka et al.* Appeal Judgement, *supra* note 326, para. 261 (listing elements of murder as a violation of the laws or customs of war); see also *supra* note 325 and accompanying text.

331 *Semanza* Trial Judgement, *supra* note 97, para. 373.

332 See *Military I* 98 *bis* Decision, *supra* note 220, para. 25 ('Murder is the intentional killing of a person, or intentional infliction of grievous bodily harm with knowledge that such harm will likely cause the victim's death or with recklessness as to whether death will result[.]') (citing *Prosecutor* v. *Ndindabahizi*, Case No. ICTR-2001-71-T, Judgement, 15 July 2004, para. 487).

333 ICTR Statute, *supra* note 13, Art. 4(e) (emphasis added).

334 See, e.g., *Kunarac et al.* Trial Judgement, *supra* note 138, para. 498 (noting that Common Article 3(1)(c) specifically prohibits 'outrages upon personal dignity, in particular humiliating and degrading treatment'); *Aleksovski* Appeal Judgement, *supra* note 151, paras. 21–22 (upholding a conviction of outrages upon personal dignity under Article 3).

On its face, 'outrages upon personal dignity' would appear to be a label, similar to inhuman or cruel treatment, that refers to a number of potential underlying offences.[335] The definitions that have been offered by *ad hoc* chambers support that interpretation, because they refer generally to a range of conduct that shares certain characteristics.[336] For example, the *Kunarac* Appeals Chamber held that the Trial Chamber in that case 'was not obliged to define the specific acts which may constitute outrages upon personal dignity. Instead it properly presented the criteria which it used as a basis for measuring the humiliating or degrading character of an act or omission.'[337] Those criteria, in turn, were relatively simple and tautological: the *Kunarac* Trial Chamber had defined outrages upon personal dignity as 'an act or an omission which would be generally considered to cause serious humiliation, degradation or otherwise be a serious attack on human dignity'.[338] The Appeals Chamber found that these criteria set an objective standard that was not dependent on the individual victim's perception of the conduct in question, and noted that the Trial Chamber had concluded that 'the humiliation of the victim must be so intense that any reasonable person would be outraged'.[339] Although there had been some question in the earlier *Aleksovski* case as to whether the mental element for outrages

[335] Indeed, the *Aleksovski* Trial Chamber concluded that 'outrages upon personal dignity' are a subcategory of inhuman treatment as proscribed by Common Article 3. See *Aleksovski* Trial Judgement, *supra* note 88, para. 54 (referring to inhuman treatment as the 'genus' and outrages upon personal dignity as the 'species'). This conclusion was upheld by the Appeals Chamber, see *Aleksovski* Appeal Judgement, *supra* note 151, para. 26 and followed in at least two subsequent trial judgements, see *Kunarac et al.* Trial Judgement, *supra* note 138, para. 502; *Kvočka et al.* Trial Judgement, *supra* note 316, para. 166, but no further clarification or detailed analysis of the relationship between the two subcategories of underlying offences for war crimes has been forthcoming from the ICTY. If such clarification is attempted, it will most likely be in the context of a cumulative convictions analysis for multiple convictions under Article 3 of the ICTY Statute. See generally Chapter 5 for a full discussion of cumulative convictions in the *ad hoc* Tribunals.

[336] See, e.g., *Musema* Trial Judgement, *supra* note 97, para. 285 (suggesting that 'outrages upon personal dignity' and 'humiliating or degrading treatment' are plural terms that cover more than one offence).

[337] *Kunarac et al.* Appeal Judgement, *supra* note 97, para. 162.

[338] *Kunarac et al.* Trial Judgement, *supra* note 138, para. 514. While this interpretation of outrages upon personal dignity defines them in terms of humiliation or degradation, one early ICTR judgement appeared to have viewed them as separate offences. In the course of its telegraphic summary of the 'required elements' for the underlying offences of war crimes under Article 4 of the ICTR Statute, the *Musema* Trial Judgement noted:

> a) Humiliating and degrading treatment: Subjecting victims to treatment designed to subvert their self-regard. *Like outrages upon personal dignity*, these offences may be regarded as a lesser forms of torture; moreover ones in which the motives required for torture would not be required, nor would it be required that the acts be committed under state authority.
>
> ...
>
> c) Indecent assault: The accused caused the infliction of pain or injury by an act which was of a sexual nature and inflicted by means of coercion, force, threat or intimidation and was non-consensual.

Musema Trial Judgement, *supra* note 97, para. 285 (emphasis added). The interpretation of the relationship between the types of conduct specified in Article 4(e) that is suggested by this part of the judgement does not appear to have been adopted by later ICTR jurisprudence. See, e.g., *Military I* 98 *bis* Decision, *supra* note 220, para. 39 n. 84 (adopting the *Kunarac* definition).

[339] *Kunarac et al.* Appeal Judgement, *supra* note 97, para. 162 (referring to *Kunarac et al.* Trial Judgement, *supra* note 138, para. 504, which noted that the earlier *Aleksovski* Trial Judgement had 'concluded that a purely subjective assessment would be unfair to the accused because the accused's culpability would be made to depend not on the gravity of the act but on the sensitivity of the victim').

upon personal dignity required specific intent to inflict the humiliation, degradation, or attack on dignity,[340] the *Kunarac* Appeals Chamber was content with a more relaxed standard, and upheld the Trial Chamber's conclusion that all that is required is knowledge that the act or omission *could* cause serious humiliation, degradation, or affront to human dignity.[341]

Although at least one ICTY trial chamber believed that outrages upon personal dignity required the infliction of lasting suffering, later judgements have implicitly or explicitly disagreed, noting either that there is no minimum temporal duration or that the determination of whether the criteria have been satisfied is fact-dependent.[342] Chambers of the *ad hoc* Tribunals appear to view outrages upon personal dignity as falling somewhere between cruel treatment and torture in terms of the severity of the suffering that results from the physical perpetrator's conduct.[343] In line with this understanding, the *Kvočka* Trial Judgement noted that 'the focus of violations of dignity is primarily on acts, omissions, or words that do not necessarily involve long-term physical harm, but which nevertheless are serious offences deserving of punishment'.[344] Accordingly, the Trial Chamber held that murder is not 'in and of itself' an outrage upon personal dignity, but that the treatment inflicted on non-Serb detainees of the Omarska camp in Bosnia and Herzegovina – including 'inappropriate conditions of confinement' and being forced to 'perform subservient acts demonstrating Serb superiority ... relieve bodily functions in their clothing, and ... endure [ ] the constant fear of being subjected to

340 See *Aleksovski* Appeal Judgement, *supra* note 151, para. 27 ('The Trial Chamber's indication that the *mens rea* of the offence is the "intent to humiliate or ridicule" the victim may ... impose a requirement that the Prosecution was not obliged to prove and the Appeals Chamber does not, by rejecting this ground of appeal, endorse that particular conclusion.').

341 See *Kunarac et al.* Appeal Judgement, *supra* note 97, para. 165, affirming *Kunarac et al.* Trial Judgement, *supra* note 138, para. 512. Both the Trial and Appeals Chambers used the term 'the accused' in their definitions. For the reasons explained elsewhere in this chapter, however, there should be no requirement that the accused be the person to satisfy the elements of the crimes with which he is charged. Instead, this requirement may be satisfied by the physical perpetrator or another relevant actor. See *supra* text accompanying notes 123, 174–176 (similar discussion with regard to the relevant actor for knowledge of existence and nature of armed conflict).

342 Compare *Aleksovski* Trial Judgement, *supra* note 88, para. 56 ('It is not necessary for the act to directly harm the physical or mental well-being of the victim. It is enough that the act causes real and lasting suffering to the individual arising from the humiliation or ridicule.') with *Kunarac et al.* Trial Judgement, *supra* note 138, para. 501 ('So long as the humiliation or degradation is real and serious, the Trial Chamber can see no reason why it would also have to be "lasting" ... Obviously, if the humiliation and suffering caused is only fleeting in nature, it may be difficult to accept that it is real and serious.'); *Kvočka et al.* Trial Judgement, *supra* note 316, para. 168 (echoing the *Kunarac* Trial Chamber); *Kunarac et al.* Appeal Judgement, *supra* note 97, para. 166 (confirming the Trial Chamber's conclusion that 'the nature of the acts committed by the Appellant against [certain named victims] undeniably reaches the objective threshold for the crime of outrages upon personal dignity set out in the Trial Judgement').

343 See *Aleksovski* Trial Judgement, *supra* note 88, para. 54 (holding that '[a]n outrage upon personal dignity ... occasion[s] more serious suffering than most prohibited acts falling within' the category of inhuman treatment); *Musema* Trial Judgement, *supra* note 97, para. 285 (holding that outrages upon personal dignity and humiliating and degrading treatment 'may be regarded as lesser forms of torture').

344 *Kvočka* Trial Judgement, *supra* note 316, para. 172.

physical, mental, or sexual violence in the camp' – constituted outrages upon personal dignity as violations of the laws or customs of war.[345]

Other acts that have been held to qualify as outrages upon personal dignity include rape and other sexual violence;[346] and using detainees as human shields or trench-diggers.[347] In addition, the ICTR Trial Chamber trying the '*Military I*' case accepted the prosecution's assertion that 'forced incest; burying corpses in latrine pits; leaving infants without care after killing their guardians; and removing fetuses from the womb' constituted outrages upon personal dignity within the meaning of Article 4(e) of the ICTR Statute, by concluding that 'a reasonable trier of fact could, if the evidence were believed' convict the accused under this provision 'for one or more of the criminal acts described'.[348]

4.2.2.6 Plunder, pillage, or extensive appropriation

The physical perpetrator intentionally took possession, or assumed control, of private or public property without justification under international law.

The conduct that constitutes plunder as a violation of the laws or customs of war under Article 3(e) of the ICTY Statute is identical to that which underlies extensive unjustified appropriation as a grave breach under Article 2(d) of that Statute, and both terms capture what has been traditionally known as 'pillage' in armed conflict.[349] Under the jurisprudence of the ICTY,[350] plunder has generally been defined as the intentional appropriation of private or public property without justification

[345] *Ibid.*, paras. 172–173 (quotations at para. 173). See also *ibid.*, para. 170 (noting that earlier cases had held that 'forced public nudity' and detainees' 'constant fear of being robbed or beaten' could also qualify as outrages upon personal dignity).

[346] See, e.g., *Akayesu* Trial Judgement, *supra* note 67, para. 688; *Furundžija* Trial Judgement, *supra* note 67, paras. 172–173. See also *Military II* 98 *bis* Decision, *supra* note 109, para. 60 (concluding that a reasonable trier of fact could conclude that two of the accused in that case bore superior responsibility for rape under Article 4(e) of the Statute). For the elements of rape as an underlying offence, see Chapter 2, section 2.2.3.7.

[347] See, e.g., *Aleksovski* Trial Judgement, *supra* note 88, para. 229; *Military I* 98 *bis* Decision, *supra* note 220, para. 39 n. 84. But cf. *Blaškić* Appeal Judgement, *supra* note 96, para. 597 (noting that forced labour, including the digging of trenches, is not cruel treatment *per se*, though it would qualify for that subcategory of underlying offences in certain circumstances). See also *supra* note 318 (quoting the relevant section from the Appeal Judgement).

[348] *Military I* 98 *bis* Decision, *supra* note 220, para. 40.

[349] See *Čelebići* Trial Judgement, *supra* note 67, para. 591 (finding that the terms 'pillage,' 'plunder,' and 'spoliation' varyingly have been used to describe the unlawful appropriation of public and private property during armed conflicts, and that 'plunder' should be understood as encompassing acts traditionally described as 'pillage'); accord, e.g., *Kordić and Čerkez* Appeal Judgement, *supra* note 101, para. 77; *Martić* Trial Judgement, *supra* note 120, para. 101; *Simić et al.* Trial Judgement, *supra* note 96, para. 98; *Naletilić and Martinović* Trial Judgement, *supra* note 57, para. 617; *Blaškić* Trial Judgement, *supra* note 57, para. 184. See also *ibid.*, para. 234 (noting that as an underlying offence of persecution as a crime against humanity, plunder 'is defined as the unlawful, extensive and wanton appropriation of property belonging to a particular population, whether it be the property of private individuals or of state or "quasi-state" public collectives').

[350] Article 4(f) of the ICTR Statute lists 'pillage' as an underlying offence punishable as a war crime within the jurisdiction of that Tribunal, but it appears that no substantive discussion of the elements of this crime has been offered by ICTR chambers. One of the accused in the '*Media*' case, Jean-Bosco Barayagwiza, was charged with pillage under Article 4(f), but the Trial Chamber acquitted him of the crime after the prosecution conceded at the midpoint of the case that no evidence supporting that count of the indictment had been presented. See *Prosecutor* v. *Barayagwiza*, Case No. ICTR-97-19-I, Decision on the Prosecutor's Request for Leave to File

under international law.[351] As the *Simić* Trial Chamber recognised in its final judgement, international humanitarian law permits the seizure of public or private property by the parties to an armed conflict under certain limited circumstances:

> These circumstances are defined by [t]he Hague Regulations and are limited to the following: taxes and dues imposed within the purview of the existing laws, or requisitions for the needs of the army of occupation, which shall be proportional to the resources of the country. Private property also may be seized if it is needed for the conduct of military operations and should be returned and compensated upon termination of the conflict. Monetary contributions may be collected only under a written order issued by the commander-in-chief in accordance with the tax rules in force and for every contribution a receipt should be issued.[352]

Outside of those circumstances, appropriation is unlawful, and may constitute a war crime punishable by the *ad hoc* Tribunals if the applicable general requirements or jurisdictional criteria are satisfied.[353]

In particular, under current ICTY case law, in order for the conduct in question to qualify as a grave breach under Article 2(d), the appropriated property must be afforded general protection under the Geneva Conventions regardless of its location, or must be located in occupied territory under the actual authority of the opposing side in the armed conflict.[354] In order to qualify as a violation of the laws or customs of war under Article 3(e), the plunder must satisfy the *Tadić* criteria – that is, it must be a violation of a rule of conventional or customary international law that attracts individual criminal responsibility, and which meets the gravity requirement.[355] Accordingly, both appropriation under Article 2(d) and plunder under Article 3(e) entail consideration of the scale of the alleged criminal

an Amended Indictment, 11 April 2000; *Prosecutor* v. *Nahimana, Barayagwiza, and Ngeze*, Case No. ICTR-99-52-T, Judgement and Sentence, 3 December 2003, para. 12 (recalling the Trial Chamber's earlier decision on the accused's motions for judgements of acquittal).

351 See, e.g., *Kordić and Čerkez* Appeal Judgement, *supra* note 101, para. 84 (affirming *Kordić and Čerkez* Trial Judgement, *supra* note 57, para. 352); *Martić* Trial Judgement, *supra* note 120, paras. 101–102, 104 (noting, in the latter paragraph, that 'the unlawful appropriation of property must have been perpetrated with either direct or indirect intent'); *Hadžihasanović and Kubura* Trial Judgement, *supra* note 57, para. 50; *Simić et al.* Trial Judgement, *supra* note 96, para. 99; *Naletilić and Martinović* Trial Judgement, *supra* note 57, paras. 612, 617. As a legal term of art, appropriation is typically understood as taking possession or assuming control of property. See, e.g., *Black's Law Dictionary* (8th edn. 2003), p. 110.

352 *Simić et al.* Trial Judgement, *supra* note 96, para. 100 (citing 1907 Hague Regulations, *supra* note 6, Arts. 48–49, 51–53). Accord *Naletilić and Martinović* Trial Judgement, *supra* note 57, para. 616 ('According to the Hague Regulations forcible contribution of money, requisition for the needs of the army of occupation, and seizure of material obviously related to the conduct of military operations, though restricted, are lawful in principle.'); *Martić* Trial Judgement, *supra* note 120, para. 102.

353 See *supra* sections 4.2.1, 4.2.1.3–4.2.1.5 (discussing the general requirements for all war crimes, additional general requirements for the subcategories of war crimes within the jurisdiction of the *ad hoc* Tribunals, and jurisdictional criteria for Article 3 of the ICTY Statute).

354 See *supra* notes 209–217, 276–279 and accompanying text (discussing the 'actual authority' test and its application). See especially the latter section for discussion of factual findings concluding that the elements of the crime of extensive appropriation as a grave breach had not been established, because the general requirement of protected status under the Geneva Conventions was not satisfied.

355 See *supra* section 4.2.1.5 for a discussion of the *Tadić* criteria in the context of additional general requirements for violations of the laws or customs of war.

activity. Under the former provision, the conduct must be 'extensive', which seems to have been interpreted as referring to the aggregate effect of the conduct on its victims or targets.[356] Under the latter provision, the requirement of grave consequences for the victims may be satisfied by proof of confiscation of property of sufficient monetary value in either large-scale, systematic, or organised seizures; or uncoordinated or opportunistic looting by individual physical perpetrators.[357] Sufficient monetary value, in turn, may be measured individually or collectively, and is assessed according to the facts in each case.[358]

4.2.2.7 Rape

This underlying offence may be charged as a grave breach under subparagraphs (b) or (c) of Article 2 of the ICTY Statute,[359] a violation of the laws or customs of war under Article 3 of that Statute,[360] or an outrage upon personal dignity under Article 3 of that Statute or Article 4(e) of the ICTR Statute.[361] Indeed, the elements of the underlying offence are the same, no matter whether rape is charged as a war crime or as an underlying offence of crimes against humanity or genocide.[362] A full discussion of these elements is included in Chapter 2.[363]

356 See *supra* text accompanying notes 272–275 (discussing this issue in the context of extensive destruction under Article 2(d)).

357 See, e.g., *Kordić and Čerkez* Appeal Judgement, *supra* note 101, paras. 80–83; *Martić* Trial Judgement, *supra* note 120, para. 103; *Simić et al.* Trial Judgement, *supra* note 96, paras. 99, 101; *Naletilić and Martinović* Trial Judgement, *supra* note 57, paras. 612–614; *Kordić and Čerkez* Trial Judgement, *supra* note 57, para. 352; *Blaškić* Trial Judgement, *supra* note 57, para. 184.

358 See, e.g., *Kordić and Čerkez* Appeal Judgement, *supra* note 101, para. 82 (citing *Čelebići* Trial Judgement, *supra* note 67, para. 1154, in which that Trial Chamber had concluded that 'the evidence … fail[ed] to demonstrate that any property taken from the detainees in the Čelebići prison-camp was of sufficient monetary value for its unlawful appropriation to involve grave consequences for the victims'); accord *Martić* Trial Judgement, *supra* note 120, para. 103 ('This requirement could be met in cases where appropriations take place *vis-à-vis* a large number of people, even though they do not lead to grave consequences for each individual. What needs to be considered here is the overall effect on the civilian population and the multitude of offences committed.') (internal quotation marks and footnotes omitted); *Hadžihasanović and Kubura* Trial Judgement, *supra* note 57, para. 55; *Naletilić and Martinović* Trial Judgement, *supra* note 57, para. 614.

359 See, e.g., *Prosecutor* v. *Bralo*, Case No. IT-95-17-S, Sentencing Judgement, para. 28 & n. 26 (noting that Bralo had pleaded guilty to, *inter alia*, torture as a grave breach under Article 2(b) of the ICTY Statute for his rape and brutal treatment of a Bosnian female detainee). Although it does not appear that rape has been specifically charged as an underlying offence under Article 2(c) of the ICTY Statute – wilfully causing great suffering or serious injury to body or health – such an allegation would be consistent with the manner in which rape is treated in the context of genocide and torture: in all three situations, rape is the means by which the physical perpetrator intentionally inflicts the suffering or harm. See Chapter 2, text accompanying note 346; *ibid.*, note 434; Chapter 3, text accompanying note 239.

360 See, e.g., *Kunarac et al.* Trial Judgement, *supra* note 138, paras. 886, 888 (convicting the accused Kovač and Vuković of torture as a violation of the laws or customs of war for rapes they committed against Muslim victims).

361 See, e.g., *Prosecutor* v. *Furundžija*, Case No. IT-95-17/1-T, Decision on the Defendant's Motion to Dismiss Counts 13 and 14 of the Indictment (Lack of Subject Matter Jurisdiction), 29 May 1998, paras. 13–14, 18; *Musema* Trial Judgement, *supra* note 97, para. 285.

362 See, e.g., *Kvočka* Appeal Judgement , *supra* note 326, para. 395 (upholding an application of the *Kunarac* definition of rape, which was developed in the context of crimes against humanity, to an allegation of rape as a violation of the laws or customs of war); *Musema* Trial Judgement, *supra* note 97, para. 285.

363 See Chapter 2, section 2.2.3.7.

4.2.2.8 Slavery or unlawful labour

The elements of slavery as a potential violation of the laws or customs of war are identical to those underlying the crime against humanity of enslavement, and a full discussion of the definition is included in Chapter 2.[364] ICTY chambers have frequently noted that forced labour may constitute slavery as both a crime against humanity and a war crime if the elements of slavery are satisfied under the circumstances of the case.[365] In the context of armed conflict, however, ICTY judgements have noted that there are limited circumstances in which international humanitarian law permits forced or compulsory labour.[366]

Nevertheless, as the *Naletilić and Martinović* Trial Chamber noted, forcing prisoners of war to perform labour proscribed by international humanitarian law may constitute a crime punishable under Article 3 of the Statute if 'the perpetrator had the intent that the victim would be performing prohibited work'.[367] It is not clear whether this *mens rea* requirement means that the physical perpetrator or another relevant actor[368] must have been aware that the labour in question is specifically prohibited under international humanitarian law, or whether it is sufficient that the prisoner of war is intentionally ordered to perform the work.

4.2.2.9 Terror

The physical perpetrator committed acts of violence against a civilian population, or threatened such acts, and the primary purpose of the physical perpetrator's conduct was to spread fear in that population.

[364] See, e.g., *Simić et al.* Trial Judgement, *supra* note 96, para. 85; *Krnojelac* Trial Judgement, *supra* note 315, para. 356. For the elements of enslavement, see Chapter 2, section 2.2.3.3.

[365] See Chapter 2, text accompanying notes 263–265. See also *Simić et al.* Trial Judgement, *supra* note 96, paras. 85–87.

[366] See, e.g., *Simić et al.* Trial Judgement, *supra* note 96, paras. 88–90 (recalling that Articles 50–52 of Geneva Convention III, Article 51 of Geneva Convention IV, and Article 5 of Additional Protocol II explicitly provide for the circumstances and conditions under which compulsory labour may legitimately be required of prisoners of war or civilians); accord *Blaškić* Appeal Judgement, *supra* note 96, paras. 593, 597. Note, however, that even persons required to work in those circumstances where international humanitarian law permits compulsory labour must be compensated. See, e.g., Geneva Convention III, *supra* note 3, Arts. 54, 62; Geneva Convention IV, *supra* note 3, Art. 51.

[367] *Naletilić and Martinović* Trial Judgement, *supra* note 57, paras. 250, 260 (quotation at para. 260). See also *ibid.*, paras. 271–272, 310–311, 313, 334 (convicting Martinović of unlawful labour for ordering prisoners of war to work in dangerous conditions, ordering prisoners to turn a privately owned building into military headquarters, and for the use of detainees to assist in the looting of private property), partially affirmed in *Naletilić and Martinović* Appeal Judgement, *supra* note 96, paras. 439, 466, 479–480. Although slavery and forced labour are not specifically enumerated in the subparagraphs of Article 3, they fall under the residual jurisdiction of this open-ended provision.

[368] Cf. *supra* text accompanying notes 123, 174–176, 262 (noting that certain of the mental state or knowledge requirements for war crimes should be susceptible of satisfaction by a relevant actor other than the physical perpetrator).

Article 4(d) of the ICTR Statute lists 'acts of terrorism' as a breach of Additional Protocol II falling within the jurisdiction of that Tribunal,[369] but neither Article 2 nor Article 3 of the ICTY Statute specifically lists terror, terrorism, or any similar term among their enumerated underlying offences.[370] Nevertheless, it appears that acts of terrorism have not been prosecuted at the ICTR to date, while at least two cases at the ICTY have included allegations of the intentional infliction of terror on the civilian population of Sarajevo during the siege of that Bosnian city between 1992 and 1995. In both ICTY cases – *Galić* and *Dragomir Milošević* – the underlying offence of terror was charged as a violation of the laws or customs of war under the residual jurisdiction of Article 3 of the Statute.[371] Notably, a provision on 'acts of terrorism' in the SCSL Statute identical to that in the ICTR Statute has also been the subject of considerable judicial exposition, relying heavily on the *Galić* Trial and Appeal Judgements; this Special Court jurisprudence is discussed in a subsequent section of this chapter.[372]

The *Galić* Trial Judgement was the first in the *ad hoc* Tribunals to consider the elements of the underlying offence of terror.[373] After noting that the prosecution had alleged that the accused Stanislav Galić, the commander of the Bosnian Serb Army in the Sarajevo area between 1992 and 1994, was responsible for the 'infliction of terror' on the civilian population of the city through the extended sniping and shelling campaign that captured international attention,[374] a majority of the Trial Chamber concluded that under applicable international law, the crime of terror as a violation of the laws or customs of war did not require a particular result in the targeted population, and so no proof that terror was actually inflicted was necessary.[375] After considering the parties' arguments, and emphasising that it was only

[369] See *supra* text accompanying note 13 for the full text of Article 4 of the ICTR Statute. The subparagraphs of this Article combine the underlying offences listed in Common Article 3 and Article 4 of Additional Protocol II. See *supra* text accompanying note 13. The offence of 'acts of terrorism' is listed in the latter IHL treaty provision, but is not explicitly included in Common Article 3.

[370] See *supra* text accompanying notes 2, 5 for the full text of Articles 2 and 3 of the ICTY Statute.

[371] See *Prosecutor* v. *Galić*, Case No. IT-98-29-I, Indictment, 26 March 1999, Count 1 (charging 'unlawfully inflicting terror upon civilians as set forth in Article 51 of Additional Protocol I and Article 13 of Additional Protocol II to the Geneva Conventions of 1949'); *Prosecutor* v. *Dragomir Milošević*, Case No. IT-98-29/1-PT, Amended Indictment, 18 December 2006, Count 1 (charging simply 'terror' as a breach of the same provisions of the Additional Protocols).

[372] See *infra* text accompanying notes 552–560.

[373] See *Galić* Trial Judgement, *supra* note 232, para. 66 ('The charge … of terror against the civilian population is one that until now has not been considered in a Tribunal judgement, although evidence of terrorization of civilians has been factored into convictions on other charges. This is also the first time an international tribunal has pronounced on the matter.').

[374] See *ibid*., para. 65.

[375] See *ibid*., paras. 65, 134; see also *ibid*., paras. 113–129 (applying the *Tadić* criteria and considering whether the 'intent to spread terror', a violation of IHL, attracts individual criminal responsibility). Judge Nieto-Navia dissented from the majority's conclusions with regard to the underlying offence of terror. See *ibid*., Separate and Partially Dissenting Opinion of Judge Nieto-Navia, para. 103.

The majority also held that the underlying offence of terror was well established in conventional international law binding on the parties to the conflict, and so there was no need to consider whether it was also recognised in customary international law. See *Galić* Trial Judgement, *supra* note 232, paras. 96–98; see especially *ibid*., para. 98 (completing the analysis of this *Tadić* factor by concluding that 'the rule against terror neither conflicts

required to determine whether the specific alleged conduct in the case constituted a violation of the laws or customs of war punishable under Article 3,[376] the *Galić* majority concluded that the elements of the underlying offence of terror were:

1. Acts of violence directed against the civilian population or individual civilians not taking direct part in hostilities causing death or serious injury to body or health within the civilian population.
2. The offender wilfully made the civilian population or individual civilians not taking direct part in hostilities the object of those acts of violence.
3. The above offence was committed with the primary purpose of spreading terror among the civilian population.[377]

On appeal, Galić asserted that the international agreement on which the Trial Chamber majority had relied to conclude that the offence was recognised by the parties to the conflict was neither binding law nor provided for the imposition of individual criminal responsibility,[378] and that its holding that the underlying offence does not require proof of the effects of the alleged conduct on the targeted population violated his rights as a criminal defendant.[379] A majority of the ICTY Appeals Chamber concluded that the first challenge was moot, because the prohibition of 'terror against the civilian population' as enshrined in the Additional Protocols was a part of customary international law, which also provided for the imposition of criminal sanctions on individuals.[380] On the second challenge, the Appeals Chamber upheld the Trial Chamber majority, and confirmed that the actual infliction of terror on a civilian population is not an element of the underlying offence of terror.[381]

with nor derogates from peremptory norms of international law'). As discussed below, the Appeals Chamber disagreed, and undertook an extensive analysis of the status of the underlying offence under customary international law. See *infra* text accompanying note 380.

376 See *ibid.*, para. 87 (emphasis added):

> [T]he Majority is not required to decide whether an offence of terror in a *general* sense falls within the jurisdiction of the Tribunal, but only whether a *specific* offence of killing and wounding civilians in time of armed conflict with the intention to inflict terror on the civilian population, as alleged in the Indictment, is an offence over which it has jurisdiction. While the Tribunal may have jurisdiction over other conceivable varieties of the crime of terror, it will be for Trial Chambers faced with charges correspondingly different from Count 1 of the present Indictment to decide that question.

377 *Ibid.*, para. 133.

378 See *Galić* Appeal Judgement, *supra* note 90, para. 86 (referring to an agreement between the parties to the conflict concluded under the aegis of the ICRC, which the majority in the Trial Chamber had concluded was an implementing instrument for Additional Protocol I).

379 See *ibid.*, paras. 70, 99.

380 See *ibid.*, paras. 86–98 (presenting an excellent and extensive analysis of whether customary international law prohibited the conduct constituting the underlying offence, and provided for individual criminal responsibility) (quotation at para. 86). Judge Schomburg dissented from the majority's conclusions. See *ibid.*, para. 86; *ibid.*, Separate and Partially Dissenting Opinion of Judge Schomburg, paras. 2, 4–24.

381 See *Galić* Appeal Judgement, *supra* note 90, paras. 72, 99, 104. This conclusion would suggest that, like direct and public incitement to commit genocide and the other genocide-related crimes, terror is also an inchoate offence that does not require proof of a particular result in order to be punished. See Chapter 3, note 24 (discussing inchoate crimes in general). But see *Galić* Appeal Judgement, *supra* note 90, para. 101 (noting, puzzlingly, that 'extensive trauma and psychological damage form part of the acts or threats of violence').

Relying on the text of the Additional Protocols, the Appeals Chamber majority presented a slightly expanded and modified definition of the elements of the underlying offence.[382] First, it incorporated the text of Article 51(2) of Additional Protocol I, and held that the underlying offence covered 'acts *or threats* of violence' directed at a civilian population.[383] Second, conduct qualifying as the *actus reus* of the offence was not limited to direct attacks on the civilian population, but also included indiscriminate or disproportionate acts of violence or threats thereof.[384] Finally, the appellate majority confirmed that terror as a violation of the laws or customs of war is a specific intent crime, and the *mens rea* is the intent to spread terror among the civilian population, which must be the primary purpose for the physical perpetrator's conduct.[385] Thus while terror as an underlying offence may be viewed as a form of the broader offence of attacks on civilians,[386] it is distinguished by such specific intent, which may be inferred from the nature, manner, timing, and duration of the acts or threats.[387]

Applying this definition to the evidence adduced at trial, the Appeals Chamber majority upheld the Trial Chamber majority's conclusion that 'attacks by sniping and shelling on the civilian population and individual civilians not taking part in the hostilities constitute acts of violence',[388] and noted that the Trial Chamber majority 'relied on a plethora of evidence to demonstrate that terrorisation of the civilian population was the primary purpose of the campaign of sniping and shelling and that Galić ordered the commission of the underlying acts with the same specific intent'.[389]

4.2.2.10 Torture

Torture is a grave breach of the Geneva Conventions punishable under Article 2 of the ICTY Statute, and a violation of Common Article 3 and Additional Protocol II

[382] As a result of that adherence to the treaty text, the Appeals Chamber majority referred to the underlying offence as 'acts or threats of violence the primary purpose of which is to spread terror among the civilian population'. See, e.g., *ibid.*, para. 104. As long as the elements of the underlying offence are clearly defined, this level of detail in the name of the underlying offence itself is unduly cumbersome and seems unnecessary.

[383] *Ibid.*, para. 101 (emphasis added). [384] *Ibid.*

[385] *Ibid.*, para. 104 (upholding *Galić* Trial Judgement, *supra* note 232, para. 136). For reasons similar to those explored elsewhere in this chapter, see, e.g., *supra* notes 121–124 and accompanying text, it would be consistent with the logic and structure of international crimes for another relevant actor to be able to supply the *mens rea* for the offence, if the physical perpetrator is acting only as a tool implementing that other person's criminal intent).

[386] See *ibid.*, para. 87; *Galić* Trial Judgement, *supra* note 232, para. 133. In his partial dissent, Judge Schomburg concluded that Galić could only be convicted for the underlying offence of attacks on civilians, and that the intent to spread terror should have counted as an aggravating factor for sentencing. See *Galić* Appeal Judgement, *supra* note 380, Separate and Partially Dissenting Opinion of Judge Schomburg, para. 2.

[387] *Galić* Appeal Judgement, *supra* note 90, para. 104.

[388] *Ibid.*, para. 106 (citing *Galić* Trial Judgement, *supra* note 232, para. 596).

[389] *Ibid.*, para. 107 (citing some of that evidence, including the fact that the attacks on civilians were numerous, but 'not consistently so intense as to suggest an attempt … to wipe out or even deplete the civilian population through attrition') (quoting *Galić* Trial Judgement, *supra* note 232, para. 593).

punishable under Article 3 of the ICTY Statute and Article 4(a) of the ICTR Statute.[390] Like rape,[391] the elements of this underlying offence are the same, no matter which international crime is charged.[392] A full discussion of its elements is included in Chapter 2.[393]

4.2.2.11 Unlawful attack on civilians and civilian objects

The physical perpetrator intentionally or wilfully committed acts of violence against a civilian population, individual civilians, or civilian objects, which caused death, serious injury to body or health, or a result of equal gravity to civilians.

Unlawful attacks on civilians and civilian objects are perhaps the most fundamental breaches of international humanitarian law, because they violate the basic principles of distinction and proportionality that underlie the law regulating the conduct of armed conflict; that is, such attacks do not observe the distinction between legitimate military targets and persons or objects that play no active part in the hostilities, or they are not undertaken with adequate precautions to reduce or avoid injury, loss, or damage to such persons and objects.[394] Neither of the *ad hoc* Statutes explicitly includes 'unlawful attacks on civilians' or 'unlawful attacks on civilian objects' among the underlying offences for war crimes. However, Article 3 (c) of the ICTY Statute lists 'attack, or bombardment, by whatever means, of undefended towns, villages, dwellings, or buildings' as an offence within that Tribunal's jurisdiction, and trial and appeals chambers have recognised that attacks on both civilians and real or personal property pertaining to civilians or civilian populations are violations of the laws or customs of war generally falling under the residual jurisdiction of Article 3 of the Statute.[395]

Relying primarily on Additional Protocol I,[396] the jurisprudence of the ICTY has identified three elements to the offences of attacks on civilians and attacks on civilian objects under customary international law:[397] (1) acts of violence committed against a

[390] Although torture is not specifically enumerated in the subparagraphs of Article 3 of the ICTY Statute, it falls under the residual jurisdiction of that open-ended provision.

[391] See *supra* section 4.2.2.7.

[392] See, e.g., *Limaj et al.* Trial Judgement, *supra* note 103, para. 235; *Brđanin* Trial Judgement, *supra* note 111, paras. 481–482.

[393] See Chapter 2, section 2.2.3.6.

[394] See, e.g., *Kordić and Čerkez* Appeal Judgement, *supra* note 101, paras. 52, 54.

[395] See *supra* note 254; see also *Galić* Appeal Judgement, *supra* note 90, paras. 123, 125; *Kordić and Čerkez* Appeal Judgement, *supra* note 101, paras. 47–68.

[396] See especially Additional Protocol I, *supra* note 3, Art. 51(2) ('The civilian population as such, as well as individual civilians, shall not be the object of attack.'); *ibid.*, Art. 52(1) ('Civilian objects shall not be the object of attack or of reprisals.'). See also Additional Protocol II, *supra* note 3, Art. 13(2), cited in *Martić* Trial Judgement, *supra* note 120, para. 67.

[397] There are two separate underlying offences with almost identical elements, one focused on individuals, the other on property. Most decisions and judgements discuss the offences together when both are charged. While the term 'unlawful' is useful in the context of IHL to distinguish between legitimate uses of military force and those which violate international law, it seems tautological in the context of international criminal law.

civilian population, individual civilians, or civilian objects; (2) causing death, serious injury to body or health, or a result of equal gravity to civilians; (3) with the intent to make the civilians, civilian population, or civilian objects the targets of the attack.[398] Under current ICTY appellate jurisprudence, the chambers apply the same definition for 'civilian' in the contexts of war crimes and crimes against humanity; a full discussion of that definition is included in Chapter 2.[399] Among the factors used to determine civilian status are 'the clothing, activity, age, or sex of a person'.[400] Civilian objects are defined as any property that is not a military objective under Article 52(2) of Additional Protocol I, that is, does not 'by [its] nature, location, purpose or use make an effective contribution to military action and whose total or partial destruction, capture or neutralization, in the circumstances ruling at the time, offers a definite military advantage'.[401] In case of doubt, combatants are expected to err on the side of assuming an individual is a civilian, or that property does not effectively contribute to military action; in the context of criminal proceedings, of course, the prosecution bears the burden of proof on this element of the crime.[402]

The prohibitions against attacking civilians and civilian objects are absolute, and may not be avoided by claiming military necessity.[403] Accordingly, indiscriminate acts of violence that do not or cannot distinguish between military targets and civilians or civilian objects may qualify as violations of the laws or customs of war, and trial chambers may consider the nature of the weapons used in order to determine whether the elements of the underlying offence have been established.[404]

Applying these guidelines to the evidence presented at trial, the *Martić* Trial Chamber concluded that the shelling of Zagreb in May 1995, which was ordered by

398 See, e.g., *Kordić and Čerkez* Appeal Judgement, *supra* note 101, paras. 47–48, 57; *Martić* Trial Judgement, *supra* note 120, paras. 66–72; *Strugar* Trial Judgement, *supra* note 51, para. 283; *Galić* Trial Judgement, *supra* note 232, paras. 56, 62 (defining the *mens rea* as wilful action, and adopting the position in the ICRC Commentary to Article 85 of Additional Protocol I, which notes that reckless action may also qualify as wilfulness), affirmed in *Galić* Appeal Judgement, *supra* note 90, para. 140.

399 See Chapter 2, text accompanying notes 126–127, 130–132, 135. See also *supra* note 179 for the listing of members of the armed forces that is included in the first three Geneva Conventions.

400 *Galić* Trial Judgement, *supra* note 232, para. 50. See also *ibid.*, para. 48 (noting that anyone who would otherwise qualify for civilian status is not protected under IHL for the duration of any direct participation in hostilities); accord *Kordić and Čerkez* Appeal Judgement, *supra* note 101, para. 50.

401 See, e.g., *Kordić and Čerkez* Appeal Judgement, *supra* note 101, para. 53; *Galić* Trial Judgement, *supra* note 232, para. 51.

402 See, e.g., *Kordić and Čerkez* Appeal Judgement, *supra* note 101, paras. 48, 53; *Strugar* Trial Judgement, *supra* note 51, para. 282; *Galić* Trial Judgement, *supra* note 232, para. 51.

403 See *Galić* Appeal Judgement, *supra* note 90, para. 130; *Kordić and Čerkez* Appeal Judgement, *supra* note 101, para. 54 (as corrected by the subsequent corrigendum); *Blaškić* Appeal Judgement, *supra* note 96, para. 109.

404 See, e.g., *Galić* Appeal Judgement, *supra* note 90, para. 132 (citing earlier jurisprudence that used the examples of cluster bombs, or which concluded from the types of weapons used that the physical perpetrators intended to target the civilian population); *Galić* Trial Judgement, *supra* note 96, para. 60 (noting that disproportionate attacks may give rise to the inference that civilians are the true targets, but cautioning that such evaluations must be made on a case-by-case basis in light of the evidence adduced at trial); *Martić* Trial Judgement, *supra* note 120, para. 69 (noting also that in order to avoid violating IHL, '[civilian] casualties must not be disproportionate to the concrete and direct military advantage anticipated before the attack').

the accused Milan Martić,[405] was an unlawful attack on civilians. Its findings were unusually detailed, and provide a useful example of the manner in which some trial chambers support their determinations. After explaining the specifications of the type of weapon used in the shelling, the Trial Chamber concluded:

> The evidence shows that the M-87 Orkan was fired on 2 and 3 May 1995 from the Vojnić area, near Slavsko Polje, between 47 and 51 kilometres from Zagreb. However, the Trial Chamber notes in this respect that the weapon was fired from the extreme of its range. Moreover, the Trial Chamber notes the characteristics of the weapon, it being a non-guided high dispersion weapon. The Trial Chamber therefore concludes that the M-87 Orkan, by virtue of its characteristics and the firing range in this specific instance, was incapable of hitting specific targets. For these reasons, the Trial Chamber also finds that the M-87 Orkan is an indiscriminate weapon, the use of which in densely populated civilian areas, such as Zagreb, will result in the infliction of severe casualties. By 2 May 1995, the effects of firing the M-87 Orkan on Zagreb were known to those involved. Furthermore, before the decision was made to once again use this weapon on Zagreb on 3 May 1995, the full impact of using such an indiscriminate weapon was known beyond doubt as a result of the extensive media coverage on 2 May 1995 of the effects of the attack on Zagreb.[406]

Rejecting the accused's arguments that the attack was a legitimate reprisal under international law,[407] the Trial Chamber found that these attacks resulted in death and serious injury to members of the civilian population of Zagreb, recalled its findings on the nature of the M-87 Orkan and Martić's knowledge of its effects, concluded that Martić 'wilfully made the civilian population of Zagreb the object of this attack', and convicted him of unlawful attack on civilians as a violation of the laws or customs of war.[408] As this finding demonstrates, unlawful attacks on civilians or civilians objects are quintessential 'leadership' crimes, where the *actus reus* of the underlying offence is typically carried out by mid-level or senior accused.[409]

4.2.2.12 Unlawful confinement

The underlying offence for unlawful confinement – which is punishable as a grave breach under Article 2 of the ICTY Statute and a violation of the laws or customs of war under the residual jurisdiction of Article 3 of that Statute – is identical to that for imprisonment as a crime against humanity.[410] As a grave breach, however, unlawful confinement is restricted by the provisions of the Geneva Conventions. In particular, confinement of civilians is unlawful in two situations: first, when the initial arrest or detention is arbitrary in the context of international humanitarian law, that is, it

[405] See *Martić* Trial Judgement, *supra* note 120, para. 460. [406] *Ibid.*, para. 463.
[407] *Ibid.*, paras 464–468. [408] *Ibid.*, para. 472.
[409] See *infra* text accompanying notes 426–433, 497–506 (discussing other such leadership war crimes in the jurisdiction of the *ad hoc* Tribunals and the ICC).
[410] See *Simić et al.* Trial Judgement, *supra* note 96, para. 63. For a full discussion of the elements of imprisonment, see Chapter 2, section 2.2.3.5.

occurs in violation of Article 42 of Geneva Convention IV, because the detainee is not a threat to the security of the Detaining Power; and second, even if the initial detention is valid, when the individual's continued detention is not compliant with procedural safeguards under Article 43 of Geneva Convention IV.[411] The *mens rea* for this underlying offence may be satisfied by proof that the detention in breach of these provisions was committed intentionally, or with reckless disregard for whether the procedural safeguards and protections were observed.[412]

4.2.2.13 Unlawful deportation or transfer

The underlying offence for unlawful deportation or unlawful transfer as grave breaches is the offence we have termed 'forcible displacement', which is also the underlying offence for the crimes against humanity of deportation and forcible transfer as an inhumane act.[413] A full discussion of the elements of forcible displacement appears in Chapter 2.[414]

4.2.2.14 Violence to life and person

Article 4(a) of the ICTR Statute grants jurisdiction over '[v]iolence to life, health and physical or mental well-being of persons, in particular murder as well as cruel treatment such as torture, mutilation or any form of corporal punishment'.[415] While there is no similar provision in the ICTY Statute, the ICTY Prosecutor brought charges of violence to life and person under Article 3 of that Tribunal's Statute in at least three cases.[416]

411 See *Čelebići* Appeal Judgement, *supra* note 162, paras. 322, 327; accord *Kordić and Čerkez* Appeal Judgement, *supra* note 101, paras. 69–70, 73.

412 See *Čelebići* Appeal Judgement, *supra* note 162, para. 378. It appears that the *Čelebići* Appeals Chamber disapproved of allegations that accused were responsible for unlawful confinement by their mere participation in the running of a prison camp, and preferred instead that evidence of intent or wilful conduct with regard to the detention be adduced. See *Čelebići* Appeal Judgement, *supra* note 162, para. 342:

> [T]o establish that an individual has committed the offence of unlawful confinement, something more must be proved than mere knowing 'participation' in a general system or operation pursuant to which civilians are confined … Such [primary] responsibility [for commission] is more properly allocated to those … who actually place an accused in detention without reasonable grounds to believe that he constitutes a security risk; or who, having some powers over the place of detention, accept [ ] a civilian into detention without knowing that such grounds exist; or who, having power or authority to release detainees, fail [ ] to do so despite knowledge that no reasonable grounds for their detention exist, or that any such reasons have ceased to exist.

As such, the Appeals Chamber seems to have disapproved of allegations of responsibility for this crime that rely only on the second category of joint criminal enterprise. See Boas, Bischoff, and Reid, *supra* note 30, pp. 34–51, 57–67 (discussing the elements of this form of responsibility).

413 See *Naletilić and Martinović* Trial Judgement, *supra* note 57, paras. 519–521.

414 See Chapter 2, section 2.2.3.4. 415 See *supra* text accompanying note 13.

416 See *Prosecutor* v. *Vasiljević*, Case No. IT-98-32-PT, Amended Indictment, 20 July 2001, Counts 13, 17; *Prosecutor* v. *Blaškić*, Case No. IT-95-14-PT, Second Amended Indictment, 25 April 1997, Count 9; *Prosecutor* v. *Hadžihasanović, Alagić, and Kubura*, Case No. IT-01-47-I, Amended Indictment, 11 January 2002, Count 2. Although violence to life and person is not specifically enumerated in the subparagraphs of Article 3 of the ICTY Statute, the prosecution brought these charges under the residual jurisdiction of this open-ended provision.

Like inhumane acts, cruel treatment, inhuman treatment, and wilfully causing great suffering or serious injury,[417] violence to life or person appears to be a subcategory of underlying offences that may qualify as an international crime if the necessary general requirements are satisfied.[418] Unlike the first three examples, however, violence to life or person does not appear to have any specific requirements that characterise the subcategory.[419] Instead, it seems to function as a loosely defined label that may be applied to a wide range of potentially criminal conduct. In light of this lack of precision or independent substantive content, at least one ICTY trial chamber has expressed concern with regard to the amorphous nature of 'violence to life and person'.[420] At the ICTR, this concern is lessened or resolved by the prosecution's charging practices, where indictments alleging conduct falling under Article 4(a) generally charge only the listed examples, which are clearly established as violations of the laws or customs of war under the jurisprudence of both Tribunals.[421]

[417] See Chapter 2, section 2.2.3.9 (inhumane acts); *supra*, section 4.2.2.3 (inhuman or cruel treatment); *infra*, section 4.2.2.15 (wilfully causing great suffering).

[418] See *supra* text accompanying note 415; see also, e.g., *Blaškić* Trial Judgement, *supra* note 57, para. 182 (noting that murder, mutilation, and torture fall within the concept of violence to life or person); *Prosecutor* v. *Hadžihasanović and Kubura*, Case No. IT-01-47-PT, Decision on the Form of the Indictment, 17 September 2003, para. 40 (noting that 'the crime of "cruel treatment" is therefore only one of the forms that the broader offence of "violence to life and person" may assume'); *ibid*., paras. 40–42 (permitting the prosecution to replace the count of 'violence to life and person' with the narrower count of 'cruel treatment').

[419] See Chapter 1, text accompanying notes 44–45 (explaining the term 'specific requirements', and giving examples).

[420] See, e.g., *Vasiljević* Trial Judgement, *supra* note 136, paras. 201–204 (concluding that there was no sufficiently precise definition under customary international law for the alleged offence of 'violence to life and person', and acquitting the accused on that count); accord *Prosecutor* v. *Ntakirutimana and Ntakirutimana*, Case No. ICTR-96-10-T & ICTR-96-17-T, Judgement, 21 February 2003, paras. 860–861 (noting also that no definition of the elements of 'violence to life and person' had been developed in the ICTR by 2003). This concern is not misplaced. The *Blaškić* Trial Chamber, for example, had convicted the accused for violence to life and person as a violation of the laws or customs of war, without identifying the legal elements that had to be satisfied in order for a factfinder to conclude that the crime had been committed, or what factual findings underlay the conviction. See *Blaškić* Trial Judgement, *supra* note 57, para. 182 & p. 268. Despite the pointed criticism this approach received from the *Vasiljević* Trial Chamber, see *Vasiljević* Trial Judgement, *supra* note 136, para. 194, the *Blaškić* Appeals Chamber did not specifically address the problems with the definition of the offence underlying the conviction for violence to life and person. It did, however, overturn the conviction on other grounds. See *Blaškić* Appeal Judgement, *supra* note 96, para. 677 & p. 261 (overturning Blaškić's conviction for this and numerous other counts on the basis of his lack of responsibility, not whether the crime had been proved).

[421] See *supra* sections 4.2.2.4, 4.2.2.3, 4.2.2.10 (respectively discussing murder, cruel treatment, and torture as war crimes). But see *Prosecutor* v. *Karemera*, Case No. ICTR-98-44-T, Decision on Count Seven of the Amended Indictment – Violence to Life, Health and Physical or Mental Well-Being of Persons – Article 4(a) of the Statute, 5 August 2005 (rejecting the accused's challenge to an indictment alleging 'killing and causing violence to health and physical or mental well-being as serious violations of Article 3 Common to the Geneva Conventions and Additional Protocol II', and only ordering the prosecution to replace the term 'killing' with another term – like murder – to 'bring the pleading into conformity with the statutory provisions') (quotation at para. 9). As of 1 December 2007, the prosecution had not yet completed its case in chief against Karemera and his co-accused, so it remains to be seen what the Trial Chamber in the case will decide with regard to these charges.

4.2.2.15 *Wilfully causing great suffering or serious injury to body or health*

The physical perpetrator intentionally caused great suffering or serious injury to body or health, including mental health, of an individual ('the victim').

This grave breach, punishable under Article 2(c) of the ICTY Statute, is almost identical to inhuman treatment or cruel treatment,[422] because it has been defined as 'an intentional act or omission consisting of causing great suffering or serious injury to body or health, including mental health'.[423] As the *Kordić and Čerkez* Trial Judgement emphasised, however, wilfully causing great suffering 'is distinguished from … inhuman treatment in that it requires a showing of serious mental or physical injury. Thus, acts where the resultant harm relates solely to an individual's human dignity are not included within this offence.'[424] In its 2003 final judgement, the *Naletilić and Martinović* Trial Chamber summarised the jurisprudence on 'serious harm' for the purposes of evaluating whether this underlying offence – and by extension, inhuman or cruel treatment – had been proved:

> This offence includes those acts that do not fulfil the conditions set for torture even though acts of torture may also fit the definition given … In the *Krstić* Trial Judgement, the Chamber considered how the term serious should be interpreted [in the context of genocide] and stated: ['s]erious harm need not cause permanent and irremediable harm, but it must involve harm that goes beyond temporary unhappiness, embarrassment, or humiliation. It must be harm that results in a grave and long-term disadvantage to a person's ability to led a normal and constructive life.' The gravity of the suffering is determined on a case by case basis taking into account the circumstances of the case.[425]

4.2.2.16 *Other underlying offences*

Other underlying offences, though specifically provided for in the Statutes of the *ad hoc* Tribunals, have not been the subject of any reasoned discussion in a trial or appeal judgement. These include the ostensibly inchoate offences of threats to commit any of the enumerated underlying offences in Article 4 of the ICTR Statute;[426] collective punishments;[427] arbitrary sentences and

[422] See *supra* section 4.2.2.3.

[423] *Čelebići* Appeal Judgement, *supra* note 162, para. 424; accord, e.g. *Naletilić and Martinović* Trial Judgement, *supra* note 57, para. 339; *ibid.*, para. 246 ('The degree of physical or mental suffering required to prove either [inhuman or cruel treatment] is lower than the one required for torture, though at the same level as the one required to prove a charge of "wilfully causing great suffering or serious injury to body or health".'); *Blaškić* Trial Judgement, *supra* note 57, para. 156.

[424] *Kordić and Čerkez* Trial Judgement, *supra* note 57, para. 245.

[425] *Naletilić and Martinović* Trial Judgement, *supra* note 57, paras. 341–343 (citing *Kordić and Čerkez* Trial Judgement, *supra* note 57, para. 244; *Čelebići* Trial Judgement, *supra* note 67, para 510; *Krstić* Trial Judgement, *supra* note 97, para. 513).

[426] See ICTR Statute, *supra* note 13, Art. 4(h). See also Chapter 3, note 24 (discussing this ostensibly inchoate war crime and noting others from the Rome Statute of the ICC); *infra* notes 520, 554 (discussing this inchoate war crime in the SCSL).

[427] ICTR Statute, *supra* note 13, Art. 4(b).

executions;[428] forced military service in the armed forces of the enemy;[429] deprivation of fair trial rights;[430] and employment of poisonous weapons.[431] As discussed below, collective punishments and threats to commit acts of terrorism have been considered to some extent in the SCSL, and convictions for collective punishments have been imposed.[432] As also noted below with respect to the ICC, many of these yet-to-be-charged war crimes would appear to be quintessential leadership crimes in which the *actus reus* is typically fulfilled not by the foot soldier on the ground, but by his intermediate- or high-level commander.[433]

4.3 War crimes in the International Criminal Court and Internationalised Tribunals

4.3.1 The International Criminal Court

4.3.1.1 The Rome Statute

The Rome Statute's article on war crimes has a very different structure and a more extensive catalogue of underlying offences than its analogues in the ICTY and ICTR Statutes. Article 8 sets forth four separate listings of offences, which can be divided into two categories: subparagraphs (2)(a) and (b) list international armed conflict war crimes, and subparagraphs (2)(c) and (e) list non-international armed conflict war crimes. Each of these categories is further divided into two subcategories. For international armed conflict war crimes, Article 8(2)(a) lists the grave breaches of the 1949 Geneva Conventions in language virtually identical to that of Article 2 of the ICTY Statute.[434] Article 8(2)(b) contains twenty-six subparagraphs listing 'other serious violations of the laws or customs applicable in international armed conflict'; these offences derive from a number of different

[428] *Ibid.*, Art. 4(g) ('the passing of sentences and the carrying out of executions without previous judgement pronounced by a regularly constituted court, affording all the judicial guarantees which are recognised as indispensable by civilised peoples').

[429] See ICTY Statute, *supra* note 2, Art. 2(e) ('compelling a prisoner of war or a civilian to serve in the forces of a hostile power').

[430] See *ibid.*, Art. 2(f) ('wilfully depriving a prisoner of war or a civilian of the rights of fair and regular trial').

[431] See *ibid.*, Art. 3(a) ('employment of poisonous weapons or other weapons calculated to cause unnecessary suffering').

[432] See *Prosecutor* v. *Brima, Kamara, and Kanu*, Case No. SCSL-04-16-T, Judgement, 20 June 2007 ('*AFRC* Trial Judgement'), paras. 676–671 (proffering two elements for collective punishments: (1) 'A punishment imposed indiscriminately and collectively upon persons for acts that they have not committed', and (2) '[t]he intent on the part of the perpetrator to indiscriminately and collectively punish the persons for acts which form the subject of the punishment.'); *Prosecutor* v. *Fofana and Kondewa*, Case No. SCSL-04-14-J, Judgement, 2 August 2007 ('*CDF* Trial Judgement'), para. 180 (proffering similar elements); *infra* notes 533, 535, 537 (noting charges and convictions in these cases for collective punishments); *infra* note 554 and accompanying text (*CDF* Trial Chamber's remarks on threats to commit acts of terror).

[433] See *infra* text accompanying notes 497–506. See also *supra* text accompanying notes 405–408 for an example of factual findings for such a leadership crime.

[434] See *supra* text accompanying note 2 (quoting Article 2 of the ICTY Statute).

treaties, most importantly the Regulations annexed to Hague Convention IV of 1907,[435] on one hand, and Additional Protocol I of 1977, on the other.[436] For non-international armed conflict war crimes, the list in Article 8(2)(c) finds its origins in Common Article 3 of the 1949 Geneva Conventions.[437] Article 8(2)(e) contains twelve sub-paragraphs listing other 'violations of the laws and customs applicable in armed conflicts not of an international character'; these come mainly from Additional Protocol II.[438]

There is a wealth of literature on this long and complex provision of the Rome Statute; the origins, meaning, and scope of the offences listed therein; the difficult and often disappointing compromises that were reached in the course of its drafting;

435 See 1907 Hague Regulations, *supra* note 6, Arts. 23–25, 27–28 (containing precursors for Rome Statute, *supra* note 1, Art. 8(2)(b)(vi)–(vii), (ix), (xi)–(xiii), (xv)–(xvii)). This list partially overlaps with Article 3 of the ICTY Statute, *supra* note 2.

436 See Additional Protocol I, *supra* note 3, Art. 85(3)–(4) (grave breaches provision of Additional Protocol I, containing precursors for Rome Statute, *supra* note 1, Art. 8(2)(b)(i), (ii), (iv)–(x), (xii), and (xxiv)–(xxvi)). Not all of the grave breaches of Additional Protocol I were included in Article 8(2)(b) of the Rome Statute, which omits unjustifiable delay in repatriation of prisoners of war or civilians, and apartheid. See *ibid.*, Art. 85(4)(b)–(c). The twenty-six subparagraphs of Article 8(2)(b) can be roughly divided into four categories. First, prohibited *methods* of warfare: (i)–(ii), (iv) attacks on civilians and civilian objects; (v) attacks on undefended places; (vi) killing or wounding persons *hors de combat*; (vii) and (xi) improper use of insignia and perfidy; (xii) declaring no quarter; (xiii) destruction or seizure of enemy property; (xvi) pillage; (xxiii) using human shields; and (xxv) starvation. Second, prohibited *means* of warfare: (xvii)–(xviii) poison; (xix) dumdum bullets; and (xx) weapons that cause unnecessary suffering, superfluous injury, or are inherently indiscriminate. Third, attacks on specially protected persons and objects: (iii) humanitarian or peacekeeping personnel; (ix) protected buildings and monuments; and (xxiv) medical personnel and units. Fourth, other human rights violations: (viii) transfer of a civilian population into or out of occupied territory; (x) mutilation or scientific experiments; (xiv) denial of justice; (xv) compelling a breach of loyalty; (xxi) outrages on personal dignity; (xxii) sexual violence; and (xxvi) conscripting, enlisting, or using child soldiers.

437 See Common Article 3, *supra* note 3. Article 8(2)(c)'s list partially overlaps with Article 4 of the ICTR Statute, *supra* note 13. Article 8(2)(c) consists of four subparagraphs: (i) violence to life and person; (ii) outrages upon personal dignity; (iii) hostage-taking; and (iv) denial of justice and extralegal executions.

438 See Additional Protocol II, *supra* note 3, Arts. 4, 5, 11, 13, 16, 17, 18. Not all violations of Additional Protocol II were included in Article 8(2)(e), such as using starvation as a method of warfare and attacking works containing dangerous forces. See *ibid.*, Arts. 14–15. Article 8(2)(e)'s list partially overlaps with Article 4 of the ICTR Statute, *supra* note 13. The twelve subparagraphs of Article 8(2)(e) can be roughly divided into three categories. First, prohibited methods of warfare: (i) attacks on civilians; (v) pillage; (ix) perfidy; (x) declaring no quarter; and (xii) destroying or seizing adversary property. Second, attacks on specially protected persons and objects: (ii) medical personnel and units; (iii) humanitarian or peacekeeping personnel; and (iv) protected buildings and monuments. Third, other human rights violations: (xi) mutilation or scientific experiments; (vi) sexual violence; (vii) conscripting, enlisting, or using child soldiers; and (viii) displacement of the civilian population. Articles 8(2)(d) and (f) define the threshold for the applicability of Articles 8(2)(c) and (e), respectively, and Article 8(3) incorporates a proviso: 'Nothing in paragraph 2(c) and (e) shall affect the responsibility of a Government to maintain or re-establish, law and order in the State or to defend the unity and territorial integrity of the State, by all legitimate means. Rome Statute, *supra* note 1, Art. 8(3). There were intense negotiations at the Rome Statute drafting meetings concerning non-international armed conflict war crimes and the threshold for their applicability. Predictably, many states opposed restricting the means they may use in quelling rebellions and in dealing with individual rebels. See Michael Bothe, 'War Crimes', in Antonio Cassese, Paola Gaeta, and John R. W. D. Jones (eds.), *The Rome Statute of the International Criminal Court: A Commentary* (2001), vol. I, pp. 419, 423–424 (describing the scope of application of Articles 8(2)(c) and (e), and Article 8(3)'s 'savings clause'); Herman von Hebel and Darryl Robinson, 'Crimes with the Jurisdiction of the Court', in Roy S. Lee (ed.), *The International Criminal Court: The Making of the Rome Statute* (1999), pp. 119–122 (describing the negotiations).

and the elaboration of the elements of war crimes in the ICC Elements of Crimes.[439] As in the previous chapters of this book, we will not attempt to reproduce these discussions or opine generally on the merits and flaws of Article 8. Instead, we briefly highlight some of the ways in which Article 8 compares to its analogues in the *ad hoc* Statutes as interpreted in ICTY and ICTR jurisprudence.

First, Article 8 begins with a jurisdictional provision not present in either the *ad hoc* Statutes or in the statutes of the internationalised tribunals that patterned their war crimes provisions on Article 8: 'The Court shall have jurisdiction in respect of war crimes *in particular* when committed as part of a plan or policy or as part of a large-scale commission of such crimes.'[440] The United States, seeking to safeguard military personnel from ICC prosecution for isolated instances of war crimes, initially proposed an absolute bar to the exercise of jurisdiction for war crimes unless committed on a large scale or as part of a plan or policy.[441] A clear majority opposed any restriction at all.[442] The majority position comports with that of the *ad hoc* Tribunals, which have never expounded any such requirement.[443] Ultimately,

[439] See Assembly of States Parties to the Rome Statute of the International Criminal Court, First Session: Official Records, Part II(B): Elements of Crimes, UN Doc. ICC-ASP/1/3 (2002) ('ICC Elements of Crimes'), pp. 125–155 (setting forth Article 8). Indeed, the complexity of Article 8 and its corresponding provision in the Elements of Crimes, along with the desire to provide 'a complete picture, which is necessary for an accurate and faithful interpretation of the crimes', led the ICRC to issue an entire volume of interpretive comments. See Knut Dörmann, *Elements of War Crimes Under the Rome Statute of the International Criminal Court: Sources and Commentary* (2003) (quotation at p. 6). Other commentaries include the following: Michael Cottier, William J. Fenrick, Patricia Viseur Sellers, and Andreas Zimmerman, 'War Crimes', in Otto Triffterer (ed.), *Commentary on the Rome Statute of the International Criminal Court* (1999), pp. 173–288; Bothe, *supra* note 438, pp. 379–426; von Hebel and Robinson, *supra* note 438, pp. 103–122; Herman von Hebel, Knut Dörmann, Eve la Haye, Daniel Frank, Didier Pfirter, Charles Garraway, and Hans Boddens Hosang, 'The Elements of War Crimes', in Roy S. Lee (ed.), *The International Criminal Court: Elements of Crimes and Rules of Procedure and Evidence* (2001), pp. 109–216; Robert Cryer, *Prosecuting International Crime: Selectivity and the International Criminal Law Regime* (2005), pp. 268–283; Peter Rowe, 'War Crimes', in Dominic McGoldrick, Peter Rowe, and Eric Donnelly (eds.), *The International Criminal Court* (2004), pp. 203–232; William A. Schabas, *An Introduction to the International Criminal Court* (2nd edn 2004), pp. 51–66; Thomas Graditzky, 'War Crime Issues Before the Rome Diplomatic Conference on the Establishment of an International Criminal Court', (1999) 5 *U.C. Davis Journal of International Law and Policy* 199; Christopher Keith Hall, 'The Fifth Session of the Preparatory Committee for an International Criminal Court', (1998) 92 *American Journal of International Law* 331.

[440] Rome Statute, *supra* note 1, Art. 8(1) (emphasis added). See also *infra* text accompanying note 565 (discussing the absence of this restriction from the constitutive instrument of the East Timor SPSC); text accompanying note 594 (discussing its absence from the SICT).

[441] von Hebel and Robinson, *supra* note 438, p. 107. This restriction resembles similar restrictions inserted into the Statute and Elements of Crimes with respect to crimes against humanity and genocide; these are discussed in the previous two chapters of this volume. See Chapter 2, text accompanying notes 490–497 (discussing the Rome Statute's high threshold for the exercise of jurisdiction over crimes against humanity); Chapter 3, text accompanying notes 349–353 (discussing the high threshold for the exercise of jurisdiction over genocide in the Elements of Crimes).

[442] See von Hebel and Robinson, *supra* note 438, p. 107. This position was in line with ICTY jurisprudence. See *Tadić* Trial Judgement, *supra* note 103, para. 573 ('It is not … necessary to show that [the crimes were] part of a policy or of a practice officially endorsed or tolerated by one of the parties to the conflict[.]').

[443] See *Čelebići* Trial Judgement, *supra* note 67, para. 591 (holding that plunder and other war crimes against property may be committed by perpetrators motivated by personal greed); *Prosecutor* v. *Hadžihasanović and Kubura*, Case No. IT-01-47-T, Decision on Motions for Acquittal Pursuant to Rule 98 *bis* of the Rules of Procedure and Evidence, 27 September 2004, para. 128 (same); *Kupreškić et al.* Trial Judgement, *supra* note 321, para. 698 ('[M]urder, torture or rape of enemy civilians normally constitute war crimes; however, if these acts are part of a widespread or systematic practice, they may also be defined as crimes against humanity.').

the US-led minority won what would appear, at first glance, to be something of a concession in the compromise language quoted above.[444] One wonders, however, whether this language was truly necessary, as the Rome Statute obliges the Court in any event to reject cases that are 'not of sufficient gravity to justify further action'.[445]

Second, there are many offences in Article 8 of the Rome Statute that do not explicitly appear in the Statutes of the ICTY and ICTR. For example, the Rome Statute contains an innovative catalogue of sexual offences punishable in both international and non-international armed conflict: rape, sexual slavery, enforced prostitution, forced pregnancy, enforced sterilisation, and 'any other form of sexual violence' meeting a certain threshold.[446] Of these, the ICTR Statute explicitly lists only rape and enforced prostitution,[447] and the ICTY Statute explicitly lists none of them. Nonetheless, the ICTY has convicted accused of various forms of sexual violence by virtue of the 'shall include, but shall not be limited to' language in the

444 von Hebel and Robinson, *supra* note 438, p. 108. But see *ibid.*, p. 124 (describing Article 8(1) as a '"non-threshold threshold", or a guideline rather than a threshold'); Graditzky, *supra* note 439, pp. 211–212 (pointing out that the compromise language 'does not [absolutely] forbid the Court to prosecute any "minor" war crimes'); Cryer, *supra* note 439, p. 269 (arguing that the original U.S. proposal would have 'collapse[d] the definition of war crimes into that of crimes against humanity too easily, and would have led to the court having to prove the additional elements, which are not present in war crimes law'). There is, however, a danger that Article 8(1) could be misinterpreted as expressing some sort of international consensus against the prosecution of isolated or minor war crimes. See, e.g., *Prosecutor* v. *Tadić*, Case No. IT-94-1-T*bis*-R117, Sentencing Judgement, 11 November 1999, Separate Opinion of Judge Robinson, p. 7 (examining Article 8(1) and a similar provision in the 1996 ILC Draft Code, along with the instruments' respective provisions on crimes against humanity, and concluding that, '[i]f these two … instruments are seen as reflecting a customary norm requiring that crimes against humanity be committed on a widespread or systematic basis, it would seem that they also reflect a norm requiring that war crimes be committed, if not on a similar basis, then on one that is akin to it'). See also Ruth Wedgwood, 'The International Criminal Court: An American View', (1999) 10 *European Journal of International Law* 93, 94 (arguing that the compromise language 'makes an appropriate distinction between the defalcations that are often committed in war and the truly extraordinary situations that merit international attention').

445 Rome Statute, *supra* note 1, Art. 17(1). Some commentators have also suggested that the United States may be expected to satisfactorily secure the prosecution in its own courts – or allow for prosecution in foreign courts under a status of forces agreement – of the aberrant soldier who commits an isolated rape, murder, or beating, and thereby avoid the exercise of ICC jurisdiction (assuming it eventually joins the Court) by operation of the principle of complementarity. See, e.g., Thomas Wayde Pittman and Matthew Heaphy, 'Does the United States Really Prosecute Its Service Members for War Crimes? Implications for Complementarity Before the International Criminal Court', (2008) 21 *Leiden Journal of International Law* 165, 181 ('[T]he ICC's work focuses on the most serious atrocities and the most senior leaders. The United States has a working legal system, unlike many of the first … countries [with respect to which ICC investigations have been undertaken], which willingly and ably prosecutes service members.').

446 Rome Statute, *supra* note 1, Art. 8(2)(b)(xxii) ('any other form of sexual violence also constituting a grave breach of the Geneva Conventions'); *ibid.*, Art. 8(2)(b)(vi) ('any other form of sexual violence also constituting a serious violation of article 3 common to the four Geneva Conventions'). See also von Hebel and Robinson, *supra* note 438, p. 117 (noting that 'the primary purpose [of the proposal to include these sexual offences] was to recognize [them] explicitly … which as such are already implicitly covered by such more general concepts as torture and inhuman treatment'). But see Michael Cottier, 'Rape and Other Forms of Sexual Violence', in Triffterer (ed.), *supra* note 439, p. 249 ('Fitting rape within other categories of crimes such as "inhuman or degrading treatment" as was often the case in past judicial decisions … trivializes the extreme physical and psychological harm caused by rape.').

447 ICTR Statute, *supra* note 13, Art. 4(e).

chapeau of Article 3 of the Tribunal's Statute,[448] and as manifestations of other war crimes, such as torture.[449] Other noteworthy war crimes set forth for the first time in the Rome Statute include conscripting, enlisting, or using child soldiers;[450] intentionally directing attacks against humanitarian or peacekeeping personnel 'as long as they are entitled to the protection given to civilians … under the international law of armed conflict';[451] '[e]mploying weapons, projectiles and material and methods of warfare which are of a nature to cause superfluous injury or unnecessary suffering or which are inherently indiscriminate';[452] and 'transfer, directly or indirectly, by the Occupying Power of parts of its own civilian population into the territory it occupies, or the deportation or transfer of all or parts of the population of the occupied territory within or outside this territory'.[453]

448 See, e.g., *Kunarac et al.* Appeal Judgement, *supra* note 97, paras. 127–133; *Kvočka et al.* Trial Judgement, *supra* note 316, para. 578; *Furundžija* Trial Judgement, *supra* note 67, paras. 172, 185, 271–275. See also *supra* text accompanying notes 228, 232 (noting the open-ended nature of the lists in Article 3 of the ICTY Statute and Article 4 of the ICTR Statute).

449 See, e.g., *Čelebići* Trial Judgement, *supra* note 67, para. 965; *Furundžija* Trial Judgement, *supra* note 67, paras. 268–269.

450 Rome Statute, *supra* note 1, Art. 8(2)(b)(xxvi) (international armed conflict); *ibid.*, Art. 8(2)(e)(vii) (non-international armed conflict). This norm is drawn from the Convention on the Rights of the Child and Additional Protocol I. See Convention on the Rights of the Child, 20 November 1989, entered into force 2 September 1990, 1577 UNTS 3, Art. 38(3); see also Additional Protocol I, *supra* note 3, Art. 77(2). See also von Hebel and Robinson, *supra* note 438, pp. 117 (noting the U.S. view at the drafting meetings that Article 8(2)(b)(xxvi) 'did not reflect customary international law and was more a human rights provision than a criminal law provision'). In a May 2004 interlocutory decision, the Appeals Chamber of the SCSL held that customary international law recognised the imposition of criminal liability for conscripting, enlisting, or using child soldiers by 1996; Justice Robertson dissented, opining that the norm did not become criminal under custom until the conclusion of the Rome Statute in July 1998. This decision is discussed at text accompanying notes 525–526, *infra*. The definition and application of this crime in two SCSL trial judgements is discussed at text accompanying notes 542–551, *infra*.

451 Rome Statute, *supra* note 1, Art. 8(2)(b)(iii) (international armed conflict); *ibid.*, Art. 8(2)(e)(iii) (non-international armed conflict). This norm is drawn from the Convention on the Safety of United Nations and Associated Personnel. See Convention on the Safety of United Nations and Associated Personnel, 9 December 1994, entered into force 15 January 1999, UN Doc A/49/49 (1994), 34 ILM 482 (1995), Arts. 7, 9. See also Cryer, *supra* note 439, pp. 271–272 (noting criticism that this conduct did not constitute a war crime under customary international law by the time the Rome Statute was concluded, but asserting that, since the conduct is only punishable 'if those persons are entitled to protection as civilians … the provision is simply an application of the unquestioned crime of intentionally attacking civilians').

452 Rome Statute, *supra* note 1, Art. 8(2)(b)(xx) (international armed conflict only). The provision continues: '… provided that such weapons, projectiles and materials and methods of warfare are the subject of a comprehensive prohibition and are included in an annex to this Statute, by an amendment in accordance with the relevant provisions set forth in Articles 121 and 123.' *Ibid.* This unsatisfactory outcome resulted from a deadlock among states at the drafting meetings over which weapons to include in the list. See von Hebel and Robinson, *supra* note 438, pp. 113–116 (noting that this solution was described as 'Solomon-esque'); Schabas, *supra* note 439, p. 62 ('The result … is a shameful situation where poisoned arrows and hollow bullets are forbidden [elsewhere in Article 8 of the Rome Statute] yet nuclear, biological and chemical weapons, as well as anti-personnel land mines, are not.'). This norm has roots in several treaties. See 1899 Hague Regulations, *supra* note 48, Art. 23(e); 1907 Hague Regulations, *supra* note 6, Art. 23(e); Additional Protocol I, *supra* note 3, Art. 35(2).

453 Rome Statute, *supra* note 1, Art. 8(2)(b)(viii) (international armed conflict only). This norm is drawn from the Fourth Geneva Convention and Additional Protocol I. See Geneva Convention IV, *supra* note 3, Art. 49(6); Additional Protocol I, *supra* note 3, Art. 85(4)(a). Its inclusion in the Rome Statute was controversial, and led Israel to vote against the Statute. See Schabas, *supra* note 439, p. 61 n. 128.

Third, somewhat ironically in light of its considerable length, Article 8 of the Rome Statute also lacks some offences listed in the Statutes of the *ad hoc* Tribunals or otherwise determined to fall within their jurisdiction. Perhaps the most obvious of these are war crimes related to terrorism. Additional Protocol II proscribes 'acts of terrorism' in non-international armed conflict;[454] both Additional Protocols also contain a prohibition on '[a]cts or threats of violence the primary purpose of which is to spread terror among the civilian population'.[455] 'Acts of terrorism' are explicitly listed as a war crime in the ICTR and SCSL Statutes[456] and, as discussed below, this crime has been considered at length in two judgements of the SCSL.[457] Moreover, the ICTY Appeals Chamber has held that '[a]cts or threats of violence the primary purpose of which is to spread terror' were punishable as a war crime in customary international law by 1992, and that they fell within the ICTY's jurisdiction under Article 3 of the Statute.[458] The reasons for the exclusion from the Rome Statute of terrorism-related war crimes are not entirely clear,[459] although the omission can probably be traced to the majority's rejection of terrorism as a freestanding crime in the ICC's jurisdiction,[460] which itself stemmed in part from states' enduring failure to reach consensus on the definition and scope of terrorism.[461] Unlike

454 Additional Protocol II, *supra* note 3, Art. 4(2)(d).

455 *Ibid.*, Art. 13(2). See also Additional Protocol I, *supra* note 3, Art. 51(2) (identical language).

456 ICTR Statute, *supra* note 13, Art. 4(d); Statute of the Special Court for Sierra Leone, 2178 UNTS 138, UN Doc. S/2002/246, 16 January 2002, Appendix II ('SCSL Statute'), Art. 3(d). As far as can be determined, no accused in the ICTR has ever been charged with acts of terrorism, and there is consequently no aspect of that Tribunal's jurisprudence dealing with this war crime.

457 See *infra* text accompanying notes 552–560.

458 See *Galić* Appeal Judgement, *supra* note 90, paras. 91, 98. The Chamber accordingly upheld Stanislav Galić's conviction for ordering the commission of this crime during the siege of Sarajevo. See *ibid.*, paras. 108–109, 390. See also *supra* section 4.2.2.9 (discussing the elements of this crime).

459 See Hall, *supra* note 439, p. 336 n. 29 (noting that, while the non-international armed conflict war crime of 'intentionally directing attacks against the civilian population as such', in Article 13(2) of Additional Protocol II, was being debated for inclusion in the Rome Statute as of the December 1997 drafting meeting, 'acts or threats of violence the primary purpose of which is to spread terror', also in Article 13(2), was not on the table).

460 That is, as a crime in its own right, instead of or in addition to being listed as an underlying offence of war crimes or crimes against humanity.

461 See Report of the Preparatory Committee on the Establishment of an International Criminal Court, UN Doc. A/51/22, 13 September 1996, vol. I, para. 107 (noting some reasons for delegations' opposition to including terrorism as a freestanding crime, including concerns over the lack of a general definition for terrorism and the delay that would be caused in attempting to come up with one; that the inclusion of terrorism would put a substantial burden on the Court and detract from prosecutions of the core crimes; and that terrorism 'could be more effectively investigated and prosecuted by national authorities under existing international cooperation arrangements'); *Galić* Appeal Judgement, *supra* note 90, Separate Opinion of Judge Shahabuddeen, para. 3 (agreeing with the Appeals Chamber majority that terror as specifically charged in Galić's indictment was a war crime recognised under custom at the relevant time, but remarking that '[t]he international community is divided on important aspects of the [definition of "terror"], with the result that there is neither the required *opinio juris* nor state practice to support the view that customary international law knows of a comprehensive definition'); John Dugard, 'Terrorism and International Law: Consensus at Last?', in Emile Yakpo and Tahar Boumedra (eds.), *Liber Amicorum Judge Mohammed Bedjaoui* (1999), pp. 159–171 (discussing the history of the crime of international terrorism and some reasons behind states' inability to agree on a comprehensive definition). 'Acts of terrorism' as a non-international armed conflict war crime was included as late as the March 1997 draft of the Rome Statute, but had disappeared by April 1998. Compare Decisions Taken by the Preparatory Committee at Its Session Held from 11 to 21 February 1997, UN Doc. A/AC.249/1997/L.5, 12 March 1997, Annex I, p. 12 with Report of the Preparatory Committee on the Establishment of an International Criminal Court, UN Doc. A/CONF.183/2/Add.1, 14 April 1998, p. 22.

Article 3 of the ICTY Statute and Article 4 of the ICTR Statute, which both have open-ended lists,[462] the various lists of war crimes in the Rome Statute were deliberately made exhaustive,[463] so it will likely not be possible for the Court to read the Statute as implicitly granting jurisdiction over terrorism-related war crimes.[464]

4.3.1.2 The Elements of Crimes

As discussed in Chapter 2,[465] the Rome Statute gives the Court recourse to an instrument setting forth non-binding elements of crimes to 'assist … in the interpretation and application of articles 6, 7 and 8' – that is, the respective articles on genocide, crimes against humanity, and war crimes.[466] The war crimes provision of the Elements of Crimes is, like the crimes against humanity provision, very detailed, replete with explanatory footnotes setting forth definitions, caveats, and provisos.[467] Again, we will focus on a few salient features.[468]

All the offences in Article 8 share several common elements: (1) that an individual referred to as the 'perpetrator' engaged in certain physical conduct; (2) that '[t]he conduct took place in the context of and was associated with' an armed conflict; and (3) that '[t]he perpetrator was aware of factual circumstances that established the existence of an armed conflict'.[469] Setting aside for the moment the question of which precise participant in a given criminal transaction may qualify as the 'perpetrator' under the Elements,[470] the first two elements appear to correspond

462 See *supra* text accompanying notes 228, 232, 448 (describing the open-ended nature of the war crimes lists in Article 3 of the ICTY Statute and Article 4 of the ICTR Statute).

463 William Schabas laments this exhaustiveness: 'In the future, judges will have greater difficulty undertaking the kind of judicial law-making that the Yugoslav Tribunal performed in the [*Tadić* Jurisdiction Appeal Decision, *supra* note 4], and this will make it harder for justice to keep up with the imagination and inventiveness of war criminals.' Schabas, *supra* note 439, p. 54 (also suggesting that the exhaustive lists in Article 8 may have been a reaction on the part of states 'frightened' by what the ICTY Appeals Chamber had done in *Tadić*, 'who then resolved that they would leave far less room for such developments' at the ICC); see also *ibid.*, p. 55 (opining that the 'extremely precise and complex provisions of Article 8 … arguably have the effect of narrowing the potential scope of prosecutions').

464 Commentators have criticised the exclusion from the Rome Statute of other activities that may well qualify as war crimes under customary international law. See, e.g., von Hebel and Robinson, *supra* note 438, p. 125 (chemical and biological weapons, and starvation as a weapon in non-international armed conflict); Cryer, *supra* note 439, p. 283 (chemical weapons and indiscriminate attacks in non-international armed conflict).

465 See Chapter 2, text accompanying note 519. 466 Rome Statute, *supra* note 1, Art. 9(1).

467 See ICC Elements of Crimes, *supra* note 439, pp. 125–155.

468 The war crimes provision of the Elements of Crimes has been considered at great length elsewhere. See especially Dörmann, *supra* note 439; see also von Hebel, Dörmann, la Haye, Frank, Pfirter, Garraway, and Hosang, *supra* note 439, pp. 109–217.

469 See, e.g., ICC Elements of Crimes, *supra* note 439, Art. 8(2)(a)(i), Elements 1, 4–5. For the international armed conflict crimes, the conduct must take place in the context of and be associated with an international armed conflict; for the non-international armed conflict crimes, the conduct must take place in the context of and be associated with 'an armed conflict not of an international character'. See, e.g., *ibid.*, Art. 8(2)(c)(i), Element 4.

470 This question is examined at text accompanying notes 491–495, *infra*.

with *ad hoc* jurisprudence,[471] and indeed were inspired by judicial pronouncements in the early *Tadić* and *Čelebići* cases.[472] The question of whether the third element is consistent with *ad hoc* jurisprudence is more complicated. Three introductory paragraphs to Article 8 in the Elements put a crucial gloss on this element:

> There is no requirement for a legal evaluation by the perpetrator as to the existence of an armed conflict or its character as international or non-international;
>
> In that context there is no requirement for awareness by the perpetrator of the facts that established the character of the conflict as international or non-international;
>
> There is only a requirement for the awareness of the factual circumstances that established the existence of an armed conflict that is implicit in the terms 'took place in the context of and was associated with'.[473]

The commentators on this part of the Elements of Crimes explain that the third element and these introductory paragraphs were inserted at the insistence of certain delegations that argued that, because it is the existence of an armed conflict that most distinguishes a war crime from an ordinary crime under national law, fairness demanded that the perpetrator have some awareness of the armed conflict before he may be convicted of a 'war crime'.[474] As a result, a requirement that the perpetrator be aware of factual circumstances that established the existence of the armed conflict was included in the Elements.[475] The delegations stopped short, however, of insisting that the perpetrator actually be aware that the conflict was international or non-international in character, or that he even be aware of factual circumstances that established the conflict as international or non-international.[476] As the commentators point out, the inclusion of the introductory paragraphs quoted above 'did not meet substantial difficulties and agreement was reached with relative ease'.[477]

For much of its existence, the ICTY appears to have been silent on whether an accused charged with war crimes must be aware of the existence of an armed conflict or its character as international or non-international.[478] As discussed

[471] See, e.g., *Brđanin* Trial Judgement, *supra* note 111, paras. 121–123 (nexus requirement for Article 2 of the ICTY Statute); *Limaj et al.* Trial Judgement, *supra* note 103, para. 91 (nexus requirement for Article 3 of the ICTY Statute); *Rutaganda* Appeal Judgement, *supra* note 92, paras. 569–570 (nexus requirement for Article 4 of the ICTR Statute). The nexus requirement in the *ad hoc* Tribunals is discussed in section 4.2.1.2, *supra*.

[472] See Knut Dörmann, Eve la Haye, and Herman von Hebel, 'The Context of War Crimes', in Lee (ed.), *supra* note 439, p. 120. See also *Tadić* October 2005 Appeal Decision, *supra* note 4, para. 70; *Čelebići* Trial Judgement, *supra* note 67, paras. 185, 193–195; *Tadić* Trial Judgement, *supra* note 103, para. 572; see also *supra*, sections 4.2.1.1–4.2.1.2.

[473] ICC Elements of Crimes, *supra* note 439, p. 125 (Introduction).

[474] See Dörmann, la Haye, and von Hebel, *supra* note 472, p. 121.

[475] See *ibid.*, p. 123.

[476] See *ibid.*, p. 122 (also remarking that '[r]equiring a perpetrator to know about the character of a certain conflict and requiring the Prosecutor to prove such knowledge would have been too high a threshold, not required by existing law.').

[477] *Ibid.*

[478] See Schabas, *supra* note 4, p. 239 ('[T]he Prosecutor appears to have essentially let the judges deduce that the accused knew of the existence of the conflict, and this does not seem to have been denied in defence.').

above,[479] nearly four years after the conclusion of the ICC Elements of Crimes, the ICTY Appeals Chamber in *Naletilić and Martinović* directly addressed the matter, and rejected the Elements' formulation as not sufficiently protective of the rights of the accused,[480] concluding that '[t]he principle of individual guilt … demands sufficient awareness of *factual* circumstances establishing the armed conflict and its (international or internal) character'.[481] The Appeals Chamber acknowledged the difference of opinion in the drafting meetings of the ICC Elements of Crimes, and concluded that the principle of *in dubio pro reo* obliged it to go along with the (small) minority of ICC delegates on this question.[482]

The grave breaches in Article 8(2)(a) of the Elements of Crimes have two further elements in common: (1) the victim or property 'w[as] protected under one or more of the Geneva Conventions of 1949'; and (2) '[t]he perpetrator was aware of the factual circumstances that established that protected status'.[483] Although chambers of the ICTY also require that the first element be established before they will impose liability for a grave breach,[484] they do not appear to have stated an express view on whether the accused must have knowledge of the factual circumstances that established the protected status of the victim or targeted property.[485] The Appeals Chamber's position in *Naletilić and Martinović* with respect to awareness of the armed conflict, along with views of Judge Shahabuddeen in a different case,[486] suggest that the Chamber would find such a requirement to exist if ever faced squarely with the question. The non-international armed conflict war crimes in Article 8(2)(c), which derive from Common Article 3 of the Geneva Conventions, have two similar additional elements: (1) the victim or victims 'were either *hors de combat*, or were civilians, medical personnel or religious personnel taking no active

479 See *supra* text accompanying notes 116–120, 172–173.

480 *Naletilić and Martinović* Appeal Judgement, *supra* note 96, para. 113 (quoting *Kordić and Čerkez* Appeal Judgement, *supra* note 101, para. 311).

481 *Ibid.* (emphasis in original). 482 See *ibid.*, para. 120.

483 See, e.g., ICC Elements of Crimes, *supra* note 439, Art. 8(2)(a)(i), Elements 2–3. For war crimes against protected persons, the perpetrator need not know the nationality of the victim, but merely that he or she 'belonged to an adverse party to the conflict'. *Ibid.*, Element 3 n. 33. See also Dörmann, la Haye, and von Hebel, *supra* note 472, p. 117 (noting that '"protected property" is not generally defined in the Geneva Conventions, but they do contain a description of property that cannot be attacked, destroyed or appropriated').

484 See, e.g., *Tadić* Jurisdiction Appeal Decision, *supra* note 4, para. 81; *Brđanin* Trial Judgement, *supra* note 111, paras. 155–156. See also *supra* section 4.2.1.3.2 (describing this requirement in ICTY jurisprudence).

485 See Mettraux, *supra* note 151, p. 66.

486 See *Prosecutor* v. *Jelisić*, Case No. IT-95-10-A, Judgement, 5 July 2001, Partial Dissenting Opinion of Judge Shahabuddeen, para. 40:

> [Under] Article 2 of the Statute … [t]he prosecution has to prove that the act of the accused was one which was 'against persons … protected [under the Geneva Conventions]. That cannot be proved unless there is evidence that the victim had that status and that the accused was aware that the victim had it. This awareness would seem to be an inseparable element of the intention with which the accused acted.

The accused's awareness of the victim's protected status was not an issue on appeal in *Jelisić*. Judge Shahabuddeen cited it as support for his views on cumulative convictions. These are discussed in more detail in Chapter 5 of this volume, text accompanying notes 111–116.

part in the hostilities', and (2) '[t]he perpetrator was aware of the factual circumstances that established this status'.[487] Again, the chambers of the *ad hoc* Tribunals have held that both elements are a requirement for the imposition of liability where the war crime at issue derives from Common Article 3.[488] By contrast, there is no common element for the offences in Articles 8(2)(b) and (e) that requires that the targeted victim or property enjoy a special status,[489] although certain of the specific offences seem to incorporate such an element.[490]

As noted in Chapters 2 and 3,[491] the delegates drafting the Elements appear to have had some appreciation for the general notion that the various elements of an international crime may be fulfilled by different actors.[492] This appreciation is reflected in an explicit provision in the General Introduction to the Elements defining 'perpetrator' as a term of art:

> As used in the Elements of Crimes, the term 'perpetrator' is neutral as to guilt or innocence. The elements, including the appropriate mental elements, apply *mutatis mutandis* to all those whose criminal responsibility may fall under articles 25 and 28 of the Statute [setting forth the forms of responsibility].[493]

As we concluded in Chapters 2 and 3, when faced with an accused who did not physically perpetrate the crimes with which he is charged, the Court will likely have to adopt a broad and varying interpretation of the term 'perpetrator'. Consider, for example, an accused general who orders soldiers under his command to kill persons *hors de combat*, a war crime under Article 8(2)(b)(vi) of the Rome Statute. The Elements of Crimes provide as follows:

1. The perpetrator killed or injured one or more persons.
2. Such persons or persons were *hors de combat.*
3. The perpetrator was aware of the factual circumstances that established this status.

[487] See, e.g., ICC Elements of Crimes, *supra* note 439, Art. 8(2)(c)(i)-1, Elements 2–3. Neither Common Article 3 nor the *chapeau* of Article 8(2)(c) make explicit mention of 'civilians, medical personnel or religious personnel'; this listing of persons 'taking no active part in the hostilities' was added on the prompting of some delegations. See Dörmann, la Haye, and von Hebel, *supra* note 472, pp. 118–119.

[488] See, e.g., *Limaj et al.* Trial Judgement, *supra* note 103, para. 176; *Rutaganda* Trial Judgement, *supra* note 103, para. 438 (in the ICTR, the victim may be protected under Common Article 3 or Additional Protocol II). See also *supra* sections 4.2.1.4, 4.2.1.5.4 (describing these requirements in *ad hoc* jurisprudence).

[489] See Schabas, *supra* note 439, p. 60 (noting, with respect to Article 8(2)(b), that '[t]here is no requirement, unlike the situation for "grave breaches", that the victims be "protected persons". Indeed, the overall focus of Hague law is on combatants themselves as victims').

[490] See, e.g., ICC Elements of Crimes, *supra* note 439, Art. 8(2)(b)(iii), Element 4 (requiring that targeted humanitarian and peacekeeping personnel and units be 'entitled to that protection given to civilians or civilian objects under the international law of armed conflict'); *ibid.*, 8(2)(e)(iii), Element 4 (same).

[491] See Chapter 2, text accompanying notes 522–528; Chapter 3, text accompanying notes 360–364.

[492] See Maria Kelt and Herman von Hebel, 'The Making of the Elements of Crimes', Lee (ed.), *supra* note 439, pp. 17–18 (discussing the debate over what term should be used in this position, that delegates rejected 'accused' because the accused is not always the physical perpetrator, and that they also rejected 'actor' as too vague a term).

[493] ICC Elements of Crimes, *supra* note 439, General Introduction, para. 8.

4. The conduct took place in the context of and was associated with an international armed conflict.
5. The perpetrator was aware of the factual circumstances that established the existence of the armed conflict.[494]

Where the accused being tried is the general, does it make sense to require his lower-level foot soldier who actually pulled the trigger to fulfil Elements 3 and 5 himself, or may these elements instead be fulfilled by the accused or another relevant participant in the criminal transaction, such as the mid-level commander who passes on the general's order and supervises the killings? Our analysis above, and in the preceding chapters of this book, would suggest the latter is the sounder interpretation in the types of leadership cases that can be expected to be tried by the ICC.[495]

Finally, it is worth noting that many of the war crimes in the Rome Statute, as defined therein and in the Elements of Crimes, appear to be quintessential 'leadership' crimes in which the *actus reus* is fulfilled by the mid- or high-level commander himself, and not by the foot soldier.[496] These include, for example, intentionally directing attacks against civilians or the civilian population;[497] intentionally directing attacks against buildings dedicated to religion or charity;[498] declaring that no quarter will be given;[499] declaring abolished the judicial rights of nationals of the hostile party;[500] and conscripting, enlisting, or using child soldiers.[501] For other war crimes, it would appear that the *actus reus* may be fulfilled by either the commander or the foot solder, depending on the circumstances. These include, for example, attacking or bombarding undefended towns;[502] making improper use of a flag of truce;[503] and employing poisoned weapons.[504] Not unlike the genocide-related inchoate crimes discussed in Chapter 3,[505] the ICC Prosecutor may be able to eschew reliance on the forms of accomplice and accessory liability in Article 25

[494] *Ibid.*, Art. 8(2)(b)(vi), Elements 1–5.
[495] See *supra* section 4.2.1.1.1; see also *supra* notes 174–177; Chapter 2, section 2.2.2.1; Chapter 3, section 3.2.1.1.
[496] See also *supra* text accompanying notes 426–433 (noting other leadership war crimes in the jurisdiction of the *ad hoc* Tribunals); text accompanying notes 405–408 (example of factual findings for such a leadership crime).
[497] See ICC Elements of Crimes, *supra* note 439, Art. 8(2)(b)(i), Element 1 ('The perpetrator *directed* an attack.') (emphasis added).
[498] See *ibid.*, Art. 8(2)(b)(ix), Element 1 ('The perpetrator *directed* an attack.') (emphasis added).
[499] See *ibid.*, Art. 8(2)(b)(xii), Element 1 ('The perpetrator *declared or ordered* that there shall be no survivors.'). See also Michael Cottier, 'Quarter', in Triffterer (ed.), *supra* note 439, p. 227 ('The declaration, order or threat must stem from a person in command who had forces under his command.'). See also Chapter 3, note 24 (noting that declaring that no quarter be given is an inchoate crime).
[500] See ICC Elements of Crimes, *supra* note 439, Art. 8(2)(b)(xiv), Element 1.
[501] See *ibid.*, Art. 8(2)(b)(xxv), Element 1. [502] See *ibid.*, Art. 8(2)(b)(v), Element 1.
[503] See *ibid.*, Art. 8(2)(b)(vii)-1 , Element 2 ('The perpetrator made such use in order to feign an intention to negotiate when there was no such intention on the part of the perpetrator.').
[504] See *ibid.*, Art. 8(2)(b)(xvii), Element 1.
[505] See Chapter 3, text accompanying notes 365–368; see also Boas, Bischoff, and Reid, *supra* note 30, p. 303 (questioning whether imposing accomplice liability for the genocide-related inchoate crimes comports with the principle of culpability).

of the Rome Statute,[506] and superior responsibility in Article 28, in seeking to prove the link between mid- or high-level accused and the perpetration of these crimes.

The Prosecutor has sought to charge war crimes against all of the persons publicly implicated in proceedings before the Court thus far, in the situations in the Democratic Republic of the Congo (DRC),[507] Uganda,[508] and Darfur, Sudan.[509] The only case in which charges have been confirmed is *Prosecutor* v. *Lubanga*. The Prosecutor sought to charge Thomas Lubanga with co-perpetrating the conscription and enlistment of children under the age of fifteen into the Forces Patriotiques pour la Libération du Congo – an armed group operating in the Ituri district of eastern DRC – and using them to participate actively in a non-international armed conflict, in violation of Article 8(2)(e)(vii) of the Rome Statute.[510] In its 'Decision on the Confirmation of Charges', the Pre-Trial Chamber found, in reliance on ICTY appellate jurisprudence on what constitutes an 'international armed conflict', that there were substantial grounds to believe that an international armed conflict existed in the relevant area of eastern DRC during part of the time period alleged in the

506 As noted in Volume I of this series, we use the term 'accomplice liability' to encompass forms of common-purpose liability (such as joint criminal enterprise), planning, instigating, ordering; in the Rome Statute, inducing and soliciting in Article 25(b) are also included in this group. 'Accessory liability' refers to aiding and abetting. See Boas, Bischoff, and Reid, *supra* note 30, pp. 3 n. 9, 279–280, 422 n. 27.

507 See *Situation in the Democratic Republic of the Congo*, Case No. ICC-01/04-01/07, Warrant of Arrest for Germain Katanga, 2 July 2007, pp. 6–7 (Pre-Trial Chamber finding reasonable grounds to believe that Katanga was responsible for various war crimes committed during an attack on the village of Bogoro in the Ituri district in early 2003, and charging these crimes in alternative international/non-international pairs: wilful killing under Article 8(2)(a)(i) or murder under Article 8(2)(c)(i); inhuman treatment under Article 8(2)(a)(i) or cruel treatment under Article 8(2)(c)(i); using child soldiers under Article 8(2)(b)(xxvi) or Article 8(2)(e)(vii); sexual slavery under Article 8(2)(b)(xxii) or Article 8(2)(e)(vi); intentionally directing attacks against the civilian population under Article 8(2)(b)(i) or Article 8(2)(e)(i); and pillage under Article 8(2)(b)(xvi) or Article 8(2)(e)(v)); see also *ibid*., Decision to Unseal the Warrant of Arrest Against Germain Katanga, 18 October 2007, pp. 3–4 (lifting the confidentiality of the arrest warrant). The charges against DRC accused Thomas Lubanga are discussed at text accompanying notes 510–519, *infra*.

508 See *Situation in Uganda*, Case No. ICC-02/04-01/05, Warrant of Arrest for Joseph Kony issued on 8 July 2005 as amended on 27 September 2005, 27 September 2005, paras. 42–44, 47–48 (Pre-Trial Chamber finding reasonable grounds to believe Kony was responsible for ordering various non-international armed conflict war crimes: rape under Article 8(2)(e)(vi); intentionally directing attacks against the civilian population under Article 8(2)(e)(i); conscripting, enlisting, or using child soldiers under Article 8(2)(e)(vii); cruel treatment under Article 8(2)(c)(i); pillage under Article 8(2)(e)(v); and murder under Article 8(2)(c)(i)). See also *ibid*., Warrant of Arrest for Vincent Otti, 8 July 2005, paras. 42–44, 47–48 (similar); *ibid*., Warrant of Arrest for Okot Odhiambo, 8 July 2005, paras. 32–34, 37–38 (similar); *ibid*., Warrant of Arrest for Dominic Ongwen, 8 July 2005, paras. 30–32, 35–36 (similar).

509 See *Situation in Darfur, Sudan*, Case No. ICC-02/05, Warrant of Arrest for Ahmad Harun, 27 April 2007, pp. 6–15 (Pre-Trial Chamber finding that the information provided by the Prosecutor demonstrated reasonable grounds to believe Harun, the Sudanese Minister of State for Humanitarian Affairs, bore common-purpose responsibility for various non-international armed conflict war crimes committed by the Sudanese armed forces and the Janjaweed militia against Fur, Zaghawa, and Masalit civilians in Darfur: murder under Article 8(2)(c)(i); intentionally directing attacks against the civilian population under Article 8(2)(e)(i); destroying or seizing the property of an adversary under Article 8(2)(e)(xii); rape under Article 8(2)(e)(vi); pillage under Article 8(2)(e)(v); and outrages upon personal dignity under Article 8(2)(c)(ii)); *ibid*., Warrant of Arrest for Ali Kushayb, 27 April 2007, pp. 6–16 (similar charges against Kushayb, a major Janjaweed militia leader).

510 *Prosecutor* v. *Lubanga*, Case No. ICC-01/04-01/06, Document Containing the Charges: Article 61(3)(a) (public redacted version), 28 August 2006, p. 24.

charging document.[511] The Chamber took note of the elements of conscripting, enlisting, or using child soldiers in the Elements of Crimes[512] and held, by reference to the dissenting opinion of Justice Robertson in an important SCSL Appeals Chamber decision on child soldiers, that 'conscripting' entails forcible recruitment, while 'enlisting' 'pertains more to voluntary recruitment'.[513] Ultimately, the Pre-Trial Chamber confirmed the charges against Lubanga, including charges in relation to a crime not included in the Prosecutor's charging document.[514] The Chamber held that, since the prohibition on conscripting, enlisting, or using child soldiers in international armed conflict under Article 8(2)(b)(xxvi) 'is similar in scope' to the same crime in non-international armed conflict under Article 8(2)(e)(vii), the Chamber need not adjourn the proceedings and request the Prosecutor to consider amending its charging document to include charges under Article 8(2)(b)(xxvi); instead, the Chamber may simply add such charges itself.[515] This course of action would appear to contradict the unambiguous mandate set forth in the Rome Statute;[516] indeed, the Prosecutor sought to challenge on appeal the Pre-Trial Chamber's ability to intervene in its decision-making in this manner.[517] Regrettably, the Pre-Trial Chamber denied leave to appeal.[518] Lubanga's trial was scheduled to begin on 31 March 2008.[519]

[511] See *Prosecutor* v. *Lubanga*, Case No. ICC-01/04–01/06, Decision on the Confirmation of Charges (public redacted version), 29 January 2007 ('*Lubanga* January 2007 Pre-Trial Decision'), para. 220 (holding that the conflict was international from July 2002 to 2 June 2003, owing to Ugandan army involvement). See also *ibid.*, paras. 208–211 (endorsing the ICTY *Tadić* Appeals Chamber's definition of what constitutes an international armed conflict); *supra* section 4.2.1.3.1 (discussing this ICTY jurisprudence). For a general analysis and critique of this decision, see Matthew Happold, '*Prosecutor* v. *Thomas Lubanga*, Decision of Pre-Trial Chamber I of the International Criminal Court, 29 January 2007', (2007) 56 *International and Comparative Law Quarterly* 713.

[512] *Lubanga* January 2007 Pre-Trial Decision, *supra* note 511, para. 240.

[513] *Ibid.*, para. 246 (endorsing the definitions in *Prosecutor* v. *Norman*, Case No. SCSL-2004-14-AR72(E), Decision on Preliminary Motion Based on Lack of Jurisdiction (Child Recruitment), 31 May 2004 ('*Norman* 31 May 2004 Appeal Decision'), Dissenting Opinion of Justice Robertson, para. 5).

[514] See *ibid.*, pp. 156–157. [515] See *ibid.*, para. 204.

[516] See Rome Statute, *supra* note 1, Art. 61(7) (providing, on its face, just three options to the pre-trial chamber: (1) confirm the charges and commit the accused for trial; (2) decline to confirm the charges; and (3) '[a]djourn the hearing and request the Prosecutor to consider … [p]roviding further evidence or conducting further investigation with respect to a particular charge; or … [a]mending a charge because the evidence submitted appears to establish a different crime within the jurisdiction of the Court'). Matthew Happold has opined that this issue reflects 'a struggle between the Office of the Prosecutor and Chambers over the extent to which each controls proceedings before the Court, or perhaps, more generally, whether those proceedings are to be primarily adversarial or inquisitorial in character'. Happold, *supra* note 511, p. 724.

[517] See *Prosecutor* v. *Lubanga*, Case No. ICC-01/04-01/06, Application for Leave to Appeal Pre-Trial Chamber I's 29 January 2007 'Décision sur la confirmation des charges', 5 February 2007, para 2 (arguing that, as a result of the Pre-Trial Chamber's addition of charges under Article 8(2)(b)(xxvi), 'the Prosecution is forced to proceed with a crime that it had already determined, after careful examination of the evidence in its possession, should not be charged, and to devote time and resources to supplement that evidence, if possible, in order to adequately substantiate that crime at trial').

[518] *Prosecutor* v. *Lubanga*, Case No. ICC-01/04-01/06, Decision on the Prosecution and Defence Applications for Leave to Appeal the Decision on the Confirmation of Charges, 24 May 2007, para. 45 (considering that 'that the matter raised [by the Prosecutor] is not an issue that would affect the fair and expeditious conduct of the proceedings or the outcome of the trial').

[519] *Prosecutor* v. *Lubanga*, Case No. ICC-01/04-01/06, Decision Regarding the Timing and Manner of Disclosure and the Date of Trial, 9 November 2007, para. 29.

4.3.2 The Internationalised Tribunals

4.3.2.1 Special Court for Sierra Leone (SCSL)

Two separate articles of the Statute of the Special Court for Sierra Leone are dedicated to war crimes. The first, Article 3, is a virtual reproduction of Article 4 of the ICTR Statute,[520] with one exception: the list of offences appears closed.[521] The second, Article 4, is a selection of three war crimes probably taken from Article 8(2)(e) of the Rome Statute:

1. Intentionally directing attacks against the civilian population as such or against individual civilians not taking direct part in hostilities;
2. Intentionally directing attacks against personnel, installations, material, units or vehicles involved in a humanitarian assistance or peacekeeping mission in accordance with the Charter of the United Nations, as long as they are entitled to the protection given to civilians or civilian objects under the international law of armed conflict;
3. Conscripting or enlisting children under the age of 15 years into armed forces or groups or using them to participate actively in hostilities.[522]

In a May 2004 interlocutory decision, the SCSL Appeals Chamber held that, while 'the Statute was drawn up with an internal armed conflict in mind',[523] the war crimes in Articles 3 and 4 are punishable whether committed in international or non-international armed conflict.[524] The late Samuel Hinga Norman, who was

[520] See *supra* text accompanying note 13 (quoting Article 4 of the ICTR Statute). As a consequence of the near-verbatim adoption of Article 4 of the ICTR Statute, the SCSL Statute contains the inchoate war crime of 'threats to commit' any of the other war crimes in Article 3 of the SCSL Statute. See *supra* note 426 and Chapter 3, note 24, for a discussion of this inchoate crime in the ICTR Statute.

[521] Compare SCSL Statute, *supra* note 456, Art. 3 ('These violations shall include: …') with ICTR Statute *supra* note 13, Art. 4 ('These violations shall include, but *shall not be limited to*: …') (emphasis added).

[522] SCSL Statute, *supra* note 456, Art. 4.

[523] See *Prosecutor* v. *Fofana*, Case No. SCSL-2004–14-AR72(E), Decision on Preliminary Motion on Lack of Jurisdiction *Materiae*: Nature of the Armed Conflict, 25 May 2004 ('*Fofana* 25 May 2004 Appeal Decision'), para. 18 (noting the *travaux* of the Statute, along with a 2000 statement of the Sierra Leonean president, a Security Council Resolution, and the Report of the Secretary-General cited at note 526, *infra*). Commentators prior to this May 2004 decision justifiably – and surely correctly – took the view that Articles 3 and 4 were intended to apply only in non-international armed conflict. See, e.g., Bert Swart, 'Internationalized Courts and Substantive Criminal Law', in Cesare P. R. Romano, André Nollkaemper, and Jann K. Kleffner (eds.), *Internationalized Criminal Courts and Tribunals: Sierra Leone, East Timor, Kosovo, and Cambodia* (2004), p. 301; see also Nicole Smith and Alison Fritz, 'Current Apathy for Coming Anarchy: Building the Special Court for Sierra Leone', (2001) 25 *Fordham International Law Journal* 391, 408 (noting that the grave breaches were left out of the SCSL Statute, and that 'their omission signals that the conflict in Sierra Leone has, in effect, been predetermined as one of a non-international armed character', and calling this predetermination 'shortsighted' in light of the involvement of Liberia and Burkina Faso in the conflict).

[524] See *Fofana* 25 May 2004 Appeal Decision, *supra* note 523, paras. 25, 30. Fofana argued that the three war crimes in Article 4 of the SCSL Statute – intentionally directing attacks against the civilian population, intentionally directing attacks against humanitarian or peacekeeping personnel or units, and conscripting, enlisting, or using child soldiers – were copies of those same crimes in Articles 8(2)(e)(i), (iii), and (vii) of the Rome Statute, and thus were intended to apply only in non-international armed conflict. The prosecution responded that they could just as well be copies of the same crimes in Articles 8(2)(b)(i), (iii), and (xxvi) of the Rome Statute, thus applying to international armed conflict. The SCSL Appeals Chamber acknowledged that Article 4(3)'s reference to enlistment 'into armed forces or groups'

charged with enlisting or using child soldiers from as early as November 1996, challenged the jurisdiction of the Special Court to try him for this crime. In another important May 2004 interlocutory decision, a 3:1 majority of the Appeals Chamber rejected Norman's challenge, holding that customary international law permitted the imposition of individual criminal responsibility for conscripting, enlisting, or using child soldiers by 1996.[525] In dissent, Justice Robertson argued that custom did not recognise the existence of such a war crime until the conclusion of the Rome Statute in July 1998.[526]

Every accused before the SCSL has been charged with war crimes.[527] Former Liberian President Charles Taylor, the highest-ranking of the Special Court's indictees, faces responsibility for murder, cruel treatment, pillage, outrages upon personal dignity (in respect of 'widespread acts of sexual violence'), child recruitment, and acts of terrorism.[528] Consistent with their mandate to 'be guided by' the

made its language identical to Article 8(2)(e)(vii) of the Rome Statute – and not Article 8(2)(b)(xxvi), which speaks of enlistment 'into the national armed forces' – but concluded dismissively and unconvincingly that 'the chosen wording [in Article 4(3)] may simply have been designed to reflect most accurately the circumstances of the acts of child recruitment alleged to have occurred in Sierra Leone'. *Ibid.*, para. 29.

525 *Norman* 31 May 2004 Appeal Decision, *supra* note 513, paras. 50, 53.

526 *Ibid.*, Dissenting Opinion of Justice Robertson, paras. 38, 47. In his report on the Special Court's establishment, the Secretary-General recommended against including in the Statute the ICC's formulation of conscripting, enlisting, or using child soldiers, opining that it had a 'doubtful customary nature'; he instead recommended including 'abduction and forced recruitment of children under the age of 15 years into armed forces'. Report of the Secretary-General on the Establishment of a Special Court for Sierra Leone, UN Doc. S/2000/915, 4 October 2000, paras. 15, 18 (quotation at para. 15). Justice Robertson gave significant weight to this statement: 'If it was not clear to the Secretary-General and his legal advisers that international law had by 1996 criminalized the enlistment of child soldiers, could it really have been any clearer to Chief Hinga Norman or any other defendant at that time, embattled in Sierra Leone?' *Norman* 31 May 2004 Appeal Decision, *supra* note 513, Dissenting Opinion of Justice Robertson, para. 6. It is interesting to note, however, that subsequent SCSL jurisprudence has defined 'conscripting' child soldiers as the abduction or other coercion of such children. See *infra* notes 546–547 and accompanying text.

527 See *Prosecutor* v. *Sesay, Kallon, and Gbao*, Case No. SCSL-2004-15-PT, Corrected Amended Consolidated Indictment, 2 August 2006 ('*RUF* Indictment') (charging the war crimes of acts of terrorism, collective punishments, murder, outrages upon personal dignity, mutilation, child recruitment, pillage, attacking humanitarian and peacekeeping personnel, and hostage-taking); *Prosecutor* v. *Koroma*, Case No. SCSL-2003–03-I, Indictment, 7 March 2003 (war crimes charges largely the same as those in the *RUF* Indictment). See also *infra* notes 528–560 and accompanying text (discussing war crimes in the other SCSL cases).

528 See generally *Prosecutor* v. *Taylor*, Case No. SCSL-2003-01-PT, Second Amended Indictment, 29 May 2007 ('*Taylor* Indictment'). See also *supra* text accompanying notes 454–464 (discussing the absence of terrorism-related war crimes in the Rome Statute). As discussed in Chapter 2, the drafters of the SCSL Statute included a longer list of sexual crimes against humanity – rape, sexual slavery, enforced prostitution, forced pregnancy, and 'any other form of sexual violence' – than appears in the ICTY or ICTR Statutes, as a response to the rampant occurrence of sexual violence as one of the hallmarks of the conflict in Sierra Leone. See Chapter 2, text accompanying notes 564–565. This list was not reproduced in the SCSL Statute's articles on war crimes, which instead include the traditional Common Article 3 formulation: 'Outrages upon personal dignity, in particular humiliating and degrading treatment, rape, enforced prostitution and any form of indecent assault'. SCSL Statute, *supra* note 456, Art. 3(e). Taylor's indictment charges him through this provision with liability for raping and making sexual slaves of 'an unknown number of' women and girls. *Taylor* Indictment, *supra*, paras. 14–16 (quotation at paras. 15–17). Taylor's alleged crimes are charged through all the forms of responsibility in the SCSL Statute, including joint criminal enterprise. See *ibid.*, paras. 33–34.

decisions of' the *ad hoc* Tribunals,[529] the two SCSL trial judgements issued as of 1 December 2007 – in the so-called *AFRC* and *CDF* cases – reveal the heavy influence of *ad hoc* Tribunal precedent in their respective war crimes discussions. Nonetheless, the Chambers' respective lists of the general requirements of war crimes differ from one another in some respects;[530] this is likely because, even though the *CDF* Judgement was rendered some weeks after the *AFRC* Judgement, it was drafted contemporaneously and thus does not cite or otherwise acknowledge the conclusions of its SCSL predecessor. Similarly, the Chambers' respective lists of elements of particular offences also differ somewhat, with the *CDF* Trial Chamber relying mainly – but not entirely – on definitions in ICTY and ICTR jurisprudence,[531] and the *AFRC* Trial Chamber relying mainly on the ICC Elements of Crimes.[532]

In the *CDF* case, Moinina Fofana and Allieu Kondewa were charged with responsibility for a number of war crimes – murder, cruel treatment, pillage, acts of terrorism, collective punishments, and enlisting or using child soldiers – for the most part physically perpetrated by pro-government fighters known as Kamajors.[533] After determining that the general requirements for war crimes had been satisfied for all the crimes the Trial Chamber found to have been committed,[534] the Chamber

529 As discussed in Chapter 2, the SCSL Statute provides that the judges of the Appeals Chamber shall be guided by the appellate jurisprudence of the ICTY and ICTR, see SCSL Statute, *supra* note 456, Art. 20(3), and this statement has since been held equally applicable to trial chambers. See *AFRC* Trial Judgement, *supra* note 432, para. 639 n. 1269. See also Chapter 2, text accompanying notes 571–577.

530 Compare *CDF* Trial Judgement, *supra* note 432, paras. 122–137 (relying on an array of ICTY and ICTR judgements to come up with four general requirements for Article 3 of the SCSL Statute: (1) an armed conflict existed; (2) a nexus existed between the conduct in question and the armed conflict; (3) the victim was a person not taking direct part in the hostilities; and (4) the accused knew or had reason to know that the person was not taking a direct part in the hostilities) with *AFRC* Trial Judgement, *supra* note 432, paras. 242–248 (also relying on ICTY and ICTR jurisprudence in a more cursory discussion, and concluding that there are three general requirements: (1) an armed conflict; (2) a nexus; and (3) the victim was not taking direct part in the hostilities). Compare also *CDF* Trial Judgement, *supra* note 432, paras. 138–139 (listing just two general requirements for Article 4–requirements (1) and (2) above–with no discussion for why requirements (3) and (4) do not apply to Article 4) with *AFRC* Trial Judgement, *supra* note 432, para. 257 (holding that the general requirements for Article 4 are the same as those the Trial Chamber articulated for Article 3).

531 See, e.g., *CDF* Trial Judgement, *supra* note 432, para. 146 (murder, relying on, *inter alia*, *Kordić and Čerkez* Trial Judgement, *supra* note 57, para. 236); *ibid.*, para. 156 (cruel treatment, relying on, *inter alia*, *Limaj et al.* Trial Judgement, *supra* note 103, para. 231); *ibid.*, paras. 163, 165 (pillage, citing, *inter alia*, *Kordić and Čerkez* Appeal Judgement, *supra* note 101, para. 84). But see *infra* note 542 and accompanying text (*CDF* Trial Chamber relying on the ICC Elements of Crimes for the elements of conscripting, enlisting, or using child soldiers).

532 See, e.g., *AFRC* Trial Judgement, *supra* note 432, para. 716 (outrages upon personal dignity, relying on ICC Elements of Crimes, *supra* note 439, Art. 8(2)(b)(xxi)); *ibid.*, para. 724 (mutilation, relying on ICC Elements of Crimes, *supra* note 439, Art. 8(2)(c)(i)-2); *ibid.*, para. 729 (child recruitment, relying on ICC Elements of Crimes, *supra* note 439, Art. 8(2)(b)(xxvi)).

533 See *Prosecutor* v. *Norman, Fofana, and Kondewa*, Case No. SCSL-03-14-I, Indictment, 5 February 2004, paras. 23–29; *CDF* Trial Judgement, *supra* note 432, paras. 2, 60–75, 751, 903. All charges against the third *CDF* accused, Samuel Hinga Norman, were dropped following his 22 February 2007 death. *Ibid.*, para. 5.

534 See *CDF* Trial Judgement, *supra* note 432, paras. 696–697, 699–700 (finding that an armed conflict existed in Sierra Leone from March 1991 to January 2002, that all the victims enjoyed protected status as civilians or captured enemy combatants, that the 'perpetrators' were aware of this protected status, and that a nexus existed between each crime and the armed conflict); see also *ibid.*, paras. 751, 753, 762, 787, 792, 831, 836, 840, 884, 891, 897 (repeating some of these findings with relation to specific incidents).

held the accused responsible for many instances of murder, cruel treatment, pillage, and collective punishments committed across Sierra Leone, mostly as superiors who failed to prevent or punish the commission of these crimes by subordinates.[535] It also found Kondewa responsible for enlisting one child soldier.[536]

In the *AFRC* case, Alex Tamba Brima, Brima Bazzy Kamara, and Santigie Borbor Kanu were charged with responsibility for acts of terrorism, collective punishments, murder, outrages upon personal dignity, mutilation, pillage, and conscripting, enlisting, or using child soldiers; these crimes were alleged to have been physically carried out, in the main, by Armed Forces Revolutionary Council (AFRC) forces or forces of the so-called AFRC/RUF 'Junta'.[537] Like the *CDF* Trial Chamber, the *AFRC* Trial Chamber rather summarily concluded that the general requirements of war crimes had been satisfied in respect of all the crimes it found to have been committed.[538] It held the three accused responsible for several war crimes – including sexual slavery as an outrage upon personal dignity[539] and mutilation as an act of terrorism[540] – usually because the accused in question ordered such crimes or failed as superiors to prevent and punish them.[541]

[535] See *ibid.*, paras. 722–732, 763 (Fofana aided and abetted murder, cruel treatment, and collective punishments in the towns of Tongo Field); *ibid.*, paras. 735–744, 764 (same for Kondewa); *ibid.*, paras. 772–783, 798 (Fofana failed as a superior to prevent murder, cruel treatment, and collective punishments in Karibondo); *ibid.*, paras. 816–827, 846 (Fofana failed to prevent murder, cruel treatment, pillage, and collective punishments in Bo District); *ibid.*, paras. 868–880, 903 (Kondewa failed to prevent and punish murder, cruel treatment, pillage, and collective punishments in Bothe Town); *ibid.*, paras. 951–955 (Kondewa failed to punish pillage in Moyamba District). See also *ibid.*, para. 919 (neither accused liable for any crime committed in Kenema District); *ibid.*, paras. 929–930, 937 (neither accused liable for any crime committed in Talia or Base Zero).

[536] See *ibid.*, paras. 968–972 (Kondewa personally enlisted a child soldier). See *infra* text accompanying notes 544–545 (discussing these findings).

[537] See *Prosecutor* v. *Brima, Kamara, and Kanu*, Case No. SCSL-2004-16-PT, Further Amended Consolidated Indictment, 18 February 2005, paras. 41–50, 63–65, 74–79. The RUF was the 'Revolutionary United Front', a rebel group that joined forces with the AFRC after the AFRC seized power from the government in a coup.

[538] See *AFRC* Trial Judgement, *supra* note 432, paras. 249–251, 254, 258 (finding that an armed conflict existed in Sierra Leone from March 1991 to January 2002, that it was non-international in character, that none of the victims were taking active part in the hostilities, and that a nexus existed between each crime and the armed conflict).

[539] See *ibid.*, paras. 1109, 1133, 1145, 1170, 1187 (finding that AFRC or AFRC/RUF Junta forces committed sexual slavery as an outrage upon personal dignity in Kono, Koinadugu, Bombali, and Loko Districts, as well as in Freetown and the Western Area); *ibid.*, para. 1835 (Brima planned sexual slavery in Bombali District, Freetown, and the Western Area); *ibid.*, para. 2096 (Kanu planned sexual slavery in Bombali District and the Western Area); *ibid.*, para. 2113 (Brima guilty 'pursuant to Article 6(1)' of the SCSL Statute); *ibid.*, para. 2121 (same for Kanu). The Chamber also convicted Kamara of sexual slavery as an outrage upon personal dignity 'pursuant to Article 6(1)', *ibid.*, para. 2117, although it did not make a clear finding that he was responsible for this crime in the section of the judgement applying the law to the facts; this confusion is discussed at note 548, *infra*. See also *ibid.*, para. 719 (holding that 'sexual slavery is an act of humiliation and degradation so serious as to be generally considered an outrage upon personal dignity'); *ibid.*, para. 708 (setting forth elements of sexual slavery). See also Chapter 2, text accompanying notes 582–587 (noting the Trial Chamber's disappointing and dubious decision to strike from the indictment the count charging sexual slavery as a crime against humanity as 'bad for duplicity').

[540] See *infra* notes 558–559 and accompanying text.

[541] See, e.g., *infra* notes 546–551 and accompanying text (discussing the *AFRC* accused's responsibility for conscripting child soldiers); notes 557–559 and accompanying text (discussing their responsibility for acts of terrorism).

The Trial Chambers' respective findings on the crime of conscripting, enlisting, or using child soldiers are noteworthy. After examining a number of sources, the *CDF* Chamber came up with a set of elements that largely resembles those of the ICC Elements of Crimes.[542] The *AFRC* Chamber borrowed its elements directly from the ICC Elements, and elaborated individual definitions for the three activities in Article 4(3) of the SCSL Statute: 'conscription' means compelling or coercing a person, including through abductions, to join the armed group; 'enlistment' means accepting and enrolling persons who volunteer to join the group; and 'use' entails not only the use of the person in active hostilities, but also for logistical tasks, such as carrying food and marking trails.[543] The *CDF* Chamber found that an eleven-year-old boy known by the pseudonym TF2-021 was abducted, along with some twenty other boys, and taken to the Civil Defence Forces (CDF) base. There Kondewa, the CDF 'High Priest', performed an initiation ritual, told the boys they would be powerful for fighting, and gave them a potion to rub on their bodies before going into battle. TF2-021 subsequently fought alongside the Kamajors in a number of CDF missions.[544] Kondewa later participated in a second initiation of TF2-021; a document bears Kondewa's signature and notes the boy's age as twelve. The *CDF* Trial Chamber found that this conduct on the part of Kondewa fulfilled the *actus reus* of 'enlistment', that the facts established beyond a reasonable doubt Kondewa's knowledge or reason to know that TF2-021 was under fifteen, and that he was thus guilty of enlisting a child soldier.[545] For its part, the *AFRC* Trial Chamber found that AFRC/RUF forces routinely abducted children and used them for military purposes;[546] this conduct qualified as 'conscription' because it involved the abduction and coercion of the victims.[547] The Chamber found all three accused

[542] See *CDF* Trial Judgement, *supra* note 432, paras. 182–196. These elements were the following: (1) the accused enlisted one or more persons, either voluntarily or compulsorily, into an armed force or group; (2) such person or persons were under the age of fifteen; (3) the accused knew or had reason to know that such person or persons were under the age of fifteen; and (4) the accused intended to enlist the person or persons. *Ibid.*, para. 195. Cf. ICC Elements of Crimes, *supra* note 439, Arts. 8(2)(b)(xxvi), 8(2)(e)(vii).

[543] See *AFRC* Trial Judgement, *supra* note 432, para. 729 (elements); *ibid.*, para. 734 (conscription); *ibid.*, para. 735 (enlistment); *ibid.*, para. 737 (use). Interestingly, the *AFRC* Trial Chamber cited the ICC *Lubanga* Pre-Trial Chamber's January 2007 confirmation of charges decision as one of its sources for these definitions. As discussed above, the *Lubanga* Chamber itself gleaned these definitions from Justice Robertson's May 2004 dissenting opinion on conscripting, enlisting, and using child soldiers. See *supra* text accompanying note 513 (discussing *Lubanga*); text accompanying note 526 (discussing the Robertson dissent).

[544] See *CDF* Trial Judgement, *supra* note 432, para. 968.

[545] *Ibid.*, para. 970. Since 'use' of child soldiers in hostilities was charged in the indictment as an alternative to 'enlistment', the Trial Chamber declined to analyse Kondewa's responsibility for using TF2–021 in hostilities. *Ibid.*, para. 971. For reasons unclear, the Chamber made no findings with respect to other child soldiers initiated by Kondewa. It found that the evidence had not established Fofana's responsibility for conscripting, enlisting, or using child soldiers. See *ibid.*, para. 967.

[546] See *AFRC* Trial Judgement, *supra* note 432, paras. 1276–1278 (finding that child soldiers were used in Kenema District, Kono District, Koinadugu, Bombali District, Freetown, and the Western Area); see also *ibid.*, paras. 1449–1450 (finding that the AFRC's primary purpose for abducting children was military in nature).

[547] *Ibid.*, para. 1276.

responsible for this crime.[548] It is interesting to note that the *CDF* Chamber and the *AFRC* Chamber appear to have taken different views on what constitutes 'conscription' on the one hand and 'enlistment' on the other. The *CDF* Chamber did not explicitly define 'conscription', and held that 'enlistment' includes 'both voluntary enlistment and forced enlistment';[549] the *AFRC* Chamber defined 'conscription' as involving abduction or some other form of coercion, and confined 'enlistment' to voluntary enrolment.[550] This apparent conflict will presumably have to be resolved in future jurisprudence.[551]

Both Trial Chambers also had occasion to define and apply the war crime 'acts of terrorism'. As mentioned above, this crime is derived from Additional Protocol II and also appears in the ICTR Statute, but has yet to be the subject of judicial analysis in that Tribunal.[552] Both Trial Chambers equated it to 'acts or threats of violence the primary purpose of which is to spread terror among the civilian population', a crime held by the Trial and Appeals Chambers in *Galić* to fall within the jurisdiction of the ICTY.[553] According to the *CDF* Chamber, the prohibition includes both acts and threats, and requires only that the accused have the specific intent to spread terror, not that the civilian population be actually threatened – thus, presumably, permitting inchoate liability.[554] The *CDF* Trial Chamber's findings on whether this crime was committed, and whether the three accused could bear liability for it, are haphazard. Although it made no explicit finding that the Kamajor fighters or anyone else committed this crime in any of the

[548] Brima and Kanu were clearly found responsible for planning conscription in the Bombali District and the Western Area. See *ibid*., paras. 1836, 2113 (Brima); *ibid*., paras. 2097, 2121 (Kanu); see also *ibid*., para. 1719 (Brima ordered conscription in Rosos in Bombali District). As with sexual slavery as an outrage upon personal dignity described at note 539 *supra*, the Trial Chamber's findings on Kamara's responsibility for conscription are confusing. In its specific findings relating to Kamara, it appears to conclude that he cannot bear liability for conscripting children or sexual slavery under a form of responsibility in Article 6(1) of the SCSL Statute (such as planning) because he did not substantially contribute to the commission of this crime, and that he also cannot be held responsible for failing to prevent or punish either crime as a superior because he lacked effective control over the relevant actors. See *ibid*., paras. 1972, 1974–1975. Nevertheless, in the disposition, the Chamber convicted Kamara of both crimes 'pursuant to Article 6(1)'. *Ibid*., para. 2117. It may be that the Chamber inadvertently left out a portion of its analysis of Kamara's Article 6(1) liability immediately following paragraph 1972.

[549] *CDF* Trial Judgement, *supra* note 432, para. 192 (emphasis removed).

[550] See *AFRC* Trial Judgement, *supra* note 432, paras. 734–735, 737.

[551] See *supra* text accompanying notes 530–531 (noting that the two judgements were drafted contemporaneously and arrive at mutually independent legal conclusions).

[552] See *supra* text accompanying notes 370–372. See also *supra* notes 454–456 and accompanying text (also noting that this crime is absent from the Rome Statute); *supra* text accompanying note 528 (noting that Charles Taylor is also charged with this crime).

[553] See *CDF* Trial Judgement, *supra* note 432, paras. 169–175; *AFRC* Trial Judgement, *supra* note 432, paras. 665–669. See also *supra* section 4.2.2.9, text accompanying note 458 (discussing *Galić*).

[554] See *CDF* Trial Judgement, *supra* note 432, paras. 172, 174; see also *ibid*., para. 172 n. 216 (making specific reference to the subparagraph in Article 3 of the SCSL Statute prohibiting 'threats to commit' any of the war crimes in the other subparagraphs, including 'acts of terrorism'); see also *supra* note 520 (discussing 'threats to commit' a war crime in the SCSL Statute); *supra* note 426; Chapter 3, note 24 (discussing this crime in the ICTR Statute and inchoate crimes in general).

towns or districts under analysis,[555] it nonetheless examined the accused's superior responsibility for failing to prevent or punish it with respect to a few (but not all) of the implicated locales, finding them not responsible.[556]

The *AFRC* Trial Chamber, by contrast, found that acts of terrorism had been perpetrated by AFRC or AFRC/RUF Junta forces in many towns and villages throughout Sierra Leone.[557] These included the systematic amputation of civilians' limbs, usually to 'teach them a lesson' for supporting the government instead of the AFRC.[558] The Trial Chamber held the three accused responsible for these and a number of other acts of terrorism.[559] Yet the Chamber also determined that many of the atrocities perpetrated by AFRC or Junta forces were not acts of terrorism because their primary purpose was something other than to spread terror among the civilian population; among these was the conscription of child soldiers, the primary purpose of which was to strengthen the AFRC's military forces.[560]

4.3.2.2 East Timor: Special Panels for Serious Crimes (SPSC)

The International Commission of Inquiry established to investigate human rights abuses committed prior to, during, and after the 1999 popular consultation in East Timor determined that 'breaches of humanitarian law' had occurred,[561] and that most of these had been perpetrated by pro-Indonesia militias acting at the direction

[555] The closest the Trial Chamber appears to have come to making an explicit finding that 'acts of terrorism' were physically perpetrated was its statement that 'the Kamajors had terrorized the civilians' of Bonthe Town. See *CDF* Trial Judgement, *supra* note 432, para. 554.

[556] See *ibid.*, para. 731 (Fofana not guilty of aiding and abetting acts of terrorism in Tongo Field because it had not been established that he knew of Norman's intent to spread terror); *ibid.*, para. 743 (same for Kondewa); *ibid.*, paras. 779–780 (Fofana not responsible as a superior for acts of terrorism in Koribondo because it had not been established that he knew or had reason to know of his subordinates' commission of this crime); *ibid.*, paras. 823–824 (same with respect to Fofana and Bo Town); *ibid.*, para. 879 (same with respect to Kondewa and Bonthe Town). For unknown reasons, the Chamber did not examine the accused's potential liability for acts of terrorism through any of the forms of responsibility other than aiding and abetting and superior responsibility, even though these forms were charged in respect of this crime. It would also appear that certain findings on this crime are simply missing, perhaps deleted in the process of revising the draft judgement in the wake of former accused Norman's death just a few months before judgement was to be rendered. See *supra* note 535.

[557] See *AFRC* Trial Judgement, *supra* note 432, paras. 1464, 1475, 1495, 1538–1539, 1571, 1609–1610, 1633.

[558] See *ibid.*, para. 1464; see also *ibid.*, para. 1463 (primary purpose of amputations was to spread terror among the civilian population, and 'served as a visible and lifelong sign to all other civilians not to resist the AFRC'); *ibid.*, paras. 1538–1539, 1609–1610 (findings on amputation as terrorism with respect to specific locales).

[559] See *ibid.*, para. 1711 (Brima ordered acts of terrorism in Bombali District); *ibid.*, para. 1773 (Brima ordered acts of terrorism in Freetown); *ibid.*, para. 1893 (Kamara failed as a superior to prevent and punish acts of terrorism in Kono District); *ibid.*, para. 1928 (same for Bombali District); *ibid.*, para. 1950 (same for Freetown); *ibid.*, para. 2044 (Kanu failed as a superior to prevent and punish acts of terrorism in Bombali District); *ibid.*, para. 2080 (Kanu failed as a superior to prevent and punish acts of terrorism in Western Area); *ibid.*, para. 2113 (Brima responsible for acts of terrorism 'pursuant to Article 6(1)' of the SCSL Statute); *ibid.*, para. 2118 (Kamara responsible for acts of terrorism 'pursuant to Article 6(3)'); *ibid.*, para. 2122 (same for Kanu).

[560] See *ibid.*, para. 1450. See also *ibid.*, paras. 1454, 1500 (forced labour of abductees not an act of terrorism because the primary purpose behind it was 'primarily utilitarian or military') (quotation at para. 1454); *ibid.*, para. 1459 (sexual slavery not an act of terrorism because the primary purpose was 'to satisfy [the AFRC troops'] sexual desires and to fulfil other conjugal needs').

[561] Report of the International Commission of Inquiry on East Timor to the Secretary-General, UN Doc. A/54/726, S/2000/59, 31 January 2000 ('East Timor Commission of Inquiry Report'), para. 123. See also Chapter 2, note 588 (discussing this report and the establishment of the Special Panels).

of the Indonesian armed forces and civilian authorities in Jakarta and Dili, who sought to 'provide the impression that the East Timorese were fighting among themselves'.[562] Perhaps as a result of these findings, the drafters of the constitutive document for East Timor's Special Panels for Serious Crimes included within the Panels' jurisdiction not only war crimes committed in non-international armed conflict, but also those committed in international armed conflict.[563] Section 6 of Regulation No. 2000/15 on the Establishment of Panels with Exclusive Jurisdiction over Serious Criminal Offences ('UNTAET Regulation') reproduces the whole of the Rome Statute's lengthy provision on war crimes,[564] with two important exceptions. First, the provision that jurisdiction over war crimes be exercised 'in particular when committed as part of a plan or policy or as part of a large-scale commission of such crime' has been omitted.[565] Second, the prohibition on using 'weapons, projectiles and material and methods of warfare which are of a nature to cause superfluous injury or unnecessary suffering or which are inherently indiscriminate in violation of the international law of armed conflict'[566] was not made to depend on those means and methods being 'the subject of a comprehensive convention'.[567]

As noted in Chapter 2, the Security Council withdrew UN support for the Special Panels in May 2005, effectively terminating them before they had tried the vast majority of their indictees.[568] No accused was ever charged with war crimes.[569] As Caitlin Reiger and Marieke Wierda point out, '[t]he question of whether the situation in Timor-Leste during 1999 satisfied the legal definition of an armed conflict was never tested'.[570]

[562] See East Timor Commission of Inquiry Report, *supra* note 561, paras. 135–140 (quotation at para. 136). See also *ibid.*, para. 140 ('The Commission is of the view that ultimately the Indonesian army was responsible for the intimidation, terror, killings, and other acts of violence experienced by the people of East Timor before and after the popular consultation.'). The Commission acknowledged that pro-independence militias 'were also involved in violent attacks', but concluded that these incidents 'were relatively fewer in number'. *Ibid.*, para. 141.

[563] See *supra* text accompanying notes 157–159 (discussing *ad hoc* jurisprudence on when involvement by a foreign government or forces in an otherwise non-international armed conflict renders the conflict international).

[564] See United Nations Transitional Administration in East Timor, Regulation No. 2000/15 on the Establishment of Panels with Exclusive Jurisdiction over Serious Criminal Offences, UN Doc. UNTAET/REG/2000/15, 6 June 2000 ('UNTAET Regulation'), Section 6. See also *supra* text accompanying notes 434–464 (discussing Article 8 of the Rome Statute).

[565] Compare *ibid.*, Section 6 with Rome Statute, *supra* note 1, Art. 8(1). This jurisdictional restriction and the negotiations resulting in its inclusion in the Rome Statute are discussed at text accompanying notes 440–444, *supra*.

[566] UNTAET Regulation, *supra* note 564, Section 6.1(b)(xx).

[567] Rome Statute, *supra* note 1, Art. 8(2)(b)(xx). See also *supra* note 452 and accompanying text (discussing this provision in the Rome Statute).

[568] See Chapter 2, text accompanying notes 593–596.

[569] Caitlin Reiger and Marieke Wierda, *The Serious Crimes Process in Timor-Leste: In Retrospect*, International Centre for Transitional Justice, March 2006, available at www.ictj.org/static/Prosecutions/Timor.study.pdf, p. 23. The charges against the accused before the SPSC consisted exclusively of crimes against humanity and ordinary crimes under domestic law.

[570] *Ibid.* See also *ibid.* ('The reasons for [not charging war crimes] are not entirely known, but may lie in the fact that prosecutors preferred to charge the crimes of 1999 as a widespread campaign against a civilian population than as crimes in the context of an armed conflict.'). See Chapter 2, section 2.3.2.2 (discussing the considerable jurisprudence of the SPSC on crimes against humanity).

4.3.2.3 The Extraordinary Chambers in the Courts of Cambodia (ECCC)

The Group of Experts tasked with determining the nature and scope of the crimes committed by the Khmer Rouge concluded that only a 'small portion' of the regime's atrocities could be characterised as war crimes.[571] According to the Group, Cambodian forces likely committed grave breaches of the 1949 Geneva Conventions, to which Cambodia and Vietnam were parties at the relevant time, against Vietnamese nationals during the protracted war between those states.[572] The Group found, however, that because violations of Common Article 3 probably did not incur individual criminal responsibility under customary international law in 1975, and Additional Protocol II was not concluded until 1977, it was 'more difficult to characterize the [regime's] acts during the internal conflict [with certain domestic resistance forces] as war crimes under the law at that time'.[573] Since war crimes 'would divert the attention of the court from the bulk of the atrocities', the Group recommended against including them in the jurisdiction of a future tribunal.[574] In spite of this recommendation, the Law on the Establishment of the Extraordinary Chambers in the Courts of Cambodia for the Prosecution of Crimes Committed During the Period of Democratic Kampuchea ('ECCC Law') gives the Chambers jurisdiction over grave breaches of the 1949 Geneva Conventions in terms largely identical to those of Article 2 of the ICTY Statute.[575]

The Group of Experts concluded that as part of its systematic attack on organised religion, the Khmer Rouge had destroyed many mosques, churches, and Buddhist temples, as well as sacred objects and texts.[576] While Cambodia became a party to the 1954 Hague Convention for Protection of Cultural Property in the Event of

571 Report of the Group of Experts for Cambodia Established Pursuant to General Assembly Resolution 52/135, annexed to UN Doc. A/53/850, S/1999/231, 16 March 1999 ('Cambodia Group of Experts Report'), para. 72.

572 *Ibid.*, para. 73; see also *ibid.*, para. 74 (determining with respect to Vietnamese civilians in Vietnam that 'the Cambodian army appears to have committed wilful killing, torture or inhuman treatment, wilful causing of great suffering, unlawful deportation or confinement and extensive destruction of property' in violation of Article 147 of the Fourth Geneva Convention). See also Ratner and Abrams, *supra* note 53, p. 291 (discussing armed tensions between Cambodia and Vietnam between 1975 and 1979); *ibid.*, p. 292 (suggesting that Cambodian forces may also have committed grave breaches against Thais and Laotians during incursions into Thai and Lao territory).

573 Cambodia Group of Experts Report, *supra* note 571, para. 75. Accord Ratner and Abrams, *supra* note 53, p. 293.

574 Cambodia Group of Experts Report, *supra* note 571, para. 151.

575 Law on the Establishment of the Extraordinary Chambers in the Courts of Cambodia for the Prosecution of Crimes Committed During the Period of Democratic Kampuchea, as amended on 27 October 2004, Doc. No. NS/RKM/1004/006, unofficial translation by the Council of Jurists and the Secretariat of the Task Force, revised on 26 August 2007 ('ECCC Law'), Art. 6, available at www.eccc.gov.kh/english/cabinet/law/4/KR_Law_as_amended_27_Oct_2004_Eng.pdf. See also *supra* text accompanying note 2 (quoting ICTY grave breaches provision). The period '17 April 1975 to 6 January 1979' is also listed in Article 6's *chapeau*; this is the duration of the Khmer Rouge regime. See Cambodia Group of Experts Report, *supra* note 571, para. 149.

576 See Cambodia Group of Experts Report, *supra* note 571, para. 28. See also Ratner and Abrams, *supra* note 53, p. 294 (noting that the Khmer Rouge destroyed most of Cambodia's 3,000 Buddhist pagodas, inflicted 'irreparable damage on statues, sacred literature, and other religious items', inflicted '[s]imilar damage … on Moslem mosques of the Cham people', and 'also attacked Christian places of worship').

Armed Conflict in 1962,[577] however, '[t]he Convention's nexus to armed conflict means … that despite the record of such destruction … only desecrations in connection with Cambodia's conflict with Viet Nam (or perhaps also of an internal armed conflict) would trigger criminal responsibility' for war crimes.[578] Again notwithstanding the absence of a recommendation to do so, the Extraordinary Chambers have been given jurisdiction over 'destruction of cultural property during armed conflict' pursuant to the 1954 Hague Convention.[579] Expressed in these terms, this provision is unique among international and internationalised courts and tribunals, although it resembles and likely overlaps with the war crime of seizing or destroying institutions dedicated to religion, charity, education, the arts and sciences, and historic monuments, which appears in the Statutes of the ICC,[580] the ICTY,[581] the SPSC,[582] and the SICT.[583] Although certain parts of the 1954 Hague Convention apply to non-international armed conflicts as well as international armed conflicts,[584] it is questionable whether individual criminal responsibility attached to the destruction of cultural property in civil war at the time of the Khmer Rouge's abuses.[585] In any event, this war crime will probably never be interpreted in the jurisprudence or applied in an actual case, as none of the five accused before the ECCC has been charged with it.

As noted in Chapter 2, on 18 July 2007, the ECCC Co-Prosecutors released a brief statement informing the public that they had filed before the Co-Investigating Judges an 'Introductory Submission' identifying five suspects thought to have committed 'crimes against humanity, genocide, [and] grave breaches of the Geneva Conventions'.[586] All five had been arrested by the end of November

577 See 1954 Hague Cultural Property Convention, *supra* note 295. The Convention's penal provision is Article 28: 'The High Contracting Parties undertake to take, within the framework of their ordinary criminal jurisdiction, all necessary steps to prosecute and impose penal or disciplinary sanctions upon those persons, of whatever nationality, who commit or order to be committed a breach of the present Convention.' Cambodia ratified the Convention on 4 April 1962. See www.erc.unesco.org/cp/convention.asp?KO=13637&language=E (listing states parties and dates of ratification). See also John Henry Merryman, 'Two Ways of Thinking About Cultural Property', (1986) 80 *American Journal of International Law* 831, 833–842 (detailed discussion of the 1954 Hague Convention, its precursors, and its penal provision).

578 Cambodia Group of Experts Report, *supra* note 571, para. 76.

579 ECCC Law, *supra* note 575, Art. 7.

580 Rome Statute, *supra* note 1, Art. 8(2)(b)(ix) (international armed conflict); *ibid.*, Art. 8(2)(e)(iv) (non-international armed conflict).

581 ICTY Statute, *supra* note 2, Art. 3(d) (international armed conflict). See also Hirad Abtahi, 'The Protection of Cultural Property in Times of Armed Conflict: The Practice of the International Criminal Tribunal for the Former Yugoslavia', (2001) 14 *Harvard Human Rights Journal* 1.

582 UNTAET Regulation, *supra* note 564, Section 6.1(b)(ix) (international armed conflict); *ibid.*, Section 6.1(e)(iv) (non-international armed conflict).

583 Law No. 10 (2005), Law of the Iraqi Higher Criminal Court, 18 October 2005 ('SICT Statute'), English translation available at www.law.case.edu/saddamtrial/documents/IST_statute_official_english.pdf, reprinted in Michael P. Scharf and Gregory S. McNeal (eds.), *Saddam on Trial: Understanding and Debating the Iraqi High Tribunal* (2006), pp. 283 *et seq.*, Art. 13(2)(J) (international armed conflict); *ibid.*, Art. 13(4)(D) (non-international armed conflict).

584 See 1954 Hague Cultural Property Convention, *supra* note 295, Art. 19(1).

585 See Swart, *supra* note 523, p. 296.

586 Extraordinary Chambers in the Courts of Cambodia, Statement of the Co-Prosecutors, 18 July 2007, p. 4. See also Chapter 2, text accompanying notes 661–666.

2007.[587] All have been charged with crimes against humanity,[588] and three have been charged with grave breaches under Article 6 of the ECCC Statute.[589] It is hoped that the trial of these accused will begin without undue delay, particularly given their advanced age.[590]

4.3.2.4 Supreme Iraqi Criminal Tribunal (SICT) (also known as the Iraqi High Tribunal (IHT))

Article 12 of the Statute of the Supreme Iraqi Criminal Tribunal[591] follows the ICC formulation in its definition of war crimes, although it features a number of important additions and omissions.[592] First, like its analogue in the UNTAET Regulation,[593] the restriction that jurisdiction be exercised over war crimes 'in particular when committed as part of a plan or policy or as part of a large-scale

[587] See Seth Mydans, 'Cambodia Arrests Former Khmer Rouge Head of State', *New York Times*, 20 November 2007, available at www.nytimes.com/2007/11/20/world/asia/20cambo.html?_r=1&oref=slogin (stating that Khieu Samphan, who was arrested on 19 November 2007, was 'the last of five top figures targeted by prosecutors in advance of trials expected [in 2008] for the atrocities of the late 1970s').

[588] See Chapter 2, notes 667–672 and accompanying text (discussing crimes against humanity charges against Kaing Guek Eav (alias 'Duch'), Nuon Chea, Ieng Sary, Ieng Thirith, and Khieu Samphan).

[589] See *Co-Prosecutors* v. *Nuon*, Investigation No. 002/19-09-2007, Order on Provisional Detention, 19 September 2007, paras. 1, 5 (charging Nuon, Pol Pot's second-in-command, with the grave breaches of wilful killing, torture, inhuman treatment, wilfully causing great suffering or serious injury to body or health, wilfully depriving a prisoner of war or a civilian the rights of a fair and regular trial, unlawful confinement of a civilian, and unlawful deportation or transfer of a civilian); *Co-Prosecutors* v. *Ieng Sary*, Investigation No. 002/19-09-2007, Provisional Detention Order, 14 November 2007, paras. 1, 15 (charging Ieng Sary, minister of foreign affairs of the Khmer Rouge regime, with the grave breaches of wilful killing, wilfully causing great suffering or serious injury to body or health, wilfully depriving a prisoner of war or a civilian the rights of a fair and regular trial, unlawful confinement of a civilian, and unlawful deportation or transfer of a civilian); *Co-Prosecutors* v. *Khieu*, Investigation No. 002/19-09-2007, Provisional Detention Order, 19 November 2007, paras. 1, 5 (charging Khieu, head of state of the Khmer Rouge regime, with the grave breaches of wilful killing, wilfully causing great suffering or serious injury to body or health, wilfully depriving a prisoner of war or a civilian the rights of a fair and regular trial, unlawful confinement of a civilian, and unlawful deportation or transfer of a civilian).

[590] Nuon and Ieng Sary are 82, Ieng Thirith is 75, Khieu is 76, and Duch is 64. Two of those thought to be most responsible for the regime's atrocities – Pol Pot and Ta Mok – have already died. Seth Mydans, 'Prosecutors Identify Suspects in Khmer Rouge Trial', *New York Times*, 18 July 2007, available at www.nytimes.com/2007/07/19/world/asia/19cambodia.html.

[591] Also known as the Iraqi High Tribunal (IHT). See Chapter 1, note 2 (discussing the different English translations of the Tribunal's name).

[592] See SICT Statute, *supra* note 583, Art. 13. See also *supra* text accompanying notes 434–464 (discussing Article 8 of the Rome Statute). There are many differences with the ICC formulation that do not change its substance. For example: (1) American spellings are used instead of British spellings for words such as 'wilful' and 'defence'; (2) the verb 'use' appears throughout, instead of the verb 'employ'; (3) the Rome Statute's respective provisions on '[d]eclaring that no quarter will be given' corresponding to international and non-international armed conflict have been awkwardly rendered '[d]eclaring that no one remained alive', and '[d]eclaring that no person is still alive', compare Rome Statute, *supra* note 1, Arts. 8(2)(b)(xii), 8(2)(e)(x) with SICT Statute, *supra* note 583, Arts. 13(2)(M), 13(4)(J); (4) the grave breach 'unlawful confinement' appears in a separate subparagraph from 'unlawful deportation or transfer', compare SICT Statute, *supra* note 583, Arts. 13(1)(G) (unlawful confinement), 13(1)(H) (unlawful deportation or transfer) with Rome Statute, *supra* note 1, Art. 8(2)(vii) (single subparagraph with all three crimes); and (5) the SICT Statute prohibits wilfully impeding relief supplies 'as provided for under international law', while the Rome Statute prohibits wilfully impeding such supplies 'as provided for under the Geneva Conventions', compare SICT Statute, *supra* note 583, Art. 13(2)(Y) with Rome Statute, *supra* note 1, Art. 8(2)(b)(xxv).

[593] See *supra* text accompanying note 565.

commission of such crime' has been omitted.[594] Second, as with the Tribunal's provision on crimes against humanity,[595] certain of the Rome Statute's listed offences have been excluded entirely: enforced sterilisation,[596] and using 'weapons, projectiles and material and methods of warfare which are of a nature to cause superfluous injury or unnecessary suffering or which are inherently indiscriminate in violation of the international law of armed conflict'.[597] Third, the two definitions of 'conflicts not of an international character'[598] have also been curiously left out.

M. Cherif Bassiouni and Michael Wahid Hanna point to a more fundamental problem, arising from the wholesale importation of the Rome Statute's definition of war crimes, which hearkens back to the similar observation made by the Cambodia Group of Experts:[599]

> The [SICT's] definition of war crimes … is problematic … because the commission of such crimes in non-international armed conflicts has only recently become an indisputable tenet of customary international law … [C]ommon Article 3 … does not categorically establish that violations of this provision are war crimes. While scholarly opinion and ICTY and ICTR decisions have overcome this jurisdictional gap and have firmly established that such violations are war crimes under customary international law, this provides an insufficient basis on which to argue that such crimes were part of customary international law during the entire period covered by the [SICT's] temporal jurisdiction [that is, 17 July 1968 to 1 May 2003].[600]

There is also at least one international armed conflict war crime in the SICT Statute that would give rise to *nullum crimen sine lege* problems if an accused were ever charged with it, as it likely did not exist in custom during the period of the Tribunal's temporal jurisdiction. '[T]ransfer, directly or indirectly, by the Occupying Power of parts of its own civilian population into the territory it occupies, or the deportation or transfer of all or parts of the population of the occupied territory within or outside this territory'[601] has been altered by replacing 'Occupying Power' with the words 'Government of Iraq or any of its instrumentalities (which includes for clarification

[594] Compare SICT Statute, *supra* note 583, Art. 13 with Rome Statute, *supra* note 1, Art. 8(1). This jurisdictional restriction and the negotiations resulting in its inclusion in the Rome Statute are discussed at text accompanying notes 440–444, *supra*.

[595] See Chapter 2, text accompanying notes 674–685.

[596] Rome Statute, *supra* note 1, Art. 8(2)(3)(vi). Enforced sterilisation was also omitted as an underlying offence of crimes against humanity in the SICT Statute. See Chapter 2, text accompanying note 682.

[597] Rome Statute, *supra* note 1, Art. 8(2)(b)(xx). See also *supra* note 452 and accompanying text (discussing this provision in the Rome Statute).

[598] See *ibid.*, Arts. 8(2)(d), 8(2)(f); see also *supra* note 438 (discussing these provisions in the Rome Statute).

[599] See *supra* note 573 and accompanying text.

[600] M. Cherif Bassiouni and Michael Wahid Hanna, 'Ceding the High Ground: The Iraqi High Criminal Court Statute and the Trial of Saddam Hussein', (2006–07) 39 *Case Western Reserve Journal of International Law* 21, 74–75 (footnotes omitted). The two cases for which there have been trials and convictions concerned, respectively, crimes committed in 1982 and 1988. See *infra* text accompanying notes 607–614.

[601] Rome Statute, *supra* note 1, Art. 8(2)(b)(viii). See also *supra* note 453 and accompanying text (discussing this provision in the Rome Statute).

any of the instruments of the Arab Ba'ath Socialist Party)'.[602] It is unclear what the drafters of the SICT Statute intended by this substitution, or in what contexts they intended this provision to apply. The law on occupation of territory, extensively set out in the Fourth Geneva Convention, concerns the occupation by one state of territory that does not form part of that state,[603] and knows no analogue in non-international armed conflict. There would consequently be no basis in international law for the imposition of liability on a member of Saddam Hussein's regime who, for example, ordered the transfer of parts of the Sunni Iraqi population into majority Kurdish regions of Iraq. This provision also suggests the general inappropriateness of copying the portion of the Rome Statute dealing with international armed conflict war crimes when trials before the SICT were anticipated to involve, and indeed have involved, atrocities committed by Hussein's Ba'ath Party government against members of the Iraqi population.[604]

As discussed in Chapter 2, the SICT has recourse to a document setting forth the elements of the crimes within its jurisdiction.[605] The elements of war crimes in the SICT Elements of Crimes are essentially the same as those of the ICC Elements of Crimes, although they reflect the differences between the respective Statutes.[606]

In the *Dujail* case – the Tribunal's first – Saddam Hussein and his seven co-accused were charged with crimes against humanity only; as a result, neither the *Dujail* Trial or Appeal Judgement deals in any way with war crimes, or attempts to address the difficult questions raised above relating to *nullum crimen sine lege*.[607] The second trial before the SICT concerned alleged massacres and forced removals involving perhaps 200,000 Kurds in the 'Anfal' campaign carried out by Hussein's regime in 1988.[608] Perhaps as a result of waning interest in the Tribunal's work in the wake of Hussein's execution,[609] as of 1 December 2007 the charging instruments and judgements in the *Anfal* case had not been made publicly available

602 SICT Statute, *supra* note 583, Art. 13(2)(I). 603 See Geneva Convention IV, *supra* note 3, Arts. 47–78.

604 A similar problem may arise from the substitution of the ICC international armed conflict war crime of 'subjecting persons who are in the power of an adverse party to physical mutilation or to medical or scientific experiments', Rome Statute, *supra* note 1, Art. 8(2)(b)(x), with 'subjecting persons *of another nation* to physical mutilation or to medical or scientific experiments', SICT Statute, *supra* note 583, Art. 13(2)(K) (emphasis added).

605 See Iraqi Special Tribunal, Elements of Crimes, Section 4 ('SICT Elements of Crimes'), available at www.law.case.edu/saddamtrial/documents/IST_Elements.pdf, reprinted in Scharf and McNeal (eds.), *supra* note 583, pp. 327 *et seq*. See also Chapter 2, text accompanying notes 681–685 (discussing the status of the SICT Elements and the reliance on them by the Trial Chamber in the *Dujail* case).

606 See, e.g., SICT Elements of Crimes, *supra* note 605, Art. 13(b)(9), Element (b) ('The perpetrator was acting for or on behalf of the Government of Iraq or any of its instrumentalities, including an instrumentality of the Arab Socialist Ba'ath Party[.]').

607 See Chapter 2, text accompanying notes 686–708 (discussing the *Dujail* charges and judgements in detail).

608 See *ibid*., notes 709–710 and text accompanying text.

609 See John F. Burns, 'Hussein's Cousin Sentenced to Die for Kurd Attacks', *New York Times*, 25 June 2007, available at www.select.nytimes.com/search/restricted/article?res=F20E10F8355B0C768EDDAF0894DF404482 (noting that 'Iraqi public interest in the [SICT's] trials has flagged'; that few Iraqi and no Kurdish reporters attended the hearing at which the judges handed down the *Anfal* verdict; and that 'only a handful of Western reporters' were in attendance).

in English, although the Prosecutor's closing argument was available. It appears to show that five accused – the highest-ranked of whom was Ali Hassan al-Majid, also known as 'Chemical Ali'[610] – were charged with ordering, inciting, aiding and abetting, and failing as superiors to prevent and punish five non-international armed conflict war crimes, as well as crimes against humanity and genocide.[611] The Prosecutor argued that, '[i]nstead of focusing military efforts against the Peshmerga forces [that is, Kurdish armed fighters], these defendants ordered the soldiers to attack civilians, and they gave them the freedom to commit acts of theft, rape, and torture, in conjunction with the destruction of the villages'.[612] The Tribunal convicted the five accused on 23 June 2007.[613] Media reports indicate that Majid was convicted of genocide, war crimes, and crimes against humanity, while the other four were convicted only of war crimes and crimes against humanity.[614]

610 See 'Prosecutorial Closing Argument in the Anfal Case', available at www.iraq-iht.org/en/doc/ppb.pdf (date unknown, on file with authors), pp. 2–3, 7. All charges against Saddam Hussein in the *Anfal* case were dropped following his execution by hanging. See Chapter 2, text accompanying note 711.

611 'Prosecutorial Closing Argument in the Anfal Case', *supra* note 610, pp. 4–7, 15, 17, 23. These war crimes were the following: (1) intentionally directing attacks against the civilian population or civilians not taking direct part in the hostilities (Article 13(4)(A)); (2) intentionally directing attacks against buildings dedicated to religious, educational, artistic, scientific, or charitable purposes that are not military objectives (Article 13(4)(D)); (3) pillage (Article 13(4)(E)); (4) rape (Article 13(4)(F)); and (5) ordering the displacement of the civilian population for reasons related to the conflict (Article 13(4)(H)). See also *ibid.*, pp. 17–19 (discussing the elements of these war crimes in terms seemingly inspired by the SICT Elements of Crimes, *supra* note 605, and discussing some of the evidence that purportedly fulfilled such elements).

612 *Ibid.*, p. 15. The Prosecutor continued: 'In one of the evil crimes, these defendants committed a war crime that no other state has committed, as history tells us. Military forces in a sovereign state have never in human history used chemical weapons against its citizens.' *Ibid.* Despite this statement, the Prosecutor does not appear to have charged the use of chemical weapons *per se* as a war crime, possibly because none of the non-international armed conflict war crimes listed in the SICT Statute concerns prohibitions on the use of certain weapons. See generally SICT Statute, *supra* note 583, Art. 13(3)–(4).

613 See, e.g., Burns, *supra* note 609; BBC News, '"Chemical Ali" Sentenced to Hang', 24 June 2007, at www.news.bbc.co.uk/2/hi/middle_east/6233926.stm.

614 Majid and two others were sentenced to death. A sixth accused was acquitted. Other trials before the SICT are apparently being prepared or are underway. See Chapter 2, note 718 and accompanying text (also noting that, as of 30 November 2007, none of the death sentences had been carried out, and explaining why).

5

Cumulative convictions and sentencing

This chapter examines several unique challenges involved in prosecuting and adjudicating international crimes, and highlights some of the pitfalls of the approach chosen by the *ad hoc* Tribunals. A recurrent issue in the *ad hoc* jurisprudence has been whether and in what circumstances the Prosecutor may bring charges for more than one crime in respect of the same underlying conduct (for example, the beating of a certain victim) and whether and in what circumstances the trial chamber may enter convictions for more than one crime (for example, cruel treatment as a violation of the laws or customs of war and inhumane treatment as a crime against humanity). While the chambers have long permitted cumulative and alternative charging in indictments without much debate or controversy, the question of when a trial chamber may convict an accused for more than one crime in respect of the same conduct is more complicated and contentious. Section 5.1 sets forth the Tribunals' law and practice on cumulative and alternative charging, and Section 5.2 addresses cumulative convictions. Section 5.3 then looks at sentencing practice, focusing in particular on the lack of a coherent sentencing practice in the *ad hoc* Tribunals, the treatment of categories of crimes for sentencing purposes, and the interventionist role of the *ad hoc* Appeals Chambers in sentencing determinations. Unlike the previous chapters of this volume, this chapter does not include a comparative survey of the practice of the other international or hybrid courts and tribunals because, with the exception of the Special Court for Sierra Leone (SCSL), they have either not included significant examinations of these issues in their jurisprudence, or have not yet issued relevant decisions and judgements. As of 1 December 2007, the chambers of the SCSL had issued two trial judgements,[1] the relevant discussions of which do not differ markedly from settled precedent of the *ad hoc* Tribunals. For this reason, they will be addressed where relevant in the general analysis below and not in their own separate subsection.

5.1 Cumulative and alternative charging

A number of early trial chambers of the *ad hoc* Tribunals were called upon to determine whether the prosecution may charge an accused in the indictment with different crimes on the basis of the same conduct. The positions adopted were often inconsistent, resulting in one line of authority that appeared to be generally sympathetic to cumulative charging without restriction,[2] and another that allowed it only in

[1] See *Prosecutor* v. *Fofana and Kondewa*, Case No. SCSL-04-14-J, Judgement, 2 August 2007 ('*CDF* Trial Judgement'); *Prosecutor* v. *Brima, Kamara, and Kanu*, Case No. SCSL-04-16-T, Judgement, 20 June 2007 ('*AFRC* Trial Judgement').

[2] See *Prosecutor* v. *Niyitegeka*, Case No. ICTR-96-14-T, Decision on Defence Motion on Matters Arising from Trial Chamber Decisions and Preliminary Motion Based on Defects in the Form of the Indictment and Lack of Jurisdiction, 20 November 2000, para. 43 ('[T]he issue of cumulative charges can only be raised at trial and not at this stage of the proceedings.'); *Prosecutor* v. *Naletilić and Martinović*, Case No. IT-98-34-PT, Decision on Defendant Vinko Martinović's Objection to the Indictment, 15 February 2000 ('*Naletilić and Martinović* February 2000 Pre-Trial Decision'), para. 12 (noting the more restrictive approach taken by some trial chambers, but declining to decide on whether certain charges were impermissibly cumulative with others 'since the defendant will not be prejudiced if cumulativeness is decided after the evidence has been presented'); *Prosecutor* v. *Krnojelac*, Case No. IT-97-25-PT, Decision on the Defence Preliminary Motion on the Form of the Indictment, 24 February 1999, para. 5; *Prosecutor* v. *Ntabakuze*, Decision on the Defence Preliminary Motions Relating to Defects in the Form and Substance of the Indictment, 5 October 1998, para. 14; *Prosecutor* v. *Ntagerura*, Decision on the Preliminary Motion Filed by the Defence Based on Defects in the Form of the Indictment of 28 November

some circumstances.[3] The most thoroughly reasoned discussion appears in the January 2000 *Kupreškić* Trial Judgement, in which the Trial Chamber weighed the different interests involved and arrived at a relatively elaborate formula. Where the prosecution contends that the same conduct constitutes two crimes and a conviction for both would be permissible under the cumulative-convictions test created by the same Chamber earlier in the Judgement, the crimes may be charged cumulatively.[4] On the other hand, where a conviction for both would not be permissible, the prosecution must charge the crimes in the alternative,[5] and in any event 'should refrain as much as possible from making charges based on the same facts but under excessive multiple heads, whenever it would not seem warranted to contend … that the same facts are simultaneously in breach of various provisions of the Statute.'[6]

1997, para. 26; *Prosecutor* v. *Nahimana*, Decision on the Preliminary Motion Filed by the Defence Based on Defects in the Form of the Indictment, 24 November 1997, para. 37; *Prosecutor* v. *Delalić, Mucić, Delić, and Landžo*, Case No. IT-96-21-AR.72.5, Decision on Application for Leave to Appeal by Hazim Delić (Defects in the Form of the Indictment), 6 December 1996, para. 36; *Prosecutor* v. *Delalić, Mucić, Delić, and Landžo*, Case No IT-96-21-T, Decision on Motion by the Accused Hazim Delić Based on Defects in the Form of the Indictment, 15 November 1996, para. 22; *Prosecutor* v. *Delalić, Mucić, Delić, and Landžo*, Case No IT-96-21-T, Decision on Motion by the Accused Zejnil Delalić Based on Defects in the Form of the Indictment, 2 October 1996, para. 24; *Prosecutor* v. *Tadić*, Case No. IT-94-1-T, Decision the Defence Motion on the Form of the Indictment, 14 November 1995, para. 17; *Prosecutor* v. *Krstić*, Case No. IT-98-33-PT, Decision on Defence Preliminary Motion on the Form of the Amended Indictment, 28 January 2000, p. 5. The *Krstić* Trial Chamber noted a number of benefits that may result from determining before trial whether cumulative charges should be permitted, including that a more focused and efficient trial may result from clarifying such issues at the outset, and that the accused may be in a better position to prepare his defence. Yet the Chamber ultimately concluded that, given the difficulty in analysing the potential overlap in particular charges before trial – particularly in light of the then-embryonic state of the jurisprudence on the elements of the crimes – only 'clear-cut' cases of 'unduly cumulative charging' would require action by the trial chamber at the pre-trial stage. The Trial Chamber did not explain what a 'clear-cut' case might look like, merely finding that Radislav Krstić had not presented one. *Ibid.*, pp. 6–7.

3 See *Prosecutor* v. *Kupreškić, Kupreškić, Kupreškić, Josipović, Papić, and Šantić*, Case No. IT-95-16-T, Judgement, 14 January 2000 ('*Kupreškić et al.* Trial Judgement'), para. 727; *Prosecutor* v. *Kayishema and Ruzindana*, Case No. ICTR 95-1-T, Judgement, 21 May 1999 ('*Kayishema and Ruzindana* Trial Judgement'), para. 649; *Prosecutor* v. *Kvočka, Kos, Radić, and Žigić*, Case No. IT-98-30-PT, Decision on Defence Preliminary Motions on the Form of the Indictment, 12 April 1999 ('*Kvočka et al.* April 1999 Pre-Trial Decision'), para. 25 (holding that 'cumulative charging is … permissible in certain circumstances'); *ibid.*, para. 47 (specifying these circumstances – 'the Articles of the Statute referred to [must be] designed to protect different values and … each Article [must] require [ ] proof of a legal element not required by the others' – and concluding that 'both these requirements are met here, where the charges alleged to be cumulated fall under Article 3 and Article 5'); *Prosecutor* v. *Kupreskić, Kupreskić, Kupreskić, Šantić, Alilović, Josipović, Katava, and Papić*, Case No. IT-95-16-PT, Decision on Defence Challenges to Form of the Indictment, 15 May 1998, p. 3 (considering that 'the Prosecutor may be justified in bringing cumulative charges when the Articles of the Statute referred to are designed to protect different values and when each Article requires proof of a legal element not required by the others').

4 See *Kupreškić et al.* Trial Judgement, *supra* note 3, para. 727(a). The Trial Chamber held that cumulative convictions for two or more crimes are only permissible where 'the offences contain elements uniquely required by each provision'. *Ibid.*, para. 718. In such a circumstance, a trial chamber must convict the accused for both crimes, but it must also order that the sentences for each must be served concurrently. See *ibid.* If this test is not fulfilled, the chamber mustf choose the crime for which to convict the accused. See *ibid.*, para. 719.

5 See *ibid.*, para. 727(b).

6 *Ibid.*, para. 727(c).See also *ibid.*, para. 823 (Trial Chamber applying its cumulative-charging standard to conclude that murder and cruel treatment as violations of the laws or customs of war had been charged impermissibly with murder and inhumane treatment as crimes against humanity).

The divergence in the jurisprudence of the International Criminal Tribunal for the former Yugoslavia (ICTY) was resolved by the Appeals Chamber in a single paragraph of the February 2001 *Čelebići* Judgement:

> Cumulative charging is to be allowed in light of the fact that, prior to the presentation of all of the evidence, it is not possible to determine to a certainty which of the charges brought against an accused will be proven. The Trial Chamber is better poised, after the parties' presentation of the evidence, to evaluate which of the charges may be retained, based upon the sufficiency of the evidence. In addition, cumulative charging constitutes the usual practice of both this Tribunal and the ICTR.[7]

In the November 2001 *Musema* Judgement, the Appeals Chamber of the International Criminal Tribunal for Rwanda (ICTR) endorsed this holding as 'equally applicable to the ICTR'.[8] As the *Semanza* Appeals Chamber later clarified, if at the end of trial the chamber determines that the elements of two or more cumulatively charged crimes have been established, it must then apply the *Čelebići* Appeals Chamber's cumulative-convictions test (discussed in detail in the following section of this chapter) to determine whether it may convict the accused for all the cumulatively charged crimes, or only some or one of them.[9] Notwithstanding repeated reaffirmations in trial and appeal judgements of what the *Semanza* Appeals Chamber called the '*Čelebići-Musema* principle',[10] accused at both

7 *Prosecutor* v. *Delalić, Mucić, Delić and Landžo*, Case No. IT-96-21-A, Judgement, 20 February 2001 ('*Čelebići* Appeal Judgement'), para. 400. As explained in Volume I of this series, the chambers have applied similar reasoning in consistently allowing the prosecution to charge an accused with liability for the same crime simultaneously under more than one form of responsibility. See Gideon Boas, James L. Bischoff, and Natalie L. Reid, *Forms of Responsibility in International Criminal Law* (2007), p. 383.

8 *Musema* v. *Prosecutor*, Case No. ICTR-96-13-A, Judgement, 16 November 2001 ('*Musema* Appeal Judgement'), para. 369.

9 *Prosecutor* v. *Semanza*, Case No. ICTR-97-20-A, Judgement, 20 May 2005 ('*Semanza* Appeal Judgement'), para. 309. See also *ibid.* (rejecting, as 'plainly meritless in light of the *Čelebići-Musema* principle', Semanza's argument that he was improperly charged in the indictment with genocide, complicity in genocide, and various crimes against humanity on the basis of the same conduct).

10 See *Prosecutor* v. *Galić*, Case No. IT-98-29-A, Judgement, 30 November 2006 ('*Galić* Appeal Judgement'), para. 161; *Prosecutor* v. *Naletilić and Martinović*, Case No. IT-98-34-A, Judgement, 3 May 2006 ('*Naletilić and Martinović* Appeal Judgement'), para. 103; *Semanza* Appeal Judgement, *supra* note 9, para. 308; *Prosecutor* v. *Kupreškić, Kupreškić, Kupreškić, Josipović, Papić, and Šantić*, Case No. IT-95-16-A, Appeal Judgement, 23 October 2001 ('*Kupreškić et al.* Appeal Judgement'), para. 386 (overturning the Trial Chamber's findings on cumulative charging described at *supra* note 6). See also *Prosecutor* v. *Ndindabahizi*, Case No. ICTR-01-71-T, Judgement and Sentence, 15 July 2004 ('*Ndindabahizi* Trial Judgement'), para. 491; *Prosecutor* v. *Galić*, Case No. IT-98-29, Judgement, 5 December 2003 ('*Galić* Trial Judgement'), para. 156; *Prosecutor* v. *Nahimana, Barayagwiza, and Ngeze*, Case No. ICTR-99-52-T, Judgement and Sentence, 3 December 2003 ('*Media* Trial Judgement'), para. 1089 ('Cumulative charging is generally permissible, as it is not possible to determine which charges will be proven against an Accused prior to the presentation of the evidence.'); *Prosecutor* v. *Semanza*, Case No. ICTR-97-20-T, Judgement and Sentence, 15 May 2003 ('*Semanza* Trial Judgement'), para. 60; *Prosecutor* v. *Naletilić and Martinović*, Case No. IT-98-34, Judgement, 31 March 2003 ('*Naletilić and Martinović* Trial Judgement'), para. 510; *Prosecutor* v. *Ntakirutimana and Ntakirutimana*, Case Nos. ICTR-96-10 and ICTR-96-17-T, Judgement and Sentence, 21 February 2003 ('*Ntakirutimana and Ntakirutimana* Trial Judgement'), para. 863. But see *Prosecutor* v. *Rukundo*, Case No. ICTR-01-70-I, Separate Declaration of Pavel Dolenc regarding Decision on Preliminary Motion, 4 March 2003, para. 10 (arguing that the *Čelebići* Appeals Chamber's reasoning 'is more applicable to alternative charges based on different alternate set of facts and not to cumulative charges based on the same set of facts').

Tribunals have continued to challenge cumulative charges in their indictments. Such challenges have been routinely and summarily dismissed.[11]

The rather sparse reasoning of the *Čelebići* Appeals Chamber was supplemented by two lengthier concurring discussions released on the same day, one in a separate opinion of Judges Hunt and Bennouna in *Čelebići*, and the other in a *Brđanin and Talić* pre-trial decision in which one of the judges was also Judge Hunt. Running through both discussions was the concern that the restrictions imposed on the prosecution by the *Kupreškić* formula were unduly onerous. These judges elaborated the view that:

> it is not possible to know with precision, prior to [the presentation of all the evidence], which offences among those charged the evidence will prove, particularly in relation to proof of differing jurisdictional prerequisites – such as, for example, the requirement that an international armed conflict be proved for Article 2 offences but not for those falling under Article 3.[12]

According to these judges, the problem was compounded by the still-developing jurisprudence on the elements of crimes: it would be unrealistic to expect the prosecution to predict with any degree of certainty which of several potential crimes have at least one mutually exclusive element – thus making it possible for the accused to be convicted of both in respect of the same conduct[13] – and to charge any crimes not meeting this standard in the alternative or not at all.[14] On balance, the judges regarded the potential prejudice to the prosecution resulting from the *Kupreškić* formula as considerably more significant than any possible prejudice to the accused: 'There is no readily identifiable prejudice to an accused in permitting cumulative charging, when the issues arising from an accumulation of offences are determined after all of the evidence has been presented, whereas the very real

[11] See, e.g., *Prosecutor* v. *Rašević and Todović*, Case No. IT-97-25/1-PT, Decision on Todović Defence Motion on the Form of the Joint Amended Indictment, 21 March 2006, para. 25; *Prosecutor* v. *Delić*, Case No. IT-04-83-PT, Decision on Defence Motion Alleging Defects in the Form of the Indictment and Order on Prosecution Motion to Amend the Indictment, 13 December 2005, para. 25; *Prosecutor* v. *Bagosora, Kabiligi, Ntabakuze, and Nsengiyumva*, Case No. ICTR-98-41-T, Decision on Kabiligi Request for Particulars of the Amended Indictment, 27 September 2005, para. 7; *Prosecutor* v. *Mpambara*, Case No. ICTR-01-65-I, Decision on the Defence Preliminary Motion Challenging the Amended Indictment, 30 May 2005 ('*Mpambara* May 2005 Pre-Trial Decision'), paras. 4, 6; *Prosecutor* v. *Limaj, Bala, and Musliu*, Case No. IT-03-66-PT, Decision on Prosecution's Motion to Amend the Amended Indictment, 12 February 2004, para. 27; *Prosecutor* v. *Rukundo*, Case No. ICTR-01-70-I, Decision on Preliminary Motion, 26 February 2003, para. 17; *Prosecutor* v. *Blagojević, Obrenović, Jokić, and Nikolić*, Case No. IT-02-60-PT, Decision on Motion of Accused Blagojević to Dismiss Cumulative Charges, 31 July 2002, pp. 3–4; *Prosecutor* v. *Hadžihasanović, Alagić, and Kubura*, Case No. IT-01-47-PT, Decision on Form of Indictment, 7 December 2001, para. 40.

[12] *Čelebići* Appeal Judgement, *supra* note 7, Separate and Dissenting Opinion of Judge David Hunt and Judge Mohamed Bennouna, para. 12. Accord *Prosecutor* v. *Brđanin and Talić*, Case No. IT-99-36-PT, Decision on Objections by Momir Talić to the Form of the Amended Indictment, 20 February 2001 ('*Brđanin and Talić* February 2001 Pre-Trial Decision'), para. 39.

[13] See *infra* text accompanying notes 39–42, 56–57 (discussing the *Čelebići* cumulative-convictions test).

[14] See *Čelebići* Appeal Judgement, *supra* note 7, Separate and Dissenting Opinion of Judge David Hunt and Judge Mohamed Bennouna, para. 12; *Brđanin and Talić* February 2001 Pre-Trial Decision, *supra* note 12, para. 41.

possibilities of prejudice to the prosecution in restricting such charging are manifest.'[15]

While the *Čelebići* Appeals Chamber did not explicitly address whether the prosecution may charge crimes in the alternative in respect of the same conduct, the *Naletilić and Martinović* Trial Chamber held that such a conclusion is implied in *Čelebići* 's reasoning,[16] and several other trial chambers have also held that alternative charging is allowable.[17] Vinko Martinović appealed against this holding and the Trial Chamber's conclusion that the alternative charging of certain crimes in his indictment did not violate his fair-trial rights,[18] arguing, *inter alia*, that 'he could not know against which criminal act he must defend himself'.[19] The Appeals Chamber quoted *Čelebići* 's consideration that 'prior to the presentation of all of the evidence, it is not possible to determine to a certainty which of the charges brought against the accused will be proven',[20] and added summarily that '[t]he same reasoning allows for alternative charging'.[21] Yet curiously, although it upheld the Trial Chamber's finding in respect of the alternative charges in Martinović's indictment, the Appeals Chamber was not unequivocal in its support of the practice: '[W]hile alternative charging on the basis of the same conduct is generally permissible, it depends on the circumstances of the case.' [22] The Chamber did not elaborate on the circumstances in which alternative charging would not be permissible, nor has any subsequent chamber.

[15] *Ibid.*, para. 40 (footnote removed). Accord *Čelebići* Appeal Judgement, *supra* note 7, Separate and Dissenting Opinion of Judge David Hunt and Judge Mohamed Bennouna, para. 12.

[16] *Naletilić and Martinović* Trial Judgement, *supra* note 10, para. 510 ('The Chamber finds that the permission of cumulative charges includes alternative charges *a maiore ad minus* ').

[17] See *Mpambara* May 2005 Pre-Trial Decision, *supra* note 11, para. 4; *Naletilić and Martinović* February 2000 Pre-Trial Decision, *supra* note 2, para. 24 (considering an indictment charging two crimes – cruel treatment as a violation of the laws or customs of war and wilfully causing great suffering or serious injury as a grave breach – as alternatives to three others – murder as a crime against humanity and as a violation of the laws or customs of war, and wilful killing as a grave breach – and concluding that '[t]he indictment is sufficient to put Mr. Martinović on notice of the nature of the Prosecution's case'); *Kvočka et al.* April 1999 Pre-Trial Decision, *supra* note 3, para. 25. Similarly, the *Musema* Trial Chamber allowed genocide and complicity in genocide to be charged in the alternative based on the holding in the *Akayesu* Trial Judgement that 'an individual cannot be both the principal perpetrator of a particular act and the accomplice thereto'. *Prosecutor* v. *Musema*, Case No. ICTR-96-13-T, Decision on the Prosecutor's Request for Leave to Amend the Indictment, 18 November 1998, paras. 7–9 (paragraph 7 invoking and quoting *Prosecutor* v. *Akayesu*, Case No. ICTR-96-4-T, Judgement, 2 September 1998 ('*Akayesu* Trial Judgement'), para. 532). Accord *Prosecutor* v. *Niyitegeka*, Decision on Prosecutor's Request for Leave to File an Amended Indictment, 21 June 2000, para. 46 (holding that genocide and complicity in genocide in such circumstances 'should' be alternatively charged). As noted in Volume I of this series, although this premise of the *Akayesu* Trial Chamber has been repeated on a number of occasions by chambers of the *ad hoc* Tribunals and of the SCSL, it would appear to be fundamentally inconsistent with the ICTR Appeals Chamber's stance that convictions for more than one form of responsibility Article 6(1) of the ICTR Statute in respect of the same crime are permissible. See Boas, Bischoff, and Reid, *supra* note 7, p. 393; see also *infra* note 23 (distinguishing 'cumulative convictions' from 'concurrent convictions'). See also *Ndindabahizi* v. *Prosecutor*, Case No. ICTR-01-71-A, Judgement, 16 January 2007, para. 122 (Appeals Chamber affirming unequivocally that 'an accused can be convicted for a single crime on the basis of several modes of liability').

[18] See *Naletilić and Martinović* Trial Judgement, *supra* note 10, para. 510.

[19] *Naletilić and Martinović* Appeal Judgement, *supra* note 10, para. 101 (internal quotation marks removed).

[20] *Ibid.*, para. 103 (quoting *Čelebići* Appeal Judgement, *supra* note 7, para. 400).

[21] *Ibid.* [22] *Ibid.*, para. 102.

5.2 Cumulative convictions

5.2.1 Pre-Čelebići jurisprudence

Few judgments prior to the February 2001 *Čelebići* Appeal Judgement contain explicit discussions of whether and in what circumstances an accused may be convicted for crimes charged cumulatively in respect of the same conduct. Indeed, the pre-*Čelebići* Appeals Chamber jurisprudence suggested that cumulative convictions[23] were permissible as long as the respective sentences imposed for the convictions in question were ordered to run concurrently.[24] The September 1998 *Akayesu* Trial Judgement was the first in which the rationale behind a possible prohibition on some cumulative convictions was expounded:

> The reason for posing this question is that it might be argued that the accumulation of criminal charges offends against the principle of double jeopardy or a substantive *non bis in idem* principle in criminal law. Thus an accused who is found guilty of both genocide and crimes against humanity in relation to the same set of facts may argue that he has been twice judged for the same offence, which is generally considered impermissible in criminal law.[25]

After quoting certain language of the Rwandan Penal Code on the doctrine of *concours d'infractions*, the Trial Chamber came to a rather detailed conclusion:

> On the basis of national and international law and jurisprudence … it is acceptable to convict the accused of two offences in relation to the same set of facts in the following circumstances: (1) where the offences have different elements; or (2) where the provisions creating

[23] We follow the uniform practice in the *ad hoc* Tribunals in using the term 'cumulative convictions' to describe simultaneous convictions for more than one crime in respect of the same conduct. As discussed in Volume I of this series, the term 'concurrent convictions' describes a related, but distinct concept: convictions pursuant to different forms of responsibility in respect of the same crime. See Boas, Bischoff, and Reid, *supra* note 7, pp. 387–388. Concurrent convictions are discussed at length in Volume I.

[24] See, e.g., *Prosecutor* v. *Aleksovski*, Case No. IT-95-14/1-A, Judgement, 24 March 2000 ('*Aleksovski* Appeal Judgement'), para. 153 (finding that, even if the Appeals Chamber were to enter convictions for two grave breaches in respect of which the Trial Chamber had acquitted Aleksovski after applying an erroneous test to determine whether an international armed conflict existed, these convictions would have to run concurrently with the Trial Chamber's conviction of Aleksovski for outrages upon personal dignity as a violation of the laws or customs of war because '[t]he material acts … underlying the charges are the same"); *Prosecutor* v. *Tadić*, Case Nos. IT-94-1-A & IT-94-1-A *bis*, Judgement in Sentencing Appeals, 26 January 2000, para. 76 (ordering that respective twenty-year sentences for three convictions – for wilful killing as a grave breach, murder as a violation of the laws or customs of war, and murder as a crime against humanity – in respect of the same killings in the village of Jaskići be served concurrently); *Prosecutor* v. *Tadić*, Case No. IT-94-1-A, Judgement, 15 July 1999, paras. 235–237 (entering these convictions pursuant to the doctrine of joint criminal enterprise). See also *infra* note 30 (discussing the similar views of Judge Khan in his dissent from the *Kayishema and Ruzindana* Trial Judgement). The jurisprudence on cumulative convictions predating the *Čelebići* Appeal Judgement has been thoroughly considered elsewhere. See *Čelebići* Appeal Judgement, *supra* note 7, Separate and Dissenting Opinion of Judge David Hunt and Judge Mohamed Bennouna, paras. 7–10; Hong S. Wills, 'Cumulative Convictions and the Double Jeopardy Rule: Pursuing Justice at the ICTY and the ICTR', (2003) 17 *Emory International Law Review* 341, 356–361; Nisha Valabhji, 'Cumulative Convictions Based on the Same Acts under the Statute of the ICTY', (2002) 10 *Tulane Journal of International and Comparative Law* 185, 186–193.

[25] *Akayesu* Trial Judgement, *supra* note 17, para. 462.

the offences protect different interests; or (3) where it is necessary to record a conviction for both offences in order fully to describe what the accused did.[26]

In January 2000, the *Kupreškić* Trial Chamber adopted a test incorporating something akin to the first two *Akayesu* factors, but only after a complicated and lengthy survey of various international and national sources, including the Nuremberg Judgement, various cases before the Inter-American and European Courts of Human Rights, the 1932 US Supreme Court opinion in *Blockburger* v. *United States*, and other national jurisprudence and statutory provisions.[27] The Trial Chamber arrived at the view that the test set forth in *Blockburger* – which it referred to as the 'reciprocal speciality' doctrine – reflects a 'principle [] of criminal law common to the major legal systems of the world'.[28] Under this test as adapted by the *Kupreškić* Chamber, if a trial chamber finds that the facts establish the elements of two of the charged crimes on the basis of the same conduct, the chamber may enter convictions for both crimes as long as each crime requires proof of an element that the other does not.[29] In such a scenario, the chamber must order that the sentences run concurrently, although it may aggravate the sentence of the 'more serious' crime if the 'less serious' crime 'significantly adds to [its] heinous nature'.[30] On the other hand, where one crime does not require proof of an element required by the other, the former crime 'falls entirely within the ambit of the other', and the chamber may only convict the accused of this latter crime.[31] The Trial Chamber also identified a

[26] *Ibid.*, para. 468. The Trial Chamber concluded that the three statutory crimes in the ICTR Statute – genocide, crimes against humanity, and violations of Common Article 3 to the 1949 Geneva Conventions and of Additional Protocol II of 1977 – all contain different elements, are intended to protect different interests, and that it may in a given case be necessary to record a conviction for more than one of these crimes in respect of the same conduct in order to reflect the full criminality of the accused. Cumulative convictions for two or all three statutory crimes are therefore permissible. See *ibid.*, para. 469–470. The Chamber gave no express consideration to whether cumulative convictions could be entered for more than one underlying offence of the same statutory crime. The Trial Chamber in the May 1999 *Kayishema and Ruzindana* Judgement repeated the first and second factors without acknowledging the *Akayesu* precedent. See *Kayishema and Ruzindana* Trial Judgement, *supra* note 3, para. 627.

[27] See *Kupreškić et al.* Trial Judgement, *supra* note 3, para. 673–692. The Trial Chamber noted that it undertook such an extensive analysis because 'this issue has a broad import and great relevance, all the more so because it has not been dealt with in depth by an international criminal court'. *Ibid.*, para. 668.

[28] See *ibid.*, paras. 680–687 (quotation at para. 680). See also *Blockburger* v. *United States*, 284 U.S. 299, 304 (1932).

[29] *Kupreškić et al.* Trial Judgement, *supra* note 3, para. 682. Accord *ibid.*, para. 718.

[30] *Ibid.* In his dissenting opinion in *Kayishema and Ruzindana*, Judge Khan opined that a chamber should be able to enter cumulative convictions in all circumstances provided the elements of the crimes in question are fulfilled. In such a scenario, however, only one, unitary sentence should be imposed: '[C]oncurrent sentencing based upon the proven criminal conduct is a satisfactory way of ensuring that the accused do[es] not suffer prejudice.' *Kayishema and Ruzindana* Trial Judgement, *supra* note 3, paras. 6, 23, 37 (quotation at para. 37). See also *ibid.*, para. 34 ('[I]t us unfair that an accused is punished more than once for culpable conduct where the facts and victims are the same. However, any real prejudice in the instant case would arise from the *sentence* imposed rather than the *pronouncement of conviction*.') (emphasis in original). Judge Khan characterised the majority's approach as a 'legal quagmire of overlapping acts, elements and social interests'. *Ibid.*, para. 52.

[31] *Kupreškić et al.* Trial Judgement, *supra* note 3, para. 683 ('In these cases the choice between the two provisions is dictated by the maxim *in toto iure generi per speciem derogatur* (or *lex specialis derogat generali*), whereby the more specific or less sweeping provisions should be chosen.'). Accord *ibid.*, para. 719.

'further test' recognised in both common-law and civil-law systems, consisting in 'ascertaining whether the various provisions at stake protect different values':[32] 'Under this test, if an act or transaction is simultaneously in breach of two criminal provisions protecting different values, it may be held that that act or transaction infringes *both* criminal provisions.'[33] 'However', the Trial Chamber added, 'the test is hardly ever used other than in conjunction with, and in support of, the [*Blockburger* and reciprocal-speciality] tests', and it 'is therefore unlikely to alter the conclusions reached' by applying those tests.[34] In reiterating its conclusions on this subject, the Chamber mentioned only the first test.[35]

5.2.2 The February 2001 Čelebići *Appeal Judgement*

The ICTY Appeals Chamber was faced squarely with the issue of cumulative convictions for the first time in *Čelebići* in February 2001. Zdravko Mucić and Hazim Delić complained that the Trial Chamber should not have convicted them cumulatively for several pairs of grave breaches in Article 2 of the ICTY Statute and violations of the laws or customs of war in Article 3 for the same underlying conduct.[36] The Appeals Chamber undertook a perfunctory comparative analysis of national approaches,[37] and arrived rather summarily at a simple two-pronged test apparently inspired by *Blockburger*.[38] The first prong requires the trial chamber to assess whether 'each statutory provision involved has a materially distinct element not contained in the other'.[39] According to the Appeals Chamber, '[a]n element is materially distinct if it requires proof of a fact not required by the other'.[40] Where, in

[32] *Ibid.*, para. 693. [33] *Ibid.*, para. 694.

[34] *Ibid.*, para. 695. The Chamber determined that cumulative convictions would be permissible for murder as a crime against humanity and persecution as a crime against humanity – regardless of whether the specific form of persecution in question was also murder – because both crimes '*may* have unique elements'. *Ibid.*, para. 706 (emphasis added). Although the *actus reus* of persecution may be effected through killing, it may also be effected through conduct falling short of killing, such as the destruction of homes, and murder as a crime against humanity does not require discriminatory intent. See *ibid.*, paras. 706, 708. Moreover, murder as a crime against humanity and persecution as a crime against humanity protect different interests: the former aims at protecting civilians 'from being obliterated on a large scale', while the latter 'is designed to reaffirm and impose respect for the principle of equality between groups and human beings'. *Ibid.*, para. 709. The *Kupreškić* Trial Chamber's conceptualisation of the relationship between forms of persecution and the other underlying offences of crimes against humanity foreshadowed a series of majority and dissenting opinions of the Appeals Chamber. See *infra* at text accompanying notes 95–165.

[35] See *ibid.*, paras. 718–719.

[36] See *Čelebići* Appeal Judgement, *supra* note 7, paras. 389–394. These were, respectively, wilful killing and murder; wilfully causing great suffering or serious injury to body or health and cruel treatment; and inhuman treatment and cruel treatment.

[37] The Appeals Chamber looked at a German treatise, the Zambian Penal Code, and the US Supreme Court cases of *Blockburger* and *Rutledge* v. *United States*, 517 U.S. 292, 297 (1996).*Čelebići* Appeal Judgement, *supra* note 7, paras. 407–409.

[38] The subsequent *Kunarac* Appeals Chamber stated that the *Čelebići* test was 'heavily indebted to the *Blockburger* decision of the Supreme Court of the United States'. *Prosecutor* v. *Kunarac, Kovač, and Vuković*, Case Nos. IT-96-23 & IT-96-23/1-A, Judgement, 12 June 2002 ('*Kunarac et al.* Appeal Judgement'), para. 168.

[39] *Čelebići* Appeal Judgement, *supra* note 7, para. 412. [40] *Ibid.*

relation to two crimes, the first prong of the test is not met, the second prong obliges the trial chamber to convict only for the crime with the 'additional materially distinct element'.[41] The result in practical terms is that the accused may only be convicted of the crime that is harder to prove, and he must be acquitted of all lesser included offences.[42] The Appeals Chamber invoked two curt rationales for the use of this particular test: 'reasons of fairness to the accused and the consideration that only distinct crimes may justify multiple convictions';[43] later Appeals Chambers have added the rationale that '[t]he more specific offence subsumes the less specific one, because the commission of the former necessarily entails the commission of the latter'.[44] Oddly, the *Čelebići* Appeals Chamber did not cite the *Kupreškić* Trial Judgement as precedent for the invocation and application of *Blockburger*, and it did not mention or endorse *Kupreškić* 's 'further test' of ascertaining whether each statutory provision protects different values.

Applying this test, the Appeals Chamber determined that a grave breach charged in Article 2 of the Statute necessarily contains at least one element that a violation of the laws or customs of war in Article 3 does not: the victim of a grave breach must be a protected person within the meaning of the particular Geneva Convention or Protocol in which the grave breach finds its origins, and not merely a person taking no active part in the hostilities,[45] as required by those violations of the laws or customs of war that derive from Common Article 3 of the Geneva Conventions.[46] Since none of the three violations of the laws or customs of war at issue contained an element not contained by the three grave breaches at issue, the convictions of Mucić and Delić under Article 3 of the ICTY Statute – along with those of their co-accused Esad Landžo, which the Appeals Chamber examined *proprio motu* – had to be vacated.[47]

Judges Hunt and Bennouna issued a lengthy opinion dissenting from certain parts of the majority's holding on cumulative convictions, and providing additional reasoning for others.[48] To this day, this opinion remains the most thoughtful and

[41] *Ibid.*, para. 413.

[42] See *Kunarac et al.* Appeal Judgement, *supra* note 38, para. 170 ('[I]t is not possible to commit the more serious offence without also committing the lesser included offence.'). However, as acknowledged by the *Kunarac* Appeals Chamber in the course of the same discussion, *Kunarac et al.* Appeal Judgement, *supra* note 38, para. 171, the ICTY and ICTR Appeals Chambers have refused to endorse a hierarchy of gravity among the crimes in their respective Statutes. For more on the notion of a hierarchy of crimes, see Chapter 3, text accompanying notes 11–18 and accompanying text; see also *infra* section 5.3.2.

[43] *Čelebići* Appeal Judgement, *supra* note 7, para. 412.

[44] *Galić* Appeal Judgement, *supra* note 10, para. 163 (quoting *Prosecutor* v. *Krstić*, Case No. IT-98-33-A, Judgement, 19 April 2004 ('*Krstić* Appeal Judgement'), para. 218). See also *Prosecutor* v. *Kordić and Čerkez*, Case No. IT-95-14/2-A, Judgement, 17 December 2004 ('*Kordić and Čerkez* Appeal Judgement'), para. 1033 ('The cumulative convictions test serves twin aims: ensuring that the accused is convicted only for distinct offences, and at the same time, ensuring that the convictions entered fully reflect his criminality.').

[45] See Chapter 4, section 4.2.1.3.2.

[46] See *Čelebići* Appeal Judgement, *supra* note 7, paras. 420, 423–426; Chapter 4, section 4.2.1.4.

[47] *Ibid.*, para. 427.

[48] *Ibid.*, Separate and Dissenting Opinion of Judge David Hunt and Judge Mohamed Bennouna, para. 1.

well-reasoned discussion on cumulative convictions in the *ad hoc* jurisprudence. Although Judges Hunt and Bennouna agreed with the majority that 'reasons of fairness to the accused' dictate that cumulative convictions for indistinct crimes not be permitted, they saw the need to elaborate this proposition. First, even if an accused's sentences for cumulative convictions are to run concurrently, there is still a degree of social stigmatisation inherent in being convicted of a crime.[49] Second, the number of crimes for which an accused has been convicted may have an impact on when that accused is eligible for early release.[50] Third, by operation of recidivist or 'habitual offender' statutes, cumulative convictions before the Tribunal may expose the accused to increased sentences if convicted in a national court for a future offence.[51]

Furthermore, although Judges Hunt and Bennouna agreed with the majority's general conclusion that an accused should only be convicted of more than one crime in respect of the same conduct where each crime has a unique element the other lacks,[52] they considered that contextual elements should be disregarded as irrelevant to this determination: 'Although matters such as the protected person status or the internationality of the armed conflict provide the context in which the offence takes place, it is … artificial to suggest that the precise nature of the conflict or the technical status of the victim … has any bearing on the accused's conduct.'[53] The focus should instead be on the accused's conduct and mental state:

> The fundamental function of the criminal law is to punish the accused for his criminal conduct, and only for his criminal conduct. We believe that taking into account such abstract elements creates the danger that the accused will also be convicted – with, as discussed, the penalty inherent in that conviction alone – in respect of additional crimes which have a distinct existence only as a purely legal and abstract matter, effectively through the historical accidents of the way in which international humanitarian law has developed in streams having distinct contextual requirements.[54]

While taking into account contextual elements did not result in cumulative convictions in the circumstances of the case before them because, in the majority's view,

49 *Ibid.*, para. 23. 50 *Ibid.* 51 *Ibid.* 52 *Ibid.*, para. 24.

53 *Ibid.*, para. 26 (emphasis removed). Judges Hunt and Bennouna also disapproved of the majority's resort to national jurisdictions as 'highly problematic in light of the lack of a uniform approach to this issue, which is complex even in well developed national jurisdictions, requiring solutions peculiar to a specific national system.' *Ibid.*, para. 20. Indeed, the great deal of US Supreme Court opinions on so-called 'same offence' double jeopardy issued in the seventy-five years since *Blockburger* has rendered the test much more nuanced and complicated than the *ad hoc* Appeals Chambers make it appear to be. See Wayne R. LaFave, Jerold H. Israel, and Nancy J. King, *Criminal Procedure* (4th edn 2004), 849–856 (discussing some of these opinions and the circumstances in which certain deviations from *Blockburger* may apply). In the view of Judges Hunt and Bennouna, 'no useful, *common* principle' could be gleaned from national jurisdictions, especially since none had ever had to face a problem of similar scope to the one at issue in *Čelebići.Čelebići* Appeal Judgement, *supra* note 7, Separate and Dissenting Opinion of Judge David Hunt and Judge Mohamed Bennouna, para. 20 (emphasis in original).

54 *Ibid.*, para. 27.

Article 3 contains no materially distinct contextual element that Article 2 does not, Judges Hunt and Bennouna foresaw the undesirable result of the majority's approach for future cases: when the crimes at issue fall under a pair of separate articles of the ICTY Statute other than Articles 2 and 3 – that is, Articles 2 and 4, 3 and 4, 2 and 5, 3 and 4, or 4 and 5 – taking into account contextual elements 'will have the result that crimes such as torture, rape, and murder/wilful killing will necessarily and in every case be considered to be distinct crimes … , and therefore two convictions will have to be entered for what is in reality the same offence'.[55] In the view of the dissenters, the majority's approach held 'the potential to produce outcomes which are, in the circumstances of any given case, arbitrary and artificial'.[56]

Judges Hunt and Bennouna also disagreed with the majority on how a trial chamber should go about choosing between two crimes after it has determined that cumulative convictions for both are impermissible. While they agreed that the choice should be made with reference to specificity, they argued that a chamber should not merely look at the legal elements in the abstract. Instead, 'the crime that more specifically describes *what the accused actually did* in the circumstances of the particular case should be selected', and this process 'involve[s] a consideration of the totality of the circumstances … and of the evidence given in relation to the crimes charged'.[57] The dissenters then proceeded to apply their version of the test to the facts before them, concluding as had the majority that none of the pairs of crimes in question had mutually distinct elements, but arriving at this conclusion by looking only at the elements of the underlying offences, and not the contextual elements of Articles 2 and 3.[58] They reached several conclusions distinct from those of the majority, however, upon applying their 'totality of the circumstances' approach to choosing between the two crimes, for reasons grounded in specific factual findings that had been made by the Trial Chamber in its judgement.[59]

[55] *Čelebići* Appeal Judgement, *supra* note 7, Separate and Dissenting Opinion of Judge David Hunt and Judge Mohamed Bennouna, para. 29. Judges Hunt and Bennouna provided an example of the desirable outcome that would be reached if jurisdictional and contextual elements were disregarded in a cumulative convictions inquiry: where rape is charged simultaneously under Articles 2, 3, and 5, and all the requirements for each statutory provision is fulfilled, the accused could be convicted only for the crime against humanity in Article 5 because it contains an additional, specific element: knowledge of the widespread or systematic attack on a civilian population. *Ibid.*, para. 33.

[56] *Ibid.*, para. 45. In a separate opinion appended to the July 2001 *Jelisić* Appeal Judgement, Judge Shahabuddeen defended the *Čelebići* Appeals Chamber's consideration of contextual elements. Using as an example the general requirement that the victim of a grave breach must be a protected person under the Geneva Conventions, he stated as follows:

> What is important is that the requirement does not lie outside of the crime; it is an integral part of the crime itself. It is consistent with customary international law to say that, unless facts are proved to show that the victim was in the position of a 'protected' person, there simply was no crime under that provision. Such a requirement is therefore an element of the crime.

Prosecutor v. *Jelisić*, Case No. IT-95-10-A, Judgement, 5 July 2001 ('*Jelisić* Appeal Judgement'), Partial Dissenting Opinion of Judge Shahabuddeen, para. 38.

[57] *Ibid.*, para. 37 (emphasis in original). [58] *Ibid.*, paras. 48–50. [59] *Ibid.*, paras. 46–58.

We have provided this detailed summary of the *Čelebići* dissent not only because these views are insightful, but also because they have been accurately predictive of what has happened in the seven years since *Čelebići*. The ICTY Appeals Chamber has routinely reaffirmed the *Čelebići* majority's test, usually without any elaboration of its reasoning,[60] and with one significant expansion.[61] The *Čelebići* test has also been the applicable standard in the ICTR since its endorsement in the November 2001 *Musema* Appeal Judgement,[62] and it has been summarily endorsed and applied in the two SCSL judgements as of 1 December 2007.[63] The result has been the compelled[64] entry by trial chambers of a great number of cumulative convictions where the conduct of the accused, physical perpetrator, or other relevant actor in fulfilment of the elements is the same.[65]

[60] See *Galić* Appeal Judgement, *supra* note 10, para. 163; *Naletilić and Martinović* Appeal Judgement, *supra* note 10, para. 562; *Prosecutor* v. *Stakić*, Case No. IT-97-24-A, Judgement, 22 March 2006 ('*Stakić* Appeal Judgement'), para. 355; *Prosecutor* v. *Vasiljević*, Case No. IT-98-32-A, Judgement, 25 February 2004 ('*Vasiljević* Appeal Judgement'), para. 145; *Prosecutor* v. *Krnojelac*, Case No. IT-97-25-A, Judgement, 17 September 2003 ('*Krnojelac* Appeal Judgement'), para. 188; *Kupreškić et al.* Appeal Judgement, *supra* note 10, paras. 387–388; *Jelisić* Appeal Judgement, *supra* note 56, paras. 78–79. The noteworthy exceptions are the June 2002 *Kunarac* Appeal Judgement and the April 2004 *Krstić* Appeal Judgement. In *Kunarac*, the Appeals Chamber acknowledged the risk of prejudice to the accused from the social stigma that attaches to multiple convictions, that such an accused may lose eligibility for early release under the law of the state of incarceration, and that this prejudice is not cured even where the sentences are served concurrently. *Kunarac et al.* Appeal Judgement, *supra* note 38, para. 169. It also provided some elaboration on why it is impermissible to convict an accused for both a greater offence and a lesser included offence. *Ibid.*, para. 170. The Appeals Chamber went on to state that while the *Čelebići* test appears to be 'deceptively simple', '[i]n practice it is difficult to apply in a way that is conceptually coherent and promotes the interests of justice.' *Ibid.*, para. 172. The Chamber declared its intention to 'scrutinise with the greatest caution multiple or cumulative convictions[,] ... guided by the considerations of justice for the accused[.]' *Ibid.*, para. 173. It concluded that 'the chamber must take into account the entire situation so as to avoid a mechanical or blind application of its guiding principles'. *Ibid.*, para. 174. Despite this statement, the Appeals Chamber proceeded to apply the *Čelebići* test in what might be described as a mechanical way. See *ibid.*, para. 176. The Chamber also proffered views on why it is appropriate to consider jurisdictional and contextual elements. See *infra* text accompanying notes 67–71. The *Krstić* Appeal Judgement's elaboration on *Čelebići* is discussed at notes 104–110.

[61] See *Kordić and Čerkez* Appeal Judgement, *supra* note 44, paras. 1039–1043. See also *infra* text accompanying notes 121–126 (discussing *Kordić and Čerkez*).

[62] *Musema* Appeal Judgement, *supra* note 8, para. 363 ('The Appeals Chamber confirms that this is the test to be applied with respect to multiple convictions arising under the ICTR Statute.'). See also *Prosecutor* v. *Nahimana, Barayagwiza, and Ngeze*, Case No. ICTR-99-52-A, Arrêt, 28 November 2007 ('*Media* Appeal Judgement'), para. 1019; *Prosecutor* v. *Ntagerura, Bagambiki, and Imanishimwe*, Case No. ICTR-99-46-A, Judgement, 7 July 2006 ('*Cyangugu* Appeal Judgement'), para. 425; *Semanza* Appeal Judgement, *supra* note 9, para. 315; *Prosecutor* v. *Ntakirutimana and Ntakirutimana*, Case Nos. ICTR-96-10-A and ICTR-96-17-A, Judgement, 13 December 2004 ('*Ntakirutimana and Ntakirutimana* Appeal Judgement'), para. 542; *Prosecutor* v. *Rutaganda*, Case No. ICTR-96-3-A, Judgement, 26 May 2003 ('*Rutaganda* Appeal Judgement'), para. 582.

[63] See *CDF* Trial Judgement, *supra* note 1, para. 974 (citing the *Čelebići*, *Musema*, and *Naletilić and Martinović* Appeal Judgements); *AFRC* Trial Judgement, *supra* note 1, para. 2099 (citing only *Čelebići*).

[64] See *Stakić* Appeal Judgement, *supra* note 60, para. 358 (clarifying that, where the crimes at issue contain materially distinct elements, trial chambers have no choice but to enter a conviction for each, and trial chambers commit reversible legal error when they choose to enter only one conviction). This holding of *Stakić* is discussed in more detail at text accompanying notes 199–209, *infra*.

[65] See, e.g., *Prosecutor* v. *Brđanin*, Case No. IT-99-36-T, Judgement, 1 September 2004 ('*Brđanin* Trial Judgement'), para. 1088; *Prosecutor* v. *Vasiljević*, Case No. IT-98-32-T, Judgement, 29 November 2002 ('*Vasiljević* Trial Judgement'), para. 268; *infra* notes 127, 160 and judgements cited therein; *infra* note 202 and judgements cited therein. It should be borne in mind that, where the conduct in fulfilment of the elements of the crimes at issue is not the same, or where the victims are not the same, no question of cumulative convictions arises. Hence, the *Galić* Trial Chamber held that it need not engage in a cumulative-convictions analysis with

5.2.3 *Application of the* Čelebići *test to different statutory crimes ('inter-article' convictions)*

Notwithstanding the contention of Judges Hunt and Bennouna that jurisdictional and contextual elements should be disregarded in a cumulative-convictions analysis, post-*Čelebići ad hoc* chambers have invariably compared the two crimes at issue by examining all their elements, including the general requirements and the elements of the underlying offences.[66] In what was an apparent rebuttal to Judges Hunt and Bennouna, the June 2002 *Kunarac* Appeals Chamber expressly sanctioned such an approach,[67] and attempted an explanation of why it is proper. The Chamber emphasised that the '*chapeau* elements' are an integral part of the substantive definition of the crimes in the Statute;[68] genocidal intent, for example, converts conduct that might otherwise qualify only as a war crime into the crime of genocide.[69] The Appeals Chamber also asserted, without citing any support, that the Security Council intended the *chapeau* elements to be taken into account: 'Surely the Security Council, in promulgating the Statute and listing in it the principal offences against International Humanitarian Law, did not intend these offences to be mutually exclusive. Rather, the *chapeau []* elements disclose the animating desire that all species of such crimes be adequately described and punished.'[70] Yet the

respect to the murder of civilians as a crime against humanity resulting from the shelling and sniping of Sarajevo, on the one hand, and serious injury to civilians as a result of the same attack, which was charged as an inhumane act as a crime against humanity, because the two groups of victims were mutually exclusive. See *Galić* Trial Judgement, *supra* note 10, para. 164, affirmed by *Galić* Appeal Judgement, *supra* note 10, para. 167. See also *Semanza* Appeal Judgement, *supra* note 9, para. 319; *Kupreškić et al.* Appeal Judgment, *supra* note 10, para. 393; *Vasiljević* Trial Judgement, *supra*, para. 266 (similarly holding that the accused may be convicted of murder for five men killed in the course of one criminal incident and of inhumane acts in relation to the two survivors, and that no issue of cumulation arises); *Prosecutor* v. *Mrkšić, Radić, and Šljivančanin*, Case No. IT-95-13/1-T, Judgement, 27 September 2007, para. 680 (similar); *AFRC* Trial Judgement, *supra* note 1, para. 2109 (similar).

66 See *Musema* Appeal Judgement, *supra* note 8, para. 363 ('In applying this test, *all* the legal elements of the offences, including those contained in the provisions' introductory paragraph, must be taken into account.') (emphasis in original). See also, e.g., *Stakić* Appeal Judgement, *supra* note 60, paras. 359–364 (comparing the elements of various underlying offences of crimes against humanity); *Semanza* Appeal Judgement, *supra* note 9, paras. 318–321; *ibid.*, para. 320 (comparing murder as a crime against humanity with torture as a crime against humanity and holding that, due to their mutually distinct elements, Semanza's conviction for both in respect of the same conduct could stand); *Kordić and Čerkez* Appeal Judgement, *supra* note 44, para. 1032 ('Whether the same conduct violates two distinct statutory provisions' – and thus whether a trial chamber may proceed to convict an accused under both – 'is a question of law.'); *ibid.*, paras. 1035–1038 (comparing general requirements of Articles 2, 3, and 5 of the ICTY Statute); *ibid.*, paras. 1041–1043 (comparing the elements of various underlying offences of crimes against humanity); *Ntakirutimana and Ntakirutimana* Appeal Judgement, *supra* note 62, para. 542 (comparing the elements of murder and extermination as crimes against humanity); *Kunarac et al.* Appeal Judgement, *supra* note 38, para. 176 (comparing general requirements of violations of the laws or customs of war and crimes against humanity); *Jelisić* Appeal Judgement, *supra* note 56, para. 82 (same). See also *CDF* Trial Judgement, *supra* note 1, paras. 977–978 (comparing elements of various underlying offences); *AFRC* Trial Judgement, *supra* note 1, paras. 2017–2109 (comparing general requirements and elements of underlying offences).

67 *Kunarac et al.*Appeal Judgement, *supra* note 38, para. 177 ('[T]he legal prerequisites describing the circumstances of the relevant offences as stated in the *chapeaux* of the relevant Articles of the Statute constitute elements which enter the calculus of permissibility of cumulative convictions.').

68 *Ibid.*, para. 177 n. 239 (noting that the ICC Elements of Crimes incorporate the *chapeau* elements of the crimes in that Court's Statute).

69 See *ibid.*, para. 177 n. 240.

70 *Ibid.*, para. 178.

Kunarac Chamber appears to have overlooked an important caveat in the analysis of Judges Hunt and Bennouna: these judges did not argue that *none* of the *chapeau* elements of a crime should be considered, but merely those that constitute jurisdictional and contextual elements. These judges would take account of *chapeau* elements that describe the conduct or mental state of the accused, such as knowledge of the widespread or systematic attack for crimes against humanity.[71]

As a result of the uniform consideration of the general requirements of the crimes in the *ad hoc* Statutes as well as the elements of the underlying offences, it is immaterial whether the underlying offences have mutually identical elements as long as the statutory crimes under analysis have at least one mutually distinct general requirement. The most obvious example is murder: the underlying offences of wilful killing as a grave breach (Article 2(a) of the ICTY Statute), murder as a violation of the laws or customs of war (Article 3), killing as genocide (Article 4(2)(a)), and murder as a crime against humanity (Article 5(a)) generally share the same elements.[72] Nevertheless, a Trial Chamber may still enter cumulative convictions for multiple instances of the same underlying offence as long as the statutory crime through which each instance of the offence is charged is different – with the important exception of Articles 2 and 3 – because each of these crimes contains at least one mutually distinct general requirement. For example:

- Grave breaches in Article 2 of the ICTY Statute: an international armed conflict existed during the period relevant to the indictment;[73] and there was a nexus between the conduct of the physical perpetrator and the armed conflict.[74]
- Violations of the laws or customs of war in Article 3 of the ICTY Statute: a state of internal or international armed conflict existed during the period relevant to the indictment;[75] and there was a nexus between the acts of the physical perpetrator and the armed conflict.[76]

[71] See *Čelebići* Appeal Judgement, *supra* note 7, Separate and Dissenting Opinion of Judge David Hunt and Judge Mohamed Bennouna, para. 33.

[72] See *Kordić and Čerkez* Appeal Judgement, *supra* note 44, para. 1035; *Prosecutor* v. *Strugar*, Case No. IT-01-42-T, Judgement, 31 January 2005 ('*Strugar* Trial Judgement'), para. 236; *Prosecutor* v. *Blagojević and Jokić*, Case No. IT-02-60-T, Judgement, 17 January 2005, ('*Blagojević and Jokić* Trial Judgement'), paras. 556, 642; *Brđanin* Trial Judgement, *supra* note 65, paras. 382, 388; *Prosecutor* v. *Kordić and Čerkez*, Case No. IT-95-14/2-T, Judgement, 26 February 2001 ('*Kordić and Čerkez* Trial Judgement'), paras. 229, 236; *Prosecutor* v. *Delalić, Mucić, Delić and Landžo*, Case No. IT-96-21, Judgement, 16 November 1998 ('*Čelebići* Trial Judgement'), para. 24. See also Chapter 3, text accompanying notes 218–223 (discussing jurisprudence holding that killing as genocide can only be committed where the physical perpetrator intends to cause the victim's death).

[73] *Prosecutor* v. *Blaškić*, Case No. IT-95-14-A, Judgement, 29 July 2004 ('*Blaškić* Appeal Judgement'), para. 170; *Brđanin* Trial Judgement, *supra* note 65, para. 121.

[74] *Brđanin* Trial Judgement, *supra* note 65, para. 121; *Kordić and Čerkez* Trial Judgement, *supra* note 72, para. 32. See also Chapter 4, section 4.2.1.2.

[75] *Prosecutor* v. *Tadić*, Case No. IT-94-1-AR72, Decision on the Defence Motion for Interlocutory Appeal on Jurisdiction, 2 October 1995, para. 67; *Prosecutor* v. *Limaj, Bala, and Musliu*, Case No. IT-03-66-T, Judgement, 30 November 2005 ('*Limaj et al.*Trial Judgement'), paras. 83, 92; *Strugar* Trial Judgement, *supra* note 72, para. 216.

[76] *Galić* Appeal Judgement, *supra* note 10, para. 165; *Kunarac et al.* Appeal Judgement, *supra* note 38, para. 58. See also Chapter 4, section 4.2.1.2 (discussing the nexus requirement); *ibid.*, section 4.2.1.4 (discussing the war crimes provisions in Article 4 of the ICTR's Statute).

- Genocide in Article 4 of the ICTY Statute: the physical perpetrator or other relevant actor had the intent to materially destroy all or part of a distinct group defined by nationality, ethnicity, race, or religion.[77]
- Crimes against humanity in Article 5 of the ICTY Statute: there was a widespread or systematic attack against a civilian population;[78] and the conduct of the physical perpetrator formed part of this attack.[79]

The result has been the creation of a regime that is conducive to cumulative convictions. Cumulative convictions for genocide and crimes against humanity are always permissible, even when based on the same conduct and regardless of the underlying offence through which each is charged, because each statutory crime requires proof of a materially distinct general requirement that the other does not.[80] Likewise, cumulative convictions for violations of the laws or customs of war and crimes against humanity are always permissible,[81] as are cumulative convictions for grave breaches and crimes against humanity.[82] Furthermore, although neither *ad hoc* Tribunal appears yet to have specifically addressed whether cumulative convictions can be entered where one crime is a violation of the laws or customs of war or a grave breach and the other is a form of genocide, application of the *Čelebići* test

[77] *Krstić* Appeal Judgement, *supra* note 44, paras. 222–223; *Ntakirutimana and Ntakirutimana* Appeal Judgement, *supra* note 62, para. 542. See also Chapter 3, section 3.2.1.2.

[78] *Blaškić* Appeal Judgement, *supra* note 73, para. 98; *Kunarac et al.* Appeal Judgement, *supra* note 38, para. 85.

[79] *Galić* Appeal Judgement, *supra* note 10, para. 165; *Vasiljević* Appeal Judgement, *supra* note 60, para 145. See also Chapter 2, sections 2.2.2.4–2.2.2.5.

[80] *Media* Appeal Judgement, *supra* note 62, para. 1029; *Semanza* Appeal Judgement, *supra* note 9, para. 318 (genocide requires genocidal intent while crimes against humanity require a widespread or systematic attack on a civilian population); *Cyangugu* Appeal Judgement, *supra* note 62, para. 426 (same); *Ntakirutimana and Ntakirutimana* Appeal Judgement, *supra* note 62, para. 542; *Krstić* Appeal Judgement, *supra* note 44, paras. 222–223, 226–227, 229; *Musema* Appeal Judgement, *supra* note 8, paras. 366–367; *Ntakirutimana and Ntakirutimana* Trial Judgement, *supra* note 10, para. 542; *Ndindabahizi* Trial Judgement, *supra* note 10, paras. 491–493. Applying this principle, chambers of the ICTR have repeatedly rejected arguments by accused that they cannot be convicted for genocide and extermination as a crime against humanity in respect of the same conduct. See, e.g., *Cyangugu* Appeal Judgement, *supra* note 62, para. 427; *Ntakirutimana and Ntakirutimana* Appeal Judgement, *supra* note 62, para. 542; *Musema* Appeal Judgement, *supra* note 8, paras. 366–367; see also *Krstić* Appeal Judgement, *supra* note 44, paras. 219–227 (same). The same is true for any of the three genocide-related inchoate crimes, on the one hand, and a crime against humanity, on the other. See *Media* Appeal Judgement, *supra* note 62, paras. 1034–1035 (cumulative convictions for direct and public incitement to commit genocide and persecution as a crime against humanity are permissible).

[81] *Jelisić* Appeal Judgement, *supra* note 56, para. 82 (violations of the laws or customs of war require a nexus to an armed conflict while crimes against humanity require that the conduct occurred as part of a widespread or systematic attack on a civilian population); *Galić* Appeal Judgement, *supra* note 10, para. 165; *Cyangugu* Appeal Judgement, *supra* note 62, para. 427; *Kordić and Čerkez* Appeal Judgement, *supra* note 44, para. 1036; *Vasiljević* Appeal Judgement, *supra* note 60, para. 145; *Kunarac et al.* Appeal Judgement, *supra* note 38, para. 176; *Kupreškić et al.* Appeal Judgment, *supra* note 10, para. 388; *Blagojević and Jokić* Trial Judgement, *supra* note 72, para. 800; *Brđanin* Trial Judgement, *supra* note 65, para. 1086. *Accord AFRC* Trial Judgement, *supra* note 1, para. 2107.

[82] *Naletilić and Martinović* Appeal Judgement, *supra* note 10, paras. 561–562; *Kordić and Čerkez* Appeal Judgement, *supra* note 44, para. 1037 (observing that Article 2 requires a nexus to an international armed conflict while Article 5 requires that the criminal conduct have occurred part of a widespread or systematic attack on a civilian population; '[t]hus, cumulative convictions for inhuman treatment (under Article 2(b) …) and other inhumane acts (under Article 5(i) …) are permissible, as are cumulative convictions for unlawful confinement of civilians (under Article 2(g) …) and imprisonment (under Article 5(e) …).').

leads to the same result: materially distinct general requirements of each – for example, a nexus to an armed conflict for violations of the laws or customs of war or grave breaches, and genocidal intent for genocide – render cumulative convictions undoubtedly permissible.

The exception, which does not apply to the ICTR or the SCSL because those Tribunals' Statutes lack a provision on grave breaches, was first recognised by the *Čelebići* Appeals Chamber itself: a grave breach in Article 2 will subsume a violation of the laws or customs of war, even though the two provisions occupy different articles in the Statute, unless the underlying offences in question have at least one materially distinct element. The ICTY Appeals Chamber has held repeatedly that any criminal conduct fulfilling the stringent general requirements of Article 2 necessarily also satisfies the general requirements of Article 3, but the opposite is not true.[83] For example, Article 3 requires that the victim has taken no active part in the hostilities, while Article 2 requires more: the victim must have enjoyed protected status under the Geneva Convention or Protocol from which the grave breach in question is derived.[84] By operation of the second prong of the *Čelebići* test, the Article 3 violation will be subsumed into the Article 2 violation.[85] Applying this rule, the *Kordić and Čerkez* Appeals Chamber held that, since the underlying offences of 'wilful killing' in Article 2 and 'murder' in Article 3 share the same elements, the accused may only be convicted for wilful killing as a grave breach.[86]

5.2.4 *Application of the* Čelebići *test to different underlying offences of the same statutory crime ('intra-article' convictions)*

Applying the *Čelebići* test across articles of the Statute is today an easy procedure. Trial chambers face a more difficult task, however, when they must determine the permissibility of so-called 'intra-article' cumulative convictions. This question typically arises when the pair of provisions under examination are two different manifestations of the same statutory crime because the underlying offence differs, such as murder as a crime against humanity versus extermination as a crime against humanity. As described below,[87] for genocide there is another possible class of

[83] *Kordić and Čerkez* Appeal Judgement, *supra* note 44, para. 1035; *Čelebići* Appeal Judgement, *supra* note 7, para. 420.
[84] *Kordić and Čerkez* Appeal Judgement, *supra* note 44, para. 1035; *Čelebići* Appeal Judgement, *supra* note 7, para. 420.
[85] *Kordić and Čerkez* Appeal Judgement, *supra* note 44, para. 1036. The Article 3 violation is subsumed into the Article 2 violation even when a third statutory crime, such as a crime against humanity, has also been proven in respect of the same conduct. See *ibid.* (where criminal conduct simultaneously fulfils requirements of Articles 2, 3, and 5, 'the Article 3 crime must fall away').
[86] *Ibid.*, para. 1038 (upholding the Trial Chamber's dismissal of the Article 3 charge).
[87] See *infra* text accompanying notes 175, 182–198.

'intra-article' cumulative convictions: when one crime is a manifestation of genocide (for instance, killing as genocide) or one of the genocide-related inchoate crimes (such as conspiracy to commit genocide), and the other is a different genocide-related inchoate crime. As the jurisprudence on intra-article cumulative convictions has been developed most extensively with respect to intra-article cumulative convictions for crimes against humanity, we begin there.

5.2.4.1 Intra-article convictions for crimes against humanity

Where the statutory provisions under examination are different crimes against humanity, the trial chamber must compare the elements of the respective underlying offences to determine whether each contains a materially distinct element; if each underlying offence does not contain such an element, the crime whose underlying offence contains the additional element subsumes the other crime.[88] For example, where the two crimes are torture as a crime against humanity and rape as a crime against humanity, the trial chamber may enter convictions for both even though they arise out of the same conduct perpetrated against the same victim: rape uniquely requires sexual penetration and torture must be inflicted for a prohibited purpose, such as coercing the victim or a third person.[89] Hence, the *Kunarac* Appeals Chamber upheld the Trial Chamber's conviction of two of the accused for torture and rape as crimes against humanity in respect of the same acts against the same victims.[90] The application of the same principle yields a different result when the two crimes are murder as a crime against humanity and extermination as a crime against humanity: extermination contains all the elements of murder and at least one additional element: a large number of persons must have died.[91] Likewise, cumulative

[88] *Kunarac et al.* Appeal Judgement, *supra* note 38, para. 179.

[89] *Ibid.*, paras. 142, 144. See also *Prosecutor* v. *Krnojelac*, Case No. IT-97-25-T, Judgement, 15 March 2002, para. 179; *Prosecutor* v. *Furundžija*, Case No. IT-95-17/1-T, Judgement, 10 December 1998, p. 112 (convicting the accused cumulatively of rape as a violation of the laws or customs of war and torture as a violation of the laws or customs of war on the basis of the same conduct involving the same victims). See also Chapter 2, sections 2.2.3.6.2 and 2.2.3.7 (especially text accompanying note 381).

[90] *Kunarac et al.* Appeal Judgement, *supra* note 38, para. 179 (upholding *Prosecutor* v. *Kunarac, Kovač, and Vuković*, Case No. IT-96-23-T & IT-96-23/1-T, Judgement, 22 February 2001 ('*Kunarac et al.* Trial Judgement'), paras. 557, 883, 888). The Appeals Chamber also held that rape and enslavement as crimes against humanity have materially distinct elements and that cumulative convictions for each are therefore permissible. *Ibid.*, para. 186. This is presumably because although forced sex – particularly on a repeated basis – may be a manifestation of a 'power [ ] attaching to the right of ownership of a person', see *ibid.*, para. 118, enslavement does not require sexual penetration as a matter of law, and rape does not require as a matter of law that the physical perpetrator exercise powers attaching to the right of ownership over the victim. See *ibid.*, paras. 127–129.

[91] *Ntakirutimana and Ntakirutimana* Appeal Judgement, *supra* note 62, para. 542; *Blagojević and Jokić* Trial Judgement, *supra* note 72, paras. 571, 573, 802; *Brđanin* Trial Judgement, *supra* note 65, paras. 388–389. See also Chapter 2, text accompanying notes 224–231. See also *Semanza* Trial Judgement, *supra* note 10, para. 505 (observing that, in theory, murder and extermination contain mutually distinct elements because the former uniquely requires premeditation while the latter uniquely requires mass killing, but that the *mens rea* distinction is not 'material' because 'it is difficult to imagine how a person could intend to perpetrate a mass killing … without a level of intent very closely approaching or identical to premeditation'); *ibid.*, para. 505 (holding that Semanza's conviction for the murder of certain victims must be subsumed in his conviction for extermination).

convictions may not be entered for torture as a crime against humanity and inhumane acts as a crime against humanity: while both crimes require that the physical perpetrator intentionally inflict severe physical or mental pain or suffering, torture uniquely requires a prohibited purpose behind such infliction, while inhuman acts contains no additional material element.[92] Accordingly, the *Martić* Trial Chamber declared that it would 'enter a conviction for the crime of torture only' in respect of criminal conduct perpetrated against certain civilian detainees,[93] although it appears to have proceeded to enter cumulative convictions for both crimes, presumably in error.[94]

While the application of the *Čelebići* test would appear to be straightforward with respect to intra-article convictions for crimes against humanity, there has been considerable disagreement among the judges of the ICTY Appeals Chamber over what to do when the evidence establishes an underlying offence other than persecution, on the one hand, and that same offence as a form of persecution, on the other.[95] As explained in Chapter 2, persecution is perhaps best understood as a category of offences that constitute crimes against humanity if the general requirements are met, and are classified as persecution if the specific requirements of discriminatory intent, discrimination in fact, and equal gravity are satisfied.[96] Although a given form of persecution does not have to appear in the Statute or even be a crime under international law,[97] the Offices of the Prosecutor at the *ad hoc* Tribunals have tended to charge the other underlying offences in Article 5 of the ICTY Statute and Article 3 of the ICTR Statute cumulatively as forms of persecution: murder, extermination, enslavement, deportation, imprisonment, torture, rape, and other inhumane acts.[98]

[92] *Prosecutor* v. *Martić*, Case No. IT-95-11-T, Judgement, 12 June 2007 ('*Martić* Trial Judgement'), paras. 74, 83. See also *Kunarac et al.* Appeal Judgement, *supra* note 38, paras. 142, 144 (defining torture); *Kordić and Čerkez* Appeal Judgement, *supra* note 44, para. 117 (defining inhumane acts). Chapter 2, section 2.2.3.6.2 and text accompanying notes 451–455.

[93] *Martić* Trial Judgement, *supra* note 92, para. 477.

[94] *Ibid.*, para. 480 (cross-referencing paragraphs finding Martić potentially responsible for torture and inhumane acts as crimes against humanity in respect of the same conduct against the same individuals, entering guilty findings for both crimes, and omitting a caveat that the torture conviction subsumes the inhumane acts conviction while making such a caveat in respect of different crimes relating to a different incident); *ibid.*, para. 518 (reiterating these guilty findings). As of 1 December 2007, no appeal judgement had been rendered in *Martić*.

[95] Surprisingly, the only ICTR Appeal Judgement thus far to address intra-article cumulative convictions for crimes against humanity is *Semanza*, and there persecution was not involved. See *Semanza* Appeal Judgement, *supra* note 9, para. 321 (upholding the Trial Chamber's cumulative convictions for murder and extermination as crimes against humanity because the factual scenarios and victims differed); *ibid.*, paras. 319–320 (upholding cumulative convictions for rape and torture as crimes against humanity on the one hand, and murder and torture as crimes against humanity on the other) (upholding *Semanza* Trial Judgement, *supra* note 10, paras. 500–507).

[96] See Chapter 2, text accompanying notes 388–392.

[97] See *Prosecutor* v. *Kvočka, Radić, Žigić, and Prcać*, Case No. IT-98-30/1-A, Judgement, 28 February 2005 ('*Kvočka et al.* Appeal Judgement'), para. 323; *Semanza* Trial Judgement, *supra* note 10, paras. 348–349. See also Chapter 2, text accompanying note 397.

[98] See, e.g., *Blaškić* Appeal Judgement, *supra* note 73, para. 153 (forcible transfer as an inhumane act and deportation); *Blagojević and Jokić* Trial Judgement, *supra* note 72, para. 585 (murder); *Brđanin* Trial Judgement, *supra* note 65, para. 1002 (torture); *ibid.*, para. 1008 (rape). See also *Kupreškić et al.* Trial

To determine the elements of a particular form of persecution where this form consists of one of the other underlying offences, the chambers add together three sets of elements: (1) the general requirements of crimes against humanity; (2) the specific requirements of persecution (physical perpetrator or other relevant actor must have had discriminatory intent,[99] and the perpetrator must have believed his victim belonged to a protected group);[100] and (3) the elements of the underlying offence constituting the form of persecution – for example, for murder, the physical perpetrator must have caused the death of the victim, and he must have intended to kill the victim or inflict serious injury or grievous bodily harm on him in reckless disregard of human life.[101] One question, thus, is where the prosecution has proven the accused's responsibility for murder as a crime against humanity and murder as a form of persecution as a crime against humanity on the basis of the same conduct (involving the same victims), does the latter subsume the former? In three separate judgements prior to the December 2004 *Kordić and Čerkez* Appeal Judgement – *Krnojelac* in September 2003, *Vasiljević* in February 2004, and *Krstić* in April 2004 – the Appeals Chamber held that it did.[102]

In *Krstić* the prosecution contended, *inter alia*, that the Trial Chamber had erred in holding that murder as a form of persecution as a crime against humanity perpetrated against Muslim civilians in Potočari subsumed murder as a crime against humanity perpetrated against these same victims.[103] The *Krstić* Appeals Chamber explained the precedent set by *Krnojelac* and *Vasiljević* :

In *Vasiljević*, the Appeals Chamber disallowed convictions for murder and inhumane acts under Article 5 as impermissibly cumulative with the conviction for persecution under Article 5 where the persecution was accomplished through murder and inhumane acts. The Appeals Chamber concluded that the offence of persecution is more specific than the offences of murder and inhumane acts as crimes against humanity because, in addition to the facts necessary to prove murder and inhumane acts, persecution requires the proof of a

Judgement, *supra* note 3, para. 621 (observing that '[i]n their interpretation of persecution courts have included acts such as murder, extermination, torture, and other serious acts on the person such as those presently enumerated in Article 5'); *Semanza* Trial Judgement, *supra* note 10, para. 349 ('[P]ersecution may include acts enumerated under other sub-headings of crimes against humanity, such as murder or deportation, when they are committed on discriminatory grounds.').

99 *Kvočka et al.* Appeal Judgement, *supra* note 97, para. 320. See also Chapter 2, text accompanying notes 423–427 (discussing who among the persons involved in the commission of persecution must possess the discriminatory intent).

100 *Blagojević and Jokić* Trial Judgement, *supra* note 72, para. 583; *Brđanin* Trial Judgement, *supra* note 65, para. 992. See also Chapter 2, text accompanying notes 416–418.

101 See Chapter 2, section 2.2.3.1 (discussing the elements of murder as a crime against humanity); Annex, section 2.2 (same).

102 See *Krnojelac* Appeal Judgement, *supra* note 60, para. 188; *Vasiljević* Appeal Judgement, *supra* note 60, para. 146; *Krstić* Appeal Judgement, *supra* note 44, paras. 228–229. The Appeals Chamber had at least one previous opportunity to address the question of intra-Article 5 cumulative convictions where persecution was involved – in *Kupreškić* in October 2001 – but declined to rule on the question because one affected accused 'abandoned' this ground of appeal and the other never raised it. *Kupreškić et al.* Appeal Judgement, *supra* note 10, para. 395.

103 See *Krstić* Appeal Judgement, *supra* note 44, para. 230.

materially distinct element of a discriminatory intent in the commission of the act. The same result was reached by the Appeals Chamber in *Krnojelac*, which concluded that 'the crime of persecution in the form of inhumane acts subsumes the crime against humanity of inhumane acts.'[104]

The Chamber continued:

The Prosecution argues at length that the crime of persecution can be committed in many ways other than through murders … This observation is accurate, but entirely inapposite. Where the charge of persecution is premised on murder … and such charge is proven, the Prosecution need not prove any additional fact in order to secure the conviction for murder … as well. The proof that the accused committed persecution through murder … *necessarily* includes proof of murder … under Article 5. Th[is] offence [] become[s] subsumed within the offence of persecution.[105]

… The Trial Chamber correctly recognised this principle, and the Prosecution's appeal on these issues is therefore dismissed.[106]

With only one apparent exception,[107] every trial chamber to face this question prior to the *Kordić and Čerkez* Appeal Judgement arrived independently at this construction of the *Čelebići* test,[108] followed a previous trial judgement so construing *Čelebići*,[109]

[104] *Ibid.*, para. 231 (footnotes omitted) (quoting *Krnojelac* Appeal Judgement, *supra* note 60, para. 188). Contrary to the assertion of the *Krstić* Appeals Chamber, however, the *Vasiljević* Appeals Chamber did not give an explicit reason for its holding, and it did not cite the *Krnojelac* Appeal Judgement as precedent. Instead, it summarily upheld the Trial Chamber's refusal to convict the accused of persecution as a crime against humanity taking the form of the murder of five men and the inhumane treatment of two survivors, on the one hand, and murder and inhumane treatment as crimes against humanity in their own right, on the other. *Vasiljević* Appeal Judgement, *supra* note 60, para. 146 (upholding *Vasiljević* Trial Judgement, *supra* note 65, para. 267). See also *Vasiljević* Trial Judgement, *supra* note 65, paras. 208–211 (holding that the acts committed against the five men who died fulfilled the elements of murder as a crime against humanity in Article 5(a) of the ICTY Statute); *ibid.*, paras. 239–240 (holding that the acts committed against the two survivors fulfilled the elements of inhumane acts as a crime against humanity in Article 5(i)); *ibid.*, paras. 254–255 (holding that these incidents of murder and inhumane acts were committed with discriminatory intent and were in fact discriminatory, and thus constituted persecution as a crime against humanity in Article 5(h)).

[105] *Krstić* Appeal Judgement, *supra* note 44, para. 232 (emphasis in original; footnotes omitted).

[106] *Ibid.*, para. 233 (upholding *Prosecutor* v. *Krstić*, Case No. IT-98-33-T, Judgement, 2 August 2001 ('*Krstić* Trial Judgement'), para. 676).

[107] See *Kordić and Čerkez* Trial Judgement, *supra* note 72, paras. 814–826 (not acknowledging the possible impermissibility of cumulative convictions for a form of persecution and that same form as an independent crime against humanity); *ibid.*, pp. 305–306 (cumulatively convicting Kordić of persecution and several other crimes against humanity).

[108] See *Prosecutor* v. *Stakić*, Case No. IT-97-24-T, Judgement, 29 October 2003 ('*Stakić* Trial Judgement'), paras. 879–882 (murder, torture, rape, deportation); *Prosecutor* v. *Simić, Tadić, and Zarić*, Case No. IT-95-9-T, Judgement, 17 October 2003, para. 1058 (deportation); *Vasiljević* Trial Judgement, *supra* note 65, para. 267 (murder and other inhumane acts); *Krstić* Trial Judgement, *supra* note 106, para. 676 (murder and other inhumane acts).

[109] See *Naletilić and Martinović* Trial Judgement, *supra* note 10, para. 724 (relying on the *Krstić* Trial Judgement); *Prosecutor* v. *Kvočka, Kos, Radić, Žigić, and Prcać*, Case No. IT-98-30/1-T, Judgement, 2 November 2001, paras. 220–221 (murder, relying on the *Krstić* Trial Judgement); *ibid.*, para. 227 (torture); *ibid.*, para. 228 (other inhumane acts); *ibid.*, para. 233–234 (rape and torture); *ibid.*, para. 238 (other inhumane acts). As noted below, the holdings in *Stakić* and *Naletilić and Martinović* were later ruled erroneous by the Appeals Chamber in judgements postdating the *Kordić and Čerkez* Appeal Judgement. See *infra* note 130 and accompanying text.

or followed one or more of these three appeal judgements.[110] Accordingly, these chambers entered a conviction only for the form of persecution and not for that same form as a crime against humanity in its own right.

Judge Shahabuddeen issued a partially dissenting opinion in *Krstić*, in which he 'accepts' the Appeals Chamber's holding on cumulative convictions where persecution is involved, but only because of the precedent in *Krnojelac* and *Vasiljević*: '[H]ad it not been for those decisions I should have had difficulty in joining in with the decision of the Appeals Chamber.'[111] In his view, it 'seems curious' that it is not possible to convict an accused separately for murder as a crime against humanity 'if, under [Article 5(h) of the Statute], there is also a conviction for persecution'.[112] Judge Shahabuddeen would place the focus of the analysis on the 'gist or gravamen' of persecution *vis-à-vis* that of murder:

> In the present matter, the gist or gravamen of one case is that the appellant murdered civilians; in the other case, the different gist or gravamen is that the appellant persecuted those victims as evidenced by the murders. The focus is different; the first crime, together with the circumstances in which it occurred, is evidence of the second crime but it is not the same as the second.[113]

Judge Shahabuddeen also opined that murder and persecution have legal elements that do not overlap: murder uniquely requires the intent to cause death, and persecution uniquely requires the denial of a fundamental right on discriminatory grounds.[114] The elements of the underlying offence of crimes against humanity that happens to coincide with the form of persecution under analysis should not also be considered legal elements of persecution:

[110] See *Brđanin* Trial Judgement, *supra* note 65, para. 1085 (footnotes omitted) (relying on the *Krstić* and *Vasiljević* Appeal Judgements, and the *Kvočka*, *Simić*, and *Krstić* Trial Judgements):

> Convictions for charges of torture, deportation and inhumane acts (forcible transfer) brought under Article 5 of the Statute are impermissibly cumulative with convictions for charges of persecution. While, the underlying acts of torture, deportation and inhumane acts (forcible transfer) all overlap with the corresponding underlying acts of persecution, persecution contains additional discriminatory elements both in the *mens rea* and in the *actus reus* that are not required for torture, deportation and inhumane acts (forcible transfer). These three charges are subsumed by the repository charge of persecution. A conviction may therefore be entered for persecution (Count 3) but not for torture (Count 6), deportation (Count 8) or inhumane acts (forcible transfer) (Count 9).

[111] *Krstić* Appeal Judgement, *supra* note 44, Partial Dissenting Opinion of Judge Shahabuddeen, para. 80. It is interesting to note that Judge Shahabuddeen was a party to both *Krnojelac* and *Vasiljević* and joined the Chamber's discussion on cumulative convictions in both judgements without dissent.

[112] *Ibid.*, para. 85.

[113] *Ibid.*, para. 88 (looking at the Australian cases of *Pearce* v. *The Queen*, [1998] 194 CLR 610, paras. 34–42 (High Court of Australia) and *R.* v. *Dudko*, [2002] 132 A. Crim. R. 371, paras. 110–115 (New South Wales Court of Criminal Appeal)). According to Judge Shahabuddeen, the allegation of murder that appears in the paragraph of the *Krstić* indictment charging persecution merely speaks of murder 'by way of stating a "means" through which persecution was committed'. *Ibid.*, para. 89 (referring to *Prosecutor v. Krstić*, Case No. IT-98-33-PT, Amended Indictment, 27 October 1999, para. 31).

[114] *Ibid.*, para. 90.

Were it otherwise, the legal elements of the crime of persecution would vary according to the legal elements of the particular crime on which the persecution is based. The legal elements of the crime of persecution would include the legal elements of the crime of enslavement if enslavement were alleged to be the basis of the persecution charged. Similarly with respect to deportation, imprisonment, torture and rape. The legal elements of a charge for persecution would thus vary from case to case; in the present case, they would include the legal elements of all the crimes on which the persecution is alleged to have been based. That variability is not reconcilable with the stability, definitiveness and certainty with which the legal elements of a crime should be known. Those elements must not depend on accidents of prosecution; they must clearly appear once and for all from a reading of the provision defining the crime.[115]

'In short, all the legal elements of the crime of murder lie outside of the legal elements of the crime of persecution: the facts of the murder are only evidence on which the charge of persecution is based [and *Čelebići*] does not mandate non-cumulation in this case.'[116]

With due respect to Judge Shahabuddeen, this view of how the chambers determine whether the elements of a particular form of persecution have been met is at odds with actual practice. As discussed in Chapter 2,[117] the forms of persecution are not merely ways of committing persecution; like the underlying offences of crimes against humanity, genocide, or war crimes, they are instead discrete offences with their own *actus reus* and *mens rea* elements.[118] Properly understood, persecution is unique among crimes against humanity because it is itself a sub-category of offences – with their own unique *actus reus* and *mens rea* elements – that share certain common characteristics when they rise to the level of persecution. These common characteristics are the specific requirements of persecution: the physical perpetrator or another relevant actor intended to discriminate on one or more of the grounds of race, religion, or politics, and the perpetrator subjectively believed that the victim was a member of the target population.[119] As a consequence, in order to determine whether murder as a form of persecution has been committed, a chamber has no choice but to examine whether the elements of murder have been fulfilled, and must then make the additional determination of whether the specific requirements of persecution have also been fulfilled.[120] Therefore, contrary to the suggestion of Judge Shahabuddeen, the elements that must be proven to convict an accused of persecution as a crime against humanity do indeed depend on the particular form

[115] *Ibid.*, para. 91.
[116] *Ibid.*, para. 93. Judge Shahabuddeen extended this reasoning to 'the question whether a conviction for persecution under article 5(h) … may be cumulated with a conviction for inhumane acts (in relation to forcible transfers) under article 5(i).' *Ibid.*, para. 94.
[117] See Chapter 2, text accompanying notes 388–392.
[118] See Chapter 3, text accompanying notes 94–98, for an analogous discussion with respect to the underlying offences of genocide.
[119] See Chapter 2, section 2.2.3.8.1.
[120] This consequence was suggested above. See *supra* text accompanying notes 100–101.

of persecution charged in the indictment in the case at hand; and it is impossible to ascertain the elements of a form of persecution without examining the *actus reus* and *mens rea* elements of the offence that constitutes the form. The chambers appear implicitly to understand this notion and do not appear to have had particular difficulties coming to grips with it.

Nevertheless, a 3:2 majority[121] of the Appeals Chamber in the December 2004 *Kordić and Čerkez* Judgement appears to have adopted Judge Shahabuddeen's interpretation of *Čelebići* and converted it into the binding law of the *ad hoc* Tribunals. The Chamber found 'cogent reasons' to depart from the contrary precedent of *Krstić*, *Vasiljević*, and *Krnojelac*:[122]

> These cases are in direct contradiction to the reasoning and proper application of the test by the Appeals Chambers in *Jelisić, Kupreškić, Kunara[c], and Musema* … [T]he Appeals Chamber in *Čelebići* expressly rejected an approach that takes into account the actual conduct of the accused as determinative of whether multiple convictions for that conduct are permissible. Rather, what is required is an examination, as a matter of law, of the elements of each offence in the Statute that pertain to that conduct for which the accused has been convicted. It must be considered whether each offence charged has a materially distinct element not contained in the other; that is, whether each offence has an element that requires proof of a fact not required by the other offence.[123]

On the basis of this sparse rationale, the majority determined that cumulative convictions for persecution as a crime against humanity and murder as a crime against humanity are indeed permissible in all circumstances, because persecution does not require an act or omission causing the death of the victim, and murder does not require a discriminatory act or omission or discriminatory intent; the majority considered it immaterial that the particular instances of persecution charged in the indictment had been perpetrated through the form of murder.[124] It extended this reasoning to inhumane acts and imprisonment as crimes against humanity,[125] and accordingly dismissed Čerkez's claims that his convictions for various forms of persecution were impermissibly cumulative with his convictions for murder, inhumane acts, and imprisonment on the basis of the same conduct.[126]

121 Judges Güney and Schomburg dissenting. See *infra*,text accompanying notes 133–142, for a discussion of this dissent and subsequent dissents by these two judges.

122 See *Kordić and Čerkez* Appeal Judgement, *supra* note 44, para. 1040 (invoking *Aleksovski* Appeal Judgement, *supra* note 24, para. 107 ('[T]he Appeals Chamber should follow its previous decisions, but should be free to depart from them for cogent reasons in the interests of justice.')). *Aleksovski* and other cases applying the 'cogent reasons' standard are discussed at notes 144–148 and accompanying text, *infra*. Interestingly, Judge Shahabuddeen was not on the bench in *Kordić and Čerkez*.

123 *Ibid*., para. 1040. The Chamber had earlier recalled that the elements of the crimes in question must be examined in the abstract: '[W]hen applying the *Čelebići* test, what must be considered are the legal elements of each offence, not the acts or omissions giving rise to the offence. What each offence requires, as a matter of law, is the pertinent inquiry.' *Ibid*., para. 1033.

124 *Ibid*., para. 1041. 125 See *ibid*., paras. 1042–1043.

126 *Ibid*., para. 1044 (upholding *Kordić and Čerkez* Trial Judgement, *supra* note 72, pp. 305–306).

Under this new construction of *Čelebići*, when a chamber considers the particular form of persecution for which the accused has been found responsible, it goes beyond an examination of the legal elements of the crime and delves impermissibly into how the crime was brought about. Subsequent trial chambers have followed this rule, as they are obliged to do.[127] And it has since been reaffirmed at least twice in the ICTY – in the March 2006 *Stakić* Appeal Judgement and the May 2006 *Naletilić and Martinović* Appeal Judgement[128] – and endorsed by a majority of the ICTR Appeals Chamber in the *Media* case as applicable in that Tribunal.[129] The majorities in *Stakić* and *Naletilić and Martinović* accordingly overturned the relevant holdings of their respective Trial Chambers as contrary to the *Kordić and Čerkez* approach.[130] It is important to recall that these trial judgements were, at the time of their rendering, in line with binding appellate jurisprudence.[131] Like *Kordić and Čerkez*, neither *Stakić* nor *Naletilić and Martinović*, nor the ICTR Appeals Chamber in the *Media* case, enjoyed unanimity on this question.[132]

Judges Güney and Schomburg dissented from the majority's cumulative-convictions discussion in *Kordić and Čerkez*.[133] They reiterated their disagreement

[127] See *Martić* Trial Judgement, *supra* note 92, paras. 475, 480, 518; *Prosecutor* v. *Krajišnik*, Case No. IT-00-39-T, Judgement, 27 September 2006 ('*Krajišnik* Trial Judgement'), paras. 1129–1130; *Blagojević and Jokić* Trial Judgement, *supra* note 72, para. 810 (noting the recent *Kordić and Čerkez* Appeal Judgement and '[r]ecalling the binding force of decisions of the Tribunal's Appeals Chamber upon the Trial Chambers'). See also *Aleksovski* Appeal Judgement, *supra* note 24, para. 113 (establishing the principle that the *ratio decidendi* of ICTY Appeals Chamber decisions are binding on ICTY trial chambers); Boas, Bischoff, and Reid, *supra* note 7, p. 26 n. 94 (discussing how the decisions of the respective Appeals Chambers of the ICTY and the ICTR have generally been treated as authoritative by the trial chambers of both Tribunals). See also *infra* text accompanying notes 199–209 (discussing the consequences for trial chambers of failing to follow the *Kordić and Čerkez* approach).

[128] *Naletilić and Martinović* Appeal Judgement, *supra* note 10, para. 589; *Stakić* Appeal Judgement, *supra* note 60, paras. 359–366. The *Naletilić and Martinović* Appeals Chamber determined that the accused 'ha[d] not presented the Appeals Chamber with any cogent reasons in the interests of justice for departing from its jurisprudence on cumulative convictions', and that '[t]he Appeals Chamber finds no reasons to do so on its own.' *Naletilić and Martinović* Appeal Judgement, *supra* note 10, para. 586 (invoking the *Aleksovski* standard described at note 122 *supra*).

[129] See *Media* Appeal Judgement, *supra* note 62, para. 1026.

[130] See *Naletilić and Martinović* Appeal Judgement, *supra* note 10, paras. 589–591 (overturning *Naletilić and Martinović* Trial Judgement, *supra* note 10, para. 724); *Stakić* Appeal Judgement, *supra* note 60, paras. 359–366 (overturning *Stakić* Trial Judgement, *supra* note 108, paras. 879–882). The prosecution did not appeal the similar holding of the *Brđanin* Trial Judgement, discussed *supra* at note 110, and the Appeals Chamber accordingly declined to address the question. See *Prosecutor* v. *Brđanin*, Case No. IT-99-36-A, Judgement, 3 April 2007, para. 505 n. 1051. The same appears to be the case in *Kvočka* and *Simić*. See generally *Kvočka* Appeal Judgement, *supra* note 97 (making no mention of cumulative convictions); *Prosecutor* v. *Simić*, Case No. IT-95-9-A, Judgement, 28 November 2006 ('*Simić* Appeal Judgement') (same). See also *ibid.*, Dissenting Opinion of Judge Schomburg, para. 9 n. 16 (noting, in a different context, that the *Simić* Trial Chamber's decision not to enter cumulative convictions for deportation as a crime against humanity and deportation as a form of persecution as a crime against humanity was correct under then-binding appellate jurisprudence).

[131] See *supra* notes 107–110 and accompanying text.

[132] In *Stakić*, the majority was 4 to 1, with Judge Güney dissenting. In *Naletilić and Martinović* it was 3 to 2, with Judges Güney and Schomburg dissenting. In the *Media* case it was 4 to 1, with Judge Güney dissenting.

[133] See generally *Kordić and Čerkez* Appeal Judgement, *supra* note 44, Joint Dissenting Opinion of Judge Schomburg and Judge Güney on Cumulative Convictions.

in a short dissenting opinion in *Naletilić and Martinović*, [134] and Judge Güney also dissented in *Stakić* [135] and the *Media* case;[136] in neither of these latter cases did Judge Schomburg sit on the appeals bench. They argued that cogent reasons did not exist for departing from *Krstić*, *Vasiljević*, and *Krnojelac*, as these cases had correctly interpreted and applied *Čelebići* to the specific scenario where a form of persecution must be compared with that same form as a crime against humanity in its own right.[137] Judges Güney and Schomburg characterised persecution as an 'empty hull ... designed to cover all possible underlying offences of persecution':[138]

> [T]o merely take the wording of the definition and convict the accused for a denial of a fundamental right is not what a criminal court can do ... Instead, one has to ask: what is the fundamental right that has been denied[?] In the present case, the answer is: the fundamental right to life. It is only by incorporating this element in persecutions that the empty hull amounts to ... a crime against humanity.[139]

According to Judges Güney and Schomburg, an approach taking account of the elements of the particular form of persecution under analysis comports with

[134] See generally *Naletilić and Martinović* Appeal Judgement, *supra* note 10, Joint Dissenting Opinion of Judge Güney and Judge Schomburg on Cumulative Convictions;

[135] See generally *Stakić* Appeal Judgement, *supra* note 60, Opinion dissidente du Juge Güney sur le cumul de déclarations de culpabilité.

[136] *Media* Appeal Judgement, *supra* note 62, Opinion partiellement dissident du Juge Güney.

[137] *Kordić and Čerkez* Appeal Judgement, *supra* note 44, Joint Dissenting Opinion of Judge Schomburg and Judge Güney on Cumulative Convictions, para. 1. Judges Güney and Schomburg argued that *Aleksovski* establishes a 'high threshold' for departing from settled precedent, and that '[i]t should not happen that due to shifting majorities the Appeals Chamber changes its jurisprudence from case to case'. *Ibid.*, para. 13. In *Krnojelac*, the bench was composed of Judges Jorda, Schomburg, Shahabuddeen, Güney, and Agius, with no judge dissenting on cumulative convictions. In *Vasiljević*, the bench was composed of Judges Meron, Shahabuddeen, Güney, Schomburg, and Weinberg de Roca, with no judge dissenting on cumulative convictions. In *Krstić*, the bench was Judges Meron, Pocar, Shahabuddeen, Güney, and Schomburg, with Judge Shahabuddeen now dissenting on cumulative convictions. In *Kordić and Čerkez*, the bench was Judges Schomburg, Pocar, Mumba, Güney, and Weinberg de Roca, with Judges Schomburg and Güney dissenting. The 'shift' in the majority in *Kordić and Čerkez* may have been the presence of Judges Pocar and Mumba to vote along with Judge Weinberg de Roca in favour of the new approach, but if so, it is curious that Judge Weinberg de Roca did not join Judge Shahabuddeen's dissent in *Krstić*, or issue her own dissent. Cf. *Prosecutor* v. *Kordić and Čerkez*, Case No. IT-95-14/2-A, Decision Authorising Respondent's Brief to Exceed the Limit Imposed by the Practice Direction on the Length of Briefs and Motions and Granting an Extension of Time to File Brief, 30 August 2001, para. 8 (Pre-Appeal Judge Hunt citing the *Aleksovski* 'cogent reasons' principle and remarking that, in his view, 'the need for certainty in international criminal law means that the Appeals Chamber should never disregard a previous decision simply because the members of the Appeals Chamber at that particular time do not personally agree with it.').

[138] *Kordić and Čerkez* Appeal Judgement, *supra* note 44, Joint Dissenting Opinion of Judge Schomburg and Judge Güney on Cumulative Convictions, para. 6.

[139] *Ibid.* Accord *Stakić* Appeal Judgement, *supra* note 60, Opinion dissidente du Juge Güney sur le cumul de déclarations de culpabilité, para. 2 ('Ce n'est qu'en qualifiant l'acte sous-jacent constituant la persécution que le crime sanctionné à l'article 5(h) du Statut prend corps. Sans l'acte sous-jacent, la coquille que constitue la disposition relative aux persécutions demeure vide.'); *ibid.*, para. 4 ('[O]n ne peut considérer le crime de persécutions sans l'acte sous-jacent que lui donne corps.'); accord *Media* Appeal Judgement, *supra* note 62, Opinion partiellement dissident du Juge Güney, paras. 2–3.

Čelebići 's mandate to determine whether each crime has a *materially* distinct element. Where the crimes being analysed are murder and murder as a form of persecution, the latter requires all the elements of the former, including 'proof of an act of murder', and at least one more: discriminatory intent.[140] Under *Čelebići*, then, the latter should subsume the former and the accused should only be convicted of murder as a form of persecution.[141] In *Naletilić and Martinović*, Judges Güney and Schomburg stressed that their future silence on this matter should not be construed as approval of the current majority position.[142]

It is indeed curious that a 3:2 majority in *Kordić and Čerkez* took the extraordinary step of departing from the Appeals Chamber's previous jurisprudence on cumulative convictions, and that it explained its reasoning in just one brief paragraph.[143] The March 2000 *Aleksovski* Appeal Judgement established the principle that the Appeals Chamber should only depart from its own precedent after 'the most careful consideration',[144] and only for 'cogent reasons in the interests of justice,'[145] such as where the previous decision was wrongly decided because the judges were ill-informed about the law.[146] By and large, both Appeals Chambers have respected the exceptional nature of departures from previous appellate jurisprudence. Cases in which the Appeals Chambers have found 'cogent reasons' to exist are exceedingly

[140] See *Kordić and Čerkez* Appeal Judgement, *supra* note 44, Joint Dissenting Opinion of Judge Schomburg and Judge Güney on Cumulative Convictions, paras. 5, 7. Accord *Stakić* Appeal Judgement, *supra* note 60, Opinion dissidente du Juge Güney sur le cumul de déclarations de culpabilité, para. 4.

[141] *Stakić* Appeal Judgement, *supra* note 60, Opinion dissidente du Juge Güney sur le cumul de déclarations de culpabilité, para. 5. Judge Güney opined that this reasoning applies equally to other crimes against humanity that may also constitute forms of persecution, such as deportation, forcible transfer as an inhumane act, and extermination. *Ibid.*

[142] *Naletilić and Martinović* Appeal Judgement, *supra* note 10, Joint Dissenting Opinion of Judge Güney and Judge Schomburg on Cumulative Convictions, p. 211.

[143] See *Kordić and Čerkez* Appeal Judgement, *supra* note 44, para. 1040 (quoted at text accompanying note 123 *supra*).

[144] *Aleksovski* Appeal Judgement, *supra* note 24, para. 109. *Aleksovski* also established a number of other basic principles regarding the binding or persuasive nature of trial and appellate precedent on later chambers. See, e. g., *ibid.*, para. 113 (trial chambers bound to follow *ratio decidendi* of Appeals Chamber rulings); *ibid.*, para. 114 (trial chambers not bound to follow each other's decisions, although a trial chamber may follow the decision of another that it finds persuasive). See also Boas, Bischoff, and Reid, *supra* note 7, p. 26 n. 94 (discussing how the decisions of the respective Appeals Chambers of the ICTY and the ICTR have generally been treated as authoritative by the trial chambers of both Tribunals); *Semanza* v. *Prosecutor*, Case No. ICTR-97-20-A, Decision, 31 May 2000 ('*Semanza* May 2000 Appeal Decision'), Separate Opinion of Judge Shahabuddeen, paras. 1–38 (Judge Shahabuddeen, who was not on the *Aleksovski* bench, detailing his views on whether the Appeals Chamber should follow its own previous decisions, and providing criteria for determining when cogent reasons for departure may be found to exist).

[145] *Aleksovski* Appeal Judgement, *supra* note 24, para. 107 (arriving at this formula after a brief analysis of British, Australian, US, French, and Italian law, as well as the practice of the European Court of Human Rights and the International Court of Justice).

[146] *Ibid.*, para. 108 (quoting *Black's Law Dictionary* (7th edn 1999)). The ICTR Appeals Chamber endorsed this rule in a May 2000 interlocutory decision in *Semanza*. See *Semanza* May 2000 Appeal Decision, *supra* note 144, para. 92.

rare,[147] and nearly all requests by a party to depart from previous jurisprudence have been rejected.[148]

It is difficult to reconcile *Kordić and Čerkez*'s tersely explained departure from *Krnojelac*, *Vasiljević*, and *Krstić* with the *Aleksovski* standard.[149] While the appeals benches in *Krnojelac* and *Vasiljević* gave virtually no reasoning behind their respective relevant holdings, the *Krstić* Appeals Chamber engaged in a thorough and well-articulated discussion as to why the elements of the form of persecution in question must be taken into account in determining whether cumulative convictions are permissible; it acknowledged and explicitly rejected the prosecution's argument that the form of persecution is irrelevant to the analysis.[150] Moreover, the *Kordić and Čerkez* Appeals Chamber disingenuously asserts that it was the *Krstić* line of judgements that went against *Čelebići* and four subsequent appeal judgements rendered before *Krnojelac*: *Kunarac*, *Kupreškić*, *Jelisić*, and *Musema*. In reality, none of these earlier judgements dealt with the specific and conceptually different question addressed in the *Krstić* line. Indeed, the *Kupreškić* Appeals Chamber expressly declined to examine how the cumulative-convictions test functions

[147] Indeed, we know of only one case in the ICTY besides *Kordić and Čerkez*, and just one in the ICTR. See *Prosecutor* v. *Žigić*, Case No. IT-98-30/1-A, Decision on Zoran Žigić's 'Motion for Reconsideration of Appeals Chamber Judgement IT-98-30/1-A Delivered on 28 February 2005', 26 June 2006 ('*Žigić* June 2006 Appeal Decision'), para. 9 (4:1 majority, including Judges Güney and Schomburg, departing from a previous ruling allowing Appeals Chamber reconsideration of previous appeal judgements in certain circumstances, and holding that 'there is no power to reconsider a final judgement'); *Semanza* May 2000 Appeal Decision, *supra* note 144, paras. 92–98 (departing from a previous ruling on when the time limit for the provisional detention of a suspect begins to run, where the Appeals Chamber in the previous decision had apparently relied erroneously on an earlier version of the relevant provision in the Rules of Procedure and Evidence, which had since been amended); *ibid.*, Separate Opinion of Judge Shahabuddeen, para. 38 (concurring in such departure).

[148] See, e.g., *Prosecutor* v. *Jović*, Case No. IT-95-14 & 14/2-R77-A, Judgement, 15 March 2007, paras. 20–23 (order prohibiting divulgence of evidence given in closed session applies not only to parties to a given proceeding, but also to press and public at large); *Galić* Appeal Judgement, *supra* note 10, paras. 117–120 (violations of the laws or customs of war may be committed against persons, and not just property, and may be committed in internal armed conflict); *Naletilić and Martinović* Appeal Judgement, *supra* note 10, paras 585–586 (no cogent reasons to depart from the *Kordić and Čerkez* approach to cumulative convictions); *Prosecutor* v. *Deronjić*, Case No. IT-02-61-A, Judgement on Sentencing Appeal, 20 July 2005, paras. 135–138 (rehabilitation a secondary consideration in sentencing, behind retribution and deterrence); *Blaškić* Appeal Judgement, *supra* note 73, para. 62 (accused superior must have had information available to him which put him on notice of subordinate criminal conduct; mere negligence will not suffice); *Prosecutor* v. *Milutinović, Šainović, and Ojdanić*, Case No. IT-99-37-AR72, Decision on Dragoljub Ojdanić's Motion Challenging Jurisdiction – Joint Criminal Enterprise, 21 May 2003, para. 30 (joint criminal enterprise exists in customary international law and is provided for in the ICTY Statute); *Kupreškić et al.* Appeal Judgement, *supra* note 10, paras. 418–423 (while sentencing practice of the courts of the former Yugoslavia should be considered, a trial chamber is not bound to act exactly as a court of the former Yugoslavia would); *Čelebići* Appeal Judgement, *supra* note 7, paras. 6–26 (extensive discussion reaffirming the 'overall control' test for determining when an armed conflict qualifies as international); *ibid.*, para. 84 (nationality of victims for purposes of Geneva Convention IV determined not on formal national characterisations, but on 'substantial relations', including ethnicity of victims and perpetrators); *ibid.*, paras. 123–136 (common Article 3 of the Geneva Conventions included in the scope of Article 3 of the ICTY Statute).

[149] Cf. *Žigić* June 2006 Appeal Decision, *supra* note 147, Declaration of Judge Shahabuddeen, para. 2 (criticising the majority for failing to adequately explain the 'cogent reasons' demanding departure from the principle established by a well-reasoned earlier Appeals Chamber ruling).

[150] See *Krstić* Appeal Judgement, *supra* note 44, para. 232 (discussed at notes 103–106, *supra*).

when persecution is involved because one affected accused 'abandoned' this ground of appeal and the other failed to raise it.[151]

More fundamentally, the *Krstić* approach is much more convincing in light of the consistent law and practice of the *ad hoc* Tribunals concerning how the elements of persecution are established; the *Kordić and Čerkez* approach is, in our view, legally incorrect. If either line of judgements can be said to have been rendered based on an unconsidered interpretation of the law, it is certainly the latter. Judges Güney and Schomburg aptly characterise persecution as an 'empty shell'. The crime cannot be described, and an accused cannot be convicted under it, without identifying the specific form of persecution – murder, torture, rape, and so forth. The determination of whether the elements of a form of persecution have been proven is an almost mathematical process. As noted above,[152] the trial chamber adds together the general requirements of crimes against humanity,[153] the specific requirements of persecution,[154] and – crucially – the elements of the offence making up the form of persecution in question: for example, where the form in question is murder, an act causing the death of the victim accompanied by the intent to kill or to inflict serious injury or grievous bodily harm on the victim in reckless disregard of human life.[155] Contrary to the assertion of the *Kordić and Čerkez* Appeals Chamber, this process *is* a comparison of legal elements in the abstract. For instance, once the trial chamber has found on the facts that the accused could bear liability for murder as a form of persecution, it need not look back to the facts – such as the identity of the victim or how the killing was brought to fruition – to compare the elements of this crime with those of murder as a crime against humanity in its own right. Instead, it need merely compare the legal elements of these two crimes as they have been defined and developed in the jurisprudence. In other words, this portion of the analysis is not seeking to answer *how* the crime was committed; instead, it seeks to answer a more fundamental question: what *is* the crime?

Perhaps the most serious problem with the *Kordić and Čerkez* approach, however, is its real-world implications. When the prosecution charges a certain underlying offence (murder, torture, rape, and so forth) as a form of persecution in the indictment, it typically includes a separate count charging the same offence for the same conduct as a 'simple' crime against humanity. This is done presumably as a

[151] See *Kupreškić et al.* Appeal Judgement, *supra* note 10, para. 395.

[152] See *supra* text accompanying notes 99–101, 117–120. See also Chapter 2, note 314.

[153] There must have been a widespread or systematic attack directed against a civilian population, the acts of the physical perpetrator must have formed part of the attack, and the perpetrator or another relevant actor must have known of the pattern of widespread or systematic crimes directed against a civilian population, and that his acts fit into such a pattern. See Chapter 2, section 2.2.2.

[154] The physical perpetrator or another relevant actor intended to discriminate on one or more of the grounds of race, religion, or politics, and the perpetrator subjectively believed that the victim was a member of the target population. See *ibid.*, section 2.2.3.8.1.

[155] See *ibid.*, section 2.2.3.1.

safeguard: if, after the presentation of evidence, the trial chamber cannot find beyond a reasonable doubt that a given act was committed with discriminatory intent, it still has the option of convicting the accused of the simple crime against humanity, which is easier to prove because it has fewer elements.[156] As long as the specific requirements of persecution are present in addition to the general requirements of crimes against humanity and the elements of the underlying offence, the prosecution has necessarily proven both the form of persecution and the simple crime against humanity.[157] In the wake of *Kordić and Čerkez*, if the trial chamber does find that the specific requirements of persecution have been fulfilled, it not only has the option of convicting the accused of both persecution and the simple crime against humanity but – as the Appeals Chamber has since confirmed[158] – is compelled to do so.[159] In essence, then, the prosecution gets a 'two for one' conviction whenever it manages to prove the commission of a form of persecution where it has also charged the simple crime against humanity in the indictment.[160]

While it could be argued that cumulative convictions in this situation vindicate the 'interests of the international community',[161] the Appeals Chamber has also stressed that the objective of the exercise is to strike the delicate balance between fairness to the accused and the need to reflect his full criminality.[162] In our view, *Kordić and Čerkez* has skewed this balance in the wrong direction. A conviction for murder as a form of persecution as a crime against humanity brands the accused with responsibility for the discriminatory killing of a civilian as part of a widespread or systematic attack on a civilian population; a second conviction for killing this same civilian as part of a widespread or systematic attack adds nothing to the description of the accused's criminality. The double conviction here does, however, hold the very real potential of significant detriment for the convicted person: the trial chamber can justifiably impose on him a harsher sentence than it otherwise would

156 See, e.g., *Prosecutor* v. *Popović, Beara, Nikolić, Borovčanin, Miletić, Gvero, and Pandurević*, Case No. IT-05-88-T, Indictment, 4 August 2006 ('*Popović et al.* Indictment'), paras. 46, 48–49 (charging murder and forcible transfer as forms of persecution as a crime against humanity cumulatively with murder and forcible transfer as crimes against humanity in their own right); *Prosecutor* v. *Martić*, Case No. IT-95-11-PT, Amended Indictment, 14 July 2003, para. 24 (charging various forms of persecution cumulatively with other crimes against humanity); *Martić* Trial Judgement, *supra* note 92, paras. 480, 518 (entering many of these cumulative convictions).

157 See *Krstić* Appeal Judgement, *supra* note 44, para. 232 ('The proof that the accused committed persecution through murder or inhumane acts *necessarily* includes proof of murder or inhumane acts under Article 5 [of the ICTY Statute].') (emphasis in original).

158 See *Stakić* Appeal Judgement, *supra* note 60, para. 358.

159 See *infra* text accompanying notes 199–209 (discussing the effect of a trial chamber's erroneous failure to cumulatively convict).

160 See, e.g., *Naletilić and Martinović* Appeal Judgement, *supra* note 10, paras. 589–591, p. 211; *Martić* Trial Judgement, *supra* note 92, paras. 475, 480, 518; *Krajišnik* Trial Judgement, *supra* note 127, paras. 1129–1130, p. 1182; *Blagojević and Jokić* Trial Judgement, *supra* note 72, para. 810, pp. 311–312.

161 *Krstić* Appeal Judgement, *supra* note 44, Partial Dissenting Opinion of Judge Shahabuddeen, para. 85.

162 See *Kunarac et al.* Appeal Judgement, *supra* note 38, paras. 169, 173.

have. Moreover, as Judges Hunt and Bennouna cautioned[163] and a full bench of the Appeals Chamber later reiterated,[164] he is less likely to be awarded early release, and he may be exposed to an increased sentence by the operation of a career-offender sentencing enhancement if later convicted in a national court.

Kordić and Čerkez mandates trial chambers to engage in the very sort of 'mechanical [and] blind' procedure warned against by the Appeals Chamber in *Kunarac* [165] While the chambers of the *ad hoc* Tribunals must unfortunately follow *Kordić and Čerkez*[166] – at least until the majority shifts again – we believe that the *Krstić* approach should be favoured by other international and internationalised tribunals adopting the *Čelebići* test.

5.2.4.2 Intra-article convictions for war crimes

Intra-article convictions for war crimes are relatively straightforward. In order to determine whether cumulative convictions are permissible for a given pair of grave breaches or violations of the laws or customs of war, the trial chamber simply compares the elements of the underlying offences in question to determine if each has a materially distinct element. Accordingly, the *Galić* Trial Chamber held that cumulative convictions for terror against a civilian population as a violation of the laws or customs of war, and attacks on civilians as a violation of the laws or customs of war, were impermissible: the underlying offence of the latter contains all the elements of the former, but lacks the additional element of intent to spread terror.[167] Likewise, the *Limaj* Trial Chamber held that cumulative convictions for torture as a violation of the laws or customs of war and cruel treatment as a violation of the laws or customs of war were impermissible: while both require the intentional infliction of serious bodily or mental harm, torture requires additionally that such harm be inflicted for a prohibited purpose.[168]

The January 2005 *Strugar* Trial Chamber's holding on intra-article cumulative convictions for war crimes deserves brief mention because it hearkens back to Judge

[163] *Čelebići* Appeal Judgement, *supra* note 7, Separate and Dissenting Opinion of Judge David Hunt and Judge Mohamed Bennouna, para. 23.

[164] See *Prosecutor* v. *Mucić, Delić, and Landžo*, Case No. IT-96-21-A*bis*, Judgement on Sentence Appeal, 8 April 2003, para. 25. See also *Jelisić* Appeal Judgement, *supra* note 56, Partial Dissenting Opinion of Judge Shahabuddeen, para. 34 ('[E]ven if no material penalty is imposed, as is well known, a conviction can have certain consequences for the accused.').

[165] *Kunarac et al.* Appeal Judgement, *supra* note 38, para. 174.

[166] As noted above, the ICTR Appeals Chamber has adopted the *Kordić and Čerkez* approach. See *Media* Appeal Judgement, *supra* note 62, para. 1026.

[167] *Galić* Trial Judgement, *supra* note 10, para. 162. The prosecution apparently did not appeal this holding, and the Appeals Chamber did not address intra-Article 3 cumulative convictions in its discussion of cumulative convictions. See *Galić* Appeal Judgement, *supra* note 10, paras. 162–168.

[168] *Limaj et al.* Trial Judgement, *supra* note 75, para. 719. See also *Kunarac et al.* Appeal Judgement, *supra* note 38, para. 196 (rape as a violation of the laws or customs of war and torture as a violation of the laws or customs of war permissibly cumulative because rape uniquely requires sexual penetration and torture uniquely requires a prohibited purpose).

Shahabuddeen's 'gravamen' approach and almost certainly misapplies both *Čelebići* and *Kordić and Čerkez*. The Trial Chamber found that the elements of three violations of the laws or customs of war – attacks on civilians, murder, and cruel treatment – had all been satisfied in respect of shelling of the Old Town of Dubrovnik. It acknowledged that a 'strict application' of the *Čelebići* test as interpreted in the *Kordić and Čerkez* Appeal Judgement would allow cumulative convictions for attacks on civilians and murder for those who died, and attacks on civilians and cruel treatment for those who were injured and survived, because each contains, as a matter of law, a unique element.[169] Nevertheless, without explicitly stating that it was deviating from *Kordić and Čerkez*'s exhortation not to go beyond the elements of the crimes in the abstract, the Trial Chamber proceeded to look at the facts of the case:

> The essential criminal conduct of the perpetrators is directly and comprehensively reflected in [the count of the indictment charging attacks on civilians]. The offence of attacks on civilians, involved an attack directed against a civilian population, causing death, and also serious injury, with the intent of making the civilian population the object of the attack. Given these circumstances, in the present case, the offence of murder adds no materially distinct element, nor does the offence of cruel treatment the gravamen of which is fully absorbed by the circumstances in which this attack on civilians occurred.[170]

Although this approach seems sensible, it will most likely be overturned on appeal.[171]

5.2.4.3 *Intra-article convictions for genocide*

As discussed in Chapter 3 and in Volume I of this series,[172] Article 4 of the ICTY Statute and Article 2 of the ICTR Statute ('Article 4/2') contain two distinct listings of genocidal activities, deriving respectively from Articles II and III of the 1948 Genocide Convention.[173] Article 4/2(2) lists six underlying offences that rise to the level of genocide if certain general requirements are satisfied.[174] Article 4/2(3) lists three species of inchoate conduct preparatory to the commission of genocide: conspiracy to commit genocide, direct and public incitement to commit genocide, and attempt to

[169] See *Strugar* Trial Judgement, *supra* note 72, paras. 449–450. [170] *Ibid.*, para. 449.

[171] See *Prosecutor* v. *Strugar*, Case No. IT-01-42-Misc, Decision on Strugar's Request to Reopen Appeal Proceedings, 7 June 2007, para. 3 (noting that the prosecution originally appealed the Trial Chamber's holding on cumulative convictions); *ibid.*, para. 13 (noting that, on 15 September 2006, both parties withdrew their appeals); *ibid.*, para. 31 (reopening appeal proceedings upon Strugar's request). It should also be borne in mind that the *Strugar* Trial Judgement was rendered on 30 January 2005, barely one month after the *Kordić and Čerkez* Appeal Judgement, and the Trial Chamber may not have had the opportunity to fully appreciate the import of the Appeals Chamber's approach.

[172] See Chapter 3, text accompanying note 103; Boas, Bischoff, and Reid, *supra* note 7, pp. 281–283.

[173] See Convention on the Prevention and Suppression of the Crime of Genocide, 9 December 1948, entered into force 12 January 1951, 78 UNTS 277, Arts. II–III.

[174] As noted in Chapter 3, causing serious bodily harm and causing serious mental harm are two separate underlying offences, even though both reside in Article 4/2(2)(b). See Chapter 3, note 208 and accompanying text.

commit genocide.[175] As a consequence of this structure, there are two different types of 'intra-article 4/2' cumulative convictions. In the first type, the two crimes under analysis are different manifestations of genocide because the Article 4/2(2) underlying offence differs, such as killing as genocide versus causing serious bodily harm as genocide; this type is parallel to intra-article convictions for crimes against humanity or war crimes as set forth above. In the second type, one or both of the crimes under analysis is an Article 4/2(3) inchoate crime. We begin with the first type.

To date, it would appear that the *ad hoc* chambers have not produced any jurisprudence analysing the permissibility of intra-Article 4/2(2) cumulative convictions. This absence is likely due to most chambers' implicit treatment of genocide as a single crime and its underlying offences merely as ways in which the *actus reus* of this crime can be realised.[176] This view is perhaps influenced by the *ad hoc* Prosecutors' practice of charging several different manifestations of genocide under a single count, instead of placing each in its own separate count, as they tend to do with crimes against humanity and war crimes.[177]

For the reasons explained in Chapter 3, however, we believe this interpretation of the relationship between genocide and its underlying offences is incorrect, and that

[175] As noted in Chapter 3 and in Volume I of this series, complicity in genocide, the conduct listed in Article 4/2(3)(e), is a hybrid of a crime and a form or forms of accomplice liability. See Chapter 3, note 161; *ibid.*, note 331 and accompanying text; Boas, Bischoff, and Reid, *supra* note 7, pp. 290–291.

[176] See, e.g., *Prosecutor* v. *Simba*, Case No. ICTR-01-76-T, Judgement and Sentence, 13 December 2005, paras. 412–418; *Prosecutor* v. *Muhimana*, Case No. ICTR- 95-1B-T, Judgement and Sentence, 28 April 2005, paras. 494–519; *Prosecutor* v. *Gacumbitsi*, Case No. ICTR-2001-64-T, Judgement, 14 June 2004 ('*Gacumbitsi* Trial Judgement'), paras. 251, 293; *Prosecutor* v. *Kajelijeli*, Case No. ICTR-98-44A-T, Judgement and Sentence, 1 December 2003 ('*Kajelijeli* Trial Judgement'), paras. 812, 818; *Prosecutor* v. *Niyitegeka*, Case No. ICTR-96-14-T, Judgement, 16 May 2003 ('*Niyitegeka* Trial Judgement'), para. 420; *Ntakirutimana and Ntakirutimana* Trial Judgement, *supra* note 10, paras. 784, 790–795, 831, 835–836; *Kayishema and Ruzindana* Trial Judgement, *supra* note 3, paras. 551–571, 637. The absence of a discussion of intra-Article 2(2) cumulative convictions in the *Gacumbitsi* Trial Judgement might be explained by the Trial Chamber's apparent finding that the victims of killing as genocide were different from the victims of causing serious bodily harm as genocide. See *Gacumbitsi* Trial Judgement, *supra*, paras. 261–262, 272–276, 284, 292.

[177] For example, the indictment in *Popović* charges four different manifestations of genocide in the paragraphs organised under Count 1: killing, causing serious bodily harm, causing serious mental harm, and imposing fatal conditions. It also charges five different manifestations of crimes against humanity – extermination, murder, persecution (in various forms), deportation, and forcible transfer as an inhumane act – but each of these has its own separate count. See *Popović et al.* Indictment, *supra* note 156, paras. 26, 33, 45–46, 48–49, 84. Similarly, the indictment in *Simba* charged three different manifestations of genocide – killing, causing serious bodily harm, and causing serious mental harm – under the same count, while charging two different manifestations of crimes against humanity – extermination and murder – under two separate counts. See *Prosecutor* v. *Simba*, Case No. ICTR-2001-76-I, Amended Indictment, 10 May 2004, pp. 2, 11, 12. Of course, the (very often confusing) manner in which the prosecution chooses to organise its charging instrument is not binding on trial chambers. As acknowledged by the very Trial Chamber in *Popović*, chambers must instead look beneath the counts to the substance of the charges in the indictment to determine how many crimes have actually been charged and in respect of what conduct. *Prosecutor* v. *Popović, Beara, Nikolić, Borovčanin, Tolimir, Miletić, Gvero, Pandurević, and Trbić*, Case No. IT-05-88-PT, Decision on Further Amendments and Challenges to the Indictment, 13 July 2006 para. 11 n. 26; accord *Prosecutor* v. *Haradinaj, Balaj, and Brahimaj*, Case No. IT-04-84-PT, Decision on Motion to Amend the Indictment and Challenges to the Form of the Amended Indictment, 25 October 2006, para. 13. The *Popović* Trial Chamber should thus consider four different crimes to be charged pursuant to Article 4(2), notwithstanding their grouping together under Count 1: killing as genocide in Article 4(2)(a), causing serious bodily harm as genocide in Article 4(2)(b), causing serious mental harm as genocide in Article 4(2)(b), and imposing fatal conditions as genocide in Article 4(2)(c).

genocide is best understood as constituting a category of six different offences, instead of a single crime.[178] Killing as genocide in Article 4/2(2)(a), causing serious bodily harm as genocide in Article 4/2(2)(b), causing serious mental harm as genocide in Article 4/2(2)(b), imposing fatal conditions as genocide in Article 4/2 (2)(c), imposing measures intended to prevent births as genocide in Article 4/2(2) (d), and forcibly transferring children as genocide in Article 4/2(2)(e) are distinct crimes, just as murder as a crime against humanity and torture as a crime against humanity are distinct crimes. As such, where a trial chamber finds that all the elements of two of these crimes have been fulfilled in respect of the same conduct, it should apply the *Čelebići* test to determine whether it is permissible to convict the accused of both.

Since Article 4/2(2) does not contain a complex underlying offence with its own specific requirements analogous to persecution as a crime against humanity, a trial chamber applying the *Čelebići* test would simply compare the elements of the respective underlying offences of any two manifestations of genocide, and ascertain whether each contains a materially distinct element. The least complicated example is killing versus causing serious bodily harm. Killing requires the victim's death;[179] causing serious bodily harm requires serious harm to the organs, senses, or physical health of the victim.[180] Killing has a materially distinct element – death – but causing serious bodily harm does not have a materially distinct element; causing a person's death necessarily entails serious harm to his or her organs, senses, or physical health. Thus, under *Čelebići*, killing subsumes causing serious bodily harm and the trial chamber may only convict the accused of the former where both are found to have been committed in respect of the same conduct and the same victims. Unfortunately, not all analyses of intra-Article 4/2(2) cumulative convictions will be this clear-cut: as explained in Chapter 3,[181] the jurisprudence has yet to develop a coherent set of elements for most of the underlying offences in Article 4/2(2).

Several chambers – all in the ICTR[182] – have had occasion to discuss one or more of the inchoate crimes in Article 4/2(3).[183] Most of these have convicted the accused

[178] See Chapter 3, text accompanying notes 94–98, 208.

[179] See *Blagojević and Jokić* Trial Judgement,*supra* note 72, para. 642; Chapter 3, text accompanying note 216.

[180] See *Kayishema and Ruzindana* Trial Judgement, *supra* note 3, para. 109; Chapter 3, text accompanying note 228.

[181] See Chapter 3, text accompanying notes 245, 269, 271.

[182] Before August 2006, the ICTY Prosecution had only charged an inchoate crime in one case; this case is still at trial. See *Popović et al.* Indictment, *supra* note 156, paras. 34–44. Two accused were severed from this case before trial proceedings began, and their individual indictments also charge conspiracy to commit genocide. See *Prosecutor* v. *Trbić*, Case No. IT-05-88/1-PT, Indictment, 18 August 2006, paras. 25–29; *Prosecutor* v. *Tolimir*, Case No. IT-05-88/2-PT, Indictment, 28 August 2006, paras. 25–29. Trbić's case was subsequently referred to the State Court of Bosnia and Herzegovina pursuant to Rule 11*bis* of the ICTY Rules of Procedure and Evidence. See *Prosecutor* v. *Trbić*, Case No. IT-05-88/1-PT, Decision on Referral of Case Under Rule 11 *bis*, 27 April 2007 ('*Trbić* Referral Decision'). Tolimir is still in pre-trial proceedings.

[183] The judgements in which the crime was discussed but the accused found not guilty are the following: *Prosecutor* v. *Seromba*, Case No. ICTR-2001-66-T, Judgement, 13 December 2006, paras. 344–351 (conspiracy); *Kajelijeli* Trial Judgement, *supra* note 176, paras. 785–798 (conspiracy); *Ntakirutimana and*

of conspiracy to commit genocide, direct and public incitement to commit genocide, or both.[184] Yet only two chambers have squarely addressed the second type of intra-Article 4/2 cumulative convictions mentioned above – that is, convictions for a manifestation of genocide and an inchoate crime, or for two different inchoate crimes, in respect of the same conduct. These chambers arrived at different conclusions.[185]

The first was the January 2000 *Musema* Trial Judgement, which predated the ICTR Appeals Chamber's adoption of the *Čelebići* test by nearly two years.[186] Addressing possible cumulative convictions for genocide and conspiracy to commit genocide, the Trial Chamber asserted – without any citation to authority – that in civil law systems 'an accused can only be convicted of conspiracy if the substantive offence has not been realized or if the [a]ccused was part of a conspiracy which has been perpetrated by his co-conspirators, without his direct participation'.[187] The Chamber then declared that, in common-law systems, 'an accused can, in principle, be convicted of both conspiracy and a substantive offence … However, this position has incurred much criticism.'[188] The Trial Chamber opted for what it considered the result most favourable to Musema, stating in *dicta* that:

Ntakirutimana Trial Judgement, *supra* note 10, paras. 800–801, 838–841 (conspiracy); *Prosecutor* v. *Musema*, Case No. ICTR-96-13-T, Judgement and Sentence, 27 January 2000 ('*Musema* Trial Judgement'), paras. 184–198 (conspiracy).

184 The judgements in which the crime was discussed and the accused found guilty are the following: *Prosecutor* v. *Serugendo*, Case No. ICTR-2005-84-T, Judgement and Sentence, 12 June 2006, paras. 9, 20–30 (incitement, guilty plea); *Prosecutor* v. *Muvunyi*, Case No. ICTR-00-55A-T, Judgement, 11 September 2006 ('*Muvunyi* Trial Judgement'), paras. 500–510 (incitement); *Media* Trial Judgement, *supra* note 10, paras. 978–1039 (incitement); *ibid.*, paras. 1040–1055 (conspiracy); *Kajelijeli* Trial Judgement, *supra* note 176, paras. 848–861 (incitement) ; *Niyitegeka* Trial Judgement, *supra* note 176, paras. 422–429 (conspiracy); *ibid.*, paras. 430–437 (incitement); *Prosecutor* v. *Ruggiu*, Case No. ICTR-97-32-T, Judgement and Sentence, 1 June 2000, p. 19 (incitement, guilty plea); *Akayesu* Trial Judgement, *supra* note 17, paras. 549–562, 672–675 (incitement); *Prosecutor* v. *Kambanda*, Case No. ICTR-97-23-S, Judgement and Sentence, 4 September 1998 ('*Kambanda* Sentencing Judgement'), para. 40 (conspiracy, guilty plea). The Appeals Chamber in the *Media* case acquitted one of the accused, Jean-Bosco Barayagwiza, of direct and public incitement to commit genocide. It also acquitted Hassan Ngeze of some incidents of instigation, but upheld his conviction for others. All three accused, including Ferdinand Nahimana, were acquitted of conspiracy. See *Media* Appeal Judgement, *supra* note 62, paras. 857, 862, 883, 886, 892, 912. As noted in Chapter 3, attempt to commit genocide in Article 4/2(d) has never been examined by any chamber in either Tribunal. See Chapter 3, text accompanying note 321.

185 The Trial Chamber in the September 1998 *Kambanda* Judgement – which predated the *Akayesu* Trial Judgement by a month and the *Musema* Appeals Chamber's adoption of the *Čelebići* test by three years – appears simply to have ignored the issue. Jean Kambanda, Prime Minister of the Interim Government of Rwanda from April to July 1994, pleaded guilty to a number of crimes, including several manifestations of genocide (killing, causing serious bodily harm, and causing serious mental harm), conspiracy to commit genocide, and direct and public incitement to commit genocide, in respect of the same incidents and victims. *Kambanda* Sentencing Judgement, *supra* note 184, para. 40. The Trial Chamber accepted the guilty plea and convicted Kambanda of these crimes without any analysis as to the permissibility of cumulative convictions. *Ibid.*, pp. 24–25. Cumulative convictions were apparently not raised on appeal. See generally *Prosecutor* v. *Kambanda*, Case No. ICTR-97-23-A, Judgement, 19 October 2000. In the judgements cited in note 183 *supra*, the accused were found not guilty of conspiracy to commit genocide; it was thus unnecessary for the trial chamber to address the issue of cumulative convictions where an inchoate crime is involved, although none of these chambers acknowledged this fact.

186 See *Musema* Appeal Judgement, *supra* note 8, para. 363 (adopting the *Čelebići* test for the ICTR).

187 *Musema* Trial Judgement, *supra* note 183, para. 196.

188 *Ibid.*, para. 197 (citing commentary in a single Canadian treatise).

an accused cannot be convicted of both genocide and conspiracy to commit genocide on the basis of the same acts. Such a definition is in keeping with the intention of the Genocide Convention. Indeed, the '*Travaux Préparatoires*' show that the crime of conspiracy was included to punish acts which, in and of themselves, did not constitute genocide. The converse implication of this is that no purpose would be served in convicting an accused, who has already been found guilty of genocide, for conspiracy to commit genocide, on the basis of the same acts.[189]

The Chamber acquitted Musema of conspiracy to commit genocide, not because such a conviction would have been impermissibly cumulative with his conviction for genocide, but because the prosecution had failed adequately to allege conspiratorial conduct on the part of Musema.[190] The prosecution did not appeal this acquittal or the Trial Chamber's conceptualisation of the relationship between genocide and conspiracy to commit genocide, and neither issue was addressed on appeal.[191]

The second judgement to address cumulative convictions where an inchoate crime is concerned was the December 2003 *Media* Trial Judgement. Without acknowledging the *Musema* precedent, the Chamber provided the following sparse and perplexing rationale and holding:

[P]lanning is an act of commission of genocide, pursuant to Article 6(1) of the Statute. The offence of conspiracy requires the existence of an agreement, which is the defining element of the crime of conspiracy. Accordingly, the Chamber considers that the [a]ccused can be held criminally responsible for both the act of conspiracy and the substantive offence of genocide that is the object of the conspiracy.[192]

Although the *Media* Trial Chamber also dealt with direct and public incitement to commit genocide at length, it did not opine specifically on whether a chamber could permissibly convict an accused for incitement and genocide, or incitement and conspiracy, but merely invoked *Čelebići* and concluded as follows:

In this case, the three Accused are guilty of conspiracy to commit genocide, genocide, direct and public incitement to commit genocide and crimes against humanity (persecution and extermination). As these offences comprise materially distinct elements, discussed above in this chapter, convictions on these counts will be entered against the three Accused.[193]

On appeal, the three accused challenged their cumulative convictions for killing as genocide and direct and public incitement to commit genocide; they also challenged their cumulative convictions for killing as genocide and conspiracy to commit genocide. Noting that it had vacated several convictions in another part of the

[189] *Ibid.*, para. 198 (not citing the portion of the Convention *travaux* referred to). [190] *Ibid.*, para. 940.

[191] See *Musema* Appeal Judgement, *supra* note 8, paras. 358–369 (addressing cumulative convictions, but not for genocide and conspiracy to commit genocide).

[192] *Media* Trial Judgement, *supra* note 10, para. 1043.

[193] *Ibid.*, para. 1090. See also *ibid.*, paras. 954–977A, 1016–1039, 1049–1055, 1092–1094 (describing the conduct of the three accused).

judgement, the ICTR Appeals Chamber declined to address these challenges, as no accused now stood cumulatively convicted of a genocide-related inchoate crime in Article 4(3) of the ICTR Statute and genocide through one of the underlying offences in Article 4(2).[194] The Appeals Chamber expressed no view on the *Media* Trial Chamber's legal conclusion with respect to the permissibility of intra Article 4/2(3) cumulative convictions.

Nevertheless, the *Media* Trial Chamber's conclusion would appear to be correct under *Čelebići*, notwithstanding the unfortunate reasoning. Conspiracy to commit genocide requires proof of an agreement, an element not required for any of the manifestations of genocide in Article 4/2(2).[195] Similarly, direct and public incitement to commit genocide requires public prompting or provocation, an element not present in the definition of conspiracy or any of the Article 4/2(2) manifestations.[196] By contrast, unlike conspiracy or incitement, all of the manifestations in Article 4/2 (2) require the actual occurrence of an act or omission amounting to genocide; for killing as genocide, for example, the physical perpetrator must have engaged in conduct resulting in the victim's death.[197] Cumulative convictions for conspiracy and incitement, conspiracy and one of the Article 4/2(2) manifestations, or incitement and one of the Article 4/2(2) manifestations should therefore be permissible.[198]

5.2.5 Effect of trial chamber error in failing to convict cumulatively when cumulative convictions are available

As noted above, the practical effect of *Čelebići* and its progeny is that trial chambers are compelled to enter cumulative convictions whenever they are available – that is, when two or more crimes have been properly charged in the indictment in respect of the same conduct, proved at trial, and each has a materially distinct element.[199] The

[194] See *Media* Appeal Judgement, *supra* note 62, paras. 1022–1023; see also *ibid.*, Section XVIII (disposition showing the convictions that remained as a result of the Appeal Judgement).

[195] See *Ntakirutimana and Ntakirutimana* Trial Judgement, *supra* note 10, para. 798; *Niyitegeka* Trial Judgement, *supra* note 176, para. 423.

[196] See *Muvunyi* Trial Judgement, *supra* note 184, para. 500; *Akayesu* Trial Judgement, *supra* note 17, para. 559.

[197] See *Blagojević and Jokić* Trial Judgement, *supra* note 72, para. 642; Chapter 3, text accompanying note 216.

[198] With respect to conspiracy, this conclusion accords with the general rule laid down by the US Supreme Court in *Ianelli* v. *United States*, although the latter was reached through reasoning similar to that in Judge Shahabuddeen's 'gist or gravamen' approach. The Supreme Court held that, because 'conspiracy poses distinct dangers quite apart from those of the substantive offense' – that is, the greater likelihood of success that comes from concerted action and the lesser likelihood that the individuals involved will abandon the path of criminality – 'the conspiracy to commit an offense and the subsequent commission of that crime normally do not merge into a single punishable act'. *Ianelli* v. *United States*, 420 U.S. 770, 777 (1975). They do merge, however, where the completed offence necessarily requires the participation and cooperation of two or more persons, absent clear legislative intent to the contrary. See *ibid.*, pp. 782–786 (discussing 'Wharton's rule'). It should also be noted that, as attempt to commit genocide in Article 4/2(3)(d) has never been charged in the *ad hoc* Tribunals and no chamber has proffered a set of elements for that inchoate crime, it is not possible to compare them to those of conspiracy, incitement, or the manifestations in Article 4/2(2) to determine whether each has a materially distinct element.

[199] See *supra* text accompanying notes 64, 159.

Stakić Appeals Chamber accordingly held that the Trial Chamber's purported exercise of discretion 'to convict only in relation to the crime that most closely and most comprehensively reflects the totality of the accused's criminal conduct'[200] was an error of law:

> When the evidence supports convictions under multiple counts for the same underlying acts, the test as set forth in *Čelebići* and *Kordić* does not permit the Trial Chamber discretion to enter one or more of the appropriate convictions, unless the two crimes do not possess materially distinct elements.[201]

When overturning trial chambers for failing to cumulatively convict where cumulative convictions are available, the Appeals Chamber has tended to enter the missing convictions itself.[202] Curiously, however, the *Stakić* Appeals Chamber expressly declined to enter new convictions,[203] even though it 'resolved' that the Trial Chamber had erred in failing to enter convictions for a number of crimes against humanity.[204] In so doing, *Stakić* followed the precedent of the *Krstić* Appeals Chamber, which also found error in the Trial Chamber's failure to cumulatively convict but declined to register the additional conviction.[205] Recalling the Appeals Chamber's authority to enter new convictions pursuant to Article 25 of the ICTY Statute,[206] Judges Vaz and Meron recorded their understanding that the approach in *Stakić* 'should not be read to suggest that the Appeals Chamber lacks

[200] *Stakić* Trial Judgement, *supra* note 108, para. 236.
[201] *Stakić* Appeal Judgement, *supra* note 60, para. 358.
[202] See, e.g., *Naletilić and Martinović* Appeal Judgement, *supra* note 10, para. 591, p. 211; *Rutaganda* Appeal Judgement, *supra* note 62, para. 584, p. 168; *Krnojelac* Appeal Judgement, *supra* note 60, para. 188, p. 113 ('Allows the Prosecution's third ground of appeal and reverses Krnojelac's acquittal on counts 2 and 4 of the Indictment (torture as a crime against humanity and a violation of the laws or customs of war)[.]'); *Kupreškić et al.* Appeal Judgement, *supra* note 10, para. 388, p. 176. The *Cyangugu*, *Semanza*, *Kordić and Čerkez*, *Ntakirutimana and Ntakirutimana*, *Vasiljević*, *Jelisić*, and *Čelebići* Appeals Chambers all addressed accused's appeals against cumulative convictions entered by the trial chamber, not prosecution appeals against a trial chamber's refusal to enter cumulative convictions. The Appeals Chamber has entered new convictions against an accused on a number of occasions in other scenarios. See *Semanza* Appeal Judgement, *supra* note 9, Separate Opinion of Judge Shahabuddeen and Judge Güney, paras. 5–9 (voicing approval for the Appeals Chamber's power to enter new convictions, and discussing a few instances in which it has done so). But see *ibid.*, Dissenting Opinion of Judge Pocar, paras. 1–4 (disapproving because 'such an approach is in violation of an accused's fundamental right to an appeal as enshrined in Article 14(5) of the International Covenant on Civil and Political Rights … given that the Appeals Chamber is the court of last resort in this Tribunal'; and noting two alternative options: (1) remand to the trial chamber; and (2) mere pronouncement by the Appeals Chamber that the trial chamber erred, without entering a new conviction or remanding, as was done by the *Krstić* Appeals Chamber). *Krstić* is mentioned at note 205, *infra*.
[203] *Stakić* Appeal Judgement, *supra* note 60, pp. 141–142.
[204] *Ibid.*, paras. 359–364, pp. 141–142 (using 'resolve' language in the disposition).
[205] *Krstić* Appeal Judgement, *supra* note 44, paras. 227, 229, p. 88 ('Resolves that the Trial Chamber incorrectly disallowed Radislav Krstić's convictions as a participant in extermination and persecution (Counts 3 and 6) committed between 13 and 19 July 1995').
[206] Statute of the International Criminal Tribunal for the Prosecution of Persons Responsible for Serious Violations of International Humanitarian Law Committed in the Territory of the former Yugoslavia since 1991, 32 ILM 1159 (1993), *as amended* by Security Council Resolution 1660 of 28 February 2006, Art. 25(2) ('The Appeals Chamber may affirm, reverse or revise the decisions taken by the Trial Chambers.'); accord Statute of the International Criminal Tribunal for Rwanda, (1994) 33 ILM 1602, *as amended by* Security Council Resolution 1534 of 26 March 2004, Art. 24(2) (same).

the power to enter a new conviction'.[207] Judge Shahabuddeen – who had also criticised the Chamber's failure to enter a new conviction in *Krstić* [208] – concurred with Judges Vaz and Meron, stating ironically: 'I do not read the [non-entry of new convictions in this case] as suggesting that the Appeals Chamber does not have the power to make such convictions. In my view, the Appeals Chamber *has merely declined to exercise its discretion* to exercise the power in this case.'[209]

5.3 Sentencing

In *Čelebići*, the Appeals Chamber stated:

> Public confidence in the integrity of the administration of criminal justice (whether international or domestic) is a matter of abiding importance to the survival of the institutions which are responsible for that administration. One of the fundamental elements in any rational and fair system of criminal justice is consistency in punishment.[210]

While the *ad hoc* Tribunals have managed over time to deliver some limited degree of consistency in their sentencing practice and in the individual sentences imposed on the convicted,[211] at the same time they have never really resolved some

207 *Stakić* Appeal Judgement, *supra* note 60, Joint Separate Opinion of Judges Vaz and Meron, p. 171.

208 *Krstić* Appeal Judgement, *supra* note 44, Partial Dissenting Opinion of Judge Shahabuddeen, paras. 77–78.

209 *Stakić* Appeal Judgement, *supra* note 60, Partially Dissenting Opinion of Judge Shahabuddeen, para. 1 (emphasis added). See also *ibid.*, Opinion dissidente du Juge Güney sur le cumul de déclarations de culpabilité, para. 6 n. 7:

> Les considérations de la majorité des juges de la Chambre d'appel sur la question du cumul de déclarations de culpabilité en vertu de l'article 5 du Statut pour persécutions et autres crimes à raison des mêmes faits n'ayant finalement pas entraîné l'introduction de nouvelles condamnations en appel – aussi curieux que cela puisse me paraître –, j'ai pu rejoindre les autres juges de la Chambre d'appel pour ce qui est la détermination de la peine.

210 *Čelebići* Appeal Judgement, *supra* note 7, para. 756. The purpose of this section is to analyse specific concerns relating to sentencing practice in the international and internationalised criminal courts and tribunals, and particularly the *ad hoc* Tribunals. There is a significant array of issues relating to sentencing in international criminal law, a full account of which is outside of the ambit of our analysis. For a more exhaustive account of some of these, see, e.g., Mark B. Harmon and Fergal Gaynor, 'Ordinary Sentences for Extraordinary Crimes', (2007) 5 *Journal of International Criminal Justice* 683; Robert D. Sloane, 'Sentencing for the "Crime of Crimes": The Evolving "Common Law" of Sentencing of the International Criminal Tribunal for Rwanda', (2007) 5 *Journal of International Criminal Justice* 713; Ralph Henham, 'Developing Contextualized Rationales for Sentencing in International Criminal Trials', (2007) 5 *Journal of International Criminal Justice* 757; Fergal Gaynor and Barbara Goy, 'Current Developments at the Ad Hoc International Criminal Tribunals', (2007) 5 *Journal of International Criminal Justice* 544; Nancy Amoury Combs, 'Procuring Guilty Pleas for International Crimes: The Limited Influence of Sentence Discounts', (2006) 59 *Vanderbilt Law Review* 69; Mark A. Drumbl, 'Collective Violence and Individual Punishment: The Criminality of Mass Atrocity', (2005) *Northwestern University Law Review* 539; Andrea Carcano, 'Sentencing and the Gravity of the Offence in International Criminal Law', (2002) 51 *International Criminal Law Quarterly* 583; Allison Marston Danner, 'Constructing a Hierarchy of Crimes in International Criminal Law Sentencing', (2001) 87 *Virginia Law Review* 415.

211 See James Meernik, 'Victor's Justice and the Law', (2003) 47 *Journal of Conflict Resolution* 140, 143; James Meernik and Kimi King, 'The Sentencing Determinants of the International Criminal Tribunal for the Former Yugoslavia: An Empirical and Doctrinal Analysis', (2003) 16 *Leiden Journal of International Law* 717, 718. The ICTR has undoubtedly handed down consistently higher sentences for those it has convicted, as well as relatively consistent sentences across the range of those convicted for genocide. See Sloane, *supra* note 210, pp. 716–719.

of the crucial issues relating to consistency in sentences meted out under their *sui generis* jurisdiction.[212] No real sentencing scales or guidelines exist;[213] sentences and the bases upon which they are justified vary widely, a consequence of the broad discretion purportedly given to trial chambers in determining sentences;[214] and, fundamentally, no real attempt has been made to determine and reason whether a crime committed in the context of an armed conflict is worth a sentence commensurate with the same or similar crime in an ordinary domestic context.[215] Indeed, one of the hallmarks of the ICTY's sentencing practice – at least until very recently – has been the remarkable levity of the sentences handed down to individuals found to have played a role in mass atrocities;[216] many of these persons end up spending far

[212] See, e.g., Mary M. Penrose, 'Lest We Fail: The Importance of Enforcement in International Criminal Law', (2000) 15 *American University Law* Review 321, 334; Scott T. Johnson, 'On the Road to Disaster: The Rights of the Accused and the International Criminal Tribunal for the Former Yugoslavia', (1998) 10 *International Legal Perspectives* 111, 115.

[213] See Robert Cryer, Håkan Friman, Darryl Robinson, and Elizabeth Wilmshurst, *International Criminal Law and Procedure* (2007), p. 396; Adrian Hoel, 'The Sentencing Provisions of the International Criminal Court: Common Law, Civil Law, or Both?', (2007) 33 *Monash University Law Review* 264.

[214] See *Galić* Appeal Judgement, *supra* note 10, Separate and Partially Dissenting Opinion of Judge Meron, para. 11 & nn. 22–24.

[215] Chambers have, as Article 24(1) of the ICTY Statute requires, persistently referred to the applicable sentencing provisions in the former Yugoslavian Criminal Code, although only as 'indicative and not binding', or even highly persuasive. *Prosecutor* v. *Blaškić*, Case No. IT-95-14-T, Judgement, 3 March 2000 ('*Blaškić* Trial Judgement'), para. 75. See also Statute of the International Criminal Tribunal for the Prosecution of Persons Responsible for Serious Violations of International Humanitarian Law Committed in the Territory of the former Yugoslavia since 1991, 32 ILM 1159 (1993), as amended by Security Council Resolution 1660 of 28 February 2006, Art. 24(1) ('The penalty imposed by the Trial Chamber shall be limited to imprisonment. In determining the terms of imprisonment, the Trial Chambers shall have recourse to the general practice regarding prison sentences in the courts of the former Yugoslavia'); *Blaškić* Appeal Judgement, *supra* note 73, paras 681–682; *Čelebići* Appeal Judgement, *supra* note 7, paras 813, 816; *Kunarac et al.* Appeal Judgement, *supra* note 38, para. 377; *Jelisić* Appeal Judgement, *supra* note 56, paras 116–117; *Čelebići* Trial Judgement, *supra* note 72, para. 1192. The ICTR and SCSL have analogous rules. See Rules of Procedure and Evidence of the International Criminal Tribunal for Rwanda, UN Doc. ITR/3/Rev.15 (10 November 2006), Rule 101(b)(iii) ('In determining the sentence, the Trial Chamber shall take into account the factors mentioned in Article 23(2) of the Statute, as well as such factors as … [t]he general practice regarding prison sentences in the courts of Rwanda[.]'); Statute of the Special Court for Sierra Leone, 2178 UNTS 138, UN Doc. S/2002/246, Appendix II, Art. 19 ('In determining the terms of imprisonment, the Trial Chamber shall, as appropriate, have recourse to the practice regarding prison sentences in the International Criminal Tribunal for Rwanda and the national courts of Sierra Leone.'). See also William A. Schabas, *The UN International Criminal Tribunals: The Former Yugoslavia, Rwanda, and Sierra Leone* (2006) , pp. 552–554; Meernik and King, *supra* note 211, pp. 726–727.

[216] See, e.g., *Aleksovski* Appeal Judgement, *supra* note 24, para. 191 (increasing the Trial Chamber's two-year sentence of prison warden for outrages upon personal dignity as a violation of the laws or customs of war to seven years); *Prosecutor* v. *Furundžija*, Case No. IT-95-17/1-A, Judgement, 21 July 2000 ('*Furundžija* Appeal Judgement'), p. 83 (confirming the Trial Chamber's sentence of paramilitary leader to ten years for co-perpetrating torture and aiding and abetting rape); *Kvočka et al.* Appeal Judgement, *supra* note 97, paras. 684, 725 (confirming sentence of five years for accused Prcać and Kvočka for various crimes committed in the Omarska prison camp); *Prosecutor* v. *Orić*, Case No. IT-03-68-T, Judgement, 30 June 2006, paras. 782–783 (imposing sentence of two years on Bosnian Muslim army commander for failing to discharge duty as a superior to prevent the murder of five Serb prisoners and cruel treatment of ten others, both as violations of the laws or customs of war); *Prosecutor* v. *Hadžihasanović and Kubura*, Case No. IT-01-47-T, Judgement, 15 March 2006, p. 640 (sentencing Kubura, a senior Bosnian Muslim army commander, to two and a half years for failing to prevent or punish plunder committed by troops under his command). For a list of ICTY convicted persons who have already served their sentences, see International Criminal Tribunal for the former Yugoslavia, 'Indictees Booklet: Individuals Publicly Indicted since the Inception of ICTY', 13 December 2005, pp. 16–17 (listing seventeen persons, including Aleksovski, Furundžija, Kvočka, and Prcać).

less time in prison than someone who rapes or murders one victim in domestic jurisdictions such as the United States or Australia. Many ICTY convicts have already served their sentences and have been released.[217]

There is considerable literature on the inconsistency between the gravity of international crimes and the comparatively light weight of sentences,[218] and a general dissatisfaction among scholars, also reflecting the views of victims, with the efforts of the *ad hoc* Tribunals to rationalise sentencing practices.[219] This point is well summarised by Guénaël Mettraux:

> [I]t is ... premature to speak of an emerging 'penal regime' and the coherence in sentencing practice that this denotes. The degree of pre-visibility of sentences handed down by both *ad hoc* tribunals is indeed still at a very low level and many of their sentences appear to be coloured as much by the national sentencing practices of the judges sitting on any particular bench as by any rules and principles specific to international criminal tribunals.[220]

These are not new concerns in international criminal law. The post-Second World War tribunals suffered from problems of incoherency, relative inconsistency, and allegations of injustice.[221] The International Criminal Court (ICC), without any detailed sentencing guidelines, will also likely be subject to the same concerns and the target of similar criticism.[222]

With this broad overview in mind, we will consider in this section some specific areas of sentencing practice within the *ad hoc* Tribunals: the lack of a coherent sentencing practice; the explicit rejection by the Tribunals of a hierarchy of crimes in

[217] See *Galić* Appeal Judgement, *supra* note 10, Separate and Partially Dissenting Opinion of Judge Meron, para. 9, nn. 22–24 (detailed account of sentences at the ICTY and some account of the ICTR). See also Harmon and Gaynor, *supra* note 210, pp. 686–687 (discussing the comparatively light sentences handed down by ICTY chambers in comparison to some notorious domestic murder cases in the United States and the United Kingdom).

[218] See, e.g., Meernik and King, *supra* note 211, p. 726; Cryer, Friman, Robinson, and Wilmshurst, *supra* note 213, pp. 397–399; Schabas, *supra* note 215, pp. 554–561; Christoph Safferling, *Towards an International Criminal Procedure* (2001), pp. 314–318.

[219] See, e.g., John R. W. D. Jones and Steven Powles, *International Criminal Practice* (3d edn 2003), pp. 778–780. See also the discussion in the sources in note 210, *supra*.

[220] Guénaël Mettraux, *International Crimes and the Ad Hoc Tribunals* (2005), p. 356. See also Stuart Beresford, 'Unshackling the Paper Tiger: The Sentencing Practices of the Ad Hoc International Criminal Tribunals for the Former Yugoslavia and Rwanda', (2001) 1 *International Criminal Law Review* 33, 38; Andrew N. Keller, 'Punishments for Violation of International Criminal Law: An Analysis of Sentencing of the ICTY and ICTR', (2001) 12 *Indiana International and Comparative Law Review* 53, 65.

[221] See Hoel, *supra* note 213, pp. 1–9; Evan J. Wallach, 'The Procedural and Evidentiary Rules of the Post-World War II War Crimes Trials: Did They Provide an Outline for International Legal Procedure?', (1998) 37 *Columbia Journal of Transnational Law* 851, 867; Telford Taylor, *Final Report to the Secretary of the Army on The Nuremberg War Crimes Trials Under Control Council Order No. 10* (1949), pp. 90–93, 107; Airey Neave, *Nuremberg: A Personal Record of the Trial of the Major Nazi War Criminals in 1945–6* (1978), pp. 388–96; B.V. A. Röling, *The Tokyo Trial and Beyond: Reflections of a Peacemonger* (1993), p. 112.

[222] See generally Hoel, *supra* note 213; see also William A. Schabas, *An Introduction to the International Criminal Court* (2d edn 2004), pp. 162–166; Claus Kress and Göran Sluiter, 'Imprisonment', in Antonio Cassese, Paulo Gaeta, and John R.W. D. Jones (eds.), *The Rome Statute of the International Criminal Court: A Commentary* (2002), vol. I, pp. 1757, 1762–1764.

sentence determination; and the (now well-noted) interference by the Appeals Chamber in the discretion of trial chambers' sentence determination.

5.3.1 No coherent sentencing practice

The *ad hoc* Tribunals have had a different experience in the sentencing of convicted persons in their jurisdictions. While the ICTY has had a patchwork of sentences that – overall – reflect a profoundly lenient approach to sentencing in respect of crimes under its jurisdiction, the ICTR, at least in respect of its genocide convictions, has been more consistently harsh in its approach.[223] Robert Sloane notes that, of the twenty-seven persons convicted and sentenced by the ICTR as at April 2007, '12 had been sentenced to life imprisonment; two to a term of 35 years; five to 25 years; two to 15 years; two to 6 years; and the others to terms of 7, 10, 12, 27 and 45 years, respectively'.[224] That is, over 44 per cent of those sentenced received life imprisonment; 70 per cent were sentenced to twenty-five years or more; and over 77 per cent to fifteen years or more. By contrast, as of November 2006, the ICTY had sentenced fifteen convicted persons to less than ten years;[225] nineteen to sentences of between ten and nineteen years;[226] and twelve to sentences of twenty years or greater.[227]

The wide divergence in ICTY sentences highlights one of the greatest concerns in its sentencing practice. Judge Meron explains that this divergence occurs 'partly in consequence of the ICTY's emphasis on individualized sentencing'.[228] While chambers have invariably referred to similar sentences given for similar categories of offenders and crimes, the broad discretion apparently ascribed to trial chambers has led to significant discrepancies in sentencing. For example, while the majority of the Appeals Chamber agreed that Stanislav Galić's involvement in the siege of Sarajevo merited revising the Trial Chamber's sentence of twenty years up to a life sentence, Milomir Stakić had his life sentence reduced by the Appeals Chamber to forty years for his involvement in an extermination campaign that killed approximately 1,500 people in the Prijedor municipality of Bosnia.[229] Momir Nikolić's role in the crime against humanity of the murder, as a form of persecution, of thousands of Bosnian Muslims and the cruel treatment of others earned him a twenty-year sentence.[230] Dragan Nikolić received twenty years for persecutions as crimes

[223] See, for example, the life sentences imposed for genocide in *Kambanda* Sentencing Judgement, *supra* note 184; *Musema* Trial Judgement, *supra* note 183; *Niyitegeka* Trial Judgement, *supra* note 176. See also generally, Sloane, *supra* note 210.

[224] Sloane, *supra* note 210, p. 716.

[225] *Galić* Appeal Judgement, *supra* note 10, Separate and Partially Dissenting Opinion of Judge Meron, para. 9 n. 22.

[226] *Ibid.*, para. 9 n. 23. [227] *Ibid.*, para. 9 n. 24. [228] *Ibid.*, para. 9.

[229] *Stakić* Appeal Judgement, *supra* note 60, para. 375.

[230] *Prosecutor* v. *Momir Nikolić*, Case No. IT-02-60/1-A, Judgement on Sentencing Appeal, 8 March 2006 ('*Momir Nikolić* Judgement on Sentencing Appeal'), paras. 2–3, p. 51.

against humanity, including murder, rape, and torture.[231] While Momčilo Krajišnik received a twenty-seven-year sentence for his leadership in a widespread campaign of ethnic cleansing in Bosnia,[232] Biljana Plavšić received a sentence of just eleven years after pleading guilty to a vast array of crimes against humanity involving the same events, which even the Trial Chamber described as 'of utmost gravity … illustrated by: the massive scope and extent of the persecutions; [and] the numbers killed, deported and forcibly expelled'.[233] On the other hand, Drazen Erdemović received a mere five-year sentence for executing, with his own hand, up to 100 Bosnian Muslims during the Srebrenica massacre.[234]

In his opinion partially dissenting from the November 2006 *Galić* Appeal Judgement, Judge Meron criticised the majority for increasing Galić's sentence to life imprisonment, which it justified on the basis that a 'sentence of only 20 years was so unreasonable and plainly unjust, that it underestimated the gravity of Galić's criminal conduct'.[235] The *Galić* majority held that the Trial Chamber had 'committed an error in finding that the sentence imposed adequately reflects the level of gravity of the crimes committed by Galić and his degree of participation'.[236] Judge Meron's dissent is important for two reasons: it raises the particularly vexatious issue of inappropriate appellate interference with a Trial Chamber's discretion,[237] and it highlights the broad divergence in sentences imposed by the *ad hoc* Tribunals. In Judge Meron's view, to satisfy the test for interference with the trial chamber's discretion – that a 'discernible error' has occurred[238] – the Appeals Chamber would have to find one of two conditions met: (1) the sentence would have to be clearly out of proportion with sentences given by the Tribunal in similar situations, or (2) the sentence would have to be otherwise so low that it demonstrably shocked the conscience.[239] Judge Meron considered that neither of these conditions had been met in Galić's case. In coming to that conclusion, he indicated that sentences tended to vary so widely at the Tribunal that it was extremely difficult for an appellate court to be able to conclude that a sentence given in any particular context was outside of a trial chamber's discretion. Indeed, the only example given was the case of a prison

[231] *Prosecutor* v. *Dragan Nikolić*, Case No. IT-02-60/1-A, Judgement on Sentencing Appeal, 4 February 2005 ('*Dragan Nikolić* Judgement on Sentencing Appeal'), paras. 4, 30.
[232] *Krajišnik* Trial Judgement, *supra* note 127, para. 1183..
[233] *Prosecutor* v. *Plavšić*, Case No. IT-00-39 & 40/1-S, Sentencing Judgement, para. 134.
[234] *Prosecutor* v. *Erdemović*, Case No. IT-96-22-T*bis*, Sentencing Judgement, para. 23. It should be noted, however, that duress was accepted as mitigating the sentence given. See *ibid.*, para. 17.
[235] *Galić* Appeal Judgement, *supra* note 10, para. 455. [236] *Ibid.*
[237] See *infra* text accompanying notes 284–301 (discussing the *ad hoc* Appeals Chambers' interference in sentence determination by trial chambers).
[238] *Ibid.*, Separate and Partially Dissenting Opinion of Judge Meron, para. 4 (citing, *inter alia*, *Krstić* Appeal Judgement, *supra* note 44, para. 242; *Naletilić and Martinović* Appeal Judgement, *supra* note 10, para. 593; *Kvočka et al.* Appeal Judgement, *supra* note 97, para. 669; *Kordić and Čerkez* Appeal Judgement, *supra* note 44, para. 1047).
[239] *Ibid.*, para. 6.

warden, Zlatko Aleksovski, whose sentence had been raised from two and a half years to seven years by the Appeals Chamber on the basis that the sentence was so manifestly unreasonable that it shocked the conscience.[240]

Sentences have varied for a range of reasons, including the nature of the particular crimes for which the accused is found responsible, the nature of his participation in these crimes,[241] and whether or not he has entered a plea of guilty.[242] However, if – as the Appeals Chamber has often held – 'the gravity of the offence is the primary consideration when imposing a sentence and is the "litmus test" for determining an appropriate sentence',[243] then the few examples provided above[244] raise the considerable question of whether the ICTY[245] has given sufficient weight in its sentencing practice to the gravity of crimes.[246] This concern receives some focus in the sentencing judgement of Dragan Nikolić, in which the Trial Chamber commissioned a German expert to provide an opinion on the range of sentences and sentencing practices in the former Yugoslavia and other states.[247] Although the expert concluded that, in the states of the former Yugoslavia and others, crimes of this nature would attract the death penalty or life imprisonment, the Trial Chamber accepted that the operation of mitigating factors mandated a lesser sentence of twenty-three years[248] – which was further reduced on appeal to twenty years.[249]

As suggested above with respect to the ICC,[250] one of the profound difficulties faced by all international criminal tribunals is the lack of any sentencing guidelines. In the early *Furundžija* Appeal Judgement, the prosecution requested the Appeals Chamber to create a set of guidelines. Regrettably the Chamber refused, stating that it would be 'inappropriate to establish a definitive list of sentencing guidelines for future reference, when only certain matters relating to sentencing are at issue before it now'.[251] In the subsequent *Čelebići* Appeal Judgement, the Appeals Chamber

[240] See *Aleksovski* Appeal Judgement, *supra* note 24, paras. 175, 183–188.

[241] See Boas, Bischoff, and Reid, *supra* note 7, pp. 406–414.

[242] For a discussion of these issues, see generally Harmon and Gaynor, *supra* note 210; Combs, *supra* note 210; Stephen M. Sayers, 'Defence Perspectives on Sentencing Practice in the International Criminal Tribunal for the Former Yugoslavia', (2003) 16 *Leiden Journal of International Law* 751.

[243] *Momir Nikolić* Judgement on Sentencing Appeal, *supra* note 230, para. 11 (footnote omitted). Accord *Čelebići* Appeal Judgement, *supra* note 7, para. 731; *Krstić* Appeal Judgement, *supra* note 44, para. 267 n. 431; *Kupreškić et al.* Appeal Judgement, *supra* note 10, para. 442. This view has also been adopted in the SCSL. See *Prosecutor* v. *Fofana and Kondewa*, Case No. SCSL-04-14-T, Judgement on the Sentencing of Moinina Fofana and Allieu Kondewa, 9 October 2007, para. 33.

[244] For an exhaustive enumeration of cases and sentences, see *Galić* Appeal Judgement, *supra* note 10, Separate and Partially Dissenting Opinion of Judge Meron, para. 9 nn. 22–24.

[245] As discussed above, the ICTR has done a better job at reflecting the gravity of crimes committed in its sentences, although it has still failed to develop and apply coherent sentencing guidelines. See *supra* text accompanying note 223.

[246] The ICTY Appeals Chamber has referred to retribution as expressing the 'outrage of the international community' at the behaviour in question, and an unwillingness on the part of that community 'to tolerate serious violations of international humanitarian law'. *Aleksovski* Appeal Judgement, *supra* note 24, para. 185.

[247] See *Prosecutor* v. *Dragan Nikolić*, Case No. IT-94-2-S, Sentencing Judgement, 18 December 2003, paras. 166–173.

[248] *Ibid*, para. 214.

[249] *Dragan Nikolić* Judgement on Sentencing Appeal, *supra* note 231, p. 45.

[250] See *supra* text accompanying note 222.

[251] *Furundžija* Appeal Judgement, *supra* note 216, para. 238.

opined that 'often the differences are more significant than the similarities, and the aggravating and mitigating factors dictate different results';[252] later still, in *Blaškić*, it reiterated that it felt it 'inappropriate to set down a definitive list of sentencing guidelines'.[253] The early and repeated failure to establish sentencing guidelines, however broad, is appropriately described by Mark Harmon and Fergal Gaynor as 'a missed opportunity',[254] one which looks set to haunt the international criminal courts and tribunals for some time.

For the reasons set out above, it is impossible to conclude that the *ad hoc* Tribunals, in particular the ICTY, have developed a coherent and consistent policy on sentencing, although the ICTR has clearly done better. A clear message that emerges from an assessment of the ICTY sentencing practice is that the Tribunal has not really attributed sufficient weight to the stated primary factor: the gravity of the offence. Harmon and Gaynor suggest that a proper assessment of gravity in a particular case should engage consideration of three principal elements:

> (i) the abstract gravity of the crime (i.e. a recognition that *any* conviction for genocide, a crime against humanity or a war crime is an inherently serious conviction); (ii) the concrete gravity of the crime (i.e. an assessment of the total quantum of suffering inflicted on, and social and economic harm caused to, direct and indirect victims of the crime, taking into account the number of victims, and the nature and duration of their suffering at the time of the crime, since the crime, and that which they are likely to continue to experience) and (iii) the level of intent and the level of participation of the convicted person in the commission of the crime.[255]

Iain Bonomy, a judge of the ICTY, has observed in an academic article that '[i]n war crimes trials the sentences may be shorter than those imposed in an equivalent domestic context'.[256] One of the great unanswered questions that emerges from a review of the international criminal tribunal jurisprudence is why this should be a characteristic of sentences for massive and widespread crimes committed in armed conflict, when compared with crimes committed in a peacetime domestic context.[257] Is it because the context of war renders less meaningful or more justifiable the harm done, or because the normal constructs of social behaviour accepted in a domestic criminal justice system operating in a state of peace do not apply in war? The implication is that different sentencing practices and comparatively lower

[252] *Čelebići* Appeal Judgement, *supra* note 7, para.719.
[253] *Blaškić* Appeal Judgement, *supra* note 73, para. 680.
[254] See Harmon and Gaynor, *supra* note 210, pp. 710–712. See also *supra* note 213 and sources cited therein.
[255] *Ibid.*, pp. 698–699. See also Danner, *supra* note 210, pp. 462–467.
[256] Iain Bonomy, 'The Reality of Conducting a War Crimes Trial', (2007) 5 *Journal of International Criminal Justice* 348, 351.
[257] Schabas argues that differences between national and international criminal punishment make comparison between the two inappropriate. William A. Schabas, 'Sentencing by International Tribunals: A Human Rights Approach', (1997) 7 *Duke Journal of Comparative and International Law* 461, 477.

sentences are appropriate for crimes committed in armed conflict. It is questionable, when viewed in this context, whether the Tribunals, particularly the ICTY, have in this respect fully served the victims and the broader international community.

5.3.2 No hierarchy of crimes

An issue that reinforces this sense of incoherence in sentencing practice is the refusal by the *ad hoc* Tribunals to acknowledge the existence of a hierarchy of crimes: from the first case before the ICTY, the Appeals Chamber explicitly rejected the Trial Chamber's holding that, all things being equal, a crime against humanity should get a heavier sentence than a war crime.[258] As discussed in Chapter 3, the *ad hoc* chambers, despite early rulings to the contrary,[259] have stated that there is no distinction in seriousness among the different crimes under their jurisdiction,[260] whether comparing crimes against humanity with war crimes,[261] or genocide with other crimes in the *ad hoc* Statutes.[262] The Appeals Chamber has also held that cases cannot be categorised systematically,[263] and that no difference in sentence can accordingly be inferred from the category into which a crime falls; instead, 'the level of gravity in any particular case must be fixed by reference to the circumstances of the case'.[264]

Salvatore Zappalà is critical of the Tribunal's approach to this issue. While accepting that, 'at this rudimentary stage of international criminal law, it might be acceptable that a hierarchy of crimes has not yet been established', he takes the view that:

[t]he reference contained in the [ICTY] Statute to the 'gravity of the offence' was not intended to enable the judges to add a *blank provision on aggravating circumstances*. On the

[258] *Prosecutor* v. *Tadić*, Case No. IT-94-1-A and IT-94-1-A*bis*, Judgement in Sentencing Appeals, 26 January 2000 ('*Tadić* Judgement on Sentencing Appeal'), para. 69.

[259] See, for example, the early decision of the ICTR Trial Chamber in *Kambanda*, where war crimes were described as 'lesser crimes' compared with genocide and crimes against humanity. *Kambanda* Sentencing Judgement, *supra* note 184, para. 14; see also *Prosecutor* v. *Erdemović*, Case No. IT-96-22-A, Judgement, 7 October 1997 ('*Erdemović* Judgement on Sentencing Appeal'), Joint Separate Opinion of Judge McDonald and Judge Vohrah, paras. 20–21 (arguing that crimes against humanity must be regarded as of greater gravity than war crimes); *infra* note 271 and sources cited therein.

[260] See Chapter 3 text accompanying notes 11–18.

[261] See, e.g., *Tadić* Judgement on Sentencing Appeal, *supra* note 258, para. 69; *Kunarac et al.* Appeal Judgement, *supra* note 38, para. 171 (citing *Tadić* with approval); *Furundžija* Appeal Judgement, *supra* note 216, paras. 243, 247; *Dragan Nikolić* Judgement on Sentencing Appeal, *supra* note 231, para. 14 n. 25. See also, generally, Micaela Frulli, 'Are Crimes Against Humanity More Serious than War Crimes?', (2001) 12 *European Journal of International Law* 329; Carcano, *supra* note 210.

[262] See, e.g., *Trbić* Referral Decision, *supra* note 182, para. 19; *Rutaganda* Appeal Judgement, *supra* note 62, para. 590.

[263] *Galić* Appeal Judgement, *supra* note 10, para. 442.

[264] *Ibid.* Accord *Furundžija* Appeal Judgement, *supra* note 216, paras. 242–243 (citing *Tadić* Judgement on Sentencing Appeal, *supra* note 258, para. 69); *Dragan Nikolić* Judgement on Sentencing Appeal, *supra* note 231, para. 14 n. 25.

contrary, it was aimed at inviting the judges to identify a hierarchy of gravity among the offences within the jurisdiction of the Court.[265]

The approach adopted by the Tribunals has also attracted criticism from other scholars,[266] and even some judges. Judge Cassese, in a separate opinion in the *Tadić* Judgement on Sentencing Appeal, criticised the majority view that crimes against humanity are not manifestly more serious than war crimes.[267] His opinion, written early in the ICTY's work on sentencing, stands as a simple yet compelling approach:

> Clearly, the reaction of the international community to [crimes against humanity] must be more severe than in cases where the same conduct attributed to the accused amounts to a war crime. For, if classified as a crime against humanity, the murder possesses an objectively greater magnitude and reveals in the perpetrator a subjective frame of mind which may imperil fundamental values of the international community to a greater extent than in the case where that offence should instead be labelled as a war crime. The international community and the judicial bodies responsible for ensuring international criminal justice therefore have a strong societal interest in imposing a heavier penalty upon the author of such a crime against humanity, thereby also deterring similar crimes.[268]
>
> … [I]t follows that whenever an offence committed by an accused is deemed to be a 'crime against humanity', it must be regarded as inherently of greater gravity, all else being equal (*ceteris paribus*), than if it is instead characterised as a 'war crime'. Consequently, it must entail a heavier penalty (of course, the possible impact of extenuating or aggravating circumstances is a different matter which may in practice nevertheless have a significant bearing upon the eventual sentence).[269]
>
> The above remarks also apply to other similar cases. For instance, the murder of a group of civilians perpetrated in an armed conflict, if classified as genocide, clearly is more serious than if defined as a war crime or as a grave breach of the 1949 Geneva Conventions. For in the case of genocide, the same *actus reus* (the killing of multiple persons) must be accompanied by a specific intent (that of destroying a group or members of a group on national, ethnical, racial or religious grounds). This mental element renders the crime more abhorrent and reprehensible. Indeed, the *dolus* is more grave than that required for murder as a war crime or as a grave breach: what is now required is not only the intent to kill other human beings but the aggravated intent to destroy them because they belong to a particular group. Hence, a heavier penalty should be imposed.[270]

[265] Salvatore Zappalà, *Human Rights in International Criminal Proceedings* (2003), pp. 202–203 (emphasis in original).

[266] See, e.g., Danner, *supra* note 210, p. 420 (arguing that 'contrary to the current practice of the ICTY, judges sentencing defendants convicted of violations of international law should consider the elements of the chapeau in evaluating the harm caused by the defendants' acts'); Carcano, *supra* note 210, p. 593 (examining whether the same conduct should be punished more severely when charged as a crime against humanity rather than as a war crime); Richard May and Marieke Wierda, 'Is there a Hierarchy of Crimes in International Law?', in Lal Chand Vohrah, Fausto Pocar, Yvonne Featherstone, Olivier Fourmy, Christine Graham, John Hocking, and Nicholas Robson (eds.), *Man's Inhumanity to Man: Essays on International Law in Honour of Antonio Cassese* (2003), pp. 513–514, 529–532.

[267] *Tadić* Judgement on Sentencing Appeal, *supra* note 258, Separate Opinion of Judge Cassese, para. 16.

[268] *Ibid.*, para. 15 (underlining in original).

[269] *Ibid.*, para. 16 (underlining in original).

[270] *Ibid.*, para. 17.

It is the very fact that humanity is a collective target that renders crimes against humanity of inherently greater gravity than war crimes, a point acknowledged by ICTY judges in earlier decisions.[271] A year after *Tadić*, however, the *Kunarac* Trial Chamber took a different position:

> The Trial Chamber is unable to accept that a so-called *in personam* evaluation of the gravity of the crime could or should also concern the effect of that crime on third persons, as submitted by the Prosecutor. Such effects are irrelevant to the culpability of the offender, and it would be unfair to consider such effects in determining the sentence to be imposed.[272]

This view appears now to be an established feature of sentencing approaches on these issues. Yet, as Danner argues, '[i]t is this knowing participation in an act of greater criminality that makes the crime more dangerous and deserving of greater punishment',[273] a perspective that is further magnified by crimes requiring a particular discriminatory intent, such as persecution.[274]

The relevance of this argument to genocide is even more obvious.[275] Judge Wald, dissenting in the *Jelisić* Appeal Judgement, stated that 'genocide is at the apex' of seriousness in the crimes within the ICTY's jurisdiction.[276] This position has

[271] See, e.g., *Erdemović* Judgement on Sentencing Appeal, *supra* note 259, Joint Separate Opinion of Judge McDonald and Judge Vohrah, paras. 20–21 (opining that a prohibited act committed as a crime against humanity – that is, with an awareness that the act formed part of a widespread or systematic attack on a civilian population – is, all else being equal, more serious than an ordinary war crime, and 'should ordinarily entail a heavier penalty than if it were proceeded upon on the basis that it were a war crime') (quotation at para. 21). This passage was cited with approval by the Trial Chamber in the *Tadić* Sentencing Judgement. The Chamber stated: 'This follows from the requirement that crimes against humanity be committed on a widespread or systematic scale, the quantity of the crimes having a qualitative impact on the nature of the offence which is seen as a crime against more than just the victims themselves but against humanity as a whole.' *Prosecutor* v. *Tadić*, Case No. IT-94-1-T*bis*- R117, Sentencing Judgement, 11 November 1999, para. 28. Support for this proposition was also borrowed from the ICTR. See *Kayishema and Ruzindana* Trial Judgement, *supra* note 3, Sentence, para. 9; *Prosecutor* v. *Akayesu*, Case No. ICTR-96-4-T, Sentence, 2 October 1998, paras. 6–10; *Prosecutor v. Serushago*, Case No. ICTR-98-39-S, Sentence, 5 February 1999 ('*Serushago* Sentencing Judgement'), paras. 13–14; *Kambanda* Sentencing Judgement, *supra* note 184, para. 14. See also *Kordić and Čerkez* Trial Judgement, *supra* note 72, para. 207. For scholarly analysis, see Aryeh Neier, *War Crimes: Brutality, Genocide, Terror, and the Struggle for Justice* (1998), p. 213; Mark A. Drumbl, 'Rule of Law Amidst Lawlessness: Counseling the Accused in Rwanda's Domestic Genocide Trials', (1998) 29 *Columbia Human Rights Law Review* 545, 546. See also Danner, *supra* note 210, p. 476 (opining that the argument that crimes against humanity affect the whole of humanity is theoretical or rhetorical in terms of sentence determination for normal crimes, but is far from inappropriate when dealing with the sort of massive-scale criminality that is the subject of the *ad hoc* Tribunals' jurisdiction).

[272] *Kunarac et al.* Trial Judgement, *supra* note 90, para. 852. [273] Danner, *supra* note 210, p. 477 n. 257.

[274] See Frederick M. Lawrence, *Punishing Hate* (1999), p. 196; Richard Goldstone, 'The United Nations' War Crimes Tribunals: An Assessment', (1997) 12 *Connecticut Journal of International Law* 727, 730.

[275] See Frank Chalk and Kurt Jonassohn, *The History and Sociology of Genocide* (1990), p. 28.

[276] *Jelisić* Appeal Judgement, *supra* note 56, Partial Dissenting Opinion of Judge Wald, para. 13. See also Patricia M. Wald, 'General Radislav Krstić: A War Crimes Case Study', (2003) 16 *Georgetown Journal of Legal Ethics* 445, 472 n. 66, stating:

> There had been an ongoing issue in Tribunal jurisprudence as to whether crimes against humanity outranked crimes against war in a gravity hierarchy. The Appeals Chamber eventually decided that no such hierarchy was contemplated by the Statute or international law … . There is, however, widespread consensus, though no specific Appeals Chamber ruling, that if a sentencing hierarchy existed, genocide would be at its apex. The Trial Chamber here, however, recognized that even within the contours of genocide, there are different degrees of culpability that may justify different penalties.

considerable support from a number of compelling earlier statements in the *ad hoc* jurisprudence that genocide is the 'crime of crimes'.[277] As we argue at greater length in Chapter 3 of this volume, the critical aspect of the crime of genocide that suggests its supreme gravity is the specific intention of the accused or other relevant actor to destroy an identified human group. This notion gives genocide its normative place at the pinnacle of international crimes,[278] and there is every reason to expect that the notion should be reflected not only in the sentences imposed by international tribunals, but also in their explicit sentencing policies. While the ICTR has at least reflected, on the whole, the gravity of the offence of genocide in its sentencing practice, the Appeals Chambers of both Tribunals have failed to explain or justify the rationale for genocide having no special place in the sentencing regime.

It is difficult to justify the position that crimes characterised by additional elements suggesting they are part of a widespread and massive criminal activity, and accompanied by particular discriminatory intentions (especially the destruction of a group), are not necessarily more serious or deserving of a higher sentence than other international crimes that lack these characteristics. Nevertheless, this 'case-by-case' approach[279] has been reaffirmed as recently as the *Galić* Appeal Judgement, where the Appeals Chamber rejected any notion that the different crimes in the ICTY's jurisdiction have a particular gravity: 'Trial Chambers have an overriding obligation to individualise a sentence to fit the circumstances of the accused and the gravity of the crime'.[280] Indeed, the ICTY has not only maintained this position but has gone further, asserting that crimes resulting in the loss of life are not necessarily more serious, or deserving of longer sentences, than other crimes. According to the Appeals Chamber, such a conclusion is 'too rigid and mechanistic'.[281]

The explicit rejection of sentencing guidelines, the refusal to acknowledge a hierarchy of crimes, and the divergence in sentences meted out all leave one with a sense that issues of gravity and coherence are being sacrificed at the altar of flexibility and discretion 'in the circumstances of the case at hand'. The somewhat ironic comment of the Chamber in the *Furundžija* Appeal Judgement in 2000, that it

[277] See, e.g., *Prosecutor* v. *Niyitegeka*, Case No. ICTR-96-14-A, Judgement, 9 July 2004, para. 53; *Krstić* Appeal Judgement, *supra* note 44, Partial Dissenting Opinion of Judge Shahabuddeen, para. 95; *Stakić* Trial Judgement, *supra* note 108, para. 502; *Musema* Trial Judgement, *supra* note 183, para. 981; *Blaškić* Trial Judgement, *supra* note 215, para. 800; *Prosecutor* v. *Rutaganda*, Case No. ICTR-96-3-T, Judgement and Sentence, 6 December 1999, para. 451; *Kambanda* Sentencing Judgement, *supra* note 184, para. 16. But see *Serushago* Sentencing Judgement, *supra* note 271, para. 14 (stating that 'it is difficult to rank genocide and crimes against humanity as one being the lesser of the other in terms of their respective gravity').

[278] See Chapter 3, text accompanying notes 20–22.

[279] Cryer, Friman, Robinson, and Wilmshurst, *supra* note 213, p. 397.

[280] *Galić* Appeal Judgement, *supra* note 10, para. 442. See also *Simić* Appeal Judgement, *supra* note 130, para. 238; *Čelebići* Appeal Judgement, *supra* note 7, para. 717.

[281] *Furundžija* Appeal Judgement, *supra* note 216, para. 246. Indeed, Judge Meron notes that a review of the jurisprudence reveals that murder-related convictions are not strongly correlated with high-end sentences at the ICTY. See *Galić* Appeal Judgement, *supra* note 10, Separate and Partially Dissenting Opinion of Judge Meron, para. 8 n. 20.

would be 'premature to speak of an "emerging penal regime", and the incoherence of sentencing practice that this denotes,'[282] is, as noted by Sloane, applicable 'with equal, if not greater, force' today.[283]

5.3.3 The Appeals Chamber's interference in sentence determination by trial chambers

The ICTY Appeals Chamber has stated that sentencing 'is essentially a discretionary process on the part of a Trial Chamber',[284] which is in the best position to identify the appropriate sentence.[285] It is for this reason that the Appeals Chamber, according to its own precedent, will only reverse a sentence imposed by a trial chamber where a 'discernible error' has occurred.[286] To show that the trial chamber committed a discernible error in exercising its discretion:

> the Appellant has to demonstrate that the Trial Chamber gave weight to extraneous or irrelevant considerations, failed to give weight or sufficient weight to relevant considerations, made a clear error as to the facts upon which it exercised its discretion, or that the Trial Chamber's decision was so unreasonable or plainly unjust that the Appeals Chamber is able to infer that the Trial Chamber must have failed to exercise its discretion properly.[287]

Appeals against sentence, like those arising from a trial chamber's finding of guilt or innocence, are appeals *stricto sensu* – that is, they are of a corrective nature rather than trials *de novo*.[288] As noted above, Judge Meron has explained that interference in the trial chamber's sentence should only occur where one of two conditions are met: there is a disproportion with sentences imposed in similar situations, or the sentence demonstrably shocks the conscience: 'Any more stringent review denies the Trial Chamber the broad discretion vested in it.'[289]

On occasion, the Appeals Chambers of both *ad hoc* Tribunals have intervened to modify sentences where such an error is said to occur. In *Gacumbitsi*, the ICTR Appeals Chamber corrected a sentence of thirty-five years' imprisonment for genocide to life imprisonment. The Chamber held that the gravity of the offences and the accused's role in them were so profound that 'the margin of discretion to

[282] *Furundžija* Appeal Judgement, *supra* note 216, para. 237.

[283] Sloane, *supra* note 210, p. 715. While Sloane is referring to ICTR sentencing practice, this comment no doubt applies with greater force to the ICTY.

[284] *Kvočka et al.* Appeal Judgement, *supra* note 97, para. 669.

[285] *Galić* Appeal Judgement, *supra* note 10, Separate and Partially Dissenting Opinion of Judge Meron, para. 4.

[286] *Ibid*. See also *Krstić* Appeal Judgement, *supra* note 44, para. 242; *Naletilić and Martinović* Appeal Judgement, *supra* note 10, para. 593; *Momir Nikolić* Judgement on Sentencing Appeal, *supra* note 230, para. 8; *Čelebići* Appeal Judgement, *supra* note 7, para. 725.

[287] *Galić* Appeal Judgement, *supra* note 10, para. 394 (internal quotation marks omitted) (citing *Prosecutor* v. *Babić*, Judgement on Sentencing Appeal, Case No. IT-03-72-A, 18 July 2005, para. 44; *Momir Nikolić* Judgement on Sentencing Appeal, *supra* note 230, para. 95).

[288] *Ibid*, para. 393; *Kupreškić et al.* Appeal Judgement, *supra* note 10, para. 408.

[289] *Galić* Appeal Judgement, *supra* note 10, Separate and Partially Dissenting Opinion of Judge Meron, para. 6.

which Trial Chambers are entitled in sentencing' – which is not unlimited – was inappropriately exercised in that case; in this instance, 'the Appeals Chamber's prerogative to substitute a new sentence when the one given by the Trial Chamber simply cannot be reconciled with the principles governing sentencing at the Tribunal' had to be exercised.[290] The ICTY Appeals Chamber in *Galić* also took this approach. The Chamber overturned the Trial Chamber's sentence of twenty years' imprisonment, and substituted a life sentence, on the basis that it was 'unreasonable and plainly unjust, in that it underestimated the gravity of Galić's criminal conduct'.[291] Although it held that the Trial Chamber 'did not err in its factual findings and correctly noted the principles governing sentencing', the Appeals Chamber was able to 'infer that the Trial Chamber failed to exercise its discretion properly'.[292]

The *Galić* Appeals Chamber's reasoning highlights the difficulty associated with an incoherent sentencing policy. While paying lip service to the established principle that the 'Trial Chamber's duty remains to tailor the penalty to fit the individual circumstances of the accused and the gravity of the crime',[293] it is apparent that this discretion is open to attack by an Appeals Chamber that simply disagrees with the weight of the sentence given by a trial chamber on its assessment of the facts before it. The *Galić* Appeal Judgement itself is the best example: to reach its conclusion that Galić deserved a life sentence and that the Trial Chamber had erred in not imposing one, the Appeals Chamber engaged in a brief analysis over just a few paragraphs, provided very little reasoning,[294] and did not refer to principles established or discussed in any prior cases.[295] Indeed, Judge Meron in dissent noted that not only was there no useful comparative analysis available for the Appeals Chamber to identify whether the Trial Chamber's sentence was clearly out of proportion with similar cases,[296] but there was also little to back up the proposition that the Trial Chamber's twenty-year sentence was 'so low that it demonstrably shocks the conscience'.[297] His dissent concludes:

[290] *Prosecutor* v. *Gacumbitsi*, Case No. ICTR-2001-64-A, Judgement, 7 July 2006, para. 205.
[291] *Galić* Appeal Judgement, *supra* note 10, para. 455.
[292] *Ibid.*, para. 455. [293] *Ibid.*, para. 442.
[294] See *ibid.*, paras. 454–456 (setting forth the substance of the Appeals Chamber's reasoning for the substitution of sentence).
[295] Judge Meron noted this in his dissent. See *Galić* Appeal Judgement, *supra* note 10, Separate and Partially Dissenting Opinion of Judge Meron, para. 8 n. 19.
[296] *Ibid.*, paras. 4–9.
[297] *Ibid.*, para. 10 (noting that only once has the ICTY Appeals Chamber arguably revised a sentence upward for such reasons, in the *Aleksovski* case); see also *supra* note 216 (citing *Aleksovski* and mentioning the increase in sentence). Judge Meron also refers to the *Kordić and Čerkez* case, where the Appeals Chamber declined to increase the twenty-five-year sentence ordered by the Trial Chamber, noting that there is 'no meaningful difference' between the two cases. See *ibid.*, para. 12 (discussing *Kordić and Čerkez* Appeal Judgement, *supra* note 44, paras. 1057–1065).

> [The increase in sentence by the Appeals Chamber majority] disserves the principles of procedural fairness on which our legitimacy rests. As the highest body in our court system, we are not readily accountable to any other authority and thus have a particular obligation to use our power sparingly. We should not substitute our own preferences for the reasoned judgement of a Trial Chamber. A sound method for assuring that we have not fallen prey to such preferences is to measure our choices fully and comprehensively against those made in prior cases. Although precise comparisons may be of limited value, the radically different approach adopted by the majority in this case requires at least some explanation. Rather than undertaking such an analysis, however, the majority simply offers conclusory statements. I cannot accept the majority's approach. No matter what he has done, Galić is entitled to due process of law – including a fair application of our standard of review.[298]

Concerns over the *ad hoc* Appeals Chambers exceeding or abusing their powers of review are not new, and are not exclusive to the review of sentences. Appeals Chamber judges have registered sharp disagreement with their colleagues for overstepping the bounds of proper appellate review in other contexts. In her dissenting opinion in the *Blaškić* Appeal Judgement, for example, Judge Weinberg de Roca criticised the majority for 'disregarding the deference normally accorded the trier of fact' by substituting its own assessment of (only part) of the evidence led at trial, and then re-determining Blaškić's guilt or innocence.[299] Judge Hunt has also vehemently criticised the Appeals Chamber for what he described as 'destruction of the rights of the accused enshrined in the Tribunal's Statute and in customary international law', by reversing or ignoring well-considered precedent on the basis of an improper contemplation of the completion strategy.[300]

In the context of sentencing law, the interference by the Appeals Chamber, without reference to or application of clear principle, invariably contributes to the general sense that the Tribunals – and especially the ICTY – lack a coherent, fair, and consistent sentencing regime.[301] The lack of well-formulated sentencing guidelines at the ICC means that this is a problem that is likely to persist until some of the fundamentals of sentencing serious international crimes, and the standard of review and its application by appellate courts in international law, are resolved.

[298] *Ibid.*, Separate and Partially Dissenting Opinion of Judge Meron, para. 13.

[299] See *Blaškić* Appeal Judgement, *supra* note 73, Partial Dissenting Opinion of Judge Weinberg de Roca, para. 2 (referring to the Appeals Chamber's stated position that it would conduct an assessment of the accused's guilt beyond reasonable doubt because it was in possession of additional evidence not available to the Trial Chamber at trial). Judge Weinberg de Roca criticised this approach because, in her view, the Appeals Chamber cannot undertake a *de novo* review of the entirety of the evidence submitted at trial. See also generally *Kordić and Čerkez* Appeal Judgement, *supra* note 44, Separate Opinion of Judge Weinberg de Roca.

[300] See, e.g., *Prosecutor* v. *Milošević*, Case No. IT-02-54-AR73.4, Dissenting Opinion of Judge David Hunt on Admissibility of Evidence in Chief in the Form of Written Statements (Majority Decision Given 30 September 2003), 21 October 2003, paras. 20–22; *Prosecutor* v. *Nyiramasuhuko*, Case No. ICTR-98-42-A15*bis*, Decision in the Matter of Proceedings Under Rule 15*bis* (D), 24 September 2003, Dissenting Opinion of Judge David Hunt, para. 17. For a general discussion of these issues, see Gideon Boas, *The Milošević Trial: Lessons for the Conduct of International Criminal Proceedings* (2007), pp. 68–69; 288–291.

[301] See Olaoluwa Olusanya, *Sentencing War Crimes and Crimes Against Humanity Under the International Criminal Tribunal for the Former Yugoslavia* (2005), cited in Schabas, *supra* note 215, p. 563 n. 111.

6

Conclusion

The elements of the core categories of international crimes discussed in the preceding chapters are the heart of substantive international criminal law. Through these elements, the constitutive instruments and judicial decisions of the courts and tribunals surveyed in this series seek to punish the most serious violations of international human rights and international humanitarian law by identifying, with the precision and consistency required of criminal law, the circumstances in which conduct breaches those norms.

These observations are subject to certain qualifications, however, and four in particular arise from the analysis in the preceding chapters. First, the elements of crimes are only one part of the equation that is tested at trial, and a nuanced understanding of international criminal law is impossible without an appreciation of the interaction between the crimes and the forms of responsibility through which individuals are held liable. It is thus crucial to understand the role that the context in which international crimes are almost invariably committed – especially the multiplicity of actors involved in their design and execution – plays in the development and application of appropriate definitions of the crimes.

Second, even though each court or tribunal has jurisdiction over most or all of the crimes discussed in this volume, the three core categories of crimes are often seen to be of varying importance in these judicial bodies. In turn, the experiences of the courts and tribunals with the categories of crimes can vary markedly depending on the profile and complexity of the cases on their dockets.

Third, while the different courts and tribunals generally apply and develop the same body of law, each was created to fulfil particular purposes in different places or at different times, and as such, each has jurisdictional peculiarities. These unique features will at times be a deliberate consequence of the conflict or other situation they were created to address; at others, they will be an unexplained or interpretational consequence of the negotiation process that accompanied the drafting of the constitutive instrument of the court or tribunal.

Finally, although the goal of consistency and predictability is largely met in respect of the elements of the crimes, it has been sadly disregarded when it comes to sentencing practices, particularly in the International Criminal Tribunal for the former Yugoslavia (ICTY). The tasks of existing and future international criminal judicial institutions will therefore include the elaboration and maintenance of a coherent body of sentencing law. Each of these four points is considered below.

6.1 The content and context of international crimes

The elements that must be proved beyond reasonable doubt in order to convict an individual of an international crime can be divided into four groups, or components.[1] Three of the four components are the subject of this volume: the underlying offence; the general requirements that render it a crime of international concern; and any specific requirements that characterise one of the subcategories of offences represented in the Statutes of the *ad hoc* Tribunals, namely persecution, inhumane acts, cruel treatment, and inhuman treatment.[2] The fourth component, the forms of responsibility, is the subject of the first volume in this series, and a comprehensive understanding of international criminal law is not possible without an awareness of how these four components interact. Unfortunately, too many judgements do not demonstrate such an awareness; instead, they are often careless in their terminology, insufficiently rigorous in their reasoning, or inarticulate in presenting their findings. These flaws in the jurisprudence tend to obscure and complicate this area of the law, rendering it even more difficult to grasp and apply correctly.

[1] See generally Chapter 1, section 1.2. [2] See Chapter 2, sections 2.2.3.8, 2.2.3.9; Chapter 4, section 4.2.2.3.

In this series, we have sought to explain where the jurisprudence could benefit from more precise and nuanced definitions that reflect the actual circumstances giving rise to the cases before international and internationalised courts and tribunals. Three points in particular have been emphasised throughout this and the previous volume:

6.1.1 Definitions of the crimes should not refer only to the accused or the physical perpetrator

The current focus of the courts and tribunals reviewed in this series – from the *ad hoc* Tribunals, which are beginning to wind down their operations, to the International Criminal Court (ICC) and the Extraordinary Chambers in the Courts of Cambodia (ECCC), which are still at the commencement of their mandates – is on the persons alleged to be most responsible for the crimes in the cases before them.[3] In practice, this means the most senior of the individuals involved in the realisation of these crimes: military or civilian leaders, heads of militias or rebel armed factions, the alleged masterminds or warlords who are reputed to be the architects of the atrocities charged in these cases. As a result, and despite the repeated references in the definitions of the crimes to 'the accused', the accused and the physical perpetrator are now rarely one and the same person.[4] This reality is clearly reflected in the charging instruments, which now seldom allege that the accused personally physically committed any of the crimes with which he is charged.[5] Thus, instead of unthinkingly repeating definitions that assume that the accused was the person who committed the underlying offence – who tortured, or raped, or murdered the victims – international judgements should acknowledge that most of the underlying criminal conduct alleged in the cases before them will likely have been committed by someone other than the accused sitting in the dock.

Yet altering definitions to use only 'physical perpetrator' instead of 'accused' will merely replace one underinclusive term with another. One can clearly conceive of situations in which the physical perpetrator commits the underlying offence, but does not himself fulfil the other requirements necessary to transform that offence into an international crime – for example, because he is not aware of the

[3] Excluded from this group is the Special Panels for Serious Crimes in East Timor (SPSC), which is no longer functioning, and which only ever brought low and mid-level offenders to trial. See, e.g., Chapter 2, text accompanying notes 593–596.

[4] See, e.g., Gideon Boas, James L. Bischoff, and Natalie L. Reid, *Forms of Responsibility in International Criminal Law* (2007), pp. 9, 93, 140–141, 191, 416, 420–423. See also Chapter 2, section 2.2.2.1; Chapter 3, section 3.2.1.1; Chapter 4, text accompanying notes 121–123.

[5] See, e.g., Boas, Bischoff, and Reid, *supra* note 4, pp. 140–141 (noting that fifteen of the twenty-one cases that had not yet proceeded to judgement as of 1 December 2006 charged JCE as the form of 'commission').

circumstances in which the offence occurs, or does not have the requisite intent.[6] If such a physical perpetrator is dispatched to kill or injure victims or destroy their property at the behest of another person, and this other person is fully aware of the context in which that offence occurs and acts with the necessary intent, it would be illogical to conclude that the offence is not an international crime simply because the physical perpetrator does not share that knowledge or intent. In this situation, where the physical perpetrator is merely the instrument of the other relevant actor involved in the crime, the fact that the person who actually pulls the trigger does not satisfy all the specific or general requirements should not preclude a determination that an international crime has been committed.[7]

The law on the forms of responsibility provides a helpful means of discerning which actors are so intrinsically involved in the crime that their knowledge or mental state could satisfy one or more of the elements of the crime. As discussed in Chapters 2, 3, and 4, certain forms of responsibility capture the conduct of persons who may be seen as the real authors of the crime: for example, one who knowingly plans, orders, or instigates genocide or a crime against humanity sees his intentions carried out when the physical perpetrator commits the underlying offence, even if the physical perpetrator is not aware of his own role in the larger scheme. Similarly, the form of common purpose liability known in the *ad hoc* Tribunals as first-category joint criminal enterprise also describes a person who is the ultimate author of the crime, one who 'commits' the crime through the instruments of various physical perpetrators. The best manner of framing the definitions is therefore to recognise that conduct will qualify as a crime in one of two situations: either the physical perpetrator (who may or may not be the accused) satisfies each and every element of the crime; or the physical perpetrator satisfies the *actus reus* and *mens rea* of the underlying offence, but he or another relevant actor (who may or may not be the accused) meets the applicable specific or general requirements. It is important to note, however, that the forms of responsibility are merely useful means of describing which actors are relevant to the question of whether a crime was committed; they are heuristics, not requirements for proof of a crime.

6.1.2 The elements of the crimes and the elements of the forms of responsibility answer separate legal inquiries

Definitions of the crimes, particularly for crimes against humanity, frequently describe the person committing the crime as 'the accused or someone for whose

6 For discussions of this issue in light of the general and specific requirements that characterise categories of international crimes or specific international crimes, see Chapter 2, section 2.2.2.1; Chapter 3, section 3.2.1.1; Chapter 4, text accompanying notes 121–123, 174–177.

7 See, e.g., Chapter 2, text accompanying notes 103–109; Chapter 3, text accompanying note 113.

conduct he is responsible'.[8] This statement is accurate in the context of a particular trial, because the accused will not be held personally responsible unless the necessary elements from all components of the crime have been proved; that is, in addition to proof that the underlying offence was committed, and that it qualified as the particular international crime charged, the accused cannot be found guilty unless the prosecution also proves that he physically committed the crime or was responsible for the conduct of those who did. As a simple definition of the crime, however, the statement is incorrect. Elements of an international crime are the description of the circumstances in which the specific fundamental norm of international law has been breached; liability is a separate inquiry, and is answered by the law on the forms of responsibility. Trial and appeals chambers could, and frequently do, conclude that the crimes alleged in the indictment were proved beyond reasonable doubt, but the accused is not responsible for them because the elements of the charged forms of responsibility have not been proven beyond a reasonable doubt.

6.1.3 Judgements should specify, in their dispositions, the precise conduct for which the accused has been convicted

In a general manner, most trial judgements at the institutions surveyed in this series already meet this basic requirement of a fair trial, because they exhaustively review the evidence adduced at trial on the crimes charged and the forms of responsibility through which the accused are alleged to be responsible for those crimes. In their dispositions, however, the judgements frequently fail to describe accurately the bases on which the accused has been convicted, and therefore portray an oversimplified view of the content of international crimes and the interaction of the crimes and the forms of responsibility. It is not uncommon, for example, for a judgement to conclude that the accused is guilty of 'persecutions', or 'inhumane acts', or 'genocide', without specifying the underlying offences for these crimes, or the form of responsibility through which the accused is being held liable. Moreover, through the jurisprudence on cumulative convictions, this approach has a significant adverse effect on the sentences meted out at the trial and appellate levels.[9] A better approach, which would impart significantly greater clarity to the final conclusions of trial and appeals chambers, would be for chambers to specify that an accused has been convicted, for example, of aiding and abetting murder as a form of persecution as a crime against humanity, or ordering forcible transfer as an inhumane act as a crime against humanity, or instigating genocide through the deliberate infliction of

[8] See, e.g., Chapter 2, notes 100–101, 205–206, 308, 417.

[9] Cf. Chapter 5, text accompanying notes 95–166 (discussing the impact of this practice on the law regarding cumulative convictions involving persecution as a crime against humanity).

eventually fatal conditions of life. In each of these situations, all components underlying the conviction are clear: the accused's particular role in the crime, the underlying offence with the real-world effect for which the accused is being held responsible, and the features of the crime that justify an international court or tribunal's exercise of jurisdiction.

6.2 The relative importance of the crimes in the different courts and tribunals

As noted in Chapter 2, the ICTY and the Special Court for Sierra Leone (SCSL) are often described as 'war crimes tribunals' in the literature and media, while the International Criminal Tribunal for Rwanda (ICTR) and the ECCC are given the label 'genocide tribunals'.[10] From the perspective of the politician, the diplomat, or the layperson, these classifications have a certain intuitive appeal: the ICTY and the SCSL were established to try persons for crimes committed in the course of armed conflict between or among reasonably well-defined warring factions with military or paramilitary hierarchies, while the ICTR and the ECCC were set up to try persons for their involvement in widespread government-sponsored campaigns of persecution of certain disfavoured groups, in which armed conflict among warring factions did not feature prominently.[11] Yet of the four tribunals, the only one that truly deserves the label given to it is the ICTR: genocide is the most often charged category of crimes in that Tribunal, and nearly every judgement discusses its elements and applies them to facts;[12] two of the three genocide-related inchoate crimes have also been defined and applied in the ICTR.[13] The ECCC, by sharp contrast, is decidedly not a 'genocide tribunal' as international lawyers would understand that term: while the ECCC enjoys jurisdiction over genocide and its related inchoate crimes, none of the five accused under indictment has been charged with genocide or

[10] See Chapter 2, notes 651–655 and accompanying text. See also, e.g., Amy Kazmin, 'Cambodia in Agreement on UN Genocide Tribunal', *Financial Times*, 5 October 2004, p. 10; Paul Lewis, 'UN Report Comes Down Hard on Rwandan Genocide Tribunal', *New York Times*, 13 February 1997, p. A13. The ICTR has often been lumped into the category of 'war crimes tribunal' as well. The observations of Sonja Starr are apt: 'Scholarship and the popular press ubiquitously refer to the ad hoc tribunals as "war crimes tribunals" – including the ICTR, which, although there was an armed conflict in Rwanda in 1994, is not principally focused on war crimes as such. It should, if anything, be called a "genocide tribunal".' Sonja Starr, 'Extraordinary Crimes at Ordinary Times: International Justice Beyond Crisis Situations', (2007) 101 *Northwestern University Law Review* 1257, 1268 (footnotes removed).

[11] See Chapter 4, text accompanying notes 91–92 (explaining why war crimes prosecutions in the ICTR are rare); *ibid.*, text accompanying notes 571–574 (noting that the Group of Experts for the ECCC recommended against including war crimes in that institution's jurisdiction because it would distract from the other, more relevant, crimes before it); Chapter 2, text accompanying notes 654–659 (predicting that the ECCC's attention will be focused on crimes against humanity).

[12] See Chapter 3, section 3.1.3.

[13] See Chapter 5, notes 183–184 (listing all the ICTR judgements in which a genocide-related inchoate crime has been discussed). But see Chapter 3, section 3.5 (noting that no chamber of either Tribunal has defined attempt to commit genocide).

an inchoate crime, probably because the Co-Prosecutors wish to concentrate their limited resources on the Khmer-on-Khmer crimes that made up the bulk of the regime's atrocities, instead of the small portion of crimes perpetrated against non-Khmer communities with the intent to destroy them.[14] As concerns the so-called 'war crimes tribunals', war crimes have indeed been important components of most prosecutions: to be sure, some ICTY cases – most notably those against Bosnian Muslim military commanders – involve allegations of war crimes to the exclusion of crimes against humanity and genocide,[15] and both trial chambers in the two SCSL judgements issued as of 1 December 2007 have discussed and applied the elements of a number of war crimes, including 'new' ones such as conscripting, enlisting, or recruiting child soldiers.[16]

Yet the reality is that crimes against humanity – and not genocide or war crimes – have been or are expected to be the single most important weapon in the prosecutor's arsenal in all of the courts and tribunals discussed in this volume, with the exception of the ICTR.[17] Crimes against humanity are generally easier to prove than war crimes because they do not require the existence of an armed conflict or that the physical perpetrator's conduct have a nexus to it, except in the ICTY, and even there, the link to the armed conflict is broadly defined and easily satisfied.[18] They are also easier to prove than genocide, since they lack the onerous requirement of proof of intent to partially or totally destroy one of the Genocide Convention's four protected groups. Crimes against humanity have been central to most ICTY prosecutions and, where war crimes are also charged, usually predominate in the trial chamber's discussion and findings.[19] Persecution as a crime against humanity, in particular, has been a hallmark of that Tribunal's work, as have deportation and forcible transfer, capturing many of the activities associated with the practice of 'ethnic cleansing' that characterised the disintegration of the former Yugoslavia.[20] Crimes against humanity

[14] See Chapter 3, text accompanying notes 397–398.

[15] See, e.g., *Prosecutor* v. *Delić*, Case No. IT-04-83-PT, Amended Indictment, 14 July 2006 (still in trial proceedings as of 1 December 2007); *Prosecutor* v. *Orić*, Case No. IT-03-68-T, Judgement, 30 June 2006; *Prosecutor* v. *Hadžihasanović and Kubura*, Case No. IT-01-47-T, Judgement, 15 March 2006; *Prosecutor* v. *Halilović*, Case No. IT-01-48-T, Judgement, 16 November 2005. See also *Prosecutor* v. *Strugar*, Case No. IT-01-42-T, Judgement, 31 January 2005 (case concerning the Yugoslav National Army's bombardment of Dubrovnik).

[16] See Chapter 4, section 4.3.2.1; see also *ibid.*, text accompanying notes 542–551 (specifically discussing the jurisprudence on child soldiers). Most of the *CDF* Trial Chamber's application of the law to the facts focuses on war crimes to the exclusion of crimes against humanity, as the Chamber found early in its analysis that neither accused could be held liable for the latter crimes because they had not taken place as part of an attack on a civilian population. See Chapter 2, text accompanying note 578.

[17] See Chapter 2, text accompanying notes 5–6. [18] See *ibid.*, text accompanying note 78.

[19] But see *supra* note 15 (listing some of the handful of cases where only war crimes have been charged).

[20] See Chapter 2, section 2.2.3.4 (deportation); *ibid.*, section 2.2.3.8 (persecution); *ibid.*, text accompanying notes 464–466 (forcible transfer as an inhumane act). See also Patricia M. Wald, 'Genocide and Crimes Against Humanity', (2007) 6 *Washington University Global Studies Law Review* 621, 631 (quoting David Tolbert, Deputy Prosecutor at the ICTY, as saying that 'the Prosecution has used persecution as a kind of umbrella charge to cover "ethnic cleansing" as no single crime really covers it').

have been charged alongside genocide in most ICTR cases, and almost every person publicly implicated in proceedings before the ICC is suspected of liability for crimes against humanity.[21] The five accused in the ECCC are all charged with crimes against humanity, and three are also charged with war crimes.[22] The UN Group of Experts for Cambodia concluded that the 'vast majority' of the Khmer Rouge's atrocities were committed against disfavoured political and social groups outside the context of armed conflict;[23] in light of this finding, it is likely that crimes against humanity will demand the lion's share of the ECCC's attention,[24] as they did in the Special Panels for Serious Crimes in East Timor (SPSC), where genocide and war crimes were never even charged.[25] In the same vein, Saddam Hussein and his co-accused before the SICT were charged only with crimes against humanity for their roles in the Hussein regime's systematic campaign of detention, torture, murder, and forcible displacement of civilians from the Iraqi town of Dujail in 1982.[26] This pivotal role played by crimes against humanity in modern international criminal tribunals is perhaps ironic given that, of the three core categories of crimes, it is the only one that did not benefit from detailed exposition in a widely accepted international treaty until the conclusion of the Rome Statute in 1998.[27]

Despite their clear prominence in the actual practice of the international and internationalised courts and tribunals, crimes against humanity do not seem to capture the imagination of the public, or of national governments or even human rights groups, in the same way that genocide does. Many of the most abominable campaigns of terror in recent decades – including the centralised programme of human destruction in Cambodia, the horrendous and widespread crimes committed in Darfur, and the deportation and murder of hundreds of thousands of Kosovo Albanians by the Serb authorities in Kosovo – have not been considered by legal experts to constitute genocide, although they certainly fall squarely within the purview of crimes against humanity and, at times, war crimes as well. Public discomfort with the idea that such mass atrocity should be legally described and punished as crimes against humanity or war crimes, and not as genocide, is clearly

[21] See Chapter 2, notes 544–555 and accompanying text.
[22] See *ibid.*, notes 667–671 and accompanying text.
[23] Report of the Group of Experts for Cambodia Established Pursuant to General Assembly Resolution 52/135, annexed to UN Doc. A/53/850, S/1999/231, 16 March 1999, para. 71.
[24] See Chapter 2, text accompanying notes 658–659.
[25] See *ibid.*, text accompanying note 595. Indeed, war crimes were not even charged in cases against *de jure* military officers. See, e.g., *Prosecutor* v. *Wiranto, Zacky Anwar Makarim, Kiki Syahnakri, Adam Rachmat Damiri, Suhartono Suratman, Mohammad Noer Muis, Yayat Sudrajat, and Abilio José Osório Soares*, Case No. 05–2003, Indictment, 22 February 2003, pp. 36–37 (charging Wiranto and other high-level Indonesian military officers with murder, deportation, forcible transfer, and persecution as crimes against humanity, but not charging war crimes). See also Chapter 2, note 596 (noting that these accused, like virtually all mid- and high-level accused before the SPSC, remained safely at large in Indonesia for the duration of the SPSC's existence).
[26] See Chapter 2, text accompanying notes 686–687. [27] See generally *ibid.*, section 2.1.

evident in the response of some to such legal characterisation.[28] This preoccupation even reaches back into the depths of the twentieth century, with clear frictions still existing between Turkey and those governments that have labelled, or have indicated a desire to label, the 1915 Armenian massacre as 'genocide'.[29] The public attitude is certainly understandable: even among other abhorrent crimes, genocide rightly carries a special stigma because at its heart is the most extreme affront to the humanity – the intention to eradicate a human group from existence, and perhaps even from memory.[30] This stigma makes it somewhat difficult to understand why the Appeals Chambers of the *ad hoc* Tribunals continue to insist that genocide is not inherently graver from a legal standpoint than crimes against humanity or war crimes.[31] Such a position seems both nonsensical and counterintuitive, and it is our hope that the ICC and future international criminal courts and tribunals will not follow the lead of the *ad hoc* Tribunals in this regard.

Still, it is important to emphasise that mass atrocity falling short of the legal definition of genocide can be equally or, at times, more egregious than a particular instance of genocide, at least in theory. As explained in Chapter 3, there are many different means by which a genocidal intention can be carried out, including inflicting serious bodily or mental harm on members of a protected group, or preventing births within a protected group, or several kinds of related inchoate conduct such as conspiracy and unsuccessful attempts to commit the crime. None of this conduct need be committed on a massive scale to constitute genocide.[32] There are many examples of conduct clearly qualifying as crimes against humanity (such as the events in Cambodia and Darfur), or war crimes (such as the siege of Sarajevo), that rival the horror of other acts that may qualify as genocide.[33] It is critical that the international community maintain the same resolve in the face of all such crimes, reinforcing the prohibitions and supporting the prosecutions, regardless of the legal

[28] See Chapter 3, text accompanying notes 21, 55 and sources cited therein (arguing that what has happened in Darfur should be considered genocide, and that political groups should be considered as potential targets of genocide). The United States has also rejected the view that the Sudanese government has not pursued a policy of genocide. See 'US Convinced of Darfur "Genocide"', BBC News, 1 February 2005, at www.news.bbc.co.uk/1/hi/world/africa/4227835.stm.

[29] A recent example is the failed attempt of some in the United States House of Representatives to introduce a bill that would recognise what happened to the Armenian minority as 'genocide'; the failure was mainly due to pressure by Turkey and the correspondent military implications for US war efforts in Iraq. See 'U.S. and Turkey Thwart Armenian Genocide Bill', *New York Times*, 26 October 2007, available at www.nytimes.com/2007/10/26/washington/26cong.html?partner=rssnyt&emc=rss. France, on the other hand, successfully passed a bill in 2006 making it a crime to deny the Armenian genocide. See 'French in Armenia Genocide Row', *BBC News*, 12 October 2006, at news.bbc.co.uk/2/hi/europe/6043730.stm.

[30] See Chapter 3, text accompanying notes 20–21; Chapter 5, text accompanying note 278.

[31] See Chapter 3, text accompanying notes 12–18; Chapter 5, text accompanying notes 279–281.

[32] See Chapter 3, text accompanying note 165. But see *ibid.*, text accompanying notes 349–353 and *infra* note 50 (noting the requirement in the ICC Elements of Crimes that, to be triable in that Court, genocide should have taken place 'in the context of a manifest pattern of similar conduct directed against [the targeted] group or was conduct that could itself effect [the group's] destruction').

[33] See Chapter 3, note 21 and accompanying text.

characterisation that may later be given to them – genocide, war crime, crime against humanity, or otherwise – in a court of law.

6.3 Variations in the definitions of crimes in the different courts and tribunals

The international and internationalised courts and tribunals discussed in this volume have largely overlapping subject-matter jurisdiction, focusing on the core categories of crimes against humanity, genocide, and war crimes. Yet the definitions of these crimes in the various constitutive instruments also differ from one another in a number of important respects. There are three primary reasons for this divergence.

First, some of the added features of a given definition – particularly those in the earliest tribunals, the ICTY and the ICTR – embody what the drafters believed to be required by customary international law at the time, so that no accused would be convicted for conduct that was not prohibited and penalised at the time it occurred.[34] Hence, the crimes against humanity provisions of the ICTR Statute specify that the offences must occur in the context of a widespread and systematic attack against a civilian population, an element of these crimes under customary international law that was nevertheless not explicitly included in the ICTY Statute.[35] In addition, the drafters of the ICTR Statute also included the requirement that the attack be discriminatory in nature, apparently believing that it was similarly mandated under customary international law.[36] For the ICTY, at least one scholar has concluded that the failure to grant that Tribunal explicit jurisdiction over war crimes committed in non-international armed conflict was due to the drafters' understandable concern that custom may not have recognised individual criminal responsibility for such infractions by the early 1990s.[37] This concern may also have prompted the inclusion of the armed conflict requirement for crimes against humanity in the ICTY.[38] Given the temporal proximity of the drafting of the ICTY and ICTR Statutes, however, it seems likely that the different circumstances surrounding the

[34] See Chapter 1, notes 18, 24–26 and accompanying text (discussing the principles of *nullum crimen sine lege* and *nulla poena sine lege*, and the *ad hoc* Tribunals' practice of looking to what was provided for under customary international law at the time of the events charged in the indictment in a given case to avoid offending these principles).

[35] Compare Chapter 2, text accompanying note 74 with *ibid*, text accompanying note 81.

[36] See *ibid*., note 60. The *ad hoc* Appeals Chambers have since held that this requirement and the ICTY's armed conflict requirement are merely jurisdictional, and do not form part of the customary definition of crimes against humanity. See *ibid*., notes 76, 84–85 and accompanying text. Despite this clarification, the constitutive document of the ECCC curiously reproduces the requirement of a discriminatory attack. See *ibid*., text accompanying note 645.

[37] See William A. Schabas, *The UN International Criminal Tribunals: The Former Yugoslavia, Rwanda and Sierra Leone* (2006), pp. 232–236. As explained in Chapter 4, however, the ICTY Appeals Chamber has interpreted the Tribunal's Statute as granting jurisdiction over non-international armed conflict war crimes despite the likely intent of the drafters. See Chapter 4, notes 4, 80–86 and accompanying text.

[38] See Chapter 2, note 55.

establishment of each Tribunal had as much, if not more, to do with the differences in their additional jurisdictional features.

Indeed, the second explanation for much of the variation in subject-matter jurisdiction across these courts or tribunals is that it reflects an attempt to focus the work of the court or tribunal on the specific characteristics of the conflict or other circumstances giving rise to its establishment. Thus, since the conflicts in Rwanda and Sierra Leone were thought to be internal in character, the war crimes in those Tribunals' Statutes were drawn from instruments on non-international armed conflict, including Common Article 3 of the 1949 Geneva Conventions and Additional Protocol II of 1977.[39] The constitutive document of the ECCC presents the converse: grave breaches of the Geneva Conventions, but not violations of Common Article 3 or Additional Protocol II, have been included, presumably because most or all of the war crimes thought to have been committed during the Khmer Rouge's reign occurred in the course of the international armed conflict between Cambodia and Vietnam.[40] The SCSL and ECCC, moreover, have jurisdiction over certain other war crimes not explicitly listed in the ICTY and ICTR Statutes: destruction of cultural property in violation of the 1954 Hague Cultural Property Convention was included in the ECCC's jurisdiction ostensibly on the strength of the Group of Experts' conclusion that the Khmer Rouge had destroyed great numbers of temples, mosques, churches, and artefacts in the course of its organised attack on religion;[41] and the three additional war crimes in the SCSL Statute were thought to be particularly emblematic of that conflict: attacks on civilians, attacks on humanitarian and peacekeeping personnel and units, and conscripting, enlisting, or using child soldiers.[42] Similarly, each internationalised tribunal has the power to try persons for a small selection of domestic crimes chosen for their perceived relevance to the conflict in question,[43] although only the SPSC undertook prosecutions for such

[39] See Chapter 4, text accompanying notes 10–13, 520–524. Of course, as the ICTY Appeals Chamber has recognised with respect to Common Article 3 crimes, and the SCSL Appeals Chamber has recognised for all war crimes within its jurisdiction, the ICTY and the SCSL are not prohibited from prosecuting an individual for these crimes where the conflict at the time and place in question is deemed to have been international, as all of the norms also provide for individual criminal responsibility under the law governing international armed conflict. See *ibid.*, notes 4, 523–524.

[40] See *ibid.*, text accompanying notes 572, 575. As noted in Chapter 4, it is unclear whether the ECCC's additional war crime of destruction of cultural property allows for the imposition of liability for the commission of this crime in non-international armed conflict. See *ibid.*, text accompanying notes 584–585.

[41] Yet as explained in Chapter 4, despite this conclusion, the Group of Experts did not actually recommend that this crime be included in the ECCC's jurisdiction. See *ibid.*, text accompanying notes 576, 579.

[42] See *ibid.*, text accompanying note 522.

[43] See Statute of the Special Court for Sierra Leone, 2178 UNTS 138, UN Doc. S/2002/246, 16 January 2002, Appendix II, Art. 5 (abuse of girls, abduction of girls for immoral purposes, and setting fire to dwelling houses or other buildings); United Nations Transitional Administration in East Timor, Regulation No. 2000/15 on the Establishment of Panels with Exclusive Jurisdiction over Serious Criminal Offences, UN Doc. UNTAET/REG/2000/15, 6 June 2000, Sections 8–9 (murder and sexual offences); Law on the Establishment of the Extraordinary Chambers in the Courts of Cambodia for the Prosecution of Crimes Committed During the Period of Democratic Kampuchea, as amended on 27 October 2004, Doc. No. NS/RKM/1004/006, unofficial

crimes.[44] Perhaps most notably, genocide and its related inchoate crimes have been omitted from the SCSL Statute altogether, in conformity with the Secretary-General's conclusion that there was no evidence showing that any of the crimes in Sierra Leone were committed with genocidal intent.[45] With its global reach and prospective outlook at the time of its creation, the Rome Statute of the ICC is the obvious exception to this trend of tailoring subject-matter jurisdiction to accommodate a specific situation, conflict, or series of conflicts.[46]

Third, particularly in the ICC, some definitions of crimes and underlying offences were deliberately crafted to restrict the reach of prosecutions to less than would be permitted under customary international law, or – more laudably – to develop the law beyond the customary definition. Certain of the provisos and restrictions in the Rome Statute and Elements of Crimes reflect the fears of certain drafting delegations that activist prosecutors and judges would intrude too far into their domestic affairs, or would attempt to invoke the Court's jurisdiction in instances of isolated criminal activity. Thus, to be triable in the ICC, a crime against humanity must have been committed as part of a state or organisational policy,[47] and it should be 'conduct which is impermissible under generally applicable international law, as

translation by the Council of Jurists and the Secretariat of the Task Force, revised on 26 August 2007, Art. 3 new (homicide, torture, and religious persecution as defined in the 1956 Cambodian Penal Code); Law No. 10 (2005), Law of the Iraqi Higher Criminal Court, 18 October 2005, reprinted in Michael P. Scharf and Gregory S. McNeal (eds.), *Saddam on Trial: Understanding and Debating the Iraqi High Tribunal* (2006), pp. 283 *et seq*., Art. 14 (attempt to influence the judiciary, squandering national resources, abuse of position, use of armed forces against an Arab country, and any other crime 'punishable by the penal law or any other criminal law at the time of its commitment').

44 Domestic crimes were charged in the vast majority, if not all, of the cases that proceeded to trial at the SPSC. A smaller number of cases involved crimes against humanity, and in no case was genocide or war crimes charged. See Chapter 2, note 595 and accompanying text. No accused in the SCSL, ECCC, or (as far as can be determined) the SICT has been charged with domestic crimes.

45 See Chapter 3, text accompanying notes 377–378. Report of the Secretary-General on the Establishment of a Special Court for Sierra Leone, UN Doc. S/2000/915, 4 October 2000, para. 13.

46 Because their drafters largely copied the definitions of crimes from the Rome Statute, most of the crimes in the constitutive documents of the SPSC and the SICT are also non-specific, with a few exceptions: both list specific domestic crimes, see *supra* note 43, the constitutive document of the SPSC lists torture as a freestanding crime, see Chapter 1, note 9, and the SICT Statute has altered certain underlying offences and omitted others, see Chapter 2, text accompanying note 674, Chapter 4, text accompanying notes 592–598. The otherwise wholesale adoption of the Rome Statute for these Tribunals is problematic for two reasons. First, they were given jurisdiction over crimes that would likely never be prosecuted, such as genocide in the SPSC (with one erroneous exception, see Chapter 3, text accompanying note 384) and international armed conflict war crimes in the SICT, see Chapter 4, text accompanying note 604. Second, and more importantly, certain of the crimes probably did not exist in custom during at least part the Tribunals' temporal jurisdiction. This is especially true of the non-international armed conflict war crimes in the SICT Statute for cases concerning events in the 1980s, such as the *Anfal* case. See Chapter 4, text accompanying notes 599–600.

47 Rome Statute of the International Criminal Court, entered into force 1 July 2002, UN Doc. A/CONF. 183/9 (1998) ('Rome Statute'), Art. 7(2)(a). See also Chapter 2, text accompanying notes 490–494. A state or organisational policy is not required in any of the other courts or tribunals discussed in this volume except the SICT, and possibly the SPSC. See Chapter 2, note 59. The restrictive nature of this requirement stands in stark contrast to one of the consistent themes in the *ad hoc* Tribunals' jurisprudence, where the Appeals Chambers have repeatedly confirmed that none of the core categories of crimes discussed in this volume require proof of a plan or policy, even if such an organisational characteristic is strong evidence that the conduct in question was purposefully committed. See Chapter 2, text accompanying notes 180–181; Chapter 3, text accompanying note 134; Chapter 4, text accompanying note 443.

recognized by the principal legal systems of the world'.[48] Likewise, the Court should exercise jurisdiction over war crimes '*in particular* when committed as part of a plan or policy or as part of a large-scale commission of such crimes',[49] and genocide where the underlying offence 'took place in the context of a manifest pattern of similar conduct directed against [the targeted] group or was conduct that could itself effect [the group's] destruction'.[50] As a result of the inability of common-law and civil-law delegations to reach agreement on the concept of conspiracy, conspiracy to commit genocide is conspicuously absent from the Rome Statute.[51] Progressive development in the Rome Statute beyond custom can be seen in all three core categories: for crimes against humanity, for example, in the inclusion of new underlying offences, such as enforced disappearance, apartheid, and various sexual offences;[52] for genocide, in the more coherent treatment of the inchoate crimes and complicity that resulted from the decision not to import Article III of the Genocide Convention verbatim;[53] and for war crimes, in the inclusion of many offences drawn from treaties spanning the twentieth century – including some relating to non-international armed conflict – that had never before been expressly designated as attracting individual criminal responsibility.[54] Most of these restrictions and expansions can also be seen in the constitutive instruments of the SPSC and SICT, the drafters of which largely copied the ICC's definitions of crimes and underlying offences.[55]

Modern international criminal law is little over a decade old and it is inevitable that, with the rapid development of a complex body of substantive law, inconsistencies and even contradiction will inevitably occur. Yet these variations across the courts and tribunals raise a broader issue about the credibility of international criminal justice as expressed through the international criminal trial process. It is important to ensure that this divergence does not threaten the immediate and fundamental goal of delivering fair trials, or the less immediate but equally fundamental

48 Assembly of States Parties to the Rome Statute of the International Criminal Court, First Session: Official Records, Part II(B): Elements of Crimes, UN Doc. ICC-ASP/1/3 (2002) ('ICC Elements of Crimes'), Art. 7, Introduction, para. 1.

49 Rome Statute, *supra* note 47, Art. 8(1) (emphasis added). This restriction is absent from both of the subsequent constitutive instruments otherwise mostly based on the Rome Statute: those of the SPSC and the SICT. See Chapter 4, note 440.

50 ICC Elements of Crimes, *supra* note 48, Art. 6(a), Element 4; *ibid*., Art. 6(b), Element 4; *ibid*., Art. 6(c), Element 5; *ibid*., Art. 6(d), Element 5; *ibid*., Art. 6(e), Element 7. See also Chapter 3, text accompanying notes 349–353.

51 See Chapter 3, text accompanying notes 339–342.

52 See Chapter 2, text accompanying notes 508–511. The similar list of additional sexual underlying offences of crimes against humanity in the SCSL Statute can also be seen as progressive development. See *ibid*., text accompanying notes 556, 564–565.

53 See Chapter 3, text accompanying notes 330–333; see also Gideon Boas, James L. Bischoff, and Natalie L. Reid, *Forms of Responsibility in International Criminal Law* (2007), pp. 331–332.

54 See Chapter 4, text accompanying notes 446–453.

55 See *supra* note 46 and the sections on the SPSC and SICT in Chapters 2 to 4.

goal of constructing a comprehensive, consistent, and coherent criminal justice system for the international community.

In this sense, the work of the ICC is, and will continue to be, critical. We hope that, as the ICC develops jurisprudence on the elements of crimes and forms of responsibility, it does not place undue restrictions on definitions not required by its statute or customary law. Considering the war crimes provisions of the constitutive instruments and jurisprudence in the different international and internationalised criminal courts and tribunals, it is apparent that the ICC has a well-developed definition in its Statute, although the Rome Statute has perpetuated the regrettable distinction between international and non-international armed conflicts. Meanwhile, the crimes against humanity definition that comes closest to custom is not that of the ICC, but that of the SCSL, which lacks an armed conflict requirement (as required by the ICTY), a discriminatory attack requirement (as required by the ICTR), or a policy requirement (such as that required by the ICC). On the other hand, the ICC does have a more complete list of underlying offences for crimes against humanity in its Statute, including apartheid and forced disappearance. The ICC's definition of genocide is generally sound, excepting the still somewhat incoherent treatment of the genocide-related inchoate crimes and the omission of conspiracy to commit genocide from the Rome Statute altogether.

In 2009 or 2010, the states parties to the Rome Statute will consider revisions to the Statute, including its list of crimes.[56] Politics aside, this occasion is an opportunity to reconsider some of these crucial issues of substantive international criminal law, and to try to tie together the strands of jurisprudence from the different courts and tribunals to create a more solid and coherent body of law on the elements of the crimes and the forms of responsibility.

6.4 The need for a more coherent conviction and sentencing practice

In Chapter 5, we discussed the lack of a coherent sentencing practice in the relatively prodigious sentencing work of the *ad hoc* Tribunals to date. Three main factors have harmed the desirable goals of consistency and coherency in sentencing: (1) the refusal to set real scales or guidelines, a position explicitly adopted and perpetuated by the ICTY Appeals Chamber;[57] (2) the refusal to acknowledge a hierarchy of crimes; and (3) the seemingly arbitrary interference by appeals chambers in the broad discretion open to trial chambers, simply because the appellate benches disagree with the sentence given.[58] These factors have created the unwelcome

[56] See Rome Statute, *supra* note 47, Art. 123; Rolf Einar Fife, Assembly of States Parties to the International Criminal Court, 'Review Conference: Scenarios and Options', 21 November 2006, Doc. No. ICC-ASP/5/INF.2.

[57] See Chapter 5, text accompanying notes 251–254.

[58] See generally *ibid*., section 5.3.3.

impression of randomness in the *ad hoc* Tribunals' sentencing practice, an impression that is exacerbated – and perhaps confirmed – by wildly diverging sentences which, if anything, suggest a misplaced leniency toward those found responsible for mass atrocities.

At least two negative consequences flow from this situation, particularly with respect to the ICTY.[59] First, as Judge Bonomy has stated academically, '[i]n war crimes trials the sentences may be shorter than those imposed in an equivalent domestic context'.[60] This comparative leniency of ICTY sentences, which occurs with little or no explanation, does not reflect the views of the international community with regard to the gravity of the conduct it is intended to punish, and it sends the wrong message to the perpetrators, the victims, and their communities concerning the impact of such crimes and the importance of international criminal tribunals in the fight against impunity. The trend of lighter sentences is even more pronounced where accused have pleaded guilty. This strategy may serve the shorter-term goals of encouraging accused to plead guilty in the hope of attaining a shorter sentence (clearly achieved in the ICTY),[61] and is no doubt facilitated by the desire to wind up the work of the Tribunals as quickly as possible.[62] It will hardly benefit the greater aspirations of international criminal law to deliver justice for the most heinous criminality.

Second, unlike their trailblazing efforts in substantive and procedural international criminal law, the *ad hoc* Tribunals will not set a standard in sentencing practice that might serve as an example for the ICC and future international and internationalised courts and tribunals. The ICC will have to look elsewhere for guidance and, in doing so, it is hoped that the Court will develop clear sentencing guidelines, establish a practice that avoids significant and unexplained leniency when compared to domestic sentences for lesser crimes, and thus give appropriate weight to the gravity of the crimes it is bound to try.

A certain degree of confusion can also be seen in the *ad hoc* Appeals Chambers' stance on cumulative convictions, particularly where persecution is involved. The clearest example of this problem is their approach to possible cumulative convictions for murder as a crime against humanity and murder as a form of persecution as

[59] As we have acknowledged in Chapter 5, some greater consistency and harshness of punishment have evolved in respect of the crime of genocide in the ICTR. See *ibid.*, note 223 and accompanying text.

[60] Iain Bonomy, 'The Reality of Conducting a War Crimes Trial', (2007) 5 *Journal of International Criminal Justice* 348, 351.

[61] See Chapter 5, text accompanying notes 228–234 (discussing the significantly lower sentences handed down on accused who plead guilty – most notoriously, the eleven-year sentence for Biljana Plavšić for an array of crimes against humanity).

[62] On the completion strategy of the ICTY, see Gideon Boas, *The Milošević Trial: Lessons for the Conduct of International Criminal Proceedings* (2007), p. 67; Daryl A. Mundis, 'The Judicial Effects of the "Completion Strategies" on the Ad Hoc International Criminal Tribunals', (2005) 99 *American Journal of International law* 142. See also Security Council Resolution 1503, UN Doc. S/RES/1503 (2003); Security Council Resolution 1534, UN Doc. S/RES/1534 (2004).

a crime against humanity. In *Kordić and Čerkez*, a slender majority of the ICTY Appeals Chamber overturned a sensible application of the well-established principle that trial chambers may only convict the accused for the more specific crime: disregarding the structure and content of the crimes in question, the Appeals Chamber asserted that the Trial Chamber had erred in concluding that it could only convict the accused for murder as a form of persecution as a crime against humanity because that crime contains all the elements of murder as a crime against humanity simpliciter plus at least one more – discriminatory intent.[63] In the place of the Trial Chamber's nuanced understanding of the interplay between underlying offences and the general and specific requirements for international crimes, the Appeals Chamber substituted an oversimplified test which ignores the form of persecution in question and compels trial chambers to enter two convictions where the prosecution manages to prove all the elements of the crime against humanity and that it was committed with discriminatory intent.[64] This mechanical approach – now entrenched in the appellate jurisprudence of both Tribunals[65] – exemplifies poor appellate practice. The Appeals Chambers replaced a clear and logical legal principle with the rote application of a rule rooted in sparse and fallacious reasoning that misapprehends how trial chambers have actually applied the elements of persecution in practice. Moreover, the Appeals Chambers' approach glosses over the complicated nature of persecution as a subcategory of crimes against humanity, rather than a simple underlying offence of the same legal character as, for example, murder, torture, or rape.[66] While the *Kordić and Čerkez* approach is not likely to be abandoned by the *ad hoc* Tribunals in the few years they have remaining,[67] the ICC and other international and internationalised courts and tribunals would be well advised to consider fairer and more legally defensible alternatives, instead of unthinkingly following the lead of *Kordić and Čerkez* and its progeny.

* * *

The central effort of the first two volumes in this series has been to offer comprehensive and sensible explanations of the process through which individual criminal responsibility for a given international crime is constructed through a combination of elements. Our goal is to assist practitioners in the development and presentation

[63] See Chapter 5, text accompanying notes 103–110, 150 (discussing the coherent analytical approach of the once-prevailing *Krstić* line of cases).

[64] See *ibid.*, text accompanying notes 121–127. [65] See *ibid.*, text accompanying notes 128–132.

[66] See especially Chapter 5, text accompanying notes 152–155 (describing the way in which trial chambers apply the elements of persecution and the form thereof to determine if criminal liability may be imposed on the accused); see also Chapter 2, text accompanying notes 388–392 (describing the nature of persecution as a label that is applied to underlying offences when they satisfy certain specific requirements).

[67] At least two judges of the ICTY and ICTR Appeals Chambers, however, would likely abandon the *Kordić and Čerkez* approach if presented with the opportunity. See Chapter 5, text accompanying notes 133–142 (discussing a series of dissenting opinions by Judges Güney and Schomburg).

of cases; to support trial and appeals chambers in the application of an accurate and appropriately flexible approach to conviction and sentencing; and to provide all, including students and scholars, with a more precise and nuanced understanding of the elements of substantive international criminal law. The Annex to this volume sets forth the myriad of combinations of such elements for each crime and form of responsibility in the jurisdiction of the *ad hoc* Tribunals.

Annex

Elements of core international crimes and sample combinations with forms of responsibility

This annex provides a bulleted summary of the physical and mental elements of the core international crimes as defined in the jurisprudence of the *ad hoc* Tribunals. For ease of reference, it also includes separate listings of (1) the general requirements for crimes against humanity, genocide, and war crimes – that is, the elements that must be proved beyond reasonable doubt in order for an underlying offence to qualify as an international crime within each of those categories; and (2) the specific requirements for persecution as a crime against humanity, inhumane acts as crimes against humanity, inhuman treatment as a grave breach of the Geneva Conventions, and cruel treatment as a violation of the laws or customs of war – that is, the additional elements that must be proved beyond reasonable doubt in order for an underlying offence to constitute one of those international crimes.

Section 5 of this annex also includes a number of sample combinations of these elements with the forms of responsibility, in order to illustrate all the elements that must be proved beyond reasonable doubt in order to convict an accused of a particular crime through a particular form of responsibility. A separate listing of the elements of the forms of responsibility is included in the annex to Volume I in this series.[1]

1. Common underlying offences

As explained throughout this volume, several international crimes have common underlying offences. That is, the elements of the underlying offence are constant, and what distinguishes one international crime from another are the general or specific requirements that characterise the core categories of international crimes, or certain subcategories of crimes. This section of the Annex lists the elements of the common underlying offences that are most frequently charged at the *ad hoc* Tribunals.

1.1 Arbitrary deprivation of liberty

a. The physical perpetrator deprived an individual ('the victim') of his or her liberty.
b. This deprivation of liberty was imposed without legal justification.
c. The physical perpetrator either
   i. intended to deprive the victim of his or her liberty without legal justification, or
   ii. knew that his conduct was reasonably likely to result in such a deprivation.

1.2 Destruction of real or personal property

a. The physical perpetrator partially or wholly destroyed, or caused significant damage to, real or personal property.
b. The physical perpetrator either
   i. intended to destroy or damage this property, or
   ii. engaged in intentional conduct with reckless disregard for the likelihood that the property would be so destroyed or damaged.

1.3 Forcible displacement

a. The physical perpetrator caused displacement of persons ('the victims') by expulsion or other coercive conduct.
b. The persons displaced were lawfully present in the area.
c. The displacement occurred without grounds permitted under international law.

[1] See Gideon Boas, James L. Bischoff, and Natalie L. Reid, *Forms of Responsibility in International Criminal Law* (2007), pp. 426–429.

1.4 Murder

a. The physical perpetrator caused the death of an individual ('the victim') by his act or omission ('conduct').
b. The physical perpetrator either
   i. intended to cause the victim's death, or
   ii. intended to inflict harm in the knowledge that the conduct was reasonably likely to cause death.[2]

1.5 Rape

a. The physical perpetrator penetrated, without consent,
   i. the vagina or anus of an individual (the 'victim') with his penis or any other object, or
   ii. the mouth of the victim with his penis.
b. The physical perpetrator intended to effect that penetration.
c. The physical perpetrator knew
   i. that the victim did not consent, or
   ii. that coercive circumstances existed that precluded the possibility of valid consent.

1.6 Torture

a. The physical perpetrator inflicted severe mental or physical suffering on an individual ('the victim').
b. The physical perpetrator intended to inflict such suffering on the victim.
c. The suffering was inflicted on the victim for a prohibited purpose, such as punishment, coercion, or intimidation of, obtaining information or a confession from, or discrimination against the victim or a third party.

2. Crimes against humanity

2.1 General requirements for crimes against humanity

a. There was an attack.
b. The attack was directed against a predominantly civilian population.[3]
c. The attack was widespread or systematic.

[2] Under current jurisprudence of the *ad hoc* Tribunals, it is unclear whether this conduct must be premeditated. See Chapter 2, text accompanying notes 212–222; Chapter 4, section 4.2.2.4.

[3] For the definition of 'civilian' that is currently used in the *ad hoc* Tribunals for both crimes against humanity and war crimes, see Chapter 2, section 2.2.2.3.1.

d. The underlying offences were part of this attack.
e. The physical perpetrator or other relevant actor[4] knew that the underlying offences formed part of this attack.
f. The victim was a civilian.

2.2 Murder as a crime against humanity

a. All elements of the common underlying offence of murder must be proved.[5]
b. The victim was a civilian.
c. The victim's murder was part of a widespread or systematic attack on a predominantly civilian population.
d. The physical perpetrator or other relevant actor knew that the murder was part of this attack.

2.3 Extermination as a crime against humanity

a. All elements of the common underlying offence of murder must be proved.[6]
b. The victim was one of a numerically significant group of victims.
c. The physical perpetrator intended to participate in causing mass death.
d. The victim was a civilian.
e. The victim's murder was part of a widespread or systematic attack on a predominantly civilian population.
f. The physical perpetrator or other relevant actor knew that the murder was part of this attack.

2.4 Enslavement as a crime against humanity

a. The physical perpetrator exercised over another individual ('the victim') any or all of the powers attached to the right of ownership.
b. The physical perpetrator intended to exercise such power or powers over the victim.
c. The victim was a civilian.
d. The physical perpetrator's exercise of such power or powers over the victim was part of a widespread or systematic attack on a predominantly civilian population.
e. The physical perpetrator or other relevant actor knew that this exercise of such power or powers over the victim was part of this attack.

[4] For an explanation of the term of art 'other relevant actor', see, e.g., Chapter 2, text accompanying notes 90–109; Chapter 6, section 6.1.1.
[5] See *supra* section 1.4. [6] See *supra* section 1.4.

2.5 Deportation as a crime against humanity

a. All elements of the common underlying offence of forcible displacement must be proved.[7]
b. The forcible displacement of the victim took place across a *de facto* or *de jure* international border.
c. The victim was a civilian.
d. The forcible displacement of the victim was part of a widespread or systematic attack on a predominantly civilian population.
e. The physical perpetrator or other relevant actor knew that the forcible displacement was part of this attack.

2.6 Imprisonment as a crime against humanity

a. All elements of the common underlying offence of arbitrary deprivation of liberty must be proved.[8]
b. The victim was a civilian.
c. The arbitrary deprivation of the victim's liberty was part of a widespread or systematic attack on a predominantly civilian population.
d. The physical perpetrator or other relevant actor knew that the arbitrary deprivation of liberty was part of this attack.

2.7 Torture as a crime against humanity

a. All elements of the common underlying offence of torture must be proved.[9]
b. The victim was a civilian.
c. The torture of the victim was part of a widespread or systematic attack on a predominantly civilian population.
d. The physical perpetrator or other relevant actor knew that the torture was part of this attack.

2.8 Rape as a crime against humanity

a. All elements of the common underlying offence of rape must be proved.[10]
b. The victim was a civilian.
c. The rape of the victim was part of a widespread or systematic attack on a predominantly civilian population.
d. The physical perpetrator or other relevant actor knew that the rape was part of this attack.

[7] See *supra* section 1.3. [8] See *supra* section 1.1. [9] See *supra* section 1.6. [10] See *supra* section 1.5.

2.9 Persecution as a crime against humanity

a. Specific requirements for persecution as a crime against humanity

i. The physical perpetrator's act or omission ('conduct') must be of the same gravity as the specifically listed underlying offences of crimes against humanity.

ii. The physical perpetrator or other relevant actor intended to discriminate against an individual on the basis of the victim's political, racial, or religious identity.

iii. The conduct must actually target the members of a group defined on the basis of politics, race, or religion.[11]

The forms of persecution defined below are those most frequently charged at the *ad hoc* Tribunals. Other conduct may qualify as persecution as a crime against humanity if the specific requirements for persecution and the general requirements for crimes against humanity are satisfied.

b. Murder as a form of persecution as a crime against humanity

i. All elements of murder as a crime against humanity must be proved.[12]

ii. The victim was, or was perceived to be, a member of a group defined on the basis of politics, race, or religion.[13]

iii. The physical perpetrator or other relevant actor intended to harm or kill the victim because of the victim's political, racial, or religious identity.

- Since murder is a specifically listed underlying offence of crimes against humanity, it is of sufficient gravity to qualify as persecution.

c. Enslavement as a form of persecution as a crime against humanity

i. All elements of enslavement as a crime against humanity must be proved.[14]

ii. The victim was, or was perceived to be, a member of a group defined on the basis of politics, race, or religion.[15]

iii. The physical perpetrator or other relevant actor intended that any or all of the powers of ownership be exercised over the victim because of the victim's political, racial, or religious identity.

- Since enslavement is a specifically listed underlying offence of crimes against humanity, it is of sufficient gravity to qualify as persecution.

d. Deportation as a form of persecution as a crime against humanity

i. All elements of deportation as a crime against humanity must be proved.[16]

ii. The victim was, or was perceived to be, a member of a group defined on the basis of politics, race, or religion.[17]

iii. The physical perpetrator or other relevant actor intended to forcibly displace the victim because of the victim's political, racial, or religious identity.

[11] Under current jurisprudence of the *ad hoc* Tribunals, this requirement is given little independent weight, because if all other elements are satisfied, the conduct will qualify as persecution if the victim is either actually member of the targeted group, or is only perceived to be a member of the group. See Chapter 2, text accompanying notes 411–415.

[12] See *supra* sections 1.4, 2.2.

[13] See *supra* note 11. For purposes of these definitions, either the physical perpetrator or the other relevant actor could be the person who perceives the victim as belonging to the targeted group.

[14] See *supra* section 2.4. [15] See *supra* note 13. [16] See *supra* sections 1.3, 2.5. [17] See *supra* note 13.

- Since deportation is a specifically listed underlying offence of crimes against humanity, it is of sufficient gravity to qualify as persecution.

e. **Forcible transfer as a form of persecution as a crime against humanity**
   i. All elements of the common underlying offence of forcible displacement must be proved.[18]
   ii. The victim was displaced within the *de jure* or *de facto* borders of a state.
   iii. The victim was a civilian.
   iv. The victim was, or was perceived to be, a member of a group defined on the basis of politics, race, or religion.[19]
   v. The physical perpetrator or other relevant actor intended to forcibly displace the victim because of the victim's political, racial, or religious identity.
   vi. The forcible displacement of the victim was part of a widespread or systematic attack on a predominantly civilian population.
   vii. The physical perpetrator or other relevant actor knew that the forcible displacement was part of this attack.
   - As a matter of law, forcible transfer has been determined to be of sufficient gravity to qualify as persecution.

f. **Imprisonment as a form of persecution as a crime against humanity**
   i. All elements of imprisonment as a crime against humanity must be proved.[20]
   ii. The victim was, or was perceived to be, a member of a group defined on the basis of politics, race, or religion.[21]
   iii. The physical perpetrator or other relevant actor intended to arbitrarily deprive the victim of his or her liberty because of the victim's political, racial, or religious identity.
   - Since imprisonment is a specifically listed underlying offence of crimes against humanity, it is of sufficient gravity to qualify as persecution.

g. **Torture as a form of persecution as a crime against humanity**
   i. All elements of torture as a crime against humanity must be proved.[22]
   ii. The victim was, or was perceived to be, a member of a group defined on the basis of politics, race, or religion.[23]
   iii. The physical perpetrator or other relevant actor intended to inflict severe mental or physical suffering on the victim because of the victim's political, racial, or religious identity.
   - Since torture is a specifically listed underlying offence of crimes against humanity, it is of sufficient gravity to qualify as persecution.

h. **Rape as a form of persecution as a crime against humanity**
   i. All elements of rape as a crime against humanity must be proved.[24]
   ii. The victim was, or was perceived to be, a member of a group defined on the basis of politics, race, or religion.[25]

[18] See *supra* section 1.3. [19] See *supra* note 13. [20] See *supra* sections 1.1, 2.6. [21] See *supra* note 13.
[22] See *supra* sections 1.6, 2.7. [23] See *supra* note 13. [24] See *supra* sections 1.5, 2.8. [25] See *supra* note 13.

iii. The physical perpetrator intended to rape the victim, or another relevant actor intended that the victim be raped, because of the victim's political, racial, or religious identity.

- Since rape is a specifically listed underlying offence of crimes against humanity, it is of sufficient gravity to qualify as persecution.

i. Destruction of property as a form of persecution as a crime against humanity[26]

i. All elements of the common underlying offence of destruction of real or personal property must be proved.[27]

ii. The destruction of property must be of sufficient gravity to qualify as persecution.

iii. The owner of the property ('the victim') was, or was perceived to be, a member of a group defined on the basis of politics, race, or religion.[28]

iv. The physical perpetrator intended to damage or destroy the victim's property because of the victim's political, racial, or religious identity.

2.10 Other inhumane acts as crimes against humanity

a. Specific requirements common to <u>other inhumane acts as crimes against humanity</u>, inhuman treatment as a grave breach of the Geneva Conventions of 1949, and cruel treatment as a violation of the laws or customs of war

i. The physical perpetrator's conduct must either

  i. cause serious mental or physical suffering to the victim, or

  ii. constitute a serious attack on human dignity.

ii. Such suffering or attack must be of similar gravity to the enumerated underlying offences for that particular category of international crimes.

iii. The physical perpetrator's conduct must be performed with either

  i. the intent to inflict serious physical or mental harm upon the victim,

  ii. the intent to commit a serious attack on the victim's human dignity, or

  iii. with the knowledge that it would probably have such an effect.

The most frequently charged inhumane act is forcible transfer, the elements of which are listed below. Other conduct may qualify as inhumane acts as crimes against humanity if the specific requirements for inhumane acts and the general requirements for crimes against humanity are satisfied.

b. Forcible transfer as an inhumane act as a crime against humanity

i. All elements of the common underlying offence of forcible displacement must be proved.[29]

ii. The victim was a civilian.

[26] ICTY indictments have frequently charged destruction of cultural property as a form of persecution as a crime against humanity. See, e.g., *Prosecutor* v. *Milutinović, Šainović, Ojdanić, Pavković, Lazarević, and Lukić*, Case No. IT-05-87-PT, Third Amended Joinder Indictment, 21 June 2006, para. 77(d) (alleging that 'wanton destruction and damage of Kosovo Albanian religious sites … cultural monuments and Muslim sacred sites' constituted persecution as a crime against humanity). Unlike the war crimes specifically derived from international humanitarian treaty law, see Chapter 4, section 4.2.2.1.3, the law on persecution does not distinguish between the types of property that is destroyed.

[27] See *supra* sections 1.2. [28] See *supra* note 13. [29] See *supra* section 1.3.

iii. The physical perpetrator or other relevant actor must either
    i. intend to inflict serious physical or mental harm upon the victim by the forcible displacement of the victim,
    ii. intend to commit a serious attack on human dignity by the forcible displacement of the victim, or
    iii. know that the forcible displacement would probably have that effect.
iv. The forcible displacement of the victim was part of a widespread or systematic attack on a predominantly civilian population.
v. The physical perpetrator or other relevant actor knew that the forcible displacement was part of this attack.

- As a matter of law, forcible transfer has been determined to cause serious mental suffering to the victims, and to be of sufficient gravity to qualify as an inhumane act.

3. Genocide and related crimes

3.1 General requirements for genocide

a. The physical perpetrator or other relevant actor[30] intended to destroy a distinct group that is objectively defined on the basis of nationality, ethnicity, race, or religion.
b. The victims were, or were perceived to be, members of that distinct group. For purposes of these definitions, either the physical perpetrator or the other relevant actor could be the person who perceives the victim as belonging to the targeted group.

3.2 Genocide by killing

a. The physical perpetrator caused the death of an individual ('the victim') by his conduct.
b. The physical perpetrator intended to cause the victim's death.[31]
c. The physical perpetrator or other relevant actor intended, through this death, to contribute toward the partial or total destruction of a distinct group that is objectively defined on the basis of nationality, ethnicity, race, or religion.
d. The victim was, or was perceived to be, a member of that distinct group.

3.3 Genocide by causing serious bodily harm

a. The physical perpetrator caused harm to the organs, senses, or physical health of an individual ('the victim').
b. The physical perpetrator intended to cause such harm to the victim.

[30] For an explanation of the term of art 'other relevant actor', see, e.g., Chapter 2, text accompanying notes 90–109; Chapter 6, section 6.1.1.

[31] Note that, but for the restriction of the *mens rea* to specific intent to cause death, the elements of killing as an underlying offence of genocide are identical to those of murder as a common underlying offence. See *supra* section 1.4.

c. This harm significantly and adversely affected the victim's ability to lead a normal life.
d. The physical perpetrator or other relevant actor intended, through harming the victim, to contribute toward the partial or total destruction of a distinct group that is objectively defined on the basis of nationality, ethnicity, race, or religion.
e. The victim was, or was perceived to be, a member of that distinct group.

3.4 Genocide by causing serious mental harm

a. The physical perpetrator caused harm to the mental faculties of an individual ('the victim').
b. The physical perpetrator intended to cause such harm to the victim.
c. This harm significantly and adversely affected the victim's ability to lead a normal life.
d. The physical perpetrator or other relevant actor intended, through harming the victim, to contribute toward the partial or total destruction of a distinct group that is objectively defined on the basis of nationality, ethnicity, race, or religion.
e. The victim was, or was perceived to be, a member of that distinct group.

3.5 Genocide by deliberate infliction of eventually destructive conditions of life

a. The physical perpetrator inflicted certain conditions of life on an individual ('the victim').
b. The victim was, or was perceived to be, a member of a distinct group that is objectively defined on the basis of nationality, ethnicity, race, or religion.
c. The conditions of life were calculated to eventually cause the partial or total physical destruction of that distinct group.
d. The physical perpetrator deliberately inflicted such conditions of life on the victim.
e. The physical perpetrator or other relevant actor intended, through imposing such conditions of life on the victim, to contribute toward the partial or total destruction of a distinct group that is objectively defined on the basis of nationality, ethnicity, race, or religion.

3.6 Genocide by prevention of births

a. The physical perpetrator imposed, on an individual ('the victim'), measures to prevent births.
b. The physical perpetrator intended to impose such measures on the victim.
c. The physical perpetrator or other relevant actor intended, through the imposition of such measures on the victim, to contribute toward the partial or total destruction of a distinct group that is objectively defined on the basis of nationality, ethnicity, race, or religion.
d. The victim was, or was perceived to be, a member of that distinct group.

3.7 Genocide by forcibly transferring children to another group

a. The physical perpetrator forcibly transferred a child ('the victim') who was a member, or was perceived to be a member, of a distinct group that is objectively defined on the basis of nationality, ethnicity, race, or religion, to another group that is objectively defined on one or more of those bases.
b. The physical perpetrator intended to so forcibly transfer the victim.
c. The physical perpetrator or other relevant actor intended, through such forcible transfer of the victim, to contribute toward the partial or total destruction of the victim's distinct group.

3.8 Conspiracy to commit genocide

a. Two or more persons ('the conspirators') came to an agreement that genocide or any of its underlying offences would be committed.
b. The conspirators intended to partially or completely destroy a national, ethnic, racial, or religious group through the conduct contemplated by the agreement.

3.9 Direct and public incitement to commit genocide

a. An individual ('the inciter') publicly prompted or provoked others to commit genocide or any of its underlying offences.
b. The inciter deliberately undertook his conduct with the intention that the prompting or provocation result in the partial or total destruction of a national, ethnic, racial, or religious group.

3.10 Attempt to commit genocide

- As discussed in Chapter 3, no chamber of either *ad hoc* Tribunal has offered a definition of this inchoate crime.[32]

4. War crimes

4.1 General requirements for all war crimes

a. At the time the underlying offence was committed, there was an armed conflict, i.e., either
   i. a resort to armed force between states ('international armed conflict'), or
   ii. protracted armed violence between organised armed groups within a state ('non-international armed conflict').

32 See Chapter 3, section 3.5.

b. The underlying offence was closely related to the armed conflict ('nexus requirement').
c. The physical perpetrator or other relevant actor[33] knew that an armed conflict existed at the time the underlying offences were committed.[34]

4.2 Additional general requirements for grave breaches of the Geneva Conventions of 1949[35]

a. The armed conflict to which the underlying offence was closely related was international in character.
b. The physical perpetrator or other relevant actor knew the factual circumstances that rendered the armed conflict international in character.
c. The individuals or property targeted in the underlying offences were protected under the Geneva Conventions of 1949 ('the Geneva Conventions').

4.3 Additional general requirements for war crimes arising from breaches of Common Article 3 of the Geneva Conventions ('Common Article 3') or Additional Protocol II to the Geneva Conventions ('Additional Protocol II')[36]

a. The individual or property targeted in the underlying offence was protected under Common Article 3 or Additional Protocol II, i.e.,
   i. The individual ('the victim') was not actively participating in the hostilities at the time of the underlying offence, or
   ii. The targeted property was not a military objective, or was otherwise protected by international humanitarian law.
b. The physical perpetrator or other relevant actor knew the facts establishing the protected status of the victim or the targeted property under Common Article 3 or Additional Protocol II.

4.4 Additional general requirements for violations of the laws or customs of war under Article 3 of the ICTY Statute

a. The underlying offence must infringe a rule of customary or conventional international humanitarian law.

[33] For an explanation of the term of art 'other relevant actor', see, e.g., Chapter 2, text accompanying notes 90–109; Chapter 6, section 6.1.1.

[34] The ICTY Appeals Chamber has made this element a general requirement for war crimes, but as of 1 December 2007, it had not yet been applied as such in subsequent trial judgements. See Chapter 4, text accompanying notes 118–120.

[35] In the context of the *ad hoc* Tribunals, these crimes fall under the jurisdiction granted by Article 2 of the ICTY Statute.

[36] In the context of the *ad hoc* Tribunals, these crimes fall under the jurisdiction granted by Article 3 of the ICTY Statute or Article 4 of the ICTR Statute.

b. The violation must be 'serious' (the 'gravity requirement').[37]
c. The breach must give rise to individual criminal responsibility under customary or conventional international law.

The violations of the laws or customs of war that are listed below (with other war crimes) are those which have been defined in the jurisprudence of the *ad hoc* Tribunals. Other conduct may qualify as violations of the laws or customs of war if all the applicable general requirements are satisfied.

4.5 'Extensive destruction of property, not justified by military necessity and carried out unlawfully and wantonly' as a grave breach

a. All elements of the common underlying offence of destruction of real or personal property must be proved.[38]
b. The destruction caused was extensive.
c. At the time of the destruction, there was an international armed conflict.
d. The destruction of property was closely related to that international armed conflict.
e. The property was protected under the Geneva Conventions.
f. The physical perpetrator or other relevant actor knew that the armed conflict existed.
g. The physical perpetrator or other relevant actor knew the factual circumstances establishing the international character of the armed conflict.

4.6 'Wanton destruction' of property as a violation of the laws or customs of war

a. All elements of the common underlying offence of destruction of real or personal property must be proved.[39]
b. The destruction caused occurred on a large scale.
c. At the time of the destruction, there was an armed conflict.
d. The destruction of property was closely related to that armed conflict.
e. The destroyed property was not a military objective, or was otherwise protected under international humanitarian law.
f. The physical perpetrator or other relevant actor knew that the armed conflict existed.
g. The physical perpetrator or other relevant actor knew that the destroyed property was not a military objective, or was otherwise protected under international humanitarian law.
    - As a matter of law, wanton destruction has been held to be a violation of international humanitarian law that entails the imposition of individual criminal responsibility.

[37] As discussed in Chapter 4, this additional general requirement is probably best interpreted as a jurisdictional requirement peculiar to the ICTY, not an element of the crime that must be proved beyond reasonable doubt in all circumstances. See Chapter 4, section 4.2.1.5.2.
[38] See *supra* section 1.2. [39] See *supra* section 1.2.

4.7 *'Unjustified devastation' of property as a violation of the laws or customs of war*

a. All elements of the common underlying offence of destruction of real or personal property must be proved.[40]
b. The destruction or damage caused occurred on a large scale.
c. At the time of the destruction or damage, there was an armed conflict.
d. The destruction or damage of property was closely related to that armed conflict.
e. The destroyed or damaged property was not a military objective, or was otherwise protected under international humanitarian law.
f. The physical perpetrator or other relevant actor knew that the armed conflict existed.
g. The physical perpetrator or other relevant actor knew that the destroyed or damaged property was not a military objective, or was otherwise protected under international humanitarian law.
   - As a matter of law, devastation has been held to be a violation of international humanitarian law that entails the imposition of individual criminal responsibility.

4.8 *'Destruction or wilful damage to institutions dedicated to religion, charity and education, the arts and sciences, historic monuments and works of art and science' as a violation of the laws or customs of war*

a. The physical perpetrator caused damage to, or destruction of, real property.
b. The damaged or destroyed property was dedicated to religion, charity and education, or the arts and sciences, or was a historic monument or work of art or science.
c. The physical perpetrator intended to damage or destroy the property.
d. At the time of the destruction or damage, there was an armed conflict.
e. The destruction or damage of property was closely related to that armed conflict.
f. The destroyed or damaged property was not a military objective, or was otherwise protected under international humanitarian law.
g. The physical perpetrator or other relevant actor knew that the armed conflict existed.
h. The physical perpetrator or other relevant actor knew that the destroyed or damaged property was not a military objective, or was otherwise protected under international humanitarian law.
   - As a matter of law, destruction and damage to these types of property have been held to be violations of international humanitarian law that entail the imposition of individual criminal responsibility.

[40] See *supra* section 1.2.

4.9 Hostage-taking as a grave breach

a. The physical perpetrator seized or detained an individual (the 'victim').
b. The physical perpetrator threatened to kill, injure, or continue to detain the victim.
c. These threats were made in order to compel a third party to do or to abstain from doing something as a condition for the release of the victim.
d. The physical perpetrator intentionally seized or detained the victim for the purpose of using him or her to compel such conduct from the third party.[41]
e. At the time the victim was seized or detained, there was an international armed conflict.
f. The seizure or detention of the victim was closely related to that international armed conflict.
g. The victim was a protected person under the Geneva Conventions.
h. The physical perpetrator or other relevant actor knew that the armed conflict existed.
i. The physical perpetrator or other relevant actor knew the factual circumstances establishing the international character of the armed conflict.

4.10 Hostage-taking as a violation of the laws or customs of war

a. The physical perpetrator seized or detained an individual (the 'victim').
b. The physical perpetrator threatened to kill, injure, or continue to detain the victim.
c. These threats were made in order to compel a third party to do or to abstain from doing something as a condition for the release of the victim.
d. The physical perpetrator intentionally seized or detained the victim for the purpose of using him or her to compel such conduct from the third party.[42]
e. At the time victim was seized or detained, there was an armed conflict.
f. The seizure or detention of the victim was closely related to that armed conflict.
g. The physical perpetrator or other relevant actor knew that the armed conflict existed.
    - As a matter of law, hostage-taking has been held to be a violation of international humanitarian law that entails the imposition of individual criminal responsibility.

4.11 Inhuman treatment as a grave breach

a. All the specific requirements common to other inhumane acts as crimes against humanity, inhuman treatment as a grave breach, and cruel treatment as a violation of the laws or customs of war must be proved.[43]

[41] It is possible that a lower *mens rea* standard, that of deliberately running the risk that the victim would be seized or detained for that purpose, may also be accepted by the *ad hoc* Tribunals. See Chapter 4, text accompanying note 306.

[42] It is possible that a lower *mens rea* standard, that of deliberately running the risk that the victim would be seized or detained for that purpose, may also be accepted by the *ad hoc* Tribunals. See Chapter 4, text accompanying note 306.

[43] See *supra* section 2.10.a.

b. At the time the physical perpetrator subjected the victim to mental or physical suffering or an attack on human dignity, there was an international armed conflict.
c. The treatment of the victim was closely related to that international armed conflict.
d. The victim was a protected person under the Geneva Conventions.
e. The physical perpetrator or other relevant actor knew that the armed conflict existed.
f. The physical perpetrator or other relevant actor knew the factual circumstances establishing the international character of the armed conflict.

4.12 Cruel treatment as a violation of the laws or customs of war

a. All the specific requirements common to other inhumane acts as crimes against humanity, inhuman treatment as a grave breach, and cruel treatment as a violation of the laws or customs of war must be proved.[44]
b. At the time the physical perpetrator subjected the victim to mental or physical suffering or an attack on human dignity, there was an armed conflict.
c. The treatment of the victim was closely related to that armed conflict.
d. The physical perpetrator or other relevant actor knew that the armed conflict existed.
   - As a matter of law, cruel treatment has been held to be a violation of international humanitarian law that entails the imposition of individual criminal responsibility.

4.13 Wilful killing as a grave breach

a. All elements of the common underlying offence of murder must be proved.[45]
b. At the time of the physical perpetrator's conduct causing the victim's death, there was an international armed conflict.
c. The physical perpetrator's conduct was closely related to that international armed conflict.
d. The victim was a protected person under the Geneva Conventions.
e. The physical perpetrator or other relevant actor knew that the armed conflict existed.
f. The physical perpetrator or other relevant actor knew the factual circumstances establishing the international character of the armed conflict.

4.14 Murder as a violation of the laws or customs of war

a. All elements of the common underlying offence of murder must be proved.[46]
b. At the time of the physical perpetrator's conduct causing the victim's death, there was an armed conflict.
c. The physical perpetrator's conduct was closely related to that armed conflict.
d. The victim was not taking active part in the hostilities.
e. The physical perpetrator or other relevant actor knew that the armed conflict existed.

[44] See *supra* section 2.10.a. [45] See *supra* section 1.4. [46] See *supra* section 1.4.

f. The physical perpetrator or other relevant actor knew that the victim was not taking active part in the hostilities.
   - As a matter of law, murder has been held to be a violation of international humanitarian law that entails the imposition of individual criminal responsibility.

4.15 Outrages upon personal dignity as a violation of Additional Protocol II / the laws or customs of war

a. The physical perpetrator treated an individual ('the victim') in a manner that would be generally considered to cause serious humiliation, degradation, or otherwise be a serious attack on the human dignity of the victim.
b. The physical perpetrator acted or failed to act in the knowledge that his conduct could cause serious humiliation, degradation, or otherwise be a serious attack on the human dignity of the victim.
c. At the time of the physical perpetrator's conduct, there was an armed conflict.
d. The physical perpetrator's conduct was closely related to that armed conflict.
e. The victim was not taking active part in the hostilities.
f. The physical perpetrator or other relevant actor knew that the armed conflict existed.
g. The physical perpetrator or other relevant actor knew that the victim was not taking active part in the hostilities. (Additional Protocol II)
   - As a matter of law, outrages upon personal dignity have been held to be violations of international humanitarian law that entail the imposition of individual criminal responsibility.

4.16 'Extensive appropriation of property, not justified by military necessity and carried out unlawfully and wantonly' as a grave breach

a. The physical perpetrator(s) took possession or assumed control of public or private property.
b. This possession or assumption of control was not justified under international law.
c. The physical perpetrator(s) intended to take possession or assume control of this property.
d. The physical perpetrator(s) or other relevant actor knew that the possession or assumption of control was not justified under international law.[47]
e. The taking of possession or assumption of control of property was extensive.
f. At the time of the taking of possession or assumption of control of property, there was an international armed conflict.

[47] At least one judgement has held that indirect intent is acceptable, so that presumably the *mens rea* for this crime would be satisfied if the physical perpetrator or other relevant actor either acted with reckless disregard for whether the appropriation was lawful, or acted in the knowledge that it was likely to be unlawful. See Chapter 4, note 351.

g. The taking of possession or assumption of control of property was closely related to that international armed conflict.
h. The property was protected under the Geneva Conventions.
i. The physical perpetrator or other relevant actor knew that the armed conflict existed.
j. The physical perpetrator or other relevant actor knew the factual circumstances establishing the international character of the armed conflict.

4.17 Plunder as a violation of the laws or customs of war

a. The physical perpetrator took possession or assumed control of public or private property.
b. This possession or assumption of control was not justified under international law.
c. The physical perpetrator intended to take possession or assume control of this property.
d. The physical perpetrator or other relevant actor knew that the possession or assumption of control was not justified under international law.[48]
e. At the time of the taking of possession or assumption of control of property, there was an armed conflict.
f. The taking of possession or assumption of control of property was closely related to that armed conflict.
g. The physical perpetrator or other relevant actor knew that the armed conflict existed.
    - As a matter of law, plunder has been held to be a violation of international humanitarian law that entails the imposition of individual criminal responsibility.

4.18 Rape as a grave breach

a. All elements of the common underlying offence of rape must be proved.[49]
b. At the time of the rape, there was an international armed conflict.
c. The rape was closely related to that international armed conflict.
d. The victim was protected under the Geneva Conventions.
e. The physical perpetrator or other relevant actor knew that the armed conflict existed.
f. The physical perpetrator or other relevant actor knew the factual circumstances establishing the international character of the armed conflict.

4.19 Rape as a violation of the laws or customs of war

a. All elements of the common underlying offence of rape must be proved.[50]
b. At the time of the rape, there was an armed conflict.
c. The rape was closely related to that international armed conflict.
d. The physical perpetrator or other relevant actor knew that the armed conflict existed.
    - As a matter of law, rape has been held to be a violation of international humanitarian law that entails the imposition of individual criminal responsibility.

[48] See *supra* note 47. [49] See *supra* section 1.5. [50] See *supra* section 1.5.

4.20 Slavery as a violation of the laws or customs of war

a. The physical perpetrator exercised over another individual ('the victim') any or all of the powers attached to the right of ownership.
b. The physical perpetrator intended to exercise such power or powers over the victim.
c. At the time of the exercise of such powers over the victim, there was an armed conflict.
d. The exercise of such powers over the victim was closely related to that armed conflict.
e. The victim was not taking active part in the hostilities.
f. The physical perpetrator or other relevant actor knew that the armed conflict existed.
   - As a matter of law, slavery has been held to be a violation of international humanitarian law that entails the imposition of individual criminal responsibility.

4.21 Unlawful labour as a violation of the laws or customs of war

a. The physical perpetrator compelled an individual ('the victim') to perform tasks or otherwise undertake labour.
b. Such performance of these tasks or labour by the victim was prohibited by international humanitarian law.
c. The physical perpetrator intended that the victim perform such tasks or labour.[51]
d. At the time of the victim's labour, there was an armed conflict.
e. The victim's labour was closely related to that armed conflict.
f. The physical perpetrator(s) or other relevant actor knew that the armed conflict existed.

4.22 Terror as a violation of the laws or customs of war

a. The physical perpetrator committed or threatened acts of violence against a predominantly civilian population.
b. The primary purpose of the physical perpetrator's conduct was to spread fear in that population.
c. At the time of the physical perpetrator's conduct, there was an armed conflict.
d. The physical perpetrator's conduct was closely related to that armed conflict.
e. The physical perpetrator or other relevant actor knew that the armed conflict existed.

[51] As noted in Chapter 4, the manner in which chambers have discussed the *mens rea* requirement for unlawful labour makes it unclear whether there is an additional requirement that the physical perpetrator or another relevant actor must have been aware that the labour in question was specifically prohibited under international humanitarian law, or whether it is sufficient that the victim was intentionally ordered to perform the work. See Chapter 4, text accompanying notes 367–368.

4.23 Torture as a grave breach

a. All elements of the common underlying offence of torture must be proved.[52]
b. At the time of the torture, there was an international armed conflict.
c. The victim's torture was closely related to that international armed conflict.
d. The victim was protected under the Geneva Conventions.
e. The physical perpetrator or other relevant actor knew that the armed conflict existed.
f. The physical perpetrator or other relevant actor knew the factual circumstances establishing the international character of the armed conflict.

4.24 Torture as a violation of the laws or customs of war

a. All elements of the common underlying offence of torture must be proved.[53]
b. At the time of the torture, there was an armed conflict.
c. The victim's torture was closely related to that armed conflict.
d. The victim was not taking active part in the hostilities.
e. The physical perpetrator or other relevant actor knew that the armed conflict existed.
f. The physical perpetrator or other relevant actor knew that the victim was not taking active part in the hostilities.

4.25 Unlawful attack on civilians as a violation of the laws or customs of war

a. The physical perpetrator committed acts of violence against a civilian population or individual civilians ('the victims').[54]
b. The physical perpetrator's conduct caused death, serious injury to body or health, or a result of equal gravity to the victims.
c. The physical perpetrator either
    i. intended to make the victims the targets of his acts of violence, or
    ii. acted with reckless disregard for whether the victims would be harmed by his conduct.
d. At the time of the physical perpetrator's conduct there was an armed conflict.
e. The physical perpetrator's conduct was closely related to that armed conflict.
f. The physical perpetrator or other relevant actor knew that the armed conflict existed.
g. The physical perpetrator or other relevant actor knew that the targets of the physical perpetrator's conduct were civilians.

[52] See *supra* section 1.6. [53] See *supra* section 1.6.
[54] For the definition of 'civilian' that is currently used in the *ad hoc* Tribunals for both crimes against humanity and war crimes, see Chapter 2, section 2.2.2.3.1.

4.26 *Unlawful attack on civilian objects as a violation of the laws or customs of war*

a. The physical perpetrator committed acts of violence against property.
b. The physical perpetrator's conduct caused death, serious injury to body or health, or a result of equal gravity to civilians.
c. The physical perpetrator either
   i. intended to make the property the target of his acts of violence, or
   ii. acted with reckless disregard for whether the property would be damaged by his conduct.
d. At the time of the physical perpetrator's conduct there was an armed conflict.
e. The physical perpetrator's conduct was closely related to that armed conflict.
f. The property was not a military objective.
g. The physical perpetrator or other relevant actor knew that the armed conflict existed.
h. The physical perpetrator or other relevant actor knew that the property was not a military objective.

4.27 *Unlawful confinement of a civilian as a grave breach*

a. All elements of the common underlying offence of arbitrary deprivation of liberty must be proved,[55] with specific reference to the Geneva Conventions to determine the lawfulness of the arrest or continued detention.[56]
b. At the time of the deprivation of liberty, there was an international armed conflict.
c. The deprivation of liberty was closely related to that international armed conflict.
d. The victim was a civilian.[57]
e. The physical perpetrator or other relevant actor knew that the armed conflict existed.
f. The physical perpetrator or other relevant actor knew the factual circumstances establishing the international character of the armed conflict.

4.28 *Unlawful confinement as a violation of the laws or customs of war*

a. All elements of the common underlying offence of arbitrary deprivation of liberty must be proved.[58]
b. At the time of the deprivation of liberty, there was an armed conflict.
c. The deprivation of liberty was closely related to that armed conflict.
d. The victim was not taking active part in the hostilities.
e. The physical perpetrator or other relevant actor knew that the armed conflict existed.
f. The physical perpetrator or other relevant actor knew that the victim was not taking active part in the hostilities.

[55] See *supra* section 1.1. [56] See Chapter 4, text accompanying notes 410–412.
[57] For the definition of 'civilian' that is currently used in the *ad hoc* Tribunals for both crimes against humanity and war crimes, see Chapter 2, section 2.2.2.3.1.
[58] See *supra* section 1.1.

4.29 Unlawful deportation or transfer as a grave breach

a. All elements of the common underlying offence of forcible displacement must be proved.[59]
   i. For deportation, the victim was forcibly displaced across a *de facto* or *de jure* international border.
b. At the time of the forcible displacement, there was an international armed conflict.
c. The forcible displacement was closely related to that international armed conflict.
d. The victim was protected under the Geneva Conventions.
e. The physical perpetrator or other relevant actor knew that the armed conflict existed.
f. The physical perpetrator or other relevant actor knew the factual circumstances establishing the international character of the armed conflict.

4.30 Wilfully causing great suffering or serious injury to body or health as a grave breach[60]

a. The physical perpetrator's conduct caused serious mental or physical suffering to the victim.
b. Such suffering was of similar gravity to the enumerated underlying offences for grave breaches.
c. The physical perpetrator's conduct was performed with either
   i. the intent to inflict serious physical or mental harm upon the victim, or
   ii. with the knowledge that it would probably have such an effect.
d. At the time of the physical perpetrator's conduct, there was an international armed conflict.
e. The physical perpetrator's conduct was closely related to that international armed conflict.
f. The victim was protected under the Geneva Conventions.
g. The physical perpetrator or other relevant actor knew that the armed conflict existed.
h. The physical perpetrator or other relevant actor knew the factual circumstances establishing the international character of the armed conflict.

5. Sample combinations of elements of crimes and forms of responsibility

In order to convict an accused of any crime within the jurisdiction of the *ad hoc* Tribunals on the ground that he physically committed the crime, a trial chamber need only examine and apply the elements discussed above, combining the elements

[59] See *supra* section 1.3.

[60] Very little attention has been paid to defining the elements or specific requirements of this apparent subcategory of underlying offences. The elements listed here are indirectly derived from statements in the existing jurisprudence.

of the underlying offence with the general requirements for the charged category or subcategory of international crimes, and any applicable specific requirements. In this scenario, the concept of the 'other relevant actor' is irrelevant, as the physical perpetrator-accused fulfils all the elements himself.[61]

The approach is different, however, where the accused and the physical perpetrator are not one and the same person. To convict an accused of a crime on the basis of any of the other forms of responsibility provided for in the statutes of the international and internationalised courts and tribunals examined in this series, a trial chamber must conclude that all the elements of the crime *and* all the elements of the relevant form of responsibility have been proved beyond reasonable doubt.[62] As an illustration of this process, we consider five crimes below; under each crime, we list all the elements necessary to convict an accused through each of the forms of responsibility applied at the *ad hoc* Tribunals.

5.1 Torture as a crime against humanity

5.1.1 Joint Criminal Enterprise, First Category (JCE I)

a. The physical perpetrator inflicted severe mental or physical suffering on an individual ('the victim').
b. The physical perpetrator intended to inflict such suffering on the victim.
c. The suffering was inflicted on the victim for a prohibited purpose, such as punishment, coercion, or intimidation of, obtaining information or a confession from, or discrimination against the victim or a third party.
d. The victim was a civilian.
e. The torture of the victim was part of a widespread or systematic attack on a predominantly civilian population.
f. The physical perpetrator or other relevant actor knew that the torture was part of this attack.
g. The accused and at least one other person came to an express or implied agreement that torture as a crime against humanity would be committed ('the common plan, design, or purpose').
h. The accused participated in this common plan, design, or purpose.
i. The accused's participation in the common plan, design, or purpose was voluntary.
j. The accused shared the intent to commit torture as a crime against humanity.

5.1.2 Joint Criminal Enterprise, Second Category (JCE II)

a. The physical perpetrator inflicted severe mental or physical suffering on an individual ('the victim').
b. The physical perpetrator intended to inflict such suffering on the victim.

[61] For an explanation of the term of art 'other relevant actor', see, e.g., Chapter 2, text accompanying notes 90–109; Chapter 6, section 6.1.1.
[62] See, e.g., Chapter 1, text accompanying notes 33–34.

c. The suffering was inflicted on the victim for a prohibited purpose, such as punishment, coercion, or intimidation of, obtaining information or a confession from, or discrimination against the victim or a third party.
d. The victim was a civilian.
e. The torture of the victim was part of a widespread or systematic attack on a predominantly civilian population.
f. The physical perpetrator or other relevant actor knew that the torture was part of this attack.
g. The accused participated in a system of ill-treatment ('the common plan, design, or purpose') that amounted to or involved the commission of torture as a crime against humanity.
h. The accused's participation in the common plan, design, or purpose was voluntary.
i. The accused had personal knowledge of the criminal nature of the system of ill-treatment.
j. The accused intended to further the criminal purpose of the system of ill-treatment.
k. The accused shared the intent to commit torture as a crime against humanity.

5.1.3 Joint Criminal Enterprise, Third Category (JCE III)

a. The physical perpetrator inflicted severe mental or physical suffering on an individual ('the victim').
b. The physical perpetrator intended to inflict such suffering on the victim.
c. The suffering was inflicted on the victim for a prohibited purpose, such as punishment, coercion, or intimidation of, obtaining information or a confession from, or discrimination against the victim or a third party.
d. The victim was a civilian.
e. The torture of the victim was part of a widespread or systematic attack on a predominantly civilian population.
f. The physical perpetrator or other relevant actor knew that the torture was part of this attack.
g. The accused and at least one other person came to an express or implied agreement that a crime within the jurisdiction of the relevant Tribunal would be committed ('the common plan, design, or purpose').
h. The accused participated in this common plan, design, or purpose.
i. The accused's participation in the common plan, design, or purpose was intentional and voluntary.
j. The accused intended to further the criminal purpose of the joint criminal enterprise.
k. The commission of torture as a crime against humanity was a natural and foreseeable consequence of the execution of the common plan, design, or purpose.
l. The accused was aware that the commission of torture as a crime against humanity was possible.

5.1.4 Superior Responsibility

a. The physical perpetrator inflicted severe mental or physical suffering on an individual ('the victim').
b. The physical perpetrator intended to inflict such suffering on the victim.

c. The suffering was inflicted on the victim for a prohibited purpose, such as punishment, coercion, or intimidation of, obtaining information or a confession from, or discrimination against the victim or a third party.
d. The victim was a civilian.
e. The torture of the victim was part of a widespread or systematic attack on a predominantly civilian population.
f. The physical perpetrator or other relevant actor knew that the torture was part of this attack.
g. A superior-subordinate relationship existed between the accused and the physical perpetrator.
h. Where appropriate, a superior-subordinate relationship also existed between the accused and the other relevant actor.[63]
i. The accused either
    i. knew that torture as a crime against humanity was about to be, was being, or had been realised by the physical perpetrator, and where appropriate, the other relevant actor; or
    ii. had reason to know that torture as a crime against humanity was about to be, was being, or had been realised by the physical perpetrator, and where appropriate, the other relevant actor.
j. The accused failed to take all measures within his material ability to either
    i. prevent the physical perpetrator and, where appropriate, the other relevant actor, from carrying out torture as a crime against humanity; or
    ii. ensure that punishment was dispensed upon the physical perpetrator and, where appropriate, the other relevant actor, for carrying out torture as a crime against humanity.

5.1.5 Aiding and Abetting

a. The physical perpetrator inflicted severe mental or physical suffering on an individual ('the victim').
b. The physical perpetrator intended to inflict such suffering on the victim.
c. The suffering was inflicted on the victim for a prohibited purpose, such as punishment, coercion, or intimidation of, obtaining information or a confession from, or discrimination against the victim or a third party.
d. The victim was a civilian.
e. The torture of the victim was part of a widespread or systematic attack on a predominantly civilian population.
f. The physical perpetrator or other relevant actor knew that the torture was part of this attack.

[63] Through superior responsibility, an accused is held liable for the criminal conduct of his subordinates. If an actor other than the physical perpetrator (the 'other relevant actor') supplies one or more of the elements of the crime, an accused cannot be held responsible for that person's participation in the crime if the other relevant actor is not also a subordinate subject to his effective control.

g. The accused lent practical assistance, encouragement, or moral support to the physical perpetrator in committing torture as a crime against humanity.
h. The practical assistance, encouragement, or moral support had a substantial effect on the commission of torture as a crime against humanity.
i. The accused acted intentionally with knowledge or awareness that his act would lend assistance, encouragement, or moral support to the physical perpetrator.
j. The accused was aware of the essential elements of the crime, including the intent of the physical perpetrator to inflict suffering on the victim.

5.1.6 Planning

a. The physical perpetrator inflicted severe mental or physical suffering on an individual ('the victim').
b. The physical perpetrator intended to inflict such suffering on the victim.
c. The suffering was inflicted on the victim for a prohibited purpose, such as punishment, coercion, or intimidation of, obtaining information or a confession from, or discrimination against the victim or a third party.
d. The victim was a civilian.
e. The torture of the victim was part of a widespread or systematic attack on a predominantly civilian population.
f. The physical perpetrator or other relevant actor knew that the torture was part of this attack.
g. The accused either
    i. designed criminal conduct constituting torture as a crime against humanity with the intent that this crime be committed; or
    ii. designed an act or omission, aware of the substantial likelihood that torture as a crime against humanity would be committed in the realisation of that act or omission.
h. The accused's conduct substantially contributed to the perpetration of torture as a crime against humanity.

5.1.7 Instigating

a. The physical perpetrator inflicted severe mental or physical suffering on an individual ('the victim').
b. The physical perpetrator intended to inflict such suffering on the victim.
c. The suffering was inflicted on the victim for a prohibited purpose, such as punishment, coercion, or intimidation of, obtaining information or a confession from, or discrimination against the victim or a third party.
d. The victim was a civilian.
e. The torture of the victim was part of a widespread or systematic attack on a predominantly civilian population.
f. The physical perpetrator or other relevant actor knew that the torture was part of this attack.

g. The accused either
   i. prompted criminal conduct constituting torture as a crime against humanity with the intent that this crime be committed; or
   ii. prompted an act or omission, aware of the substantial likelihood that torture as a crime against humanity would be committed in the realisation of that act or omission.
h. The accused's conduct substantially contributed to the perpetration of torture as a crime against humanity.

5.1.8 Ordering

a. The physical perpetrator inflicted severe mental or physical suffering on an individual ('the victim').
b. The physical perpetrator intended to inflict such suffering on the victim.
c. The suffering was inflicted on the victim for a prohibited purpose, such as punishment, coercion, or intimidation of, obtaining information or a confession from, or discrimination against the victim or a third party.
d. The victim was a civilian.
e. The torture of the victim was part of a widespread or systematic attack on a predominantly civilian population.
f. The physical perpetrator or other relevant actor knew that the torture was part of this attack.
g. The accused either
   i. instructed another[64] to commit torture as a crime against humanity with the intent that this crime be committed; or
   ii. instructed another to engage in an act or omission, aware of the substantial likelihood that torture as a crime against humanity would be committed in the realisation of that act or omission.
h. The accused enjoyed formal or informal authority over the person to whom the order was given.
i. The accused's conduct had a direct and substantial effect on the perpetration of torture as a crime against humanity.

5.2 Murder as a form of persecution as a crime against humanity

5.2.1 Joint Criminal Enterprise, First Category (JCE I)

a. The physical perpetrator caused the death of an individual ('the victim') by his act or omission ('conduct').
b. The physical perpetrator either
   i. intended to cause the victim's death, or
   ii. intended to inflict harm in the knowledge that the conduct was reasonably likely to cause death.

[64] For example, the accused could instruct the physical perpetrator directly, or he could instruct someone else – an intermediate commander, for example – who himself instructs the physical perpetrator.

c. The victim was a civilian.
d. The victim's murder was part of a widespread or systematic attack on a predominantly civilian population.
e. The physical perpetrator or other relevant actor knew that the murder was part of this attack.
f. The victim was, or was perceived to be, a member of a group defined on the basis of politics, race, or religion.[65]
g. The physical perpetrator or other relevant actor intended to harm or kill the victim because of the victim's political, racial, or religious identity.
h. The accused and at least one other person came to an express or implied agreement that murder as a form of persecution as a crime against humanity would be committed ('the common plan, design, or purpose').
i. The accused participated in this common plan, design, or purpose.
j. The accused's participation in the common plan, design, or purpose was voluntary.
k. The accused shared the intent to commit murder as a form of persecution as a crime against humanity, including the physical perpetrator's intent to commit murder, and the specific intent of the physical perpetrator or other relevant actor to discriminate against the victim because of the victim's political, racial, or religious identity.

5.2.2 Joint Criminal Enterprise, Second Category (JCE II)

a. The physical perpetrator caused the death of an individual ('the victim') by his act or omission ('conduct').
b. The physical perpetrator either
    i. intended to cause the victim's death, or
    ii. intended to inflict harm in the knowledge that the conduct was reasonably likely to cause death.
c. The victim was a civilian.
d. The victim's murder was part of a widespread or systematic attack on a predominantly civilian population.
e. The physical perpetrator or other relevant actor knew that the murder was part of this attack.
f. The victim was, or was perceived to be, a member of a group defined on the basis of politics, race, or religion.[66]
g. The physical perpetrator or other relevant actor intended to harm or kill the victim because of the victim's political, racial, or religious identity.
h. The accused participated in a system of ill-treatment ('the common plan, design, or purpose') that amounted to or involved the commission of murder as a form of persecution as a crime against humanity.
i. The accused's participation in the common plan, design, or purpose was voluntary.
j. The accused had personal knowledge of the criminal nature of the system of ill-treatment.
k. The accused intended to further the criminal purpose of the system of ill-treatment.

[65] See *supra* note 13. [66] See *ibid*.

l. The accused shared the intent to commit murder as a form of persecution as a crime against humanity, including the physical perpetrator's intent to commit murder, and the specific intent of the physical perpetrator or other relevant actor to discriminate against the victim because of the victim's political, racial, or religious identity.

5.2.3 Joint Criminal Enterprise, Third Category (JCE III)

a. The physical perpetrator caused the death of an individual ('the victim') by his act or omission ('conduct').
b. The physical perpetrator either
   i. intended to cause the victim's death, or
   ii. intended to inflict harm in the knowledge that the conduct was reasonably likely to cause death.
c. The victim was a civilian.
d. The victim's murder was part of a widespread or systematic attack on a predominantly civilian population.
e. The physical perpetrator or other relevant actor knew that the murder was part of this attack.
f. The victim was, or was perceived to be, a member of a group defined on the basis of politics, race, or religion.[67]
g. The physical perpetrator or other relevant actor intended to harm or kill the victim because of the victim's political, racial, or religious identity.
l. The accused and at least one other person came to an express or implied agreement that a crime within the jurisdiction of the relevant Tribunal would be committed ('the common plan, design, or purpose').
m. The accused participated in this common plan, design, or purpose.
h. The accused's participation in the common plan, design, or purpose was intentional and voluntary.
i. The accused intended to further the criminal purpose of the joint criminal enterprise.
j. The commission of murder as a form of persecution as a crime against humanity was a natural and foreseeable consequence of the execution of the common plan, design, or purpose.
k. The accused was aware that the commission of murder as a form of persecution as a crime against humanity was possible.

5.2.4 Superior Responsibility

a. The physical perpetrator caused the death of an individual ('the victim') by his act or omission ('conduct').
b. The physical perpetrator either
   i. intended to cause the victim's death, or
   ii. intended to inflict harm in the knowledge that the conduct was reasonably likely to cause death.

[67] See *ibid.*

c. The victim was a civilian.
d. The victim's murder was part of a widespread or systematic attack on a predominantly civilian population.
e. The physical perpetrator or other relevant actor knew that the murder was part of this attack.
f. The victim was, or was perceived to be, a member of a group defined on the basis of politics, race, or religion.[68]
g. The physical perpetrator or other relevant actor intended to harm or kill the victim because of the victim's political, racial, or religious identity.
h. A superior-subordinate relationship existed between the accused and the physical perpetrator.
i. Where appropriate, a superior-subordinate relationship also existed between the accused and the other relevant actor.[69]
j. The accused either
    i. knew that murder as a form of persecution as a crime against humanity was about to be, was being, or had been realised by the physical perpetrator, and where appropriate, the other relevant actor; or
    ii. had reason to know that murder as a form of persecution as a crime against humanity was about to be, was being, or had been realised by the physical perpetrator, and where appropriate, the other relevant actor.
k. The accused failed to take all measures within his material ability to either
    i. prevent the physical perpetrator and, where appropriate, the other relevant actor, from carrying out murder as a form of persecution as a crime against humanity; or
    ii. ensure that punishment was dispensed upon the physical perpetrator and, where appropriate, the other relevant actor, for carrying out murder as a form of persecution as a crime against humanity.

5.2.5 Aiding and Abetting

a. The physical perpetrator caused the death of an individual ('the victim') by his act or omission ('conduct').
b. The physical perpetrator either
    i. intended to cause the victim's death, or
    ii. intended to inflict harm in the knowledge that the conduct was reasonably likely to cause death.
c. The victim was a civilian.
d. The victim's murder was part of a widespread or systematic attack on a predominantly civilian population.
e. The physical perpetrator or other relevant actor knew that the murder was part of this attack.
f. The victim was, or was perceived to be, a member of a group defined on the basis of politics, race, or religion.[70]

[68] See *ibid.* [69] See *supra* note 63. [70] See *supra* note 13.

g. The physical perpetrator or other relevant actor intended to harm or kill the victim because of the victim's political, racial, or religious identity.
h. The accused lent practical assistance, encouragement, or moral support to the physical perpetrator in committing murder as a form of persecution as a crime against humanity.
i. The practical assistance, encouragement, or moral support had a substantial effect on the commission of murder as a form of persecution as a crime against humanity.
j. The accused acted intentionally with knowledge or awareness that his act would lend assistance, encouragement, or moral support to the physical perpetrator.
k. The accused was aware of the essential elements of the crime, including the intent of the physical perpetrator to kill or harm the victim, and the intent of the physical perpetrator or other relevant actor to harm or kill the victim because of the victim's political, racial, or religious identity.

5.2.6 Planning

a. The physical perpetrator caused the death of an individual ('the victim') by his act or omission ('conduct').
b. The physical perpetrator either
    i. intended to cause the victim's death, or
    ii. intended to inflict harm in the knowledge that the conduct was reasonably likely to cause death.
c. The victim was a civilian.
d. The victim's murder was part of a widespread or systematic attack on a predominantly civilian population.
e. The physical perpetrator or other relevant actor knew that the murder was part of this attack.
f. The victim was, or was perceived to be, a member of a group defined on the basis of politics, race, or religion.[71]
g. The physical perpetrator or other relevant actor intended to harm or kill the victim because of the victim's political, racial, or religious identity.
h. The accused either
    i. designed criminal conduct constituting murder as a form of persecution as a crime against humanity with the intent that this crime be committed; or
    ii. designed an act or omission, aware of the substantial likelihood that murder as a form of persecution as a crime against humanity would be committed in the realisation of that act or omission.
i. The accused's conduct substantially contributed to the perpetration of murder as a form of persecution as a crime against humanity.

[71] See *ibid.*

5.2.7 Instigating

a. The physical perpetrator caused the death of an individual ('the victim') by his act or omission ('conduct').
b. The physical perpetrator either
   i. intended to cause the victim's death, or
   ii. intended to inflict harm in the knowledge that the conduct was reasonably likely to cause death.
c. The victim was a civilian.
d. The victim's murder was part of a widespread or systematic attack on a predominantly civilian population.
e. The physical perpetrator or other relevant actor knew that the murder was part of this attack.
f. The victim was, or was perceived to be, a member of a group defined on the basis of politics, race, or religion.[72]
g. The physical perpetrator or other relevant actor intended to harm or kill the victim because of the victim's political, racial, or religious identity.
h. The accused either
   i. prompted criminal conduct constituting murder as a form of persecution as a crime against humanity with the intent that this crime be committed; or
   ii. prompted an act or omission, aware of the substantial likelihood that murder as a form of persecution as a crime against humanity would be committed in the realisation of that act or omission.
i. The accused's conduct substantially contributed to the perpetration of murder as a form of persecution as a crime against humanity.

5.2.8 Ordering

a. The physical perpetrator caused the death of an individual ('the victim') by his act or omission ('conduct').
b. The physical perpetrator either
   i. intended to cause the victim's death, or
   ii. intended to inflict harm in the knowledge that the conduct was reasonably likely to cause death.
c. The victim was a civilian.
d. The victim's murder was part of a widespread or systematic attack on a predominantly civilian population.
e. The physical perpetrator or other relevant actor knew that the murder was part of this attack.
f. The victim was, or was perceived to be, a member of a group defined on the basis of politics, race, or religion.[73]

[72] See *ibid.* [73] See *ibid.*

g. The physical perpetrator or other relevant actor intended to harm or kill the victim because of the victim's political, racial, or religious identity.
h. The accused either
    i. instructed another[74] to commit murder as a form of persecution as a crime against humanity with the intent that this crime be committed; or
    ii. instructed another to engage in an act or omission, aware of the substantial likelihood that murder as a form of persecution as a crime against humanity would be committed in the realisation of that act or omission.
i. The accused enjoyed formal or informal authority over the person to whom the order was given.
j. The accused's conduct had a direct and substantial effect on the perpetration of murder as a form of persecution as a crime against humanity.

5.3 Genocide by killing

5.3.1 Joint Criminal Enterprise, First Category (JCE I)

a. The physical perpetrator caused the death of an individual ('the victim') by his conduct.
b. The physical perpetrator intended to cause the victim's death.
c. The physical perpetrator or other relevant actor intended, through this death, to contribute toward the partial or total destruction of a distinct group that is objectively defined on the basis of nationality, ethnicity, race, or religion.
d. The victim was, or was perceived to be, a member of that distinct group.[75]
e. The accused and at least one other person came to an express or implied agreement that genocide by killing would be committed ('the common plan, design, or purpose').
f. The accused participated in this common plan, design, or purpose.
g. The accused's participation in the common plan, design, or purpose was voluntary.
h. The accused shared the intent to commit genocide by killing, including the physical perpetrator's intent to cause the victim's death and the intent of the physical perpetrator or other relevant actor to partially or totally destroy the distinct group.

5.3.2 Joint Criminal Enterprise, Second Category (JCE II)

a. The physical perpetrator caused the death of an individual ('the victim') by his conduct.
b. The physical perpetrator intended to cause the victim's death.
c. The physical perpetrator or other relevant actor intended, through this death, to contribute toward the partial or total destruction of a distinct group that is objectively defined on the basis of nationality, ethnicity, race, or religion.
d. The victim was, or was perceived to be, a member of that distinct group.[76]

[74] For example, the accused could instruct the physical perpetrator directly, or he could instruct someone else – an intermediate commander, for example – who himself instructs the physical perpetrator.

[75] For purposes of these definitions, either the physical perpetrator or the other relevant actor could be the person who perceives the victim as belonging to the targeted distinct group.

[76] See *supra* note 75.

e. The accused participated in a system of ill-treatment ('the common plan, design, or purpose') that amounted to or involved the commission of genocide by killing.
f. The accused's participation in the common plan, design, or purpose was voluntary.
g. The accused had personal knowledge of the criminal nature of the system of ill-treatment.
h. The accused intended to further the criminal purpose of the system of ill-treatment.
i. The accused shared the intent to commit genocide by killing, including the physical perpetrator's intent to cause the victim's death and the intent of the physical perpetrator or other relevant actor to partially or totally destroy the distinct group.

5.3.3 Joint Criminal Enterprise, Third Category (JCE III)

a. The physical perpetrator caused the death of an individual ('the victim') by his conduct.
b. The physical perpetrator intended to cause the victim's death.
c. The physical perpetrator or other relevant actor intended, through this death, to contribute toward the partial or total destruction of a distinct group that is objectively defined on the basis of nationality, ethnicity, race, or religion.
d. The victim was, or was perceived to be, a member of that distinct group.[77]
e. The accused and at least one other person came to an express or implied agreement that a crime within the jurisdiction of the relevant Tribunal would be committed ('the common plan, design, or purpose').
f. The accused participated in this common plan, design, or purpose.
g. The accused's participation in the common plan, design, or purpose was intentional and voluntary.
h. The accused intended to further the criminal purpose of the joint criminal enterprise.
i. The commission of genocide by killing was a natural and foreseeable consequence of the execution of the common plan, design, or purpose.
j. The accused was aware that the commission of genocide by killing was possible.

5.3.4 Superior Responsibility

a. The physical perpetrator caused the death of an individual ('the victim') by his conduct.
b. The physical perpetrator intended to cause the victim's death.
c. The physical perpetrator or other relevant actor intended, through this death, to contribute toward the partial or total destruction of a distinct group that is objectively defined on the basis of nationality, ethnicity, race, or religion.
d. The victim was, or was perceived to be, a member of that distinct group.[78]
e. A superior-subordinate relationship existed between the accused and the physical perpetrator.
f. Where appropriate, a superior-subordinate relationship also existed between the accused and the other relevant actor.[79]

[77] See *ibid.* [78] See *ibid.* [79] See *supra* note 63.

g. The accused either
   i. knew that genocide by killing was about to be, was being, or had been realised by the physical perpetrator, and where appropriate, the other relevant actor; or
   ii. had reason to know that genocide by killing was about to be, was being, or had been realised by the physical perpetrator, and where appropriate, the other relevant actor.
h. The accused failed to take all measures within his material ability to either
   i. prevent the physical perpetrator and, where appropriate, the other relevant actor, from carrying out genocide by killing; or
   ii. ensure that punishment was dispensed upon the physical perpetrator and, where appropriate, the other relevant actor, for carrying out genocide by killing.

5.3.5 *Aiding and Abetting*

a. The physical perpetrator caused the death of an individual ('the victim') by his conduct.
b. The physical perpetrator intended to cause the victim's death.
c. The physical perpetrator or other relevant actor intended, through this death, to contribute toward the partial or total destruction of a distinct group that is objectively defined on the basis of nationality, ethnicity, race, or religion.
d. The victim was, or was perceived to be, a member of that distinct group.[80]
e. The accused lent practical assistance, encouragement, or moral support to the physical perpetrator in committing genocide by killing.
f. The practical assistance, encouragement, or moral support had a substantial effect on the commission of genocide by killing.
g. The accused acted intentionally with knowledge or awareness that his act would lend assistance, encouragement, or moral support to the physical perpetrator.
h. The accused was aware of the essential elements of the crime, including the physical perpetrator's intent to cause the victim's death and the intent of the physical perpetrator or other relevant actor to partially or totally destroy the distinct group.

5.3.6 *Planning*

a. The physical perpetrator caused the death of an individual ('the victim') by his conduct.
b. The physical perpetrator intended to cause the victim's death.
c. The physical perpetrator or other relevant actor intended, through this death, to contribute toward the partial or total destruction of a distinct group that is objectively defined on the basis of nationality, ethnicity, race, or religion.
d. The victim was, or was perceived to be, a member of that distinct group.[81]
e. The accused either
   i. designed criminal conduct constituting genocide by killing with the intent that this crime be committed; or
   ii. designed an act or omission, aware of the substantial likelihood that genocide by killing would be committed in the realisation of that act or omission.
f. The accused's conduct substantially contributed to the perpetration of genocide by killing.

[80] See *supra* note 75. [81] See *ibid.*

5.3.7 *Instigating*

a. The physical perpetrator caused the death of an individual ('the victim') by his conduct.
b. The physical perpetrator intended to cause the victim's death.
c. The physical perpetrator or other relevant actor intended, through this death, to contribute toward the partial or total destruction of a distinct group that is objectively defined on the basis of nationality, ethnicity, race, or religion.
d. The victim was, or was perceived to be, a member of that distinct group.[82]
e. The accused either
    i. prompted criminal conduct constituting genocide by killing with the intent that this crime be committed; or
    ii. prompted an act or omission, aware of the substantial likelihood that genocide by killing would be committed in the realisation of that act or omission.
f. The accused's conduct substantially contributed to the perpetration of genocide by killing.

5.3.8 *Ordering*

a. The physical perpetrator caused the death of an individual ('the victim') by his conduct.
b. The physical perpetrator intended to cause the victim's death.
c. The physical perpetrator or other relevant actor intended, through this death, to contribute toward the partial or total destruction of a distinct group that is objectively defined on the basis of nationality, ethnicity, race, or religion.
d. The victim was, or was perceived to be, a member of that distinct group.[83]
e. The accused either
    i. instructed another[84] to commit genocide by killing with the intent that this crime be committed; or
    ii. instructed another to engage in an act or omission, aware of the substantial likelihood that genocide by killing would be committed in the realisation of that act or omission.
f. The accused enjoyed formal or informal authority over the person to whom the order was given.
g. The accused's conduct had a direct and substantial effect on the perpetration of genocide by killing.

5.4 Extensive destruction of property as a grave breach

5.4.1 *Joint Criminal Enterprise, First Category (JCE I)*

a. The physical perpetrator partially or wholly destroyed, or caused significant damage to, real or personal property.

[82] See *ibid.* [83] See *ibid.*
[84] For example, the accused could instruct the physical perpetrator directly, or he could instruct someone else – an intermediate commander, for example – who himself instructs the physical perpetrator.

b. The physical perpetrator either
   i. intended to destroy or damage this property, or
   ii. engaged in intentional conduct with reckless disregard for the likelihood that the property would be so destroyed or damaged.
c. The destruction caused was extensive.
d. At the time of the destruction, there was an international armed conflict.
e. The destruction of property was closely related to that international armed conflict.
f. The property was protected under the Geneva Conventions.
g. The physical perpetrator or other relevant actor knew that the armed conflict existed.
h. The physical perpetrator or other relevant actor knew the factual circumstances establishing the international character of the armed conflict.
i. The accused and at least one other person came to an express or implied agreement that extensive destruction of property as a grave breach would be committed ('the common plan, design, or purpose').
j. The accused participated in this common plan, design, or purpose.
k. The accused's participation in the common plan, design, or purpose was voluntary.
l. The accused shared the intent to commit extensive destruction of property as a grave breach.

5.4.2 Joint Criminal Enterprise, Second Category (JCE II)

- Since the predicate for this form of responsibility is the existence of a system of ill-treatment, it is unlikely that any indictment would ever charge an accused with responsibility through JCE II for destruction of real property. Indeed, no indictment at either *ad hoc* Tribunal has ever alleged the combination of a war crime targeting property and this category of JCE.

5.4.3 Joint Criminal Enterprise, Third Category (JCE III)

a. The physical perpetrator partially or wholly destroyed, or caused significant damage to, real or personal property.
b. The physical perpetrator either
   i. intended to destroy or damage this property, or
   ii. engaged in intentional conduct with reckless disregard for the likelihood that the property would be so destroyed or damaged.
c. The destruction caused was extensive.
d. At the time of the destruction, there was an international armed conflict.
e. The destruction of property was closely related to that international armed conflict.
f. The property was protected under the Geneva Conventions.
g. The physical perpetrator or other relevant actor knew that the armed conflict existed.
h. The physical perpetrator or other relevant actor knew the factual circumstances establishing the international character of the armed conflict.
k. The accused and at least one other person came to an express or implied agreement that a crime within the jurisdiction of the relevant Tribunal would be committed ('the common plan, design, or purpose').

l. The accused participated in this common plan, design, or purpose.
m. The accused's participation in the common plan, design, or purpose was intentional and voluntary.
n. The accused intended to further the criminal purpose of the joint criminal enterprise.
o. The commission of extensive destruction of property as a grave breach was a natural and foreseeable consequence of the execution of the common plan, design, or purpose.
p. The accused was aware that the commission of extensive destruction of property as a grave breach was possible.

5.4.4 *Superior Responsibility*

a. The physical perpetrator partially or wholly destroyed, or caused significant damage to, real or personal property.
b. The physical perpetrator either
    i. intended to destroy or damage this property, or
    ii. engaged in intentional conduct with reckless disregard for the likelihood that the property would be so destroyed or damaged.
c. The destruction caused was extensive.
d. At the time of the destruction, there was an international armed conflict.
e. The destruction of property was closely related to that international armed conflict.
f. The property was protected under the Geneva Conventions.
g. The physical perpetrator or other relevant actor knew that the armed conflict existed.
h. The physical perpetrator or other relevant actor knew the factual circumstances establishing the international character of the armed conflict.
i. A superior-subordinate relationship existed between the accused and the physical perpetrator.
j. Where appropriate, a superior-subordinate relationship also existed between the accused and the other relevant actor.[85]
k. The accused either
    i. knew that extensive destruction of property as a grave breach was about to be, was being, or had been realised by the physical perpetrator, and where appropriate, the other relevant actor; or
    ii. had reason to know that extensive destruction of property as a grave breach was about to be, was being, or had been realised by the physical perpetrator, and where appropriate, the other relevant actor.
l. The accused failed to take all measures within his material ability to either
    i. prevent the physical perpetrator and, where appropriate, the other relevant actor, from carrying out extensive destruction of property as a grave breach; or
    ii. ensure that punishment was dispensed upon the physical perpetrator and, where appropriate, the other relevant actor, for carrying out extensive destruction of property as a grave breach.

[85] See *supra* note 63.

5.4.5 Aiding and Abetting

a. The physical perpetrator partially or wholly destroyed, or caused significant damage to, real or personal property.
b. The physical perpetrator either
   i. intended to destroy or damage this property, or
   ii. engaged in intentional conduct with reckless disregard for the likelihood that the property would be so destroyed or damaged.
c. The destruction caused was extensive.
d. At the time of the destruction, there was an international armed conflict.
e. The destruction of property was closely related to that international armed conflict.
f. The property was protected under the Geneva Conventions.
g. The physical perpetrator or other relevant actor knew that the armed conflict existed.
h. The physical perpetrator or other relevant actor knew the factual circumstances establishing the international character of the armed conflict.
i. The accused lent practical assistance, encouragement, or moral support to the physical perpetrator in committing extensive destruction of property as a grave breach.
j. The practical assistance, encouragement, or moral support had a substantial effect on the commission of extensive destruction of property as a grave breach.
k. The accused acted intentionally with knowledge or awareness that his act would lend assistance, encouragement, or moral support to the physical perpetrator.
l. The accused was aware of the essential elements of the crime, including the physical perpetrator's intent.

5.4.6 Planning

a. The physical perpetrator partially or wholly destroyed, or caused significant damage to, real or personal property.
b. The physical perpetrator either
   i. intended to destroy or damage this property, or
   ii. engaged in intentional conduct with reckless disregard for the likelihood that the property would be so destroyed or damaged.
c. The destruction caused was extensive.
d. At the time of the destruction, there was an international armed conflict.
e. The destruction of property was closely related to that international armed conflict.
f. The property was protected under the Geneva Conventions.
g. The physical perpetrator or other relevant actor knew that the armed conflict existed.
h. The physical perpetrator or other relevant actor knew the factual circumstances establishing the international character of the armed conflict.
g. The accused either
   i. designed criminal conduct constituting extensive destruction of property as a grave breach with the intent that this crime be committed; or

ii. designed an act or omission, aware of the substantial likelihood that extensive destruction of property as a grave breach would be committed in the realisation of that act or omission.

h. The accused's conduct substantially contributed to the perpetration of extensive destruction of property as a grave breach.

5.4.7 Instigating

a. The physical perpetrator partially or wholly destroyed, or caused significant damage to, real or personal property.
b. The physical perpetrator either
   i. intended to destroy or damage this property, or
   ii. engaged in intentional conduct with reckless disregard for the likelihood that the property would be so destroyed or damaged.
c. The destruction caused was extensive.
d. At the time of the destruction, there was an international armed conflict.
e. The destruction of property was closely related to that international armed conflict.
f. The property was protected under the Geneva Conventions.
g. The physical perpetrator or other relevant actor knew that the armed conflict existed.
h. The physical perpetrator or other relevant actor knew the factual circumstances establishing the international character of the armed conflict.
g. The accused either
   i. prompted criminal conduct constituting extensive destruction of property as a grave breach with the intent that this crime be committed; or
   ii. prompted an act or omission, aware of the substantial likelihood that extensive destruction of property as a grave breach would be committed in the realisation of that act or omission.
h. The accused's conduct substantially contributed to the perpetration of extensive destruction of property as a grave breach.

5.4.8 Ordering

a. The physical perpetrator partially or wholly destroyed, or caused significant damage to, real or personal property.
b. The physical perpetrator either
   i. intended to destroy or damage this property, or
   ii. engaged in intentional conduct with reckless disregard for the likelihood that the property would be so destroyed or damaged.
c. The destruction caused was extensive.
d. At the time of the destruction, there was an international armed conflict.
e. The destruction of property was closely related to that international armed conflict.
f. The property was protected under the Geneva Conventions.
g. The physical perpetrator or other relevant actor knew that the armed conflict existed.

h. The physical perpetrator or other relevant actor knew the factual circumstances establishing the international character of the armed conflict.
h. The accused either
   i. instructed another[86] to commit extensive destruction of property as a grave breach with the intent that this crime be committed; or
   ii. instructed another to engage in an act or omission, aware of the substantial likelihood that extensive destruction of property as a grave breach would be committed in the realisation of that act or omission.
i. The accused enjoyed formal or informal authority over the person to whom the order was given.
j. The accused's conduct had a direct and substantial effect on the perpetration of extensive destruction of property as a grave breach.

5.5 Plunder as a violation of the laws or customs of war

5.5.1 Joint Criminal Enterprise, First Category (JCE I)

a. The physical perpetrator took possession or assumed control of public or private property.
b. This possession or assumption of control was not justified under international law.
c. The physical perpetrator intended to take possession or assume control of this property.
d. The physical perpetrator or other relevant actor knew that the possession or assumption of control was not justified under international law.[87]
e. At the time of the taking of possession or assumption of control of property, there was an armed conflict.
f. The taking of possession or assumption of control of property was closely related to that armed conflict.
g. The physical perpetrator or other relevant actor knew that the armed conflict existed.
i. The accused and at least one other person came to an express or implied agreement that plunder as a violation of the laws or customs of war would be committed ('the common plan, design, or purpose').
j. The accused participated in this common plan, design, or purpose.
k. The accused's participation in the common plan, design, or purpose was voluntary.
l. The accused shared the intent to commit plunder as a violation of the laws or customs of war.

[86] For example, the accused could instruct the physical perpetrator directly, or he could instruct someone else – an intermediate commander, for example – who himself instructs the physical perpetrator.
[87] See *supra* note 47.

5.5.2 Joint Criminal Enterprise, Second Category (JCE II)

a. The physical perpetrator took possession or assumed control of public or private property.
b. This possession or assumption of control was not justified under international law.
c. The physical perpetrator intended to take possession or assume control of this property.
d. The physical perpetrator or other relevant actor knew that the possession or assumption of control was not justified under international law.[88]
e. At the time of the taking of possession or assumption of control of property, there was an armed conflict.
f. The taking of possession or assumption of control of property was closely related to that armed conflict.
g. The physical perpetrator or other relevant actor knew that the armed conflict existed.
j. The accused participated in a system of ill-treatment ('the common plan, design, or purpose') that amounted to or involved the commission of plunder as a violation of the laws or customs of war.
k. The accused's participation in the common plan, design, or purpose was voluntary.
l. The accused had personal knowledge of the criminal nature of the system of ill-treatment.
m. The accused intended to further the criminal purpose of the system of ill-treatment.
n. The accused shared the intent to commit plunder as a violation of the laws or customs of war.

5.5.3 Joint Criminal Enterprise, Third Category (JCE III)

a. The physical perpetrator took possession or assumed control of public or private property.
b. This possession or assumption of control was not justified under international law.
c. The physical perpetrator intended to take possession or assume control of this property.
d. The physical perpetrator or other relevant actor knew that the possession or assumption of control was not justified under international law.[89]
e. At the time of the taking of possession or assumption of control of property, there was an armed conflict.
f. The taking of possession or assumption of control of property was closely related to that armed conflict.
g. The physical perpetrator or other relevant actor knew that the armed conflict existed.
h. The accused and at least one other person came to an express or implied agreement that a crime within the jurisdiction of the relevant Tribunal would be committed ('the common plan, design, or purpose').
i. The accused participated in this common plan, design, or purpose.

[88] See *supra* note 47. [89] See *supra* note 47.

j. The accused's participation in the common plan, design, or purpose was intentional and voluntary.
k. The accused intended to further the criminal purpose of the joint criminal enterprise.
l. The commission of plunder as a violation of the laws or customs of war was a natural and foreseeable consequence of the execution of the common plan, design, or purpose.
m. The accused was aware that the commission of plunder as a violation of the laws or customs of war was possible.

5.5.4 Superior Responsibility

a. The physical perpetrator took possession or assumed control of public or private property.
b. This possession or assumption of control was not justified under international law.
c. The physical perpetrator intended to take possession or assume control of this property.
d. The physical perpetrator or other relevant actor knew that the possession or assumption of control was not justified under international law.[90]
e. At the time of the taking of possession or assumption of control of property, there was an armed conflict.
f. The taking of possession or assumption of control of property was closely related to that armed conflict.
g. The physical perpetrator or other relevant actor knew that the armed conflict existed.
h. A superior-subordinate relationship existed between the accused and the physical perpetrator.
i. Where appropriate, a superior-subordinate relationship also existed between the accused and the other relevant actor.[91]
j. The accused either
    i. knew that plunder as a violation of the laws or customs of war was about to be, was being, or had been realised by the physical perpetrator, and where appropriate, the other relevant actor; or
    ii. had reason to know that plunder as a violation of the laws or customs of war was about to be, was being, or had been realised by the physical perpetrator, and where appropriate, the other relevant actor.
k. The accused failed to take all measures within his material ability to either
    i. prevent the physical perpetrator and, where appropriate, the other relevant actor, from carrying out plunder as a violation of the laws or customs of war; or
    ii. ensure that punishment was dispensed upon the physical perpetrator and, where appropriate, the other relevant actor, for carrying out plunder as a violation of the laws or customs of war.

[90] See *supra* note 47. [91] See *supra* note 63.

5.5.5 Aiding and Abetting

a. The physical perpetrator took possession or assumed control of public or private property.
b. This possession or assumption of control was not justified under international law.
c. The physical perpetrator intended to take possession or assume control of this property.
d. The physical perpetrator or other relevant actor knew that the possession or assumption of control was not justified under international law.[92]
e. At the time of the taking of possession or assumption of control of property, there was an armed conflict.
f. The taking of possession or assumption of control of property was closely related to that armed conflict.
g. The physical perpetrator or other relevant actor knew that the armed conflict existed.
h. The accused lent practical assistance, encouragement, or moral support to the physical perpetrator in committing plunder as a violation of the laws or customs of war.
i. The practical assistance, encouragement, or moral support had a substantial effect on the commission of plunder as a violation of the laws or customs of war.
j. The accused acted intentionally with knowledge or awareness that his act would lend assistance, encouragement, or moral support to the physical perpetrator.
k. The accused was aware of the essential elements of the crime, including the intent of the physical perpetrator to commit plunder as a violation of the laws or customs of war.

5.5.6 Planning

a. The physical perpetrator took possession or assumed control of public or private property.
b. This possession or assumption of control was not justified under international law.
c. The physical perpetrator intended to take possession or assume control of this property.
d. The physical perpetrator or other relevant actor knew that the possession or assumption of control was not justified under international law.[93]
e. At the time of the taking of possession or assumption of control of property, there was an armed conflict.
f. The taking of possession or assumption of control of property was closely related to that armed conflict.
g. The physical perpetrator or other relevant actor knew that the armed conflict existed.
h. The accused either
    i. designed criminal conduct constituting plunder as a violation of the laws or customs of war with the intent that this crime be committed; or

[92] See *supra* note 47. [93] See *supra* note 47.

   ii. designed an act or omission, aware of the substantial likelihood that plunder as a violation of the laws or customs of war would be committed in the realisation of that act or omission.

i. The accused's conduct substantially contributed to the perpetration of plunder as a violation of the laws or customs of war.

5.5.7 Instigating

a. The physical perpetrator took possession or assumed control of public or private property.
b. This possession or assumption of control was not justified under international law.
c. The physical perpetrator intended to take possession or assume control of this property.
d. The physical perpetrator or other relevant actor knew that the possession or assumption of control was not justified under international law.
e. At the time of the taking of possession or assumption of control of property, there was an armed conflict.
f. The taking of possession or assumption of control of property was closely related to that armed conflict.
g. The physical perpetrator or other relevant actor knew that the armed conflict existed.
h. The accused either
   i. prompted criminal conduct constituting plunder as a violation of the laws or customs of war with the intent that this crime be committed; or
   ii. prompted an act or omission, aware of the substantial likelihood that plunder as a violation of the laws or customs of war would be committed in the realisation of that act or omission.
i. The accused's conduct substantially contributed to the perpetration of plunder as a violation of the laws or customs of war.

5.5.8 Ordering

a. The physical perpetrator took possession or assumed control of public or private property.
b. This possession or assumption of control was not justified under international law.
c. The physical perpetrator intended to take possession or assume control of this property.
d. The physical perpetrator or other relevant actor knew that the possession or assumption of control was not justified under international law.
e. At the time of the taking of possession or assumption of control of property, there was an armed conflict.
f. The taking of possession or assumption of control of property was closely related to that armed conflict.
g. The physical perpetrator or other relevant actor knew that the armed conflict existed.

h. The accused either
    i. instructed another[94] to commit plunder as a violation of the laws or customs of war with the intent that this crime be committed; or
    ii. instructed another to engage in an act or omission, aware of the substantial likelihood that plunder as a violation of the laws or customs of war would be committed in the realisation of that act or omission.
i. The accused enjoyed formal or informal authority over the person to whom the order was given.
j. The accused's conduct had a direct and substantial effect on the perpetration of plunder as a violation of the laws or customs of war.

[94] For example, the accused could instruct the physical perpetrator directly, or he could instruct someone else – an intermediate commander, for example – who himself instructs the physical perpetrator.

Index